SECRET SCIENCE

SECRET SCIENCE

A CENTURY OF POISON WARFARE AND HUMAN EXPERIMENTS

ULF SCHMIDT

OXFORD
UNIVERSITY PRESS

OXFORD
UNIVERSITY PRESS

Great Clarendon Street, Oxford, OX2 6DP,
United Kingdom

Oxford University Press is a department of the University of Oxford.
It furthers the University's objective of excellence in research, scholarship,
and education by publishing worldwide. Oxford is a registered trade mark of
Oxford University Press in the UK and in certain other countries

Published in the United States of America by Oxford University Press
198 Madison Avenue, New York, NY 10016, United States of America

British Library Cataloguing in Publication Data
Data available

Library of Congress Control Number: 2014959974

ISBN 978–0–19–929979–9

Printed in Great Britain by
Clays Ltd, St Ives plc

Links to third party websites are provided by Oxford in good faith and
for information only. Oxford disclaims any responsibility for the materials
contained in any third party website referenced in this work.

For Katia, Luca, and Bella

Acknowledgements

The world was a different place ten years ago when I started work on this book; the second Iraq war was about to be launched to rid the international community of the threat of Saddam Hussein's alleged stockpiles of weapons of mass destruction; in the United States and Britain, especially, the subject of deadly chemical weapons shaped part of the political thinking and national security strategies in what was to become known as a global war on terror; it was a world which had not yet woken up to the uncomfortable realities governing our post-modern lives, in which the delusion of endless growth and prosperity and the uncritical admiration of a liberal market economy made it seemingly impossible for national governments to even contemplate a global banking crisis of the proportions of the one we experienced in 2008. Since then the world around us has changed beyond recognition and with it our sense of place and security. As former certainties have given way to profound uncertainties, most of us have come to realize that the fragility of our existence cannot be overcome through material goods alone, but that stability and inspiration are instead to be found in a community of likeminded people. As a senior scholar at a British university, and the founding director of the University of Kent's Centre for the History of Medicine, Ethics and Medical Humanities, I have enjoyed the particular privilege of being part of an international community of scholars who have been a source of strength and constant encouragement to me, and without whom this book could not have been written.

Over the years, I have incurred many debts from friends and colleagues who have supported the project with their ideas, sources, and helpful guidance. Amongst these, some clearly stand out: Alan Care, a personal injury lawyer with a moral conscience, a kind of British 'Erin Brockovich', who over a fifteen-year period became one of the leading legal representatives of Britain's chemical warfare veterans; without his stubborn determination 'never to give up' righting the wrongs committed against British and Allied servicemen during the Cold War period, many of the key documents used in this study would never have seen the light of day. What started as a working relationship on a complex legal case soon turned into one of friendship. Special mention too must be made of Kenneth Earl who in May 1953 was exposed to the nerve agent Sarin at Porton Down, only two days before the death of Leading Aircraftman Ronald Maddison. A real gentleman who made you want to hear about the fate of the British chemical warfare veterans, Kenneth quickly became the public face of the Porton Down Veterans Support Group. His sense of optimism and belief in justice infected and buoyed everyone around him. On several occasions he came to Kent to share his story with my Special Subject students in what were clearly some of the best seminars I have had the privilege to chair. I am also grateful to all the many veterans, including Terry Alderson, Mike Cox, and Eric Gow, who over many years supplied me with information about their time as experimental subjects at Porton Down, Edgewood Arsenal, and other secret research facilities: subjects who knew very little, if anything, about the substances being tested on them or the risks they were incurring. Next on the list of people to whom I owe a particular debt of gratitude are my research assistants Ryan Hills and David Willcox; both did a tremendous job in conducting dozens of interviews with veterans and former scientists, and in creating the foundation of what is today known as Kent's Porton Down archive. However, there is one scholar to whom I owe a greater debt than to anyone else: Julian Perry Robinson of the Science Policy Research Unit (SPRU) at the University of Sussex. He provided my assistants and me with unfettered access over a prolonged period to a wealth of historical and contemporary sources. His expertise in the field of chemical and biological warfare policy is simply second to none. I would like to thank him for not only supporting the project from its inception but for making detailed comments on earlier drafts of the manuscript, which have significantly improved the scope and quality of the book.

I am grateful to a number of senior officials and scientists for agreeing to share their experiences and expertise in a series of tape-recorded interviews, especially Lord Butler of Brockwell, then Master of University College Oxford, for discussing his review of secret intelligence on weapons of mass destruction; David Langley, a senior government adviser on chemical and biological warfare, for his invaluable insights into the often contentious relationship between secret science and policy; and Robert Maynard, a leading expert on toxic chemicals from the Health Protection Agency, for helping me to better understand the personal networks and long-term continuities within Britain's chemical warfare community. These conversations provided me with essential background information which allowed me to gain a 'sense' of the research culture in top-secret Allied research facilities.

This book would not have been possible without generous support from various funding bodies. I am especially grateful to the Wellcome Trust for granting me a major project grant entitled 'Cold War at Porton Down: Medical Ethics and the Legal Dimension of Britain's Biological and Chemical Warfare Programme, 1945–1989', which provided me with much-needed resources, time, and flexibility for pursuing this study wherever the evidence took me. I am grateful to Anthony Woods, David Clayton, and the staff of the Trust for all their helpful advice throughout the life of the grant; it is thanks to James Peto that key findings of the study have previously been presented to a wider public as part of the *War and Medicine* exhibition organized by Wellcome Collection in 2008–2009. I am likewise indebted to the Chemical Heritage Foundation in Philadelphia for awarding me a Herbert D. Doan Fellowship at a critical juncture in the life of the project; special thanks go to Ronald Brashear, Carin Berkowitz, and the friendly staff of the Othmer Library of Chemical History. My stay there not only enabled me to examine key archival collections, but allowed me to engage in creative conversations with scholars from the University of Pennsylvania's Department of History and Sociology of Science, especially Mark B. Adams, Susan Lindee, and Ruth Schwartz Cowan, whose warm welcome was greatly appreciated. Angela and Rolf Dessauer's generous hospitality at their beautiful home in Greenville, Delaware, made this trip especially memorable. Towards the end of the project, two Visiting Fellowships from the Swiss-based Brocher Foundation allowed me to write up the findings of the book in a particularly supportive and collegiate atmosphere; Cécile Caldwell Vulliéty, Anyck Gérard, Marie Grosclaude, and Elliot Guy made my stay a real success. I am also grateful for all the constructive feedback I have received from colleagues in response to papers given at the Universities of Cambridge, Glasgow, Kent, Oxford, and Pennsylvania, University College London, the Brocher Foundation, the Chemical Heritage Foundation, and the World Health Organization, Geneva.

A study of this size and nature has benefited greatly from the professionalism and expertise of countless archivists around the world. I am particularly indebted to the staff of the German Federal Archives in Berlin, Koblenz, and Freiburg. At the Imperial War Museum, London, Stephen Walton and Kay Gladstone helped me to identify and access important private papers and film material, and at its Duxford branch, Alan Wakefield was most helpful in making available to me, at rather short notice, the previously classified Porton Down photographic collection. The staff at Churchill College Cambridge (Churchill Archives Centre), King's College London (Liddell Hart Centre for Military Archives), the National Archives and Records Administration, Washington, DC, the National Archive, London, the University of Liverpool (Special Collections and Archives), the University of Sussex (Science Policy Research Unit), the Wellcome Trust Library (Archives and Manuscripts Section), and the World Medical Association likewise went beyond their call of duty in making their respective collections available to me.

This might also be the appropriate—perhaps even the only—place where credit can be given to those police officers who had the determination and courage to investigate allegations made by former servicemen to the effect that they had been 'duped' into taking part in potentially deadly chemical warfare experiments at Porton and to re-examine the Maddison case after more than fifty years in an inquiry known as Operation Antler and established thanks to Detective Superintendent Gerry Luckett. He and his team of dedicated officers provided me with access to relevant sources as far as was permissible. David Masters, HM Coroner for Wiltshire and Swindon, conducted—without fear or favour—one of the most challenging inquests in Britain's recent legal history, and I am grateful to him for having contributed to our conference on Porton Down in 2006. Although I will probably continue to disagree with Gerwyn Samuel, QC, who acted on behalf of Maddison's family, about the correct dress code for court-appointed experts, I came to respect his professional judgement during the Maddison inquest. I would also like to thank André Marin, the then Ombudsman for the Department of National Defence and Canadian Forces, and Gareth Jones (Special Adviser, Office of the Ombudsman) for providing me with valuable insights into the origins of the Canadian compensation scheme and for helping me to obtain relevant Canadian documents for the princely sum of 5 Canadian dollars—one of the best investments I have made in a long time.

The initial idea for the book was conceived in close collaboration with Christopher Wheeler from Oxford University Press, whose intellectual input was instrumental in framing the overall study. My commissioning editors Robert Faber and Cathryn Steele supported me throughout the entire production processes and were always on hand when I needed additional guidance; it has been a wonderful experience working with them.

I would also like to thank Manikandan Chandrasekaran from SPi Global for his flexibility in adjusting some of the schedules; Rosie Chambers, my in-house production editor; Lorna Richerby, my marketing manager; and Clare Hoffmann, the cover designer. Sarah Patey did a fantastic job in turning what was barely a manuscript into a book; I am grateful for all her critical comments and suggestions. Edward Corse, my former doctoral student, and his brother James readily offered their help in designing the figures, and Markus Wahl was so kind as to take time off to help me with the index. Their contributions were key to the overall success of the book's production. Special thanks must go to Virginia Catmur, though, one of the most meticulous and knowledgeable copy-editors I have come to know in my career; if a topic or debate required clarification it would be pursued, no matter what. Her working schedule and pace were often relentless, her list of queries almost endless, but they were always fair and justified. I owe her enormous gratitude for having shown such exceptional commitment to the project.

Finally, many friends and colleagues have played an active role in the genesis of this study, and I am grateful to them all for having had the patience to engage with, and shape, the ideas now presented in this book; foremost among them is Jonathan Moreno, who has been a constant source of inspiration as one of the world's leading scholars in the field of biomedical ethics and human experiments in the twentieth and twenty-first centuries. Not for the first time, I am indebted to Jo Fox for her support and friendship when it was sorely needed during preparations for the Maddison inquest and, above all, to David Welch, my long-standing mentor and friend, for all his critical and highly perceptive comments; all these friends have read parts of the manuscript, and they have all in their own way improved the quality of the book. I am likewise indebted to all my colleagues at the University of Kent for their unwavering support for such a sensitive and potentially controversial project, especially to Dame Julia Goodfellow, our vice-chancellor at Kent, Keith Mander and John Baldock, pro-vice-chancellors, and Kenneth Fincham, my head of department. I would also like to thank Julie Anderson, Robert Baker, Brian Balmer, Antony Beevor, Richard Bessel, Christian Bonah, Timothy Bowmann, Robert Bud, Don Carrick, Mark Connelly, Dominiek Dendooven, Rob Evans, Robert Field, Andreas Frewer, Stefan Goebel, Michael Gross, Mark Hall, Mark Harrison, Alastair Hay, Karen Jones, Thomas Keegan, Mike Kenner, Otmar Kloiber, Egmont Koch, Catriona McLeish, Margaret Pelling, Andreas Reis, Marc Rodwin, Florian Schmaltz,

Margit Szöllösi-Janze, Kate Venables, and John Walker for discussing, and exchanging valuable information about, the subject matter on numerous occasions. Whilst all the above-named have helped in the genesis, development, and production of this book, I must include the usual disclaimer to the effect that any errors are of course mine alone.

I leave till the end acknowledgement of my greatest debt: to my wife Katia who, more than anyone, must be looking forward to seeing the book in print; as a professional art historian with expertise in the field of painting and modern photography, she opened my eyes to the wider cultural history of modern art and its reflection of, as well as response to, international debates revolving around the subject of chemical and biological warfare, deterrence, and disarmament; and to our beloved son Luca Francis Arthur, who often sat on my lap patiently and perceptively observing the chronicler of historical developments as he attempted to make sense of the complex material in front of him; and of course to our rescue dog Bella, our constant companion. The book is dedicated to them—my family.

Canterbury, February 2015

Contents

If we tell them that the experiments could be lethal there would inevitably be a sharp fall-off in numbers, and probably a degree of embarrassing publicity. On the other hand, if no more warning of the danger is given than at present, we may be quite rightly accused of deliberate misrepresentation in the future. (J.F. Mayne, Permanent Secretary to Secretary of State for Air, 15 September 1959)

List of Figures

List of Images

Abbreviations

A-2	US Air Force intelligence agency
ABC	Applied Biology Committee
ACIGS	Assistant Chief of the Imperial General Staff
ACSRTD	Advisory Council on Scientific Research and Technical Development
AEF	American Expeditionary Force
AFES	Australian Field Experimental Station
AFHQ	Allied Force Headquarters
AFMPC	Armed Forces Medical Policy Council
AG	anti-gas
AHRC	Arts and Humanities Research Council
AMA	American Medical Association
AMSSO	Air Ministry, Special Signals Office
APIL	Association of Personal Injury Lawyers
ARC	Agricultural Research Council
ARP	Air Raid Precautions
ASA	Applied Science and Analysis, Inc.
ATS	Auxiliary Territorial Service
BAB	Bundesarchiv-Berlin
BAK	Bundesarchiv-Koblenz
BAL	British anti-lewisite (ointment)
BA-MA	Bundesarchiv-Militärarchiv
BAOR	British Army of the Rhine
BAS	British Army Staff, Washington DC
BBC	bromo-benzyl-cyanide (a tear gas); British Broadcasting Corporation
BEF	British Expeditionary Force
BIOS	British Intelligence Objectives Subcommittee
BJSM	British Joint Service Mission, Washington DC
BMA	British Medical Association
BMJ	*British Medical Journal*

BMRC Beit Memorial Research Council
BRAB Biological Research Advisory Board
BSHS British Society for the History of Science
BTWC Biological and Toxin Weapons Convention
BW biological warfare/weapon(s)
BZ 3-quinuclidinyl benzilate, an anticholinergic glycolate
CBW chemical and biological weapons/warfare
CCDD Controller, Chemical Defence Development
CCG, BE Control Commission for Germany, British Element
CCRU Common Cold Research Unit
CDAB Chemical Defence Advisory Board (Ministry of Supply)
CDEE Chemical Defence Experimental Establishment
CDES Chemical Defence Experimental Station
CDRD Chemical Defence Research Department
CDRE(I) Chemical Defence Research Establishment in India
CG phosgene
ChE cholinesterase
CHF Chemical Heritage Foundation
CIA Central Intelligence Agency
CIC Counter Intelligence Corps
CIOS Combined Intelligence Objectives Subcommittee
CN chloracetophenone (a tear gas)
CND Campaign for Nuclear Disarmament
COSHE Committee on the Safety of Human Experiments
CPA Crown Proceedings Act
CPS Crown Prosecution Service
CS a tear gas, named after its creators Corson and Stoughton
CWC Chemical Weapons Convention
CW chemical warfare/weapon(s)
CWS Chemical Warfare Service
DBCD Directorate of Biological and Chemical Defence
DCDEE Director, Chemical Defence Experimental Establishment
DCDRD Director of Chemical Defence Research and Development
DCW Director of Chemical Warfare
DERA Defence Evaluation and Research Agency
DGAMS Director General of Army Medical Services
DGMS Director General of Medical Services

DHSS	Department of Health and Social Security
DM	adamsite (an arsenical irritant)
DMI	Director of Military Intelligence
DMO	Director of Military Operations
DMT	Director of Military Training
DoD	US Department of Defense
DoH	Declaration of Helsinki
DRA	Director of Royal Artillery
DRPC	Defence Research Policy Committee
DSWV	Director(ate) of Special Weapons and Vehicles
DTH	dimercaptopropyl alcohol or Dithiol
ECHR	European Court of Human Rights
ECIC	European Command Interrogation Center
FBI	Federal Bureau of Investigation
FCO	Foreign and Commonwealth Office
FIAT	Field Information Agency, Technical
FRS	Fellow(s) of the Royal Society
G-2	US Army intelligence agency
G-agents	nerve gases
GA	Tabun
GB	Sarin
GD	Soman
GF	Cyclosarin
HC	House of Commons
HCN	hydrogen cyanide
HMG	His/Her Majesty's Government
HS	mustard gas
ICC	International Criminal Court
ICI	Imperial Chemical Industries
ICMMP	International Committee on Military Medicine and Pharmacy
ICRC	International Committee of the Red Cross; Imperial Cancer Research Council
IG	*Interessen Gemeinschaft*, the so-called IG cartel of chemicals companies
ILO	International Labour Organization
IMT	International Military Tribunal
IRB	Institutional Review Board
ISCCW	Inter-Service Committee on Chemical Warfare

IWM	Imperial War Museum
JAMA	*Journal of the American Medical Association*
jg	junior grade
JIC	Joint Intelligence Committee
JMIS	Joint Medical Intelligence Subcommittee
JPS	Joint Planning Staff
LAC	Leading Aircraftman; large area coverage
LSD	lysergic acid diethylamide
LSHTM	London School of Hygiene and Tropical Medicine
MI	Maddison Inquest
MI5	Britain's domestic intelligence service
MI6	Britain's overseas intelligence agency
MID	Military Intelligence Detachment
MIT	Massachusetts Institute of Technology
MJC	Medico-Juridical Commission
MLO	Military Liaison Officer
MoD	Ministry of Defence
MoH	Ministry of Health
MoS	Ministry of Supply
MP	Member of Parliament
MPA	multi-party action
MRC	Medical Research Council
MRD	Microbiological Research Department
MRDB	Medical Research and Development Board (US Army)
MRE	Microbiological Research Establishment
MRI	magnetic resonance imaging
NARA	National Archives and Records Administration
NASA	National Aeronautics and Spaces Administration
NCO	non-commissioned officer
NDCF	National Defence and Canadian Forces
NDT	Nuremberg Doctors' Trial: NDT Documents, in Dörner and Ebbinghaus 1999
NHS	National Health Service
NIH	National Institutes of Health
NSA	National Security Agency
ONI	US Navy intelligence agency
OPCW	Organization for the Prohibition of Chemical Weapons

OSA	Official Secrets Act
OSI	Office of Scientific Intelligence (CIA)
OSS	Office of Strategic Services
OTP	one-time pad (encryption technique)
PCS	Project Coordination Staff
PDSR	Principal Director of Scientific Research (Ministry of Supply)
PDVSG	Porton Down Veterans Support Group
PHLS	Public Health Laboratory Service
PI	personal injury
PRO	Public Records Office
Ptn.	Porton Note
PTP	Porton Technical Paper
R&D	Research and Development
RAMC	Royal Army Medical Corps
RCP	Royal College of Physicians
REC	Research Ethics Committee
RN	Royal Navy
RUSI	Royal United Services Institute
SAC	Scientific Advisory Council (Ministry of Supply)
SEAC	South East Asia Command
SHAEF	Supreme Headquarters Allied Expeditionary Forces
SHAPE	Supreme Headquarters Allied Powers Europe
SIPRI	Stockholm International Peace Research Institute
SIS	Secret Intelligence Service
SOE	Special Operations Executive
SROs	Station Routine Orders
T3436	a psychological incapacitant
T3456	LSD
TL2636	an oripavine derivative
TL2833	a short-acting oripavine derivative
TNA	The National Archives
UCL	University College London
UoK	University of Kent
UoL	University of Liverpool
USSTAF	United States Strategic and Tactical Air Forces
V-agents;VX	nerve gases
WAAF	Women's Auxiliary Air Force

WHO   World Health Organization
WL   Wellcome Trust Library
WMA   World Medical Association
WWI   First World War
WWII   Second World War

Prologue
The Girl in the Gas Mask

Towards the end of this project, I was privileged to be given time off to spend in an old nineteenth-century villa on the shores of Lake Geneva, a place as surreal in luminosity and ambience as its mountainous surroundings. I was the temporary occupant of a room with a view, sleepless, image-drunk, unable to grasp the enormous beauty of my immediate environment, where the rhythm of daily existence slowed down to create space for reflection. I was surrounded by experts from the fields of medicine, law, and ethics in a place where it seemed natural to share experiences over a glass of wine with colleagues. One of these told me a story he had heard about an accomplished young scholar from northern Europe. It was hardly credible, but it struck a particular chord with my own work, not so much as matter of verifiable historical fact, but because of its powerful iconic meaning about the status of medical science in our time. She was a leading expert in the philosophy and ethics of medical jurisprudence, and her specialist field, I was told, was human subject protection in Anglo-Saxon law. She tackled complicated questions such as informed consent and the dividing lines between different types of criminal law, and had a personality that combined highly complex, yet well considered, thought-processes with a certain childishness. At the request of a group of physicist colleagues, she had apparently agreed to subject herself to a human experiment to study the image resolution of various artificially induced brain activities during an MRI scan. It might well be claustrophobic, the scientists had apparently told her, perhaps even a little traumatic, given the confines of the machine, but it was perfectly safe. She had been told that, to ensure her brain activity could be artificially modified during the scanning process, and thus made visible, she would be breathing carbon monoxide through a gas mask. I had just spent ten years of research trying to capture the political and cultural milieu of experimental scientists in some of the most secretive research facilities on earth, Porton Down in Great Britain and Edgewood Arsenal in the United States, and documenting the lives and suffering of thousands of servicemen exposed to toxic agents, in a 400-page manuscript which became the book you are now holding in your hands, so at that moment I had difficulty in masking my surprise at the foolhardiness of what I was hearing. Was such behaviour, if indeed it had occurred, reckless, I wondered? It was probably safe, but why would an intelligent young women, barely in her mid thirties, her entire life in front of her, do such a thing? Why would *anyone* do such a thing? Her rationale for subjecting herself to such a toxic trial, I was told, was that it was an exciting, novel experience, something she had apparently not done before. Besides, she would be getting an MRI scan of her brain for free. The story, disconcerting as it may have been, raised a series of pertinent ethical questions about ownership and agency. It was her body. She owned it and could decide what to do with it. Her mannerisms were perhaps those of a girl of seventeen years of age, but she was fully competent and know-ledgeable in her chosen field; she knew what she was doing far better than the men I had studied. They had rarely known what would happen to them, and had trusted their superiors, military officials, and expert scientists not to take any risks with their lives, but had been badly let down.

The story reminds me of Tracy Chevalier's historical novel *The Girl with a Pearl Earring* (1999), which describes the origins of Johannes Vermeer's masterpiece, said to have been painted in the late seventeenth century and often referred to as the 'Mona Lisa of the North'. The gaze of the observer is directed, as the name implies, to a shining-white pearl earring. In the novel, the Dutch painter has asked his fictional young servant to assist him by serving as a model for his envisaged piece of fine art. Their social and professional status seem clearly defined, yet as the story progresses, it becomes clear that she is not just the subject wearing his wife's pearl earrings, but rather an equal partner, one our fictional Vermeer has to treat with respect if their joint project is to succeed. His increased dependence on her pres-ence, as a model and as a woman he desires, requires him to forfeit his social and class privileges and regard her for what she is, a human being. The work of art has become a catalyst for bridging class divides, momentarily, as long as the process of its construction is ongoing. Once it is completed, however, each returns to their previous social space, content in the knowledge that their only possible point of contact remains the artefact itself. The story provides a powerful, albeit idealized metaphor for understanding parts of the dynamics of the relationship between research scientists and trial participants. Though they do not know each other, and would ordinarily not interact with one another, were it not for the experiment, they are both required to invest time and effort for the procurement of new knowledge. One without the other will not work. A human experiment without the human being is destined to fail, in the same way as Vermeer's painting would fail without a sitting model, unless it were constructed from the imagination. Likewise, trial participants in and by themselves are likely to achieve very little—if anything at all—for their lack of technical expertise prevents them from appropriating the role of the scientist. The servant by herself remains a servant, as the end of the book makes plain. Only in coming together as equal partners who respect each other's role will artist and servant be able to produce something worthwhile. Each needs to trust the other. Today, as we move further into the twenty-first century, there are a plethora of ethical guidelines backed up by national laws and regulations to protect human participants, yet that bond between the two continues to be an important ingredient in allowing medical science to flourish.

The image of the girl in the gas mask breathing in carbon monoxide gas while lying on her back in the metal tube of an MRI scanner is emblematic of some of the ethical challenges faced by modern medical science, highlighting the ambivalent relationship between the individual and a highly specialized, technological approach to health and disease in the Western world, yet also throwing into relief the role of the scientist. How do we describe the kind of power relationship the two actors entered into? The girl was unable to move, turn over, or leave, had she wished to do so; her consciousness—if not her life—was reliant on the level of toxic gas being released into the plastic tubes connecting her lungs with the outside world. The image shows her utter dependence on the investigating researcher, her defencelessness and utter vulnerability; it suggests servants and slaves at the mercy of their master, in this case of the machine and its controller. How can this be exciting? Have citizens become so desensitized and detached from themselves in a free civil society that they perceive moments of voluntary imprisonment as an interesting experience? A novel 'experience' it may well have been, but was it also one that enriched our physical and intellectual well-being, one that provided us, in the German philosophical tradition, with *Erkenntnisgewinn* (best translated as 'enriched cognition')? What happened to the girl with the pearl earring? The equal partnership did not last.

And what was the return for the gas–mask girl who invested her time, and risked her health, her life? Plenty of scientific data may have been collected, and a successful experiment may have offered an opportunity to improve an existing technology. For her, what remained was a brain scan—in colour, one would suspect—but not much more.

So why do human beings take part in such experiments? What are their underlying motives? In such cases, the scientist takes on the role of the seemingly selfless father figure, assuring his subjects that their joint enterprise will ultimately, in some distant future, be of benefit to the greater good; resources and human sacrifice are an apparently inevitable necessity. At a metaphorical level, one is reminded of Velázquez's painting *Las Meninas*, in which the association with members of the Spanish royal household boosts the social status of the painter to such an extent that he becomes the dominant figure in the painting. The viewer joins those observing him— the royal couple, whose reflection can be seen only in the mirror hanging on the wall behind the painter—and in imagination gains equal status with the Spanish royal family, and yet all eyes are directed at the painter himself. He, and he alone, is at the heart of Velázquez's painting. Likewise, the gathering of research data provides the scientist with the material evidence from which to construct his professional and pecuniary success. Ostensibly, he operates behind the scenes, yet it places him centre stage. The quality and interpretation of the data defines his relation to his peer group and the public at large; it is what makes or breaks his career, in some cases also those of his collaborators. The scientists involved in the research this book investigates, knowing full well that any attempt to lure even the most susceptible participant into the researchers' den would require more than lofty promises of a better future, offered the subject one or more further incentives: different types of financial rewards and payments in kind; an 'unusual experience' to overcome the boredom of modern life; privileged access to new knowledge, medical care, and treatment. For military personnel, a weekend pass to see their loved ones may have been on offer. In almost all cases, the participant was allowed to believe that his or her action *might* contribute to some greater good, to the advancement of science, for instance, yet it was also coupled with real, tangible benefits. It is this interaction between illusion and reality that made the offer especially attractive for prospective participants. One could hardly refuse such a deal, since it satisfied both intellectual and material desires, a willingness to contribute to the life of the community and a longing for individual recognition and reward. For some, the rationale for agreeing to take part in tests may even have been a wish for self-discovery, seeing the experiment as an inexpensive way of discovering themselves through the observations of others, as a scientifically grounded, seemingly objective form of self-reflection. In the same way that 'we are observing ourselves being observed by the painter' in Velázquez's painting, as Foucault puts it, the test subject hoped to receive a reward of a different kind, motivated not by any charitable impulse or sense of social duty, but by the timeless desire to find out who we are as humans. The girl in the gas mask may have volunteered because she believed that any external stimuli would benefit her sense of self. Yet, why would thousands of servicemen have agreed to take part in the testing of unknown toxic substances? Theirs was not a story of men—and men they almost exclusively were—engaged in self-absorbed navel gazing, but one in which willingness to serve Crown and country turned into a prolonged campaign to highlight human and civil rights violations at the hands of a powerful state. Amidst justified claims for compensation, their main demand was simple: an apology.

The image of the girl in the gas mask has become for me an iconic symbol of the extent to which we, as individuals and as a society, have become detached from ourselves, separated from our bodies and one another, a reminder that we have lost our place and balance in the world. We are living in a society which is profoundly wrong, Tony Judt has poignantly pointed out, with its relentless consumerism and material interests. Ideas and ideologies do not seem to matter any longer. In our world today, people no longer ask whether a thing is good, fair, or just or whether it improves the lives of the many, not the few. Our postmodern, post-Cold War world has not only left behind ideologies and theories, but it has become 'postethical', he argues. The culturally constructed image of a world in which people remained connected to themselves and their surroundings is, as we know, a distant memory, one that exists only in our imagination, yet this does not negate the justified claims of stability and social justice that shaped much of the collective discourse of the postwar period, when people hoped and worked for another, better world, one in which those who had served their country, in whatever way, would be treated fairly and justly.

I

Introduction

Porton Down, England, 1953

On Wednesday 6 May 1953, at around 10.00 a.m., twenty-year-old Leading
Aircraftman (LAC) Ronald Maddison, a wireless mechanic from Consett,
County Durham, and five other subjects entered a 100 m³ gas chamber in
Building 11 at Porton Down, Britain's chemical and biological warfare
research establishment, unaware that they were to be exposed to the nerve
agent Sarin.[1] All were wearing general service respirators. They were dressed
in their standard military uniform, and each had two identical pieces of
cloth (serge and flannel) tied loosely over the forearm. Present with the men
were senior technician W.N. Truckle and Herbert W. Lacon, a retired lieutenant from the Royal Navy, who administered the agent, while a medical
officer, Major Richard H. Adrian, son of the Cambridge scientist Edgar
D. Adrian, observed the experiment from outside the chamber. A dose of
200 mg of pure Sarin was applied from a calibrated pipette onto the layers
of cloth, on the inside of the left forearm. Maddison was the fourth of the
six to be treated, at around 10.17 a.m. Each was to remain in the chamber
for thirty minutes from the time of contamination, and permitted to play
draughts or noughts and crosses. But at 10.40 a.m., Maddison said he felt
'pretty queer.'[2] Sweating, he was sent from the chamber with one of the
scientists. Once he was outside, Adrian took charge of the situation.
Maddison's respirator and the contaminated cloth were removed and he
walked to a bench about 30 yards away, still sweating. Two minutes later an
ambulance was called. Over the phone, Adrian informed Alfred L. Leigh
Silver, the Establishment Medical Officer, that he had 'an observer at the
gas chamber who might need attention'.[3] A minute later Maddison said
he could not hear. As tremors to his hand set in, Adrian administered an

intravenous injection of atropine sulphate, used as a treatment of nerve gas poisoning, and then a further injection, intramuscularly. Maddison became unconscious shortly thereafter.

At 10.47 a.m., his arms in spasm and his fists clenched, Maddison arrived at the Station Medical Centre, where his condition deteriorated further. He was put to bed and given oxygen.[4] But very soon his respiration became irregular, infrequent; he started gasping. Then he stopped breathing. Resuscitation attempts began immediately. Alerted by his assistant Lacon, who had administered the nerve gas, Harry Cullumbine, head of the Physiology Section and therefore responsible for Porton's human experiments, rushed to the Medical Centre with Charles Lovatt Evans, one of Britain's most senior chemical warfare scientists. They found Leigh Silver and Adrian desperately trying to save Maddison's life through artificial respiration.[5] More and more medical officers were called to the scene, which was fast spiralling out of control. Those witnessing the unfolding events, such as the ambulance driver Alfred Thornhill, were clearly shocked by what they saw:

> It was like he was being electrocuted, his whole body was convulsing... The skin was vibrating and there was all this terrible stuff coming out of his mouth, it looked like frogspawn or tapioca. I saw his leg rise up from the bed and I saw his skin turning blue. It started from his ankle and started spreading up his leg. It was like watching someone pouring a blue liquid into a glass, it just began filling up.[6]

By 11.00 a.m. Maddison's colour had become ashen grey and no pulse could be detected, indicating complete circulatory collapse. He was placed on the floor with his lower limbs raised; the team frantically massaged his limbs towards his heart, and applied hot water bottles to his trunk while maintaining artificial respiration. Anacardone, a drug used to stimulate respiratory centres in acute respiratory failure, was injected and he was given further doses of atropine.[7] As a last resort, liquid adrenaline was injected directly into his heart. Unsure what to do next, Leigh Silver telephoned Porton's medical consultant Dr Gubbins, but nothing more could be done for Maddison. At 1.30 p.m., with the electrocardiogram showing no signs of life, Maddison was pronounced dead.[8] His cholinesterase inhibition recorded 99 per cent by one method of measurement, and 93 per cent by another, the most severe case of nerve gas poisoning ever recorded in the Western world.[9]

A Century of Poison Warfare and Human Experiments

This book traces the long history of chemical and biological weapons research involving experiments on humans and animals by the former Allied powers during the twentieth century, particularly Britain, the United States, and Canada.[10] It charts the ethical trajectory and culture of military science, from its initial development in response to Germany's first use of chemical weapons in the First World War to the ongoing attempts by the international community in the twenty-first century to ban these types of weapons once and for all. Above all, the study aims to throw new light onto the evolving field of military medical ethics, not exclusively from a philosophical or bioethical perspective, but by exploring continuity and change in the understanding and application of military medical ethics over a hundred-year period. A *longue durée* perspective allows for greater recognition of important developments in often contentious medical ethics debates, sometimes across national boundaries and research cultures, as is the case in the chemical and biological warfare field examined here.

This study asks whether material changes in military medical ethics have been brought about by enforced external pressures from professional groups and the agencies of the state, for example in response to unforeseen accidents or embarrassing trial revelations, or through a process of measured reform. Are changes in military medical ethics, if and when they occur, driven forward by major paradigm shifts, historical turning points, and moments of institutional upheaval, or by a calibrated evolutionary process which, grounded in the Hippocratic medical tradition, has been supported because of the long-term material interests and privileges of the governing classes? Some experts reached a point in their careers in which a break with the past was seen as inevitable, as a way of fostering a radically new medical ethics culture within both military and civilian science. Others favoured tradition and continuity—change, if it was needed at all, had in their view to be carefully managed and controlled. It is the interplay between different historical actors who pursued and resisted proposals for lasting change in applied research ethics which lies at the heart of this book.

From the early 1990s, allegations that servicemen had been duped into taking part in trials of toxic agents at top-secret Allied research facilities throughout the twentieth century featured with ever greater frequency in the media. Porton Down, Britain's chemical and biological warfare facility, established during the First World War, had quickly become the main focus of public and political speculation. Investigative journalists and television crews interviewing former 'guinea pigs' reported that many had believed they were taking part in tests for the common cold, and that no informed consent had been obtained. These were far from isolated incidents. Although a whole army of British soldiers, a total of 21,752 to be precise, had participated in Porton's research programme between 1939 and 1989, the number of veterans coming forward numbered in the tens and hundreds rather than the thousands.[11] Most of the veterans' complaints related to the 1950s and 1960s, some to the 1970s and, in a few cases, even the 1980s. Many remembered their stay at Porton as relatively harmless, but there were large numbers of men for whom the experience had been anything but pleasant, sometimes harmful, and in isolated cases deadly. To this day, many are trying to come to terms with why the government tested highly toxic chemicals on their bodies without informing them of at least some of the basic risks involved. Relatives of veterans, their parents, wives, partners, and children, often forgotten in official histories, struggled to understand the idiosyncratic behaviour and health problems of their loved ones, only to be told, years after the event, that their child, husband, partner, or father had taken part in top-secret and potentially lethal warfare experiments. For some, news of the tests came as a shock. Many felt that the experiments had a 'huge impact' upon their working lives and family. Most looked to the authorities to provide them with emotional guidance and explanations for lives lost. Often, their reasonable expectations remained unfulfilled. In 2008, after a sustained campaign that had lasted over a decade and involved the combined efforts of politicians, journalists, medical experts, and historians, myself included, the UK government awarded compensation to about 670 veterans and issued an official apology, a milestone in Britain's attempt to come to terms with her inglorious past.

My own involvement started in May 2001 with an unexpected phone call from Lieutenant Colonel Bolton from the Ministry of Defence (MoD), who asked for advice about the development of ethics standards in the conduct of research at Porton Down. Although I considered myself an unlikely candidate to act as a consultant to the MoD, and I did not in fact do so, I asked Bolton to put his request in writing. His letter gives a rare insight into the position of the UK government at a critical juncture in its dispute with the Porton veterans, which lasted roughly fifteen years between the mid 1990s and about 2010.[12] By the time I received Bolton's letter, hundreds of servicemen were alleging that they had been led to believe that they were taking part in tests to find a cure for the common cold, but instead had been involved in nerve agent and other related chemical warfare trials. A second complaint revolved around 'persistent claims' by veterans that they had suffered ill-health as a result of the tests. That is why, according to Bolton, the MoD had adopted a 'policy of openness' after shortcomings had been revealed in medical record-keeping for Gulf War veterans. In a period marked by geopolitical *Glasnost*, it did no harm to acknowledge administrative errors and provide citizens with access to relevant evidence, but the government wanted to go further and conduct expert-led medical assessment programmes for both Gulf War and Porton veterans. A final area of concern focused on the paucity of explanatory information about the trials given to the servicemen upon their arrival at Porton. Consent, if it had been obtained, had apparently not been informed and thus, according to the veterans, had been invalid. Bolton acknowledged that the 'overall history' of Britain's research programme into chemical and biological weapons had not yet been written despite an existing, though barely known, repository of sources; this repository would be made available to a specially selected team of MoD civil servants and expert medical ethicists. The MoD wanted to gain greater insight into the role of informed consent as a moral and legal requirement in human experimentation, not for reasons of scholarly interest, as it turned out, but as a means of knowing, prior to any case coming to court, the conceptual dividing lines between ethical and unethical military research throughout much of the twentieth century. In a second step, it was planned to make an assessment about the extent to which the 'Porton Down programme [had] adhered to the principles extant at the time'.[13]

It all sounded too good to be true. Military officials in open conversation with scholars from the humanities and medical sciences, a government willing to embrace transparency, and an apparent desire to seek constructive solutions for soldiers who had suffered ill-health as part of their military service? Even if, as Bolton represented it, UK government policy had been made in good faith, the reality, as experienced by Porton and other UK veterans over several decades, looked remarkably different. As if to underline an unspoken assumption that the veterans were confused about events which had taken place up to fifty years earlier, MoD officials repeatedly pointed out that a search of archival records had not uncovered 'any documentary evidence' that could corroborate the veterans' allegations that they had been duped into taking part in warfare experiments. Since both establishments, Porton Down and the Common Cold Research Unit (CCRU), were located near Salisbury, albeit on opposite sides of the town, there seemed to be a simple explanation as to how the confusion might have arisen. Given that nerve agents could cause a discharge of excess of fluid from the nose, it was, according to MoD officials, 'easy to see' how the association with common cold research would have been made. Experts had also been unable to discover any 'discernible pattern' among the 'few' complaints the MoD had received. On the basis of the small sample size, officials concluded that there was 'no scientific or medical evidence to support claims of unusual or excessive ill health'. While the MoD acknowledged that 'all volunteers *should* [emphasis added] have been fully informed', it was apparently impossible to verify this since written consent forms were introduced only in the 1980s. Some veterans may have felt misled by the experiments, officials argued, but others had understood the nature of the trials. The whole affair was portrayed as an unfortunate misunderstanding, albeit one which came at a colossal cost to the health and well-being of thousands of participants. In 2006—three years into the disastrous Iraq war—the MoD finally published the long-awaited Historical Survey, which aimed to document Porton's Human Volunteer Research Programme from 1939 to 1989; by this time official interest in studying the history of Porton's past had waned, yet the issues raised remain pertinent.[14]

Less than four months after Bolton's call, the 9/11 terrorist attack on the United States not only transformed the global security environment, but challenged the military and strategic orthodoxy that had underpinned the national security policies of Western governments throughout much of the Cold War and post-Cold War period. All of a sudden, the tectonic plates holding the global security system together began to shift in unpredictable directions and, with them, Britain's willingness to deal constructively with her Cold War past. The UK government's stated policy of transparency quickly turned into one of greater entrenchment on matters related to national security, especially in the field of atomic, chemical, and biological weapons. Whereas an open access policy may have had certain 'merits' for historians, it provided the media and those critical of Allied defence policies with a resource for the dissemination of 'ill-informed concern', as Hammond and Carter put it, which, it was alleged, played into the hands of those opposed to the ideals of Western democracy.[15] Current affairs correspondents were brushed aside as belonging to a powerless 'reality-centred community' unable to keep up with the rapidly constructed reality of the present, a view expressed most forcefully in 2002 by a senior adviser to former President George W. Bush, believed to have been his deputy chief of staff Karl Rove, as the country was preparing to invade Iraq: 'We're an empire now, and when we act, we create our own reality. And while you're studying that reality—judiciously, as you will—we'll act again, creating other new realities, which you can study too, and that's how things will sort out. We're history's actors . . . and you, all of you, will be left to just study what we do.'[16] He mocked the idea that one could develop solutions to emerging problems by studying 'discernible reality', whether historical or contemporary, since those with the true power to construct new realities would leave those studying those realities behind, with no role to play in creating a common future.

Today, the hubris of the United States, along with most empires once they are financially bankrupt and politically divided, has been replaced by an extended nemesis. Its military fire-power still remains beyond most people's imagination, yet with its dysfunctional health and welfare system, massive unemployment, child poverty, and social and educational inequalities, the US government is struggling to prevent the former superpower from sliding into global insignificance. Worse still, not only has evidence come to light which suggests that the US Central Intelligence Agency (CIA) used methods of torture on al-Qaida terror suspects, and that health professionals seem to have played not only a central but an 'essential role' in such practices which violated 'U.S. and international law and fundamental principles of medical ethics',[17] but serious allegations have recently been levelled against the US military for showing a 'disregard for the safety, health, and welfare of military personnel', who discovered, handled, or detonated chemical weapons munitions during their deployment in Iraq. Over 600 US service personnel are said to have been exposed to stocks of chemical weapons, most dating from the 1980s, including mustard gas and nerve agents, yet for years the Pentagon has apparently failed to monitor their symptoms and provide them with adequate medical care.[18] For Jeff Miller, chairman of the Committee on Veterans Affairs in the US House of Representatives, the allegations, if shown to be correct, 'undercut the very foundation of our military principles'.[19]

Subsequent events and recent revelations have proved Rove wrong. Yet, there is another dimension to his delusional, postmodernist hyperbole which helps explain the complex dynamics in top-secret Allied research establishments: the desire and ability of the chemical and biological warfare corps, largely comprised of military officials, scientists and expert civil servants, to construct and identify a never-ending stream of national security threats which served as flexible justification strategies for the allocation of enormous resources to conducting experimental research with some of the most deadly agents known to man.

For almost half a century, experts and the public alike have engaged in a highly charged debate about the extent to which Allied and especially British warfare trials were ethical, safe, and justified within the prevailing conditions and values of the time. Whereas the Porton veterans, and those representing them, argued for a public inquiry into 'this dark episode of human experimentation', others, such as the *Lancet* writer David Sharp, were less convinced that a sufficiently strong case for an 'unavoidably long and expensive public inquiry' had been made.[20] The MoD's decision to exclude the testimony of Porton scientists and civil servants from the Historical Survey, however, was universally seen as a 'serious gap' which could create further imbalances, possibly even prejudices, about their place in history.[21] Porton veterans, meanwhile, dismissed it as a 'hysterical survey' because the sources used lacked transparency and contextualization. Against this backdrop, this book offers a nuanced, non-judgemental analysis of the contributions made by servicemen, scientists, and civil servants to military research in Britain and elsewhere, and shows them not as passive, helpless victims 'without voices', or as perpetrators 'without a conscience', but as history's actors and agents of their own destiny. It does not aim to 'speak for them', to project ideas and concepts onto an imagined experience, but to unearth material which enables them to 'speak for themselves' through the emerging contours of their personalities and expert networks. It was their loyalty to the British realm which brought and kept these men—and they almost all were men—together in rather complicated ways; though their interests and individual memories differed widely, they have a common history which is worth excavating. Rather than taking a tried and tested, yet narrow approach, which overlooks these dimensions, this study attempts to construct a finely knit tapestry of life and power relations in some of the most secretive research facilities in the Western world; the aim is to reconceptualize the previous understanding of twentieth-century human research ethics.

This book addresses a series of interrelated questions. To what extent are medical ethics applied, and are they applied equally, in all research contexts, including those that are generally hidden from public view because of their national security classifications? What is the relationship between secrecy, science, and medical ethics? Does secrecy serve as a justification strategy for ethical decision-making in military science, or, conversely, does it give scientists the opportunity to conduct their research unhindered by external forms of control and ethical oversight? In other words, are medical ethics standards monitored and enforced uniformly in both civilian and military science? Historically, we still know surprisingly little about the factors and forces responsible for shaping the formation of different medical ethics cultures and practices in past societies. For example, do the risks involved for those participating in human experiments increase during times of war, and if so, how are these risks justified by military and medical experts or the agencies of the state? How does the potential threat of war, a recurring feature of the Cold War, affect military and civilian research ethics? What are the similarities and differences in applied research ethics in war, in which military forces are involved in active combat operations, compared to periods of heightened military preparedness? Can we detect a decline in the upholding of professional ethics standards in research on humans during national emergencies, especially in relation to bioethical principles such as consent, beneficence, and non-maleficence (to do no harm)? Put in more general terms, is it true that 'things can happen in war that would not be tolerated in peace-time'?[22] Although scholars no longer see war as separate from, but rather as a state of, society, the question remains, as Moreno puts it, whether 'wartime dictates its own morality'.[23]

Latterly, scholars have come to look more closely at how existing medical ethics regimes relate to, and develop as a result of, national security considerations, wartime conditions, and contingency planning. Experts have questioned, for instance, the extent to which human experiments can be performed under conditions of great secrecy, and whether such experiments can be ethical, transparent, and accountable.[24] Others have examined the shifting boundaries between accident and experiment in the context of biological weapons trials by stressing the role of secrecy in guiding the conduct of military officials and scientists.[25] This book aims to enhance our understanding of the complex history of military medical ethics and nonconventional weapons research as practised by various state actors and political regimes.[26]

This work is located within the broader literature on the history and ethics of human experimentation in the twentieth and twenty-first centuries.[27]

Since the mid 1990s, largely as a result of commemorative events to mark the fiftieth anniversary of the Nuremberg Code—the set of ten ethics principles written in response to Nazi medical atrocities carried out during the Second World War—we have witnessed a surge in studies examining the politics and ethics of experimental research performed on thousands of inmates in government prisons, asylums, orphanages, and prisoner-of-war camps, and on members of the military.[28] A considerable body of literature has examined medical war crimes committed by Axis scientists during the Second World War, including Japan's medical atrocities.[29] These studies have highlighted the effect of human experiments on contemporary research ethics and the relative effectiveness of ethical codes and human rights in protecting human participants in modern medical science.[30]

Although the World Medical Association (WMA) categorically prohibits physician-scientists from participating in offensive chemical and biological warfare research, or from contributing to their 'conception and manufacture', the subject nonetheless produces, as Gross has argued, an 'overwhelming tension between military necessity and humanitarian obligations'.[31] This is reflected not only in the historical debates leading up to the Geneva Protocol, promulgated in 1925 and outlawing chemical and biological warfare, but also in contemporary debates over the use of incapacitating weapons in modern warfare. By examining professional and scientific developments in chemical weapons research that were informed by, and occurred in response to, shifting military doctrines, this book hopes to inform wider debates about the relationship between military medical ethics and national security.

Few subjects are as fraught with such vested interests as chemical and biological weapons, which are seen as evidence of mankind's self-destructive capability. For much of the twentieth century, writers have engaged with the subject in order to explain, condemn, or justify their use from different perspectives and traditions. Over the last decade, there has been an explosion of public and scholarly interest in military medicine and the ethics of secret science—science carried out away from the public eye— triggered in part by the emergence and perception of new security threats resulting from radical innovation in the life sciences, concerns about biosecurity, and the role and limits of science in society, yet our historical understanding about internal modes of operation in secret research and development facilities has been limited at best.[32] Most histories have tended to focus on how international politics and the military have responded to evolving chemical and biological warfare capabilities, and have overlooked the role of hundreds of trial participants and different science communities, including members of the civil service corps, in shaping the character and culture of military research. The existing literature ranges from general histories of chemical and biological warfare to whiggish studies dealing with weapons technologies, policies, and personalities or levels of military preparedness.[33] Histories of nonconventional weaponry during the First and Second World Wars continue to enjoy a renaissance, not necessarily for their explanatory potential, but for their seemingly attractive interpretation of Western democracies fighting Imperial or Nazi Germany, a story of good versus evil.[34]

Backed up by the findings of official advisory committees in the United States, Canada, and Australia, the general argument in studies dealing with military science was that veterans had been, in Pechura and Rall's words, put at risk.[35] Their book, *Veterans at Risk*, published in 1993, not only raised greater public awareness about long- and short-term injuries sustained by US servicemen in secret wartime research programmes, but highlighted a lack of follow-up studies to monitor the health effects. As the injured servicemen had risked their health and well-being, the authors argued that the US government should have monitored them as a way of justifying much-needed medical care. Pechura and Rall's study also drew attention to the complex relationship between the politics of secrecy, research environments, and military medical ethics which has been particularly pertinent to the present study.

Goodwin's book *Keen as Mustard* arguably exposed Britain's 'horrific' chemical warfare experiments in Australia during the Second World War, and Evans' journalistic account *Gassed* accused the British government of unethical research at Porton throughout the twentieth century.[36] In the United States, meanwhile, Eileen Welsome's explosive revelations in *The Plutonium Files*, based on her Pulitzer Prize reporting in *The Albuquerque Tribune*, and Moreno's acclaimed book *Undue Risk*, both published in 1999, placed the ethics of secret government experiments at the centre of an ongoing debate about the human and environmental legacies of militarized medicine and war.[37] These studies joined forces with the efforts of self-appointed campaigners who proclaimed that servicemen and the general public had suffered adverse health effects from exposure to chemical and biological warfare agents.[38] This body of work followed in the footsteps of scholars who, since the 1970s, had shown a growing interest in atomic, chemical, and biological weapons research and the environmental impact of military testing. The six volumes published by the Stockholm International Peace Research Institute (SIPRI) between 1971 and 1975 on the problem of chemical and biological warfare still rank among the most comprehensive studies on the subject, and they placed the 1972 Biological and Toxin Weapons Convention (BTWC) into context.[39] They addressed, with great thoroughness, the complexities of chemical and biological warfare and proposed possible disarmament measures. Aimed at a general readership, Harris and Paxman's study *A Higher Form of Killing*, first published in 1982, provided a revelatory account of the 'secret story' of chemical and 'germ' warfare during a period of deterrence and disarmament.[40] Most histories were meant to serve broader ideological and political objectives, especially the global reduction and destruction of nonconventional weapons. Against this background, Cole's *Clouds of Secrecy* (1988) caused widespread alarm about public and environmental safety.[41]

At the other end of the scale were those defending the development of Cold War science as a way of counter-balancing inaccurate and biased media reporting. Their studies, despite greater access to scientific intelligence, were however often limited by institutional loyalties and national security considerations. Others drew disproportionate attention to Porton's role in developing defensive technologies. In 1960, Lieutenant Colonel A.E. Kent, who had coordinated chemical warfare operations during the First World War, produced a first descriptive 'history of Porton', although public access to this work and to its published version remained restricted for several decades.[42] Another institutional insider, Carter, offered in his history of chemical and biological 'defence' a chronological narrative of Britain's weapons programme.[43] More ambitious, though not more convincing, has been Hammond and Carter's attempt retrospectively to construct a linear development from Britain's biological warfare programme to present-day health care.[44] Avery's study *Pathogens for War*, on the other hand, which looks at Canada's biological warfare programme, adds to an increasingly sophisticated and transnational field of study.[45]

The relationship between science and war has been of scholarly interest for some time, from attempts to chart the influence of—mostly nuclear—research on military and civil affairs to Craughwell's recent book on *War Scientists*, which claims to examine the 'brains' behind modern technologies of destruction and defence.[46] Parker's uncritical narrative portrays Porton as embedded within a global network of 'killing factories' in which tens of thousands of animals and humans were 'sacrificed' by faceless, immoral scientists.[47] Edgerton, on the other hand, has simply placed Porton within the context of government-funded 'specialized inventing institutions' staffed by 'boffins' who were trying to support the war effort.[48] In another study he focused his attention on members of the scientific civil service corps who, in addition to creating a postwar welfare system, apparently constructed an all-powerful warfare state.[49] This recent literature has shifted the parameters of the debate, but much of it has lacked historicization and nuanced, impartial analysis. Perhaps because chemical and biological weapons have been perceived as immoral and illegitimate, the subject has also long been ignored, with notable exceptions, by military historians and historians of science and medicine.[50] Recently, the work of local historians with an interest in Cold War industrial archaeology has offered a novel approach to the study of Britain's chemical warfare community. McCamley's *Secret History of Chemical Warfare* explores the process of the public and political paranoia which led to the accumulation of ever more deadly chemical weapon stockpiles, and assesses their long-term environmental legacy.[51] Balmer, meanwhile, has used the relationship between secrecy and science as a conceptual framing device to write a sociological history of chemical and biological warfare.[52]

Secrecy may have been helpful as a marketing device for scholars and publishers alike, but it has presented historians of military medical ethics with sometimes insurmountable methodological and conceptual problems. Access to textual and visual sources, notebooks, government minutes, technical reports, statistical information, patient files, photographs, and films has all too often been restricted; relevant material has been withheld, deemed lost, and at times known to have been destroyed. Of all the sources listed in the MoD's Historical Survey about 'psychological incapacitating agents', approximately 80 per cent are not in the public domain and cannot currently be verified.[53] This does not only apply to Britain. To this day, large numbers of previously open files about chemical and biological weapon technology and threat assessments, located in the US National Archives in Washington DC, which is generally known for its liberal public access policy, remain closed for the foreseeable future. Those which are still open are often heavily redacted, at times to such an extent that almost all content on a page has been blacked out, or the pages themselves have been removed and replaced by a rider informing the reader that the content has been removed under national security legislation. Anyone trying to read up on the history of the US Chemical Corps since the Second World War, and its successor agency, the US Army Materiel Command, is likely to be disappointed and will need to return in perhaps fifty years.[54] Such restrictive policies apply not only to Western governments but also elsewhere. In the Russian Federation, for example, an extended 'top-secret' security classification of files relating to the history of medicine and science during the Cold War makes the study of Soviet chemical and biological weapons research a most challenging enterprise.[55] In the former Eastern bloc, secrecy could function on multiple levels. In the bureaucratic maze of the Soviet Union, security classifications were not only meant to protect state secrets, but often provided civil servants with an effective vehicle to secure a decision at higher political levels; as one insider put it, 'secrecy was used to push files up the hierarchical ladder'.[56] The present study thus agrees with Balmer's wider argument that 'secrecy cannot simply be regarded as a negative phenomenon that obscures knowledge, but is, instead, an active tool that allows governments to define reality through the exercise of spatial-epistemic power'.[57]

All this should come as no surprise. Chemical and biological weapons, because of their destructive and odious nature, have long been the subject of strict controls by the international community, as the firm response to the alleged use of chemical weapons by the Syrian regime in 2013 made plain.[58] Attempts at controlling nonconventional weapons made significant progress during the Iran–Iraq conflict, especially after images of Iraq's chemical attack on the Kurdish town of Halabja shocked the United Nations into action. The indiscriminate use of Sarin nerve gas by terrorists in a Japanese underground network a couple of years later likewise caught the public's attention. The 1993 Chemical Weapons Convention (CWC), which came into force in 1997, created an internationally agreed framework, administered by the Organization for the Prohibition of Chemical Weapons (OPCW), for the systematic monitoring, verification, and destruction of chemical weapon stockpiles in the world. The recent award of the Nobel Peace Prize to the OPCW in recognition of its global disarmament efforts has clearly placed international arms control high on the political agenda.[59] For most governments, the use of such weapons is seen as 'morally indefensible', a 'repugnant crime', which neither state nor non-state actors— whatever their motivation—can be permitted to commit without impunity. It is a subject deemed to be so sensitive that it can prompt politicians to act in the name of 'human civilization' beyond the national limits of their political mandate. At the same time, it touches upon areas of secrecy that nations guard most closely. In Britain, the institutions involved, their location, and the identity of military officials and senior scientists all too often remain shrouded in secrecy. Throughout most of the twentieth century, the British government neither denied nor officially confirmed the existence of Porton Down. Its address in Wiltshire was classified; staff and civil servants were prohibited from using it in any records to which the public had access.[60] At times, Whitehall officials, operating within a pervasive culture of secrecy, saw the level of misinformation displayed in the media as a measure of their success in preserving state secrets, even if this clashed with the requirement for democratic accountability.[61] In 2013, Edward Snowden, former NSA contractor, drew the world media's attention to the gathering and storage of personal data by Allied intelligence agencies. The subject of human experimentation with nonconventional weaponry bears similarities to the Snowden affair in that it involves multiple and often insurmountable sensibilities at the highest levels of government. It is a subject no government, whatever its political outlook, is keen to explore in public for fear of jeopardizing national security interests. The potential political fallout from revelations about chemical weapons research, even if only for defensive purposes, together with the complexities involving the ethics of military science, is often sufficient to provoke a curt response from officials to any request for information.

Despite such generic problems, it has been possible to base the argument of this book on a satisfactory evidential basis. Owing to his appointment as an expert witness to HM Coroner for Wiltshire and Swindon at the 2004 inquest into the death of Leading Aircraftman Ronald Maddison from nerve gas exposure in 1953, and with his brief to comment on the history of informed consent, which had been requested by the families' legal representatives, the author was provided with access to a sound body of sources.[62] In addition to unclassified military, political, and scientific records, he was able to gain full access to the exhibits and transcripts of the inquest proceedings, including extracts from the Porton chamber test book, the cover of which was marked in ink with the word 'Observers'; the Porton summary book; the day book; the physiological measurements book; Porton Technical Papers, known as PTPs; reports on Tripartite Conference meetings attended by representatives from the United States, Britain, and Canada; and an invaluable cache of witness statements.[63] The sheer weight and size of some of these records posed their own intricate problems: each of the bulky inquest folders containing hundreds of exhibits printed on A3 paper first needed to be carefully examined; given its fragility, storage and preservation of this material was sometimes challenging. Evidence from senior civil servants, scientists, and servicemen, government papers and reports, newspaper clippings, oral history interviews, and films, to name a few, all helped to construct a nuanced tapestry of research activity within the walls of the secret science community. Sometimes, the absence of evidence on aspects of military research ethics turned out not to be a problem, but an important part of my conclusions.

This has therefore not been a study in the conventional sense; instead it has revealed certain limitations in examining the application of ethical principles in research contexts that are generally concealed from public scrutiny. Secrecy has been able, under certain circumstances, to impact upon research ethics. The efficient monitoring and recording of unethical research conduct was not necessarily in the national interest, nor were ethical procedures and safeguards always seen to be conducive to the advancement of military science. Yet how does one examine the perception of, and responses to, ethical dilemmas in the military—such as the exploitation of accidents for research purposes—if the empirical evidence is incomplete or non-existent, or itself classified, and if those who participated in this kind of work are either no longer alive or have been sworn to secrecy? How can one gain insight into the nature of military research ethics without being seen to endanger national security? How can one be sure that the material one is permitted to see or hear is relevant and representative of military medical ethics as a whole, and not a smokescreen to camouflage ethically more problematic work? These are exceedingly difficult issues to tackle, which is why, perhaps, they are often ignored.

Another important route into the subject has been a prosopographical study, both geographically diverse and chronologically expansive, of military scientists involved in nonconventional weapon testing. This helped in the detection and reconstruction of generational patterns, scientific 'schools', modes of knowledge exchange, innovation, and tradition in Allied chemical warfare work. Britain's tightly knit group of chemical warfare scientists called themselves the 'Portonians', a relatively small group of expert scientists often with professional backgrounds in both the military and civilian spheres. Members of the older First World War generation aptly called themselves 'Old Portonians'.[64] The bond between them not only helped in the efficient production and preservation of what was deemed to be sensitive knowledge, or in the construction of informal research networks, but in the expansion of vital professional interests. Influenced by years of government employment, this group of—almost exclusively male—experimental scientists managed to align military and national security concerns with their overriding objective to advance basic scientific research (known in Germany as *Grundlagenforschung*), particularly in the fields of experimental physiology and pathology, pharmacology, biochemistry, and toxicology. Porton, in short, provided—and probably continues to provide—an ideal platform from which to launch their professional careers, an opportunity to create government-funded research centres and laboratories, many of which still exist today.

Some scholars have hitherto applied a quasi-circular argument in assessing the motivational factors and justification strategies of those involved in chemical and biological weapons research.[65] As a starting point, an apparently universally accepted normative framework among the scientific community is used to label nonconventional weapons as 'uncontrollable and indiscriminate', a 'deliberate perversion' of science, before demonstrating that things are more 'complex'. Likewise, scientists working in the field apparently enter 'uncharted moral territory', an unknown and hardly understood 'moral economy', in which 'exceptional factors' must exist—research interests, professional advancement, overriding national security considerations, better pay, and so on—to compel scientists to violate the 'norms of the scientific community'.[66] Seen from a historical perspective, however, it becomes apparent that neither did the normative and apparently universally accepted framework exist in the first place, which obviates any need to debunk it, nor can the factors which scientists employed to justify their role in chemical and biological weapons research be seen as in any way 'exceptional'. On the contrary, these factors were widely applicable to civilian and military scientists alike; they constituted an important part of the armoury in the recruitment and long-term motivation of qualified research staff. Military scientists, not unlike their civilian colleagues, developed different justification strategies if and when it suited their interests. In other words, warfare scientists did not necessarily violate the existing norms of their peer group, because ethical standards were subject to negotiation, compromise, and historical change throughout the research community. What we can see is not so much an alternative ethical universe in which researchers constructed unique moral codes to explain seemingly immoral research, but quite ordinary science and scientists at work.

Yet, how unique is Britain's military medical ethics culture as reflected in work at Porton? How do the findings for Britain's secret science facilities compare with other Allied military research establishments? By examining the actors and agencies responsible for introducing changes in military

medical ethics and policy, this study identifies national and cultural variations. It shows that the uniqueness of Britain's military medical ethics culture, as reflected in Porton's work, needs to be contextualized: not only
within Britain's position as an empire that was as ramshackle as it was controlling and powerful, and in her established links to the commonwealth
nations—India, Australia, and Canada especially—but also by taking account
of her 'special relationship' with the United States in all matters of national
security since the Second World War. Such a history highlights the process
of Britain's changing national identity in the twentieth century and the role
of Anglo-Saxon law as a powerful servant of stability. International medical
ethics codes may have played their part in informing public and professional
debates on clinical research, especially in the 1950s and 1960s; their impact
on military science, though, other than gradually changing the culture and
ambience in which research was seen as permissible, remains difficult to
assess. Scholars are on a firmer footing once the relationship between military science and the law is addressed. The ethics of military medicine was
shaped not so much by established or emerging medical ethics standards but
by the rule of law. Porton's work, however secret and important, was not
above the law of the land.

What this book suggests is that medical ethics, far from being applied
equally, has in the past evolved inconsistently and at times unpredictably,
particularly in those research facilities in which national security considerations were given priority over humanitarian obligations. At the same time,
it challenges the notion that military medical ethics is utterly 'unique', in
light of the occasional demands on military physicians to compromise their
Hippocratic medical ideals to preserve their nations' fighting capacity.[67] It
also questions the assumption that military medical ethics is a rather recent
phenomenon or that it is seemingly disconnected from civilian medical
ethics, with the two cultures in fact existing side by side. Secrecy in military
facilities, including Porton, was socially and temporally constructed and
rarely, if ever, absolute. Secrecy was not only unable to function as an impenetrable wall between the military and civil society—it was not supposed to
do so. As such, the material presented supports Balmer's argument that the
boundaries between secrecy and openness can be 'fluid and negotiable'.[68]
Research and innovation in military science and medicine, however classified, required knowledge from, and negotiations with, civilian scientists and
research organizations. As Edgerton has pointed out, although Porton
produced a 'strong long-serving scientific community', it benefited from

expertise and input from Britain's academic elite, most notably in the fields of physiology, pathology, toxicology, chemistry, and microbiology.[69] By reconstructing the various interconnections and complex networks between these different worlds, it has been possible to show how expert scientists contributed to both civilian and military medicine, and thus shaped the creation of modern biomedical research ethics. This work thus reveals the extent to which civilian and military scientists, research organizations, and universities contributed to, and benefited from, Britain's nonconventional warfare programme.

During times of heightened international tension and armed conflict, scientists and senior officials were more likely to take greater risk with the lives of test subjects to expedite the development of modern weaponry and suspend, for the time being, the key bioethical principles of informed consent and non-maleficence. As I have argued elsewhere, in a perceived or real national emergency 'concern for human rights and the inviolability of the experimental subjects, be they patients or service personnel, came second to the strategic considerations of most Western governments'.[70] Recent scholarship lends additional support to the argument that 'war makes actions wholly impermissible during normal times appear more acceptable', especially to those researchers, as Weiss has argued, for whom the interests of society had higher priority than the health and welfare of the individual.[71] Physician–scientists, who today are morally prohibited from taking part in offensive chemical weapons research, took a leading role in shaping the nature of chemical warfare trials. Their loyalties, whether as military medical scientists or medically qualified soldiers, often conflicted with their professional duty to protect the well-being of participants. In the absence of internationally accepted ethics standards governing human experiments, and conscious of the apparent ambiguity of national ethics rules, military medical experts felt that the exigencies of war justified their ethical decision-making. In this, the safety of human participants was all too often of secondary concern, and their autonomy and right to self-determination was at times severely curtailed.

2

Justifying Chemical Warfare

Ypres 1915

For the German army, it had been little more than a large-scale military experiment. Yet for thousands of Allied soldiers it was a painful reminder that modern chemical warfare had begun.[1] On 22 April 1915 at about 5.00 p.m., around the village of Langemarck near the Belgian town of Ypres, German military engineers released 160 tons of pressurized liquid chlorine from 6,000 steel cylinders that had been positioned along a four-mile front; the moment the liquid was depressurized it vaporized and formed a dense, greenish-yellow cloud, five feet high, which began to drift towards the French and Canadian trenches. For weeks, the Germans had waited for the wind to change direction; it had been blowing steadily from west to east, and they were fearful of exposing their own troops to the poison gas. On the afternoon of 22 April, the wind suddenly began to shift and blow from the northeast. Within minutes, the chlorine cloud had enveloped tens of thousands of Allied soldiers, who began fighting for breath. Utterly disoriented, coughing and choking, blinded, frightened, and overcome by violent sickness, they buried their faces in the mud or ran to escape the trenches. On 4 May 1915, while recovering from battle wounds at the Royal Hospital in Huddersfield, Lance Corporal John Keddie told his mother:

> We went out on the 20th to take up Reserve trenches north of Ypres, we had practically nothing to do for the first two days then it was on the afternoon of my birthday that we noticed volumes of dense yellow smoke rising up and coming towards the British trenches, as I said my Coy. [Company] was not in the firing line and we did not get the full effect of it, but what we did was enough for me, it makes your eyes smart and run, I became violently sick, but it passed off fairly soon, by this time the din was something awful, where we

were, we were under a crossfire of rifles and shells, we had to lie flat in the trenches; The next thing I noticed was a horde of those Turcos [French Colonial Soldiers] making for our trenches, some were armed, some unarmed, the poor devils were absolutely paralysed with fear, they were holding a trench west to a Sec: of 48th—so 48th had to hold it also, until some of their officers came and made them all go back.[2]

By the time the first major chemical warfare attack in modern history came to an end, the Allies had lost hundreds, if not thousands, of soldiers. Allied propaganda estimated that 5,000 soldiers had been killed and 10,000 had been wounded, though these numbers are generally accepted to have been exaggerated.[3] Whatever the exact casualty figures, witness accounts confirmed that Allied troops had been exposed to one of the first weapons of mass destruction, which killed men slowly and painfully from within rather than wounding them on the outside. Total panic had gripped thousands of seasoned soldiers and civilians who fled from the toxic fumes; the modern battlefield had become a site of unimaginable horror and untold human suffering.

Despite a four-mile hole in the Western Front, and an enemy army in disarray, the German military, having failed to anticipate the effects of the 'new infernal invention', as some called it, and lacking the necessary reserves to break through Allied defences, was unable to exploit their sudden strategic advantage.[4] Among those disappointed by the German lack of planning was the head of the Kaiser Wilhelm Institute in Berlin, Fritz Haber, who was instrumental in developing German chemical warfare agents. If only the military authorities had launched a full-scale offensive, he complained, 'instead of the experiment at Ypres, the Germans would have won'.[5] According to Harris and Paxman, writing in 1982, he is supposed to have described chemical warfare as a 'higher form of killing', yet while scholars have been unable to attribute the phrase reliably to Haber, it is indisputable that he saw gas warfare as a more 'humane' weapon of war: 'The gas weapons are surely not more horrible than flying metal fragments, on the contrary, the percentage of deadly gas injuries is comparably smaller, there are no mutilations and nothing is known...in terms of follow-up injuries.'[6] In 1919, much to the shock of the civilized world, Haber was awarded the Nobel Prize for Chemistry.[7]

From the moment chemical weapons appeared on the stage of armed conflict, Just War theorists opposed the use of this new weapon and campaigned for an internationally enforced legal ban. Chemical weapons, they argued, violated the requirement for non-combatant immunity because they indiscriminately killed and injured children, women, and the elderly. In the 1920s, however, military and political exigencies forced the advocates of the Just War tradition to construct new arguments and principles that would make this type of war morally and militarily acceptable. Responding to an international legal ban on poison gas, government experts began to condemn the inhumanity of armed conflict, while simultaneously accepting the need for this type of warfare in certain circumstances. There is therefore a need to examine the ways in which military strategists, scientists, diplomats, and government officials attempted to justify the development, possession, and use of chemical weapons through different means and methods of propaganda, and to contextualize Britain's delicate balancing act between deterrence and disarmament in the postwar period. More broadly, this chapter looks at the changing criteria under which military force was seen to be justified—the *jus ad bellum*; explores conflicting expert opinions with regard to acceptable conduct of war—the *jus in bello*; and provides a hitherto neglected perspective on debates about war crimes, peace-building, and reconciliation after the end of the First World War—the *jus post bellum*.[8] In attempting to justify multiple objectives simultaneously, though not necessarily in concert and often in secret, and by avoiding public scrutiny on the sensitive subject of chemical warfare, the British government pursued a pragmatic political approach that was aimed at positioning the country diplomatically and militarily in a highly volatile international environment, while it prepared itself for yet another major conflict on the European continent.

Rejected as immoral and illegal by many, the new weaponry was greatly feared by the soldiers on the battlefield. Gas warfare became as much a psychological as a physical weapon. Often the experience of being gassed led to real and imagined clinical symptoms for years to come. The possibility of being killed by asphyxiating gases triggered deep-seated emotional responses and occasional nervous breakdowns which psychiatrists classified as 'gas neurosis'; in other cases, soldiers exposed to blistering agents were classed as suffering from 'gas hysteria', since the substances could cause conjunctivitis and temporary blindness.[9] Not unlike soldiers suffering from shell shock, victims of gas war exhibited a range of respiratory and other medical symptoms, including 'functional photophobia, aphonia, hysterical cough, vomiting and palpitations'.[10] Eyewitnesses recalled that 'gas shock was as frequent as shellshock'.[11]

Medical experts were at first reluctant to acknowledge the psychological symptoms of gas war. For Charles Wilson, Churchill's future doctor, the use of gas 'usurped the role of high explosives in bringing to a head a natural unfitness for war'.[12] Echoing this assessment, a Cambridge scientist classified most cases of 'gas shock' as 'hysterical' and called on the authorities 'to prevent the impression gaining ground that men who have inhaled a little mustard gas will get 3 or 4 months away in England'.[13] Those suffering from 'gas neurosis' were often seen as mentally and emotionally unstable, men who were weak to begin with and unable to cope with the stresses and strains of modern life. Showing sympathy for gassed soldiers was surely not to everyone's liking. In 1916, Captain Henry W. Kaye from No. 8 Casualty Clearing Station noted in his diary: 'ours were a pitiful collection of human beings; gassed patients certainly seem to inspire all who see them with more pity, indignation and horror than any other atrocity of warfare'.[14] The fear that gas war could undermine the morale of the troops, and weaken the home front, however, forced the military to establish expert medical centres for the treatment of the physical and psychological effects of poison gas.

No one had been prepared for this kind and scale of warfare; few had ever imagined that poison gas would be used; almost all were shocked that the world would never be the same, that armed conflict would forever be tainted by what many perceived to be an unmanly, dirty form of warfare. As early as 22 April 1915, Michel Toudy, a soldier of the Belgian Grenadiers tasked with strengthening front-line defences in the immediate aftermath of the first gas attack, noted in his war diary: 'Throughout the entire night French territorials arrive in our trenches coughing and saying that it is not permitted to attack aged family fathers with asphyxiating gas.'[15] Many Allied servicemen believed at this point that Germany had violated international conventions governing the conduct of war, which in many ways it had—if not the letter of the law, then certainly its spirit.

Since the outbreak of war, the military had gradually accepted that their fighting forces were ill-equipped for modern trench warfare. In Britain, regimental officers were given orders to sharpen their swords, whereas in France, the army went into combat in red trousers. The failure to anticipate the effects of modern military technology on the conduct of the war resulted in the death of hundreds of thousands of soldiers. Increased fire-power, in the form of automatic weapons, barbed wire, and later machine guns and heavy field guns, made unsupported infantry offensives all but impossible; the modern fighting machine now needed a rationalized, coordinated war economy which was managed by professionals and technical experts. Breaking the deadlock in the war of attrition became a major strategic objective. Technological and military innovations, logistical planning, transportation, efficient communication, and new types of ammunition changed the face of modern warfare beyond recognition.[16]

In Germany, the authorities began to appreciate the power of chemistry. Less affected than other businesses by the Allied blockade, Germany's chemical industry was among the most advanced in the world. Under the leadership of Carl Duisberg, 'an imperious Prussian who could not tolerate dissent', the *Interessen Gemeinschaft*, known as the IG cartel, a conglomerate of eight chemical companies located in the Ruhr region and the world's biggest manufacturer of dyestuffs, launched research into chemical warfare. Expert scientists were tasked with searching for new incapacitating and lethal agents which could be used in preparing an all-out military attack. The testing and employment of incapacitating agents during the Battle of Neuve Chapelle in October 1914, and in early 1915 at the Eastern Front, at first failed to achieve the intended military objectives. In January, according to military sources, 18,000 rounds of artillery shells filled with liquid tear gas were placed at the disposal of the Ninth Army for an attack against the Russians at Bolimóv, some 30 miles south-west of Warsaw.[17] The result was all but disappointing; instead of poisoning enemy forces and preparing the offensive, the German scientists had not taken into account the freezing temperatures, which prevented the agent from vaporizing into a lethal cloud. Technically, none of the belligerents had at this stage broken international law, because all of the weapons contained a combination of high explosives and chemical agents, and were thus not covered by the 1899 Hague Declaration banning the use of 'poisoned arms'.[18]

Attention now turned to the Western Front, where temperatures and environmental conditions were more favourable; with artillery shells in short supply, experts argued that an alternative, and perhaps more devastating, mode of delivery could be to release the gas from pressurized cylinders, thus ensuring that a larger area would be cleared for a ground offensive once the gas had dissipated. Because the IG cartel was producing large quantities of liquefied chlorine for the manufacture of dyestuffs, Haber eventually proposed using chlorine as a lethal weapon. At the end of January, the chief of the German General Staff, General Erich von Falkenhayn, instructed the Fifteenth Army Corps stationed at Ypres to prepare a gas attack by using steel cylinders filled with chlorine. To kill the enemy by poisoning, 'just as one poisons rats', was perceived by many to be 'unchivalrous' and 'repulsive'. Yet, according to the memoirs of the commanding officer, General von Deimling, personal objections had to be suppressed if Germany was to achieve military victory: 'War is necessity and knows no exception.'[19]

The German use of steel cylinders for the delivery of poison gas had yet another, more profound rationale. Since the end of the nineteenth century, international law had prohibited the use of poison gas. Fearing that the ongoing arms race with Germany could weaken the fledgling Russian economy, and further destabilize the regime through strikes and revolutionary activities, Tsar Nicholas II had initiated the First Peace Conference in The Hague to revise and ratify the declarations about the laws and customs of war that had been negotiated in 1874 in Brussels. In 1899, representatives of twenty-six countries, including Britain, France, Russia, and Germany, had signed The Hague Convention Respecting the Laws and Customs of War, which not only regulated the treatment of prisoners of war and the care of sick and wounded, but also banned certain types of warfare and the use of modern technology, including aerial bombardment, chemical warfare, and hollow point bullets. Article 23(a) specifically prohibited the employment of 'poison or poisoned arms'.[20] In a separately signed document, The Hague Declaration Concerning Asphyxiating Gases, the contracting states also pledged to outlaw the use of poison gas as a means of future warfare by 'abstaining from the use of projectiles, the sole object of which is the diffusion of asphyxiating or deleterious gases'.[21] Attempting to ban weapons which did not yet exist, The Hague Declaration contained three major loopholes which the belligerents exploited during the First World War: the use of irritants, the employment of gas through means other than by using projectiles, and the use of gas-filled, yet shrapnel-causing bombs, were not covered by The Hague Declaration. Faced with a war of attrition, the German army was less concerned about the inherent legality or morality of gas warfare but more about semantics. Whereas the use of gas-filled *projectiles* was against international law, the German military considered the use of poison gas released from cylinders to be lawful. Days after Germany's first gas attack, the *Kölnische Zeitung* claimed that 'the letting loose of smoke clouds, which, in a gentle wind, move quite slowly towards the enemy, is not only permissible by international law, but is an extraordinarily mild method of war'.[22] The Allied powers, however, described it as an act of inhumanity which violated 'all codes of civilized behaviour'.[23] It certainly

did not bode well that the German military had given the poisonous cloud
the code-name 'Disinfection', a cover to confuse Allied intelligence, surely,
but also one which portrayed enemy soldiers and civilians as vermin to be
exterminated.[24]

Twenty-four hours after Germany's first gas attack, Sir John French, the
Commander of the British Expeditionary Force, inquired about the existing supply of respirators and requested from London that 'immediate steps
be taken in retaliation to supply similar means of the most effective kind for
the use of our own troops'.[25] In his reply, Lord Kitchener, the War Minister,
called for caution: 'The use of asphyxiating gases is, as you are aware, contrary to the rules and usages of war. Before we fall to the level of the
degraded Germans I must submit the matter to the government.'[26] To investigate the matter, Kitchener called upon two civilian scientists: John S.
Haldane (1860–1936), a former reader in physiology at Oxford University
who, as director of a research laboratory in Doncaster, had worked with the
mining industry in developing respirators against the toxic effects of mine
gases;[27] and Herbert B. Baker (1862–1935), a professor of chemistry at
Imperial College. Both were immediately dispatched to France by Alfred
Keogh, the Director General of the Army Medical Service (DGAMS) and
Rector of Imperial College, to find out what kind of gas had been used and
inspect the site of the first gas attack. As a leading expert who was politically
well connected, and personally known to Keogh, Haldane was an ideal candidate for the mission. His brother, the Viscount Haldane, had introduced
military reforms as Secretary of State for War and was serving as Lord
Chancellor. Baker was likewise an obvious choice, given Keogh's position as
Rector of Imperial College.[28] At St Omer, close to the general headquarters
in France, they managed to identify the gas which had been used as chlorine
through the use of a school laboratory.[29] For all concerned, it was clear that
'immediate defensive measures were required'.[30] On their return to Britain,
Haldane submitted a full report to Prime Minister Herbert Asquith, while
Baker briefed Lord Kitchener about the situation; the latter told him to 'do
his damnedest' to ensure that Britain could soon retaliate.[31]

Despite these bold declarations of intent there was considerable uncertainty among members of the British government as to whether Germany
had actually contravened the terms of The Hague Declaration. On 26 April,
Asquith told King George V: 'As the gases are apparently stored in and
drawn from cylinders, and not "projectiles", the employment of them is
not perhaps an infraction of the literal terms of The Hague Convention.'[32]

Given that Germany was widely perceived as having violated the spirit of the Declaration, however, and with pressure mounting on the War Office to retaliate, the government knew that such legal sophistry would have little truck with the British public.

Within days, after graphic accounts of gas casualties had been published by *The Times* and other newspapers, anti-German sentiment reached fever-pitch.[33] On 29 April, *The Times* commented:

> The wilful and systematic attempt to choke and poison our soldiers can have but one effect upon the British people and upon all the non-German people of the earth. It will deepen our indignation and our resolution, and it will fill all races with a new horror of the German name.[34]

On the same day, the *Daily Mirror* reported that the German military had again used 'asphyxiating gases' contrary to The Hague Declaration.[35] In Germany, meanwhile, gas warfare was portrayed as a modern weapon which was not only lawful but humane, one which produced a 'rapid end', rather than the misery which resulted from turning the German trenches 'into a terrible hell'.[36] A week later, on 7 May, the sinking of the *Lusitania* off the coast of Ireland by a German U-boat, killing 1,198 civilians on board, including American citizens, caused further international outrage and turned public opinion firmly against Germany.[37] With no end in sight to German 'frightfulness', the satirical *Punch* magazine called it an 'explosion of calculated ferocity. Last month it was poison gas; now it is the sinking of the *Lusitania*.'[38] By portraying Germany as an 'inhuman enemy', and German soldiers as barbaric criminals, hell-bent on committing atrocities against civilians by means of poison gas and submarine warfare, and in flagrant violation of the rules of war, Allied officials managed to bring the United States into the conflict and justify, in the eyes of the public, Britain's retaliatory measures.

In the meantime, British troops were becoming impatient. In May 1915, Captain E.S. Chance, stationed near Ypres with the Second Dragoon Guards, told a friend that the 'poisonous gases used by the Germans are exceedingly trying to our men and I hope it will not be long before we have some equally effective stuff to use ourselves'.[39] Britain's ability to retaliate, however, if only in kind, first needed to be authorized, developed, and tested. The man placed in charge of British gas warfare at the end of May, Major Charles Howard Foulkes, a forty-something, no-nonsense soldier from the Royal Engineers, who had been brought up to serve the British Empire, was

given five months to establish a full-scale British chemical warfare programme for the autumn offensive.[40] On 31 May, Foulkes recommended a
detailed programme to prohibit further public discussion of gas reprisals,
an immediate ban on the use of gas along the front line to maintain an
element of surprise, the employment of a range of existing agents, rather
than further experiments, and an attack by means of gas clouds and gas-
filled projectiles, 'the latter to be large, so as to produce appreciable effects;
long-range, to safeguard our own men; and filled with the deadliest gases
procurable'.[41] International law and accepted customs of war notwithstanding, for the Allies it was only a matter of time before they began offensive
chemical warfare.

Germany's premeditated gas attack initiated a Europe-wide chemical
arms race on an unprecedented scale, one in which there was 'no time to
worry about ethics'.[42] Even neutral Netherlands got involved in the production of hundreds of tons of poison gas.[43] The German gas attack 'both
inspired and provoked the British into retaliating with illegal weaponry,
thereby opening the door to a virtually unlimited chemical warfare'.[44]
After recovering from the initial shock, Britain and France wasted little
time in establishing large-scale programmes for the testing of toxic substances, and in preparing their armies for all-out technological warfare
to be fought irrespective of any moral or legal boundaries. At the end of
September 1915, British forces attempted, but largely failed, to use poison
gas in a major offensive at Loos in Belgium.[45] Despite months of preparation, the training of special gas brigades, the employment of chemical experts,
and the shipment and positioning of thousands of gas-filled cylinders along
the front line, military planners began to appreciate the enormous problems
associated with chemical warfare. Gas warfare was highly unpredictable,
scientifically complex, and dependent on prevalent weather and environmental conditions, and it quickly turned into a nightmare for military
strategists. Whereas the human cost of the Battle of Loos was substantial,
strategic gains were almost negligible. The British had captured some
3,000 German prisoners of war. Yet with over 50,000 British casualties,
and hundreds of troops gassed by their own side—after the toxic cloud
had changed direction—together with 3 miles of ground taken and then
lost again, the military agreed that the machinery of war needed to be
modernized if Britain and her Empire were to sustain a prolonged military campaign. Moreover, by using the newly developed Stokes mortar,
the *sole* purpose of which was the delivery of chemical projectiles into and

behind enemy lines, Britain had become the first nation to contravene the literal terms of The Hague Convention, and thus international law.[46]

Porton Down

During the course of the war, the role of experimental science moved from the periphery to the centre of the conflict. Although traditionally sceptical towards technical innovation and the involvement of civilians in war, the military establishment felt compelled to exploit civilian scientists for the war effort.[47] Whereas the Royal Society had made little progress in persuading the War Office to use civilian expertise, Haldane and Baker's commission set a precedent in establishing the role of British scientists in chemical warfare research. Their war-related work ushered in a period of scientific innovation and reform which saw the employment of chemists and physiologists to conduct research into offensive and defensive aspects of chemical warfare.[48] British scientists, many of them Fellows of the Royal Society (FRS), felt duty-bound and honoured to place their expertise at the service of the realm, and had little, if any, moral objections in developing new weapons of mass destruction.

Although responsibility for chemical warfare research rested with different departments, British scientists did not follow this division of labour in practice; instead, they established informal networks and channels of communication which allowed them to coordinate, as best they could, their work throughout the war, and advance their professional careers thereafter.[49] Appreciating the potential limitations of being integrated into the military and ministerial hierarchy, scientists used some of the newly created departments and expert committees on chemical warfare for the exchange of information and avoidance of duplication, for example at the War Office, the Ministry of Munitions, the Royal Society, and the Medical Research Committee, the predecessor of the Medical Research Council (MRC), founded under Royal Charter in 1920.[50]

In 1914, the Royal Society had set up a number of subsidiary committees of its War Committee. Members included Haldane and Ernest Henry Starling (1866–1927), distinguished professor of physiology at University College London. After Germany's gas attack, the War Committee also created a Sectional Committee on Physiology to assess the physiological effects of toxic substances, and liaise with the War Office's Anti-Gas Department in the design and development of respirators. Under Starling's leadership, the Anti-Gas Department recruited a number of civilian scientists, among them J.A. Sadd, E.F. Harrison, Charles Lovatt Evans, H.S. Raper and H.W. Dudley, who played an influential role in building up Britain's chemical warfare programme in the twentieth century.[51]

In June 1915, in an attempt to overcome the chronic shortage of ammunitions, the government transferred responsibility for the development, production, and procurement of weapons from the War Office to the newly established Ministry of Munitions. Under the leadership of Lloyd George, the Ministry was responsible for the development of Britain's offensive chemical warfare capability. This particular change in governmental structures during the war had profound implications for Britain's chemical warfare programme. As someone who believed in the innovative power, creativity, and efficiency of private business, Lloyd George not only welcomed the contributions of experts in the day-to-day running of his Ministry, but established independent scientific advisory bodies which shaped the relationship between science and policy long after the war. At the end of 1915, officials in the Ministry of Munitions concluded that the modern war machine needed nothing less than a fully equipped, large-scale testing ground to keep abreast of rapid developments in science, technology, and medicine.[52] In September, the Trench Warfare Department duly instructed the Scientific Advisory Committee to find and requisition a suitable 'ground for experimental purposes'.[53] A few months later, in early 1916, after trials at a site on Cannock Chase had proved unsatisfactory, some 2,886 acres of land near the villages of Idmiston, Idmiston Down, and Porton, on the southern edge of Salisbury Plain in Wiltshire, formed the basis of what came to be known as Porton Down (see Image 1).[54]

Porton rapidly expanded to take over 6,200 acres of largely woodland and farmland, accessible through a complex network of roads and a light railway that interlinked the administrative headquarters, army huts, workshops, laboratories, munitions depot, open-air testing station, and animal farm, a place teeming with service personnel and civilian scientists working under the leadership of Porton's commandant, Lieutenant Colonel Arthur W. Crossley, a Mancunian, who had made his career as a chemist at King's College London (see Image 2).[55] As sign that Porton was there to stay, certainly for the duration of the war, the organization soon saw the creation of more permanent laboratories, photographic and meteorological units, barracks, and welfare facilities. By 1918, Porton had become a large-scale

Image 1. Porton Down

Source: IWM, Photographic Collection, Photographs of Camp, no date. © Imperial War Museums (L 1991/0).

research facility with over 900 members of staff, many of them officers, thirty-three women from the Queen Mary Army Auxiliary Corps, who were employed as typists, and some 500 civilian workmen who maintained the workshops and laboratories.[56] At first, much of the work was directed towards developing new weapons of mass destruction.

In September 1916, the first use of the Livens Projector, an ad-hoc device consisting of a steel tube, about 3 feet in length and 8 inches wide, dug into the ground at an angle of 45 degrees in batteries of twenty, and detonated remotely through an electrical charge, opened a new chapter in gas warfare. It was no longer necessary to rely on the right meteorological conditions: bombs containing 30 pounds (15 kg) of chemical agents, generally phosgene (CG), could be fired directly into enemy lines, resulting in high numbers of casualties and deaths. The power of the new weapon lay in the number of projectiles that could be fired simultaneously, sometimes more than 1,000 at a time.[57] In April 1917, at the Battle of Arras, the British used the Livens Projector for a full-scale, deadly attack. Although inexpensive and inaccurate, with a range limited to one mile, it was an effective but also terrifying weapon that served as a technological precursor to 'multiple rocket launchers and...aircraft cluster bombs'.[58] Gas shells, on the other hand, used by

Image 2. Lieutenant Colonel A.W. Crossley, CMG, FRS, RE, Porton Down
Commandant, 17 April 1917–28 May 1919
Source: IWM, Photographic Collection. © Imperial War Museums (A.W. Crossley).

Germany and France from 1916, required less preparation, offered greater targeting precision, and were able to be fired over longer distances. In Germany, the symbols on the shell cases represented the different chemical agents: a white cross stood for tear gas, a green cross for phosgene, and a yellow cross for mustard gas (HS).[59] Often, these shell markings served to wrongfoot enemy troops: different types of agents were fired simultaneously or in quick succession. With an estimated total of 66 million gas shells fired during the war, chemical warfare had turned into an ever-present threat for Allied and German forces.

As part of their involvement in the development of weapons of mass destruction, Porton's scientists were also tasked with developing known organic and inorganic compounds to create the most deadly gases possible. In December 1915, the German military used phosgene for the first time, an almost colourless and odourless gas, eighteen times more toxic than chlorine, which, when inhaled, caused serious lung damage from excessive fluid accumulation, and death within a few hours.[60] Toxicologists called it an 'inner drowning' of the lungs.[61] Retaliating in June 1916, the Allies employed phosgene with devastating effect during the battles of the Somme; by firing 4,000 gas-filled shells simultaneously, and thus releasing a total of 54 tons of gas over the target area, the Allies wiped out hundreds, if not thousands, of German soldiers, horses, and wild animals.

The close proximity of Porton's laboratories to one another allowed scientists and service officers to conduct integrated research across disciplinary boundaries. Except for a few scientists who wanted to protect their academic independence, most researchers were given military ranks.[62] Physiologists, chemists, pathologists, meteorologists, and a range of technical and military experts all collaborated in designing and executing experiments, both outdoors on the test range and indoors in the laboratory, sampling station, or gas chamber; by sharing their research data, they managed to improve protective clothing, diagnostic tools, and forms of treatment. Sometimes, relevant expertise had to be brought in from the outside. Porton's first respirator and gas tests, for instance, were conducted by civilian rescue workers from Derbyshire, where mining accidents from gas explosions were not uncommon.[63] Teamwork was an essential ingredient of Porton's developing research culture. It provided scientists and military personnel with an incentive to join the establishment and work long, exhausting hours, late at night, or during weekends. Field trials could start as early as 4.30 a.m. and finish as late as 11.30 p.m. Members of staff initially

worked seven days a week, but were later granted a break on Sunday after-
noons. Porton's collaborative 'spirit and unity of purpose', as Crossley put it,
strengthened their belief that they belonged to an exclusive group of professionals who were tasked by the government to develop defensive and
offensive chemical weapon technologies.[64]

There was one rather unusual, if not unique, facility which subsequently
influenced the Porton research culture, the loyalty of the staff, and the tradition of the establishment more than anything else: the Porton Mess.
Founded in 1916, the Porton Mess was not a mess in the ordinary sense,
serving senior-ranking military officers, for its membership was largely
made up of civilian scientists. Membership was nonetheless organized along
strict hierarchical lines, and restricted to the scientific officer class and the
chief and senior grades of the experimental officer class.[65] The Mess provided these men with a distinct sense of identity and professional purpose;
it facilitated the informal exchange of knowledge and the collaborative
involvement of groups and individuals in cross-disciplinary projects, but it
was also a forum for idle chit-chat, social intercourse, and relaxation, akin
more to a gentleman's club or a senior common room at Oxbridge,[66] where
members invented certain acronyms to depict the elite character of an
organization they had vowed to serve with life-long loyalty. It was as much
an integral part of the life inside Porton as its own cricket club or drama
society. The 'Old Portonians', those service officers who had been at Porton
during the First World War, as well as 'Portonians' generally, saw the Mess as
a 'focal point' of the establishment that 'perpetuated the concept of the
Porton tradition', the nerve centre which connected different strands of
activity to facilitate the flow of information.[67] Later generations of scientists
called themselves the 'cognoscenti', those few in the know about Britain's
top-secret chemical warfare work. Given the strict security classifications of
most of their work, the Mess gave the staff a much-needed professional and
social space to discuss their work freely, raise scientific or methodological
issues over lunch or tea, or relax with friends and colleagues. It allowed
them to get to know and trust each other, not unlike a band of brothers,
charged by the Crown with defending the realm against some external evil.
Here at the Porton Mess, the senior staff would celebrate important occasions in the annual calendar, organize dinners, ladies' nights, and the annual
cocktail party. The Mess also offered accommodation for distinguished
guests and former members of staff.[68] Porton's Mess created an informal,
collegiate atmosphere which facilitated interdisciplinary team work, despite

its intensity and secrecy. It made staff feel at home. When in 1940/1941 the Suffield Experimental Station was set up as a joint UK–Canadian defence establishment, the Chief Superintendent, a man from Porton, insisted that its Mess should be modelled along the same lines.[69]

New challenges brought about by modern chemical warfare also led to advances at Porton in defensive technologies for both soldiers and civilians, for example in the design and development of more efficient respirators.[70] The Anti-Gas Department introduced the Haldane cotton respirator, a black cloth soaked in a solution of sodium thiosulphate, washing soda, and glycerine.[71] The respirator was sufficient for low concentrations of chlorine, but provided little protection against other toxic substances. Further studies improved the efficiency of respirators, among them the 'H [hypo] helmet' from 1915, a flannel bag impregnated with a hypo solution and a small, rectangular window, the 'PH helmet' from 1916, a helmet impregnated with a solution containing both sodium phenate and hexamine to protect soldiers from phosgene poisoning, and the 'small box' respirator from June 1916, which protected soldiers against airborne toxic particles. Over 13 million small box respirators and some 14 million PH helmets were distributed during the war.[72] In 1917, the Anti-Gas Department of the Royal Army Medical College was transferred to Porton to evaluate 'British and foreign respirators in the field under realistic conditions, especially the vulnerability of the German respirator to British gases'.[73] Research conducted under the leadership of Captain H. Hartley, a senior figure in Britain's chemical warfare programme, strengthened the role of physiology in better understanding the effects of toxic agents on humans, knowledge that was central in advancing Allied protective and therapeutic measures.

Realizing that Allied respirators offered improved protection against certain gases, chlorine and phosgene especially, German scientists developed ever more lethal and incapacitating agents that attacked the body from the outside. Dichlorethyl sulphide, or mustard gas as it became known in Britain because of its distinct garlicky, mustard-like smell, attacked the skin, causing severe burns and blisters within a couple of hours.[74] If inhaled, mustard gas could cause serious inflammation of the lungs, followed by a slow and painful death from asphyxiation. In Germany, the agent was called 'Lost' in recognition of the two scientists (Lommel and Steinkopf) who synthesized it, and in France it was called 'Ypérite' in reference to Germany's first mustard gas attack in July 1917, when the military employed the agent to deadly effect in the area around, yet again, the heavily embattled Ypres. The onset of symptoms was delayed, and thousands of soldiers were unaware of having been exposed to a toxic agent, yet developed severe blisters on their hands and neck, and in armpits, groin, and buttocks. The blisters often became infected, leaving soldiers totally incapacitated and in need of medical treatment. Impregnated leather gloves and suits drenched in linseed oil provided some degree of protection, yet these could be worn only temporarily. British scientists quickly came to realize that the complex scientific problems linked to mustard gas, and the means to protect the human skin from it, needed to be studied in great detail after the end of hostilities. As the 'King' or 'Queen' of war gases,[75] contaminating Allied troops and their equipment for prolonged periods of time, mustard gas stood at the forefront of Porton's research until the end of the Second World War.

Servants of the Realm

The generation of civilian scientists and service officers associated with Porton during the Great War had grown up in Victorian and Edwardian Britain, came from middle-class or more modest social backgrounds, studied at elite universities such as Cambridge, Oxford, or University College London, and occasionally married into the British establishment. Porton's origin as a defence establishment during the Great War was intricately connected with a generation of male researchers who were driven by a deep-seated desire for advancement and social prestige, an emerging 'intellectual aristocracy' with strong social and professional bonds, determined to unlock the secrets of the world through science and experiment and thus realize their visionary ideas of modern society (see Image 3).[76] Those who believed in the power of science were men such as Lieutenant Colonel Charles Lovatt Evans (1884–1968) who, according to a friend, 'possessed the great qualities of some of the most zealous and distinguished of the Victorians, who accomplished their life's work by an immense capacity for hard work and a burning zeal for achievement'.[77] Born in 1884 into a Birmingham family of modest means, Lovatt Evans got interested in physiology, physiological chemistry, and histology as a student at the Municipal Technical School. Given that his father, a music teacher, had 'somewhat rigid views on religion, life and death', and his mother an 'aloof nature', he seems to have had a rather lonely childhood in which he had to earn his chemistry set through good performance in school. Despite the lack of emotional support, or perhaps because of it, he later adopted his father's deeply held belief that 'the more you do for people the less they do for themselves', a reflection of the Victorian idea of individual responsibility, which was coupled with an implicit criticism of emerging welfare measures for the poor and needy.[78] At the age of thirteen, he knew that he wanted to pursue a scientific career, in chemistry if possible, for he was mesmerized by the 'wizardry' of chemistry experiments. He was likewise fascinated by new forms of transport that altered beyond recognition the urban landscape and the experience of travel: motor cars, steamships, and steam trains. Steam trams, in particular, caught his imagination and influenced his life-long interest in gas clouds and toxic substances.[79] In 1910, Lovatt Evans took up a position in the department of physiology at University College London. As Starling's protégé, and at the forefront of research, he quickly advanced and established professional networks in Britain and Europe.[80] During the war, both Starling and Lovatt Evans, like their US colleagues, ran gas schools (in which servicemen and military staff received chemical warfare training) and conducted research on offensive chemical agents as part of their military assignments.[81] They recommended mustard gas, but it was turned down

Image 3. Servants of the realm

Source: IWM. © Imperial War Museums (HU 102408).

Annual Cricket Match between Porton staff and the Chairmen of the various subcommittees serving the Chemical Warfare Committee, *c.* 1929. The besuited gentleman in the middle of the front row is the physiologist Joseph Barcroft.

by the Army as an offensive weapon. Starling's team was furious when the Germans employed it in 1917. Quickly rising through the ranks, Major Lovatt Evans was transferred to Aldershot Command Headquarters from where he organized field trials at Porton, thereby witnessing one of the few visits to the establishment by British royalty.[82]

In the mid 1920s, Lovatt Evans returned to University College London to succeed Archibald Vivian Hill, who himself had succeeded Starling as Jodrell Professor of Physiology. Lovatt Evans now found himself in charge of a department that provided office space and laboratories for the two strong-minded men who had been his most important mentors, a situation which required considerable diplomatic skill. It was this closely knit network of experimental scientists in the field of physiology, chemistry, and related disciplines, together with his first-hand knowledge of chemical warfare, to be gained during a lifetime of research, that placed Lovatt Evans centre stage as a power broker and mediator between Britain's military authorities, including those stationed at Porton, and gave him ready access to some of the leading research scientists of the day for almost half a century, from the mid 1910s to the mid 1960s, when he retired.

At Porton, Lovatt Evans' colleagues included the Cambridge physiologist Joseph Barcroft. Born in 1872 into a Quaker family from Northern Ireland, Barcroft had been educated at the Friends' School at Bootham, York, and then at the Leys School in Cambridge, where he met many of his future colleagues including Henry Dale, later President of the Royal Society, and John Clapham, later President of the British Academy. Studying at King's College Cambridge introduced him to the academic elite of the day, working alongside men such as Ernest Rutherford, who was among the first to split the atom. His colleague and subsequent competitor was John S. Haldane's son, J.B.S. Haldane, at the time a biochemist at Cambridge, with whom he worked on different methods of blood-gas analysis, and whose theories about the effects of high altitude on human blood he later refuted.[83] On the eve of the First World War, following his marriage to Mary Agnetta Ball, daughter of Sir Robert Ball, a famous astronomer and Professorial Fellow at King's College, and after publishing his acclaimed book on *The Respiratory Function of the Blood*, Barcroft had become a highly respected and influential member of the scientific elite with close links to the British establishment.

Despite his Quaker upbringing, Barcroft felt the need to contribute to the war effort after Germany's premeditated gas attack. Colleagues portray him as a religious man who applied the lessons of the New Testament to his own expert field, from the theory of hormones to the correct 'spirit which should exist in a physiological laboratory'. Family recollections suggest that his mind was apparently 'haunted by the parable of the Good Samaritan' in deciding whether he should get involved in chemical warfare research.[84] Later, he is said to have remarked: 'In war I find it very hard to reconcile my instincts as an Irishman with my convictions as a Quaker.'[85] Whether a man like Barcroft really had to battle with his conscience, and if so, for how long, is difficult to say in retrospect, though we do know that he accepted the appointment as Porton's chief physiologist to study the 'medical aspects of gas poisoning'. However, he agreed to serve only as civilian scientist. As someone who wore a bowler hat during front-line inspection tours, Barcroft believed that his civilian status allowed him to 'tell generals and other military bigwigs exactly what he thought of them'.[86]

In January 1917, prompted by the devastating effects of Germany's mustard gas attack, Porton established a permanent laboratory for physiological tests on humans at nearby Boscombe Down Farm.[87] The department seems to have been limited at first to a single hut, measuring 30 feet by 15 feet, which was converted into an office and physiological laboratory. To ensure close liaison with the Royal Army Medical Corps (RAMC), medical officers were attached to Porton, among them Barcroft's assistant, Captain Rudolph Peters, known as 'Bunny', who had witnessed gas casualties in France.[88] Conditions were austere, to say the least, with Peters not only living in the hut but taking his bath in a round tin on the floor of the post-mortem room where the animals were dissected.[89] Other accounts mention a better-equipped outfit: an old brick building, laboratories, offices, and even a gas chamber for various animal experiments.[90] Whether staff deliberately played down the existing working conditions to highlight their scientific achievements is difficult to tell in retrospect, yet what seems to be certain is that facilities were relatively simple, even by the standards of the day. Under Barcroft's leadership, and in collaboration with British universities, for example with Cambridge's Chemistry Department, itself engaged in the preparation of toxic agents under the leadership of Sir William Jackson Pope (1870–1939), these men set out to investigate the effects of chlorine, phosgene, adamsite (DM), an arsenical irritant, and mustard gas in experimental gas chambers and to analyse the results in improvised laboratories.[91]

One person who joined Barcroft's team of physiologists—teasingly
described by Porton's members of staff as 'the b[loody] body snatchers'—
was the subsequent Inspector General John Murray. Working under
A.E. Boycott who, as a committed pacifist, saw the war as the 'greatest man-
ifestation of Anglo-German folly', yet who also wanted to do his utmost to
secure an Allied victory, Murray engaged in animal and human experiments
as a way of charting the 'relative killing power' of toxic substances. Here, in
the confines of ramshackle farm buildings, British scientists studied microscopic slides of the lungs of gassed animal and collaborated with fine artists
in the construction of coloured representations of organs damaged by warfare agents. The aim was to understand and visualize the incapacitating
effects of these agents on the principal organs of the body. So-called 'working tea breaks' in the afternoon, introduced by Barcroft, helped to establish
a collegiate environment that was conducive to the sharing of ideas and
technical expertise, often in the presence of Allied chemical scientists from
the United States and France.

The Allied failure to anticipate, and appropriately appreciate, the blistering potential of mustard gas had placed scientists on notice not to 'miss an
obvious trick' in the race for the most deadly weapon of war. Research had
at first concentrated on assessing toxic agents for their ability to kill within
forty-eight hours, though experts soon discovered the 'casualty producing
effects' of certain gases. Chemical warfare, they realized, was not so much
about killing people but about incapacitating them for the duration of combat activity. Toxicity trials had revealed that the length of exposure to certain
substances, and their concentration, were key in determining the degree to
which agents were harmless or dangerous. By the end of the war, Barcroft's
team had examined the toxicity and the possible remedies for 160 substances, including mustard gas and lewisite, which became known among
Allied propagandists as the 'dew of death', a description which overempha-
sized its actual killing potential.[92] Among the more unusual weapons tests
was the idea of blowing powdered glass into the faces of different animals
or the use of concentrated cayenne pepper as an alternative to toxic gas.[93]
Phosgene and mustard gas, on the other hand, were treated with the 'greatest respect'. Sometimes unintended accidents had to substitute for planned
experiments, for example when a group of 'Indo-Chinese labourers' was
accidentally exposed to a drifting cloud of arsenical smoke near the French
Gas Experimental Station at Entresen near Arles in the Bouches du Rhône.

For Porton, the 'tearful lamentations in Chinese' were sufficient proof that the gas was doing what it was supposed to do.

Porton also developed curative measures and treatment guidelines for front-line medical officers who, at times, resented the sudden interference of civilian scientists in their field of expertise. Disagreements over different treatments surfaced as early as 1915, when leading British physiologists warned the authorities about the risks of oxygen deprivation in gas casualties. Treatment, they argued, required the administration of oxygen in order to keep men alive until the body had partially recovered, yet in spite of this recommendation it took several years for oxygen therapy to become widely accepted practice.[94] In collaboration with the RAMC, Porton also established standardized methods of assessing the degree of incapacity of servicemen who had been exposed to toxic agents, tests which later determined their eligibility for pensions.[95]

In a much publicized and subsequently embellished self-experiment to refute the idea that one could use animals as a reliable measure to assess the effects of chemical agents on man, Barcroft locked himself with a dog into a chamber containing hydrocyanic acid gas to demonstrate that the sensitivity to poisonous agents varied among different species. Neither of them wore respirators. Whereas the dog was unconscious after ninety seconds, but then recovered, Barcroft left the chamber almost unaffected.[96] The experiment demonstrated in rather stark fashion not only that humans and different species of animals reacted differently to chemical agents, but that there were likely to be significant variations in sensitivity to toxic gases among humans as well. In general, researchers do not seem to have spent much time worrying about or assessing the levels of risk involved in their work; theirs was a rather casual, at times careless approach. Most believed that there 'was no real risk of suffering serious damage unless you did something silly and allowed familiarity to breed contempt of the poisons we handled'.[97]

Although Porton encountered difficulties in retaining some of the civilian scientists after the war, with men such as Barcroft, Lovatt Evans, and Starling returning to their university positions, often as FRS, almost all of them continued to conduct research which was informed by their work on chemical warfare.[98] In the interwar period, and thereafter, the 'Old Portonians' formed a closely knit group of experimental scientists who continued to have close links to the British defence community at Porton

Down.[99] This was the generation of military men and civilian researchers for whom the experience of the Great War, and of tens of thousands of gassed soldiers, marked a watershed in their determination to prepare the country for a future war, protect the army and civilians from the anticipated fallout, and supply the military with the means and methods to retaliate. On the eve of the Second World War, many of those who had fought in the previous war were ready to recommence research on chemical warfare to protect the United Kingdom and her allies.

Images of Gas Warfare

During the war, Allied strategists had exploited the imagery of gas war as a powerful propaganda weapon by levelling accusations of war crimes at the German military, which subsequently affected postwar peace negotiations. Visual depictions of chemical warfare also played an important role in a thriving postwar artistic culture that was highly critical of war as a means of conflict resolution.[100] Gas shells made up only a small percentage of the overall ordnance which had been used, yet had caused an estimated 5.7 per cent of non-life-threatening injuries and 1.32 per cent of deaths on the battlefield. These statistics were cited by supporters of chemical warfare as evidence of a more humane form of weaponry, yet the images of gas warfare played a disproportionate role in the artistic representations of the horrors of war, and this left a lasting legacy in the popular conscience of the world. Modern warfare became synonymous with gas warfare, its images an iconographic shorthand for a detached, humiliating, and dishonourable death, and the gas mask a modern symbol of *memento mori*, a reminder of man's own mortality.[101]

Writers and poets such as Wilfred Owen and Siegfried Sassoon, in an attempt to reflect upon and come to terms with nervous breakdowns and traumatic experiences in an 'undisguisedly mechanical and inhuman' conflict, and give artistic expression to the suffering of millions, immersed themselves in the subject of modern warfare. Owen's famous war poem *Dulce et Decorum Est* (1917) portrayed the existential fears of a man choking helplessly to death, as if drowning in a green sea, and thus challenged cultural constructions of beauty and honour in war, and artists such as John Singer Sargent produced lasting representations of blinded and exhausted soldiers in his painting *Gassed* (1918).[102] Far from depicting war as just and honourable, revitalizing the biological make-up of human society in a gigantic, cataclysmic, and cathartic process, artists and pacifists attacked war for its inherent inhumanity and immorality. Remarque's bestselling novel *Im Westen Nichts Neues*, which was translated into English in 1929 as *All Quiet on the Western Front*, provided postwar readers with a realistic, though deeply depressing account of the suffering of gas casualties.[103] Whether gas was seen to turn wars into 'a nightmare' affecting Allied and Axis soldiers in equal measure, or as an emotive vehicle to influence international public opinion on chemical and biological weapons, one of the themes running through almost all artistic genres was the primeval fear of asphyxiation.

In Weimar Germany, expressionist artists such as Otto Dix and George Grosz, also known as 'proletarian realists' or Verists, whose provocative and often satirical form of realism was aimed at exposing the ugliness of war and postwar society, gave fresh impetus to a wave of artistic productivity in the *Neue Sachlichkeit* (new objectivity) school, which came to have a major influence on pictorial art, literature, music, photography, film, and modern architecture.[104] In 1924, lamenting rather than commemorating the tenth anniversary of the outbreak of war, Karl Nierendorf published a series of fifty of Otto Dix's etchings, entitled *Der Krieg* (The War), in which the artists portrayed a 'harrowing panorama' of war, 'the trenches of the Western Front, the corpses, the wounded, the fatigue, the brothels in Belgium, aerial bombardment, civilian victims, destroyed cities', a brutal, bloodthirsty slaughter-house of modernity in which science and technology, far from fostering prosperity and happiness, had become the engines driving humanity into the abyss (see Image 4).[105] The detailed titles of poignant images such as *Gastote: Templeux-la-Fosse, August 1916* (*Gas Victims: Templeux-la-Fosse, August 1916*) or *Leiche im Drahtverhau, Flandern* (*Corpse in Barbed Wire, Flanders*) emphasized that Dix had witnessed these disturbing events.[106] Inspired by Henri Barbusse's socialist anti-war novel *Le feu* (*Under Fire*, 1916), his etchings made compelling reference to *The Disasters of War*, Francisco de Goya's eye-witness depiction of the atrocities of the Peninsular War.[107] Rather than offering an artistic commentary on or explanation of modern warfare, Dix and many other artists depicted 'states of affairs', the ugly consequences of war, an 'apocalyptic hell of reality'.[108] Images of gas warfare, whether in poems, songs, novels, drawings, or cartoons, or in any other form of popular representation, turned into a powerful indictment of the inherent criminality, immorality, and meaninglessness of modern wars. In such a politically charged, pacifist atmosphere, in which the presence of war-wounded on the

Image 4. The image of gas warfare

Source: Otto Dix, *Sturmtruppe geht unter Gas vor* (Shock Troops Advance under Gas) from *Der Krieg* (The War) (1924). © 2011 MoMA/Scala/DACS.

The entire caption of the image is as follows: Dix, Otto (1891–1969), *Sturmtruppe geht unter Gas vor* (Shock Troops Advance under Gas) from *Der Krieg* (The War) (1924). New York, Museum of Modern Art (MoMA). Etching, aquatint, and drypoint from a portfolio of fifty etchings, aquatints, and drypoints, plate: 7 5/8 × 11 5/16″ (19.3 × 28.8 cm); sheet: 13 11/16 × 18 5/8″ (34.8 x 47.3 cm). Publisher: Karl Nierendorf, Berlin. Printer: Otto Felsing, Berlin. Edition: 70. Gift of Abby Aldrich Rockefeller. Acc. no.: 159.1934.12. © 2011 MoMA, New York/Scala, Florence/DACS, London.

streets of Europe was a constant reminder of human suffering and war-time casualties, the British government was forced to tread a careful line between deterrence and disarmament, sanctioning—largely in secret—the development of the nation's chemical warfare capability to protect the security of the Empire, and, at the same time, publicly supporting coordinated attempts by the League of Nations to outlaw those same weapons once and for all.[109]

Crisis of Legitimacy

Following the Armistice in November 1918, the victorious powers envis-aged the creation of a demilitarized and largely peaceful world, free from violence and weapons of mass destruction. Undermined by feelings of revenge and demands for reparations, their vision got off to a difficult start. Under the Versailles Treaty, notorious for its humiliating terms, the Allies not only annexed territory, disarmed the German army, and extracted material resources from a traumatized, politically divided society that was barely coming to terms with military defeat, but forced the government to admit sole responsibility for the war.[110] To destroy any future chemical warfare capability, Germany was strictly prohibited, under Article 171, from using, producing, or importing chemical agents, including 'asphyxiating, poisonous or other gases and all analogous liquids'.[111]

Although far from homogenous, public opinion became a powerful force in shaping the international community's protracted disarmament negotiations.[112] In 1918, representatives of the British medical profession called for a ban on chemical warfare in *The Times*, describing it as an 'unclean', uncontrollable, and malignant weapon of war which ought to be abolished.[113] Elsewhere, doctors and nurses employed by the armed forces protested against their involvement in this type of warfare. Some have argued that the interwar debate simply resulted from a 'clash' between the wartime practicalities of using chemical weapons and the experienced or perceived horrors among 'victims and observers alike', but this overlooks quite specific economic, political, and scientific factors as well as cultural traditions that shaped the discourse at a national level.[114] In the United States, where the chemical industries, like their British counterparts, launched a major publicity offensive, chemical warfare became a matter of domestic politics. Chemical warfare meant big business at a time of great economic uncertainty and guaranteed the employment of thousands of officers lecturing in US chemical warfare (CW) training facilities.[115] In a bid to improve chemical warfare preparedness and secure the postwar continuity of the Chemical Warfare Service (CWS), founded in mid 1918, stakeholders and major suppliers from the building, mining, and engineering trades, who advocated a more isolationist policy, became involved in a campaign to frustrate international disarmament negotiations. The proposed abolition of the CWS, in particular, threatened the existence of small, specialized companies supplying the US chemical warfare industry, which needed to adjust to peacetime conditions, for example through the sale of tear gas to law enforcement agencies. While Edgewood Arsenal highlighted the 'relative humaneness' of toxic agents compared to high explosives in specially designed publications, engineering firms promoted their latest air-tight steel tanks. Elsewhere, the producers of metal ores advertised their ability to deliver 'gas by the ton'.[116]

Yet the campaign also fuelled public anxieties against possible airborne attacks with toxic agents, and strengthened the resolve of organizations such as the British Association for the Advancement of Science and the International Committee of the Red Cross (ICRC) to protest against the use of poison gas in 1918 and call for an absolute ban on chemical warfare.[117] Having been criticized by the belligerents for abandoning its principle of impartiality, the ICRC subsequently took a more 'neutral' position and 'waged war on gas warfare' by campaigning for the improvement of defensive capabilities in the late 1920s in order to make the use of chemical warfare agents unworkable; there was even an ICRC-funded prize for innovative developments in the field of chemical defence. Anti-militarist groups and pacifists, however, became increasingly hostile towards the ICRC for viewing chemical weapons as an inevitable reality of future wars. In the aftermath of the Second World War, and in light of the Holocaust, the ICRC's stated policy of impartiality and non-interference became the subject of heated controversy, which has continued ever since.

Another major organization involved in shaping public opinion on the subject of chemical and biological warfare was the League of Nations. In the 1920s, it played a leading role in negotiating international agreements for the limitation and reduction of chemical weapons, and in prohibiting their use in future wars. Founded in 1920, the League of Nations was firmly committed to comprehensive disarmament, weapons control, and conflict resolution through international cooperation. Yet political setbacks during the League's formative years placed the United States in a powerful negotiating position. Held in Washington DC from November 1921 to February 1922, and attended by the Principal Allied and Associated Powers (United States, Britain, France, Italy, and Japan), as well as Belgium, China, The Netherlands, and Portugal, the Conference on the Limitation of Armament, organized by the United States to establish a new security framework in the Pacific area, sought, inter alia, a legally binding resolution for the prohibition of chemical weapons. During the negotiations, because of behind-the-scenes tensions between experts and politicians about the real and imagined power of chemical agents and the ability to control them, careful management was required to preserve a united front.[118] Article 5 of the Washington Agreement prohibited the 'use in war of asphyxiating, poisonous or other gases, and all analogous liquids, or materials, of devices', such use having been 'justly condemned by the general opinion of the civilized world'.[119] Despite reservations by Britain and France, which prevented the resolution from coming into force, the Washington Agreement marked an important milestone that galvanized public opinion and political power to work towards an international chemical weapons ban.[120]

Clearly affected by the international climate, Porton Down suffered a crisis of legitimacy after it transpired that Britain's chemical warfare programme no longer enjoyed unconditional political and public support.[121] At first, almost all research activities ceased. Parliamentary questions were now being raised about Porton's annual cost to the taxpayer.[122] Reflecting public concerns about a substantially weakened economy, the MP Hugh Morrison queried in 1920 whether the government would not be well advised to 'have it [Porton] closed down'. In his cautious reply, which avoided revealing that the total cost of the establishment had been around £90,000 in 1919–1920,[123] Winston Churchill told the House of Commons that the government aimed to keep the experimental facility open 'until the attitude of the League of Nations to chemical warfare is defined'.[124] In March 1922, prompted by the Washington Agreement, the government came under renewed pressure, but insisted that it 'would be failing in its duty if it failed to take all possible steps which might be necessary to protect the Forces of the Crown and the inhabitants of the country against gas attacks in time of war'.[125]

Unbeknown to the public, the Cabinet had accepted the recommendations of the Holland Committee in May 1920 to expedite chemical warfare research and reorganize Porton Down. Made up of experienced military and civilian experts, the committee had concluded that the 'safety of the Empire' could not be left to chance: 'A nation which is unprepared for gas warfare lays itself open to sudden and irretrievable disaster.'[126] Separating defensive from offensive research was seen to be impossible, because one could not be understood without the other. Recommended changes to the organization involved a reconstituted Chemical Warfare Committee, the attachment of experts to the Director of Military Intelligence, the consolidation of 'research, design and supply' under the control of the MoS, and improved liaison and 'intelligent cooperation' between Porton's scientists and the armed services, a subject which had caused some considerable controversy during the war.[127] It was recommended that Porton's staff should, in future, be composed 'partly of soldiers and partly of men of science', the latter to be of 'high standing' and 'independent of outside inspection and criticism'.[128] To attract scientists of the highest calibre, and because staff sacrificed parts of their careers and occasionally risked their own health in the

pursuit of knowledge, the authorities were asked to offer substantial inducements in the form of salaries, security of tenure, pensions, and the right to
publish.[129] Largely oblivious to stringent cuts to the military budget during
a period of economic austerity, the committee weighed Porton's 'considerable' running costs on the basis of national security considerations. It also
believed that Porton's discoveries were likely to have scientific and commercial value which would transform the organization into a 'very valuable
national asset'.

Porton's primary purpose remained serving the strategic needs of the
armed forces: 'Care must be taken to ensure that Porton does not become a
place apart from the military hierarchy but is looked upon as a stream which
supplies the military irrigation channels which fertilise the whole Army.'[130]
At the same time military interference with Porton's activities needed to be
kept to a minimum, provided the General Staff could 'indicate the general
lines' which appeared to be the most promising. The tension between the
ability to conduct independent research work, free from external political or
military pressures, and the practical demands by the military to defend the
country against potential chemical warfare attacks, together with the need
for a credible retaliatory capability, have characterized Porton ever since.

Close liaison between Porton's scientists and expert networks elsewhere
in Britain and overseas, essential in maintaining a first-class research facility,
was to be assured through the Chemical Warfare Committee, which was
broadly representative of the wider scientific, military, and business community.[131] To ensure the coordinated production of toxic agents, including
those for testing purposes at Porton, the committee recommended the creation of a state-controlled factory for chemical warfare products at Sutton
Oak, near St Helens in Lancashire, which later became the Chemical
Defence Research Establishment.[132] A representative of Porton liaised with
members of the committee about planned field trials. It was this coordinated approach to chemical warfare through an external body of experts
and stakeholders that other nations, the United States and Canada especially,
began to emulate.

Animal Experimentation

In order to discover new chemical warfare agents and means of treatment,
much of Porton's research involved the systematic testing of chemical

compounds and their toxicity on animals and humans, which increased public and political pressure to justify Britain's chemical warfare activities.[133] Although the prewar antivivisectionist movement had raised considerable public awareness of animal research, tests with animals, many of them lethal, were seen as vitally important to Porton's experimental programme.[134] A few miles west of the establishment, near the village of Newton Toney, and under military command, Arundel Farm, and later Allington Farm, began holding and breeding experimental animals for pharmacological and toxicological research (see Images 5 and 6).[135] The 1920s saw continued attempts by antivivisectionist groups to close Porton Down or, failing that, slow down any further expansion. Fenced off, and largely removed from public scrutiny, Porton's animal programme became the focus of considerable political debate during the interwar period.

In May 1923, Lieutenant Colonel Walter Guinness, the Under-Secretary of State for War, told Parliament that Porton had used 66 cats, 48 goats, 118 guinea pigs, 148 mice, 23 monkeys, 139 rabbits, and 209 rats in 'gas poisoning experiments' since February 1922. Attempting to dispel public concerns about animal cruelty, Guinness remarked: 'None of the experiments had consisted in dropping bombs containing poisoned gas among these animals.

Image 5. Arlington Farm cat house
Source: IWM, Photographic Collection, Arlington Farm Cat House, 28 May 1959. © Imperial War Museums (F 725/1-6).

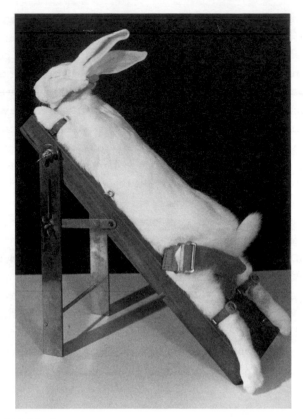

Image 6. Rabbit block
Source: IWM, Photographic Collection, Rabbit Block, no date. © Imperial War Museums (L 1943).

They were always under an anaesthetic if it was in any way possible, and they were destroyed as soon as the objects of the experiment had been attained.'[136] Two years later, Parliament was told that Porton had conducted a total of 1,001 animal experiments in 1924, the highest number of animal tests performed in any one year throughout the interwar period.[137] From 1924 onwards, as a result of savings requirements in the national economy, an ongoing antivivisectionist campaign, and the Geneva Protocol of 1925 banning the use of chemical warfare, the number of animal experiments steadily declined to an average of about 430 tests per year.

In conducting animal research, scientists began avoiding tests with animals which could harm Porton's reputation because they enjoyed the protection of the law. The Cruelty to Animals Act of 1876 limited animal experiments to those 'useful for saving or prolonging human life or alleviating human suffering', and prohibited painful experiments on dogs, cats, and horses unless there was an overriding rationale.[138] For most of the time, experiments with dogs were off-limits at Porton, although some tests with dogs were performed over the years.[139] Despite public concerns, experiments with horses were occasionally carried out, but the animals were generally not killed.[140] After the death of seventeen horses in 1925/1926, the government felt compelled to justify Porton's action on the grounds that the animals had suffered from 'some incurable disability'.[141] Five years later, it had to respond to claims by the press that Porton had experimented on 2,000 old horses, although only 25 horses had been used between 1921 and 1930.[142] For journalists and newspaper editors willing to exploit the secrecy surrounding Porton's work, experiments on animals fuelled the public imagination about state-sponsored military research. By the mid 1920s, Porton's research programme had transformed into an almost never-ending news story which would run for almost a century.[143]

Between 1921 and 1937, Porton carried out a total of 7,777 experiments on animals of which 5,374 were killed, either by the experiment or because they were subsequently destroyed (see Figure 1). Compared to over 450,000 experiments performed on animals in Britain in 1930 alone,[144] Porton's animal programme was relatively small-scale, yet it attracted all the more

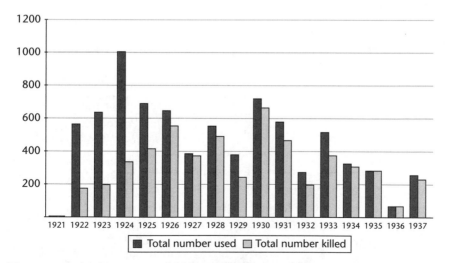

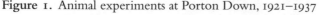

Figure 1. Animal experiments at Porton Down, 1921–1937

Source: Data compiled from Hansard, HC Debate, vol. 237 c633–5W, Chemical Warfare (Experiments on Animals), 27 March 1930; vol. 303 cc171–3, Chemical Defence Experiments, 18 June 1935; vol. 342 cc50–1W, Chemical Warfare (Experiments on Animals), 28 November 1938.

attention for its association with secret chemical warfare research. Animal
tests were generally performed on rabbits, guinea pigs, mice, and rats.[145]
Alarmed by poison gas tests, animal rights groups alleged that Porton's
research contravened the Cruelty to Animals Act, prompting one Member
of Parliament to question 'whether the use of animals in these researches
can now be dispensed with?'[146] Under pressure to justify Porton's work, the
government insisted that the tests were 'essential' in developing Britain's
defensive capability.[147] In July 1930, Thomas Shaw (1872–1938), the Secretary
of State for War and a Labour politician, stressed the value of animal research
in understanding the effects of poison gas on human beings, knowledge
which had apparently alleviated 'human suffering during the Great War'.[148]
Less than a year later, with little evidence of Porton's negative image showing any signs of improvement, Shaw attempted to reassure Parliament by
stating that 'the stories of torture [at Porton]...are quite unfounded'.[149]

Human Experimentation

Human tests involved the recording of the effects of chemical agents on the
military performance of soldiers and the testing of different types of respirators. Humans, as Carter points out, were meant to 'act as the ultimate
sensor and recorder of the effects on man', which is why the military may
have used the term 'human observer' in their description of test subjects.[150]
The term is somewhat misleading, however, given that it would have
implied an active role on the part of the subjects in the tests—as, for example, in the observation of the effects of gas on other species—yet this was
rarely the case. In general, the test subjects were the objects of the experiments, their role defined by physiological reactions in the body which
others, the medical scientists, could observe, such as changes in the colour
of the skin or the size of the pupils, or indeed the presence and severity of
certain types of physical injuries, for example blisters caused by mustard gas.
Test subjects would report the effects of certain substances on their health,
performance, and psychological well-being, but they would not observe
these in the strict sense of the term, nor would they record them; the actual
observation of the effects caused by different substances was left to the
investigators. For nineteenth-century physicians, such as the neurologist
Jean-Martin Charcot, to be seen as 'an observer, a man who knows how
to see', was a mark of professional expertise.[151] For the military authorities,

though, the term offered a convenient euphemism to refer to, as well as play down non-therapeutic research on, human subjects throughout the twentieth century.

Experiments with humans always carried the risk of injury, both physical and mental, short- and long-term discomfort, disability, or even death, something that was acknowledged by the authorities and known by the scientists who, for a variety of reasons, frequently participated in the tests themselves. 'Much of the work done here was of an unpleasant nature and some of it was dangerous', Foulkes later recalled, 'but volunteers were always to be found who exposed themselves fearlessly in the chamber tests'.[152] Another service officer stressed the contribution which 'human guinea pigs' had made to the advancement of knowledge, but also highlighted the 'pain and discomfort they suffered on many occasions'.[153] On one occasion, members of staff, their eyes completely unprotected, took part in an experiment to assess the 'neutralizing effect and persistency of two agents having acute lachrymatory properties'.[154] When tests with mustard gas revealed that the skin of volunteers became more sensitive once it had been exposed to the agent, Porton decided to use 'virgin skin' instead, as Foulkes liked to call newly appointed staff, to ensure that accurate information was obtained.[155] The issue of 'acquired sensitivity to mustard gas' continued to inform physiological research at Porton after experiments had shown that succeeding exposures to mustard gas led to increased levels of sensitivity.[156]

In the early 1920s, Porton introduced standardized procedures for the recruiting of volunteers from all three service arms, and for conducting poison gas tests on service officers and civilian personnel, a policy which was broadly endorsed by the General Staff without ever being formally authorized. Despite animal tests, researchers campaigned for a sustained experimental programme with human subjects, particularly with blistering agents such as mustard gas:

> Our knowledge is scanty as to its physiological action, means of protection against it and curative measure; and yet this gas proved in the late war to be intensely productive of casualties. In each of these directions intelligent use of human observers appears to be simply unavoidable, if progress is to be made.[157]

Around 1922, the Chemical Warfare Committee applied to the Army Council for permission to allow service personnel stationed at Porton to volunteer for 'special tests' involving deliberate exposure to toxic substances. Pending a full report detailing the nature and safety precautions in place for such tests, the Army Council at first declined permission and suspended all experiments.[158] In an attempt to lift the ban, Porton's commandant, Colonel S.W.H. Rawlins, produced a detailed memorandum in which he stressed that 'only volunteers' would be accepted in experimental trials. Since tests were largely confined to the 'officer and civil scientist ranks', who were permitted to take part in gas tests only once a month, the number of available subjects had steadily declined.[159] Officials were assured that experiments with servicemen would be done 'under the most careful supervision and with every conceivable precaution to prevent the health of the individual concerned being impaired'.[160] As a way of addressing contentious medical ethics and legal liability issues, he told the Army Council that all subjects would be made 'acquainted with the possibility of risk' before undergoing any of the tests, and would receive 'generous compensation' in case of accident or lasting disability. An abundance of recreational facilities would also enhance the 'power of resistance' against the effects of toxic agents. In general, life at the experimental station was to be rendered 'as healthy as possible' for servicemen. Conversely, a prolonged continuation of the ban, he warned ominously, could have serious consequences for Britain's gas defences. Looking into the future, Rawlins compared the history of chemical warfare agents with the production of high explosives—by companies such as Dupont in the United States, for instance—which in the past had been accompanied by 'serious and well-known risks', arguing that it was reasonable to assume that the 'risks from exposure to gas will also gradually be reduced as experience is gained', a gross miscalculation on the part of Porton's leadership, if nothing else.[161]

Rawlins' memorandum might be seen as a cynical attempt to gain government approval for chemical warfare experiments on humans without regard to long-term health and safety standards, yet such a retrospective reading would overlook the limitations at the time on accuracy in predicting developments in chemical science and modern warfare. To effectively adapt to such changes, institutions need to be prepared to constantly review and update their existing health and safety procedures, something Porton had felt no need to do for a long time. Germany's subsequent discovery of nerve agents prior to the Second World War, however, would make the work with toxic agents at Porton a great deal more dangerous than Rawlins and his contemporaries could reasonably have anticipated. The safety precautions put in place appear to have been appropriate for the level of risk faced by the servicemen in the 1920s, yet the more the toxicity of the compounds increased the more Porton's procedures became outdated. One of the most significant shortcomings in the history of Porton's 'human volunteer' programme, it would appear, was its inability to adapt to changes in the level of risk in the environment in which experiments with toxic agents were performed. In their reluctance to continuously update existing health and safety protocols, Porton, and the relevant government officials, exhibited a considerable degree of complacency until the mid 1950s.

In 1924, in an attempt to induce servicemen to volunteer, and compensate them for the 'dangerous and unpleasant nature of the work', the Treasury authorized additional 'money benefits' in return for tests with toxic agents. According to officials tasked with assessing the programme in the 1950s, by granting financial compensation for the tests the government had 'tacitly approved' the programme.[162] Permission was also given to use Porton's civilian laboratory assistants for experiments, yet this decision raised complex issues of legal liability. Who would fund medical treatment and compensation claims, if civilian staff suffered personal injuries as a result of their employment? After a lengthy debate it was decided that the activity of civilian staff who volunteered for experiments was considered to be outside their employment, and thus excluded from the Workmen's Compensation Act of 1897, and that in such cases the War Office would make an 'ex gratia payment' along the same lines as the Workmen's Compensation Act.[163] That there was a real risk of injury to staff working at Porton became graphically clear when a large-scale trial chamber exploded in the mid 1920s; on this occasion, research staff working next to the chamber had a lucky escape.[164]

In the mid 1920s, the recruitment of volunteers was first extended to the Southern Command, then to all Army Commands and, in 1929, to servicemen from the Royal Air Force and the Royal Navy.[165] In order to reassure military commanders about the safety of human experiments, the War Office told the Commander-in-Chief, Southern Command, Salisbury, that the 'risk of injury' to servicemen who volunteered for mustard gas trials at Porton was negligible: 'The tests will involve only slight discomfort to the individual, and consist simply in subjecting a small place on the arm to the action of certain chemicals.'[166] A parliamentary debate on 'Poison Gas Experiments' revealed that between January 1929 and December 1930 a total of 520 servicemen had taken part in Porton trials, yet none of the experiments had apparently posed any 'risk to the health of the volunteers'.[167] In case of accident, injury, or death, the War Office was willing to pay compensation from existing funds as 'ordinary regulations' permitted.

The RAF was also told that all experiments were conducted under expert medical supervision to ensure that none of the subjects would be exposed to any 'danger to their health'.[168] Repeated assurances about existing safety standards over the years were designed to maintain vitally important political support for Porton's experimental programme.

In general, the recruitment of experimental subjects worked as follows: Porton would notify the War Office on a regular basis about the number of test subjects needed, and the War Office would communicate these requirements, and the time service personnel would be attached to Porton, to the Army, the Admiralty, and the Air Ministry. The Commands would then transmit the requirements and invitations to volunteer to individual units, where they would be 'formally repeated in station orders'.[169] The information given to military units generally lacked specific details about the proposed tests and was couched in generalized, sometimes even euphemistic language. In the early 1930s, however, concerns were raised, perhaps for the first time, about the information brought to the attention of personnel to encourage them to volunteer. From some of the soldiers arriving at Porton it had become apparent that 'they were not fully aware of the conditions under which service personnel were asked to volunteer'.[170] In January 1931, Porton attempted to reassure the War Office of its experimental procedures by highlighting that 'great care' was taken to ensure that service personnel, especially those from outside units, would 'understand the object of each particular test' and would not get the wrong impression of 'what is being done' to them.[171]

Porton attracted further attention when it was disclosed that the cost of the facility to the taxpayer had more than doubled by the mid 1920s, expenditure which raised concerns during an economic crisis.[172] Following Britain's ratification of the Geneva Protocol, some politicians advocated the closure of Porton Down.[173] In a climate of economic austerity, in which chemical warfare had been publicly condemned by the civilized world, the public focus shifted from concerns for the rights of animals to Porton's 'human volunteer programme'.[174] In 1930, replying to questions about the number of soldiers 'gassed at Porton', Shaw insisted that no soldiers had been 'gassed' in the 'ordinary sense of the word' but admitted that an average of six 'volunteers' per week were undergoing trials to test the efficacy of treatments and the efficiency of respirators.[175] Up until about 1936, Porton's existence was legitimized on the basis that Britain needed a defensive chemical warfare capability.[176]

Britain's chemical warfare programme not only needed to be justified to the servicemen and the general public, but information about it also had to be carefully controlled for reasons of national security. Those living near Porton, some of whom had been forcibly evicted from their homes during the Great War to allow for expansion of the testing ground, generally had little, if any, access to information about ongoing field trials, even when these affected their immediate environment and in some cases their own persons. Anticipating future gas attacks from the air, Porton had, as early as 1923, developed a retaliatory aircraft spraying device, which had 'high casualty producing potential over large areas'.[177] Further trials confirmed the possibility of effectively spraying mustard gas from planes flying at altitudes of up to 10,000 feet. During these trials harmless, coloured chemicals accidentally contaminated parts of the nearby Wiltshire countryside. In one case, a woman living close to Porton found pink spots all over the perambulator carrying her new-born baby. In another, the housewives of military personnel living near Boscombe Down aerodrome, 2 miles from Porton, were furious when one of Porton's field trials stained all their washing. For the local community, the 'Porton camp', as it was known, provided employment and security for many, but it was also viewed with suspicion because of its secretive nature.

On a bilateral level, Britain and the United States joined forces in developing offensive and defensive chemical warfare capabilities that required the sharing of information and resources. In 1918, after the American Expeditionary Force (AEF) sustained disproportionately high numbers of chemical warfare casualties due to an inadequate level of preparedness, the US Army attached liaison officers to Porton to keep abreast of Britain's advances in chemical warfare work, a tradition which continued thereafter.[178] Britain's scientists, on the other hand, developed close links with their counterparts at Edgewood Arsenal, near Baltimore, Maryland, which became the United States' headquarters for chemical warfare research and development.[179] Given the exclusivity of the field, together with the need to preserve the utmost secrecy, research networks which had been established during and after the First World War were central in creating a long-term system of bilateral, and later tripartite, cooperation on chemical warfare between the Allied powers.

Still unresolved questions about the legitimacy of chemical warfare, together with the widespread public and international condemnation of toxic agents as a means of warfare, turned intelligence sharing between

Britain and the United States into a sensitive issue requiring a clear understanding about confidentiality arrangements and levels of secrecy. By assigning the highest security classification to chemical and biological warfare matters, and by avoiding the publication of details which could inform other countries about the nature and extent of the work undertaken, Britain attempted to ensure that its expanding chemical warfare programme would not become public knowledge.[180] In July 1924, Earl James Atkisson, Assistant Military Attaché at the US Embassy in London, a former commander of Edgewood Arsenal who was well connected to the chemical warfare field on both sides of the Atlantic, told Major General Amos Fries, chief of the CWS, in confidence that the British authorities were 'whole-heartedly in sympathy with the free exchange of chemical warfare information', provided it was understood that any information given was conditional upon a distinct, yet informal, agreement which restricted information to only the two countries. Whereas Britain was 'going ahead with the work with as little publicity as possible', Atkisson noted, there was some concern that the 'extent of their work' might be revealed through bilateral cooperation with the United States. To illustrate the point, he cited the case of a US military official who had replied to a foreign diplomat's question about Atkisson's whereabouts during an official lunch saying that he was 'at Porton learning about chemical warfare'.[181] As a British officer had overheard the remark, the War Office issued an official reprimand to the US official.

In another instance, the Secretary of the Chemical Warfare Committee and subsequently Controller, Chemical Warfare Research Department, Captain James Davidson Pratt (see Image 7), who came to play a highly influential and long-term role in Britain's chemical warfare programme, gave Atkisson one of the Royal Navy's gas masks, with the proviso that 'no one is to know that we have received it, not even the War Office or the Admiralty'. In summing up the arrangement, Atkisson remarked:

> We have received so much valuable information and are in such a fine position to receive more that I am certain, if all who have access to the information understand the situation clearly, nothing can possibly happen to disturb existing splendid relations... When it is understood that Great Britain is doing as much, if not more, than we are in chemical warfare, I am sure it will be appreciated that it is of greatest importance that we exercise such precautions as she desires.[182]

Britain was not only doing 'more', but it was outsourcing research, some of it offensive in nature, to British-controlled laboratories overseas to

Image 7. Sir James Davidson Pratt

Source: IWM, Photographic Collection. © Imperial War Museums (Davidson Pratt).

J. Davidson Pratt, Esq, OBE, MA, BSc, FIC; Assistant Secretary of the Chemical Advisory and Chemical Warfare Committees, 1 August 1916–31 December 1918; Secretary, Chemical Warfare Committee; Controller, Chemical Warfare Committee, 1 January 1919–30 June 1923; Controller, Chemical Warfare Research Department, 1 July 1923–31 December 1925; Chief Superintendent, Chemical Warfare Research Department, 1 January 1926–30 September 1928. Davidson Pratt was later promoted to Controller, Chemical Defence Development, in the MoS.

deflect public attention from its expanding chemical warfare programme.[183] Subsidiary research facilities in India and Australia, established in the 1920s, allowed British scientists to investigate the effect of chemical warfare agents under specific climatic conditions and among different population groups. Between 1921 and 1924, one of Porton's officers, Lieutenant Colonel W.A. Salt, ran the Military Chemical Laboratory in Dehra Dun in India, which conducted high-altitude and smoke trials to test different types of respirators suitable for bearded Sikhs.[184] Porton's service personnel and physiological staff also served as instructors to the Indian Chemical Warfare School in Begaum, a centre of the armed forces for the British Raj. In 1929, the British authorities set up a Chemical Warfare Research Establishment in Rawalpindi, in the Punjab, staffed by scientists and officers from Porton, who engaged in smoke trials for the protection of bridges and other strategic sites.[185] To forge better relations, Indian representatives were invited to Britain for an appreciation of the power of chemical warfare. Around the same time, Britain established closer links with the Australian Chemical Warfare Board to study the effects of tropical and subtropical conditions on chemical warfare, attached Australian, Canadian, and South African representatives to Porton, and organized chemical warfare courses in the Dominions. In some cases, Porton helped Allied governments to deal with civil unrest by providing defensive technologies and chemical agents; in 1930, for example, Porton supplied South Africa with specially developed bombs filled with tear gas which the government employed against opposition groups. Most of Porton's activities overseas were strictly classified, not only to protect existing expertise but to preserve Britain's political credibility in ongoing disarmament talks. At an international level, though, and in public, the subject of chemical warfare was openly discussed.[186]

Expert Opinion

Although the League of Nations almost unanimously portrayed chemical warfare as unethical and contrary to international law, expert opinion was heavily divided, especially among military officials and chemical scientists. Whereas some saw it as an inhumane terror weapon, which affected civilians and entire communities indiscriminately, others were convinced that it was 'the most powerful and the most humane method of warfare ever invented'.[187] Ironically, in the 1950s, the advocates of biological warfare argued along similar lines, namely that the development and usage of such weapons was 'humane' and could be justified on ethical grounds because the killing was performed 'without the distressing preliminaries'.[188] There were also those for whom chemical weapons were just another weapon of war—albeit a terrible one. For members of the Holland Committee, including Foulkes, chemical agents were a 'legitimate weapon in war' and the question whether they would be used in future wars a 'foregone conclusion'.[189] In the United States, in an attempt to shore up support for the CWS, Fries declared that 'civilized nations should not hesitate' to use toxic agents. For him, it was just as 'sportsman-like to fight with chemical warfare materials as it is to fight with machine guns'.[190] Having witnessed how 'small children' had suffered from a gas attack during the war, General Peyton Conway March, one of the founders of the CWS, was fiercely opposed to this assessment and campaigned for the abolition of chemical weapons. As an advocate of the 'just war' doctrine, he believed that chemical warfare violated the requirement of non-combatant immunity, because it killed and injured women, children, and the elderly, and thus stood in 'opposition to the best sense of the civilized world'.[191] Similar views were expressed by Sir John French, who had commanded British forces in France. Mourning the loss of gentlemanly warfare, in which professionals could demonstrate their skills, he found chemical warfare morally abhorrent, yet supported its use to retaliate in kind and boost the morale of Allied troops.[192]

A number of Allied scientists could not have disagreed more. Their arguments were based on the assumption that chemical agents killed fewer people and produced less severe battlefield injuries compared to other types of weaponry. Ignoring cases of blindness and often life-long respiratory problems, any prolonged health effects were apparently more of a psychological rather than physiological nature, they argued. One of the most outspoken supporters of chemical warfare was J.B.S. Haldane, who in 1925, whilst Reader in biochemistry at Cambridge, published his tract *Callinicus: A Defence of Chemical Warfare*.[193] Combining utilitarian with socialist ideas, Haldane, later renowned for his work in physiology, genetics, and evolutionary biology, was convinced that chemical warfare agents were more humane than conventional weapons. Wounds caused by artillery shells were apparently 'more distressing' than the effects suffered from chlorine or phosgene. He attacked the 'shameful ignorance' of politicians, pacifists, and 'sentimentalists' who described war as a 'noble occupation' but condemned the use of poison gas as 'unsoldierly'. Hidden under a cloak of alleged scientific objectivity, his call for greater investment in civil defence revealed underlying racial and social prejudices. Research by the US Army on the susceptibility of the human skin to different warfare agents had apparently shown that 80 per cent of 'negroes' were resistant to mustard gas, compared to 20 per cent of 'white men'. It should consequently be possible, he noted, 'to obtain coloured troops who would all be resistant to mustard gas blistering in concentrations harmful to most white men. Enough resistant whites are available to officer them.'[194]

Conveniently ignoring the fact that the German military had violated the 'spirit' of The Hague Declaration by cynically exploiting its existing loopholes, Haldane criticized the document for prohibiting the employment of projectiles filled with tear gas, but permitting the 'exceedingly cruel' use of gas cylinders.[195] To ensure more humane types of warfare in the future, he naively proposed prohibiting the worldwide use of goggles and other eye protection devices, regardless of the fact that this was totally unrealistic and unworkable, while allowing only tear gas to be used in armed conflict. Although admitting that these rules were 'unlikely' ever to be adopted, Haldane wanted to highlight the apparent—and arguably hypo-critical—contradiction between banning chemical warfare as unlawful and morally objectionable on the one hand, and permitting the use of high explosives on the other. In addressing the relationship between science and ethics, and defending the role of scientists, Haldane remarked that all applications of science can be abused, 'but none perhaps is always evil; and many, like mustard gas, when we have got over our first not very rational objection to them, turn out to be, on the whole good. If it is right for me to fight my enemy with a sword, it is right for me to fight him with mustard gas: if the one is wrong, so is the other.'[196] Paying almost no attention to the short- and long-term psychological effects of gas, Haldane's basic utilitarian argument was one of proportionality. Mustard gas, the 'most humane weapon ever invented', he argued, apparently killed only 2.6 per cent of all battlefield casualties and permanently incapacitated 0.46 per cent.[197] Not unlike many who have spoken on this subject before and since, and who have misrepresented or underestimated the potential power of chemical weapons, Haldane maintained that chemical agents killed or permanently incapacitated fewer people than conventional weaponry; Britain should therefore denounce the Washington Agreement 'at the earliest possible opportunity'.[198]

The Geneva Protocol

Irrespective of such voices, international pressure by the League of Nations to ban chemical warfare as a legitimate instrument of armed conflict increased throughout the 1920s. Convened by the League of Nations in

Geneva in 1925, the Conference for the Supervision of the International Trade in Arms, Munitions, and Implements of War was met with opposition from countries such as Brazil, which feared a widening gap between producing and non-producing nations. Economically poor and militarily weak nations came to see the possession of such weapons as a deterrent against external aggressors. Common ground could be found in prohibiting the *use* of these weapons, however. The 'Protocol for the Prohibition of the Use in War of Asphyxiating, Poisonous or other Gases and of Bacteriological Methods of Warfare', known as the Geneva Protocol, and modelled on Article 5 of the Washington Agreement, outlawed the employment of chemical and biological weapons. However, it failed to establish an international verification and enforcement system, and exposed deep-seated disagreements about disarmament. The United States was opposed to prohibiting the use of tear gas in war on the grounds that it was also used by police forces against civilians in peacetime, especially as a weapon for riot control, and they refused to ratify the Protocol until 1975. The French and the British were likewise reluctant to go ahead and ratify, and this further limited the scope of the Protocol to a 'no-first-use' agreement.[199]

When in April 1930 Britain ratified the Protocol, it attached a two-part reservation to its instrument of ratification, which read:

> (1) The said Protocol is only binding on His Britannic Majesty as regards those Powers and States which have both signed and ratified the Protocol or have finally acceded thereto. (2) The said Protocol shall cease to be binding on His Britannic Majesty towards any Power at enmity with Him whose armed forces, or the armed forces of whose allies, fail to respect the prohibitions laid down in the Protocol.[200]

Notwithstanding these qualifications by individual member states, in Geneva the groundswell of public opinion against chemical warfare merged with high politics to form a powerful declaration of intent by the leading nations of the world to ban chemical and biological weapons systems. The slick propaganda campaign deployed to achieve this ambitious commitment had the added effect of keeping within clearly defined bounds the practice of research in places such as Porton Down.

Given the level of publicity about the odious nature of chemical weapons, tests with toxic substances on humans needed not only to be carefully designed to avoid any potential risk of harm, but also to conform to existing legal and ethical guidelines relating to non-therapeutic human experiments.[201] A key feature of the Porton experiments is that they were non-therapeutic in nature, and therefore qualitatively entirely different in character from medical treatment for therapeutic purposes. By definition, none of the Porton experiments was conducted in order to benefit the research subjects or carried out in their best interest. Since the Porton experiments were not intended to benefit the subjects, the subjects possessed the right to decide whether or not they were prepared to participate in the experiment. That is why contemporary legal opinion placed considerable importance on the issue of consent, irrespective of whether or not the experiment was carried out within a military or civilian context. As early as 1933, the Treasury Solicitor, after consulting the Director of Public Prosecutions, told the MRC 'that the consent of the person on whom the experiment is made' would afford a 'complete answer' with regards to civil liability, but added:

> I assume, of course, that the nature of the risk which the person in question was being invited to incur would be explained to him, and that the experiment itself would be conducted with all due care and that all precautions suggested by medical science would be taken.[202]

The MRC was also advised that the risk of a criminal charge against it was so remote as to be negligible, assuming, of course,

> that the person responsible for performing the experiment would be able to show that it had been conducted with the full consent of the patient, given after proper appreciation of the risks involved, and that it had been performed with all due care and skill.[203]

In the late 1920s, in an attempt to alleviate public concerns about the ethics of human experiments, Porton regularly updated the government about the latest rules and regulations pertaining to human experiments, informing the War Office, for example, about the level of protection required in tests with mustard gas:

> The most scrupulous care is taken to ensure that tests are so conducted that not only no injury is incurred, but that only the minimum of discomfort is caused. Nobody but volunteers are submitted to these tests, and then only if certified fit by the Medical Officer.[204]

Although the historical record remains rather elusive as to whether servicemen were fully informed about the risks involved in experiments, and thus were true volunteers, there is greater certainty about various public and political concerns which were raised about Porton's chemical warfare

programme. For example, in 1930, after it transpired that Porton had conducted poison gas tests on 520 servicemen, the Secretary of State for War
felt compelled to inform Parliament that Porton was taking 'every care' to
protect soldiers against possible risks, and to compensate them 'if an injury
were sustained'.[205]

Experiments considered to be 'harmful' were outright refused. In January
1926, after the Geneva Protocol had been announced, but had not yet been
ratified by Britain, the War Office declined permission for breathing tests
with toxic smoke at Porton, because it was felt 'that the proposal might
prove very far-reaching in the long run and possibly result in difficulties
as regards injury to health, whether justifiable or not'.[206] If anything, the
Protocol changed public and political awareness towards chemical agents
and strengthened resolve to pursue a worldwide reduction in weapons of
mass destruction. To reflect Britain's international commitments during
a period of pacifism, the Chemical Warfare Committee was renamed the
Chemical Defence Committee, and Porton re-branded in 1925 as the new
Chemical Defence Experimental Station. However, the changes in nomen-
clature changed little, if anything, in practice. Porton, as before, continued to
carry out research on chemical weapon technologies, but was forced to
accommodate political sensitivities which stemmed from ongoing disarmament negotiations.[207]

Questions relating to chemical and bacteriological weapons routinely
surfaced in the discussions of the Preparatory Commission for the World
Disarmament Conference[208] that opened under the chairmanship of the
former British Foreign Secretary and Labour politician Arthur Henderson
(1863–1935) in Geneva in February 1932. Preliminary meetings had highlighted the relative ease with which a chemical industry could be adapted
to the production of toxic agents, and their potential delivery from the air.
Secret intelligence further suggested that almost all countries that had
signed up to the Geneva Protocol were pursuing an offensive chemical
weapons capability.[209] It therefore came as little surprise that the negotiations were beset by disagreements over what constituted 'offensive' and
'defensive' weapons and by Germany's belligerent posturing. Britain's
high-profile role during the negotiations left senior officials back in London
distinctly nervous about granting permission for human experiments
involving chemical warfare agents. Porton's proposal to conduct breathing
tests with 'small amounts of toxic smoke' was again turned down by the
Army Council. Given that Britain's international reputation was at stake,

the then Chief of the Imperial General Staff, Field Marshal George Francis Milne (1866–1948), took an uncompromising stance towards Porton: 'I consider that nothing of this kind, involving some risk, however small, should be carried out while the conference is sitting at Geneva.'[210] By the time Britain proposed a draft convention at the World Disarmament Conference in March 1933, two months after Hitler's accession as Reich Chancellor, it had become clear that Europe, if not the world, was faced with an extraordinarily brutal military dictatorship which had no intention of settling international disputes by peaceful means. The talks collapsed after Germany withdrew firstly from the Geneva World Disarmament Conference and then, in October 1933, from the League of Nations. Breathing tests with toxic substances remained prohibited until the outbreak of war in 1939 changed the ethics of human experimentation at Porton.

Whereas some have hailed the Geneva Protocol (i.e. that arising from the Conference for the Supervision of the International Trade in Arms, Munitions, and Implements of War) as 'the high-water mark of the hostility of public opinion towards CW', others have stressed the role of the international community in reasserting its authority after the contravention of The Hague Declaration during the First World War.[211] Irrespective of whether chemical weapons had been 'politicized' before, during, or after the war, whether politicians had responded to public opinion, or whether chemical weapons themselves were inhumane and immoral, the Geneva Protocol established a new international law which not only prohibited the use of chemical and biological weapons, but which, perhaps more importantly, most nations perceived to be obligatory. Concerned that any violation could lead to adverse public reactions or long-term 'stigma', even leading Nazis later expressed a certain 'respect' for the Protocol.[212]

Foreboding

Far from being a 'sudden outburst' of idealism, the Geneva Protocol was the League's 'attempt to meet a grave and increasing practical danger, viz., the insecurity of European peace and, resulting therefrom, the rise of a new competition in armaments'.[213] In the context of emerging European dictatorships, this constituted a realistic assessment. Since the early 1920s, the German *Reichswehr* and the Soviet Red Army had been involved in clandestine military operations which included weapons development and arms trade. Although the manufacture of chemical weapons was banned under the Versailles Treaty, and outlawed by national legislation, Germany's chemical industry and the military were organizing shipments of poison gas from Soviet Russia. The accidental release of phosgene from a storage tank in Hamburg in 1928 alerted the international community to the fact that Germany was flouting the Versailles Treaty. By the early 1930s, Germany's rearmament programme had reached such alarming proportions that another war in Europe seemed a realistic possibility, especially in the context of a Hitler-led regime. Hell-bent on destroying the existing democratic fabric of the Weimar Republic, the Nazis wanted to establish a terror regime against Jews and against their political opponents, to cast off the shackles of Versailles, and to pursue geopolitical aims in the east. Anyone who had hoped for a more peaceful world in which the danger of chemical weapons could be controlled soon had to acknowledge that dictatorial regimes in Italy, Germany, Spain, and the Soviet Union posed a profound threat to stability and security on the European continent.

In the context of the Europe-wide rearmament programmes that preceded the outbreak of the Second World War, issues relating to chemical warfare became absorbed into debates about national security. Almost all European governments, including the Soviet Union and Britain, employed the threat of chemical weapons as a way of accelerating the introduction of comprehensive civil defence measures. Whereas Soviet citizens received anti-gas drills in simulated gas attacks on Leningrad and Kiev in 1928, the British public was exposed to exaggerated reports about the power of chemical weapons. One estimate predicted that all men, women, and children in Central London would be killed if a large poison gas bomb were dropped onto Piccadilly Circus; another estimated the death of all Londoners if 40 tons of newly developed toxic agents were released. Italy's widely reported, but at first vehemently denied, use of chemical weapons in Ethiopia in 1935 and 1936, which involved the alleged use of mustard gas bombs against civilians and hospital patients, led to demands for sanctions by the League of Nations and increased the value of chemical weapons as a propaganda tool among anti-fascist groups.[214] In the Middle East, the British government pursued a dual strategy of attempting to broker a political settlement in conjunction with providing practical support; Porton's experimental officer was dispatched to Egypt, Aden, the Sudan, and Palestine to advise military officials about defensive chemical warfare technologies.[215] The outbreak of the Spanish Civil War in 1936 led to a fierce propaganda war over chemical warfare, with insurgents and government forces each alleging the enemy's use of poison gas. In the context of Britain's appeasement policy, official support was limited to public condemnation and the supply of respirators to aid the Spanish government. Although the Spanish military had shown few moral qualms in employing chemical weapons against Moroccans in the mid 1920s, reports confirming the use of chemical agents during the Spanish Civil War never materialized, apart from one incident involving the alleged use of tear gas.[216] At the same time, intelligence from Germany and the Soviet Union suggested increased chemical and biological warfare activities.[217]

Sufficiently alarmed by international tensions, the British government launched a large-scale civil defence programme that included the systematic distribution of millions of civilian gas masks, and the publication of propaganda material about Air Raid Precautions (ARP) that dealt with gas attacks.[218] Magazines now regularly ran news reports about different types of gas masks for civilian and military purposes.[219] While the book *On Guard Against Gas* (1938) informed 'the ordinary citizen' how to 'defend *his* family' against gas warfare, films such as *Your Book* (1938) not only depicted ordinary householders, mostly middle-class, making their windows gas proof, but showed a young girl wearing a 'floral dress with a ribbon in her blond hair and a doll in her arms' putting on and taking off her respirator, thus introducing the gas mask, a symbol of modern warfare, to mothers and children.[220] The Ministry of Health (MoH), meanwhile, distributed leaflets to doctors about *Enemy Gas Attacks* outlining various medical treatment regimes for gas casualties.[221] Of special interest for ARP and Porton officials was the development of respirators for children and infants as a way of alleviating public fears about the expected aerial and chemical attacks.[222] Under the headline 'Gas Proof Cases Save the Babies: Mothers will Pump in the Air', the *News Chronicle* tried to reassure readers that government preparations to protect the public from gas warfare were well advanced. The design and testing of gas-proof helmets and tents or the use of prams as suitable protective devices nonetheless posed unforeseen practical and psychological problems. Prams, for example, were mainly in possession of middle- and upper-class families and could not be taken for granted among the poorer sections of British society.[223] Any model Porton designed therefore needed to be distributed by the authorities free of charge. The assumed ignorance of mothers living in slums was also believed to prevent the correct use of respirators; debates about housing and welfare reform could thus become enmeshed with civil defence measures. Trials involving children and infants to assess the effectiveness and psychological impact of anti-gas helmets raised additional ethical and methodological issues.[224] Faced with a notable lack of volunteers, Porton first used the children of its staff and the armed forces stationed there for preliminary tests. After enlisting the support of selected Medical Officers of Health, Britain's gas-mask designers proceeded to conduct a series of trials at maternity and welfare clinics in London, Bristol, and Southampton, most of which were frequented by mothers and infants from the lower classes or by foster parents. Posters issued by some of the city councils asking for volunteers seemed to suggest that parents and guardians were required to attend so that children under the age of two could be 'fitted' with 'gas helmets', a not entirely correct, indeed somewhat misleading, implication.[225] The data thus gathered were hardly representative of the British public as a whole. Although infants often became terrified and overheated within a minute, or showed signs of distress when placed in a gas-proof bag that needed to be ventilated by the mother—herself often rather upset by the experience—the authorities continued to stress the level of Britain's chemical warfare preparedness in information leaflets, which the National Federation of Women's Institutes and other agencies distributed throughout the country. Powerful images of protecting the most vulnerable and innocent against a chemical attack served as a potent metaphor to shore up morale on the eve of war.

Retaliatory preparations were likewise set in train. In 1936, in addition to existing facilities which produced 20 tons of mustard gas per week, the Committee of Imperial Defence ordered the development of a pilot plant with an estimated output of 50 tons per week for the production of a new chemical warfare agent, code-named HT, better known as Runcol.[226] Less than a year later, over 5 million respirators were reported to be in storage for a national emergency. Additional storage facilities for defensive equipment were set up in Canada and South Africa.[227] Following the notorious Munich Agreement of September 1938, and Hitler's invasion of what was left of Czechoslovakia in March 1939, the government distributed over 30 million respirators. Two years into the war, Britain had at its disposal a total of almost 4 million children's respirators and anti-gas helmets alone.[228] Here was an aggressor who warranted the mobilization of all resources in preparation for a potential chemical warfare attack.

More recently, however, sources have come to light that ask whether the widespread distribution and usage of respirators before and during the war, and in some cases after it, might have come at a cost to the health of the British people. An internal report commissioned by Porton on the fiftieth anniversary of the outbreak of the war revealed that the majority of gas masks produced for civilians and service personnel contained significant amounts of asbestos.[229] Of an estimated total of ninety-seven million civilian respirators produced during the war, approximately forty million contained a merino wool–asbestos filter. The probability that children would have breathed in small fibres of asbestos through their gas mask was even greater (see Image 8). In the case of the small children's respirator, known as 'Mickey Mouse', since it was fitted with a red face-piece and a blue-coloured canister, officials concluded in 1989 that 'it must be assumed that *all* the early canisters contain asbestos'. As a result, they 'should not be worn and they should not be played with by children',[230] for example, by children re-enacting scenes at school or during museum visits. As if casting a long shadow into the postwar period, those wearing the gas masks at museum exhibitions designed to 'bring history to life' would have been

Image 8. Child with gas mask
Source: IWM, Photographic Collection, Child with Gas Mask, no date. © Imperial War Museums (L 1092).

unaware of the health risks. Indeed, women who had worked in the gas-mask factories during the war later suffered from high rates of mesothelioma, a rare form of cancer caused by exposure to asbestos.[231] Yet rather than addressing the issue of asbestos-contaminated canisters proactively, and alerting the public to the dangers of asbestos exposure as further evidence started to become available from the 1950s onwards, Porton failed to act until 1989.

Shortly before the outbreak of war, research on chemical and biological warfare accelerated at all levels. Through liaison with the ARP Subcommittee, Porton became an integral part of Britain's civil defence planning with increased access to military intelligence and hardware.[232] In 1935, an RAF 'Special Duty Flight' was put on permanent stand-by to allow scientists to study the effects of airborne gas attacks on the Porton range.[233] Research and development at Porton included the design of respirators for humans and animals, detector and decontamination devices, filtration units for ships, buildings (including air raid shelters) and armoured vehicles, methods to prevent toxic gas from infiltrating the London Underground and government buildings, impregnated garments to protect against specific agents, and the testing of anti-gas ointments. To assist the RAF in assessing wind conditions on the ground or the Royal Navy in battleship protection, Porton conducted research on smoke, including smoke curtain installations and assessments about the relation between screening effects and meteorological conditions.[234] Offensive work involved chemical shell and aircraft gas bombs, ground mustard gas bombs to contaminate whole areas, gas-filled rocket launchers, gas spraying devices, toxic smoke (arsenical) weapons, or substitute agents ('pseudo gases') to mislead the enemy.[235] Hand in hand with the rapid expansion of Porton's areas of responsibilities in the interwar period came the expansion of its research staff, who forged closer links with subsidiary research facilities in India and later Canada.[236] The number of scientists affiliated with Porton during these years is testimony to the way in which the government managed to integrate research and development into the planning process for future military operations.[237]

Although military assessments suggested that the likelihood of air attacks with high explosives, fragmentation, or incendiary bombs was greater than an attack with chemical or biological agents, civil defence planners recognized the propaganda value of chemical warfare and referred to potential airborne gas attacks to reassure and train the population about defensive measures. Yet by raising the possibility of gas war among the population, the authorities inadvertently increased public fears. In 1935, Lord Marley (1884–1952), Chief Labour Whip and Deputy Speaker in the House of Lords, criticized the government's publicity campaign designed to prepare the population for possible gas attacks, labelling it as ineffective and mis- leading; given the availability of air raid shelters, provisions for the civilian population were as yet inadequate, he argued; information about new gases was suppressed, state control of essential raw materials, especially of rubber, was non-existent, and the advice to ordinary householders to protect them- selves against gas was impractical.[238] A number of left-wing politicians and commentators supported the call for enhanced civil defence measures, among them the Cambridge scientist—and left-leaning eugenicist—J.B.S. Haldane, who in 1937 advocated greater cooperation between the armed forces and scientists.[239] His talk on 'Science and Future Warfare' was aimed at provoking public debate, as had his advocacy of chemical warfare in the 1920s, but his assessment of the limited military capabilities of future radio- active, chemical, and biological weapon systems was wide of the mark. Within the next few centuries, he argued, there was no prospect of destroy- ing the world with atomic and aerial bombs, as had been predicted by science fiction writers such as H.G.Wells in *The World Set Free* (1914) or *The Shape of Things to Come* (1933).[240] Whether it was in his assumption that scientists were unlikely to discover chemical agents more toxic than mustard gas, or his scepticism about the successful use of chemical and biological weapons in future wars, Haldane appeared—when he stressed the future role of scientists in devising new 'methods of passive defence' against known methods of warfare—to be caught up in the very 'romantic illusions' he criticized among those involved in planning for future conflicts with as yet unknown weapons of war.[241]

By the late 1920s, the notion of gas warfare and its associated imagery had become a powerful part of the collective memory of the European public; any reference to it by journalists or politicians, however far-fetched and unsubstantiated—as in the case of the sudden death of dozens of Belgian citizens from 'poisoned fog' in 1930, which turned out to be a meteorological anomaly rather than any deadly residue from former German chemical weapon stockpiles—tapped into a highly contentious narrative about the horrors of gas warfare. This applied especially to First World War memorials. Built in 1929 on Belgian soil to commemorate the suffering of thousands of victims of asphyxiation in the first chemical attack in modern history, the Steenstraate gas memorial blamed the German military for this act of inhumanity, which is why the occupying German forces duly destroyed it in 1941.[242] Whatever people's ideological or political convictions, for the majority gas warfare had turned into an emblematic shorthand to depict the ugly face of modernity, a threshold that had been irreversibly crossed. For Walter Benjamin, who in 1940 committed suicide near Spain's border with France in order to avoid capture by the Nazis, any future world war would be a 'gas war' with a 'ghostly frontline', in which the distinction between combatants and non-combatants no longer existed, and which would involve not only 'an absurd degree of risk' but, being based on 'fear' and 'annihilation', would 'bring with it the end of all civilization': a view that, in the context of the systematic extermination of the European Jewry by means of poison gas, adds poignancy to all those who had expressed dark forebodings in the 1930s.[243]

3

Research without Bounds

Schrader's Secret Compound

After the Second World War, Gerhard Schrader, the German industrial chemist who in the mid 1930s discovered the chemical warfare potential of organophosphorus compounds, wanted Allied interrogators to believe that workers in German nerve agent factories had only occasionally suffered from minor convulsions and that there had only been a 'single human fatality' among the workforce. According to Schrader, one employee died within two minutes of exposure to half a gallon of the nerve agent Tabun.[1] Although nerve gases were extremely toxic, and their handling extremely dangerous, German military manufacturing facilities had apparently complied with the latest health and safety standards. Postwar witness statements, however, painted a different picture, suggesting that accidents were more frequent and more serious, and that workers, including forced and slave labourers, suffered from severe and sometimes fatal injuries. Up until the end of 1941, a total of 324 apparently minor accidents occurred at Dyhernfurth, code-named 'Hochwerk'—a small town northwest of Breslau, in the eastern province of Silesia—where the German conglomerate IG Farben established the first ever plant for the manufacture of the nerve agent Tabun after the outbreak of war.[2] For some Allied investigators, the figure was 'in no sense spectacular; indeed, judged by experience elsewhere, it might be regarded as quite a low figure'.[3] Subsequent interrogations revealed, however, that there had been twelve serious casualties in a single accident in 1941. Despite intensive medical care, and the administration of oxygen, eight of the injured men and women died. Among those who recovered was 'one girl', who had an extremely low white blood cell count.[4] In 1945, Porton officials concluded that in German factories the 'effects upon man were observed whenever it was possible to do so; the accidents in factories, laboratories etc. offered the opportunity to study the effects as well as the proper treatment' during the war.[5] Officially, experiments with lethal dosages of nerve agents were conducted only on animals, yet military scientists were prepared to 'capitalize' on different types of accidents and forms of exposure in nerve agent factories, irrespective of the ethical implications.

Given that Germany's nerve agent programme was one of the best-kept secrets of the war—so secretive that Allied intelligence had no idea that German scientists had developed a new generation of toxic compounds—it is hardly surprising that documentation about accidents, including the ones highlighted above, and deliberate human experiments with chemical warfare agents was kept to a minimum. If such documentation was ever produced, it was probably destroyed by the end of the war. Yet an analysis of the ethics of accidents and experiments in Nazi chemical warfare research, even if based on fragmented evidence, can extend our understanding of the medical ethics standards applied in different research environments. In his study of a major biological warfare accident during the Cold War, which turned into a prolonged human experiment, Balmer has shown that 'those who are accidentally or deliberately exposed, but are not the objects of experiment, challenge not only the boundaries between accident and experiment... but, significantly, between the patron and experimenter'.[6] By looking at the role of accidents in the acquisition of military knowledge, we can also gain insights into how secrecy trumps ethics in decision-making. The material presented in this chapter explores how German military scientists addressed, ignored, or circumvented the ethical dilemmas resulting from their top-secret military assignments, and assesses some of the differences between military medical ethics and civilian research practices.[7] Such an analysis obviously needs to be embedded within the overall political and strategic context of Germany's chemical weapons programme.

Nazi Chemical Warfare Policy

It is fair to argue that Nazi Germany was one of the most ruthless and murderous regimes of modern history: it killed millions of soldiers on the battlefield; it imprisoned, starved, and tortured to death hundreds of thousands of men, women, and children in the German Gulag archipelago, that notorious system of concentration camps spread across the European continent;

it systematically planned and carried out the annihilation of the European Jewry with poison gas. It is hard to believe that it would have had any hesitation in, and even less so moral scruples about, employing chemical warfare agents against its mortal enemies. Given that Germany was in possession of nerve agents, the deadliest substances mankind had yet invented, and had mass-produced and weaponized them, it seems all the more difficult to understand why the Nazi regime never launched a full-scale chemical attack.

As the Third Reich disintegrated, there were no 'miracle weapons' in sight for a defeated and demoralized German army. All that was left was a population feeling disillusioned, betrayed, and abandoned, a command and communication structure in total disarray, and a leadership engulfed in a desperate struggle to survive. Although the use of chemical weapons would have been unlikely to change the course of the war, or delay the unconditional surrender of the German armed forces, in a strangely twisted sense the use of deadly agents would have fitted well with the country's appeal to its idealized past and fatalistic tradition, perhaps even with Hitler's own theatrical visions of death and destruction. Still, Hitler and his subordinates never authorized their employment, either in victory or in defeat, not even as a defensive measure to halt or slow down the Allied advance. In the context of one of the most brutal and morally abhorrent wars fought in modern times, Germany's decision to abstain from using its chemical weapon stockpile, including over 12,000 tons of nerve agents, requires explanation. At the same time, we need to acknowledge certain limits of historical analysis in explaining why something did not happen, even though it might have been expected to happen.

The regime's restraint in using nerve agents has fascinated and puzzled historians in equal measure. In the context of an outwardly aggressive and expansionist regime, with its attempts at world domination, some scholars have taken a counterfactual approach by classifying nerve agents as Hitler's 'secret weapon', which, had he chosen to use them, 'could conceivably have saved Germany from defeat'.[8] Others have interpreted German chemical warfare research as 'politicized' and 'perverted science', and have related it almost exclusively to the horrors of the war and ongoing camp experiments, if not the Holocaust.[9] Such assessments tap into a popular desire for seemingly unambiguous dividing lines between German and Allied science that help to claim the moral high ground for the large-scale production and human testing of chemical agents by Allied researchers as a defence against the Nazis regime during the war; yet they provide only a limited explanatory potential.

Based on the assumption that Germany's material resources and production facilities were insufficient for a sustained chemical warfare campaign, some authors have argued that the use of chemical weapons for offensive purposes was never seriously considered, and that the Nazi leadership, and Hitler in particular, had no intention of employing chemical agents except in retaliation against Allied chemical attacks.[10] Seemingly unable to exploit the more toxic nerve agents for strategic purposes, since an apparent lack of raw materials and manufacturing problems prevented their mass production, and vulnerable because of a lack of sufficiently developed defensive measures, the Nazi regime was apparently not in a position to launch a large-scale chemical attack during the entire period of the war. An uncritical reading of postwar testimonies has also led some to assume that Germany would have been unable to withstand an Allied attack.[11] According to Speer's postwar account, the military rejected the idea of using gas warfare as 'utterly insane' for fear that it would 'bring the most terrible catastrophe' upon unprotected German cities, and because it could be seen as an 'international crime' committed by the German people.[12] The Chief of the German Chemical Troops (*Nebeltruppe*), Hermann Ochsner, anxious not to implicate himself by revealing his support for offensive chemical warfare operations, also constructed a convenient retrospective narrative for his own postwar defence.[13] More recently, historians have stressed that Germany's chemical warfare programme enjoyed greater military priority, was more aggressively pursued and technologically more advanced than previously assumed, and that there were recurrent proposals to use toxic agents at different stages of the war. Having amassed stockpiles of over 41,000 tons of conventional chemical warfare agents by the end of 1941, phosgene and mustard gas especially, the German military was reportedly prepared and ready to use them in March 1943.[14]

In Germany, a detached leadership, having cultivated an informal, highly personalized system of communication, was accustomed to a fragmented, uncoordinated, and often chaotic system of decision-making, which had a detrimental effect on chemical warfare research and development. Military and civilian experts, as well as competing research laboratories, were often unaware that their secret work on scientific problems was in fact in parallel with, or overlapped, that of others.[15] Teamwork and the coordinated pooling of resources and expertise required ingenuity and considerable perseverance. At the same time, the aggressive and belligerent nature of the Third Reich created not only a self-feeding and ultimately self-destructive process of cumulative radicalization, but also a research culture that competed to develop new and more toxic compounds, innovative delivery systems, and production facilities for the mass manufacture of huge quantities of chemical warfare agents. Backed up by vague and sometimes inaccurate intelligence assessments, German chemical warfare policy was also influenced by military assumptions about Allied preparedness and capabilities. A government system in which secrecy was all-pervasive and camouflaged a plethora of criminal activities—not least a cover-up of the murder of millions of people in the Holocaust—and in which the sharing of classified information was heavily censored facilitated the successful concealment of nerve agents from Allied intelligence services: but it also produced an uncoordinated and, as the war progressed, increasingly ineffective system of communication, which hampered chemical warfare planning across the services. As a result the efficient monitoring of health and safety standards was significantly reduced. Unsupervised and largely detached from centralized government control, those in charge of German manufacturing plants often turned a blind eye to frequent accidents or the prolonged incidental exposure of staff to nerve and blistering agents. In the absence of a uniformly applied regulatory framework, secrecy began to undermine the level of transparency and accountability with which chemical warfare research was conducted in Nazi Germany.

Nerve Agents

Following the Nazi consolidation of power, the military launched a large-scale rearmament programme that included the search for new chemical weapons.[16] In Allied countries, chemical warfare work was largely centralized, state-sponsored, and integrated into the military command structure to protect national security interests. In Germany, in contrast, research was predominantly decentralized and concentrated in military and partly state-controlled research institutions.[17] In collaboration with German industry, universities, and the military, the regime pursued research into offensive chemical weapons and anti-chemical warfare protection.[18] In this complex, at times fragmented, ideologically driven, and secretive research environment, in which laboratory scientists were kept informed on a strictly need-to-know basis, German military authorities played a coordinating role in exploiting research data for the war effort, and in stimulating an aggressive, highly competitive research culture.

An estimated 450 scientific experts at the Army Gas Protection Laboratory (*Heeresgasschutzlaboratorium*) in Berlin-Spandau, officially tasked with chemical defence, synthesized thousands of chemical compounds to see whether any of them could be developed into warfare agents, performed tests on animals and humans, established collaborative networks and secret contracts with private companies, including IG Farben, conducted extensive literature reviews, and secured the support of the State Patent Office, yet up until the mid 1930s no major advances had been made.[19] In the end, the discovery of the first major new warfare agent since the First World War was largely unrelated to the allocation of government resources or to the provision of military expertise: it resulted from research into new synthetic pesticides.

In December 1936, Gerhard Schrader, a thirty-three-year-old industrial chemist heading the plant protection group at Bayer, a subsidiary of IG Farben located in Leverkusen, synthesized a new colourless substance, today known as Tabun, which was part of a research programme to develop a non-flammable pesticide.[20] Research with organophosphorus compounds had been conducted since the mid nineteenth century and systematically developed by the chemical industry in the early twentieth century. To increase its toxicity, Schrader and his team synthesized hundreds of analogue compounds, one of which included the element cyanide, which is poisonous in itself. After exposure to the fumes of the compound, Schrader suffered from 'extremely unpleasant' side-effects—severe headache, lack of breath, and poor eyesight—and had to be hospitalized for two weeks.[21] Researchers at Leverkusen examined the compound for its insecticidal properties, and quickly established its high toxicity: a drop spilled by accident by one of Schrader's assistants led to a 'strong irritation of the cornea, marked dimming of the visual field, and an oppressive feeling of tightness in the chest'.[22] For the most part, senior chemists in both civilian and military establishments accepted that their work involved certain occupational hazards, and also expected others, their staff and students especially, to take similar levels of risk when researching new chemical compounds.

Further tests on warm-blooded animals, including mice, guinea pigs, rabbits, cats, dogs, and apes, demonstrated that the compound, named Le-100, was extremely toxic when injected or inhaled in minute concentrations.

Apes exposed to vapours of Le-100 in a gas chamber gasped for air, then convulsed and died within less than thirty minutes. Although this level of toxicity made the substance unsuitable as a commercial pesticide, IG Farben officials alerted the military authorities to its potential as a chemical warfare agent.[23] The subsequent patent applications, filed by IG Farben in February and July 1937 and in September 1939, but classified by the German authorities until the early 1950s, covered the entire class of organophosphorus compounds, and thus secured IG Farben property rights for their commercial exploitation as pesticides for civilian purposes and as nerve agents for the German military.[24]

By synthesizing Tabun, Schrader's team had manufactured a product that could be used for both peaceful and offensive military purposes; yet despite the ethical issues arising from such a discovery, known as the 'dual-use' dilemma, no one—not Schrader, not any other chemical scientist from IG Farben, nor the company as a whole—seems to have expressed any reservations in collaborating with the German military to establish an offensive chemical warfare capability. It gave the Nazi regime extra confidence in pursuing its military objectives on the European continent. For the scientists, it appears that the prospect of additional research resources and investments to advance their field of expertise had priority over any ethical concerns. The Nazi regime not only lacked the necessary legal and regulatory system that could have governed the systematic exploitation of civilian science for military objectives, but there was also no normative ethical framework to prevent the misuse of chemical discoveries for hostile purposes.

Tests with Tabun-filled shells at the Army Proving Ground (*Heeresversuchsstelle*) in Raubkammer, near Münster, were immediately carried out to ensure that the German army would be ready to employ the agent in any future war.[25] After the war, in recalling some of the tests, which involved experiments on animals, Ochsner noted: 'Convulsions after a few minutes; death often occurs within ten minutes; [agent shows] immediate effect.'[26] At the end of October 1937, in a memorandum submitted to the Army General Staff, Ochsner argued for research and development into a new generation of chemical warfare agents. Given that enemy forces were no longer unprotected against poison gases, and since most of the known warfare agents could be detected by their odour, it was necessary to manufacture agents which had 'little or no odour, caused no sensory irritation, and were so toxic that one or two breaths could kill'.[27] Although field trials had highlighted problems in dispersing Tabun into a deadly cloud, Ochsner recommended it to the military. Tabun was difficult to detect, extremely toxic, and able to penetrate through the skin, which taken together made it an ideal warfare agent. A week later, on 5 November 1937, Hitler informed his senior advisers about his plans to expand the German Reich by force, first by preparing Germany for war against the European powers, possibly as early as 1938, and in a second stage through a major conflict which would take advantage of Germany's military superiority. From the military point of view, the discovery of Tabun and other deadly nerve agents such as Sarin could not have come at a better time.[28]

Accidents and Experiments

On the eve of the Second World War, the German military had formulated ambitious plans to establish one of the most deadly chemical warfare programmes in the world. This required detailed studies on human subjects under laboratory and real-life conditions, some of which were performed in Nazi concentration camps. Germany's invasion of Poland in September 1939 marked the transition from military planning to the construction of highly secret pilot plants and factories for the mass production of chemical warfare agents, especially of mustard gas and Tabun. After Hitler instructed the military to 'prepare for gas warfare', officials wasted little time in establishing a credible chemical warfare manufacturing capability with an estimated output of 19,000 tons of mustard gas by the end of 1940.[29] In collaboration with IG Farben, the military also pursued the construction of a plant for the production of Tabun. After being briefed about the discovery of a new class of warfare agents, Hitler is said to have expressed his wish to 'build as soon as possible a plant for the manufacture of the new warfare agent with an output of 1,000 tons per month'.[30]

The extreme toxicity of nerve agents exposed those individuals dealing with the substances in the laboratory, on the test range, or in the factory, to considerable health risks, when the agents accidentally came into contact with their unprotected bodies, contaminated their respirators, or adhered to their clothes and technical equipment. Researchers could even experience adverse effects from inhaling small quantities of vapours released from contaminated experimental animals. German scientists knew that nerve agents differed widely in toxicity but were likely to be 'lethal when applied to the skin' or when inhaled in the form of vapours.[31] Through animal experiments, they established variations in the lethal dosages of Tabun for cats, dogs, and apes. As a function of the concentration (c = concentration) and length of exposure (t = time), a lethal ct of Tabun ranged from 200 to 600 mg/m^3.[32] Aware of the importance of obtaining comparable data for lethal dosages of Tabun and Sarin for humans, some scientists studied chemical warfare accidents as a way of advancing biochemical and physiological knowledge about the agents. Depending on the kind of exposure, individuals suffered from 'marked contraction of the pupils, bronchospasm with respiratory distress, diarrhoea, convulsions, unconsciousness and finally death'.[33] Most of these clinical observations were made under controlled conditions in animals but there were also a number of cases, some of them fatal, in which humans were poisoned by accident.

Despite general safety regulations at Dyhernfurth, where parts of the plant were enclosed in 'double-glass-lined chambers with pressurized air circulating between', neither the Nazi regime nor the IG Farben conglomerate introduced occupational exposure limits or routine medical examinations to protect workers from the short- and long-term effects of nerve-gas poisoning. Germany's chemical warfare plants also lacked a robust system to monitor potential health risks and major incidents, as was standard practice in Britain, where serious accidents or explosions had to be immediately reported to military headquarters.[34] In general, experts believed that there was an 'inevitable' risk to the incidental exposure of small quantities of toxic gases in laboratories and production plants, yet they underestimated the cumulative effects of nerve agents. As a result, operators and mechanics, wearing full protective clothing and respirators, suffered from chemical warfare injuries which indirectly contributed to existing knowledge about the agents. Through leaking rubber seals, workers were constantly exposed to small amounts of nerve agents which over time led to serious medical complications and in some cases death.

Officials later conceded that there had been ten accidental deaths between May 1942, when mass production of Tabun began, and the end of the war. These were probably the first human beings ever to die of nerve gas poisoning.[35] Some of the few surviving records highlight the enormous hazards to which staff in chemical warfare plants had been exposed. Wilhelm Kleinhans, an IG chemist working at Dyhernfurth until 1945, later testified about an accident in which four pipe fitters were killed by Tabun leaking from pipes: 'These workmen had died in convulsions before the rubber suits could be torn off.'[36] In another terrible incident, five plant workers were killed, and two seriously injured, after their faces were exposed to large quantities of liquid Tabun: 'They became giddy, vomited, and so then removed their respirators thus inhaling more of the gas. On examination they were all unconscious…had a feeble pulse, marked nasal discharge, contracted pupils, asthmatic type of breathing, and smelled strongly of flowers.'[37] Although the attending medical officer immediately injected a solution of atropine sulphate and sympatol intramuscularly, and for the more severe cases intravenously, and although artificial respiration, heart massage, and oxygen masks were applied, only two of the men survived. Interestingly, the above measures corresponded in many ways with the kind of treatment regime British researchers applied to severe cases of nerve gas poisoning in the 1950s. An autopsy performed at the Military Medical Academy in Berlin found the lungs and brains of the dead men to be heavily congested.[38]

During the war, the industry also employed prisoners as well as forced and slave labourers who worked under appalling conditions and with almost no access to medical facilities. Often their human rights and dignity were violated; medical ethics principles of beneficence and non-maleficence were frequently ignored. After the summer of 1943, Dyhernfurth used prisoners from Dyhernfurth I, a subsidiary camp of the Gross-Rosen concentration camp.[39] Former prisoner Mikolaj Koroloko recalled that he and his fellow inmates, despite wearing protective clothing, often suffered from poisoning when filling artillery shells and aerial bombs with chemical agents at Dyhernfurth: 'The pupils became smaller, we lost our ability to see over a certain period and mucus was running from our noses.'[40] At another facility in Gendorf, which manufactured mustard gas, technicians were likewise exposed to serious health risks. According to a postwar report, 'a good deal of non-quantitative data, arising from accidental exposure of the workers concerned, must have been available even in 1939'.[41]

Given the pressing need for greater scientific understanding of the agents, Nazi officials seem to have given tacit approval for such accidents to occur in order to study their effects on the human body. Although evidence about the systematic exploitation of accidents for experimental purposes may be circumstantial, there is little to suggest that the regime was concerned about preventing such accidents from happening, or that it went to any lengths to prevent them. Except for providing extra rations of milk and fatty foods to the workforce to improve resistance against Tabun vapours, the authorities did little to reduce the risks involved in working at Dyhernfurth: 'All members of the staff working in the Dyhernfurth plant were never free at one time from the effects of Tabun; some of the members were labouring to a greater or lesser degree under the influence.'[42] For Karl Brandt, Hitler's escort physician, the enormous health risks to the workers at Dyhernfurth were all too apparent. Since the outbreak of war, Brandt's meteoric rise to power had been accompanied by his responsibility for, and involvement in, the systematic murder of tens of thousands of handicapped children and adults in the Nazi 'euthanasia' programme.[43] Appointed General Commissioner for Health and Sanitation in 1942, he was in charge of the majority of the German health care system. In the summer of 1944, shortly before his promotion to Reich Commissioner, he witnessed cases of Tabun poisoning during an inspection tour of Dyhernfurth and Gendorf.[44]

At Raubkammer, researchers also conducted various experiments on animals and human subjects: 'There was extensive testing of German CW on human volunteers—experiments to test skin decontamination agents, the miotic action [constriction of the pupil] of Tabun, possible protective suits, eye, nose and throat irritants.'[45] With up to 800 employees working at Raubkammer during the war, the scientists enjoyed ready access to a considerable number of test subjects.[46] Most of the volunteers were officers, clerks, employees, and labourers, possibly even forced and slave labourers, and sometimes students from the Army's Gas Protection Laboratory, who, for a small financial incentive, took part in nerve agent tests, sometimes wearing only rubber shorts to protect their genitals.[47] Men crawled over contaminated ground without wearing any form of protective garments, lay in shallow trenches for up to an hour downwind of toxic agents, or were exposed to them in a gas chamber. In some instances chemical agents were fired into the woods: 'Human subjects [then] entered the area to see how long they could remain there without adjusting their respirators.'[48] Over a ten-year period, from 1935 to 1945, scientists at Raubkammer performed a total of 174 aircraft weapons trials with different types of air- or ground-burst bombs, cluster bombs, and spraying devices, which in fifty-two cases involved the large-scale use of Tabun. Only a single aircraft trial was conducted with Sarin, which turned out to be three times more effective than phosgene. In addition, from 1940 to 1945, a total of 109 ground weapon trials with chemical warfare agents such as Sarin, Tabun, phosgene, HCN (hydrogen cyanide), and mustard gas were carried out.[49]

Postwar investigators later discovered a pathological museum which exhibited, among other artefacts, the organs of seven cats that had been gassed with Tabun. Photographic albums containing some 4,000 images, some of them in colour, systematically documented almost all of Raubkammer's activities, including the controlled application of mustard gas to the skin of human subjects, and also the case history of over 200 accidents, some apparently fatal, from mustard gas exposure. Somewhat uncritically, the investigators remarked: 'Due to the gruesome appearance of some half-dozen fatal cases, the suggestion has been made that political prisoners might have been used in these experiments. There was no evidence for such a contention.'[50] Yet there was also no indication that medical ethics standards had been upheld. On the contrary, there was sufficient evidence to suggest that non-therapeutic experiments on humans had led to considerable physical and psychological harm at Raubkammer.[51]

In general, the chemical warfare field saw the expansion of research to develop methods for the diagnosis and treatment of phosgene and mustard gas poisoning, and an intensification of experimental work on nerve agents. Under the directorship of Wolfgang Wirth, and in total secrecy, scientists from the Institute for Pharmacology and Toxicology at the Military Medical Academy conducted animal and human experiments, sometimes on themselves, to advance existing physiological knowledge of nerve gas poisoning and develop possible antidotes, for example through the use of atropine.[52] They also performed experiments with different types of mustard gas for hot and cold climates and with specially developed rubber sleeves and pants to protect the armpits and genitals, performed decontamination trials with various ointments, or studied blood samples obtained from victims of accidents.[53] To assess the miotic effects of nerve agents, Wirth undertook a number of experiments on himself and on medical officers who apparently volunteered for the tests, perhaps to avoid being drafted to the front line.[54] Wirth also oversaw a collaborative, highly competitive network of pharmacologists, some of whom were seconded to the Military Medical Academy; the pharmacologists included Hans Gremels from the university of Marburg, Ludwig Lendle from the university of Leipzig, and Werner Koll from the university of Münster. By performing a range of tests, they were able to establish the biochemical properties of nerve agents as 'inhibitors of cholinesterase', an enzyme which is of fundamental importance for the functioning of the peripheral and central nervous systems.[55]

Beginning in 1936, human research with known chemical warfare and nerve agents was also performed by Colonel Welde and Captain Kroeber at the Army's Gas Protection Laboratory in Berlin-Spandau. In some cases, the subjects experienced chemical warfare tests as deeply traumatic events which had a detrimental effect on their personality, leaving them with feelings of isolation and depression for years to come.[56] Postwar testimonies also suggest that some of the experiments were done on prisoners who, having been sentenced to death, were given an opportunity to 'redeem' themselves by taking part in the trials.[57] Attempting to shift responsibility away from himself, Wirth alleged that 'these special experiments' with Tabun were conducted only at Spandau, yet evidence seems to suggest that experiments with nerve agents were performed both there and at the Military Medical Academy. In one case, a metalworker, wearing a protective rubber suit, suffered a fatal accident in the course of repair work undertaken on one of the pipes when Tabun leaked directly onto the filter of his gas mask.[58] Reports later confirmed the occurrence of accidental cases of Sarin poisoning at the laboratory.[59] In April 1944, having 'witnessed one of Wirth's tests with Sarin', Brandt indirectly confirmed ongoing experiments on humans during a meeting with a senior representative of IG Farben. Although Brandt referred only to 'guinea pigs', it was apparent from the manner in which he described the experiments that 'human beings had been the subjects, not animals'.[60]

In the same year, the Military Medical Academy published a photographic volume documenting the clinical symptoms and pathology of chemical warfare injuries. Some of the subjects were dressed in striped prison garments and are likely to have been political prisoners. Other images showed the effects of mustard gas on the body and lungs of people who had died. None of the subjects appeared to have consented to the tests and some of the material appeared to suggest that crimes may have been committed. Seemingly aware that the context in which the images had been made raised serious ethical concerns, especially in relation to the voluntary consent principle, one senior Nazi official noted: 'It is not permitted to use the images for any other purpose than as illustration in lectures.'[61]

German researchers also performed a range of tests with different animals to assess the vesicant—that is, blistering—power of liquid chemical warfare agents on guinea pigs, rabbits, mice, cats, and dogs. Whereas in Britain experimental tests on dogs were generally banned under existing laws and regulations, scientists in Nazi Germany considered tests on dogs comparable—from a pharmacological perspective—with those on humans, especially when testing different substances on the skin between the dog's toes.[62] Trials involved rabbits whose bellies had been shaved and then brought into contact with different types of contaminated clothing; shaved guinea pigs were exposed to aircraft spraying trials, and caged cats were positioned inside tanks to test the extent to which chemical warfare grenades hurled against the vehicle would infiltrate the commander's position in the turret or the gunner's seat. Special arrangements were made to acclimatize the animals before the trials commenced to protect them from the cold. At the Army Gas Protection Laboratory, animals placed in cages in a gas chamber were exposed to mustard gas and other agents.

Upon discovering that most of the German research confirmed their own findings, which they had obtained in similar trials, Allied scientists highlighted Germany's 'unrealistic approach' to field assessments with toxic agents, yet refrained from assessing German research ethics. Allied investigators from Porton felt that the methodologies used were subject to considerable inaccuracies, misleading observations, and gross factual errors. It was not clear to them why German scientists had not exposed human subjects directly to aircraft spray with chemical agents, why no 'objective tests' had been used in assessing harassing agents, and why humans had not been placed inside tanks to test the effects of such substances. Germany had admittedly invested considerable resources in chemical warfare research, had employed twice as many research staff compared to Britain, and had been able to accommodate an expansion of its chemical warfare programme, but the overall research output appeared to be questionable. In conclusion, the investigators remarked:

> The outstanding achievement of German chemical warfare research has undoubtedly been the discovery of Tabun, Sarin, and Soman. Apart from this, however, there was surprising lack of originality in their work, and important phases of CW, such as micrometeorology, the vapour effect from mustard ground contamination and ointments were given small or belated attention.[63]

Although it is not impossible that they did so, there is no evidence to suggest that military experts engaging in chemical warfare research discussed or implemented the 'Regulations Concerning New Therapy and Human Experimentation' that had been formulated by the Reich Ministry of the Interior in 1931.[64] In §12, concerned with non-therapeutic research, the Regulations stated, among other things, that 'experimentation shall be prohibited in all cases where consent has not been given'. It also stipulated that human experiments should be avoided if they could be replaced by animal studies. However, since the Regulations were directed specifically, if not exclusively, at physicians in full-time hospital employment, who were asked to sign them upon taking up their position, they were not necessarily seen to be applicable to scientists or doctors working in other institutional contexts.[65] As a result, military researchers, including those trained as doctors, either were unaware of the existence of the guidelines or decided to ignore them. Some scientists may also have felt that the Reich Animal Protection Act (*Reichstierschutzgesetz*), which had been enacted in 1933, conflicted with the Regulations, which prioritized animal testing over human trials. In practice, neither the Regulations nor the Animal Protection Act seem to have been particularly effective. Shielded from the interference of civilian regulatory bodies, Nazi scientists were given access to substantial resources and personnel, yet their concern for the well-being of human subjects was limited at best; rarely, if ever, did they engage in debates about issues of informed consent, beneficence, or care. Under wartime conditions, medical ethics came second to what many perceived to be a fight for national survival.

Concentration Camps

Experiments—including those with chemical and biological warfare agents and poisoned bullets—on camp inmates coincided with a progressively worsening military situation that affected tens of thousands of German soldiers, and undermined morale among the civilian population.[66] Germany was fighting a titanic struggle for survival on the European continent and beyond, and members of the German military were suffering in their thousands from severe battle wounds, gas gangrene, malnutrition, frostbite, hypothermia, malaria, typhus, and other infectious diseases. At home, Allied bombing raids with high explosives and incendiary bombs were causing severe burns and multiple injuries among the civilian population. Sensing military defeat after the catastrophe of Stalingrad, the Nazi leadership called for ever more radical measures and sacrifices from all sections of society, and this provided the necessary rationale for experiments on camp inmates on an unimaginable scale.[67]

After the war, Allied intelligence attempted to establish the extent to which German scientists had conducted chemical warfare experiments on camp inmates. From early on, investigators expressed 'serious doubts' whether the regime would have agreed to the allocation of resources and personnel during the war for the mass production of a novel agent 'which had not been shown unequivocally to be capable of killing men'.[68] Given that the military had classified Tabun as a 'quick acting lethal agent', it appeared reasonable to assume that German scientists had exploited the opportunity presented to them in concentration camps to 'determine with some degree of accuracy the lethal dosages for man of various war gases'.[69] Researchers readily admitted the importance of obtaining such data for the military, yet when it was put to them that their 'less squeamish' colleagues in Himmler's SS might have performed such experiments on camp inmates, they 'flatly denied all knowledge of such killings ever having been carried out in Germany at all, until the end of the war when it was announced by the Allied Nations'.[70] Allied investigators were not impressed: 'The profession of such complete ignorance, advanced with wholly unnecessary vehemence, left us with some doubts regarding their veracity.'[71]

Overall, the evidence suggests that camp experiments were conducted with various well-known chemical agents, with phosgene and mustard gas, in particular, but not, it seems, with the new class of top-secret nerve agents that were strictly controlled and overseen by a relatively small group of experts.[72] The availability of a sufficient number of volunteers in military, industrial, and other well-equipped research laboratories, together with the findings gained from accidental exposure, animal, and self-experiments, is likely to have made the recourse to human experiments in concentration camps, under the auspices of the SS, on malnourished camp inmates and prisoners of war, against international law and under poor conditions, an unattractive proposition for the majority of German scientists. For them, it was more important to establish the precise properties of nerve agents in order to develop protective measures and potential antidotes.

Chemical warfare experiments with phosgene and with mustard gas, commonly known as Lost, were largely conducted at Sachsenhausen and Natzweiler camps.[73] Believing that experiments on man were the swiftest and most efficient way of obtaining data on chemical warfare injuries, and on how to treat them, German researchers generally subjected non-German nationals to the experiments: Poles and Russians, but also Jews and gypsies. Intelligence information suggesting the stockpiling of large quantities of chemical warfare agents at Tunis and Dakar by Allied forces, to be used for a large-scale attack against the Axis powers, added further pressure to expediting the development of effective therapeutic methods against poison gases.[74]

Since the summer of 1942, researchers such as August Hirt and Otto Bickenbach from the university of Strasbourg had collaborated with the SS Ancestral Heritage Research Foundation, SS-Ahnenerbe for short, and with the pathology and anatomy departments of the university, to perform animal and human experiments with phosgene and mustard gas at the Natzweiler concentration camp.[75] Joint experiments at the Dachau concentration camp with experts from the Strasbourg Institute for Physiological Chemistry and the Entomological Institute were also planned.[76] Early in 1943, after initial problems had been overcome, Hirt reported on his experiments, in which inmates were fed vitamin A to protect them against mustard gas exposure: 'Our L[ost] experiments at Natzweiler are now at last making good progress. After three fatalities, the applied therapy is producing a good healing process.'[77] Encouraged by the results, and oblivious to the lives lost, SS-Ahnenerbe proposed a large-scale follow-up experiment on hundreds of prisoners.

Between November 1942 and autumn 1944, according to estimates by Allied prosecutors, Hirt and his fellow scientists conducted poison gas experiments on approximately 220 inmates of Russian, Polish, Czech, and German nationality at the Natzweiler camp, of whom fifty reportedly died.[78] In some cases the bodies of experimental subjects were exposed to liquid mustard gas; in others prisoners were forced to inhale the agent in a gas chamber, which led to a number of deaths from suffocation.[79] Ferdinand Holl, arrested in Bordeaux in 1940 by the secret police (Gestapo), had been transferred first to Buchenwald and then to Natzweiler, where he worked as one of the medical orderlies in the infirmary. After the war, he testified about the involuntary, degrading, and often deadly experiments. After rumours about experiments in other camps spread among the prisoner population, volunteers completely stopped coming forward. Arbitrarily selected and fearing for their lives, prisoners had to report to the laboratory where Holl, under the direction of Karl Wimmer, a staff physician of the German Air Force, and Hirt's principal collaborator, administered a mustard gas solution to their arms, producing severe burns and excruciatingly painful injuries; vapours released from the gas gave rise to additional medical complications such as blindness. A report by Hirt and Wimmer referred only to 'heavy, medium and light wounds'.[80] Another witness, the internee Fritz Leo, whose alleged involvement in medical killings weakens his credibility, recalled that

there were deep areas of necrosis on the forearms, and also burns on the side
of the body where the contaminated arms had come into contact [with it].
The men also suffered [from] severe conjunctivitis and about three days later
bronchitis, which developed into bronchopneumonia.[81]

Treated with dressings of Rivanol and other boric acid or zinc oxide ointments, the subjects' wounds were photographed on a daily basis, yet after
five or six days, despite constant medical attention, the subjects started to
die.[82] Holl counted a total of seven deaths in a group of thirty subjects who
had been thus exposed to chemical agents.[83] Autopsies performed by
Wimmer revealed the internal damage poison gases could cause; in all cases,
the men had suffered from purulent bronchopneumonia. Highly unethical
and criminal, the experiments did little more than confirm existing knowledge about known chemical agents.

The Nazi medical establishment was well informed about these and
other experiments in support of the German war effort. At the end of 1943,
Professor Picker from the university of Strasbourg conducted another series
of chemical warfare experiments that caught the attention of Brandt.
Following chest X-rays, ten prisoners, all of whom were classified as 'habit-
ual criminals', were administered Urotropin (a potential antidote) in the
form of tablets or injections before being placed in a gas chamber, two men
at a time, where they were exposed to phosgene for two to three minutes.
To assess the prophylactic efficacy of Urotropin, the pairs were exposed to
increasingly higher doses of the agent and given proportionally higher doses
of the drug. Four days after exposure, the men suffered from breathing difficulties and headache, low blood pressure, raised pulse rate, and temperature, and increased respiratory rate; another X-ray showed that they had
developed pulmonary oedema, a swelling of and fluid accumulation in the
lungs that impairs breathing and can lead to death from respiratory failure.
A fortnight later, all of the men were deemed to have recovered, once their
chests showed no clinical symptoms; a couple of weeks later they were back
to work. According to Leo, who had administered the drugs to the prisoners, high-ranking SS officers, including Brandt, subsequently conducted an
inspection tour of the recovered experimental subjects in the camp. Allied
investigators, though, were not overly concerned with military medical ethics; their primary objectives were the spoils of war: 'The exact data of the
above experiments would be most valuable. We believe that Professors
Wimmer and Picker should be interviewed and this information obtained.'[84]

Whereas the use of data originating from the Dachau experiments led to public debate and some considerable embarrassment for the scientific community in the 1980s, much less is known about the extent to which Nazi chemical warfare research was exploited in developing Allied chemical weapon programmes after the war.

In March 1944, Brandt was personally informed about the ongoing Natzweiler experiments, and visited the camp a month later, yet at his subsequent trial he alleged that he had not realized that the work involved human subjects: 'I was at Hirt's place at the end of April 1944, and I did not gain the impression that we were concerned with experiments on some concentration camp inmates carried [out] in camps.'[85] Allied prosecutors undermined his credibility with evidence of yet another set of experiments he had sanctioned. In the summer of 1944, Bickenbach and his assistants, Helmut Rühl and Fritz Letz, performed criminal chemical warfare experiments 'on 40 prisoners'; these were 'on the prophylactic effect of hexamethylentetramin [Urotropin] in cases of phosgene poisoning' at Natzweiler. Most of the subjects were probably Russian prisoners of war. Twelve were given Urotropin orally, twenty intravenously, and eight were used as a control group without any form of protection against phosgene poisoning; almost all were in a weak and malnourished condition and two were suffering from localized tuberculosis. Willy Herzberg, one of those who survived the tests, recalled seeing four subjects being carried out of the gas chamber:

> They had brown foam at the mouth, which also came through the ears and nose...After we were led into the gas chamber, the professor [probably Bickenbach] stood in the entrance and had two glass ampoules...The professor [probably Bickenbach] encouraged us once again to move swiftly, and inhale strongly...Then he threw the two ampoules against the wall and rapidly closed the door...Approximately 10 minutes after the experiment had begun, I heard a noise with a thud, like someone clapping hands with the hands curved. This noise was the bursting lungs of two of the prisoners, who then fell on the ground, and who manifested the foam on mouth, nose and ears I described earlier.[86]

Around August 1944, Letz informed Brandt about the progress of the experiments, but told him that the 'dosis letalis minima [minimum lethal dose]...cannot yet be determined with certainty'.[87] Although four humans had been killed, the experiments had not yielded any conclusive results. Conscious of breaching known standards of medical ethics by taking excessive risks with lives of his subjects, Bickenbach later defended his actions by referring to the need to protect the German people against the dangers of gas warfare: 'I thought it my duty to do everything to ensure this protection and to save the lives of thousands of Germans, especially the children and women.'[88] The emergency of war, with its overriding ideological and military objectives, required improved protection for the general population which justified, in the eyes of Bickenbach and his fellow scientists, unethical experiments on human subjects. In their world view, the lives of others, of men, women, and children with different cultural and religious traditions, had lost all intrinsic value and become meaningless; imprisoned behind barbed wire, sentenced to death, and stripped of rights and dignity, they had become dispensable, useful as experimental subjects to support the war effort but no more.

Underlying many of the camp experiments were attempts to enhance diagnostic and therapeutic measures against chemical warfare agents and establish a defensive capability against extensive water, ground, and air contamination. By 1943, Ludwig Werner Haase of the Reich Office for Water, Ground, and Air Purification had developed a new procedure for decontaminating drinking water.[89] Authorization to conduct initial tests on camp inmates was duly obtained from the head of the SS, Heinrich Himmler, but experiments were initially delayed by war-related difficulties. After a number of tests 'with poisoned water' had been conducted at Munsterlager in the summer of 1944, the researchers planned a large-scale experiment at the Neuengamme concentration camp. Early in December 1944, a total of 150 prisoners were forced to drink water heavily contaminated with lewisite, yet the warfare agent had hydrolysed, so short-term harmful effects do not seem to have occurred and were therefore not recorded. Given the possibility of long-term damage, however, German scientists recommended the continuation of the experiments on another group of camp inmates, this time with mustard gas. With rumours circulating about imminent Allied chemical attacks, the military authorities felt under mounting pressure to exploit ongoing camp experiments for the protection of German civilians and soldiers. In December 1944, after inspecting Bickenbach's research facilities, Wirth and Brandt convened a conference with representatives of the Air Force, the Army, and the anti-aircraft services, which sanctioned a series of mustard gas experiments at Neuengamme.[90] Three months later, at the end of March 1945, officials of the Reich Office for Water, Ground, and Air Purification reported that human experiments with 'an agent of the Lost group, the asphyxiating gas Lost' had been conducted on prisoners at

Neuengamme.[91] However, neither these nor any other camp experiments with chemical warfare agents could have prevented the total destruction and disintegration of German society in the weeks that followed.

Germany in Retreat

As German forces retreated from the front lines, the Nazi leadership became increasingly concerned about Germany's chemical warfare capability. Since the debacle of Stalingrad, rumours had been circulating about planned chemical warfare attacks by the Western Allies—the suggestion of the stock-piling of large quantities of 'poison gas ammunition' in Tunis and Dakar, for example.[92] In December 1943, a German air raid on the Italian harbour of Bari, a central hub for Allied forces, resulted in the explosion of a US freight ship containing a secret cargo of 540 tons of mustard gas, and this fuelled further anxieties about imminent Allied gas attacks. Some of the mustard gas leaked into the water, and a considerable amount was dispersed into the air, causing over 600 military and an estimated 1,000 civilian casualties.[93]

The incident almost led to further military escalation, and possible retal-iation with chemical agents, as Allied officials at first assumed that Germany had started gas warfare. For the Nazi leadership, though, the attack high-lighted insufficient defensive preparations and a lack of protective equip-ment. The production of respirators by leading supplier Auergesellschaft of Oranienburg had fallen sharply, owing to air raids and shortages of raw materials, especially rubber; losses of gas masks on the Russian front had reached terrifying proportions: experts estimated that out of a total of about 15 million respirators, 6 to 7 million had been lost in the various military campaigns.[94] The German Red Cross alerted officials to the growing requirement for gas masks for anti-aircraft protection, fire fighting, and res-cue work, and the matter was referred to the highest levels of the govern-ment in early 1944.[95] Brandt, for example, concluded that Germany's ability to withstand an Allied chemical attack was 'disastrous'.[96] The civilian popu-lation, including women, children, and the elderly, was left without any form of protection against an Allied gas attack, and Germany's level of pre-paredness was widely regarded as 'totally inadequate'.[97] On average, there were respirators only for an estimated 30 per cent of the civilian popula-tion—10 per cent in some regions—and for only 7 per cent of children.[98]

In March 1944, Hitler extended Brandt's already wide-ranging powers by appointing him Special Plenipotentiary for Chemical Warfare, tasked with the implementation of an ambitious programme for the production of 60 million 'people's gas masks' (*Volksgasmasken*) using a newly developed filter made of activated charcoal. Brandt also was given control of offensive chemical warfare research (see Image 9).[99] The head of the Department for Raw Materials and director of the Planning Department in the Ministry for Armaments and War Production, Hans Kehrl, later confirmed that in 1944 he had received detailed plans to increase production of gas masks for the entire German population, including special tents to protect infants and babies against chemical warfare.[100] Briefed by leading officials about the existence of German 'super' gases, Brandt discussed the issue of gas warfare with Goebbels to see whether it was appropriate to inform the German public about the possible dangers ahead. On 25 March, the Propaganda Minister noted in his diary:

> Professor Brandt visits me and reports to me about our preparations for gas warfare. These are very poor. There is a lack of gas masks, and there is also a lack of information for the population. The Führer now has ordered a large programme for the production of gas masks, according to which seven million gas masks will be produced monthly from next month onwards... We would then be out of the woods in four to five months. Gas warfare has, God help us, not yet been introduced. What Professor Brandt tells me about the possibilities of gas warfare is truly horrible. But I really believe it to be possible that modern civilized humanity resorts to this instrument to destroy itself. Anyway, it would be irresponsible if we were not to prepare ourselves for such an eventuality. It is a difficult question, whether one should now inform the population about gas warfare. I don't think that is opportune... I therefore order that a sufficient number of gas masks should be produced first; we can then begin propaganda against gas warfare.[101]

For the Nazi regime, accelerating defensive chemical warfare planning to protect the civilian population was a central precondition in the transition to chemical warfare, which included the option of offensive operations with toxic agents, but it also highlighted, more than anything else, the danger of chemical warfare: 'If chemical warfare agents had been used', Brandt later told investigators, 'it would have been impossible for us to have lasted even for weeks. After the first attack with chemical warfare agents the war would have been over for us.'[102] Speer had told Hitler as early as 1943 that Allied air raids with phosphorus ammunition were taking a heavy toll on German

Image 9. Hitler and Karl Brandt at the Führer's 'Wolfsschanze' headquarters,
15 July 1944
Source: Bayerische Staatsbibliothek, Fotoarchiv Hoffmann (hoff-53867).

cities, and that the war could not be sustained if the Allies continued to
launch strategic attacks such as the one on Hamburg in July 1943.[103] For all
concerned, it was clear that chemical warfare could spell disaster for
Germany.

In April 1944, discussions between Brandt, Otto Ambros, chief chemical
adviser to the Nazi government, and his deputy, Jürgen von Klenck, about
the state of German chemical warfare preparedness revealed a lack of respirators for professional groups such as nurses and health officials.[104] Conscious
of 'the enemy's superiority in manufacturing facilities and in stocks of war
gases', Brandt told them that Germany needed to establish 'a new and more
efficient defence' through the availability of more and better gas masks, an
increase in decontaminating agents and charcoal, and the production of

offensive chemical warfare agents as a deterrent. All agreed that Germany's offensive warfare capability should be concentrated on 'the most effective materials, such as mustard gas, Tabun and Sarin'.[105]

At around the same time, a small circle of Nazi officials learned about the discovery of Soman, one of the most deadly nerve agents known to man, which still required further development.[106] Unbeknown to Schrader and many others working in the chemical warfare field, Richard Kuhn, director of the Kaiser Wilhelm Institute for Medical Research in Heidelberg, and his team of scientists had been commissioned by the military to screen various organophosphorus compounds for their level of cholinesterase (ChE) inhibition, and had discovered Soman in the process. When inhaled, Soman turned out to be twice as toxic as Sarin, was able to penetrate through the skin, and quickly affected the central nervous system. Because it inhibited cholinesterase very rapidly, the effective use of antidotes such as atropine was considerably reduced. Experiments on dogs and apes at Gross' laboratory in Elberfeld quickly established the enormous toxicity of the new substance.

In September, Kuhn's research was cut short when the military ordered the destruction of all his laboratory facilities and the transfer of his documents to a location in east Berlin.[107] Allied investigators later acknowledged his leading role in Germany's chemical warfare research, especially in the field of nerve agents. Porton scientists were especially interested in a chemical method measuring the level of cholinesterase inhibition that not only enabled Kuhn's team to estimate the degree of nerve agent exposure but also served as a basis for the development of potential medical therapies. 'Much impressed' by tests with Sarin, Brandt had apparently discussed the 'treatment of Tabun and Sarin poisoning (not Soman)' with Kuhn in the summer of 1944.[108] Although possible, it is highly unlikely that someone in his position, whose power and influence with Hitler was at its zenith in mid 1944, would not have been informed about Kuhn's discovery. For those in authority, his work highlighted the urgent need to accelerate defensive chemical warfare planning to avoid a military disaster.

More worryingly, it was realized that German civilians were vulnerable to nerve agent attacks, assuming that the Allies possessed such substances and were prepared to use them. Existing respirators, designated Type M.44, offered limited protection since nerve agents were absorbed through the skin. The same was true of mustard gas. German civilians, in short, could be exposed to the effects of nerve agents if the Allies possessed similar agents, or, if Germany itself ever used them, the Allies would be able to copy and mass-produce them. For the tightly knit circle of Nazi officials shaping German chemical warfare policy, neither of these two possibilities could be discounted. The authorities also knew that the Allies had large quantities of mustard gas ready to be used as a retaliatory measure against the German heartland at any time.[109]

However, up until the end of August 1944, the German military command, egged on by Nazi party radicals, considered that the sudden deployment of nerve agents in strategically important front-line locations was likely to produce a 'decisive [military] success'.[110] For the time being, reservations voiced by senior officials and logistics experts were brushed aside. In October, the head of the Supreme Command of the Army, General Field Marshal Wilhelm Keitel, turned down Speer's request to reduce the production of chemical warfare agents, of Tabun and mustard gas especially, in order to ensure the continued supply of vitally needed raw and explosive materials for the production of conventional weapons.[111] Others, such as Brandt, despite being Speer's friend, believed that nerve agents could function as effective countermeasures after an Allied gas attack to 'compel the adversary to halt his use of poison gas', and opposed plans to limit or slow down their production.[112] On the contrary, in June 1944 he had asked Himmler about the possibility of increasing chemical warfare production by improving the living conditions in concentration camps that supplied forced and slave factory labourers.[113] After the war, he told investigators that he, Speer, and General Kennes, Assistant Chief of the General Staff, 'had an agreement' to countermand any orders to initiate chemical warfare against the Allies by holding up the 'transport of supplies', which may have been true; on balance, however, Brandt seems to have supported the continued production and possible use of chemical agents to a greater extent than he wanted postwar investigators to believe.[114] Although the Nazi leadership was determined to maintain an offensive chemical warfare capability, in reality the strategic bombing raids by Allied forces against the German aircraft, oil, and ammunitions industries, together with the complete loss of control over German air space, reduced offensive chemical warfare planning to little more than wishful thinking.

The history of the final months of the Third Reich throws into stark relief the importance the German military and political leadership attached to the existence of nerve agents. As late as February 1945, the Army Ordnance Office set up an emergency programme involving the development of industrial manufacturing processes for the nerve agent Soman. In the same month, Hitler issued instructions prohibiting the destruction of chemical warfare agents. When, in early 1945, the advancing Russian forces came dangerously close to threatening the secrecy of, and access to, nerve agents, the regime mobilized transport facilities in the form of freight trains, trucks, and barges to transfer the existing stockpiles of nerve agents to munitions depots in German-controlled territory. In the ensuing chaos, officials removed and safeguarded essential equipment so that the future manufacture of nerve agents could be assured, and buried or destroyed secret documents implicating IG Farben and its leadership in German chemical warfare production.[115]

Determined to hold out to the end and preserve as many options as possible, perhaps to improve German's bargaining position, the Nazi leadership refused to clarify Germany's position vis-à-vis neutral countries about the possible first use of chemical agents. Two weeks before his suicide, Hitler, by now living in a fantasy world, continued to believe in Germany's ability to launch chemical warfare. As the world around him disintegrated, Hitler's ability to wage war from his bunker deep underground rapidly diminished, until the day he knew that the game was up. By the end of April 1945, the Allied forces considered any start of chemical warfare as little more than a 'nuisance' to ongoing military operations. What they did not know, though, was that they were in for a massive shock when the first German munitions depots were captured. One senior Porton official later remarked that it had been 'the one time we were really caught with our trousers down'.[116]

4

Preparing for Total Warfare

The Battle of Britain

The Second World War acted as a central catalyst in expanding and expediting chemical warfare research and development on a colossal scale, one surpassed only by the Allied programme to build an atomic bomb. The risks for those participating in human experiments with toxic agents increased exponentially, and top-secret Allied facilities around the world saw a noticeable decline in the maintenance of professional standards in non-therapeutic research on man. In peacetime, medical ethics guidelines and international conventions had served medical scientists well in keeping legal liabilities and public embarrassment under control, yet during a national emergency, the military officials running a modern war machine felt under pressure temporarily to suspend or lower the standards of certain safety principles in order to advance war-important knowledge. Defending their action retrospectively, some argued that it would have been a greater risk for the defence of the nation if the experiments had not been carried out, and that the risks which had been taken were reasonable and proportionate, a counterfactual assessment which has been challenged in recent years since details of Allied research practices have come to light.[1]

Allied political and military leaders have frequently been credited both with considerable foresight and with strategic and moral leadership for avoiding chemical warfare during the Second World War. Scholars have not, however, fully acknowledged how very close Allied forces came to launching a full-scale chemical onslaught in the European and far eastern theatres of war. Chemical warfare would not only have violated international law and morality as it was known and understood at the time, but would have changed beyond recognition the image and conduct of modern warfare for generations to come. The fact that a potentially devastating event did not happen is seen as tangible evidence of the underlying morality and humanity of Western governments in defending modern civilization. A more thorough reconstruction of Allied chemical warfare planning, as is proposed here, allows us to recognize that no 'lack of preparedness', however serious it may have been in the initial stages of the conflict, would have deterred the Allies from launching chemical warfare if the military situation had required it.[2] Allied forces were indeed planning for total warfare.

Since 1938, British senior officials had believed that the use of toxic agents in conjunction with high explosives against Nazi Germany would 'add seriously to the strain on the morale of the civil population', and divert war-essential resources and personnel to defensive operations.[3] Churchill, in particular, repeatedly pressed his Chiefs of Staff to examine 'in cold blood' the feasibility and strategic benefits of using chemical and biological weapons against the Nazi regime. For him, ethical and political considerations had no part to play in a war that indiscriminately killed women, children, and civilians in large-scale bombing raids from spring 1940.[4] Irrespective of any moral objections or international obligations, chemical warfare was seen as another weapon of war to bring about Germany's unconditional surrender.

At the start of hostilities, Britain, France, and Germany pledged to abide by the Geneva Protocol outlawing the use of chemical and biological weapons, yet none of the parties trusted that the agreement would be observed 'a moment longer than is necessary'.[5] Britain anticipated the use of chemical weapons by one or more of the belligerents. Contingency plans involved the manufacture and distribution of millions of gas masks, anti-gas ointments, and bleach for decontamination. Millions of leaflets were distributed to all households and the BBC was on stand-by to broadcast pre-arranged gas warnings in the event of gas attacks. Following Hitler's *Blitzkrieg* campaign through the Low Countries and the surrender of France in May 1940, the threat of invasion by German forces loomed large in the minds of British officials in London. Two days after the evacuation of the British Expeditionary Force (BEF) from Dunkirk, Sir John Dill, Chief of the Imperial General Staff, proposed to attack invading German forces with mustard gas on beaches and other landing sites. Although Britain was bound by the Geneva Protocol to refrain from using poison gas, except in retaliation, Dill considered that to 'break our word' was a risk worth taking.[6] In a total war, in which millions of civilians were under threat from air raids, ethics and international law ranked second to the government's obligation to protect the

British people, he argued. Support for Dill's proposal was far from unanimous, however. One senior official felt that such a departure from Britain's
'principles and traditions' was not only 'dangerous' but would lead to the
'most deplorable effects' on the British people and its armed services: 'Some
of us would begin to wonder whether it really mattered which side won.'[7]
The controversy reflected the enormous tension which affected the government regarding the issue of chemical warfare like no other; in planning
for Britain's response to an invading enemy, officials were pulled in different
directions, whether to uphold international law and morality on the one
hand, or to defend the realm and its inhabitants by all possible means on the
other. With her back to the wall, and no other options left, it is highly likely
that Britain would have chosen the latter.

Mustard gas and phosgene were Churchill's chemical weapons of choice
to attack deep within the German heartland and cause maximum casualties
and mayhem, but also as weapons which could legitimately be deployed to
defend Britain's beaches, ports, and industry against an invading army. His
retrospective assessment, made after the war, was that the Germans 'would
have used terror, and we were prepared to go all lengths'.[8] Churchill was
relatively vague when he alluded to Britain's readiness to use chemical
weapons, but gave detailed executive instructions to prepare Britain for a
full-scale chemical attack after it had become apparent that the country
possessed only 450 tons of mustard gas, sufficient for about one day of combat operations.[9] Cabinet instructions dating back to 1938 to establish a 'pro-
ductive capacity of 300 tons of mustard gas per week and a reserve of 2,000
tons' had not been implemented. With Britain believed to be in 'very great
danger', Churchill ordered an immediate inquiry to identify those responsible for such a profound error of judgement. In addition, he instructed the
military to establish a chemical warfare reserve of 13,000 tons of mustard gas
within a year, involving the employment of nearly 6,000 people in research,
development, and production of chemical weapons.[10] The failure to implement War Cabinet orders were traced to Sir William Brown, Permanent
Secretary to the MoS, which had taken control of Porton in August 1939.
Apart from being a major bureaucratic oversight, the incident reflected the
administrative and communication problems that affected chemical warfare
work in the early stages of the war.

The outbreak of war turned Porton's research and development programme into a matter of national priority. To overcome the 'semi-stagnation'
into which the station had fallen in peacetime, and break the deadlock of

petty departmental disputes, the authorities appointed Colonel G.L.Watkinson as the new commandant to make the staff 'work together as a team'.[11] A sense of urgency suddenly pervaded the organization. Security was seriously tightened, buildings were camouflaged. Researchers wanting to gain access to 'closed areas' where classified work was being carried out now required special passes. An anti-aircraft battery, manned by members of the Territorial Army (Britain's volunteer reserve force), protected the site against possible air attacks. Suggestions from intelligence sources to the effect that German forces were ready and able to launch chemical warfare 'at any time' expedited contingency plans for the swift relocation of laboratories and staff to alternative facilities in case Porton were bombed.[12] For those preparing Britain's response to German chemical attacks it was essential to have an efficient system for communicating enemy activity in the chemical warfare field. A special unit for the analysis of intelligence information provided Porton with the latest threat assessments, and liaison officers supplied Whitehall officials with bi-monthly situation reports.[13]

Porton established a number of strategically located anti-gas laboratories for the collation and analysis of chemical warfare data. In September 1939, Anti-Gas Laboratory No. 1 was set up near Arras as part of the BEF but was abandoned during the Dunkirk evacuation. A year later, in October 1940, members of Porton's Anti-Gas Laboratory No. 2 were dispatched to base laboratories in Egypt and Palestine, the latter governed by the British Mandate since 1923. In the event of a gas attack, special arrangements between technical officers and anti-gas laboratories were meant to ensure the swift transfer of suspected enemy substances to Porton for examination and identification by an expert committee.[14] In total, Porton trained up to sixty technical officers in chemical warfare matters, among them Owen Haddon Wansbrough-Jones, who later became Scientific Adviser to the Army Council before being promoted to Chief Scientist to the MoS.

The Making of Experts

For the duration of hostilities, the MoS recruited eminent university scientists, many of whom had previously worked in the chemical warfare field.[15] Porton's wartime staff quickly expanded to an estimated 700 to 1,000 employees. Their professional backgrounds had been shaped by both

the armed forces and civilian institutions.[16] Among those approached by
the MoS was Lovatt Evans, who had formerly served Porton as a physiologist
(see Image 10).[17] Others included the distinguished physiologist Sir Joseph
Barcroft (see Image 11) and his former assistant Rudolph Peters from Oxford's
biochemistry department who, together with Robert H.S. Thompson and
Lloyd A. Stocken, conducted human experiments at Porton to develop the
British anti-lewisite (BAL) ointment.[18] A good number of 'Old Portonians'—
the generation of military scientists born in the 1880s—returned to Porton
after being closely associated with the establishment during the Great War.
Claude Gordon Douglas, born in 1882, Fellow of St John's College Oxford
from 1907, joined the RAMC before collaborating with J.S. Haldane,
J. Barcroft, and J.G. Priestly in developing the field of respiratory physiology
after Germany launched its first gas attack. Like most of his former Porton
colleagues, he returned to his peacetime position at Oxford to pursue a career
in physiology during the interwar period. At the outbreak of the Second

Image 10. Sir Charles Lovatt Evans, 3 May 1967
Source: IWM, Photographic Collection. © Imperial War Museums (F 123/1).

Image 11. Sir Joseph Barcroft, *c.* 1940
Source: Wellcome Library, London (M0018946).

World War, Douglas was among many senior scientists returning to Porton
to strengthen Britain's defensive measures against chemical warfare.[19]

Porton also became the wartime workplace for expert pathologists such
as Gordon Roy Cameron, who later became chairman of the Chemical
Defence Board. Born in 1899 in Victoria, Australia, Cameron trained at
the Universities of Melbourne and Freiburg, Germany, where he developed the field of experimental pathology with Ludwig Aschoff at the
Freiburg Pathological Institute. In the 1930s, he moved to University
College Hospital Medical School, London, a bustling hub of current and
future researchers associated with Porton. In 1937, he was promoted to a
chair in pathology with an interest in the aetiology of pulmonary oedema
caused by irritant gases such as phosgene, which is why he was tasked with

devising defensive measures against chemical warfare agents on the outbreak of war.[20] Six years later, he was part of a small team assessing the
level of toxicity of the German nerve agents that the Allied forces had
discovered.[21] In addition, Porton employed a great number of chemists,
including Sir Jocelyn Thorpe, Sir Harry W. Melville, scientific adviser to
the Chief Superintendent of Chemical Defence, and Samuel Sugden, as
well as professor of pharmacology Jack Gaddum, and dozens of scientifically qualified officers and servicemen posted there for the duration of the
war, such as Captain Harry Cullumbine, a chemist, who oversaw and was
ultimately responsible for human field trials, including those which resulted
in serious injury or death, as in the case of Leading Aircraftman Ronald
Maddison in 1953.[22]

Although it is difficult to obtain reliable statistical data about Porton's
military officers, selected biographical evidence about their professional
development reveals certain patterns. Keen to advance their military medical ambitions through overseas experiences, many, if not most, served as
members of the RAMC in countries influenced by British interests, in
India, Hong Kong, Singapore, Palestine, Australia, and Canada especially, but
also in China, Iraq, Egypt, Africa, and the United States. At the same time,
as in the British armed forces generally, Porton attracted a cross-section of
servicemen from Ireland, New Zealand, and Australia, many of whom saw
their temporary appointment at Porton as a necessary rite of passage to
boost their service or civilian medical careers. A prosopographical analysis
of some of Porton's medically qualified servicemen allows us to reconstruct,
in part, certain motivations for why individual soldiers took up an assignment at Porton in the 1930s and 1940s, and highlights their long-term future
association with Britain's chemical and biological warfare programme, often
until or sometimes beyond the age of retirement.

Prior to coming to Porton, a large proportion of officers gained considerable medical experience during their tours of duty in the British Raj.
Born in 1888, Colonel E.C. Linton, RAMC, had served in France during
the Great War before being sent to India, then to China, and back to India
as Director of the Medical Laboratory in Jhansi and as Deputy Assistant
Director of Pathology of the Lucknow district in the 1920s. Upon returning
to Britain, he became the chief pathologist at Porton from 1931 to 1936.[23]
Lieutenant Colonel J.D. Cruickshank, son of the Reverend W.W. Cruickshank
and born in 1911, had studied medicine at Birmingham University before
joining the RAMC in the 1930s. From 1936 to 1945, he served with the

Sixth Indian Field Ambulance in India and Burma. After his promotion to Assistant Director of Pathology, Western Command, he started work as an expert pathologist at Porton.[24]

Group Captain Thomas Montgomery, on the other hand, passed through Porton on his way to serve as Principal Medical Officer for the Air Force in India from 1937 to 1941, and later in Northern Ireland. Born in 1886, he had joined Barcroft's department of physiology at Cambridge and Porton's School of Chemical Warfare in the mid 1920s to study the effects of toxic agents.[25] His time at Cambridge and Porton mirrored that of other high-ranking military officers, including Brigadier Robert Alexander Hepple. Like many of his peers, he had briefly served in India after the Great War but had then returned to Britain for additional chemical warfare training in Barcroft's laboratories and at Porton before returning to his military career in India. Major General Leopold Thomas Poole, the War Office director of pathology during the Second World War, a Scotsman born in Edinburgh in 1888, had likewise been selected for chemical warfare training and inde-pendent research at Porton in the 1920s after postings to Mesopotamia and northern India. In the 1930s, he had returned to India to study the aetiology of sand-fly fever, which was particularly prevalent in the region along the Khyber Pass, the main route between Pakistan and Afghanistan even today. His expertise made him one of the leading military medical advisers on disease prevention in the south-east Asian theatre of war.[26] Porton, it seems, served both as a hub to boost the science of chemical warfare at home and as an important point of reference with which military officer and civilians scientists could identify abroad. Those having worked there acquired the necessary credentials to be admitted into a global network of expert scien-tists who, for the most part, remained committed to the sharing of often highly sensitive knowledge for the rest of their lives.

A noticeable proportion of medical and military personnel passing through Porton during their careers, whether for research or training pur-poses, or both, belonged to the RAMC. In addition, serving officers, and later men doing their National Service, would sometimes be seconded to Porton to undergo their required chemical warfare training.[27] Close collab-oration between the RAMC and Porton helped to establish effective net-works of chemical warfare experts in Britain and abroad which, in turn, provided Porton with vital intelligence for Allied research. Walter Somerville, RAMC, born in Dublin in 1913, did a tour of duty on a troop ship before being sent to Porton, yet it was his two secondments to the Canadian

military and the US Chemical Corps during the war that made him an ideal
candidate to advise the government on chemical and biological warfare for
many years.[28] His career dovetailed well with that of Henry M. Adam, born
in 1911, who, after working at Porton as an RAMC pathologist, was seconded
to the US Army to gather scientific intelligence. Following the liberation of
the Buchenwald concentration camp, he was dispatched to assess German
scientists for alleged medical war crimes and exploit their knowledge, as
part of Allied reparation demands.[29]

Sir James Kilpatrick, future Dean of the London School of Hygiene
and Tropical Medicine (LSHTM), passed through Porton on his way to
becoming Director General of RAF Medical Services. Born in Belfast in
1902, and educated in Ireland, he gained overseas experience as the RAF's
principal medical officer in India, Iraq, and West Africa. His time at Porton
from 1937 to 1939 helped him to obtain important research credentials in
both tropical and preventive medicine.[30] Another Irishman who served at
Porton in the early 1940s was Joseph H.C. Walker, RAMC. Following
postings to Hong Kong, Singapore, Northern Ireland, and Malta, at the
age of 47 he took charge of Porton's Chemical Warfare School and led
it from 1940 to 1942. After the war, Walker joined the Public Health
Laboratory Service (PHLS) and served as an expert adviser for the World
Health Organization (WHO), assessing laboratory facilities in places such
as Indonesia.[31]

Others saw Porton as an ideal opportunity to conduct research. For
example, Sydney Curwen, a member of the Territorial Army, used Porton as
the base for his experimental work in the field of radiotherapy after the
outbreak of war.[32] So did Robert Douglas Harkness, who, after studying
medicine, developed civil defence measures at Porton, an important step-
ping stone for his successful postwar career in the physiology department at
University College London.[33] Among their colleagues was Trevor Charles
Stamp, Baron Stamp of Shortlands. As a member of the Emergency PHLS,
he was engaged in wartime vaccine research at Porton. After 1945, he returned
to his former post at the Postgraduate Medical School at Hammersmith
Hospital, the same school which in the 1960s was widely criticized for
alleged unethical research practices.[34] Lord Stamp later used his privileged
position to comment on subjects such as biological warfare and medical
education in the House of Lords in the 1950s and 1960s.[35] There were also
others, such as Wally Crane, who launched his career as a chemist at Porton
before moving to a more senior position in the Australian MoS.[36] For many,

it seems, Porton offered attractive prospects and laboratory facilities to begin or advance research careers in times of national crisis.

Sometimes a relatively brief period of perhaps two years was sufficient for medical experts to contribute to Porton's research activities or, for more senior staff, assist the organization in an advisory function.[37] Group Captain Gerald Struan Marshall, born in 1889, had served as a temporary lieutenant in the RAMC during the Great War.[38] After taking a diploma in public health, he advanced to become one of the first RAF medical officers doing research work at Porton during the 1920s. As Chief Assistant to the Director of Medical Research, RAF, he became interested in developing pressure suits for pilots flying at high altitudes, a field of work simultaneously attracting the attention of German physiologists who subsequently became involved in concentration camp experiments. Men such as Marshall, whose association with Porton was temporary, were nonetheless part of an expanding network of expert scientists that kept Porton in touch with the latest developments in military medicine and science.

For others, Porton became their professional home for years to come. Born in 1883, Surgeon Captain Archibald Fairley had trained in medicine in Glasgow, a 'rugged, honest and loyal' personality with a strong dislike for all kinds of 'humbug, cant and insincerity'. His otherwise stern personality apparently concealed a 'heart of gold'. He worked as a surgeon in the Royal Navy before being appointed Superintendent of Porton's physiology department in 1932, a position he held for the next twenty years.[39] He was thus, in effect, overseeing the work of men such as Barcroft, Peters, and Lovatt Evans. Aged fifty-six in 1939, Fairley was recognized on both sides of the Atlantic as a leading expert on military toxicology and chemical warfare, someone whom Porton's civilian scientists could readily accept as a superior authority in times of national crisis. Porton's chemical warfare scientists also collaborated with staff at the Biology Department, Porton, headed by Paul G. Fildes.[40]

By the time of their posting to Porton, many scientists were, or were to become, Fellows of the Royal Society, which functioned as an influential power broker of vested scientific interests. Its carefully controlled professional and political network facilitated effective negotiation and mediation between government agencies and Britain's research community. Of the roughly thirty scholars recruited to do wartime work for various government agencies, who were or would become FRS between 1939 and 1950, the MoS took on seventeen. Of these, according to Edgerton, Porton received only three, though the actual number may have been higher.[41] Fellows with close connections to Porton were, for instance, Claude Gordon Douglas (1922), Edgar D. Adrian, Baron Adrian of Cambridge (1923), Charles Lovatt Evans (1925), Paul Gordon Fildes (1934), Neil Kensington Adam (1935), Roy Cameron (1946), Gerald Struan Marshall (1947)—who became a Fellow of the Royal Society of Edinburgh—Wilson Smith (1949), Donald Devereux Woods (1952), Kenneth Bailey (1953), David W.W. Henderson (1959), and Richard H. Adrian, Second Baron Adrian of Cambridge (1977).[42] Field Marshal Viscount Montgomery later remarked: 'Never has it been so necessary for the fighting man and the scientists to work so closely together and for the Service Chief to say clearly what he wants from the scientist.'[43] In fostering this relationship, the Royal Society played a significant part, for all that it was largely invisible to the British public.

Whitehall officials quickly ran into trouble over pay, pensions, and career prospects; civilian scientists disliked red tape and being subordinated to military discipline. Asked to coordinate Porton's physiological research, Lovatt Evans told the MoS that administrative work was not his 'forte'. Besides, conditions at Porton were apparently 'so much a matter of civil service routine that I should soon be lost in the maze'.[44] As it happened, it was all a misunderstanding; after Sir Joseph Barcroft's departure from Porton, the authorities wanted to ensure that the existing lines of communication between the MoS, Porton, and the universities could continue undisturbed to avoid unnecessary duplication of work.[45]

The presence of established civilian scientists provided Porton with vitally important expert knowledge, yet it also exacerbated professional, generational, and, in some cases, gender tensions. In August 1941, after complaints had been received about the 'attitude' of senior staff towards female members of the Auxiliary Territorial Service (ATS) working in the Porton Mess, Watkinson (the commandant) felt compelled to stress the need for more professional forms of interaction: 'The girls are employed in the Mess as servants and must be treated as such.'[46] Lovatt Evans was among those receiving a confidential censure. The discrepancy between the male–dominated Edwardian culture of the Great War, in which the Mess had come to resemble a gentlemen's club, and the expectation of professional conduct between the sexes in the early 1940s must have been considerable for some.

A privileged education, preferably at Oxbridge, patronage, and old-school connections was what mattered then and seemed to matter now, especially for those whose social status was inextricably linked with their professional career.[47] Seeing it might foster his image as a benefactor in higher circles, Lovatt Evans, for example, did not shy away from helping a young Cambridge graduate, posted to Porton as 'laboratory assistant', to be transferred to a more challenging assignment.[48] Lovatt Evans was approached by Hill, President of the Royal Society, whom he had succeeded at University College in the 1920s, and between them they ensured that the matter was raised privately with the Secretary of State for War. Both felt that the authorities should provide the 'poor fellow' with a chance of doing something more interesting than 'acting as a laboratory drudge' which would be 'purgatory to an intelligent man'.[49] Even in times of war, or perhaps because of it, when it came to helping one of their own Britain's establishment knew how to wield professional and political power.

Assured of their professional status and reputation in peacetime, civilian scientists could easily feel undermined by military routine and security protocol. On frequent occasions, ruffled feathers needed to be smoothed and reputations restored. In September 1942, Lovatt Evans formally complained to his superior after being stopped and searched by the police: 'As a Fellow of the Royal Society of 17 years standing, and by far the senior scientist at Porton, I wish to protest formally against this personal affront offered by a Ministry of HM government to a scientist of distinction and good repute.'[50] To calm the situation, Air Commodore G. Combe, RAF, Porton's recently appointed Chief Superintendent, told him that measures were being put in place to avoid such occurrences from happening again.[51] This barely sufficed for Lovatt Evans, since the incident stood 'in vivid contrast to the political clap-trap about the importance and dignity of science in the prosecution of the war'.[52] Working with distinguished men of science in times of war certainly required considerable diplomatic skills.

As far as the government was concerned there was a general consensus that the expertise of Lovatt Evans and his colleagues was indispensable if gas warfare were to be initiated. In October 1941, the Director of Chemical Warfare (DCW), General Headquarters, Home Forces, inquired at the MoS about the possibility of placing him on 'Action Stations' as senior civilian adviser: 'If gas is used in this country, I think we will be expected to advise in high circles.'[53] Later, in July 1942, when arrangements for a 'possible gas blitz' were reviewed, Porton was told that Lovatt Evans had been designated to hold himself available in London to advise, in the event of gas warfare, the DCW, the Scientific Adviser of the Ministry of Home Security, and the

Controller, Chemical Defence Development (CCDD), who reported directly to the Cabinet.

Since 1940, the worsening military situation had focused military minds on strengthening Britain's chemical warfare capability, given that her defensive preparedness was more advanced than her ability to retaliate. Because offensive chemicals weapons were outlawed by international agreements, Britain's scientists and industry had lacked the necessary political support and funding to develop them in the interwar period. Retaliating in kind against an aggressor would have meant the employment of the chemical weapons technology of the Great War, a situation which was unacceptable for the government.[54] Britain needed to gear up to defend herself against gas warfare and retaliate, if necessary, with the latest chemical armoury.

Wartime liaison between Porton and the armed services was maintained through an established network of scientists and military officials, many of whom had built up a professional rapport during the interwar years. Officials from the Directorate of Special Weapons and Vehicles (DSWV), posted to the establishment in the 1930s, created efficient lines of communication between Porton and the War Office that helped researchers gain approval for the allocation of scarce resources and manpower. Although chemical warfare operations were formulated by policy committees such as the Chemical Defence Research Department (CDRD), and passed down the line of command, experiments with toxic agents were often initiated by Porton scientists in consultation with their colleagues in the armed services. High-ranking military representatives frequently visited Porton to discuss, at times over a glass of wine, progress on chemical warfare technology. Porton scientists, on the other hand, sat on joint service committees to coordinate Britain's wartime preparedness, and collaborated with the School of Artillery, the Royal Armoured Corps, and the Ordnance Board.

At a training level, Porton established a good working relationship with the service schools, especially with the Combined Gas School, located in close proximity at Winterbourne Gunner, Wiltshire. It regularly supplied Porton with research subjects from the Army and RAF in 'ad hoc user trials'.[55] Porton also maintained close contact with the Navy Gas Schools at Devonport, Portsmouth, and Chatham, and contributed to the publication of training manuals such as the 'Chemical Warfare Pocket Book', the so-called 'CW Bible'.[56] In an attempt to bring 'designers and users' closer together, and foster mutual cooperation and trust, the military gave senior scientists access to classified intelligence and operational information that helped them in constructing realistic field trials with human participants. Porton, in other words, came to enjoy an unprecedented level of independence, political influence, manpower, and resources, and this allowed it to shape Britain's chemical warfare preparedness during the war.

As far as defensive equipment was concerned, Britain was believed to be sufficiently prepared to withstand a major chemical warfare attack. Some regarded the country's 'gas defensive preparedness' as being among the 'best in the world'.[57] By 1941, Britain had manufactured 70 million civilian gas masks, of which 3.2 million were allocated for key workers. In collaboration with research laboratories and industry, Porton developed special respirators for babies and small children, for dogs and horses, a gas-proof cover for carrier pigeon baskets, and eyeshields for camels. For service personnel, the government commissioned the production of 400,000 'assault respirators'. Defensive preparations involved the development of special devices for the detection of liquid and vaporized chemical agents, and the distribution of the 'Detector Vapour Pocket' for untrained operators. To defend Britain's war-important industry, the military commissioned the development of efficient methods for the protection of industrial targets, railways, and dockyards from gas warfare. Early in 1940, when Britain expected chemical attacks from German submarines and aircraft on major ports along the East Coast, Porton took the lead in developing filtration units and the gas proofing of command posts, shelters, and ships.

Offensive preparations involved expanding and expediting the production of chemical warfare agents and their transfer to bulk-storage depots and filling stations across the country.[58] From 1937, Imperial Chemical Industries operated a series of process research and agency factories on behalf of the MoS, for example at Sutton Oak, to produce, in total secrecy, stockpiles of known and novel chemical warfare agents.[59] At an estimated total cost of 20 million pounds sterling, production capacity for mustard gas drastically increased in the agency factories on Wigg Island, near Runcorn, later known as 'Randle', now Wigg Island Community Park, which became operational in 1937; at Springfield, Lancashire, in 1940; and at the Valley Works at Rhydymwyn, North Wales, where the manufacturing and charging of toxic agents started in early 1941. Another three agency factories were established for 'intermediary' products. From 1938, Valley Works—like Randle, believed to be beyond the range of enemy bombers—also served as a secure underground storage depot for Britain's reserve stock of chemical weapons, and later doubled as a secret facility in developing the Allied nuclear programme, code-named 'Tube Alloy'. At Randle, production concentrated on a weekly output of 200 tons of 'Pyro M'. Whereas standard 'Pyro' had a 15 per cent carbon tetrachloride content to lower the freezing point of mustard gas, and thus make it more suitable for an anticipated aerial bombing attack by Allied forces, researchers at Sutton Oak had developed 'Pyro M', a compound in which the carbon tetrachloride content was replaced with monochlorobenzene to make the substance more stable at high altitudes. The emphasis on the manufacture of vesicant agents, which were resistant to the risk of freezing, as opposed to standard mustard gas, which could be delivered by artillery shells, highlighted the importance placed by the British military upon aerial warfare with chemical weapons.

From the late 1930s, Porton's scientists were intricately involved in the research and development processes of chemical agents. By designing a prototype head-filling machine, which was used at the poison gas factory at Rhydymwyn, they attempted to assist with the filling of chemical shells, yet several of Porton's 'inventions' turned out to be too complex and unreliable for their intended purpose.[60] Additionally, experts from Porton helped South Africa in setting up a full-scale manufacturing plant which produced mustard gas and phosgene to British requirements.[61] Technical and moral support reached Allied scientists from another quarter. From the outbreak of war, émigré scientists such as Curt Wachtel, founder of the Pharmacological Department of the Kaiser Wilhelm Institute and former director of the Institute of Industrial Hygiene and Professional Diseases in Berlin, tried to raise awareness about the dangers of chemical warfare through a detailed study and evaluation of the development of new gases.[62] Meanwhile, Porton tested other substances as well; between 1941 and 1942, for example, scientists conducted fifteen trials with ricin, an extremely toxic protein of natural origin, to assess its chemical warfare potential.[63] By 1943/44, the stockpile of toxic agents and munitions had reached a 'satisfactory' level and, although output was significantly reduced compared to previous years, Britain retained its large-scale production capability in order to be prepared if gas war were to be initiated.

Whereas Britain and her allies made only moderate progress in developing new and more toxic chemical warfare agents, albeit not so toxic as German nerve agents, military scientists were reasonably successful in designing more effective delivery systems. Work at Porton included the modification and evaluation of enhanced gas shells, grenades, mortar bombs, gas-filled rockets, and aircraft weapons. In 1940, the RAF urgently requested the supply of smoke devices to support day-time air raids on military facilities along the French coast. Some scientists conducted trials with lachrymatory anti-tank bullets to wage gas warfare against German tank formations; others concentrated their efforts on aircraft spraying devices and phosphorus bombs to be used against German civilians and in the Pacific. Given that Allied combat operations were affected by, and had to adapt to, geographical and meteorological conditions, research focused on different terrains, diseases, and climate zones. In 1944, a small party of Porton scientists was even dispatched to the Arctic Circle to study the 'effects of cold climates on the performance of naval smoke equipment'.[64] In putting Britain on a total war footing and conducting chemical warfare work on a global scale, military scientists believed that their work transcended national and moral boundaries. One Porton official later remarked: 'We had to be prepared to retaliate at once.'[65]

Human Experiments

To test the potency of known and novel chemical warfare agents, and develop effective measures for the treatment of gas casualties, experiments on human beings intensified throughout the war. Capitalizing on over twenty-five years of experience, Porton's physiology department, led by Fairley, stood at the forefront of providing the military with a 'final assessment' of the offensive and defensive value of chemical compounds.[66] Experiments with blistering and harassing agents, administered as individual drops on subjects' skin in field trials, chamber tests, or during training exercises, were not without risk, and in a large number of cases the participants experienced significant discomfort and pain from burns and other injuries requiring treatment.[67] Exposure to mustard gas and lewisite, among the most potent of Britain's toxic agents, frequently produced severe and painful blisters on the subject's skin. Research subjects numbered in their hundreds and thousands; an estimated twenty servicemen were required each week for various trials, and Britain's chemical warfare scientists encountered difficulties in maintaining a 'steady flow of volunteers'.[68] One Porton official later described the 'provision' of research subjects as one of the 'most important contributions' the armed services had made to the work at Porton, but acknowledged that their role was 'little known to the outside world'.[69]

Whereas the authorities had previously refused permission for experiments considered to be harmful to participants, and had taken extra safety precautions since the promulgation of the Geneva Protocol, the outbreak of war shifted the main focus to the defence of the British mainland; this increased external political and military pressure on Porton's scientific establishment to advance chemical warfare preparedness and thus decreased, albeit indirectly, the level of protection afforded to experimental subjects. Since the mid 1920s, research participants had been 'subject to conditions and safeguards approved from time to time by the Army Council'; it is not clear, however, that these were either fully applied or independently monitored. Some have argued that researchers had to follow few if any 'external constraints' that would have placed the tests within well-defined ethical bounds, and that there was no kind of verification system in place, but records seem to suggest that some form of ministerial oversight did exist, however vague it may appear in retrospect.[70]

In 1937, the head of the Chemical Warfare Department reiterated the government's cautious approach to non-therapeutic human experiments by stating that the War Office had 'repeatedly refused' to sanction the use of subjects from outside Porton for 'breathing tests against arsenical or other gases'.[71] Now, two years later, with the country under threat of invasion, the ethical landscape was redrawn as the official and unofficial parameters of risk were beginning to shift. By granting military researchers greater latitude in conducting tests involving some, and sometimes considerable, risk, it was hoped to advance chemical warfare knowledge and development.[72] This became apparent in extended test series with harassing agents. A War Committee memorandum from April 1940 about experiments with sternutators, chemicals which can cause irritation to the nasal and respiratory passages, highlighted that the framework within which human subjects were permitted to be exposed to certain risks had expanded. Having had similar tests turned down before the war, Porton's Chief Superintendent yet again requested permission for experiments with toxic smoke by stressing the 'difference between peace and war conditions and the increase in the importance of the experimental work being carried out on sternutators'.[73] Porton also asked for general approval to call on volunteers from the Chemical Companies stationed at Winterbourne Gunner for large-scale field trials with chemical warfare agents. The official in charge minuted that there was no 'objection on medical grounds to the application put forward. These tests would be carried out under expert supervision and with adequate precautions. I therefore support the application.'[74] For Britain's military, it seemed only prudent to take somewhat greater risks in understanding the action of certain warfare agents that the enemy might employ against her armed forces.

At the same time, the military raised concerns when soldiers returning to their units were deemed unfit for service, having sustained multiple injuries from mustard gas experiments. In an attempt to entice soldiers to volunteer for tests, Porton was permitted to offer financial rewards and extra leave, and to make their stay comfortable, yet some officials, anticipating lengthy litigation procedures, at first rejected the idea of making extra payments to servicemen who had suffered from 'severe mustard burns incurred during a trial which was considered to have a special risk'.[75] In the end, Whitehall acknowledged its legal duty to protect the health and well-being of its citizens, including servicemen, and, despite concerns that payments might be 'over-generous', compensated those who had suffered at the hands of the state—for example a soldier who 'had been blinded for more than three days by mustard gas'.[76]

In marked difference to the postwar period, all departments of Porton regularly participated in human experiments, although predominantly in those with harassing agents. An army of men and women working in Porton's laboratories and administrative departments, trained as medical scientists, office clerks, and engineers, had heeded the call to defend Britain. Apart from isolated incidents where scientists accidentally exposed themselves to small amounts of lewisite, for example, and suffered an 'attack of dermatitis', the risks involved in the tests were significantly lower than in those with blistering agents that were conducted almost exclusively on service personnel.[77] Subjects participating in the tests were recruited from the Royal Engineers Chemical Companies, who were trained in implementing gas defences, and later from Porton personnel.[78] All new members of staff, including women, had to undergo a sensitivity test with mustard gas, but that was all, except on two occasions when staff members were asked to detect the smell of lewisite.[79]

In looking at the relationship between the status of different experimental groups within the military hierarchy, and the risks to which the different groups were exposed in experiments, Porton seems to have applied the principle that the lower the rank and importance of the group for ongoing military operations, the greater the risk to which the participants could be exposed. Such a system of recruitment was neither explicitly sanctioned by the authorities, nor based upon clearly formulated policy directives, nor was it implemented systematically and consistently at all times; rather it reflected the diverse roles which different social classes and professional groups traditionally held within the British military. Military rank, professional status, and social class all seem to have played a defining role in deciding who would be exposed to what kind of agents at which level of toxicity. Almost all experiments involving mustard gas, nitrogen mustard, or lewisite, for example, were conducted on service personnel of the armed forces.

Many of Porton's participants belonged to the Royal Engineers, some of whom had been awarded the George Cross for their service to the British Empire.[80] One of them, Wilfred Hall, from a nearby Chemical Warfare Company, who was twice hospitalized for a week in early 1940 after being exposed to blistering agents, later remarked: 'You name it, we did it... I was coughing for about 36 hours.'[81] Reflecting on the events with the benefit of hindsight, Hall and many others stressed that they had had limited choice about taking part in the tests. Indeed, some of them had been encouraged, ordered, and in some cases misled or coerced: 'I was not a volunteer. We was [sic] in the army. It was a matter of you're going and that's it.'[82] Porton's experimental programme evoked memories of gas chamber tests in which Hall and his peers were subjected to toxic substances, but he also remembered moments of solidarity and empowering disobedience, for example when they all refused to return to the gas chamber: 'We told [the officials] that we were not going in no more [sic]. We had [had] bloody enough of it. Absolutely everyone refused. We all stood fast and said "That's it, we are not doing it any more."' [83] According to Hall, the researchers discontinued further trials, at least for the time being and with this contingent of men, but there is no corroborating evidence to back up the sequence of events. If the assumption is correct that such isolated incidents of disobedience and perhaps even resistance against some of the experiments may have occurred, for Porton it became even more essential to foster a close relationship with military commanders and their units to ensure a steady supply of human subjects. By 1941, the number of servicemen available for Porton trials had decreased to such an alarming level that the British military felt compelled to make the recruitment of subjects the responsibility of all commands, either 'in proportion, or in rotation'. Rumours circulating in military units about Porton's experimental programme had led to a general reluctance among soldiers to take part in gas warfare tests. In some cases these were nothing but 'exaggerated stories', officials noted; in others it was the 'fear of the unknown' which apparently held the men back from volunteering. Given the perceived urgency of conducting trials of 'special national importance', the government eventually granted servicemen additional privileges, payments, and extra leave in return for their participation in human experiments.[84]

Later in the war, when manpower shortages made extensive tests increasingly difficult, Porton began using Axis and other foreign nationals who had been interned at the start of hostilities. To help the war effort, many had joined the Pioneer Corps after their release in 1941. As the 'dumping ground of the British Army', the Corps enjoyed a poor reputation, as a labour force of 'illiterates and former criminals' who cleaned the nation's lavatories and dug ditches. Porton's scientists were naturally concerned about the physical fitness of some of the subjects, which, according to some, was 'too low' and could render the findings unreliable. How many members of the Pioneer Corps were recruited to take part in gas tests, and how this was done, is as yet unknown. Some tests used German scientists as participants, yet information about their identity or how they ended up at Porton remains equally vague.[85]

Trials to establish the effectiveness of blistering agents, so-called 'vesicant power tests', included 'sensitivity studies', trials with 'variants', and experiments with 'alternatives' to mustard gas, code-named H or HS, and lewisite, code-named L. Since 1931, the British military had used sensitivity studies as a safety precaution to exclude hypersensitive subjects from further participation in chemical tests.[86] During the war, Porton collaborated closely with the MRC in studying the issue of hypersensitivity and concluded that 'succeeding exposures [to mustard gas] resulted in greater sensitivity'.[87] In the summer of 1942, mustard gas trials involving thirty-four soldiers also corroborated the assumption about the relative insensitivity to the agent of the skin of the hand, evidence suggesting that the handling of mustard gas posed only a minor hazard.[88] A few months later, in December 1942, six participants developed blisters after being exposed to mustard gas on their upper arm, forearm, back, and leg. Previously, Porton's scientists had tested the normal reaction of the skin to lewisite among 250 subjects from the armed services. Given the great variations in the skin reactions recorded, the results were somewhat confusing, even more so once the tests had been repeated.[89] If anything, the experiments suggested that skin reaction to lewisite was

more unpredictable than the 'well ordered' reaction to mustard gas, evidence
that could have—but does not seems to have—informed scientists in the
1950s of potentially wide variations in how the body might react to nerve
agents. Experiments to study the effects of different types of warfare agents,
including mustard agents, on the skin of servicemen continued long after
the end of the war (see Image 12).

Trials with variants of mustard gas or lewisite involved tests with different
dilutants of one of the agents, or mixtures and chemical analogues of both
that were compared to the pure agent, whether newly synthesized or taken
from stored samples. With the majority of tests conducted during the critical
phase of the war, hundreds of soldiers were exposed to a whole range of blistering agents; between September 1939 and July 1943, a total of 293 soldiers
participated in trials with mustard gas variants, and between January 1940
and March 1941, 123 men took part in tests with variants of lewisite.[90]
Though we have little evidence of how their bodies reacted to these agents,
we can safely assume that many of them suffered from burn injuries of varying severity. In July 1943, another twenty men were exposed to different
concentrations of mustard gas in lubricating oil which was applied to their
arms, twice a day after washing, for three weeks. This time, Porton was forced

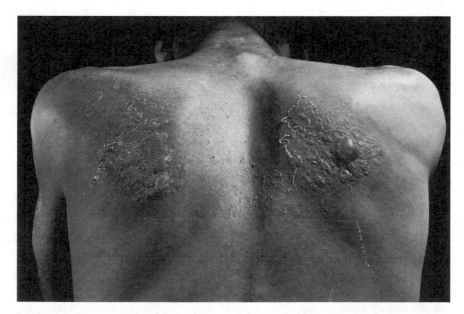

Image 12. Burns on shoulders of Porton 'observer', 1953
Source: IWM, Photographic Collection, Burns on Shoulder of 'Observers', 3 June 1953. © Imperial War
Museums (L 1545/1).

to terminate the trial prematurely, because some of the men developed severe erythema (redness) of the skin. No report of the study has yet been found.[91]

Hoping to 'pull a quick one on the Hun', Porton scientists also sought to discover alternative and more potent agents: 'Typically, a volunteer would have a drop of the new substance placed on his arm, together with a drop of either H [mustard gas] or L [lewisite] to allow a direct comparison of the effects. Hundreds of these tests were conducted.'[92] Nitrogen mustard had been considered but discarded by the General Staff before the war, but researchers developed a keen interest in it after a French delegation high-lighted certain advantages of the agent, and following receipt of intelligence information about a newly developed German agent called *Stickstofflost*, which was a nitrogen mustard gas.[93] It not only appeared to be more diffi-cult to detect by smell than mustard gas but also promised to have a more potent effect on the eyes of subjects. Trials to study the effects of various types of nitrogen mustard gas (HN-2 and HN-3) began in June 1939 and lasted until February 1943, involving a total of 281 servicemen.[94] Other than confirming the limited value of nitrogen mustard as a warfare agent, the experiments did not yield any significant results.

A subsequent test series with dozens of subjects was aimed at determin-ing the relative ease with which low concentrations of blistering agents other than mustard gas could be detected by their smell, something which turned out to be impossible for untrained personnel.[95] Terence Barnes of the Royal Engineers, who saw Porton's work as 'part of his soldierly duties', was one of those participating in the tests. For him, as for many others, there was never a question of choice. He remembered having to walk 'over unknown poison gas on a piece of ground' without any form of protection, and being questioned by a 'few bigwigs' on whether he could detect the agent by its smell.[96] Godfrey Henman, then twenty-one years old and mem-ber of a group of some thirty Sappers, was similarly instructed to walk slowly through a contaminated field, but was not given any information about the nature or purpose of the experiment: 'We were told nothing.'[97]

Many of the experiments were performed to determine the threshold dose, the point below which the agent had no or only a minor effect on the human body. Tests with the vapour of blistering agents required the arms of servicemen to be exposed to a stream of air containing the vapour of the blistering agent: 'Typically, the vapour was directed down a tube onto a small area of the arm for a few minutes and the reaction of the skin moni-tored.'[98] In August 1939, fourteen men were exposed to lewisite vapour for thirty minutes; other than a mild redness of the skin, none of the subjects showed any reaction. Four years later, in August 1943, the test was repeated on twenty-four subjects to establish the threshold dose. Four groups of six servicemen were each exposed to 250, 500, 750, and 1000 mg·min/m³. Two of the six men exposed to the highest dose suffered from blisters, the other eighteen from mild erythema.[99]

A final test series with the vapours of blistering agents concentrated on one of the most sensitive and important organs humans have to make sense of their immediate reality: the eyes. Although documentation is fragmented, and in some cases non-existent, we know that between July and October 1941 the eyes of fifty-five soldiers were exposed to varying concentrations and durations of application of mustard vapour, ranging from fifteen seconds (at 343.2 mg/m³) to eight hours on three consecutive days (at 0.102 mg/m³). A year later, Porton conducted a test to assess the effects of nitrogen mustard (HN-2) on human eyes; we know that the subjects suffered from consistent and severe pain and headache, sleep deprivation, extreme sensitivity to light, tearing, and sudden contractions of the eyelids, but that is all we know. It is not known how many servicemen took part in the test. A report summarizing the findings of the study concluded that 'an exposure level of 100 mg·min/m³ would induce casualties through eye effects alone'.[100] Another test series with nitrogen mustard, conducted in 1943, took even greater risks with the eyes of the participants; of twenty-one subjects, three men suffered from more severe symptoms: 'One of the three men was considered a casualty, and the other two had symptoms for 4–5 days and one of those had definite corneal damage.'[101] Given that nitrogen mustard had generally been found wanting as a chemical warfare agent, and had largely been discarded by the military, one may wonder why the test series was carried out over such a prolonged period, and with what appears to be increasing risk to the health of the subjects. Other than satisfying basic scientific curiosity and determining threshold doses, the tests contributed little if anything to the war effort.

Another area of investigation involving hundreds of servicemen and staff between 1940 and 1942 focused on the effectiveness of, and protection against, a range of harassing agents. Experiments included variants of known harassing agents, skin reaction tests, trials to study their effects on the eyes of volunteers, aircraft spraying tests, and simulated attacks against tanks.[102] In performance trials, participants were positioned at a distance from a generator producing a cloud of the harassing agent, waited there for a couple of minutes, and then performed certain activities such as rangefinder or pegboard tasks.[103] In all, 198 servicemen took part in field trials with harassing agents in May and June 1941 alone, and another 124 soldiers and forty-eight civilian staff members in chamber tests. In another case a 'surprise attack was mounted in the early morning against soldiers on an exercise' to study the potency of particular harassing agents.[104]

Tests did not always go according to plan. In one incident civilians living in caravans in the vicinity of Porton, in all likelihood travelling Sinti and Roma, including children aged between six weeks and ten years, were unintentionally exposed to a harassing agent. Interviewed about the accident, one of the occupants remarked 'that the children reacted to the gas first, waking up coughing and crying. He and his wife concluded they were experiencing gas but did not put on their respirators.'[105] The case was a poignant reminder of the extent to which the presence of Porton's chemical warfare trials affected the surrounding countryside and villages. Close proximity between laboratories and field range provided the scientists with an efficient infrastructure to test toxic agents under real life conditions, provided any health risk to the local population were negligible. For most of the time, local residents were blissfully ignorant of what was going on at Porton. In collaboration with the armed services, spray trials with harmless liquids were carried out over Salisbury to a height of up to 10,000 feet, in which 'inhabitants were hit by drops of an effective size without knowing it'.[106] 'Only God alone knows what's going on there', is how one of the locals living in the vicinity summarized the feelings of many.[107]

More seriously, a number of experiments were designed to cause military casualties of varying severity. In one case, a tank trial (see below), a soldier was accidentally killed. From 1941, Porton conducted mustard gas weapons trials on the field range to study the technical design and quality of dispersion of chemical weapons, which in many cases involved human subjects, some of whom had previously been exposed to blistering agents. Of ten servicemen wearing protective trousers, rubber boots, respirator, hood, and gloves, and thus exposed in October 1941 to a cloud of mustard gas, only two 'escaped any kind of skin damage'.[108] Another eight men suffered from lesions of 'casualty severity' which required immediate medical treatment, and two of the soldiers 'developed fresh blisters around the site of their previous lesions and were admitted to hospital eight and eleven days (respectively) after the trial'.[109] A year later, the scientists examined new dispersion techniques with only a handful of participants. This time, the success rate in the production of mustard gas casualties was 100 per cent. Of the three men exposed, all 'became severe casualties necessitating hospital treatment but the full effects did not develop until nearly a week after exposure'.[110] A report subsequently noted that the effects of the trial had been 'much more severe than expected'.[111]

Tests became increasingly severe and the risks involved increasingly high. In January 1942, a field trial examined the 'dissemination capabilities' of two methods for the release of mustard gas; nineteen servicemen were positioned as 'detectors' near a suspended screen onto which gas shells were fired from a range of 400 yards until 'all men were suitably contaminated'.[112] Eleven of the nineteen subjects were classified as casualties requiring medical treatment, sustaining severe burns through their battle dress. They were not permitted to return to their units until they had recovered sufficiently 'to be treated by their regimental medical officer'. Eight of the eleven men were declared 'unfit for duty for 30 or 32 days after the trial'.[113] Because cold weather reduced the potency of mustard gas, it had been decided to subject the servicemen to a particularly heavy contamination 'to ensure casualties'.[114] One can hardly imagine the agony and pain these men would have endured.

For some of the Porton staff, though, the trials were more of a nuisance when road blocks for a 'ground contamination shoot' delayed their weekly shopping in Salisbury.[115] Others enjoyed taking 'long walks' around the Wiltshire countryside or going off in groups to visit Salisbury cathedral, blissfully oblivious to ongoing warfare tests with highly toxic agents. A subsequent trial to study possible treatments for vesicant burns produced a total of thirty-one casualties, many of whom required immediate hospital treatment.[116] Lives at Porton clearly revolved around different types and experiences of reality.

One of those experiencing disproportionate pain was twenty-six-year-old Army Service Corps driver Richard Daykin, who had joined up with his 'mates' to go to Porton because they had been 'bored at the time'. It retrospect, he felt 'like a bloody fool' for volunteering for the tests in 1941. Dressed in a captured German uniform to study the level of protection afforded to enemy soldiers, he was exposed to the vapours of an exploding mustard gas shell detonated above his head on a target board, leaving him with blisters on his hand and life-long scars. Others required immediate hospital treatment following severe burns.[117]

Some trials were meant to develop defensive equipment in areas of technological vulnerability, or enhance the protection of specialized military units. Tanks and their crews, for example, were vulnerable to gas attacks. During the North Africa campaign, the Army posted a tank officer to

Porton and invited one of their representatives onto the Anti-Tank Committee.[118] In January 1942, live ammunition containing the harassing agent CN was fired at a Valentine tank travelling at normal speed and the effects on the crew were measured. It took the cloud two seconds to penetrate the inside of the tank, and this made the crew leave the tank with 'severe lachrymation'. The British doctor David Sinclair, who took part in the tests under the direction of Captain Harry Cullumbine, later recalled: 'I was the lucky one who had a respirator on, and I had to observe the reactions of the unfortunates who had not.'[119] It vividly demonstrated how harassing agents which infiltrated and incapacitated tank crews through the ventilation system posed a serious threat to combat operations, findings which Cullumbine published after the war in the *BMJ*.[120]

Porton's scientists assumed that the glass grenades fired at tanks were safe, and could not penetrate the armoured plates or damage them to the extent that 'shards of metal would be released inside the tank'. The fatal injury mentioned above occurred on 3 January 1944, when three 20 mm bullets containing a harassing agent were fired at a tank with nine people on board. The incident prompted Porton to concede that the risks involved had been underestimated: 'One of the bullets discharged a small fragment which penetrated the complicated armour defences of the tank and struck the volunteer in the neck.' In the subsequent inquest, held in secret two days later, the Coroner issued a verdict of 'death by misadventure'.[121] The handling of the case by the military authorities and the Coroner showed distinct similarities to the death of Leading Aircraftman Ronald Maddison, who died after exposure to a fatal dose of nerve agents in the early 1950s. Any public disclosure of Britain's extensive chemical warfare programme needed to be avoided by all means.

Royal Engineers tasked with repairing damaged bridges contaminated with chemical agents also needed additional protective garments and gas masks requiring extended field trials. In mid October 1941, prompted by concerns over delays in repairing damaged railways after air attacks with bombs containing warfare agents, Porton carried out a field trial with mustard gas on a disused railway line near Medbourne in Leicestershire. The experiment was akin to the farcical events portrayed in *Dad's Army*, the satirical sitcom on the British Home Guard. Those participating in the test were neither servicemen nor staff. Instead, some sixty civilian workers, many 'above military age', with no gas training, were asked to repair the damaged and contaminated line. On the day, though, a strong gust of wind blew across the railway line and over the contaminated thirty-foot-wide crater, thus contaminating neighbouring fields and cattle. Having been informed of the ground contamination, the men refused to attend the scene for two hours, and when they finally arrived they worked for short periods of time only, because the protective clothing they were required to wear was deemed to be inadequate. With no organized procedure in place, they contaminated their tools, the track, and their own clothing, which led to 'complication and definite danger'. By now the scene had descended into total chaos. A report subsequently found that the men 'had an exaggerated view of the danger' of mustard gas; whereas some of their precautions were 'overly elaborate', others were omitted, thus spreading the ground contamination further.[122] It was a rare case in which historical reality matched, perhaps even surpassed, postwar satire on wartime Britain.

Porton's scientists conducted hundreds of experiments on thousands of servicemen to examine the quality of existing protective garments, for example prolonged chamber tests with mustard vapour on servicemen wearing ordinary battle dress and protective face-pieces.[123] The men would sometimes sit in the chamber and be exposed to chemical agents for hours on end, interrupted only by brief interludes to have a meal or relieve themselves. In June and July 1941, for example, three groups of four servicemen were exposed to mustard vapour for four, six, and seven hours respectively.[124] In March 1942, prolonged tests with nitrogen vapour were carried out on six servicemen 'wearing battle dress and respirators', each being exposed to the agent for one hour per day for up to five consecutive days. After two exposures, three of the subjects had developed erythema in their armpits, scrotum, and scalp, and were 'withdrawn' from the study, and after four exposures, another two of the men were removed from the experiment. None of the servicemen was classified as a military casualty until after the scientists had yet again exposed the same individuals to mustard vapour in a separate trial, 'three being severe causalities due to scrotal burns'.[125]

In some cases, the experiment had long-term and sometimes life-long consequences for the people involved. For Harry Hogg, a corporal in his late twenties from RAF Honington in Suffolk, the experience of being a test subject in the experiments for ten or twelve days was not only deeply traumatic, but left him with a feeling of having been misled. At the end of 1942, after seeing a recruitment notice in his station, he had applied for a position to maintain chemical weapons at another army base, but was transferred to Porton. At first assuming that he was being sent to a training course on chemical weapons, he found himself being 'herded' into a small gas chamber upon his arrival: 'There was no ventilation. There were no windows. There was just a small light in the ceiling. And a thick door of course, with a peep hole in the door.'[126] Other than being told that 'no man would be let out until everyone was on their hands and knees', soldiers were given no information about the experiment. For Hogg, it was a horrific event. He heard the scientists close the door and release the gas, and was aware that they were monitoring the group through a small peep hole while every man in the chamber desperately tried to breathe in air nearer the door, believing his lungs were 'bursting':

> It seemed like an eternity. They opened the door and we all piled out. Hands and knees, groaning and moaning and crying and oh goodness... one man in particular, who was a little bit older than I was, was just like an animal. He was trying to eat grass. He was out of his mind. It was horrendous what we went through.[127]

Under pressure to produce tangible scientific data that could be used in defending the country against German gas warfare, Porton scientists sometimes showed little regard for the rights and dignity of their human subjects. Without malicious intent, they frequently breached established standards of professional medical conduct. Theirs was a wartime emergency requiring urgent and decisive action, they believed, one in which there was little time to worry about ethics.

Whenever they were asked to reassure the Allies about the prevailing conditions in experiments on 'volunteer observers', as was the case in August 1944, Porton's leadership, ever sensitive to its reputation in military circles, constructed an image of an organization in which experiments were performed in accordance with the latest research standards. Following discussions at the Inter-Service Committee on Chemical Warfare (ISCCW) about supplying soldiers from the US Strategic Air Forces in Europe for a series of mustard gas tests at Porton, Colonel A.E. Childs of the MoS told Colonel H.J. Baum, CWS, Air Service Command, that all personnel were medically supervised and that, based on past experience, severe casualties requiring hospitalization were 'very rare'.[128] According to Porton, all tests were conducted to produce only the 'minimum effects' required by a specific experiment: 'It is only very rarely that more serious results are sought and then the observer is told fully what results are expected and given full freedom to refuse.'[129] The scientists apparently exercised the 'greatest care' to ensure that human volunteers would not be exposed to any 'undue hazard' or 'unjustifiable risk', Baum was told. On the whole, Porton was portrayed as a place that British servicemen greatly appreciated, if not enjoyed, as most of them apparently regarded their visit 'as a bit of a joy ride'.[130] Rather than being a fair description of the conditions awaiting soldiers at Porton, Child's report was aimed at strengthening bilateral relations with the United States; acceptable inter-Allied propaganda, perhaps, but not more. This is not to say that Allied soldiers participating in Porton experiments were not well looked after; on the contrary, they seem to have received privileged treatment from the Porton authorities, who went out of their way to ensure a steady flow of servicemen from sources other than the British armed forces.[131]

Studies on clothing examined the level of protection afforded by ordinary but impregnated battle dress and 'anti-gas' clothing against liquid and vaporized chemical warfare agents, the irritancy of different rubber mixes to the human skin as part of ongoing gas-mask developments—tests which continued until the mid 1980s—and the effectiveness of decontamination methods.[132] Impregnated denim suits, for example, provided good protection against mustard vapour and were recommended for mechanized units of the Army. In 1941, garments impregnated with carbon were developed for men at RAF and Army units and certain civilian workers. For Kenneth Henson, a thirty-four-year-old serviceman from the Royal Engineers Chemical Warfare Company, who had volunteered to go to Porton for a day, experiments with mustard-gas-contaminated clothing, in this case an army shirt, landed him in hospital for a fortnight. In retrospect, the experience of lying there alone, without permission to receive any visitors, was deeply traumatic: 'I got it into my mind that they wanted to find out how long it would take for me to die.'[133] His physical injuries, though, compared to his psychological trauma, were far less serious; other than receiving a small rash, extra leave, and some extra cash, he left Porton relatively unscathed.

Much of the work concentrated on the 'extreme vulnerability of the scrotal region' compared to other parts of the human body. Although anti-gas ointments such as AG (Anti-Gas) No. 3 could protect servicemen's necks from mustard gas, they were unsuitable for the scrotal region, where they were 'rubbed and sweated off'. Experiments to study the 'full extent of the danger' began in March 1942, involved six participants, and resulted in scrotal injuries of 'casualty severity'.[134] All six servicemen were subsequently unfit for duty for up to four weeks.

The work led to hundreds of experiments in which the underwear of Allied men and women were impregnated under the arms, as were the closely knit knickers of the Women's Auxiliary Air Force (WAAF) and the underpants of the Army and the ATS; laboratories were filled with different types of underwear, addressing the needs of soldiers operating under temperate and tropical conditions, or reflecting cultural customs and religious traditions in Britain and the Dominions. In 1942, in an attempt to simulate a hot climate, Porton conducted a thirty-two-hour clothing trial with twenty-two workers in a melting shop at a Sheffield steel factory. Some experiments looked at levels of protection afforded by service kilts, or examined the culturally specific underwear of Indian troops.[135] Others focused on anti-gas clothing such as oilskin capes and jackets, rubber boots and gloves, and the respirator face-pieces worn by ARP wardens and by employees working in the chemical warfare industry. Porton also studied the protective clothing worn by Allied and enemy forces, in respect of decontamination and treatment.[136]

During the war, thousands of servicemen participated in trials to decontaminate skin from liquid warfare agents, assess the effectiveness and irritancy of anti-gas ointments, and study different methods of treatment. In collaboration with scientists from Oxford's biochemistry department and Suffield Experimental Station in Canada, Porton developed various ointments to protect the forces against the German use of arsenical compounds such as lewisite.[137] For Sydney Pepper from the Bedfordshire and Hertfordshire Regiment, who remembered his week-long stay at Porton in January 1940 as a dull yet 'pleasant break', the tests involved an 'experimental treatment' that 'hurt a bit' and was 'like a burn'.[138] Allied suspicion of German arsine attacks had hardened after a chance discovery revealed German respirators to be more effective against arsine. It also turned out that the Nazi regime had amassed one of the world's largest arsine stockpiles. As it turned out, the two developments were unrelated; the improved German gas mask was to protect German soldiers from Russian hydrogen cyanide, while the arsine stockpile was used in industrial production. The German authorities had intensified their research activity after capturing British-designed detector paper, which in turn propelled Porton's scientists into action, a process commonly known in the history of chemical warfare as the 'mirror image' effect.[139] Porton's research was as much shaped by perceived and suspected enemy activities as by firm intelligence about planned military operations; both influenced and stimulated each other.

It was a dynamic and largely unpredictable process of responding to the potential threat of gas warfare that determined Britain's activities in the chemical warfare field.[140]

At the outset of war, Rudolph Peters had been directed by the MoS to enlist an extra-mural team of scientists to conduct research on blistering agents with a view to developing an effective antidote. Biochemists such as H.B. Fell and C.B. Allsopp from the Strangeways Research Laboratory in Cambridge, for instance, which was in regular contact with Porton, studied on behalf of the MoS the effects of various 'toxic gases' on tissue cultures, and on animals and human serum; while their findings needed to remain secret, and could not be published, they were still widely circulated among Britain's chemical warfare experts.[141] Around 1941, following experiments on animals and successful experiments on themselves, as well as trials with medical students, Peters, Thompson, and Stocken performed a series of controlled experiments on servicemen at Porton who were treated with DTH (dimercaptopropyl alcohol or Dithiol), originally known as OX217, and later renamed 'BAL' (British anti-lewisite). Travelling from Poole in a four-engined flying boat, Thompson was dispatched to the United States to update researchers at Edgewood Arsenal and discuss plans for mass production.[142] It later turned out that BAL was potentially toxic for patients suffering from impaired liver function.[143] Another substance, hydrogen peroxide, was also tested in animal and human experiments at Porton. In the meantime, Ida Mann, head of the Ophthalmology Department at Oxford's Radcliffe Infirmary, who tested the healing potential of BAL on rabbits' eyes, showed that any effective treatment aimed at reversing the effects of lewisite needed to be applied within one minute.[144] In accordance with Porton's line of research, her work suggested the need for speed in treating skin contaminated by blistering agents. In 1943, scientists at Porton conducted further tests with sixty compounds on two to six participants each to confirm the initial findings. Between 1939 and 1943, a total of 466 servicemen participated in such studies, and, in 1944, another 192 subjects took part in experiments with different ointments for tropical conditions.[145]

Porton scientists also expended considerable energy in developing prophylactics against mustard vapours, and although we do not know how many men took part in the trials, we know that a total of 350 mustard gas exposures were performed on armpits shaved and treated with different ointments. In another instance, the skin of the face, neck, and hands was first treated with the experimental ointment before being exposed to varying concentrations of mustard vapour 'necessary to produce burns of casualty severity'.[146] A total of 290 exposures were conducted in this way. Some of the experiments, such as those performed in 1943 on sixty servicemen, with eight artificially produced mustard gas burns, four large blisters covering 6 cm², and four small ones covering 2 cm², must have been painful.[147] A subsequent test in the same year assessed existing compounds in use by Field Medical Officers among twenty-four subjects who had six blisters each, induced by liquid mustard gas.[148] Sulphanilamide powders—already widely used as a remedy against gas gangrene infections—and acriflavine emulsions, functioning as an antiseptic, generally proved to be effective compounds in treating vesicant blisters, although mustard-induced burns were prone to secondary infections.

With the country at war, nothing was left to chance, no area of potential vulnerability ignored, however time-consuming, costly or burdensome the research might be. From the water the people of Britain drank to the food they ate, for Porton's chemical investigators no area of civil society was off-limits. Since 1939, scientists had performed decontamination trials on foodstuffs contaminated with mustard vapour, and measured its effects on human skin.[149] Different types of meat, beans, and spaghetti and corned beef were decontaminated by boiling or steaming and then left on the skin for an hour; sugar, flour, butter, potatoes, or margarine, on the other hand, were decontaminated by means of airing and then placed on the skin for several hours to see whether the skin would react and show irritation. Scientists wanted to know the extent to which bacon, having been left for a week 'against the woodwork of a railway truck previously contaminated' with mustard gas, would absorb and then emanate mustard vapours. Every imaginable line of inquiry was pursued.[150] To demonstrate decontamination methods to the local population, Porton organized a series of public information events in collaboration with the Ministry of Food and officials in charge of ARPs. Sometimes these were akin to public spectacles in which passers-by, about to do their weekly shopping, observed how a group of men dressed in rubber suits, boots, and gas masks would trim a piece of meat to salvage it from gas contamination.[151] For outside observers, it looked as if Porton was preparing the country for an afterlife on a different planet, one in which the soil people walked on, every object they touched and every apple they ate were contaminated by deadly chemical agents. The authorities were surely planning for a grim future.

Anticipating the worst possible onslaught with chemical weapons in modern history, Porton's scientists, working in total secret in the Wiltshire countryside, went to enormous lengths to develop effective, albeit at times improvised, methods of treatment to help the military and civilians deal with the after-effects of chemical strikes. Their research involved considerable risks for the thousands of servicemen taking part in the trials, and this led to sometimes severe and multiple injuries and, in some cases, long-term disability. Breaches of peacetime ethical standards, of safety regulations, and of risk-assessment and informed consent protocols were not the exception but the rule. This was a country at war determined to defend itself at all costs. Seen from the perspective of the authorities, it was only right and proper that servicemen should make certain sacrifices for the safety and stability of the nation.

Important though defensive preparations were, Porton's research activities did not take place in a strategic and geopolitical vacuum. Extensive field trials had multiple, at times complementary, objectives in order to create a body of applied scientific knowledge that was of equal value for offensive and defensive operations. Human experiments seeking to study the potency of vesicant vapours, as well as possible defensive measures and treatments against them, provided officials with important data about offensive chemical warfare operations against German cities and their inhabitants, detailed, for example, in the report 'Attack on Cities with Gas' of April 1943.[152] Because of the nature of the agent, attacks with phosgene required an estimated '16 tons of gas per square mile' and had to achieve maximum surprise 'so as to catch as many of the inhabitants as possible without their respirators on', preferably after heavy bombing raids with high explosives or incendiary bombs had left buildings severely damaged, which would bring out 'a large number of people ... into the open where they would be more vulnerable to gas'.[153] Mustard gas, on the other hand, required a different military strategy since it developed its deadly potential by affecting the eyes and lungs of unprotected people, by circumventing gas masks through blisters on the human skin, and by contaminating the ground and buildings thereafter. With an estimated '15 tons of gas per square mile' in summer, and twice that amount in winter, the aim of strategic mustard gas bombing was to produce 'a prolonged danger from vapour over the whole area attacked', and thus cause the maximum numbers of casualties.[154] Apparently attacks with vesicant agents also provided disillusioned workers with an 'unprecedented opportunity for malingering' by inflicting small disabling blisters.

The danger from mustard gas resulted not so much from the number of people killed, but from the anticipated breakdown of the rescue and medical services to cope with a 'very large number of casualties' and from a 'serious loss of man hours' of injured inhabitants: 'The total moral effect would be very high.'[155]

According to Porton officials, there was no known protection against this kind of warfare other than evacuating the entire population, which would expose a city to subsequent incendiary attacks. A preliminary attack with high explosives, followed by a series of air attacks, first with phosgene, then mustard gas, and finally incendiary bombs, would, it was thought, totally contaminate and destroy the urban environment, kill tens of thousands of people, seriously injure almost the entire population, and create mayhem and organizational chaos for weeks thereafter. Another line of inquiry envisaged the construction of particularly deadly chemical bombs. In March 1943, Porton unsuccessfully tested a 250-pound experimental bomb containing a mixture of high explosives and mustard gas substitute in the evacuated village of Shingle Street in East Suffolk to improve the strategic use of chemical weapons.[156] Britain's 'legendary aircraft and bomb designer', Barnes Wallis, may well have been involved in the work, if we are to believe some of those attending the trial. A photograph depicting the lead scientist, dressed in civilian clothes, flanked by local firemen and police officers, looks remarkably like Wallis; unsurprisingly he appears to have kept no record of a top-secret assignment with which, understandably, his family would not subsequently have wanted him to be associated.[157] Be that as it may, given the perceived urgency of the situation, Porton joined forces with military engineers to construct novel and more deadly systems of chemical weaponry capable of delivering a potentially devastating gas attack against the German heartland, one which would have been in breach of international laws and customs of warfare. This kind of narrative surely did not mesh well with the postwar myth of Britain's seemingly glorious wartime past.

By April 1943, plans for total warfare were at an advanced stage of readiness. Weeks later, Allied forces launched Operation Gomorrah, one of their most destructive air raids, using high explosives and incendiary bombs on the city of Hamburg in northern Germany as part of an Allied 'moral bombing' campaign. It left the city's administration in total disarray, destroyed large parts of the infrastructure, and killed approximately 40,000 inhabitants, many of whom were burnt alive in the resulting firestorm, or suffocated in the damaged houses or bunkers to which they had fled.[158] Over 900,000 people had to be forcibly evacuated. Anyone thinking that Porton's chemical warfare plans were empty or unrealistic threats would have been badly mistaken.

Whatever the Germans threw at the people of Britain, its defensive and offensive chemical warfare capabilities were ready and waiting to ensure that life would continue as normally as possible, and that subsequent retaliatory attacks would be comprehensive and devastating. Despite disagreements within government circles over Britain's pledge to abstain from initiating chemical warfare and to abide by the Geneva Protocol, there was little doubt in the minds of senior officials that if chemical warfare were ever launched, it would be done by all sides, extensively and over a prolonged period of time. Porton's human experiments reflected this all-encompassing approach to Britain's chemical warfare programme. If anything, Britain's research and development programme into deadly chemical agents was expanding on a global scale.

Global Expansion

By collaborating with newly established research facilities in the Dominions and Allied countries, Porton extended its realm of influence at a global level. Based in the 'outposts' of the British Commonwealth—Canada, India, and Australia—Allied scientists subjected servicemen to blistering and other agents to assess their 'casualty producing power' and develop defensive and therapeutic capabilities.[159] In 1940 the surrender and subsequent occupation of France by German forces deprived Porton of access to the French chemical warfare laboratories at Le Bouchet (in the Rhône-Alpes region) and their large-scale trial range in North Africa, and British officials found themselves under pressure to establish a new testing site away from Axis-controlled territories.[160] Following representations by the British government, Canada established a new 700,000-acre testing site at Suffield, Alberta, which became operational in August 1941. Driven by wartime expediency to test 'existing chemical munitions and develop even more deadly war gases', Suffield Experimental Station was a specifically UK–Canadian joint venture. Modelled along the lines of Porton, and led by Chief Superintendent E. Lloyd Davies, who had previously worked as a chemist at Porton, the station was predominantly staffed by Canadian scientists and servicemen, a 'polyglot mixture of Army, Navy and Air Force brass with the odd visitor from Britain or the USA'.[161]

Wartime chemical warfare experiments performed in Canada involved considerable risks to soldiers. Many of the field trials were conducted by Porton scientists and at the request of the British government.[162] Researchers wanting to experiment with toxic substances would sometimes travel to Canada to conduct their tests at Suffield, as Porton's field range did not meet the necessary safety requirements.[163] From 1942 to 1945, in response to special incentives such as extra pay, better food, or better accommodation, approximately 2,500 servicemen volunteered to take part in hundreds of chemical warfare trials at Suffield, generally for a period of six weeks.[164] Most do not seem to have been adequately informed about the experiments. Crawling over contaminated bomb craters for hours or being exposed to toxic agents in gas chambers was not what these men had anticipated, nor did they expect to be used as 'guinea pigs' in aircraft spraying trials under conditions of secrecy. Test subjects suffered from severe mustard gas and lewisite burns and required hospital treatment for weeks as a result; others subsequently battled with chronic skin disorders, scarring, and respiratory illnesses, yet were refused a war pension, in one case for fifty-five years. Furthermore, as revealed by the Canadian Ombudsman in 2003, relatives struggled to comprehend why tests had continued after the end of hostilities.[165]

According to regulations governing the use of volunteers in warfare trials from August 1942, Canadian military stations had to supply officers tasked with selecting subjects with a 'statement outlining in a general way the nature and purpose of the tests'.[166] These were posted on unit notice boards: potential volunteers were told that participants were needed to study the 'effects of weapons, chemicals and defensive equipment used in war', that all tests would be performed under medically and scientifically controlled conditions, and that 'consequently no permanent injury is likely to result'.[167] In return, they were offered extra pay and extra leave. The information given to the soldiers to encourage them to volunteer lacked sufficient detail about the trials to enable them to make an enlightened decision as to whether to take part. Veterans such as Bill Tanner, who was exposed to toxic agents during the war, is adamant that 'what was done to us was done without our informed consent'.[168] Relatives also recalled that their loved ones 'did not have any idea of what was to happen, as no explanation was given'.[169]

Suffield required a maximum of 100 soldiers per month for its experimental programme. The men had to be physically fit, trustworthy, and free from venereal and infectious diseases. Once soldiers arrived at Suffield, their presence was seen as evidence that they had volunteered for the tests. No further information was given. Suffield's medical officer was charged with ensuring that the experiments involved 'no unnecessary risk', yet at the same time he was granted discretionary powers to implement safety precautions for dangerous experiments, authorize medical treatment, and award minor compensation for severe injuries.[170] However morally questionable and abhorrent the experiments may appear in retrospect, the Canadian government's intention in providing servicemen at their units with none but the most basic information—if any—and in keeping them in almost complete ignorance of what was to happen to them once they arrived at the facility should not necessarily be seen as a Machiavellian ploy deliberately to mislead or harm them, but only as an attempt to preserve utmost secrecy about Suffield's activities in times of war. In balancing the rights of individuals to make informed decisions about taking part in non-therapeutic experiments on the one hand with the demands for military security on the other, the government clearly prioritized Canada's national security interests.

Suffield's *raison d'être* was defined as conducting experimental work to assist Allied forces in winning the war: 'Nothing will be allowed to interfere with the object.' In pursuing this objective, secrecy was absolutely paramount. In 1941, the officer commanding, Major J.S. Beeman, told servicemen to be on their guard at all times to prevent the enemy 'from knowing what we are doing', and to avoid careless talk with their wives, sweethearts, or family members and, above all, with inquisitive strangers. Except in the case of a handful of official photographers, taking pictures was strictly forbidden, and everyone owning a camera had to have it registered. All service personnel were instructed to 'solemnly promise' not discuss the work of the station and to sign the Official Secrets Act. Those carelessly endangering military secrets were faced with imprisonment for up to five years.[171] Some officials wanted to go even further in deterring soldiers from gossiping. In December 1942, according to one subject, the officer in charge threatened servicemen that 'they would be shot if they ever talked about the tests'. If this incident took place, which seems possible, it constituted an act of gross professional misconduct and should have been subject to military discipline, yet no officer appears ever to have been investigated or charged.[172] Another recalled being threatened with treason 'if they ever spoke to anyone about the tests'.[173] In this case the officer in charge was British. Some senior officers clearly went too far in protecting the secrecy surrounding Canada's chemical warfare programme.

Canadian chemical warfare trials were initially beset by practical problems, ranging from difficulties in relating the 'casualty producing power', or 'killing power', as some called it, of mustard gas spray to the number of aircraft needed and the height at which a 'fair hit' could be achieved.[174] Experiments requiring the 'most superlative good luck' to achieve the desired results, namely the contamination of all participants, were not only methodologically flawed but of 'doubtful value' in drawing sound conclusions. Predicting human behaviour under battlefield conditions with some degree of accuracy posed another problem. However well trained and disciplined the troops, and irrespective of official policy, it was almost impossible to forecast how soldiers would react in real-life situations. Accidental exposures and misfortunes could also not be foreseen; in one incident, a soldier suffered severe burns to his abdomen after his belt broke and his trousers fell down, thus exposing his underwear to toxic substances; in another case, air force personnel were expected, without much protection, to 'clean up the toxic spill' from a mustard bomb which had dislodged and then exploded on the runway, resulting in 'some injuries'.[175] These incidents reflected poorly on existing safety precautions and procedures at Suffield and elsewhere.

Of six trials performed in September 1942, the first five were considered a failure since the injuries sustained by the 'observers' were 'trivial'. The last trial, which contaminated fifteen men, four so severely that they required hospital treatment, was seen as the 'least unsuccessful'.[176] It had all got off to a bad start. A month earlier, scientists had studied the health risks emanating from 'persistent ground contamination' with mustard gas by positioning sixteen soldiers in heavily contaminated areas, yet given the small number of casualties the findings were fairly disappointing. Tangible results concentrated on the importance of gas discipline among staff and service personnel, which 'left much to be desired', and on the conduct of men dressed in full protective clothing, some of whom had been found semi-conscious and 'in a state of complete heat exhaustion'. Believing that they were suffering from gas poisoning, they had ripped off their respirators in total panic, bringing home the dangers of 'ignorance' and 'gross carelessness' in defensive preparations.[177]

By producing measurable health effects through aircraft spraying and ground contamination trials, military scientists hoped to gain much-needed data to establish the 'casualty producing power' of different delivery techniques.[178] Under the leadership of Major Walter Somerville, RAMC, an Irishman seconded from Porton to the Canadian Department of Defence,[179] the Royal Canadian Air Force employed two Lysander aircraft to carry out a large-scale spraying trial with 100 servicemen of the First Battalion Winnipeg Light Infantry and the First Battalion Prince Albert Volunteers, including officers and NCOs (non-commissioned officers). The aim was to assess the extent to which mustard gas lesions impaired the performance of troops engaged in field exercises. Of ninety-four men hit by the gas who then took part in marching exercises for two consecutive days under 'unfavourable' conditions, sixty-six sustained mustard gas lesions, and for three men these were so severe that they required medical treatment.[180]

Some tests clearly went outside the bounds of acceptable ethical conduct. In July 1943, groups of five soldiers each were sent into a circular area in which twenty-five drums, each containing 50 gallons of crude mustard gas, had been detonated. Some of the exposure was so severe that the men had to be recalled immediately, two suffering from 'nausea, vomiting and weakness'. One man, called Dillen, complained of being 'very uncomfortable' and of 'lack of sleep; subsequently, he "lost all the skin" from his mid thigh to his ankles'.[181] In preparing Allied forces for all-out chemical warfare, Allied scientists became ever more inventive in their research design. Of ten men taking part in a chamber trial to assess the effects of mustard vapour, five were kept in constant motion for an hour without any form of protective underwear, and suffered severe genital burns as a result. It had been known for years that the effects of vesicant agents were more pronounced in areas of the body with higher skin temperature; the test can therefore hardly be seen as an addition to existing knowledge.[182] Since the result was highly predictable, the test was not only unnecessary but unethical.

Following the United States' entry into the war, the military launched a 'vast' research and development programme into chemical warfare. Funding for the Chemical Warfare Service at Edgewood Arsenal, the 'American Porton', having fluctuated between 1 and 2 million dollars in the interwar period, rocketed to a staggering 60 million dollars in 1941 and 1 billion dollars in 1942 before gradually decreasing once a sufficient retaliatory capability had been built up. In line with an expansion in funding and responsibilities came a marked increase in personnel, both military and civilian, from just under 1,000 officers and enlisted men in 1939 to over 46,000 in 1942. A year later, the CWS boasted over 66,000 officers and enlisted servicemen. In the same period, civilian staff increased from over 1,300 in 1939 to around 24–25,000 in the years 1942 to 1944.[183] To bridge the time until the completion of new laboratories at Edgewood Arsenal, the CWS sought assistance from the chemical industry, oil companies, and universities by signing up hundreds of civilian scientists for research and development purposes. At the Massachusetts Institute of Technology (MIT), experts conducted work on phosgene, mustard gas, and thionylchloride, and designed filling plants, field laboratories, and respirators. At Columbia University, in the Building of Mines, scientists developed incendiary bombs and studied the manufacture of napalm, an agent widely employed by US forces during the Vietnam war.[184] Elsewhere, the CWS recruited chemical engineers such as Chalmer G. Kirkbride from the Pan American Refining Company (Amoco) in Texas City, Texas, to help with the manufacture of toluene, which was urgently needed for the mass production of TNT, a high explosive.[185] Additional facilities provided the CWS with an extensive testing network, for example at Dugway Proving Ground, Utah, to advance aircraft spraying techniques, and at Bushnell, Florida, to study the effects of contaminated beaches; scientists also had unfettered access to the experimental station at San José Island, a small island in the Pacific about 70 miles west of Panama, and to Canada's trial ground. From 1940, medical and related problems were taken up by the Subcommittee on Clinical Research of the Committee on Medicine, National Research Council, including the treatment of vesicant burns and water decontamination methods. To increase awareness of defensive preparations against gas attacks in potential combat zones, the CWS launched a nationwide poster campaign, urging service members through an emotional appeal using fear and sexual imagery to take good care of their gas masks, enrol in chemical warfare courses, and be vigilant for the smell of warfare agents: green corn for phosgene, garlic for mustard gas, and geraniums for lewisite.[186] At an operational level, emergency medical field units were trained in the decontamination and treatment of civilian casualties, while chemical sections supported theatre commanders with intelligence and supply as an 'insurance against gas warfare'.[187] In short, the CWS became an integrated part of the Allied military machine.

Among those bridging the academic divide between the Western Allies was the physiologist Abner McGehee Harvey from Johns Hopkins University, who contributed to top-secret chemical warfare research during the Cold War.[188] Born in 1911 in Little Rock, Arkansas, he had enjoyed a meteoritic rise in his medical career by the time he was twenty-nine.[189] Travelling to London in the late 1930s, McGehee Harvey collaborated with experimental physiologists such as Sir Henry Dale, Joseph Barcroft, Archibald Vivian Hill, and, most probably, Charles Lovatt Evans, all of whom were intimately connected to Britain's chemical warfare community. From 1941, when he was posted to Australia and New Guinea with the 118th General Hospital, the Johns Hopkins Unit, his work focused on peripheral nerve injuries. McGehee Harvey was part of a self-selected group of elite physiologists and experimental scientists whose professional identity was shaped by a closely knit, often informal, sometimes secretive, largely male-dominated community of scholars with first-hand combat experience and close links to the military and to government authorities. During the Cold War, as senior adviser for the US Chemical Corps Advisory Council on highly secretive nerve agent research, McGehee Harvey demonstrated moral and professional leadership by accepting the principles of the Nuremberg Code as the guiding standards in non-therapeutic human experiments.[190]

Keeping Allied scientists informed of ongoing developments in the chemical warfare field without breaching military security required a small but efficient system of communication between trusted individuals. The US Assistant Military Attaché in London and members of the British Purchasing Commission in New York City at first functioned as a mechanism for the exchange of highly classified intelligence. To enhance uniformity in test procedures and avoid overlap and duplication of work, Britain joined the US–Canadian Advisory Committee that had been set up to inter-connect the chemical warfare services of Canada and the United States.[191] In 1942, the Combined Chief of Staff also established the United States Chemical Warfare Committee to coordinate all US 'chemical warfare activities'.[192] Given the scale and complexity of the work undertaken, and the desire to improve coordination and standardization, the three Allied powers eventually set up a joint policy committee at the highest military level in 1943. This was to become a precursor to the Tripartite Conferences that shaped chemical warfare policy and research during the early Cold War period. Meanwhile, Allied researchers increased their efforts to understand the potential and limitations of chemical warfare under tropical conditions in anticipation of gas attacks by Japanese forces.

In the same year, the former Superintendent of Porton, Robert Kingan, became the British representative at Edgewood Arsenal. His brief was to liaise with US scientists about field experiments with thousands of human volunteers. One of the trials required the participation of 7,000 US soldiers to explore the effectiveness of British anti-gas equipment and ointments. Recruiting volunteers for large-scale trials posed constant problems for the CWS, and affected the process of obtaining informed consent. The Naval Research Laboratory in Virginia not only enticed potential recruits with a 'change of scenery' but advised staff against telling volunteers 'too much' at the start of the experiments to avoid 'a fear reaction' that could affect the morale of the men; only after repeated gas chamber exposures was it deemed safe to inform them: 'The men take any resulting casualty extremely well.'[193] The experience of 'intense fear' nonetheless proved to be the main common denominator among veterans of chamber tests interviewed by an expert panel in the early 1990s. Not unlike many of the Porton veterans, who felt they had been misled by the authorities, many US servicemen originally believed before they arrived at the test facility that they were testing 'summer clothing' in return for extra leave. Once they were there, they were rarely informed about the agents to which they would be exposed, and in some cases they were 'threatened with court martial' if they expressed a desire to withdraw from certain experiments.[194] Uncooperative subjects were given 'a short, explanatory talk and, if necessary, a slight verbal "dressing down"'; others, described by naval scientists as 'malingerers and psychoneurotics', were sent into the chamber as a form of corporal punishment.[195] Apart from occasional threats and acts of intimidation, appalling in any environment, what frightened these men the most was a feeling of being trapped in a gas chamber in which the door could be opened only from the outside. Panic-stricken and utterly powerless, they found themselves at the mercy of unknown investigators, their bodies reduced to mere objects of the scientists' desire for experimental results. It was an experience so traumatic, so humiliating, that many rarely talked about their sense of existential *Angst*, sometimes revealing their innermost emotional past only on their deathbeds. Governments in both the US and the UK, fearing an avalanche of compensation claims, have been reluctant at best to acknowledge the deeply rooted emotional dimensions of such nonconventional weapon tests, which in some cases have had profound effects on the lives of former participants.

Soldiers trained with the CWS units, on the other hand, such as the Ninety-fourth and Ninety-fifth Medical Gas Treatment Battalions, felt less frightened by the experience of warfare tests, if we are to believe their postwar recollections, unless these involved major accidents with chemical shells.[196] Staff likewise could find themselves at the sharp end of the trials. At Edgewood Arsenal, senior scientists in need of human subjects at times 'rounded up' researchers in their laboratory. For them, minor accidents and contaminations with mustard gas were a regular occurrence. The same applied to those many uneducated, disadvantaged, and often very young men in charge of handling chemical warfare materials who experienced unforeseen exposure due to a lack of protective equipment. Severe burn injuries were sustained by many in both chamber and field tests, in some cases to such an extent that unit commanders discouraged their men from volunteering to certain research facilities, for example to Camp Sibert in Alabama. Given the paucity of and proven inconsistency in the reporting of accidental injuries from chemical warfare agents during and after the war, there has been an unsurprisingly high level of frustration among veterans who fail to qualify for a disability allowance because of a lack of historical evidence.[197]

Occasionally, warfare trials highlighted issues of race, class, and ethnicity. In 1944, in an attempt to tackle shortages of volunteers, the Army Ground Forces supplied the CWS with forty Japanese-American servicemen from Texas to study variations between Asians and Caucasians in responding to blistering agents. Proposals to recruit civilians for chemical warfare tests were shelved, however, after officials raised concerns about public sensitivities. A postwar report later noted: 'It is not unfair to say that due care was not always exercised in the application of vesicant agents and corrosive ointments to the arms and legs of volunteers and they were sometimes burned more than was necessary.'[198] US chemical warfare experiments were not unethical by nature, nor were they intended to cause harm from the outset, but many were haphazardly designed, poorly executed, not well coordinated, and insufficiently aligned with Allied military strategy, shortcomings that experts sought to rectify as the war drew to a close.

In the spring of 1944, at an international conference to establish a more unified approach in research and development, and ensure the most economical use of Allied testing facilities in preparation for chemical warfare operations in the Pacific, the three Allied countries established the Advisory Committee on the Effectiveness of Gas Warfare Material in the Tropics and the Project Coordination Staff (PCS).[199] Although American scientists were in the majority on the PCS, representatives from Britain and Canada played an equally important role.[200] Senior British officials such as Davidson Pratt and Wansbrough-Jones, for example, stressed the need for human subjects in assessing chemical warfare agents, and called on the United States to contribute to its ongoing experimental programme. Only human experiments, they argued, had revealed that the potency of lewisite and the magnitude of risks emanating from mustard gas contamination of the ground had probably been overestimated.[201]

The PCS, headed by W.A. Noyes, Jr, concentrated on correlating and disseminating chemical warfare information that had been obtained from Allied field installations in or as part of combat operations. In 1946, after its remit had been extended to include all aspects of chemical warfare, the PCS published some of its findings in a two-part chemical warfare manual entitled *Technical Aspects of Chemical Warfare in the Field*, also known as *TACWIF*.[202] Personal networks and the continued exchange of highly sensitive information meant that inter-Allied collaboration on chemical warfare matters continued long after the end of the war.[203]

Porton in India

If the research design required a tropical environment, if circumstances prevented Allied scientists from travelling to Canada, the United States, or to any of the sub-stations in the Pacific, or if tests were likely to produce severe blisters and incapacitation, and thus deemed too dangerous to be conducted on British or Allied servicemen, officials could commission field trials at Porton's subsidiary research station in India. The Chemical Defence Research Establishment in India (CDRE(I)) in Rawalpindi in the Punjab had been established in the late 1920s to support the armed forces of the British Raj, and had field ranges in Porkal and Kumbala, near Mangalore, and subsidiary stations in Coimbatore and Trichinopoly; its scientists concentrated their efforts on developing defensive technologies and chemical weapons for retaliatory purposes in the war against Japan.[204]

By the end of the First World War, Britain's involvement with chemical warfare on the Indian subcontinent had become closely associated with issues of race, class, and eugenics, and it was hoped that Britain's activities in this field would help to secure the Empire's geopolitical and financial interests in the colonies. In 1919, Churchill, then Secretary of State at the War Office, objected to the 'squeamishness' of those opposed to chemical warfare and advocated the use of toxic agents against 'Afghan rebels' and other 'uncivilized tribes'.[205] Porton's man in India, Lieutenant Colonel Salt, resisted calls to ban chemical weapons and dismissed London's argument of keeping 'clean hands' and abstaining from using 'low-down tricks against the poor ignorant tribesmen'. Moreover, since tests conducted in the United States suggested a greater degree of resistance to mustard agents among 'black' people, British officials anticipated finding variations in the 'susceptibility among the different tribes'. Research therefore concentrated on establishing whether 'Indian skin' was more susceptible to blistering agents than 'European skin', for example in a mass experiment with liquid mustard gas in 1934.[206] As part of a broad nineteenth-century eugenics movement to construct normative categories about the inequality of mankind, and in addition to studies on racial anthropology, phrenology, and craniometry, Porton scientists used their results from their examination of the physiognomy of Indian subjects to develop standardized gas masks for various Indian castes to establish seemingly objective evidence to endorse racial and social prejudices.

Much of Porton's work in India involved smoke trials with phosphorus bombs, which Allied forces planned to employ against Japanese bunker installations. Another major component was field trials with poison gas. In general, British and Indian nationals were exposed to liquid mustard gas or lewisite to assess the effects of the agents on human skin and on eyes under different climatic conditions, to examine the susceptibility of different skin types, and to develop new types of treatment.[207] Tests conducted between 1942 and 1943 produced a 'large number' of casualties among Indian and British soldiers who suffered from severe burns, 'were often very miserable and depressed and in considerable discomfort'.[208]

In 1943, researchers wanted to explore the effectiveness of mustard gas under hot weather conditions and the different factors that determined the 'nature and extent' of the gas injuries: the mass and density of the agent, the chemical itself—its viscosity and drop size; its characteristics in the prevailing atmospheric conditions; the effects of types of clothing—their texture, ventilation, and relative contact with the skin; and indeed skin types and skin sensitivity. However, they had to acknowledge that the complexity of the science made a full understanding of all the factors impossible.[209] The work went ahead regardless. To establish a 'casualty producing dosage' of certain mustard gas preparations, male participants, dressed in khaki cotton shirts and shorts, were instructed to wear contaminated clothing for four hours under tropical conditions. The results showed that under these conditions mustard gas behaved differently and could produce 'very severe lesions' compared to more temperate and less humid climates, yet there appeared to be few physiological differences between the types of injuries suffered between British and Indian participants.[210] Whereas some tests produced 'unusual lesions' among Indian volunteers, others appeared to suggest that Indian troops enjoyed a somewhat greater resistance to mustard gas vapours.[211] Rather than establishing marked ethnic or racial differences, Porton's work in India showed the need to adapt the research to cultural and religious customs.

Human experiments with impregnated garments for the protection of the scrotal regions in tropical climates highlighted cultural differences and religious sensitivities among Indian troops. In a trial carried out at Madras under tropical conditions, over 160 British and Indian troops wore various types of impregnated underwear for seven days, both day and night, before being exposed to blistering agents.[212] Although the 'pantee or bathing slip type of garment' was broadly acceptable to the soldiers, the majority of Indian troops, among them Dogras, Pathans, and Sikhs, expressed their preference for wearing a 'kacha': this is a loose garment with short legs made of thin cotton material, and one of the five articles of faith in Sikhism worn by both male and female Sikhs as a religious symbol and sign of sexual self-control.

With tens of thousands of combat troops suffering from malaria, and in liaison with the medical services of the armed forces and US entomologists, Porton scientists accelerated insecticidal research that included the manufacture of repellents and other prophylactics; technical experts developed spraying devices for the diffusion of DDT from the air and the ground to control mosquito populations in operational areas such as Malaya and Burma.[213] Shortly after the war, Porton also carried out a series of observational trials in which laboratory workers from the chemistry section responsible for the handling and manufacture of large quantities of DDT were monitored for several weeks as a way of recording the physiological effects of accidental exposure to DDT and other chemicals. Additionally, dozens of servicemen were exposed to undergarments impregnated with a DDT solution. These 'controlled accidents' seemed to indicate that the risk from DDT exposure was relatively small, except for a noticeable rise in blood calcium levels among the laboratory staff.[214] In testing effective spraying devices for DDT, and in assessing its toxicology, Porton established some of the methods and safety margins that the WHO later applied in the fight against malaria during the 1950s and 1960s.[215]

In 1944, the Chiefs of Staffs ordered the transfer of CDRE(I) to Cannanore on the Malabar coast, where it remained until Indian independence in 1947. Under the leadership of J.S. Anderson, and at the request of the CWS, Porton scientists carried out a 'very comprehensive programme' to test defensive and offensive chemical warfare technologies.[216] Meanwhile, staff at the physiology department, who had moved to Trichinopoly in South India for its consistently 'hot' and 'uncomfortable' climate, performed human experiments which stressed racial stereotypes and exposed Indian subjects to excessive risks. Driven by a sense of urgency to prepare for combat operations in the Pacific, physiologists were dissatisfied with the 'dark skinned Indian observers' (Madrassis) who apparently made the study of toxic agents difficult and time-consuming.[217] Almost all subjects of chamber trials were believed to be of 'low medical category' and unrepresentative of Allied troops, which might explain why few precautions were taken in protecting them from multiple and severe injuries. In one of the tests, an Indian sepoy, a soldier in the service of the British Empire, suffered severe burns to his eyes and face after his respirator slipped during exposure.[218] Whether Indian participants ever gave any meaningful, informed consent to the experiments cannot be answered conclusively but, given the available evidence, it does not seem likely. To this day, Britain's chemical warfare programme in India remains a 'delicate political subject'.[219]

The War in the Pacific

Following the Japanese attack on Pearl Harbor in December 1941, and the declaration of war by the United States, Allied headquarters began to pay greater attention to the possibility of waging chemical warfare under tropical conditions. This not only highlighted the military value of Porton's research facilities in the Far East, but strengthened collaborative projects and the sharing of resources, expertise and production facilities between Britain, the United States, Canada, Australia, India, and South Africa.[220] Reports alleging the use of poison gas by Japan against China since 1937 fuelled Allied fears that Japan might initiate chemical warfare operations in the Pacific. Japan, after all, was not a party to the Geneva Protocol.

In total, more than ten different agencies in the Unites States and the British Commonwealth were engaged with chemical warfare problems under tropical conditions, among them the experimental station at San José.[221] Here, military scientists from the United States, Britain, and Canada tested both defensive and offensive chemical warfare equipment under 'jungle and tropical conditions'. One of them, Lieutenant Colonel Sommervill from the RAMC, was posted to San José to assess ongoing field experiments; others seem to have used the island for recreational purposes.[222] Detailed information about human experiments carried out here is relatively scarce, yet from what we do know it appears that breaches of medical ethics standards were commonplace. Although tests were similar in design to those performed by other Allied nations, thousands of experimental subjects seem to have been ill-informed and some may have been coerced into taking part. Some participants as young as seventeen, and from disadvantaged social backgrounds, spent hours locked up in mustard-gas-filled gas chambers. Many of them later claimed that they had been misled.[223]

Around 1942, backed by the British War Cabinet, and after the Australian government had been gently reminded of its 'imperial responsibility' to enable British warfare tests, the Australian Field Experimental Station (AFES) was established at Proserpine. Under the energetic leadership of Major Frederick Samuel Gorrill, aged twenty-nine and a former Porton man, a team of half a dozen scientists and laboratory assistants began studying the effects of blistering agents under tropical conditions. Born in 1913, Gorrill had studied biochemistry at London University before joining the RAMC, which seconded him first to Porton and then to Australia to build up the AFES.[224] He later recruited many of his staff directly from Porton, including David Sinclair, an expert on the effects of mustard gas, who took over the new physiology section 'to find out what damage the gas caused in subtropical and tropical conditions'.[225] Conducted in Townsville, Queensland, Northern Australia, the trials suggested mustard gas was 'roughly four times more potent' under hot and humid conditions than in more temperate climates, and that Allied defensive capabilities would be inadequate. According to Gorrill, the entire Allied 'body of [chemical warfare] knowledge' had to be re-examined and revised.[226] By expanding and relocating the Unit to Innisfail, north of Queensland, where the terrain 'resembled the tropical

forests of islands in the south-west Pacific', Allied planners heeded his call
for greater research activity. The Australian Chemical Warfare Experimental
and Research Station at Innisfail became a 'centre of intense experimentation' on hundreds of Australian servicemen.[227] After the war, Sinclair
intimated that over a two-year period, from 1943 to 1945, he and his team
had conducted mustard gas experiments under tropical conditions on a
total of 438 'healthy young men', a figure which appears to be broadly in
line with contemporary progress reports, but excludes those exposed to
toxic agents during trials on Brook Island, a small coral atoll covered by
dense rainforest.[228]

Under pressure to preserve the utmost secrecy, the process of recruiting
experimental subjects was largely improvised, if not misleading, given that
the information contained in appeal notices referred to 'experiments in the
tropics' only.[229] To overcome the boredom of daily military routine, and
anxious not to let down their 'mates', hundreds of Australian servicemen
volunteered to take part in the tests, sometimes in complete ignorance of
the dangers involved. Once they were at the facility, few details about the
experiments were forthcoming. Major Sinclair, who was in charge of the
trials, told the men that they would be exposed to mustard gas 'in some way'
and that they could withdraw if they wanted to. In an attempt retrospectively to justify his actions, he argued that the subjects had given their consent since they had not withdrawn from the tests, but conceded that he
had not informed them 'quite as [fully] as I perhaps should have done'.[230]
Although perhaps not strictly unethical, his experiments were certainly
eccentric. Under the influence of peer pressure, mostly uninformed soldiers
were permitted to run a sweepstake in the gas chamber tests that declared
the person with the most serious injuries to be the winner who received all
the money. It was a truly bizarre set up. Egged on by female staff making
faces through the gas chamber window or singing Australian folk songs,
some men were encouraged to volunteer repeatedly to earn extra cash, but
all this effectively turned the tests into a brutal game that left many subjects
suffering severe disfigurement for years to come. In Sinclair's worldview,
wartime exigencies rendered the experiments ethical and morally legitimate, so that they required no apology on his part: 'Animals were no use to
us, it had to be humans that we used.'[231]

Other work included a 'vicious assault course' to study the endurance of
servicemen exposed to toxic agents and the formulation of normative categories to assess chemical warfare casualties. Film footage documenting

dozens of men with horrific blisters crawling in agony over contaminated ground reflected how the willingness of Australian servicemen, and the effects of peer pressure, led them to sacrifice their health for the good of the nation. The US representative at Innisfail, Captain Howard Skipper, later remarked: 'It is important to keep in mind the keen individual pride in physical prowess inbred in each Australian when comparing casualties obtained here and in other countries. The men who are classed as casualties here are truly casualties.'[232] Between November 1943 and May 1944, Sinclair and his team conducted mustard gas tests on a total of 258 servicemen, of whom ninety-eight wore no protective garments and almost all of whom suffered incapacitation.[233] On average, according to Freeman, soldiers were hospitalized for four weeks, in one case for fourteen months.[234] Some of the investigators later conceded that they would have liked to see 'less dramatic results', yet it is clear from the record that the Australian experiments were 'close to conditions' which could have had 'lethal consequences' for some subjects.[235]

In 1944, after Allied forces sustained heavy losses on Tarawa Island, and in response to plans considered by the military to expel the Japanese from fortified islands in the Pacific by means of poison gas, the Australian station performed a series of major warfare trials on Brook Island.[236] Supported by senior Allied military officials, Gorrill's team wanted to test defensive equipment and clothing, and assess the value of offensive chemical warfare in comparison to conventional weaponry.[237] In this offensive warfare experiment, the plan was to examine 'human casualties in simulated tropical battle conditions' and gather data that would allow Allied forces to 'kill or incapacitate every occupant' on the targeted Pacific islands.[238] Four tons of coloured mustard gas were to be dropped on the island, wiping out almost the entire natural habitat, to enable the study of military manoeuvres under heavily contaminated conditions. Goats and guinea pigs that had been shipped to the island were killed almost instantly. Many of the volunteers, who subsequently landed on the island with limited or no protection, suffered from major systemic effects and severe burns to their entire body and were hospitalized for prolonged periods. Despite the heavy casualties, the trial was believed to have been a success since it demonstrated the destructive power of chemical weapons. A year earlier, a secret report had concluded: 'A ruthless application of chemical weapons under tropical conditions will produce destruction and desolation upon a scale scarcely surpassed in the history of war.'[239] The Brook Island trials were crudely executed warfare tests in which the findings were largely predictable, the risks involved disproportionate, and the injuries sustained by the volunteers excessive. It had many of the hallmarks of unethical experiments on man.

Relocated to a new facility in Proserpine, Queensland, and under Gorrill's directorship, some 650 military experts continued to pursue top-secret chemical warfare work, which by 1945 had involved some 2,000 human subjects. The scientists displayed a certain carelessness and a cavalier approach in obtaining informed consent, and this, together with rather poor safety standards and large numbers of casualties among the volunteers, explains why the Australian tests, especially those on Brook Island, rank among some of the most notorious chemical warfare trials conducted by Allied forces during the Second World War.

Although they were at an advanced stage of readiness, Allied forces never initiated chemical warfare in the Pacific, for lack of military and political support. In July 1944, US and Canadian experts were tasked with assessing the feasibility and strategic advantage of chemical attacks. Their report highlighted logistic and technical problems with chemical warfare ammunitions, and uncertainties over Japanese retaliatory and defensive capabilities that had the potential to slow down Allied combat operations. Major Donald Dewar, one of the authors, later remarked that they felt they were 'being pushed into something' they did not like and concluded that chemical warfare 'doesn't matter a damn'.[240] British scientists called the report a 'deliberate distortion of data' that damaged the war effort. Ultimately Allied leaders were reluctant to authorize a form of warfare that had not only been outlawed in the 1920s, and perceived as immoral by men in uniform, but was widely seen as ineffective and difficult to control. As the war drew to a close there was little appetite for a major military gamble with toxic agents. In the end, Allied leaders concluded that the risks outweighed the potential benefits.

Ethical Relativism

By 1944, Allied military planners were growing increasingly concerned about the potential use of chemical agents by Axis forces, fearing the employment of these weapons in a desperate, last-ditch attempt to hold their positions. The large-scale decommissioning of scientific experts, who began to return to their prewar posts, added to a renewed crisis at military headquarters. Military planners warned about a lack of vigilance and the scaling down of chemical warfare preparedness which could cost Allied forces dearly in the closing stages of the war. At Porton, and elsewhere, researchers were likewise determined to finish the job at hand, however disillusioned or frustrated they were at times with their work. In April 1944, Hill, President of the Royal Society, asked Lovatt Evans in no uncertain terms: 'If your place is so rotten, why don't you clear out and do something more useful?'[241] In his reply, Lovatt Evans explained that he was best qualified to do 'war work'; all else was selfish: 'Having spent, or wasted, four-and-a-half years here... I don't wish to drop it until it is quite certain gas will not be used.'[242] On the contrary, he resisted attempts to have his 'departure accelerated' by calling in support from the MoS, but eventually resigned to take up his former position at University College London; as a sign of gratitude, he was appointed to a number of influential government committees.[243] Tensions within Britain's small chemical warfare community were mounting, however. Porton's reputation as a research facility in which science could freely flourish had suffered from a routine that was shaped by military discipline and constant service requirements; at the same time, laboratories lacked leadership and direction when senior scientists were temporarily absent.[244] In early 1944, a colleague told Lovatt Evans that he was looking forward to visiting 'the concentration camp in the happy knowledge that I won't have to stay'.[245]

Oblivious to institutional and professional sensitivities, the authorities continued incessantly to prepare servicemen and civilians for the Allied invasion which might involve or trigger the use of gas warfare. In May, Porton carried out large-scale chemical warfare exercises in conjunction with beach-head operations by service and civilian authorities; at around the same time, scientists from Porton came to the conclusion that the use of mustard gas was likely to have a 'big potential in the subjugation' of Japanese forces on the Pacific islands thousands of miles to the east.[246] With millions of soldiers and civilians killed and injured, families and children displaced, buildings burnt, and entire cities destroyed, there was little appetite among senior Allied officials to uphold standards of medical ethics and international morality if the end of combat operations would be delayed as a result.

Biological weapons were likewise seriously considered. In collaboration with the Special Operations Executive (SOE), Porton developed, and tested on goats, grenades in which metal fragments had been coated with botulinum toxin.[247] It is not known, however, whether these weapons were ever employed in Europe, for example by members of the Polish or French resistance. Other projects prepared Britain for total war. In 1942, the government authorized the Chairman of the War Cabinet Committee on Bacteriological Warfare, Lord Hankey, to 'take such measures as he might from time to time deem appropriate to enable us without undue delay to retaliate in the event of resort by the enemy to the offensive use of bacteria'.[248] The plan was to disperse large amounts of anthrax spores, code-named 'N', and anthrax-filled 'cattle cakes' over Germany to kill humans and livestock on an unprecedented scale. To test the lethal nature of these weapons, Porton fed contaminated 'cattle cakes' to various cattle, sheep, and horses before burying the dead animals on site.[249] Experiments conducted by Porton scientists on Gruinard Island, off the north-west coast of Scotland, had previously shown the viability of killing sheep with the highly infectious disease within a short space of time, albeit contaminating the island for generations to come.[250]

In February 1944, Churchill was told by his scientific adviser, Lord Cherwell, about the 'appalling potentiality' of Britain's biological weapon, which was almost 'more formidable, because infinitely easier to make, than tube alloy' (the code-name for the atom bomb project): 'Half a dozen Lancasters [bombers] could apparently carry enough, if spread evenly, to kill anyone found within a square mile and to render it uninhabitable thereafter.'[251] Britain recognized, though, that there was no 'effective defence against a large-scale attack' by enemy forces, irrespective of improved respirators or newly developed vaccines against the disease. In short, biological warfare had come to be considered on a par with and 'complementary' to atomic weapons.

In the meantime, preparations for offensive chemical warfare operations intensified. On 6 July 1944, one month after the D-Day landing of Allied forces in Normandy, Churchill returned once again to the subject by telling the House of Commons that the introduction of the German 'flying bomb' raised some 'grave questions' about the future conduct of the war. On the same day, dissatisfied by the negative assessment of the Joint Planning Staff (JPS) on the use of gas warfare as a retaliatory measure, he informed his Chiefs of Staff of his intention to employ chemical weapons if it were a matter of 'life or death' for Britain or if it would shorten the war by a year:

> It may be several weeks or even months before I shall ask you to drench Germany with poison gas, and if we do it, let us do it one hundred per cent. In the meanwhile, I want the matter studied in cold blood by sensible people

and not by that particular set of psalm-singing uniformed defeatists which one runs across now here now there. Pray address yourself to this. It is a big thing and can only be discarded for a big reason. I shall of course have to square Uncle Joe [Joseph Stalin] and the President [Franklin D. Roosevelt], but you need not bring this into your calculations at the present time. Just try to find out what it is like on its merits.[252]

Churchill considered it to be 'absurd' to worry about the 'morality on this topic' since all parties had used chemical weapons during the First World War. Whereas the bombing of large cities had formerly been regarded as a war crime, it was now done by the Axis and Allied forces on a day-to-day basis, he argued. Attempting to downplay any moral concerns of his senior military advisers, he noted: 'It is simply a question of fashion changing as she [sic] does between long and short skirts for women.'[253] For the Prime Minister, the Geneva Protocol outlawing the use of poison gas was of no relevance if the existence of British realm were at stake.

Although Allied forces appeared to possess the capability, Churchill's senior military advisers stopped short of recommending the start of chemical warfare operations.[254] The Chiefs of Staff nonetheless expressed a high degree of confidence in respect of the state of Allied readiness to initiate chemical warfare operations. By 1944, British and American stocks located in Britain were deemed sufficient, they said, to produce a 'formidable scale of gas attack on Germany during the early and most important phase after a decision has been taken to employ gas'.[255] At a cost of 24 million pounds to the taxpayer, Britain alone had produced a total of 40,719 tons of mustard gas and 14,042 tons of phosgene and tear gases during the war.[256] Instead of a prolonged use of some chemical agents by 20 per cent of Bomber Command, the Chiefs of Staff recommended the concentration of all British and American long-range bombers in a 'massive hammer blow', employing high explosives and phosgene and mustard gas bombs in quick succession on tactical and civilian targets. Phosgene would be dropped on 1,000 tactical targets or twenty German cities, causing heavy casualties and deaths among civilians and civil defence personnel. Mustard gas, on the other hand, would be employed against 1,500 tactical targets or, alternatively, against sixty specifically identified German cities covering the entire Reich that were 'best calculated to bring about a collapse of German morale'.[257] By causing death and destruction on a monumental scale, military commanders aimed to exercise intense pressure on the regime's leadership, but they were also acutely aware that the population was likely to lack the necessary 'initiative required for active revolt' against the Nazi regime following gas attacks.[258]

In France, chemical weapons could aid the war effort by helping Allied forces to 'break through the German defences', but they could also slow the military advance, affect communications, unsettle civilian labour, and negatively affect the relationship with the local population. The same was the case in the east, in southern France and in the Mediterranean, where chemical warfare was seen to be counterproductive in maintaining support from civilians and partisans. Existing chemical warfare stocks in the Far East were deemed to be insufficient to allow offensive chemical warfare to be conducted simultaneously in both theatres of war, and defensive measure were inadequate to protect the military from gas under tropical conditions.

Military officials were under no illusion that Germany would immediately retaliate against the United Kingdom, with London as the principal target, if the Allies started to use gas warfare. Although the possible effects of gas on the home front were difficult to judge, they felt that the general public, after five years of war, might be resentful of being exposed to toxic agents if it could be shown that this 'could have been avoided'.[259] The Chiefs of Staff were also concerned about the effects on public morale of potential retaliatory measures against Allied prisoners of war who might be forced to 'work in contaminated areas'.[260] All things considered, and irrespective of any political, legal, or moral considerations, Britain's military planners concluded that chemical and biological weapons were not an attractive military proposition. General Hastings Lionel Ismay, one of Churchill's closest military advisers, even suggested to the Prime Minister that the use of these types of weapons was likely to be detrimental to the Allied military campaign:

> It is true that we could drench the big German cities with an immeasurably greater weight of gas than the Germans could put down on this country. Other things being equal, this would lead to the conclusion that it would be to our advantage to use the gas weapons. But other things are not equal. There is no reason to believe that the German authorities would have any greater difficulty in holding down the cowed German population, if they were subjected to gas attack, than they have had during the past months of intensive high explosive and incendiary bombings. The same cannot be said for our own people, who are in no such inarticulate condition.[261]

However impressive the plans drawn up by the Chiefs of Staff in July 1944 may appear in retrospect, we still need to be careful not to jump to any conclusions, on the basis of the above outlined memorandum, in respect of the actual state of Allied readiness to start chemical warfare operations during the closing stages of the Second World War. Given what we now know about newly developed operational research methods which allowed experts to calculate more precisely the requirements for chemical weapons stockpiles needed for a major military attack, it seems far from certain whether the Allied military would actually have been capable of delivering the kind of 'massive hammer blow' to the German enemy within the operational realities of war conceived by the Chiefs of Staff, had the order to employ chemical and biological weapons actually been given. As plans were drawn up in the United States to employ chemical weapons as part of an invasion of the Japanese home islands, for example, it became apparent that the quantitative requirements far exceeded existing stockpiles of chemical munitions. Yet if we assume, for a moment, that the existing chemical weapons stockpiles were likely to be insufficient for the kind of attack the Chiefs of Staff had outlined to Churchill—who at this point seems to have been, by all accounts, keen to launch chemical warfare operations—then this raises a series of questions: i.e. whether the Chiefs of Staff were aware of the fact that their chemical warfare capability might not have been quite what it seemed, and if so, why they did not communicate this fact to the Prime Minister. The following scenario is certainly possible: under considerable pressure from Churchill to confirm the viability of employing such unorthodox weapons, which up to this point had not been used in the war, senior military officials—who were keen to keep it that way—might have overstated the Allied chemical warfare capability, thus preserving the impression that the current state of readiness was such that chemical weapons could be employed on a massive scale and at any time, if necessary, whilst simultaneously arguing against the immediate use of chemical weapons in the current conflict.

Although hardly convinced by the report, Churchill decided to accept the assessment of his senior officials, at least for the time being.[262] As it happened, Britain's Chiefs of Staff, and Churchill in particular, had no need to return to the subject of chemical warfare. In April 1945, after Allied forces had crossed the Lower Rhine, the Joint Intelligence Subcommittee concluded that Germany appeared unwilling and unprepared to initiate gas warfare to defend the territory of the Reich. However, it also counselled caution: 'There remains the possibility that Hitler may recklessly order its use in the final stage of disintegration.'[263] He never did. At the end of the month, Hitler ended his life in his bunker beneath the Reich Chancellery. Shortly thereafter, the unconditional surrender of the German army heralded the end of one of the most murderous regimes in modern history, and with it came the uncomfortable realization that Allied intelligence agencies had had almost no knowledge of one of the greatest military and scientific secrets of the Second World War: nerve gas.

5
Deadly New Gases

A Novel Type of 'Nuisance'

In the summer and autumn of 1944, as evidence of Nazi atrocities in the occupied eastern territories mounted, Allied officials considered, but ultimately rejected, proposals to conduct large-scale bombing raids to disrupt the gassing of millions of European Jews and other nationals at Auschwitz-Birkenau. The establishment of military bases in Italy had made the deployment of bombers to attack Auschwitz a realistic proposition, yet faced with opposition from Washington and London, where senior officials objected to diverting war-important resources for 'humanitarian purposes', the idea never got off the ground.[1] Foremost in the minds of Allied leaders was the aim of bringing the war to a conclusion as fast as possible, a desire so strong that even the use of gas chambers against millions of innocent women and children could not bring military planners to reconsider their position. The use of gas as a method to kill, however, received all the more attention if it was directed against Allied soldiers and civilians.

The discovery of nerve agents at the beginning of April 1945 propelled chemical warfare to the top of the military and political agenda, and tested the existing systems of verification and inter-Allied communication to the full. For weeks, Porton's research laboratories became the epicentre of intense activity, fuelling speculation at the highest levels of a new and far more toxic German gas weapon. Planning for such an eventuality had been in the making for years, and had continually been improved, for example through the establishment of the Gas Detection and Identification Service. Indeed, the 'early identification' of new chemical agents was classed as a 'matter of national importance'.[2] Following the landing of Allied forces in Normandy in June 1944, Porton's Anti-Gas Laboratory No. 3, which served alongside 21 Army Group, was put in charge of analysing and dispatching enemy gas samples to Porton for verification. In November, the command-ing officer was instructed to make the necessary arrangements for the 'safe transit by air' of enemy gas samples to Britain, including an officer escort tasked with delivering the sample to Porton, awaiting analysis, and reporting back to 21 Army Group.[3] As Allied forces made steady progress on the con-tinent, fear of a last-ditch German gas attack loomed large at Allied military headquarters. Launched in mid December by the German military, the Ardennes offensive spectacularly ground to a halt after some initial success. German forces were effectively in retreat. By March, Allied forces were pushing towards the Rhine and into German territory. Weeks later, the German Army withdrew from Hungary. The surrender of the city of Königsberg on 9 April further accelerated the mass migration of millions of refugees and former camp inmates attempting to flee the Red Army advanc-ing from the east. In the West, the Allies made military gains in the German industrial heartland, capturing in quick succession the cities of Münster and Hamm and, on 10 April, Essen and Hanover. Days earlier, on Friday 6 April, as ground forces were pushing towards Hanover, members of the British Eighth Corps had discovered ten truckloads of unusually coloured enemy shells at a railway marshalling yard at Espelkamp, 7 miles north of Lübbecke.[4] Following cursory examination by the US Fortieth Chemical Laboratory Company at Le Bouchet in the Rhône-Alpes region in south-eastern France, the shells were dispatched to Britain.[5] After years of planning, this was the real-world scenario for which Porton had been set up.

In the early evening of Sunday 8 April, at around 6.00 p.m., Major Karle from the British Second Army delivered 'by hand' four enemy shells to Porton for chemical analysis.[6] The senior scientist on duty decided to begin work the next day, at 9.00 a.m. on Monday 9 April, and to continue work 'by day only'. It was immediately clear that the unusual delivery contained two types of high-explosive 105 mm gas shells. Whereas the first type con-tained 75 per cent CAP (CN) and 25 per cent penthrite (PETN), a powerful high explosive, it was the second type of shell, marked with one green band and one yellow, that concerned the investigating scientists. On 10 April, Porton informed Davidson Pratt—who, as Controller, Chemical Defence Development at the MoS, was responsible for briefing the Prime Minister and the War Cabinet—firstly by telephone and then in a brief top-secret report, of the discovery of a liquid of unknown identity: 'Liquid is highly toxic; contains nitrile[7] and phosphorus. Sulphur arsenic and halogen absent. Investigation proceeds.'[8] 21 Army Group was to be advised, as a precautionary measure, that both shells contained chemical agents and that the second type especially was to be 'treated with the greatest respect'.[9] Back at military headquarters, Lieutenant Colonel S.G. Notley was to receive confirmation 'by hand' the next morning. Twenty-four hours later, Porton's senior duty scientist told London in his first progress report that the substance, which appeared to be either an 'alkyl phosphine cyanide' or a 'cyanophosphate', was 'highly toxic by injection', about as lethal as phosgene by inhalation, non-blistering, and rapidly absorbed through the eyes. Absorption through the skin was still under investigation. Various detecting devices and powders had responded positively, however. Details of the report were to be treated as preliminary only and subject to confirmation. With regard to potential protection, he noted: 'No information yet.'[10] In London and Washington alarm bells were starting to ring at the highest levels.

The next day, 12 April, after the liquid had been purified and the chemical formula provisionally established, Porton requested the assignment of a T-number or provisional code-name for the substance. Small concentrations of vapour strongly constricted the pupils and several workers had reported a 'feeling of tightness in the chest'. Further tests were performed by pharmacologist Jack Gaddum who, by injecting the substance into cats, established that it acted as an inhibitor of cholinesterase: 'The symptoms are tremors, convulsions and finally death from respiratory failure. Death is usually rapid, and takes place in a few minutes.'[11] Post-mortem examinations by expert pathologist Gordon Roy Cameron did not reveal any distinctive pathological findings other than a pronounced congestion of the liver and the lungs, which was deemed consistent 'with right[-sided] heart failure'.[12]

Despite the realization that the substance was far more toxic in minute concentrations than anything Allied researchers had seen before—four times more toxic than HCN and ten times more toxic than PF-3—the scientists were not unduly concerned at this stage. PF-3, also known as di-isopropyl fluorophosphate, a similar substance to the one discovered, had been extensively analysed in Britain and the United States. During the war, researchers at Cambridge, including Edgar D. Adrian, Wilhelm S. Feldberg,[13] B.A. Kilby and M. Kilby, examined a whole range of highly toxic and cholinesterase-inhibiting substances on behalf of the MoS. In 1946, to claim credit for their work on chemical warfare agents—which during the war could not be published for reasons of secrecy—Adrian and his team published a letter to the editor of the journal *Nature*, arguing that the 'first observations on the cholinesterase-inhibiting action of fluorophosphates were made in 1941'.[14] They argued that the substances studied, dimethyl and diethyl fluorophosphates, were less toxic than PF-3—which they examined a year later—but otherwise had 'similar effects' in terms of strongly inhibiting 'the cholinesterase activity of human plasma'.[15] Between 1942 and 1944, M. Dixon, J.F. Mackworth and E.C. Webb, also at Cambridge, continued some of the work of Adrian's group on anti-cholinesterases.[16] The findings of all the Cambridge scientists subsequently informed Porton's own assessment of PF-3: an oily, colourless liquid which, although stable, underwent hydrolysis when exposed to moisture, thus reducing its potential as a chemical weapon.[17] British researchers also tested eight substituted amine phosphoryl fluorides, one of which, a compound code-named T 2002 (bis-dimethylamino-phosphoryl fluoride), had shown an 'outstanding' degree of toxicity and stability, an assessment which in 1944 led Porton to conclude that T 2002 was 'one of the most toxic of known substances by oral administration'.[18] Given the existing knowledge among Allied scientists, this was probably a reasonable conclusion. However, it also has to be said that none of the substances tested was recommended for use as a chemical weapon. Allied scientists, in other words, believed themselves to be 'familiar', from a pharmacological perspective, with the German warfare agent they had just discovered. It was part of 'a family' of compounds that they had investigated but turned down as a warfare agent, 'though this particular member of it was a new one'.[19]

Other than 'ease of manufacture', which might have persuaded the Germans to incorporate the agent into their chemical arsenal, there were apparently no detectable advantages to the substance. German researchers appeared to have been guided by its 'toxicity and laboratory trials' rather than by its effectiveness in the field. According to the Porton scientist K. Harrison, it all seemed to have been a false alarm that needed to be downgraded: 'Judging by preliminary results, the substance has a nuisance value only; undue alarm is to be deprecated. Existing methods of protection appear to be fully adequate.'[20] If ever Porton got their findings dramatically wrong, it was on this occasion: the substance was extremely dangerous. Four days later, Porton's assessment was officially repeated, albeit somewhat more cautiously, by 21 Army Group:

> This charging, though novel, should not give rise to excessive alarm. It is perhaps going too far to say that it is of nuisance value only, since inevitably if it were used a number of troops would be killed in spectacular

fashion…chemically it is analogous, and physiologically it is similar in action, to a series of compounds in the UK whose merits as war gases are not regarded as particularly outstanding.[21]

Senior officials in London and Washington nonetheless set in train a series of high-level meetings in preparation for what had the potential to develop into a military nightmare scenario: a last-minute and large-scale attack by German forces with a hitherto unknown but highly toxic chemical warfare agent. In a flurry of top-secret cables, Allied intelligence services and top military commanders in Europe and the Far East were informed of the discovery. On 13 April, the MoS invited Major Harris from the CWS and other senior military officials to an informal meeting the next day since it was 'felt that urgent action should be taken to draft appropriate instructions for defensive measures to be taken in the event of this agent being employed'.[22] Twenty-four hours later, it was decided 'to warn theatres of its existence' and provide experts with some information.[23] On 16 April, as evidence of enemy activity to 'remove chemical ammunition' was coming in, the War Office dispatched a detailed summary of what was known of the agent, now code-named T 2104, in a secret cipher telegram to the Supreme Headquarters Allied Expeditionary Forces (SHAEF), the headquarters of South East Asia Command (HQ SEAC), and Allied Force Headquarters (AFHQ). Distribution included 21 Army Group, Allied land forces, South East Asia, general headquarters in the Middle East and India, British Army Staff Washington, the War Cabinet offices, and senior military and intelligence officials from Britain and the Commonwealth.[24] Examination of the substance had been undertaken by both Porton and US chemical warfare experts, whose agreed findings were as follow: the chemical formula, which, as it later turned out, was based on an incompletely purified sample, was $(C_6H_{13}O_2N_2P)$, provisionally identified as dialkylaminocyanophospate. The lethal dose for humans was estimated to be in the 'order of 5 gm [gram] absorbed through the skin'. Health risks emanating from an initial gas cloud were believed to be concentrated on the eyes and lungs, while 'lethal doses would probably cause tremors and convulsions followed by rapid respiratory failure'.[25] Eight days after the strangely coloured shells had been discovered, Allied forces across the world were put on alert, yet they were also told that it was unclear whether the liquid had 'any advantages' for the enemy over other known substances used in high-explosive chemical shells. Since the service respirator was believed to provide 'complete protection' to the eyes and lungs of servicemen, it was felt that the substance 'should give rise to no undue concern'.[26]

Rumours suggesting the existence of fast-acting deadly new gases 'against which the respirators are useless' had been circulating among the British population throughout the war. As early as 1940, J.B.S. Haldane had made it clear that he did 'not believe [any of] them'.[27] Rumours relating to chemical agents were nonetheless monitored by Home Office officials to counter potential enemy propaganda, but their truthfulness had rarely, if ever, been tested, nor had the intelligence behind them been passed on to the relevant agencies, or indeed to Porton itself.[28] Rumours had a life of their own, detached from the seemingly hard-nosed military intelligence gathering that informed Porton's chemical warfare corps. In those cases where vital intelligence was shared with Porton, no further action had been taken. British officials were able to glean no knowledge about the type of the newly discovered gas bomb from captured documents, other than that German prisoners of war had referred to a new substance called 'Trilon'. Evidence obtained from an unidentified German army officer captured in North Africa in 1943 revealed that the German military had developed a new warfare agent with 'astounding properties'; the officer, a former chemical scientist, had even described the symptoms of the agent he knew only by the name of 'Trilon 83', the German code-name for Tabun, yet military officials felt that the matter did not warrant further attention given the lack of 'corroborating evidence'. In retrospect, it looked like an intelligence failure of monumental proportions.[29]

For the time being, Allied commanders were advised to limit knowledge of the agent to technical chemical warfare and medical personnel only and refrain from distributing the information below the level of corps headquarters for fear of spreading panic among the troops. Until more was known, the phrase 'a new gas' would only cause undue alarm.[30] Weeks later, the War Office called for even tighter secrecy in inter-Allied communication until investigators had established the 'true military value' of the liquid and until the ISCCW had taken a policy decision as to whether these novel agents would be employed in future combat operations. Intelligence suggested that Germany's ally, Japan, had been kept in the dark about the existence of Tabun (T 2104) and associated gases. As long as the war in the Far East was ongoing, Britain preferred a 'total ban on [the] release of information' to ensure 'tactical surprise if the Japanese start chemical warfare'.[31] In a top-secret, OTP-encrypted cipher, dispatched in June 1945, the Air Ministry, Special Signals Office (AMSSO) told the British Joint Services Mission (BJSM) in Washington DC that it was 'most important that no information should reach the Japanese regarding the properties of Tabun, Sarin and Soman', three of the most deadly nerve agents that had by then been discovered and identified.[32] The Admiralty, meanwhile, proposed to distribute the information to the 'East Indies and British Pacific Fleets only'.[33] While Allied scientists in Los Alamos were frantically working on the first atomic bomb, the Allies came to the realization that German nerve agents were one of the greatest discoveries of the Second World War. Chemical warfare was suddenly elevated to, and given the status of, a tactical weapon that might be employed in the war in the Far East.

The discovery of Tabun, i.e.T 2104, the substance in the strange-coloured shells, provided an 'excellent opportunity' to test and evaluate the way new warfare agents were analysed and the collaborative arrangement between the British and US authorities. Considering that the discovery was made in 'gas peace', under 'semi-operational conditions', and at a time when the staff at Porton 'had been curtailed', the system had, on the whole, proved to be 'effective and speedy'—despite lacking in accuracy as far as the initial assessment about nerve agents was concerned.[34] Some procedural weaknesses and inter-departmental tensions were exposed, however. Military officials, for example, had inundated Porton staff with telephone calls for updates on the investigation, and although Porton understood their desire to 'get early information', the MoS felt compelled to remind the War Office to observe appropriate chains of command and communication.[35] In cases where Porton acted as the main anti-gas laboratory, however, and was asked to examine samples of 'operational importance', as it had done in this case, the War Office insisted on the submission of frequent telephone reports, at least every evening, by the Chief Superintendent or his representatives. Porton was asked to communicate with the War Office only, 'because there is no other means of communication nearly as quick, certain and secret'.[36] There was also a sense that Porton had been too slow, and inflexible, in its response. Some found it difficult to believe that it had taken two days to fly the shells to Britain, and that tests to identify the compound had not even begun until fifteen hours later because they had been delivered on a Sunday. For 21 Army Group, the procedure in similar cases 'would of course have to be much quicker' in the future.[37] Senior British officials were also told to be 'gentle', 'tactful', and not 'too critical' of the US chemical warfare machine, which they regarded as 'very odd', to ensure future inter-Allied collaboration about suspected enemy agents.[38]

As Allied forces drove ever deeper into German territory, more and more chemical warfare dumps were discovered, including on barges camouflaged with large red crosses on a white background to protect them against Allied air raids. By the end of April, Porton was working round the clock to examine the content of dozens of newly discovered chemical bombs with different types of markings.[39] Intelligence obtained from the interrogation of German scientists now suggested a probable link between the substance Le 100, code-named 'Trilon 83' by the Germans, and the compound discovered by the Allies, code-named T 2104. The two appeared to be the same: military intelligence officials urged the War Office's DSWV, headed by Major General Gerald Brunskill, to establish a 'key to German chemical charging' as fast as possible.[40] Back in Germany, the staff at the depot where the ammunition had been found told interrogators that they had been 'most afraid' of all 'three-green ring' shells since the liquid contained therein (*Spitzenkampfstoff*, as they called it) acted as a 'blood and nerve' gas. Gradually, one of Germany's most highly protected secrets of the war was being uncovered, not just by Britain and the United States, but, according Allied intelligence, also by the Soviet Union.

Soviet forces had overrun and taken possession of the Tabun plant at Dyhernfurth, near Breslau, and were believed to have captured personnel and some nerve agent stocks that were likely to provide them with good intelligence as to the novelty and high priority of German 'special gases'. Whereas the plant at Falkenhagen had been vacated before Soviet forces reached it, stocks of Tabun-filled shells were discovered in various dumps in Saxony, and there were conflicting reports as to whether the American military had been able to remove them before Soviet forces occupied Saxony. Moreover, Soviet scientists had shown an interest in organic phosphorus compounds and had published on the subject, and they were believed to have created a new war gas similar to Sarin. Some of the research, which had been translated into German, was based on work described in openly available literature and had been captured by the Combined Intelligence Objectives Subcommittee (CIOS) at Raubkammer (the German Army's proving ground).[41] British military intelligence was therefore in a position to assess the state of knowledge with regard to nerve agents in the Soviet Union. In contrast to those in Japan, it was believed to be 'more than probable' that Soviet scientists had followed up research on organic phosphorus compounds, and if they had not already produced similar substances, they were now in possession of knowledge which would enable them to produce nerve agents in the near future.[42]

Back in Britain, Porton's interim report on 'Substance T 2104', submitted on 26 April, not only provided a thorough analysis of the physical, chemical, and physiological properties of the compound, but gave insight into its deadly potential. There were horrific images, obtained from animal and human experiments, of life succumbing to convulsions, tremors, and rapid death—in the case of animals—from respiratory failure. Tests with a carefully purified sample had required the empirical formula to be revised to $(C_5H_{11}O_2N_2P)$, or ethyl dimethylamine cyanophosphate. With a distinct but faintly fruity smell, the substance was unlikely to be detected by combat troops in the field. Exposed in a gas chamber for two minutes to a small concentration of the substance, the first ten experimental subjects immediately reported tightness in the chest, visual impairments, severe headaches, and pain in their eyes, symptoms that persisted for two days. All showed a marked contraction of the pupils. In four cases, the men suffered from prolonged vomiting. Inhalation experiments with animals, however, gave the researchers a sense of what was lying in store for them, a foreboding of a future in which chemical warfare might compete with, if not surpass, other forms of warfare technology: 'Death in convulsions is preceded in most cases by a peculiar muscular twitching.'[43] Although a 'firm appreciation' of the potency of the substance was seen as premature, and could not easily be determined within the confines of the laboratory, its effects were likely to 'cause considerable persistent harassment and/or incapacitation of unprotected troops'.[44]

Raubkammer

To find out how nerve agents really worked one needed to know how those who had discovered them had tested them. In mid May, the War Office agreed to dispatch a reconnaissance party of senior military and chemical warfare experts to Germany to assess the viability of conducting field trials and experiments with German chemical shells at Raubkammer, near Münster, and to report back to London.[45] Top-secret discussions at the highest levels had made it plain that there was an urgent need to investigate and understand these new compounds more fully. The group included Air Vice Marshal G. Coombe and Lieutenant Colonel G.N. Dunlop from the Air Ministry, Brigadier E.A.E. Bolton from the War Office, Davidson Pratt from the MoS, and Brigadier R.M.A. Welchman, Chief Superintendent at

Porton (see Image 13).[46] Shortly afterwards, Churchill authorized the arrest
of the last German government led by Admiral Dönitz: 'All this should be
very popular with the papers right now. It seems a notable step in making
sure we have no one to deal with in Germany.'[47] On 23 May, the day the last
remaining members of the Reich government were taken into custody in
Flensburg and Germany ceased to exist as a sovereign nation, the reconnaissance party touched down on German soil, where they were greeted by
Lieutenant Colonel S.A. Mumford (see Image 14) and Captain R.E.F.
Edelston from Porton. Supreme authority over the whole of Germany now
rested with the Allied authority. As part of ongoing technical and scientific
intelligence gathering, Porton was given the historic opportunity to conduct extensive field trials on former enemy territory.

Image 13. Brigadier R.M.A. Welchman, Chief Superintendent Porton Down,
April 1944–August 1947
Source: IWM, Photographic Collection. © Imperial War Museums (R.M.A. Welchman)

Image 14. Lieutenant Colonel S.A. Mumford, Chief Superintendent Porton Down, September 1951–September 1955
Source: IWM, Photographic Collection. © Imperial War Museums (S.A. Mumford)

Forty-eight hours later, after the reconnaissance party had returned to London, the War Office convened a meeting with service representatives to consider plans for a three-month experimental programme with German chemical warfare agents at Raubkammer. There was general agreement between the Air Ministry and the War Office that they should exploit German research facilities and personnel for field trials. The site, with its equipment and layout, was seen as ideal and, unlike at Porton or Suffield, there was also the possibility of conducting warfare trials in wooded areas. Given the level of security restrictions by now in place, Davidson Pratt only alluded to 'German munitions' that presented 'novel features…which might lead to new ideas and development'.[48] For those in the know in the room it was clear that the subject of nerve agents could no longer be openly discussed. Key to the programme of research was the establishment of an entirely self-supporting and self-contained detachment of experts from Porton, protected by a large contingent of military guards, and in close liaison with representatives from the US CWS. Civilian staff were to be given military status. Logistical problems ranged from the supply of food, petrol, and transportation for the Porton team to the repair of the internal telephone system at Raubkammer and the provision of interpreters and typists. Researchers also needed specialized laboratory and meteorological equipment. British single-seater Typhoon fighter bombers and German Junkers JU 88s were on stand-by to conduct trials with aircraft chemical ammunition. From an intelligence perspective, concerns were raised as to whether German civilians posed a security risk since some of Porton's techniques would be revealed in the course of the trials, a point which strengthened the argument for isolating German personnel from access to raw scientific data.

Porton's programme of work at Raubkammer, signed off during an informal meeting at the MoS, aimed to investigate German experimental techniques and methods and assess the lethal and incapacitating potential of German nerve agents, Tabun especially, when dispersed by German or British shells, bombs, or spray. Researchers also wanted to examine the performance of German blistering agents, and to conduct a small number of tests with incapacitating and smoke weapons over wooded land.[49] Air Ministry officials were also keen to learn more about German tactical policy in employing air weapons. Proposals by service representatives to visit Raubkammer to witness specific experiments received a muted response; for logistical reasons, permits were granted only in exceptional circumstances. In view of the importance of experimental animals for the Porton detachment, Cullumbine was tasked to examine the possibility of supplying the team with 'small animals from German sources'. Staff detailed to go to Germany were reminded not to discuss matters of technical intelligence and to comply with the Allied non-fraternization policy.[50]

Efforts to manage public relations and press censorship moved centre stage after journalists had figured out what the Germans had stored at Raubkammer and been given permission to visit the site. Cullumbine was prepared to tell them that it was a 'CW Experimental Station' but no more; he refused to discuss or refer to agents by name or engage in any debate about whether German chemical stocks would be disposed of at sea; and he likewise declined to comment on the suggestion by one journalist to 'use these stocks against the Japanese'. These were matters to be discussed by the Allied Control Commission. Senior military officials were furious that the press had 'grossly misrepresented the facts' and asked for immediate action to be taken to control press reporting on such highly sensitive issues. The war in the Far East made any public debate about the destruction of German stocks of toxic chemical seem premature. Behind the scenes, the CWS requested that Britain should not dispose of any chemical warfare stocks but instead make them available for 'United States requirements' until the war against Japan had been brought to a conclusion.[51]

Arriving on 27 June, the Porton Down Inspection and Evaluation Team (see Image 15) or No. 1 Porton Group, as it was called, went straight to work setting up field trials and making security arrangements that prohibited German technical personnel from attending British assessment procedures. However, given their limited understanding of the science involved, German field and animal staff were permitted to take part. Despite additional logistical and technical support from 21 Army Group and Chemical Defence Laboratory No. 3, unsettled weather conditions at first slowed down the

Image 15. The Porton Down Inspection and Evaluation Team at Raubkammer, near Münster, 1945

Source: IWM, Photographic Collection. © Imperial War Museums (HU 102394).

The Porton Down Inspection and Evaluation Team at the German chemical warfare station at Raubkammer bei Münster following the German surrender at the end of the Second World War. All are wearing uniform although most were in fact civilians (and therefore wear no cap badges).

start of the trial programme; within a month of arrival, however, Porton had performed deadly nerve agent experiments on over 900 animals, mostly rabbits, cats, and guinea pigs. Whereas rabbits responded to the initial gas cloud by holding their breath, cats changed their respiration pattern; guinea pigs, on the other hand, exhibited tremors and spasms of the bronchi. By studying these three types of species it was hoped to establish a 'fair estimate of the toxicity' of different gas clouds. Tests with rabbits were meant to establish the extent to which nerve agents damaged the eyes of living beings. Even preliminary findings surpassed anything the scientists had anticipated or seen before. An initial gas cloud of Tabun passing over the cats caused '90–100 per cent mortality', about '75 per cent mortality in guinea pigs and regular but fewer rabbit deaths'.[52] Although a full assessment of the toxicity of the agents was deemed premature, for Porton scientists their deadly potential had been on display. In August, Cullumbine and his colleagues from the CWS submitted a preliminary report on German chemical air weapons and their performance. Some of their findings were equally astonishing. Air weapons charged with Tabun and Tabun mixtures could create very large areas of contamination. The 250-kg bomb, for example, with a payload of about 86 kg of agent, could produce a contaminated area of between 4,000 and 4,500 m^2. Under the heading 'Corresponding Allied Munitions', they had little to say other than 'none'.[53]

By the summer of 1945, Allied interrogations of German scientists and technical experts in de-briefing centres such as 'Dustbin', located at Kransberg Castle near Heidelberg, were gathering pace. In collaboration with the CIOS secretariat, small teams of expert investigators made up of War Office and Porton officials attempted to reconstruct the organization and underlying policies of Germany's chemical warfare programme, and identify the key personalities behind it.[54] Rather than conducting a standard interview, one official felt that the required information could best be obtained by 'setting the expert concerned a written exam, and then giving him a viva on it if necessary afterwards', and added in brackets: 'This is a serious suggestion.'[55] Armed with a list of some forty German chemical warfare experts, compiled by the Porton team at Raubkammer, and with a detailed questionnaire and aide-memoire, Mumford from Porton, Hand from Sutton Oak, and Lieutenant Colonel Kerr Muir set off to join US interrogators at Heidelberg. At the top of their list was Otto Ambros, the chief chemical adviser to the Nazi government. Later that year, Hermann Ochsner, Chief of the German

Chemical Troops (see Chapter 3 above), was apprehended and interrogated by a British Intelligence Objectives Subcommittee (BIOS) team that included A.W. Kent from Porton.[56] The official mechanisms and channels of communication between German military scientists and the Nazi administration not only turned out to be undefined and poorly demarcated, or as one interrogator put it, 'fairly flexible', but extremely complicated; to produce tangible results one needed to have 'friends in the ministry'. Yet in the midst of all the chaos and confusion, largely resulting from Hitler's personalized style of government, experts had made highly original discoveries that baffled Allied experts.

Questions of general policy focused on the role of chemical agents in an invasion of Britain and on the level of collaboration in chemical warfare between Axis countries, especially Germany and Japan. Investigators were instructed to press the German experts on production techniques, particularly in relation to chemical engineering in Tabun and Sarin plants, and document 'any production data on Soman or other analogues' as well as 'factory safety methods', necessary information for Allied nerve agent manufacture. Considerable time was spent examining Germany's offensive preparations for gas warfare, including an assessment of chemical agents and tactics and of the value attributed to ground contamination weapons and training. With regard to defensive gas warfare, the line of inquiry concentrated on impregnated clothing, the evacuation and treatment of gas casualties, decontamination methods, and different types of ointments. Concerned by unconfirmed reports of widespread camp experiments, the Porton team also wanted to establish the extent to which human 'guinea pigs' had been used in chemical warfare research and to understand the nature and ethics of human trials with nerve agents. The process of obtaining war-important information from German experts thus became enmeshed with ongoing war crimes investigations into criminal camp experiments; it transformed Porton into an agency which highlighted demands for Allied reparations and, at the same time, contributed to wider policy objectives to hold Nazi war criminals to account.[57]

Some of the technical data transmitted from Raubkammer, especially in relation to nerve agents, made British officials acutely aware of the great danger in which the country had found itself; for them, it was 'fortunate' that Nazi policy planning in relation to chemical warfare had been 'so bad'.[58] Reports compiled by military intelligence suggested that the German High Command had assigned a low priority rating to chemical warfare production in the 1930s; the old officer corps, having experienced what gas could do in the Great War, had apparently shown a persistent dislike for chemical warfare and were anxious not to tarnish Germany's standing in the world by authorizing military action that contravened the Geneva Protocol. General Field Marshal von Rundstedt, perhaps some-what disingenuously, regarded this type of warfare as 'repugnant to his feelings'; his favourite weapons of war were the horse and the lance. Smoke weapons, on the other hand, were 'unreliable' and 'treacherous'.[59] Officials were also beset by fears that the initial success of using gas weap-ons could spell disaster for Germany in the long term; any military success achieved in the East through the use of toxic agents, for example at Stalingrad, would come 'at the price of having her cities attacked with gas from the air in retaliation'. In a fast-moving military campaign, where the front lines were constantly changing, the use of chemical agents was seen as counterproductive in supporting German military offensives. Germany had reportedly held a small retaliatory capability to maintain military morale after a surprise gas attack, but had recognized her inability to com-pete with the industrial production potential of the Allies. According to von Rundstedt and other senior officials, Germany was in no position to withstand chemical warfare from the air. To avoid the unintentional initi-ation of chemical warfare, all gas weapons had apparently been stored within the borders of the German Reich. The German generals wanted the Allies to believe that they had never seriously contemplated the first use of chemical warfare for offensive purposes. In this, they were rather economical with the truth.

Porton's experimental programme at Raubkammer raised fundamental issues of policy and military strategy, since the findings suggested poten-tial vulnerabilities in the weapons arsenal of the Western Allies. Decisions as to whether to dispose of tens of thousands of tons of German chemical weapons by incineration, burial, or by dumping at sea were at first post-poned. In August, the Chiefs of Staff directed that the general policy governing the disposal of these weapons should involve the destruction of all toxic chemicals 'except for stocks of high quality mustard gas and Tabun', the disposal of all chemical shells and mortar bombs 'other than those charged with Tabun', and the retention of all 'aircraft bombs charged with Tabun'.[60] Until the Allied military had developed its own nerve agent programme, it was considered prudent to preserve German stockpiles.

The Raubkammer trials also highlighted problems of compatibility when using German stocks of nerve agents in British shells. Whereas 'the Hun' had designed shells with a large bursting charge to break Tabun down into 'very fine droplets', and had produced a 'reasonably efficient weapon', the British shells contained a charge which was 'just sufficient to rupture the casing and to liberate the contents'.[61] In short, 'our weapons are not suitable for Tabun' was how the War Office explained the situation to the Cabinet Office.[62] In early 1946, the Chiefs of Staff nonetheless recommended the retention of all stocks of Tabun as part of Britain's chemical warfare reserve. The development of efficient air and artillery weapons containing nerve agents would take up to three years in peacetime, it was estimated. Although Britain's defensive equipment 'adequately' protected against Tabun, it had become clear that no satisfactory detector had yet been developed, nor had researchers devised effective methods of treatment for Tabun casualties. On balance, the military expressed considerable reluctance to dispose of German nerve agent stocks as long as Britain had not yet developed appropriate means of production and delivery, and was not in a position to protect civilians and soldiers against these compounds.[63]

As Cold War tensions increased, military advisers concluded that the mere possession of nerve agents could function as a deterrent against the initiation of chemical warfare: 'The real danger lies with those who do not possess the gas but know that it may be used against them.'[64] In reality, though, ordnance experts encountered enormous problems with the long-term storage and disposal of nerve agents. After negotiations with the United States, which expressed greater interest in the more toxic nerve agent Sarin, Britain took possession of 71,000 250-kg bombs filled with Tabun. As soon as the first bombs arrived at Llandwrog airfield, near Caernarfon Bay in North Wales, where they were stored at first out in the open and later in Bellman hangars, it became clear that the justification for their retention had been overtaken by the nuclear age. Whether the decomposing nerve agent arsenal on the Welsh coast ever constituted a credible deterrent against Soviet forces remains questionable. In the mid 1950s, the entire 14,000-ton Tabun stockpile was dumped at sea in Operation Sandcastle.[65]

Meanwhile, at Raubkammer, Porton Group pursued the liquidation and destruction of German experimental facilities designed for chemical warfare production and research purposes. Apart from temporary difficulties in dismantling the production plant and re-erecting it at Sutton Oak, which were exacerbated by the mysterious disappearance of valuable equipment, some of it containing significant quantities of silver, Porton's researchers were keen to bring the work in Germany to an end and prepare the nation against future attacks with the latest types of chemical agents.[66] Experts were in agreement that the threat from chemical weapons, as opposed to biological weapons, had markedly increased with the discovery of nerve agents, yet the new agents also provided Porton with the scientific and military rationale for a considerable expansion of its own experimental programme, if not with the political justification for its postwar existence generally.

Porton's Nerve Agent Programme

Once Allied forces had used two atom bombs, with devastating effect, against Hiroshima and Nagasaki in the summer of 1945, military strategists recognized that the world of modern warfare would never be the same. In October, General Brunskill called for an informal, yet top-secret conference of the subcommittee of the Chemical Defence Advisory Board (CDAB) to discuss the implications of these new weapons for the future of Britain's chemical warfare preparedness. Attended by some of Britain's most senior chemical scientists and policy experts from the War Office and Porton—including Davidson Pratt, Childs, Duncan, Hartley, Lovatt Evans, Mumford, Peters, Sadd, Wansbrough-Jones, and Welchman—the meeting acknowledged that the factors determining the future of chemical warfare and its relationship to atomic and biological weapons were extremely 'complex and nebulous'.[67] Some wanted to exclude an assessment of the potential and limitations of atomic weapons from the discussions, but others, such as Major General H.W. Goldney, were adamant that the use of the atom bomb would affect the future of defensive and offensive chemical warfare operations.

General consensus existed among senior military officials to update Britain's general staff policy statement in relation to chemical warfare, last issued in 1944, to take account of the latest developments in modern weapon technology and military strategy, including the use of nuclear weapons, which, it was assumed, would render 'almost all other air weapons out of date'; the introduction of 'substances of far higher lethality' that might allow the use of 'gas as a neutralizing weapon'; the increased mobility of the modern army;

and the adoption of aerial bombing. Questions were also raised as to whether there were any future requirements for substances such as phosgene and mustard gas.[68] Rather than creating 'special offensive chemical warfare units', all chemical weapon systems had to be 'capable of use by the separate arms', and to achieve this, research into offensive chemical warfare needed to accelerate. Since any major use of gas 'will come from the air', policy experts argued, there was now a 'new requirement for the development of means of employing nerve gases from the air', principally through the use of small bombs containing high explosives and nerve agents to create the maximum number of casualties among enemy forces. Britain's military scientists were asked to conduct a comprehensive 'investigation into all new chemical compounds', nerve agents especially, which could potentially be used in waging offensive chemical warfare, and assign the highest priority to work aimed at developing defensive measures against such agents.[69]

So what was the perceived military advantage of nerve agents over conventional chemical weapons—mustard gas and phosgene especially—which propelled Allied military leaders to launch an extended nerve agent research and development programme involving large numbers of tests on animals and humans during the 1950s and 1960s? Ever since Churchill had instructed his Chiefs of Staff to study 'in cold blood' the large-scale use of chemical and biological weapons against the German enemy, and probably even before that, senior military officials on both sides of the Atlantic were acutely aware that the operational utility of these weapons not only had to be fit for purpose, if ever the order to employ them was given, but that technical and logistical requirements—in terms of the delivery systems and quantities needed to achieve the desired effect—could actually be met by the military.

For Allied military planners, the discovery of nerve agents not only changed fundamentally the feasibility of using chemical weapons in active combat operations, but they also became responsible for the 'gravity of existing and future threats' of chemical warfare. These new agents had two major advantages compared to existing chemical weapons: first, they were extremely toxic and could be easily disseminated. This meant that the efficiency of existing artillery shells could be increased significantly. Second, they were extremely rapid in action, which meant that minute quantities could kill both humans and animals quickly, either through inhalation or penetration of the skin. A person exposed to a lethal respiratory dose of one of the then most toxic chemical warfare agents—phosgene—was likely to die within four to twenty-four hours. In contrast to this, a person inhaling a lethal dose of Tabun, Sarin, or Soman was expected to die in spectacular fashion within one to ten minutes.[70] These two factors explain why, from a military perspective, nerve agents were in a league of their own. They were a 'game changer' which made the use of chemical weapons a much more attractive proposition for ground forces conducting a major offensive. As Perry Robinson has pointed out: 'The nerve agents thus combined the efficiency of mustard gas with the rapidity of the blood gases [agents], and made CW techniques far less unsuitable for fast moving land-warfare operations.'[71]

Nerve gases possessed other advantages as well; almost odourless, they were difficult to detect, thereby delaying, and thus reducing the value of, conventional means of protection. The agents were suitable for disbursement by means of high-explosive shells which broke the liquid down into fine droplets to be inhaled or absorbed through the skin. The physical and chemical properties of nerve agents, as much as their toxicological ones, meant that they could be used for a whole range of military objectives. Their volatility, for example, 'ranged from above that of water to about that of fuel oil'; those which were volatile could be delivered in the form of a spray to be inhaled by enemy forces, whereas those which were less volatile could either be used for persistent ground contamination or function as a percutaneous agent which produced its casualty effects through the skin, and thus replaced mustard gas. When used at sublethal dosages, the G-agents could also function as harassing agents on the battlefield, but with the added advantage that the field concentrations required were much smaller compared to those of known incapacitating agents.[72]

In theory, therefore, a significantly reduced quantity of nerve agents was needed to achieve a similarly lethal and/or harassing effect in conventional chemical weapons; as the Russian chemist M.M. Dubinin later pointed out, about 7,200 tons of Sarin is 'toxically equal to approximately 100,000 tons of mustard gas', a central factor which elevated nerve agents to a tactical weapon of mass destruction.[73] However, the great range of G-agents also meant that before employing these types of weapons in real-world combat operations, they had to be extensively studied and tested from various angles and on different living species to allow experts to answer a series of key scientific and technical questions, i.e. a) what dosage was needed for different types of nerve agents which, when applied to the clothing or bare skin of humans, would cause incapacitation or death? b) which of the by then

known nerve agents could best be employed in aerial, naval, and land warfare? c) were the existing delivery systems appropriate for this type of warfare agent, and, if not, what were the technical challenges involved in the
development process? d) which of the agents was the most suitable in terms
of ease of manufacture and overall cost? Nerve agents, in other words,
brought with them an urgent need to conduct animal and human experiments on a massive scale to obtain reliable data about the lethal and/or
harassing effects of these substances and, by extrapolation, information
about the quantities needed to kill and/or incapacitate large numbers of
people through the use of specially designed weapon and delivery systems.

Human experiments with deadly nerve agents had started immediately
after their discovery. Weeks before the unconditional surrender of the Nazi
regime, Porton had performed gas chamber tests on ten subjects who
responded with 'severe contraction of pupils and violent headache'. Larger
doses of the substance were all but lethal. Shortly afterwards, the war in
Europe having come to an end, Brunskill turned his attention to the war
in the Far East by requesting assistance from the War Office's Director of
Operations in setting up an urgent experimental programme with 'physiological observers' to study nerve agents at Porton and, if necessary, employ
them against Japan. Having tested and rejected similar cholinesterase-
inhibiting substances during war, 'on the grounds that the lethal concentrations required were too big, and the minor symptoms caused by smaller
ones were not of military significance', experts now expressed reservations
about the initial findings.[74] Porton, especially, was 'anxious to assess the
seriousness of these minor symptoms, the contraction of the eyes, the
headache and some loss of muscular coordination, on fit men under normal battle conditions', and see whether trained soldiers could overcome
the incapacitating effects, as was the case with 'nose gases'. If small concentrations of these compounds caused disabling symptoms, which could not
be overcome by military training, then 'an important discovery in gas warfare' had been made (see Image 16).[75]

According to Brunskill, a platoon of soldiers was required, twenty to
thirty men, strong, physically fit, and experienced, who would be dispatched
to Porton for two to four weeks to take part in experimental nerve agent
trials. With hundreds of servicemen coming to Porton on a regular basis to
participate in warfare tests, the arrangement was meant to be seen as 'simply
an extension of the normal routine', without creating any additional administrative burdens. In reality, however, and in the long term, it was far more

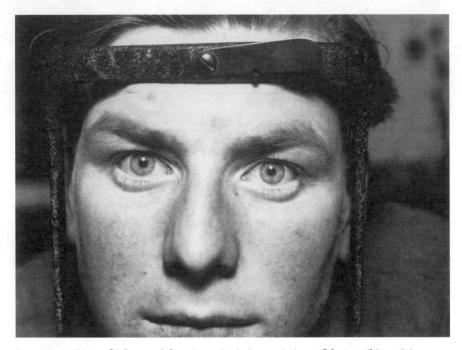

Image 16. Eyes of 'observer' showing miosis (constriction of the pupils), 25 May 1951
Source: IWM, Photographic Collection. © Imperial War Museums (L 1306/7).

than that; it established a tacit, albeit unspoken understanding that the recruitment of human subjects for tests with nerve agents—far more lethal than anything British scientists had so far encountered—and the information provided to encourage them to volunteer could essentially remain the same. The failure thoroughly to reassess not only all the processes and procedures involved in the recruitment of experimental subjects, including the information contained in the recruitment notices, but, perhaps even more significantly, the risks to which these men could legitimately be exposed, ultimately led to serious, and in one instance fatal, consequences.

Although responsibility rested with Porton 'for seeing that the men are not exposed to any concentration of gas which would do them permanent harm', Brunskill had no strong views on whether the men ought to have freedom of choice in deciding whether they wanted to take part in the trials: 'I must leave it to you to decide whether in this case the platoon should be volunteers.'[76] Military and national security interests seem to have been the overriding concern, rather than the health and well-being of individual soldiers. Since the tests were regarded as 'extremely important', there was, for the time being, little appetite to worry about the ethics of experiments:

> The experiment may have an application in the Japanese war, for we are contemplating reserving these charging[s] for ultimate use there, should gas warfare break out, and in that case it would be necessary to know considerably more about them than we do now. We have reason to believe that these charging[s] are unknown to the Japanese, in which case, were they used by us, we might achieve a major tactical surprise. If on the other hand the Japanese do know about them, it is even more important that we should know before they are used in the field what harm might result.[77]

Brunskill, it seems, had made a compelling case for launching one of Porton's most dangerous experimental programmes. In mid July 1945, the first platoon arrived at Porton as a 'special attachment' for tests involving the exposure to Tabun—a moment that reflected fundamental changes in chemical warfare research and policy.[78] In London and Washington officials were pressing ahead with initiating large-scale, inter-Allied testing programmes on animals and humans to establish, with scientific accuracy, the potency of nerve gases under different meteorological and environmental conditions. The number of animals required was significant. In the immediate postwar period, concern about animal welfare was regarded as of low priority, given the existential pressures to rebuild war-torn towns and lives, and as a result, Allington Farm, operating on over a thousand acres of land away from the public eye, became one of the leading suppliers of experimental animals, not just for Britain's chemical and biological warfare scientists, but for the RAMC, the PHLS, universities, research laboratories, and the pharmaceutical industry.[79]

Prompted by the wealth of information obtained from captured German documents, chemical scientists accelerated their research activity in the field of organophosphorus compounds. Basic research into G-agents was assigned the highest military priority. In laying down the policy governing the appointment of a new Chief Superintendent at Porton, who needed to be a 'thoroughly competent man' from either a civilian or a military background and with good contacts in British industry and universities, the government was determined to 'devote the maximum time possible to basic research' in developing new weapons and equipment.[80] While collaborative activities with civilian research institutions on broader therapeutic questions were welcome, they needed to inform the military agenda, which is why officials responded coldly to proposals to exploit Porton's research and human volunteer programme for civilian purposes. With work of medical interest under way, Porton was 'faced with a mass of fundamental research on the nerve gases'; any plans to divert attention or resources away from this objective were seen as a 'doubtful policy'.[81]

In July 1946, the CDAB launched a major programme of 'work on nerve gases' since these had shown considerable warfare potential both in the laboratory and in the field at Raubkammer. Scientists at Porton and at a number of British universities were asked systematically to study the bio-chemical properties and physiological effects of Tabun and Sarin to deter-mine which of these two substances should be selected as Britain's 'standard charging', to develop means of detection, decontamination, and protection, to investigate the physiological and biochemical modes of actions of nerve gases, to devise prophylactic and therapeutic methods against them, and to examine their 'behaviour' if dispersed in both chamber and field trials 'with the ultimate object of developing weapons for their optimum use'.[82]

To overcome Porton's shortage of expertise after the return of the major-ity of the research scientists to their peacetime positions, the government decided to seek extra-mural assistance from British researchers who either had an interest in the subject or had been affiliated to the chemical warfare field. Adam (Southampton), Bickley (Imperial College), Melville (Aberdeen), Mott (Bristol), Todd (Cambridge), and Thompson (Oxford), for instance, were asked to study the chemical and physical properties of nerve agents. Work on the 'physiology and biochemistry of GA [Tabun] and GB [Sarin]' had top priority. Since the initial experiments with 'human observers' in early 1945, no further trials had been conducted. Experts from Cambridge, Oxford, and Sheffield universities were seen as best qualified to investigate the physiological and biochemical modes of action of nerve agents, and to develop potential therapeutic measures.[83] Senior officials were particularly interested in the physiology of nerve gas poisoning—the 'fate of nerve gases in the body, assimilation, detoxification, excretion, retention [and] metabo-lism'—and in the role of atropine, curare, blood transfusion, artificial respir-ation, and other stimulants as means of treatment. These areas of work, they thought, could best be carried out by Edgar D. Adrian at Cambridge, and by Andrew Wilson, then at Sheffield. Both helped senior scientific officials to overcome the two major crises of research ethics, discussed later in the book (see Chapters 6 and 8 below), that hit Porton in the 1950s and 1960s. On the other hand, the main thrust of research assigned by the MoS to scientists at Oxford, Cambridge, and Sheffield, respectively Peters, Malcolm Dixon,[84] and Hans Krebs—the latter having conducted vitamin A and vitamin C deprivation experiments on dozens of conscientious objectors during the war—focused on the biochemistry of nerve agents, especially on the extent to which they affected certain enzyme systems of the animal and human body: this work was discussed by leading biochemists during a symposium at the London School of Hygiene and Tropical Medicine in 1947.[85] Although preliminary studies suggested that death from nerve gas poisoning ultimately resulted from respiratory failure, and that atropine and artificial respiration had some therapeutic value, more basic research was needed to better understand the deadly potential of these hitherto unknown compounds. In fulfilling a dual role of providing expertise and advice on complex scientific, ethical and warfare issues, particularly when things had gone wrong, civilian scientists managed to create powerful clusters of long-term influence within Britain's military research and development programme.

Andrew Wilson's association with Porton's work on nerve agents is of particular interest because it allows us to reconstruct not only how a collaborative relationship between a civilian scientist and Porton originated, but how it was nurtured, developed, and cultivated over the years.[86] His extra-mural research (EMR) assignment resulted from a series of informal conversations in spring and summer 1946 with Lieutenant Colonel E.F. Edson from Porton's physiology section. However, rather than Porton seeking to persuade Wilson to conduct EMR for them, he, Wilson, seems to have initiated the contact with Porton after discussing 'substances with a nicotine like action' with his colleague, the pharmacologist Jack Gaddum, who had worked for Porton during the war (see above), and had been instrumental in identifying the pharmacological properties of nerve agents in April 1945. It is highly likely, therefore, that, with his insider's knowledge of Porton, Gaddum alerted his colleague to Porton's planned work on nerve agents which could be of interest—in terms of access to new chemical compounds, knowledge, and resources—to scientists investigating substances causing cholinesterase inhibition. Edson approached Wilson in May 1946 and invited him to Porton to share 'information about the nature of the substance(s) concerned'. Shortly thereafter Wilson stated that he and Gaddum had concluded that, in light of the work done on toxic agents during the war, it would be best to 'discuss the whole subject with the people at Porton'.[87]

Seen from Edson's perspective, who worked with a greatly 'restricted staff'—which in actual fact was a euphemism for working 'single handed'—collaboration with Wilson, who had access to international networks and to scholars such as Krebs, was likewise beneficial.[88] Although Edson had worked at Sheffield between 1933 and 1939, he thought that Krebs would probably no longer 'remember' him. Wilson's overtures to Porton offered a unique opportunity for Porton's scientists, Edson especially, to establish close links—with the help of Wilson as Porton's liaison man—to senior British scientists with an interest in, and knowledge of, substances causing enzyme inhibition, which was so vital for a fuller understanding of nerve agents. There was also another reason why Wilson's expertise was welcome: Porton's staff, at this point, lacked the necessary technical knowledge of the 'Warburg apparatus' used to measure cholinesterase inhibition levels, and it was thought that Wilson might be of assistance. Porton, in other words, needed the expertise of civilian scientists as much as civilian scientists needed the expertise of Porton. In certain fields of scientific enquiry, both were, to some extent, dependent on each other to overcome temporary shortages of experienced personnel and equipment in the postwar period.

Wilson first visited Porton on 20 May 1946. Arriving by train at Salisbury Station after 7.00 p.m., he was invited to stay the night at Edson's house and enjoy his hospitality. The next day, whilst being shown around Porton's facilities, he witnessed—and took part in—a series of animal experiments with PF-3, a substance with similar pharmacological properties to but lower toxicity than nerve agents, one of which—code-named T 2106—interested him especially: this was Sarin. To develop potential means of treatment, Wilson knew, one first needed to see whether certain compounds, or forms of stimulation, would have an effect on the muscle tremors caused by nerve agents. To begin work, Porton sent him a pure sample of PF-3 tested on eight rats, which all died within between twenty-seven and forty-one minutes of exposure. On 14 June, Miss F. Uffelmann, writing on behalf of the MoS in a letter marked 'Secret', officially invited Wilson to carry out research on the 'pharmacology of nerve gases', to continue his studies with PF-3 solutions on patients suffering from chronic and excessive muscle fatigue (myastenia granis), and to provide the ministry with a rough estimate of the time and technical assistance needed and probable cost of the work.[89]

Less than a month later, Edson, who needed to get out of Porton every once in a while, or as he put it, 'to procure a breath of non-Porton scientific air', proposed to visit Wilson in Sheffield as a way of exchanging research findings on PF-3 and its 'more active analogues', which was code for nerve agents. Edson was hopeful, after the MoS had asked him to 'compile a list of research' which would be 'farmed out' to university experts, that Wilson's application for EMR resources would be granted, except that the MoS, rather than Porton, would officially employ him—'The same dwelling, but entry per front door!'[90] As a sign of their evolving cordial relationship, he remarked: 'My wife sends her best wishes; the plastic fish [which Wilson probably gave to Edson's family as a present during his visit in May] helps the nightly bathing ritual very well.'[91] Those looking at the subject of chemical and biological weapons in isolation, and distant from the nuances and shades of grey which often define personal networks and relationships, not to speak of friendships, might think that scientists would hardly discuss some of the most lethal agents on earth in the same breath as intimate family rituals, yet we need to realize that the culture and code of conduct of Britain's warfare scientists working at Porton and elsewhere did not differ significantly from those of civilian scientists, whose rules of academic etiquette would have seen the blurring of the lines between the professional and the private as perfectly acceptable, perhaps even desirable, among colleagues.

Although the meeting was postponed, the two scientists continued their conversation about the fast evolving body of knowledge in relation to nerve gas and its related substances. In September 1946, Edson finally approached Wilson in 'an almost official' capacity to tell him that Porton had requested from the MoS a total of 1,000 pounds sterling for the year to fund Wilson's proposed work on PF-3 and on nerve agents. As an 'inducement', Wilson would be given permission to publish his work on PF-3.[92] Experts at the MoS wanted to understand a) the cholinergic actions of PF-3; b) the pharmacological antagonisms between PF-3 and atropine, curare, etc.; c) the way in which PF-3 '[inhibited] enzyme systems other than cholinesterase'; d) the cholinesterase inhibition 'in vivo and in vitro in poisoned animals or tissue, brain, serum, red cells, muscle'; and, most importantly, e) the exact 'relationship between dosage, cholinesterase inhibition…and symptomatology produced, both in acute poisoning and during recovery from acute poisoning'.[93] In short, Porton was keen to produce with as much accuracy as possible reliable data about the 'relationship between human dosages, symptoms and serum cholinesterase'. Getting the necessary funds approved by the MoS, however, turned out to be rather difficult; when, in October, it turned out that no decision had yet been made, Edison alerted the ministry to the proposed work of Wilson and Krebs in a detailed memorandum. At the bottom of Wilson's copy of the memorandum, written in hand in small letters, Edson remarked: 'Fear not, we'll grind them down!'[94] At one level, this was an attempt to reassure Wilson that his requested funds would be granted eventually, but, at another, it served as a reflection of the often close relationship and professional understanding between Britain's military and civilian scientists, who could easily find common ground when the matter concerned the allocation of resources to conduct basic research with highly toxic chemical agents. After further delays, Wilson confirmed that he 'proposed to investigate the pharmacology of PF-3 and related compounds. The investigation will be conducted on experimental animals and on human subjects.'[95] Wilson's extra-mural contract with the MoS was finally agreed in March 1947. From rather tentative, informal beginnings, it marked the beginning of Wilson's close relationship with Britain's chemical warfare community. In the mid 1960s, he was among a group of senior scientists who were asked to take a view on whether the ban on Porton's human tests with incapacitating agents should be lifted.

At a more general level, we need to recognize that most of Porton's staff had close connections to universities and independent research laboratories that exposed them to, and invited them to engage in, the latest medical and ethical discourses. Throughout the 1950s and 1960s there was also a constant flow of early career scientists who spent a couple of years at the Chemical Defence Experimental Establishment (CDEE) and Microbiological Research Establishment (MRE) in order to secure senior research or university positions, or moved between organizations to improve their career opportunities—even quite literally across the street.[96] Similarly, for senior military officers and civil servants rising through the ranks during the Cold War, Porton became a necessary rite of passage for a successful military career, for example for Lieutenant General R.P. Bradshaw, successor to Lieutenant General Sir James Baird as Director General of Army Medical Services.[97] A specialist in pathology, Bradshaw had served in Ceylon and East Africa before moving to Washington and then to Porton as an adviser on chemical defence. In 1969, after a tour of duty with the British Army of the Rhine (BAOR), he returned to London to take up an appointment as professor of pathology to train the next generation of military doctors. Others, such as Thomas Simpson, a 'shrewd and kindly doctor' and career civil servant, went to Porton on active duty after joining the MoD's Medical Service.[98] There were also those who pursued a career at Porton itself, for instance Group Captain Robert John Moylan-Jones, a trained pharmacologist, who took over responsibility for recruiting suitable volunteers for chemical warfare tests in the 1960s.[99] Lovatt Evans, on the other hand, who belonged to a select group of elder statesmen with established links to Porton, remained actively involved in chemical weapon development. Following the death of his wife in 1964, and after suffering a stroke four years later, he moved into the Officers' Mess to spend the last couple of months of his life with his former colleagues and died in 1968. Despite their diverse social, professional, and generational backgrounds, this network of deeply loyal expert scientists, who, since the 1920s, used the occasional reunion to rekindle their professional and personal bonds (see Image 17), wielded considerable influence over the strategic direction of research and the allocation of resources and personnel, including the recruitment of servicemen for tests with highly toxic agents.

Another area of priority involved the construction of a pilot plant designed for production of 1 ton of Sarin per week for research purposes. No extra-mural assistance was required. Although detailed studies into organophosphorus compounds continued, experts had identified Sarin as Britain's chemical warfare agent of choice. It was not only more toxic but also more stable than Tabun. In dealing with nerve agent manufacture, maintaining high levels of secrecy remained a constant cause for concern for the authorities, not only in Britain. In 1952, during the construction of a nerve agent manufacturing facility in the United States, architects, civil engineers, and sub-contracted workmen, who did not necessarily have security clearance, could easily gain access to classified information. They were building a complex with tight security measures, massive air-tight double-door systems, large silver-lined kettles costing tens of thousands of dollars and using miles of expensive copper tubing—all indications that this was not a run-of-the-mill manufacturing facility. Add to this some local gossip among the workforce about an extremely toxic 'paralysing gas' which had originated from Germany, and the authorities could be dealing with a serious breach of security.[100] Choosing an appropriate location away from prying eyes was therefore a high priority in both the USA and Britain. Since neither Porton nor Sutton Oak were deemed suitable sites for a pilot plant, the former being conceived as a research facility and the latter posing a security and possibly even a public health risk if agents leaked into nearby populated areas, the British government decided to establish, on behalf of Porton, a new nerve agent factory on a disused airfield near the Cornish town of Portreath. Known as Nancekuke, the plant enabled Britain to maintain an offensive chemical warfare capability for over a decade, up until the mid 1950s. The decision to go it alone had been facilitated by the fact

Image 17. Reunion of staff who served at Porton during the Second World War, 6 September 1946

Source: IWM, Photographic Collection. © Imperial War Museums (HU 102389).

Those shown include Sir Owen Wansbrough-Jones, A.E. Childs, Sir Charles Lovatt Evans, Sir Harold Hartley, Sir Fredrick Baine, Professor D.D. Woods, Professor J.S. Kennedy, and Sir Paul Fildes.

that the planned purchase of 2,500 tons of nerve agents from the United States had not only turned out to be far too costly, more than the capital expenditure for an entire plant, but also by the fact that Britain's ally had made no commitment to 'meet British requirements in the event of war'. To 'rely on a distant and uncertain source of supply for a vitally important weapon' was, according to the MoS, a 'serious disadvantage'. It was therefore envisaged that Nancekuke would be expanded to become a fully automated plant producing 50 tons per week. This was never actually realized, however—indeed, it never produced more than 20 tons of Sarin nerve gas in total.[101] Still, by 1952, Britain's Director of Chemical Defence Research and Development (DCDRD) was requesting assistance from the United States in the sharing of technical intelligence after visiting the US nerve agent production sites at Muscle Shoals, Alabama, and at Rocky Mountain Arsenal, Denver, Colorado. What Britain needed, he told the US Chief Chemical Officer rather explicitly, were copies of architect drawings for its own nerve gas production facilities.[102] The British nuclear weapons programme, and an independent offensive chemical warfare programme, together underpinned Britain's aspiration to sit at the 'top table' as one of the world's leading military powers during the Cold War.[103]

In January 1947, Porton's Chief Superintendent, Brigadier Welchman, was in a position to provide a comprehensive appreciation of the value of nerve agents for offensive chemical warfare.[104] Substantially revising an earlier assessment judging nerve agents as of 'nuisance value' only, the report stressed the exceptional potential of these 'low freezing, mobile liquids', to which the human senses responded without any warning, and that were largely undetectable and extremely 'rapid in action'.[105] Scientists distinguished between three different series of nerve agents: the dialkyl fluorophosphonates such as PF-3, code-named T 1703, the dialkylamino cyanophosphonates such as GA (Tabun), code-named T 2104, and the alkane fluorophosphonates such as GB (Sarin), code-named T 2106, GD (Soman), code-named T 2107, and GE (Ethane Sarin), code-named T 2109. Whereas the effects of Tabun and, to a lesser extent, Sarin, were reasonably well understood as a result of tests undertaken using German stockpiles on both animals and humans, research into the properties of Soman and Ethane Sarin had not yet advanced. If inhaled in small dosages, nerve agents were believed to cause rapid death from 'respiratory and heart failure', and, even in lower dosages, less severe symptoms such as breathing difficulties, headaches, vomiting, and visual impairment: 'The lethal dosages are very considerably less than those of the most toxic agents hitherto used.'[106] Severe nerve gas poisoning, which involved loss of balance and coordination, muscular twitching, spasms, violent convulsions, paralysis, unconsciousness, heart muscle failure, and ultimately death by asphyxiation, was understood to result from the inhibition of cholinesterase, which led to an 'excessive accumulation of acetyl choline at various key-points of the body'.[107]

Detailed information about this new group of war gases was widely distributed among active service and civilian personnel. As early as 1947, all flag officers, captains, and commanding officers of the British Navy were briefed about possible treatments against nerve agents in specially designed pamphlets, while the Home Office distributed a civil defence manual about basic chemical warfare. The Air Ministry even commissioned the production of a training film about 'Nerve Gas' (1952).[108] Articles outlining the chief characteristics of these compounds were also published in *The Lancet* and the *BMJ* in late 1952, advising general practitioners and civil contingency planners that a drop of the liquid in the eye, or inhaled in large quantities, could 'cause incapacity or death within a few minutes'.[109] Two or three drops on the bare skin, on the other hand, could kill within thirty minutes. Written on behalf of the MoS, the articles were produced in response to similar publications in the United States, including one on nerve gas poisoning in the popular *Life* magazine.[110] There can be little doubt that leading officials and principal investigators knew or must have known about the risks that exposure to Sarin nerve gas posed to human subjects.

So far, no known first-aid treatments existed, other than soap and water to wash off any remnants of the liquid, and there were no known antidotes either, except, perhaps, for atropine and artificial respiration. Treatment, if any, was 'palliative rather than curative'. Since their lethal potential resulted from the inhalation of nerve agent vapour, or airborne droplets, engineers tasked with designing suitable weapons in the form of new rockets and mortar bombs were advised to ensure that the 'maximum possible proportion of the charging is rapidly and effectively dispersed in the air within a few feet of the ground' to cause the highest possible number of casualties among enemy forces. The manufacture of these liquids, which required specially designed equipment and an extremely complex, staged production process, posed considerable, though not insurmountable, logistical and technical problems.

From 1951 to 1955, Porton also carried out highly secret trials with 'experimental nerve agent weapons' in Sobo, Obanakoro (Obanaghoro), Nigeria, about 250 miles from Port Harcourt, so that combat operations could, if necessary, be conducted with G-agents under tropical conditions.[111] The closure of Porton's subsidiary facilities in both India and Australia, together with India's transition to political independence, had prompted the search for a site in one of Britain's remaining African colonies for the testing of nerve agents in tropical climates. In total, Porton officials undertook four 'expeditions' lasting between three and four months at a time.[112] Evidence about the scientists and personnel involved in the trials is limited, at best. One of those who, in all probability, would have been a witness to, or taken part in, the nerve agent tests was William Ladell, Director of the Hot Climate Physiology Research Unit in Lagos, located some 300 miles from where the experiments took place. We know that in 1956, a year after the last of the trials was concluded, he transferred to Porton, where he became a leading figure in Britain's human experimentation programme with the next generation of nerve and incapacitating agents.[113] In other words, the close proximity between Ladell's workplace and the site of Porton's nerve agent trials, together with his interest in physiological research under tropical conditions, makes it quite unlikely that he had no association with the experimental nerve agent tests whatsoever. Corroborating evidence about his involvement in the tests, however, has not yet come to light, and it is also not known whether the trials, if he did take part in them, helped him to secure the position at Porton. On the other hand, the circumstantial evidence linking Ladell with the African trials is also not without merit.

As far as staff were concerned, we know that the local Nigerian population was enrolled to set up sections of the experimental site, as 'local labour' for the construction of laboratories, staff facilities, and the supply of food, but it is not known at present whether Porton also used them as trial participants.[114] Given the context in which Porton had been operating in India, it certainly is possible. If this was the case, it is doubtful whether valid informed consent would have been obtained. We know further that the nerve agent munitions, different types of artillery and naval shells, mortar bombs, and aircraft 'cluster bombs' were 'handcharged', but we do not know by whom or whether sufficient safety precautions were taken. Members of the local population may have been recruited to undertake such hazardous work, and some may well have sustained short- and long-term injuries. Existing images of the experiments, recently discovered by the author at the Imperial War Museum (IWM)

Duxford, show some of the scientists and local support staff at work in improvised laboratories and preparing the trial ground at Sobo, Obanakoro, for
possible spraying trials.[115] Finally, the existing records are conspicuously silent
about the extent to which the soil in this area was contaminated, possibly for
years to come, or whether neighbouring villages and schools would have
been affected by toxic clouds blown across the land. Officials clearly had good
reasons as to why the kind of experiments undertaken in Nigeria were strictly
prohibited on the British mainland, which is why the files and photographic
records surrounding Britain's postwar nerve agent testing in Africa were
regarded as particularly sensitive.

   In summary, Porton had come to the conclusion that the 'combination
of high toxicity and rapid effect with undetectability' elevated nerve agents
to a formidable threat which, if ever employed against Britain, would 'very
probably have [the] most serious effects' on her armed forces and on the
civilian population.[116] As political tensions during the Cold War raised the
spectre of another major war in Europe, Porton assigned ever greater importance to the potential psychological effects that nerve agents might have on
the morale of the military and on civilians. It was thought that the fighting
capability of troops who witnessed 'convulsive deaths' on the battlefield, or
who believed that the onset of minor symptoms marked the beginning of
nerve gas poisoning, would be seriously impaired, and that if agents were
used against civilian targets, this could cause a major panic among the
British public, disrupting existing infrastructure and the orderly business of
government.[117] While the arms race with the eastern hemisphere placed the
military on high alert, Britain, Canada, and the United States began to
channel vast resources into research and development programmes that
were aimed at accelerating their nations' chemical warfare preparedness,
irrespective of wider ethical or moral concerns relating to the participants
in the proposed experiments.

Nuremberg

Although Porton's weapons programme in the late 1940s and early 1950s
raised fundamental questions about human testing, the high level of secrecy
surrounding the subject of chemical warfare may have shielded military
scientists, for the time being, from engaging with wider paradigm changes

in the field of research ethics. It comes perhaps as little surprise that the violent death of goats and horses exposed to poison gases in one series of tests, or the slaughter of some thirty rabbits in yet another, evoked little empathy from battle-hardened researchers whose objective was the defence of the realm: it never had since the establishment of Porton—yet experiments on humans were a different matter. Or were they? Scholars attempting to ascertain the level of ethical awareness among Porton's scientists, and their understanding of accepted codes of conduct in non-therapeutic clinical trials, including the principle of informed consent, may find themselves on difficult terrain since the majority of the evidence is conspicuously silent on the subject. Porton seems at first to have been almost impervious to the ongoing ethical discourse that engulfed the international medical profession after German doctors, including Hitler's personal escort physician Karl Brandt, and other senior officials were put on trial at Nuremberg for conspiracy, war crimes, crimes against humanity, and membership of an organization declared criminal by the International Military Tribunal (IMT).[118]

On a few occasions, however, senior military officers returning from fact-finding missions to Germany reported to the CDAB about the ethics of Nazi wartime medical experiments that German doctors had performed on camp inmates, and which were now the subject of intense debate at the Nuremberg trials. At Nuremberg, the city in which the regime staged its infamous mass rallies and promulgated the Nuremberg Race Laws, the entire German medical profession, their moral integrity, and scientific reputation were on trial, a scenario that would have been totally inconceivable during the interwar period, when German medical science led the world in fields such as biochemistry, physiology, surgery, and public health. German experts had been hailed for their innovative approach and far-reaching achievements in medical science. Now an 'odd' selection of the profession, as observers noted, was charged with murder and unspeakably cruel torture committed in the name of medical progress and wartime exigencies.

In early January 1948, Major D.C. Evans, who served as a senior military liaison officer at the BJSM in Washington DC and was therefore responsible for the exchange of top-secret chemical warfare information between the two Allied powers, was dispatched to Nuremberg to assist the US prosecution in the case against the IG Farben conglomerate. His second objective was to obtain, on behalf of the MoS, technical data about Nazi chemical warfare experiments on humans and about 'mass exterminations' through the use of hydrogen cyanide, known under IG Farben's trade name of Zyklon B. The assignment took him right to the heart of Nazi medical war crimes and the regime's attempt to exterminate European Jews and other victim groups in the Holocaust.[119]

Evans arrived in Nuremberg on a plane chartered by General Telford Taylor, the chief prosecutor of the American military tribunals, for distinguished British guests attending the opening of the Krupp trial, and was introduced to senior military and legal personnel, who helped him to gain access to classified intelligence material about Nazi chemical warfare experiments and the use of gas for exterminatory purposes. Evidence introduced at the Nuremberg trials established, beyond any reasonable doubt, that German medical scientists had conducted criminal experiments on concentration camp inmates that had resulted in severe injuries, mutilations, and deaths. Himmler's SS, which had been in charge of the camps, and Karl Brandt as General Commissioner for Health and Sanitation, had been responsible for initiating and sanctioning many of the experiments. In addition to experiments involving high altitude, hypothermia, sulphanilamide, bone transplantation, seawater, epidemic jaundice, sterilization, and typhus, chemical warfare trials were conceived at Strasbourg University and carried out on prisoners at the Natzweiler camp. British military intelligence, including officers from Porton who had interrogated staff at Raubkammer in 1945, had for some time suspected that Strasbourg University scientists were implicated in chemical warfare experiments, yet had not yet managed to apprehend their key suspects, Karl Wimmer and Professor Picker, whom they wanted for interrogation about German chemical weapons; when it transpired that Wimmer was living in a small village in Bavaria, Evans arranged his arrest so that he could be interviewed and put on trial as a war criminal.[120]

Evans' rationale for pursuing Wimmer's case with such vigour can be understood only in the context of broader strategic objectives aimed at advancing Allied chemical warfare capabilities through additional intelligence about nerve agents. As early Cold War tensions with the Soviet Union mounted, chemical warfare scientists in Britain and the United States had military clearance to step up their efforts to obtain reliable data about the required concentration of nerve gas to kill or incapacitate human beings under combat conditions. Although captured documents and interrogations had generated a wealth of information about Hitler's chemical weapon programme—including detailed data emanating from human experiments with mustard gas, phosgene, lewisite, nitrogen mustard, and other highly toxic agents, most of which confirmed rather than challenged the findings of Allied scientists—what had not yet been established was accurate information about the concentration of nerve agents that would be lethal for humans.[121] Porton's nerve agent programme, despite enjoying the full backing of Allied military and political leaders, would never, even in anyone's wildest imagination, be expanded to the point where it would include lethal human experiments with nerve agents. The potential political fallout resulting from such an undertaking, illegal and unethical in the extreme, would not only have been a public relations catastrophe if it had ever become public, but might have fatally undermined the moral high ground of Western democratic governments in their defence against communist dictatorships. Allied intelligence officials such as Evans had therefore been tasked with unearthing this information from among the documents and witness testimonies that were becoming available at Nuremberg. Although no evidence of human trials with nerve gas had so far been discovered, it was considered 'highly probable' that the Nazis had carried out such experiments. 'The results (if available) might provide invaluable data as to lethal concentrations for man', Evans remarked.[122] Wimmer was believed to be largely oblivious to the questionable conditions under which the data would have been obtained, and so was seen as 'one of the few surviving individuals' who might be in a position to supply Allied researchers with the required information. Another option, of course, was to conduct human experiments with increasingly high dosages of different nerve agents at Porton in order to extrapolate more reliable data about incapacitating and lethal dosages, a course of action with considerable consequences for large numbers of servicemen, who, during the early 1950s, were exposed to disproportionate and in some cases excessive amounts of nerve agents, putting their lives in danger.

Another equally important objective of Evans' fact-finding mission related to the use of chemical agents in the Holocaust. The evidence he collected on the subject included material from the 'Zyklon B Case' that the British military government had staged in Hamburg against men like Bruno Tesch for systematically supplying poison gas to the extermination camps in the Eastern territories. For Evans, however, the information was not so much a warning from history with which the German people might be re-educated, or a reminder of the enormous human cost of racial and political persecution in times of war, but valuable technical data about the methods and means of employing hydrogen cyanide as an instrument of mass murder. He was particularly keen to obtain reliable information about the concentrations of hydrogen cyanide gas used by the Germans to exterminate their victims in different sizes of gas chambers; in the end, though, he had to concede that 'no controlled experiments' had been performed. If anything, the methods to exterminate millions of people had been haphazard and largely improvised. There had been no uniform guidelines or agreement about the number of Zyklon B tins needed to kill the victims, with estimates diverging notably from one another, nor had data on the methods of killing been collated on a 'scientific basis'. The primary aim had apparently been to kill as many people 'as quickly as possible' and 'make room for the next batch'.[123] Indeed, when Evans and representatives from Porton examined the gas chamber at the Dachau concentration camp in March 1946, they had at first been 'puzzled' by the absence of any machinery which would produce hydrogen cyanide, and then transport it into the gas chamber. As it happened, the methods of unprecedented mass murder had been frighteningly simple.

> The accepted procedure was for the SS guards, wearing respirators, to open up the Zyklon B tins and tip out the solid contents through the holes or gratings in the roof of the chamber on the heads of the victims. On exposure to the air in a very confined space the Zyklon powder quickly evolved a sufficiently high concentration of HCN [hydrogen cyanide].[124]

The evidence suggested that the Holocaust had not been scientifically monitored or micro-managed at every level, but had been implemented to a considerable extent by camp officials according to their own expertise and initiative.

Among dozens of affidavits and witness testimonies that Evans brought back to Britain were reports relating to human experiments with chemical warfare agents, the interrogations of Rudolf Höß, Kurt Gerstein, and Joachim Mrugowsky, all of whom were intricately involved in the Holocaust, documentary material on German chemical warfare policy, and, last but not least, a series of legal documents, including the judgement in the Doctors' Trial and the Nuremberg Code. As an immediate reaction to Nazi medical crimes, and in order to distinguish between criminal physical injury on the one hand, and permissible research on humans on the other, the judges felt the need to establish a compendium of ten ethics principles that would not only serve as a reference point in assessing the level of culpability of each of the defendants, but would protect the rights of experimental subjects and other vulnerable groups in the future. The ten principles came to be known as the Nuremberg Code.[125]

In robust, but somewhat legalistic, fashion the Code made it plain that the rights and integrity of the research subject should be protected at all times. Of the ten provisions, two were designed to protect the rights of subjects of experiments, and eight to protect their welfare. Human experiments, the Code stipulated, needed to 'yield fruitful results for the good of society' that could not be procured by any other means or method of study, should not be random or unnecessary, should be based on the results of animal research, and should be designed with a sound knowledge of the problem under investigation. They had to be performed 'to avoid all unnecessary physical and mental suffering and injury', and were strictly prohibited if there was reason to believe that 'death or disabling injury' would occur. Above all, the 'degree of risk' researchers were willing to take in human experiments 'should never exceed that determined by the humanitarian importance of the problem to be solved by the experiment'. To protect subjects from 'even remote possibilities of injury, disability, or death', scientifically qualified personnel had to make 'proper preparations', provide 'adequate facilities', and conduct all stages of the experiment with the 'highest degree of skill and care'.[126] The one provision, though, that was formulated in the most uncompromising language was the requirement for informed, voluntary consent.[127]

In the Code, the judges combined the Hippocratic medical tradition with innovative human and patient rights that were integral to the development of international law in the postwar period. Hippocratic medical ethics offered a central precondition in protecting the welfare of patient-subjects, yet this professional and moral belief system appeared to be insufficient to protect human lives in human experimentation. Research subjects, the judges thought, required quite specific rights to protect them sufficiently from potential harm. Conditions under which voluntary consent should be obtained were therefore formulated more comprehensively in the Code than in any earlier or subsequent medical ethics code. The principle of voluntary consent, according to the Code, has the status of an absolute, non-negotiable, a priori principle. The judges believed in the creation of an international legal and professional framework that would empower those who had suffered harm to claim their rights against those who had violated them. The Code was in many ways a visionary and innovative medical ethics code designed to apply to all research involving human subjects.

Although experimental scientists expressed considerable scepticism towards, and in some cases outright ignorance of, the Code in the years after it had been promulgated, there were others who publicly endorsed its informed consent principle as a central tenet in non-therapeutic research. In October 1952, Robert Pulvertaft, Professor of Clinical Pathology and former Assistant Director of Pathology, Middle East, told his peers that 'there is only one safe rule—no action of a doctor must have any other objective save the individual's personal welfare, with that individual's entire and competent approval'.[128] Showing considerable foresight, he drew attention to the fact that UK servicemen might easily be misled into participating in potentially hazardous experiments without knowing the full risks involved.[129] His address was published by *The Lancet* in November 1952, three months after the MoS had warned British scientists about the risks involved in exposing humans to nerve gas. They not only knew about the various dangers of G–agents, but should also have known about the required standards of medical ethics involving potential harm. Moreover, as Porton's nerve gas experiments were gaining momentum, the Nuremberg Code was widely publicized in the journal *Science*. We can safely assume that Porton's principal investigators would have had access to the journal and would, in all likelihood, have consulted it. In February 1953, the journal included a discussion of the 'Problem of Experimentation on Human Beings'; amongst the experts taking part was Michael Shimkin, a US researcher, who stated that 'whenever human beings are to experiment on human beings, the mores of human conduct…cannot and must not be ignored or minimized'.[130] According to Shimkin, the Code constituted the most authoritative and 'clearest' set of medical ethics standards, which had to be applied irrespective of any racial, religious, social, or financial considerations, thus giving both scientist and subjects 'entirely equal, inalienable rights that supersede any considerations of science or general public welfare'.[131] His, though, was an ideal position, which in the 1950s and 1960s had not yet entered the canon of applied medical practices in Allied military research facilities.

Ethics and Experiments

Prompted by the international publicity surrounding the Nuremberg trials, senior scientists and research organizations embarked on a reflective process about the ethical legitimacy of existing research practices, often among the perceived safety of their professional peers, and away from the public eye. The issues raised by the Code were not only highly contentious, legally complex, and difficult to implement, requiring additional resources and expertise, but they also fundamentally challenged the status quo of modern experimental medicine. While some Western politicians, receptive to legal advice, attempted to catch up with the rules crafted at Nuremberg and write them into policy, some of those institutions and groups most affected by the planned changes in research governance wanted to renegotiate their contract with the agencies of the state. Their engagement in these debates has often been read as a form of resistance to the suggested changes, and while this is part of the story, we need to recognize that there was, at times, a genuine attempt to strike a balance between the desire to accommodate proposed reforms and yet at the same time achieve, through experiments on man, highly sensitive national security objectives. In assessing this ethical discourse, we need to be cautious that the analytical pendulum does not swing too far. At the same time, greater contextual nuance should not serve as convenient rationalization to legitimize or retrospectively condone work which failed to meet the moral and legal standards of civilized nations.

Although judged as highly unethical and criminal by the Nuremberg judges, there were some Nazi experiments which caught the imagination of British military officials tasked with developing new types of deadly chemical weapons. A report signed in 1944 by Joachim Mrugowsky, former Chief Hygienist of the Reich Physician to the SS and the Police and now on trial on charges of war crimes, showed how five Russian prisoners at Sachsenhausen camp were shot through the left thigh with poisoned bullets containing 38 mg of aconitine nitrate. Whereas the bullets passed right through the legs of two of the victims, who survived but were then shot in the neck, the report documented in horrific detail the two-hour-long process of dying of the three remaining victims.[132] In August 1947, while the Nazi doctors were being tried at Nuremberg, members of the MoS Offensive Equipment Committee of the CDAB, including the Scientific Adviser to the Army Council, considered the possibility of 'using certain special chemical warfare and biological warfare agents as a means of imparting extreme toxicity to bullets, shell or bomb fragments'.[133] Since it was not certain whether such weapons would have 'enhanced operational value' or could ever be produced, senior representatives from the armed services, including Brigadier Pennycook, were asked to consider two hypothetical cases before a research programme could be recommended, one in which a poisonous bullet or shell fragment, if it penetrated through the skin, would kill a man within twenty-four hours, which basically meant 'injecting a poison subcutaneously', another in which an agent would cause a man 'grave illness, probably ending fatally in the course of one of two weeks'. The latter case was based on the assumption that medical experts would find it difficult to establish whether the wounds had been caused by poison bullets or specially treated fragments, and therefore had to work on the basis 'that all wounds of this type were potentially lethal'. Attempting to restrict discussion of this highly classified research to the smallest of circles, Pennycook was asked to treat the matter as 'rather unusually secret'.[134] The War Office, although unimpressed by the findings of the Operational Research Group (Weapons & Equipment), was on the whole supportive of the idea. Provided the lethality of the penetrating objects, whether poison bullets or fragments, would be the 'maximum compatible with 100 per cent safe handling of the ammunition by the user', there appeared to be a 'definite operational value' in manufacturing a certain number of poison bullets and shell fragments since the enemy medical services would have to treat all wounds 'as though they were lethal'.[135] Although such weapons were not going to increase casualty numbers, a senior War Office official noted, their 'moral effect' on enemy troops was likely to be 'considerable', which is why the work seemed to have sizeable merits: 'On the whole I think toxic bullets might well be a useful adjunct to our armoury, provided that production problems are completely satisfactorily solved. In other words considerable research is necessary.'[136] The moral ambiguity and inconsistency in prosecuting German physicians for alleged war crimes with poison bullets on the one hand and continuing research into strikingly similar weapons of war at the same time on the other seems to have been of little concern to Whitehall officials. In responding to rising Cold War tensions, military experts felt under pressure to study new weapons of war that had hitherto been classed as immoral and illegal under international law.

The gradual expansion of what was deemed to be permissible military research significantly increased the known and unknown risks to which servicemen were exposed at Porton and other Allied facilities. In the spring of 1949, W.H.E. McKee and B. Woolcott conducted a series of Sarin vapour trials on fourteen unprotected, healthy servicemen wearing battle dress but no respirator in a 100 m³ gas chamber; rabbits served as a control group.[137] During the course of the experiment, the young men were given 'no palliative or remedial treatment', in order that the effects of nerve agents could be observed and 'threshold' dosages assessed. Although exposed to only 'low concentrations' of nerve gas vapour, the men were exposed for increasingly long durations, rising from one to forty minutes. Their symptoms ranged from persistent miosis, i.e. an excessive constriction of the pupils, to serious headaches and blurred vision; some also experienced a tightness of the chest and 'mild harassment' at higher dosages. This was despite warnings in an earlier report to the effect that 'inhalation of relatively low dosages [of Sarin] may lead to death by respiratory and heart failure'.[138]

In the United States, meanwhile, the Chemical Corps embarked on a programme of human trials with chemical and biological warfare agents which, once it had been set up and approved by the armed services, ran continuously for the next thirty years until the mid 1970s.[139] Its origins were part of much wider developments affecting the US military. Throughout the late 1940s and early 1950s, various US agencies and expert advisers engaged in protracted negotiations relating to experiments with atomic, biological and chemical weapons. In a climate influenced by national security considerations, tensions erupted between government officials, legal representatives, and research scientists over the nation's state of readiness.[140] According to some, the US retaliatory chemical and biological weapon capability was worth only a 'token effort' in a future national emergency. Further concerns raised by the US Secretary of Defense, Robert Lovett, about the country's lack of preparedness for chemical and biological warfare, prompted the armed services to document a 'serious need for increased testing of these weapons, in particular, experiments involving humans'.[141] Towards the end of 1952, after detailed debates at the Armed Forces Medical Policy Council (AFMPC), agreement was reached to use human subjects in chemical and biological weapons research, yet only on the condition that the ten rules of the Nuremberg Code would be followed as 'guiding principles', to alleviate the Pentagon's fear of legal liability. Senior legal experts such as the Pentagon's attorney Stephen S. Jackson, who, on the advice of Anna Rosenberg, Assistant Secretary of Defense for Manpower and Personnel, proposed to expand the requirements of the Code to *written consent*, felt that clinical trials on man should be conducted only according to the principles of the Code since these 'already had international juridical sanction, and to modify them would open us to severe criticism along the line—"see they use only that which suits them"'.[142] Following the realization that the Pentagon had no 'policy on the books' permitting human experiments 'in the field of atomic, biological and/or chemical warfare', the

stage was set for a major power struggle between different interest groups
within the US military establishment.

The military medical community took issue with a policy proposal
which, it was felt, not only undermined the moral authority of experienced
scientists but would probably do 'more harm than good'. Although researchers were prepared to accept a set of general ethical rules, they demanded
that the Code's restrictive principles be softened to align them with the
'capabilities of the average investigator'.[143] At the same time, there were
varying levels of enthusiasm among research groups and military agencies in
signing up to the new policy on human experimentation. There is some
indication, for instance, that the US Chemical Corps was more receptive to
the idea of incorporating the Nuremberg principles into its policy on
human research. At a meeting of the AFMPC in November 1952, for example, the chairman of the Chemical Warfare Committee broke ranks with his
professional peers by supporting the AFMPC draft policy document,
prompting one member to comment ironically: 'If they can get any volunteers after that I'm all in favour of it.'[144] On 26 February 1953, while various
advisory bodies in the Pentagon continued to debate the potential implication of the AFMPC proposal, and of the Code in particular, and after senior
advisers unilaterally endorsed the new policy to the incoming Secretary of
Defense, he, Charles E. Wilson, signed the proposed policy in a top-secret
memorandum, 'Use of Human Volunteers in Experimental Research'.[145]
The document became known as the Wilson memorandum.

Given the practical difficulties in recruiting large numbers of volunteers
from among the staff working at Edgewood and other facilities, the AFMPC
looked towards Britain for inspiration in drawing up proposals which went
'beyond the AFMPC recommendation', including a 'British-style system
of rewards for volunteers', the employment of entire units for research
purposes, and the acceptance of 'government liability in case of accident'.[146]
In the meantime, J.B. Dill from Edgewood Arsenal, who was about to
request permission for physiological experiments with military personnel,
approached Mumford, via Evans, to learn about the specific rules and procedures governing Porton's experimental programme.[147] Edgewood was
keen to know, for instance, for how long Porton had been conducting
human experiments, how many men were enrolled in each group, for how
long, how much they were paid, whether the men were segregated according to rank, whether civilians and/or officers were used, and who was legally
liable in case of serious illness or death resulting from the experiment.

Significantly, Edgewood also wanted to know 'what advance information as to the nature of the tests is given to the men in their units before they are asked to volunteer', thus indicating its awareness of the requirement for informed consent as outlined in the Code.[148] In response to the questions, Mumford and E.A. Perren, the head of Porton's chemistry section and superintendent of its research division, told Edgewood, again via Evans, that Porton had used 'service observers' since about 1930 and station employees in the years before. In general, they used about twenty men in each batch for one week, except for longer trials or treatments. The men were given no extra leave, but a 'few shillings a week', depending on the nature of the tests, and since they did not have to perform any military duties while at Porton, they were 'readily available at all times' for the experiments. No officers or civilians were used. The War Office Directorate of Weapons and Development, formerly the Directorate of Special Weapons and Vehicles, which issued instructions to the Director of Personnel, who in turn passed them down the chain of command to the units in question, functioned as the 'coordinating authority' to provide Porton with the required number of subjects from the three service arms. Whereas the processes and procedures in obtaining research subject had been refined over the years, there was little recognition in government of the need to incorporate the principles of the Code into Britain's research programmes with nuclear, chemical, or biological agents. On the matter of informed consent especially, Porton had little to say: 'No advance information as to the nature of the tests is given to the men in their units before they are asked to volunteer beyond the attached Appendix A.'[149] The information given to British servicemen to 'encourage them to volunteer', as outlined in Appendix A from November 1950, not only contained the bare minimum of what they needed to know before making an enlightened decision as to whether to participate, but was, as it turned out, misleading as far as the known risks from highly toxic substances were concerned; servicemen were told that the 'physical discomfort' they would experience as a result of taking part in the tests would be 'very slight' and that the experiments were organized under expert medical supervision to avoid the 'slightest chance of danger'.[150] At best, Porton was being rather economical with the truth.

It was partly this intelligence obtained directly from Porton, together with the recently signed Wilson memorandum, that in March 1953 informed the comprehensive discussion about the ethics of human experiments at the US Medical and Related Problems Committee of the Chemical Corps

Advisory Council. The literature has tended to imply that the policy proposed by the AFMPC, discussed previously, received a cold response from
Pentagon officials and scientific advisory boards in the months leading up
to and following its approval by the government, evidence that, by infer-
ence, supports the idea that the US military establishment largely ignored
the policy in the mid 1950s, especially in its nuclear weapons programme.
However, the debates recorded at the Medical and Related Problems
Committee paint a somewhat different picture. They suggest that the profound ethical implications resulting from the Nuremberg Code—and the
Wilson memorandum—for experiments on man were recognized and
broadly accepted by senior civilian scientists advising Edgewood Arsenal in
the early 1950s. Chaired by the physiologist Abner McGehee Harvey from
Johns Hopkins University, the meeting was attended by, among others,
Frederick B. Bang, Herbert E. Longendecker and C.B. Marquand, Secretary
of the Test Safety Panel of the Atomic Energy Commission and Executive
Director of the Chemical Corps Advisory Council.[151] Tasked with establishing how best to obtain clinical data in offensive and defensive chemical
and biological warfare research, the panel considered how a system could be
set up that would supply Edgewood with a 'steady flow of volunteers' so
that experiments could be conducted continuously, efficiently, and economically, and thus produce the greatest amount of information as fast as
possible.[152] The meeting determined the requirements of the Chemical
Corps, explored the merits of the system in place at Porton, compared contract work with what was done in government facilities, and discussed the
relevant legal implications. Much of McGehee Harvey's opening remarks,
however, centred around the Chemical Corps' desire to conduct human
experiments and the associated moral, ethical, financial, and temporal factors in using humans for potentially hazardous military tests. The practice of
modern medicine involved clinical research with patients requiring treatment, often without obtaining informed consent, but in which the potential benefits were weighed against the ill-effects of novel drugs, the type of
disease, and the comparative value of different therapies. The Chemical
Corps, however, was confronted with a different set of ethical problems,
since healthy persons would be exposed to some degree of risk. Researchers
wanting to perform potentially hazardous tests, McGehee Harvey told the
panel, had to recognize the importance of experimental procedures in safe-
guarding the health and well-being of trial subjects, which is why the ten
rules of the Nuremberg Code had not only been endorsed by the American

Medical Association (AMA), but had recently been signed into policy by the Secretary of Defense, Wilson, as the guiding principles in the field of human experimentation.

McGehee Harvey, a leading expert on organophosphorus compounds, showed considerable knowledge of, and due regard for, the Hippocratic medical tradition and research ethics, emphasizing the manner in which trial subjects needed to be selected and informed of any potential risks involved in any given experiment.[153] Having been thoroughly briefed on the Nuremberg Doctors' Trial, and the rules of the Code, he and Colonel Greer directed the panel's attention to complex legal and ethical issues, such as the question of what constituted voluntary and non-voluntary consent, the person or groups best placed to obtain written consent in an impartial fashion, the age and mental state of subjects, the professional qualification of investigators, and the type and amount of information that ought to be divulged while simultaneously preserving high levels of secrecy.[154] Trial participants, the panel was told, needed to be informed of any hazards prior to volunteering, and any form of coercion and psychological pressure, not uncommon in the military, or payments in kind, had to be avoided. There were essentially two questions the committee needed to consider: the first related to the extent to which existing Army regulations authorizing experiments on humans, issued during the war but never rescinded, ought to be extended and, arising from this, the type of safeguards which would have to be put in place to resolve any ethical or legal problems. The second issue concerned the methods by which the Chemical Corps could obtain clinical data on human subjects.

In the subsequent debate, Edgewood felt compelled to stress its safety record, stating that in the organization's history there had never been a case of permanent injury. Panel members also expressed reservations about the proposed policy changes; while some queried the definition of consent, others felt that there was nothing unusual in using a pool of servicemen for clinical research, except that some might not realize upon joining the armed forces that they might be asked to take part in an experiment. Strategically, it was thought best to obtain a general authorization for experiments already being performed that might pave the way to gaining permission for more hazardous tests. Some Edgewood scientists wanted to distinguish between hazardous and non-hazardous experiments, and exclude the latter from the discussion. For them, exposure to high concentrations of mustard gas during gas-mask training should be considered part of servicemen's military duty. The lack of human subjects seriously impaired Edgewood's work, they argued, especially in the field of nerve agent experiments, where no approved system existed to obtain research subjects. Scientists attempting to study the percutaneous toxicity of nerve gas were therefore faced with great practical difficulties. Although neither Edgewood nor Porton had so far produced a large number of 'severe systemic effects' in their experiments, David Grob, McGehee Harvey's colleague at Johns Hopkins, reminded the panel of the small margin between mild, moderate, and severe effects, which increased the risk that scientists might inadvertently expose subjects to larger dosages than they had originally intended.[155] If the Chemical Corps aimed to create 'systemic effects', Grob cautioned, it exposed itself to the criticism of harming human subjects intentionally, and thus breaching both Hippocratic medical ethics and the Nuremberg Code, something Edgewood refuted by stating that there were no plans to expose subjects to lethal or sublethal dosages. As for legal liability, the panel, not surprisingly, felt that the government should assume responsibility in case of injury or death of a subject, except in cases where there was prima facie evidence of malpractice. Whilst being receptive to such concerns, McGehee Harvey emphasized that certain fundamental principles were required by which to assess proposed experiments.

Most agreed, though, that there were fundamental differences between the perceived and real hazards in chemical as opposed to biological weapons research. Given the great number of variables, the panel regarded the utility of biological experiments with great scepticism, except in the field of vaccine research. The general public was also easily alarmed by offensive biological warfare, which created additional problems for conducting experiments. Other than supporting them financially, the Chemical Corps did not want to become involved in, or associated with, biological warfare research performed in places such as Camp (later Fort) Detrick, Maryland, and they felt that a public opinion poll should be conducted if the government's policy became public knowledge. While certain agents were clearly too dangerous, Camp Detrick officials considered human tests with other agents as feasible and the risks involved as acceptable, especially in times of war. This view was not shared by all members of the committee, some of whom felt that national security considerations were no justification for unethical experiments, as the recent Nuremberg trials had shown. At Camp Detrick, one panel member had been asked to see whether permission could be obtained to perform experiments with agents that might harm the subject temporarily or permanently, yet the incoming Secretary of Defense insisted that the rules governing biological experiments were those set out at Nuremberg.

David Grob's report on his visit to Porton two years earlier, together with Porton's answers to Edgewood's questions, channelled via Evans and Dill to McGehee Harvey, seemed to suggest that the British system of using 'excessive numbers of men' in chemical warfare experiments was rather inefficient and repetitive, and that more valuable information could be obtained by varying the 'experience' of each trial participant.[156] At the same time, the system seemed to prepare large numbers of service personnel for the use of chemical agents in war. There was scope for improving Porton's facilities, according to Grob, including the rarely used and somewhat 'simple' hospital, but he also highlighted important continuities in personnel and knowledge, and the level of independence enjoyed by Porton scientists in setting their own priorities.[157] Although Porton was, on the whole, doing an 'excellent job' in screening the agents, given its limited staff and equipment, the panel rejected the suggestion of outsourcing hazardous experiments to Britain for fear that demands might not be met in an emergency. In any event, it was thought that US representatives attending the annual Tripartite Conference meetings between United States, Britain, and Canada could recommend that certain work ought to be carried out at Porton.[158] In the meantime, Edgewood was using the Porton plan 'as a model' in drawing up a programme of work for the Research and Engineering Command, not so much in terms of an ideal, but in terms of what appeared to be a viable and reasonably efficient system of using servicemen for experiments with toxic agents.[159] Finally, the committee addressed the issue of accidents in manufacturing plants as possible sites in which much could be learned about the effects of toxic substances. Despite being willing to engage with the ethical implications of experiments in their facilities, members were less prepared to consider health and safety issues in manufacturing plants, and with production about to commence in one of them, plans were put in place to exploit future accidents for research purposes.

Although the Wilson memorandum was a landmark document in its recognition of the legal and ethical validity of the Code, scholars have tended to assume that its security classification delayed and possibly even prevented its circulation and efficient implementation by experimental scientists.[160] This is likely to have been one of the factors, yet the introduction of the principles of the Code within the military was no easy or straightforward task. Indeed, members of the Chemical Corps Advisory Council showed considerable flexibility in adapting the ethical framework of the Wilson memorandum to their specific research requirements and national security obligations. This was not an attempt at paying lip service to yet another government policy, but a sincere endeavour to consider the practical implications of applying the Code to the complexities of the US chemical warfare field, a prolonged and time-consuming process characterized by considerable conflict and occasional compromise.

Whereas the rules governing non-therapeutic clinical research were undergoing a major transformation in the late 1940s and early 1950s, partly as a result of the international condemnation of Nazi medical crimes, partly in response to substantial changes in the organization and funding of large-scale clinical trials, Allied military circles, and Porton in particular, were only gradually coming to terms with the realization that experiments on man could no longer be conducted along the same or similar ethical lines as they had been in the years before. Faced with a sudden increase in the risks servicemen were expected to take when participating in nerve agent trials, together with a certain reluctance in adapting to the shift in the culture and ethics of clinical trials, Porton scientists entered a new world of chemical warfare trials in which they were largely unaware of the dangers lying in wait for them.

Crossing the Threshold

Research by Porton up until the early 1950s largely confirmed rather than revised earlier assessments, except for a line of inquiry focusing on the speed with which liquid nerve agents were absorbed by the skin with potentially lethal consequences. Tests with different types and sizes of animals, ranging from rats to horses, had suggested that a dose of more than 0.2 g of liquid nerve gas placed on bare skin would pose a 'serious hazard, and possibly prove fatal to man. Restriction of free evaporation of the liquid, by covering, dangerously increases the hazard.'[161] As early as 1946, Porton had also established, with some degree of certainty, that gloves, dressings, and face-pieces, which limited or prevented nerve gases from evaporating, increased the 'toxic absorption ten-fold', especially in the case of the relatively volatile Sarin, yet by the late 1940s scientists had become concerned that they might have 'underestimated' the complexities of the relationship, leading Porton to conclude: 'Though primarily of value as agent to cause death by inhalation, their toxicity by absorption through the skin is of a high order and may prove to be of operational significance.'[162] Detailed follow-up studies focused on the 'penetration of clothing by liquid GB [Sarin] and GF [Cyclosarin]' and on the absorption of Sarin vapour through the skin of rabbits.[163] Extrapolating data from animal skin, even when clipped or depilated, to the skin of humans, however, raised difficult methodological questions that could not be easily overcome unless tests were carried out on humans.[164] Scientists started to appreciate the complications in estimating the 'percutaneous toxicity of liquid nerve gases', given the large number of variables such as volatility, the 'spreading characteristics' of the liquid, and the changing nature and condition of the skin.[165] Another, more practical, but no less important issue related to the availability of stocks of nerve agents for testing purposes, since Britain was not yet in a position to manufacture them in sufficient quantities. A.E. Childs, Porton's newly appointed Chief Superintendent, reported that Porton scientists were largely confined to field trials with Tabun, not considered to be representative of nerve agents generally, and with stocks of Sarin and Cyclosarin, which were in short supply, and that they therefore felt 'severely handicapped' in advancing Britain's offensive chemical warfare capability.[166]

However much scientists felt unappreciated at home, transnationally Britain's chemical warfare work was all the more valued at a time of increased ideological tensions with the Soviet Union. Ever since the First Tripartite Meeting at Edgewood in March 1947, there had been broad agreement about the free and unbureaucratic circulation of chemical warfare knowledge through the exchange of personnel and scientific progress reports.[167] At the Fourth Tripartite Coordination Meeting in September 1949, Britain highlighted important discrepancies between the three countries on the percutaneous toxicity of G-agents; whereas Porton had discovered that drops of Sarin applied to two layers of clothing made the agent 'much more toxic', Edgewood believed that one layer of clothing offered 'some protection' against liquid Sarin. Since these findings could not easily be reconciled, all three agencies agreed to 'continue work on exposure to very high concentrations of G vapour, and the hazards arising from droplets on clothing'.[168] A year later, though, a tripartite subcommittee consisting of J.M. Parker of Edgewood, S.D. Silver of Suffield and A. Muir of Porton, tasked with identifying the likely lethal dosage for clothed and unclothed men if exposed to Sarin percutaneously, concluded that toxicity levels did not increase sufficiently as a result of clothing such that they became 'militarily significant'. On the contrary, it was thought that clothing provided more protection, not less.[169] By March 1951, researchers were broadly in agreement that clothing afforded partial protection against nerve agents and that two layers 'increased the efficacy of the barrier', an assessment that three years later required essential revision once it had been established that two layers of clothing—one of serge and one of flannel—increased the hazard from Sarin contamination.[170] Rather than providing enhanced protection, the layer of flannel appeared to be responsible for a rise in percutaneous penetration of Sarin nerve gas. For Ronald Maddison, exposed through two layers of clothing six months earlier, these findings came too late.

As a sign of mutual inter-Allied cooperation, and as far as national security permitted, the United States, Britain, and Canada drew up a tripartite programme of future chemical and biological warfare research.[171] With the approval of plans to modernize and greatly expand its trial facilities, including those for a proposed space for 'seven thousand guinea pigs', Canada committed itself to investigate the dispersal and properties of nerve, mustard, and biological warfare agents through the use of high-speed photography and other technologies. 'Rockets fired from multi-rail launchers' appeared to be the most effective weapon for dispersing nerve gas over target areas. After a lapse of some years, Suffield had also been given permission to recommence trials with a 'wide range of biological warfare agents', quite possibly involving plague bacteria, but only on the condition of constructing a 'rodent proof fence' to prevent the potential spread of disease. In the field of physiology, Canada took the lead in studying the mode of action of Sarin nerve gas on 'acclimatized or clothed animals' under sub-zero conditions, although Britain and the United States planned to do similar work once appropriate facilities became available.[172] Porton, on the other hand, was assigned to 'determine the concentration of GB [Sarin] at which death ensues prior to development of warning signs'.[173] A year later, it was agreed to 'proceed with due caution but as rapidly as possible' into the realm of human experiments as a way of obtaining 'percutaneous toxicity data in man'.[174] Under the perceived threat from a new generation of chemical and biological weapons, the tripartite programme propelled Porton and its allied agencies into a largely unregulated orbit of inquiry which, although accountable to the governments of the day, aimed to determine the lethal dosages for animals and humans exposed to nerve agents (see Image 18).

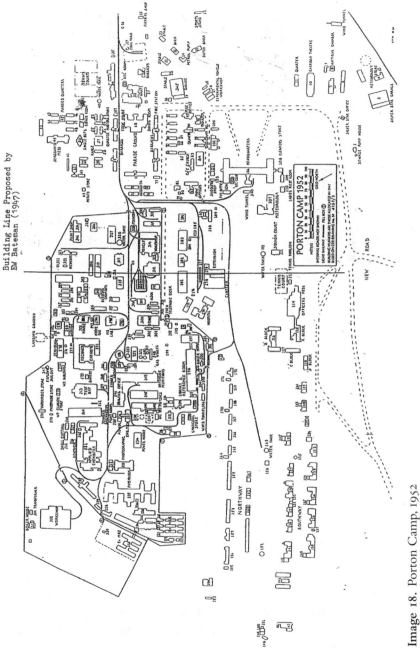

Image 18. Porton Camp, 1952

Source: MI, Folder 21, Exhibit MPG/207, Line Diagram Showing the Porton Down Establishment, Marked 1952, p. 150.

Image 19. 'Observers' on field trial, *c.* 1956
Source: IWM, Photographic Collection, Prog. 26/56. © Imperial War Museums (F 637).
The purpose of the masks was to allow for the collection of simulants during aircraft spraying trials.

In late 1952, at the height of the Korean War, research into respirators, portable resuscitators, biochemical methods of detection, and forms of treatment for nerve gas casualties accelerated on all levels (see Images 19 and 20), and this work was discussed at the tenth meeting of the Biology Committee of the CDAB in January 1953.[175] Chaired by Gordon Roy Cameron, who had been involved in identifying German nerve agents, the meeting was attended not only by the elder statesmen of Britain's chemical warfare programme such as Lovatt Evans, Peters, Gaddum, Dixon, Mumford, and Thompson, but also by a new generation of military scientists and civilian experts, such as M. de Burgh Daly from University College London, who had examined the effects of nerve gas on the pulmonary circulation of dogs.[176] The armed services were represented by Surgeon Commander J.M. Holford from the Medical Department of the Admiralty, Air Commodore P.B. Lee Potter, Director of Hygiene in the Air Ministry, and by Brigadier A. Sachs, Director of Pathology from the War Office; G.A. Clark was dispatched on behalf of the Ministry of Health (MoH). Miss F. Uffelmann, the only woman attending, acted as secretary.[177] According to Cullumbine, troops whose treatment combined the use of atropine injections

Image 20. Showing comfort of S.6 respirator, 9 May 1966
Source: IWM, Photographic Collection. © Imperial War Museums (F 1139/6).

with Porton's newly developed mechanical resuscitator enjoyed protection 'of the order of 200–300 time[s] the lethal dose', as long as resuscitation occurred over a prolonged period of time.[178] By studying variations in the level of cholinesterase in the blood of servicemen exposed to nerve agents, some experts hoped to develop a technique for diagnosing early signs of nerve gas poisoning, while others examined physiological changes in the body as possible indicators to 'predict minimum casualty producing dosage and lethal dosage for man'.[179] Porton also teamed up with a new generation of industrial toxicologists to assess individual variations in blood cholinesterase levels among healthy adults, specifically among workers exposed to organophosphorus insecticides.[180] Although a 'definite relation' between cholinesterase inhibition and Sarin appeared to exist, scientists had difficulties in predicting 'with confidence' the dosage needed for 'nearly complete inhibition of the cholinesterase'. The many unknown variables affecting cholinesterase inhibition called for great caution in using the technique as an accurate indicator of nerve gas poisoning.

A month later, in February 1953, Britain's chemical warfare preparedness was discussed at the CDAB under the chairmanship of Davidson Pratt, who had temporarily replaced Peters owing to a 'sudden indisposition'.[181] Apart from undertaking an assessment of the financial cost difference between the UK-designed 'massive' and the US-designed 'clustered' nerve gas bombs in relation to military efficiency in Porton field trials, Britain was making steady progress with the construction of the plant at Nancekuke, which was due to manufacture nerve gas at a rate of up to 1 ton per week. Production was about to commence in June 1953.[182] London and Cambridge were also scheduled to host informal workshops on the latest advances in biochemistry, especially on anti-cholinesterases and enzyme inhibitions. Porton's physiologists, on the other hand, appeared to be having difficulties in extrapolating 'lethal dosages' from 'nonlethal effects' in humans. Gaddum, reporting the latest findings of the Biology Committee, stressed that the 'possibility of assessing the lethal dosage by extrapolation from measurements of nonlethal effects had been explored', but that the work 'did not seem to be very promising, the decline in cholinesterase level not being sufficiently predictable'.[183] This prompted Edgar D. Adrian to question whether the lethal dosage of Sarin for humans was known by now. Attempting to reassure the Board, Mumford responded by saying that 'there was no great uncertainty about the human lethal dosage of GB [Sarin], as variations with species was not big', yet he provided no factual data, perhaps because Porton and Edgewood Arsenal were in the process of researching this very question.[184]

Internationally, the Seventh Tripartite Conference in September 1952, attended by over one hundred delegates, offered an ideal forum for the exchange and interpretation of trial results. Britain had found it difficult to achieve 'dangerous levels' of liquid or vapour contamination with nerve agents out in the open, but the United States had apparently detected a 'liquid hazard' resulting from nerve agents through clothing; trials planned for the autumn 1952 were meant to establish more firmly the different levels of risk resulting from Sarin vapour and liquid Sarin. Although all three countries seemed outwardly committed to engage in an extensive research and evaluation programme into the risks of nerve agents, the chronic effects of nerve gas poisoning, methods of resuscitation, the use of radioactive nerve gas, and diagnostic methods and medical treatments under different climatic conditions, tensions behind the scenes over access to the latest research data and resources began to manifest themselves.[185]

In the early 1950s, the United States attempted to strengthen bilateral collaboration and top-secret information exchange with Porton, often on an informal basis, through mutual visits, conferences, and joint projects. Despite a general willingness to share their experimental findings at high-level meetings, Porton scientists exhibited a certain degree of caution in divulging information prematurely, especially on the subject of nerve agents, which had developed into a highly competitive field of inquiry. In May 1952, Evans approached Porton on behalf of the Chemical Corps Medical Laboratories at Edgewood Arsenal in order to receive the 'latest estimates' on the toxicity of liquid Sarin and Cyclosarin as part of an 'informal exchange' with the United States.[186] Other than what had been discussed at the Tripartite Conference, Porton had 'nothing substantial to add', reiterating its inability to obtain reliable data about the correlation between cholinesterase inhibition and skin dosages of Sarin for humans. In general, it was felt that previous estimates for percutaneous toxicity had been too high and that larger dosages would in the future be applied in 'fundamental studies on man and monkeys'.[187] Porton, to all intents and purposes, was planning to expose soldiers to increasing dosages of Sarin in order to reach cholinesterase inhibition levels which were as close to 100 per cent as possible. With danger levels rapidly increasing, it was only a matter of time until either Porton or Edgewood Arsenal would have their first serious causality from nerve gas exposure.

In October 1952, having been 'needled' by Edgewood, Lieutenant Colonel Peter Franklin, the British Liaison Officer, felt obliged to contact Cullumbine at Porton. Cullumbine, as newly promoted head of the physiology section, had 'inherited this programme of ad hoc percutaneous testing', and Franklin was requesting, yet again, 'further data on liquid toxicity of the G agents' that could help the Chemical Corps in ongoing power struggles with the US Research and Development Board (RDB) over strategic research decisions. Responding to a shift towards nerve agent spray as a chemical weapon of choice, the RDB had become 'very worried' about the issue of protection, especially from percutaneous toxicity, and was applying pressure on the Chemical Corps to launch a large-scale experimental programme at their Edgewood facility. The Chemical Corps, on the other hand, felt that their authority had been challenged, since informal data obtained from Porton seemed to suggest that the problem of percutaneous toxicity was 'not serious enough to warrant a further large expenditure on research'.[188] By requesting 'factual data' from Porton's experiments, which were deemed to be 'unique in character', the Chemical Corps hoped to persuade senior US military officials to downgrade the assumed risks to troops from percutaneous nerve gas exposure, avoid duplication of work, and redirect resources elsewhere. Attempting at first to delay full disclosure of their results, Porton referred Edgewood to the relevant technical report, which would be available in 'due course'. In the meantime, Wing Commander Adam Muir, RAF Medical Officer at Porton, told the Americans:

> I understand that Bill Summerson saw some percutaneous toxicity tests during his visit here in September. Briefly these belonged to a series in which...quantities of G agents have been applied to the unprotected skin of man. On the day he took part 200 mgs GB were applied with no resulting ill-effects. Since then we have applied as much as 300 mgs—no apparent symptoms.[189]

With attention directed to providing accurate data to the Americans from Porton's percutaneous nerve agent experiments, Britain's warfare scientists, including Cullumbine, were forced to acknowledge internally that the 'reliability' of measuring cholinesterase inhibition in human red cells, the central indicator of nerve gas poisoning, was 'open to very grave doubt'.[190] Tests with a dosage of 35 mg of Sarin on the bare skin of man had started on 25 August 1952 on three servicemen aged between nineteen and twenty-five. Over a two-month period, this had gradually been increased to 300 mg.[191] Although no major symptoms had been detected, the two methods of testing cholinesterase inhibition were producing different results, not substantially, but sufficiently to 'worry' staff. In a note from May 1953, Cullumbine made it plain that 'such diverse results could not be tolerated'.[192] If Porton could no longer trust their own inhibition figures, there was a real risk of 'overcontaminating the human volunteers'.[193] After a 'certain amount of plain speaking', as Cullumbine put it, two of Porton's scientists agreed to 'restore some degree of confidence in the ChE determinations' by resolving what seemed to be an 'odd discrepancy'. They discovered that the method of measuring the enzyme inhibition was not at fault, but that measurements had to be done with greater precision. It is this broader political and ethical context which helps to explain why Porton's scientists temporarily suspended nerve agent experiments on 22 October 1952, the day Cullumbine had been approached by the Americans, thus highlighting, to its credit, Porton's determination at this point to produce data which was not only scientifically reliable but which would also not expose any servicemen to undue risk. In retrospect it may seem slightly ironic that Cullumbine's note calling for extra caution with nerve agent tests was written the day before Porton experienced one of its most spectacular fatalities, calling its entire experimental programme into doubt for years to come.

Experiments with nerve agents on bare skin and through clothing restarted on 9 January 1953. At around the same time, experts were becoming increasingly alarmed about the methodological difficulties in assessing the lethal dosage of Sarin by 'extrapolation from measurements of nonlethal effects', simply because the decline in cholinesterase levels was too unpredictable.[194] Others, though, were more confident about the 'human lethal dosage' of Sarin, arguing that there were only minor variations in the way in which humans and animals responded to Sarin. Data from animal experiments apparently allowed for reasonably accurate predictions. 'It was a very, very good guessification', Robert Lynch, who worked at Porton's physiology department at the time, told the Maddison inquest.[195] To discover the 'lethal dose to man' was seen as a vitally important objective in developing Britain's chemical warfare capabilities.

In March 1953, some five months after first approaching Porton, and in an effort to overcome its apparent intransigence, Edgewood inquired from Cullumbine through the BJSM when a copy of the long-awaited report could be expected, and failing that, whether an interim report or at least some 'notes' could be received. As Evans put it, the US scientists, who had started work along similar lines, were 'most anxious to learn of your recent results'.[196] To encourage the reciprocal exchange of data, Edgewood told Porton of a recent Sarin trial which showed an 18 per cent cholinesterase inhibition for a dose of 550 mg. In other words, evidence coming from the United States appeared to suggest that percutaneous exposure to Sarin of up to 550 mg would not lead to high levels of cholinesterase inhibition, and thus nerve gas poisoning. In responding to the request, Cullumbine told Evans that Porton had not yet used

> such large contaminations as the Edgewood people. In fact we dare not—we have often produced our 80 per cent inhibition in individual cases and have had to hospitalize, temporarily, 3 men. There is a very wide spread of response between individuals and we feel Edgewood have been lucky so far. With the same contamination on different men, the inhibition may vary from 10 to 95 per cent. We are investigating possible causes of this variation.[197]

In responding to the requests coming from the United States, and reviewing their own data, Porton's scientists may have believed that British nerve agent tests remained comparatively safe. Despite reaching inhibition levels of up to 93 per cent in Sarin tests with 226 servicemen during the previous eight months, some of whom had exhibited mild forms of nerve gas poisoning, the race between Edgewood and Porton to reach the highest level of cholinesterase inhibition—without intentionally harming or killing the participants—was about to begin.[198] Put differently, they were determined to go beyond what was then regarded as the threshold dosage of 80 per cent inhibition. As a leading British toxicologist, Professor Alexander R.W. Forrest, later pointed out during the 2004 inquest proceedings, by producing cholinesterase inhibition levels in 'excess of 80 per cent', the scientists increased the chance of 'severe adverse effects on a small and unpredictable number of experimental subjects'.[199] It is at this point that things were taking a turn for the worse at Porton. A serious accident, if not a fatality, was rapidly becoming more likely.

What the Americans had also not conveyed to their British colleagues, neither through the BJSM nor through any other channel of communication, was that they had indeed recently been 'lucky' in a dramatic incident involving exposure to Sarin nerve gas. On 7 November 1952, during a planned field trial with Sarin-filled spraying devices at Dugway Proving Ground, Tooele, in the state of Utah, to which the United States had alluded during the Seventh Tripartite Conference, a thirty-two-year-old 'white male' medical officer, by failing to 'observe elementary safety precautions', had been severely poisoned by a high dosage of nerve gas vapour. The case constituted the 'most severe' nerve gas casualty Western scientists had so far encountered.[200] About three hours after a jet aircraft had dropped its spraying tanks, each containing 90 gallons of Sarin, from a height of 2,000 feet over a deserted area, thus contaminating an estimated 38,000 square feet of ground with nerve gas, a small inspection team arrived in an ambulance at the scene. Except for the medical officer, himself a chronic smoker, and generally seen to be 'withdrawn and indifferent', all the men had by now donned their respirators. Without any protection whatsoever, perhaps to prove a point about the alleged toxicity of the substance, the medical officer calmly walked close to the shallow crater containing the liquid nerve gas which, he later recalled, smelled like petrol fumes. Then, after ten seconds, feeling 'giddy' and about to faint, he came racing back, clutching his chest, frantically calling for his respirator, stumbling and convulsing before collapsing in front of the ambulance. By now unconscious but still breathing, he was given an intramuscular injection of atropine, yet his situation rapidly deteriorated to violent, repeated spasms, irregular breathing, and respiratory paralysis. High-pitched 'screeching' noises and low-pitched 'gurgles' on expiration, followed by sporadic gasps, left the team in little doubt that he was dying. Two minutes after exposure no pulse could be found.[201]

With no medical expert in sight, the crew frantically applied artificial resuscitation with a portable respirator, but by now he was suffering from oxygen starvation owing to the accumulation of secretions in his airways, apparent from the blue colour of his peripheral skin, known as cyanosis. As a long-time heavy smoker, his nasal secretory cells had shown considerable hyperactivity, evidenced by daily postnasal discharge, for which he was now paying the price. Smoking had quite literally put his life in danger. Twenty-five minutes later, a medical officer, having intercepted the ambulance on the way to hospital, attempted to stabilize the patient by inserting an artificial airway, then manually forcing oxygen into his lungs using a rubber bag while a colleague providing first aid applied pressure to his thorax to make him breathe out. All his muscles were paralysed, he was in a coma, and his life was ebbing away fast. Once admitted to the US Army hospital, however, the man spectacularly recovered within a couple of days thanks to an 'iron lung' resuscitator, the insertion of a hard rubber artificial airway, and repeated injections of a total of 19 mg of atropine at fifteen-minute intervals. All involved agreed that artificial respiration in conjunction with high dosages of atropine and the supply of oxygen had probably saved his life. Some three weeks later, he was transferred to Oak Knoll Naval Hospital in Oakland, California, to convalesce in the company of some 2,500 military casualties from the Korean War.[202] Although more of a self-experiment under uncontrolled conditions, or indeed a self-inflicted accident, in which no quantitative data about exposure levels had been obtained, it provided the most detailed clinical observation of a case of severe nerve gas poisoning, a subsequent, successful treatment regime, and recommendations about first-aid equipment, all of which might have proven invaluable to Porton's scientists, if only they had received the information in time. The report was filed in December 1952, and Porton received a copy on 6 May 1953, the day another batch of British servicemen went into the gas chamber for a Sarin experiment. This time, luck had run out for Allied scientists. A little later, one of those servicemen was dead.

6

Flying the Atlantic

Unlawful Killing

Hidden away in the remote Wiltshire countryside, protected by barbed wire and armed guards, an international network of Allied researchers set out to uncover the latest secrets of modern warfare—deadly biological agents but also some of the most toxic chemicals man had created on planet earth. Unregulated, unsupervised, and largely uncontrolled by government, their work took place away from the public eye, in the confines of purpose-built laboratories, in gas chambers, and on a test range; others used the London Underground system, converted ships, towns and villages in Norfolk, or faraway islands in Scotland and the Bahamas to test their toxic substances. Secrecy protected them from outside interference, transparency, and democratic accountability. Initiated and developed quite independently from that of their professional peers, their work stood apart, their technical language a foreign code, undecipherable by ordinary mortals. They had been set free from society to protect the fabric of the nation state in times of crisis, protect the shores, the air, and the land from enemy invasion, yet inadvertently their activities put at risk the very fabric of society, its civility, and its moral compass. Endowed with enormous powers, privileges, and resources, Britain's warfare scientists were experiencing lift-off on a monumental scale in the climate of the Cold War. Detached from civil society and moral reality, they were quite literally 'flying the Atlantic', as one senior civil servant phrased it.[1]

Around mid morning on 7 May 1953, Leslie John Anderson, Officer Commanding, Radio Servicing Flight from RAF Ballykelly, near Londonderry—a small, friendly village in Northern Ireland, a place with few attractions, and even fewer adventures for young national servicemen—was summoned to see his Station Commander as a matter of urgency. He was told that one of his men, twenty-year-old Leading Aircraftman (LAC)

Ronald Maddison, a wireless mechanic from Consett, County Durham, had died the previous day while on detachment at Porton Down (see Image 21).[2] Instructed to change into his 'Best Blue' uniform and report to the Flying Wing Headquarters within thirty minutes, he was ordered to leave for Porton at once to do whatever was necessary on behalf of Maddison's family as a representative of the RAF. A couple of hours later, Anderson landed in a Shackleton aircraft at Boscombe Down, near Porton, where he was met by the RAF Experimental Officer, Wing Commander A. Cross, who briefed him about the funeral arrangements. As for the cause of death, he was told that Maddison had developed a 'chest complaint', which had apparently turned into pneumonia during one of the experiments. He was not told about the exact nature of the test, nor did he inquire about it, for he felt he was not entitled to do so. He knew that Porton was undertaking work of a 'classified nature', but he did not know what it was, and he was completely unaware of any chemical or biological warfare research going on. Anderson had known Maddison well before they had joined the RAF: a 'run-of-the-mill' lad from the lower working classes, popular among his peers, quite skinny, a 'seven stone weakling' with a puny physique and a 'weak chest', as those prone to tuberculosis were frequently described, which is why the stated cause of death seems not to have raised any suspicion in his mind.[3] Days later, after attending the funeral service, where he witnessed Maddison's distraught girlfriend trying to jump into the young man's grave, he returned to Ballykelly, this time by ferry and train, gathered together all of Maddison's belongings, and sent them to his family. Meanwhile, rumours had begun to spread on the station's grapevine to the effect that Maddison 'had not recovered from a cold virus given to him at Porton Down', a convenient narrative which not only ensured that the flow of human volunteers from Northern Ireland would not dry up, but one which helped to cover up the case for over half a century. Anderson, an officer of lower rank and social status who dared not challenge the official position—or at least, not until officers from Operation Antler[4] questioned him about it in 2001—seems to have been little more than a pawn in a concerted effort to conceal the circumstances surrounding Maddison's death, which sent profound shock waves through Britain's government at a time of heightened tensions with the Soviet Union and North Korea.[5]

The specific series of experiments in which Maddison died was suggested by the Tripartite Conference and authorized by the Air Ministry on 12 February 1953. 'It was agreed that we had the facilities; we should

Image 21. Ronald Maddison, *c.* 1953
Source: Lillias Craik, Private Papers.

therefore undertake it', a senior Porton official recalled.[6] Over a seven-week period, from the end of April to early June, the RAF was asked to supply '140 airmen volunteers', twenty each week, among them two from Coastal Command, where Maddison was stationed, to undergo 'physiological experiments' at Porton for additional pay.[7] Potential participants were to be given the following information to encourage them to volunteer: 'The physical discomfort resulting from the tests is usually very slight. Tests are carefully planned to avoid the slightest chance of danger and are [carried out] under expert medical supervision.'[8] They were told that they would not have to undertake any military duties during their stay and were free to do whatever they liked in the evening. Extra pay for taking part in the tests—which made no reference to nerve agents—would be between 10 and 15 shillings per week.[9]

Existing evidence shows that investigators knew that the risk of physical injury or death to participants was high and was increasing as the tests continued. In total, 396 men were contaminated with various doses of Sarin nerve gas (see Images 22a–c). Of these, fourteen men displayed cholinesterase inhibition exceeding 80 per cent (see Figure 2), and seven of these exhibited clinical symptoms requiring medical treatment and in

(a)

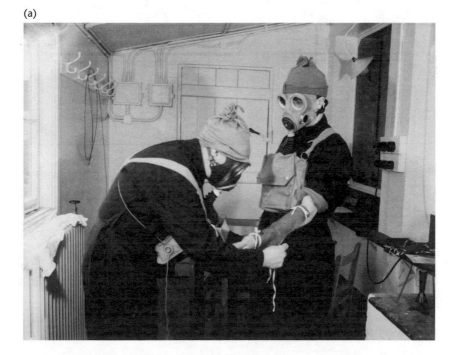

(b)

(c)

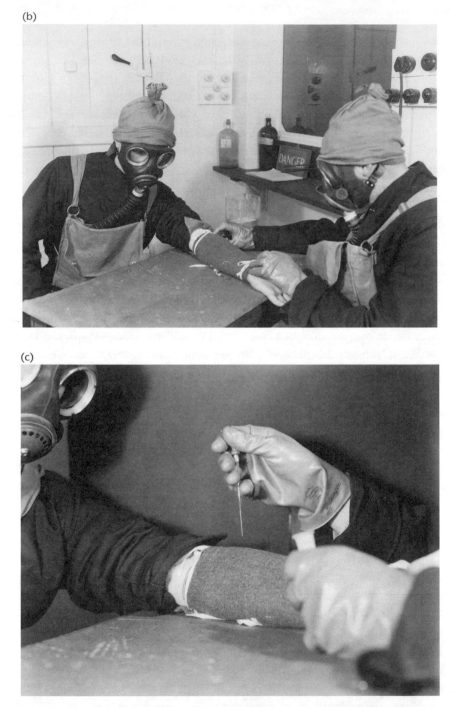

Images 22a–c. Method of nerve gas application at Porton Down, 1953

Source: IWM, Photographic Collection, Method of Application of Nerve Gas on Fore Arm, 18 May 1953. © Imperial War Museums (F 519/1–3).

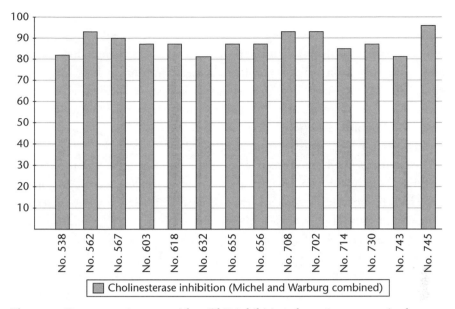

Figure 2. Porton servicemen with a ChE inhibition above 80 per cent in the run-up to Maddison's death, January–May 1953

Source: MI, Folder 2B, Exhibit MNJ/30, PTP 399, 'Percutaneous Toxicity of G-Compounds', 11 January 1954, pp. 267–318; MI, Folder 2H, Wiltshire Constabulary; Operation Antler; Data to Show ChE % Inhibitions, Symptoms, and Other Relevant Information on Volunteers during GB Tests between 19 January 1953 and 6 May 1953. Prepared by DC Goundry for HM Coroner of Swindon and Wiltshire Mr D Masters.

The participants were as follows: 'Blood Number' 538 (Joyce; 29 January); 562 (Sammons, 10 February); 567 (Perry, 16 February); 603 (Moules, 9 March); 618 (Gardiner, 16 March); 632 (Kitchener, 23 March); 655 (McMullen, 30 March); 656 (Willis, 30 March); 708 (Popplewell, 22 April); 702 (Kelly, 27 April); 714 (Allen, 27 April); 730 (Slater; 4 May); 743 (Verallo, 6 May); 745 (Maddison, 6 May). Michel and Warburg were the then existing methods of measuring cholinesterase inhibition levels.

some cases hospitalization. On 10 February, one of the participants of the previous cohort, volunteer number 562, a Mr Sammons, after exposure to 300 mg of Sarin, experienced the first recorded serious adverse reaction as part of Porton's attempt to study the percutaneous toxicity of nerve agents. Suffering from dizziness, nausea, a cold sweat, vomiting, and a feeling of 'being pressed down', he was admitted to hospital with a mean cholinesterase inhibition level of 94 per cent.[10] Testing continued.[11] Six days later, number 567, twenty-eight-year-old Mr Perry, who was exposed to 250 mg of Sarin, likewise showed adverse reactions with a depression level of 90 per cent. Feeling sick upon returning to the barracks, he began behaving erratically, laughing and crying, and talking nonsense eight hours after exposure. Following the administration of atropine for two days, his condition fortunately improved.[12] On 9 March, volunteer 603, twenty-year-old Mr Moules, believing he had gone to Porton for common cold research, 'suddenly dropped to the floor' and had to be hospitalized for six days. Sweating profusely, he recorded a mean inhibition level of 88 per cent.[13] About two weeks later, on 22 April, Porton recorded a mean inhibition level of 93 per cent for volunteer number 708, nineteen-year-old Granville Popplewell, who recalled suffering from vomiting, insomnia, and nightmares for two days.[14] Testing continued.

Then on 27 April, six subjects were given 300 mg of Sarin on one layer of serge.[15] Volunteer number 702, a man named Kelly, aged twenty-one—described by Porton's consultant psychologist Basil Clarke a week after the experiment as 'slightly on the duller side of the general mean'—suffered serious ill-effects, fell into a coma, but then recovered.[16] His pre-exposure inhibition levels had shown 52 and 82 per cent, which meant that he should have been rejected as a test subject. 'He slipped through the net', is how David Masters, HM Coroner for Wiltshire and Swindon, described the near-fatal oversight.[17] The failure to reject him was indicative of the pace and lack of reflection characterizing the experiments at this stage; vital data which should have rung alarm bells among the scientists was simply ignored. One of those present with Kelly in the gas chamber saw him trying to pull off his respirator before dropping to the floor with foam around his mouth: 'Quite frankly, it scared the living daylights out of me', he recalled.[18] Kelly's symptoms were marked by general spasms of the body—from his knees to his chin—and an inability to breathe. Shortly after he became unconscious, he was given a total of 4 mg of atropine and taken to hospital, where his breathing stopped temporarily. Mucus and saliva were immediately cleared from his mouth, and he was given oxygen and another 2 mg of atropine. Four and a half hours later, as he returned to consciousness, smiling but still producing excessive saliva, he could barely mutter 'I feel terrible' with a strong Scottish accent. To state that he was 'easily revived', as Cullumbine later claimed, could not be reconciled with his actual state of health, as the Coroner pointed out in 2004.[19] Within twenty-four hours, Kelly's inhibition level had risen to a life-threatening 94 per cent, with a further rise to 98 per cent twenty-four hours after exposure.[20] The Kelly incident was the clearest indication yet that the experiments posed a significant risk to the health of the subjects. It provided an unambiguous warning that from that moment onwards the most rigorous safeguards and standards of medical ethics needed to be applied if the investigators wanted to continue with the tests. It provided a warning to pursue the experiments, if at all, only under extreme caution. The record suggests that more rigorous safeguards were not introduced.

Porton, rather than suspending the test series and reassessing the entire experimental set-up after the 'Kelly incident', a move never seriously considered, tried to balance the need for acknowledging known hazards with a desire to proceed with exposing servicemen to Sarin. Although Mumford, as Chief Superintendent, had instructed Cullumbine and his team to confine all percutaneous tests with Sarin to the 'lowest range of dosage'— which a Porton scientist later interpreted to mean reducing the dosage to 30 mg—Cullumbine, on his own initiative, decided to continue the experiments with a 'lower' dosage, reducing it from 300 to 200 mg.[21] 'In view of the hazards involved in this investigation', he, Mumford, also asked colleagues to reconsider the 'objectives of the research and…the methods to be adopted to reach these objectives, before proceeding any further with the exposure of observers to the higher ranges of contamination'.[22] Neither the initial inquest in 1953 nor the one held in 2004 could really explain why Mumford's instructions had not only failed to specify the actual dosage the scientists were permitted to apply, but also why they had not been implemented in the way he had originally intended. His memorandum made no reference to the addition of an extra layer of clothing. One should not however jump to the conclusion that these were somehow scientists out of control. Mumford may well have couched his instructions in general terms in order to provide researchers with a certain level of discretion, thus allowing them to alter the experiment in the manner they deemed most appropriate. Experts working at Porton enjoyed considerable freedom in achieving their research objectives as long as the lives of participants were not put at unnecessary risk, but it was also a research culture in which work could be undertaken in a 'compartmentalized manner', in which a scientist, though discussing the general line of work over a cup of tea, could remained ignorant of what exactly his neighbouring colleague was doing, at some times for security reasons, at others for lack of integrated communication. Only a selected few had knowledge of the bigger picture.[23]

Another factor known at the time to have a possible effect on the risk to which the servicemen were being exposed was skin fat. In a handwritten memorandum about the 'percutaneous toxicity' of nerve agents, produced on 5 May 1953, less than twenty-four hours before Maddison went into the gas chamber, and in a copy of the same note, dated 8 May 1953, Cullumbine suggested that physiological factors affecting skin absorption and the physical distance to the dermis, i.e. the layer of skin located between the epidermis (outer skin) and subcutaneous tissues, might 'be important' in understanding how and why individuals responded to nerve agents in the way they did.[24] Existing data, he noted, seemed to suggest that human skin showed 'wide variations in penetration rate', which meant that a whole range of factors determining this rate—including the characteristics of the skin fat, the thickness, temperature, and humidity of the skin, blood flow, and amount of body hair—required closer examination. It was in this context that he remarked, in the present tense (emphasis added), 'The fat content of different skins *is* being studied', which strongly suggests that such a study had already begun and was ongoing, a point taken up by one of the experts at the Maddison inquest in 2004.[25] This expert, on examining the evidence fifty years later, was baffled by the fact that the various factors governing these types of experiments with highly toxic chemical agents were not only little understood, but were known to be little understood, which is why it seemed incomprehensible—especially from a medical ethics perspective—that the experiments were not put on hold with a view to studying and ultimately controlling for these factors. If undertaken, such an approach would have allowed Porton's scientists—in all probability—to reduce the risk to which the servicemen were exposed, but Cullumbine, for some reason, was determined to press ahead with the trial series, with fatal consequences, as we now know.

In September 1953, in an attempt to record 'as fully as possible' the known and potential factors which might have been responsible for Maddison's death four months earlier, the scientists involved concluded that it was unfortunate that so little was known about the average 'human skin' since 'a clearer picture of the relative inhibition of the enzymes of these tissues *might* [emphasis added] have provided a more precise demonstration of the manner of skin penetration'.[26] In other words, if this knowledge had existed *before* Maddison's death, then Porton scientists *might* have had a better understanding of the way in which nerve gas was absorbed through the skin, knowledge which *could* potentially have saved Maddison's life. This then raises the central question—asked by experts ever since—as to why no concerted attempt was made to procure that knowledge *before* tests with nerve gas resumed after the Kelly incident. Did Porton think it would take too long to find out? Did they have the necessary expertise to research these questions? Would they have needed to ask for external assistance? Would a temporary halt to Porton's experimental programme have affected the standing of the institution as a whole in the corridors of power, and if so, to what extent? We will probably never know why the 'controlling minds' of Porton's nerve agent programme decided against examining these and other factors more fully before conducting further trials which they were unable to control and in which the risk was known to be impossible to assess.

In the event, Cullumbine instructed his staff, on his own initiative and without further consultation, to establish whether or not clothing facilitated or restricted the penetration of liquid Sarin.[27] He seems to have believed that a reduction to a somewhat lower dosage—though not as low as that suggested by his superior Mumford—together with another layer of what he and others considered to be protective clothing—an additional inner layer of khaki flannel under the outer layer of khaki battle-dress serge—would render the experiment sufficiently safe. This extra layer of clothing, it seems, contributed to a fatal dosage, as it increased the extent to which the nerve gas penetrated through the skin of the test subjects. If Porton had not reduced the dosage from 300 to 200 mg, in other words, but also had not added another layer of clothing to all subsequent tests, Maddison, in all probability, who seems to have been particularly susceptible to the agent, might well have survived, as the nerve gas dropped onto his body would have evaporated more quickly, thus reducing the amount that penetrated through his skin.

Why Cullumbine made such a fatal error of judgement is difficult to tell in retrospect, and it seems even more difficult to understand, especially from a scientific perspective, why he changed two factors at the same time—dosage *and* layers of cloth—because he introduced thereby a serious methodological flaw into the experimental design. We do have some idea, however, why he may have believed that an additional layer of cloth increased rather than reduced protection: wartime human experiments he had carried out in 1944 to assess the 'burning power of white phosphorus' had revealed that an additional layer of clothing increased protection by almost 100 per cent.[28] The question as to whether this also applied to the family of nerve agents had been debated but not conclusively settled by Allied experts in the late 1940s and early 1950s, so Cullumbine may well have believed, wrongly as we now know, that the 'two measures' he had taken would make the experiment particularly safe, while in truth it produced an element of 'uncontrollable danger'.[29] Perhaps in an attempt to protect the integrity of his staff, and retrospectively to sanction the tests, Mumford later told the court of inquiry that Porton had believed that a reduction to 200 mg would render an experiment with two layers of clothing 'perfectly safe'.[30]

Yet if this was the case, how had Maddison found himself in a position which risked his life? On Saturday 2 May 1953, about a week after the Kelly incident, as austerity Britain was feverishly following the Stanley Matthews Cup Final football match between Blackpool and Bolton Wanderers, Leading Aircraftman Ronald George Maddison, a labourer in civilian life, and Henry J. Newman, a radar mechanic, who had volunteered in the hope of seeing a young lady in Leicestershire, left Ballykelly to catch the Belfast to Heysham overnight ferry before starting their long train journey to Salisbury in Wiltshire, from where they took a bus to Porton.[31] Their travel plans had not been a secret at the station. On the contrary, both had told their colleagues, who assumed—quite innocently and understandably—that Porton was not doing anything other than common cold research, since there were two types of Station Routine Orders (SROs) asking for volunteers, one to attend Porton, the other to go to the CCRU, with the two located in close proximity. Like many others, Maddison had wanted a change of scenery, a little adventure, a chance of getting back to England to see family and friends and, of course, his girlfriend Mary Pyle (see Image 23). His motives for going to Porton were the same as those of hundreds of

Image 23. Ronald Maddison with friends, *c.* 1953
Source: Lillias Craik, Private Papers.

other service volunteers in the 1950s and 1960s.[32] There was also the added incentive of earning some extra money while being relieved from military duties, a factor not to be underestimated, particularly by the thousands of poorly paid national servicemen from low-income families; Maddison sup-posedly even boasted about his forthcoming 'jolly' when he was found smoking in one of the Shackleton aircraft he had been instructed to service.[33]

On arrival at Porton, Maddison and Newman were allocated their billets and given a general briefing about the site the next day. Then, on Monday, a civilian scientist told them, as part of a group of about a dozen servicemen, that the purpose of their stay was to 'test various cloths with chemicals'; he then took a photograph of each of the men in the nude from the front only, which apparently was all part of the 'standard army' medical examination. Most of the men do not seem to have paid much attention to what was said; Newman certainly did not, nor could he recall that anybody was unhappy with taking part in the tests: 'Not many questions were asked. It was more a case of this is what we want you to do, and we did it.'[34] At first, life at Porton was how they had imagined it, pretty easy going, with few restrictions, army discipline, or parades, a good night's sleep, time to read and excellent food in comparison to what they had been used to in Northern Ireland. To assist in the preparation of animal experiments, they were asked to spend some of their free time feeding and shaving the skin of rabbits before their own experiments began in earnest.[35]

Then, on 6 May 1953, Maddison, Newman, and four other subjects, all wearing respirators, went into Porton's gas chamber at around 10.00 a.m., unaware that they were to be exposed to 200 mg of pure Sarin nerve gas.[36] Maddison was contaminated at around 10.17 a.m., but about twenty min-utes into the experiment, he said he felt 'pretty queer'; sweating profusely, he was led from the chamber by one of the scientists to a bench outside, where he collapsed.[37] As tremors and body convulsions set in, medical officer Major Richard H. Adrian administered atropine as an antidote, yet Maddison's condition deteriorated fast. By the time the ambulance arrived, he was unconscious. One of the ambulance drivers, Alfred Thornhill, recalled that upon arrival all he saw was a person lying on the ground not far from the entrance to the gas chamber. As he approached the three men surround-ing Maddison, Thornhill asked: 'What's happened here?' 'He's taken his mask off too soon', came the reply. At this point Maddison was 'thrashing around and his limbs were shaking violently' and he was 'making a very strange bubbling noise that sounded to be coming from his throat'.[38] It was a scene for which Thornhill and his colleague felt wholly unprepared. There was no time to get a stretcher, so they lifted Maddison onto the floor in the back of the ambulance, and drove off to the nearby Station Medical Centre. En route, Maddison was lifted onto a stretcher, still convulsing violently and making all sorts of gurgling sounds. Thornhill later recalled that the manner in which he witnessed a young man die for the first time was 'particularly traumatic'.[39] Despite concerted attempts by the Station Medical Centre to save Maddison's life, it was too late. At 1.30 p.m., Maddison was pronounced dead.[40] His cholinesterase inhibition was 99 per cent, according to one method of measurement (Michel), and 93 per cent according to another (Warburg), the most severe case of nerve gas poisoning ever recorded in the Western world (see Images 24a–b).

In accordance with procedures concerning the reporting of serious accidents involving the loss of life, those in charge wasted little time in alerting the relevant authorities in order to justify how it had come about that a man had died at Porton. At the same time, they set the wheels in motion to conceal the true cause of death from the British public for reasons of national security. The government possessed far-reaching powers to control the information given to the Coroner and to invoke press censorship in inquests involving the possible disclosure of classified information.[41] Seen from Porton's perspective, Maddison's death appeared to fulfil the relevant criteria for the invocation of such extraordinary powers. Leigh Silver, who put the first call through to the Coroner's office at around 2.00 p.m., was unwilling to discuss the case 'too freely' with anyone other than Harold Dale, the Wiltshire Coroner himself, who was absent, and told his secretary that the 'people in London want to be present at the PM [post-mortem]'.[42] When he finally spoke to Dale late in the afternoon, he told him that he needed to see him in person 'as there were facts that could not be discussed over the phone'. He got into a car with Cullumbine and Adrian, and drove to the Coroner's office in Wootton Bassett, a small Wiltshire market town well known in the early twenty-first century for its role in paying respect to the fallen soldiers from the wars in Iraq and Afghanistan.[43] Authorized by the Chief Superintendent to disclose, if necessary, the details of the case under certain conditions, Cullumbine stressed the 'secret nature of the work' to Dale, who was willing to cooperate but made it plain that he also had to perform his duties as a Coroner. This meant that Dr G. W. D. Henderson, Dale's own pathologist, would conduct

(a)

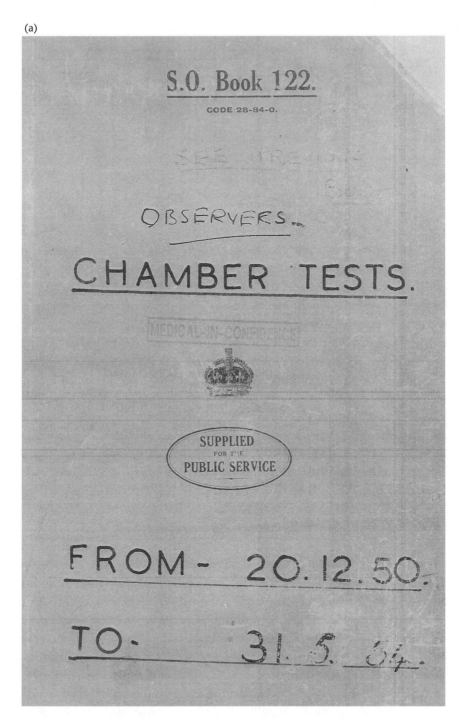

(b)

Images 24a–b. Observers' Chamber Tests Book, 1950–1954: (a) Cover; (b) Extract for 29 April–6 May 1953

Source: MI, Folder 2D, Exhibit MPG/36, Extracts from Observers' Chamber Tests Book, 20 December 1950–31 May 1954, pp. 1–16, here Cover and p. 14.

Transcription of comments next to Maddison's name: 'Felt "pretty queer" at Z [Zulu] + 23'. Walked out of chamber. Collapsed – unconscious. Given 3 x 1.2 mg Atrop[in] (3.6 mg). Breathing laboured. Salivation. Colo[u]r bad. No miosis or enlargement of pupils. Pulse volume good + regular – M.I. [Medical Inspection] Room. D/D [Discharged Dead] later –'

the post-mortem the next day and be assisted by Cameron, chairman of the Biology Committee, whom Cullumbine had proposed.[44] If Dale had assumed that this would be the end of the matter, he was mistaken, as the British establishment swung into action to protect the realm's chemical secrets and began to place this legal official under considerable pressure. The next day, the Secretary of the Coroner's Society for England and Wales, W.B. Purchase, told Dale that his 'friend' from the Treasury Solicitor's Office, B.M. Stephenson, was taking an interest in the inquest from which, it was assumed, the public would be excluded under Rule 14. He commented ominously: 'I need say no more than that.'[45] At the same time, the then home secretary, Sir David Maxwell-Fyfe, who had been Deputy Chief Prosecutor in the Nuremberg Trials, came under pressure from the War Office to take control of the case.[46] Days later, the Coroner received a telephone call from the Home Office: 'Home Secretary says essential inquest should be held in camera on grounds of national security. Must not be published.'[47] Unsure as to whether formal representations were needed from the government, Dale made inquiries of Purchase, who advised him to 'simply make up [his] own mind' once he was satisfied that it was acceptable to hold the inquest in secret, adding: 'At the present moment, the motto seems to be least said, soonest mended.'[48]

The Inquiry

To all concerned the enormous implications for the British government were immediately apparent. The case could turn out to be politically embarrassing, legally challenging, and extremely costly, if compensation had to be paid. If not managed well, it was a public relations disaster waiting to happen. Yet panic was spreading through the corridors of Whitehall for quite different reasons, for it was considered to be of paramount importance that the secrecy surrounding Britain's offensive chemical warfare capability be preserved under all circumstances, and this was far more important than satisfying the public interest which was keen to know how this man had died. Any revelations, however small, or any public debate about Britain's nerve agent experiments that detrimentally affected defensive preparations and the willingness of soldiers to volunteer for Porton trials were considered to be potentially catastrophic; and, as Porton's historical consultant, Graydon Carter, put it, 'opprobrium was certain to arise'.[49] Communication about the incident therefore needed to be restricted and tightly controlled, preferably confined to top-ranking senior officials, with high levels of security clearance, whose loyalty was beyond any doubt. That is why the fatality was reported without delay to the MoS's Principal Director of Scientific Research (PDSR), Walter Cawood, and the DCDRD, A.E. Childs.[50] To prevent sensitive information from becoming public knowledge, speed was of the essence. This meant the sooner the body was buried and a ministerial inquiry could be concluded, the better, leaving only the inquest as a potential site from which secret information could leak into the public domain— hence the heavy concentration of attention on the Coroner in the hours after Maddison's death.[51]

Back in London, news of the incident reached the highest levels of government. Duncan Sandys, responsible for Porton as Minister of Supply since 1951, alerted Prime Minister Churchill to the death of an RAF serviceman during a nerve agent trial at Porton within twenty-four hours of the incident. In an attempt to pre-empt any notion of negligence, he stressed that the tests were of 'an exceedingly mild type and are conducted under strict medical supervision'.[52] According to Sandys, some 13,000 experiments had been performed since the late 1920s, and a total of 1,500 tests with nerve agents, and this had apparently been Porton's 'first fatality'. By placing Maddison's death into the long history of Porton's research programme, and by omitting the death of at least one serviceman during the war, he hoped to downplay the significance of the incident, and thus limit the potential fallout for the government. Britain's scientists were 'greatly surprised by this accident', he told Churchill, since human subjects had been exposed to larger dosages of nerve gas 'without any lasting ill effects', an understatement at best, considering that one of the test subjects had fallen into a coma a week before Maddison's death.[53] Although the Coroner was likely to hear evidence of a secret nature in camera, Sandys anticipated that the 'general circumstances' in which Maddison 'met his death' would have to be made public, and since this might cause 'some stir in the press', and raise questions in Parliament, Churchill needed to be aware of the 'facts without delay'.[54] Most importantly, as the minister in charge, he immediately issued a temporary ban on any 'further tests on human beings with nerve gas' until a ministerial inquiry had been concluded and further instructions issued.[55] The Home Secretary, the Minister for Defence, and the Secretary of State for Air were likewise informed. Communication down the chain of command was swift; twenty-four hours later, the MoS had relayed the ban to Porton's Chief Superintendent, who passed it to Cullumbine as the head of the physiological section.[56] In addition, a carefully drafted statement about the 'fatal accident' at Porton, prepared by the Ministry, noted: 'In every case the nature of the test and the anticipated result was described to the volunteer prior to the test so that he could withdraw if he so wished.'[57] It may well be, given what we know today, that Sandys, if he was not intentionally misleading Parliament and the British public in trying to salvage the reputation of his ministry, could at least be accused of being economical with the truth on this occasion.

Evidence of Churchill's response to Sandys does not seem to have been recorded, perhaps because of certain health problems he was experiencing around that time. If there was such a response, it has not yet come to light, and we therefore need to be cautious in determining the level of priority the head of the government assigned to the matter. Likewise, we can only speculate as to whether Churchill was, or later became aware of, the full facts of the case, or questioned his minister about the way it had been handled. Other than taking note of what appeared to be an unfortunate accident at a military facility, Churchill seems to have left it to his ministers to inform Members of Parliament and the media. He also knew that challenges of greater political and strategic importance required his prime ministerial attention, not just constitutionally—with all eyes focused on the planned Coronation of Queen Elizabeth II in June—but also militarily, with Britain's development and possession of nuclear weapons seen as an essential deterrent against the Soviet Union and other communist countries.

The inquest was opened on 8 May and attended by, amongst others, Maddison's father. It was then adjourned until 16 May, this time without a family member present. In addition, those involved in the incident prepared brief reports detailing what they had seen and whether they were satisfied that all had been done to save Maddison's life, a form of collective cover-up by a highly secretive institution which suddenly found itself under intense scrutiny by government-appointed medical and legal experts. The five subjects who survived the experiment of 6 May, Henry J. Newman, Michael B. Cox, Frederick J. Verallo, W. Jenkins, and M.L. Grady, were also asked to draft statements—which all turned out to be rather similar—detailing how much they had enjoyed their stay at Porton. Although these were not dictated, the topics upon which they were permitted to write were carefully stage-managed and communication between the men was kept to a minimum, so much so that they became aware of hardly any details surrounding Maddison's death. All that Newman knew was that 'one of the lads felt a bit groggy and was taken outside'.[58]

Probing questions were nonetheless being asked by the Coroner and the Treasury Solicitor's Department about how servicemen had been recruited and how their fitness had been tested, how they had been medically examined after volunteering and before taking part in the tests, and the type of information which had been brought to their attention to encourage them to volunteer. Most importantly, had these men been informed about the nature and purpose of the experiment or the risks involved? Had they been exposed to undue risk? The Coroner's handwritten notes, disclosed in 2004 for the first time, also reveal that at least one of the Porton scientists, John Rutland, believed that Maddison was exposed to levels of Sarin nerve gas

which were 'well above the normal limits'.[59] Such testimony constituted
potentially incriminating evidence which, some felt, had to be counterbal-
anced through the submission of other material and ideally kept hidden
from public view. In an attempt to reassure the Coroner, the Treasury
Solicitor, having been briefed by the Ministry, confirmed that none of the
men had been coerced to go to Porton, it had been their 'absolute choice',
and those responsible for sending them had apparently 'known the type of
test', a statement which, days later, was flatly contradicted by a senior government legal adviser.[60] It was apparently within the discretion of those
responsible for sending the men to Porton, the Treasury Solicitor noted, to
decide whether the applicant was 'medically fit'; he himself assumed, of
course, that 'no applicant who is not fit is sent'.[61] Though not misleading the
Coroner, he was relying heavily on information supplied by the Ministry,
which was feeding various government departments with a sanitized version of events.

Porton, above all, was bracing itself for a court of inquiry by the MoS,
convened only days later to investigate the circumstances of Maddison's
death and the existing safety procedures for human experiments with highly
toxic agents.[62] Chaired by retired Air Vice Marshal T. McClurkin, who was
to report to the Controller of Supplies, the court was made up of representatives of the Chief Medical Officer, Chief Safety Officer, and legal branch
from the MoS, a member of the RAF, and an eminent medical scientist from
the MRC.[63] Proceedings began with detailed testimony from the staff
involved.[64] Like the Coroner, the court wanted to find out how the servicemen had been recruited and 'what information' they had received before
the tests. The idea that solders were told of the 'possible effects' and could
'withdraw' if they wanted to, as some witnesses claimed at the court of
inquiry, could not be corroborated by the Porton veterans. For the most
part, the scientists appear to have misled the subjects by providing them
with only a 'general idea' of the tests, and by understating the dangers
involved. Stanley Mumford, Porton's Chief Superintendent, told the court
that on arrival the subjects were 'given a broad idea and they [were] told by
the Medical Officer that there is no risk'.[65] At the same time, he conceded
that there were 'hazards involved', after one of the men had fallen into a
coma.[66] Porton officials were concerned that if they were to supply the
subjects with more detailed information, some might refuse to participate
in the experiments, or as Mumford put it: 'If you advertised for people to
suffer agony you would not get them.'[67] This was a rare instance where the

court disagreed with Porton's approach, arguing that the recruitment notices might have misled the servicemen: 'I do feel that to say there is not the slightest danger is a mis-statement as you are in fact dealing with a dangerous substance.'[68] In a remarkable climb-down, Mumford suggested that the tests were 'planned to avoid risk' but accepted that there was 'inevitably a danger of some poisoning' which, if it occurred, could be treated with an atropine antidote.[69] Summing up the position, the court felt that the servicemen should be 'told quite clearly what risks they are going to take' before travelling to Porton, a minor criticism of existing recruitment practices, perhaps, but no more.[70]

Who were, in fact, the other experts involved in Porton's fatal experiment? How had they made a career as chemical warfare scientists? Information about Porton staff at the time of Maddison's death is somewhat sketchy, but fragmentary evidence has survived. Harry Cullumbine had trained as a doctor before specializing as a chemist. His responsibilities as head of the physiology section involved the supervision of experiments with nerve agents on both animals and humans.[71] A wartime colleague recalled that Cullumbine, whom he described as 'ambitious, ruthless, and easy to get on with if you called a spade a spade', had apparently waited for the opportunity of this promotion.[72] M. Ainsworth, one of Cullumbine's colleagues at Porton, in a retrospective account, remembered feeling 'a bit unhappy' about Sarin tests with clothing since these appeared to be more dangerous than those on bare skin, yet Cullumbine continued regardless despite having been advised 'to go carefully'.[73] In addition to writing a series of scientific papers on the treatment of lewisite shock and the toxicology of atmospheric pollutants, detailing, for example, a series of deadly animal experiments with undiluted diesel fumes, Cullumbine published a carefully crafted, and officially censored, postwar summary of the chemical warfare experiments Porton had carried out with human participants during the war.[74] According to Cullumbine, 'no one' had been exposed to any toxic chemicals at Porton 'without first being told the precise nature of the test and the possible consequences to himself', a statement which, albeit lacking in credibility as far as the reality of Porton's research programme was concerned, reflected the official position that non-therapeutic experiments required the consent of the participant after full disclosure of all the risks involved.[75] For tests involving greater risks to the health and well-being of subjects, for example in offensive chemical weapon trials, Porton had apparently established a system by which 'volunteers from [among] the volunteers' were invited to take part.[76] Taken at face value, officials might have wondered about certain discrepancies between Cullumbine's procedural claims and the recruitment of servicemen exposed to highly dangerous nerve agents in the late 1940s and 1950s. Cullumbine told the court that although the terms of reference for using volunteers had received 'little alteration', the nature of the tests had changed dramatically, 'from using harmless agents to those involving very toxic substances'.[77] His assurances that Porton had responded to these changes by improving their 'precautionary measures' were later called into question by the Treasury Solicitor.[78] Reflecting perhaps on his own level of culpability as the scientist in charge at the time of Maddison's death, and thus formally responsible, he urged the court to recognize that the 'responsibility of medical staff is now a very heavy one', a strategy which had the desired effect. Cullumbine was never held accountable for continuing with the experiments after the Kelly incident.[79]

On the contrary, whilst ostensibly accepting 'full responsibility', he felt that scientists ought to be given the 'recognized right to refuse to do any human experiments which they consider unsafe', and that these rights should be firmly anchored in any future 'charter for volunteers'.[80] Grounded in the Hippocratic medical tradition and the Declaration of Geneva of 1948, these were rights every medically qualified expert possessed anyway, yet what Cullumbine appeared to imply was that Porton's scientists were some-how exempt from these rights, but placed under considerable external pressures—a not-so-veiled criticism of military interference, perhaps, or a useful ploy to shift attention to more influential actors. Through a complete reversal of perspective, he managed to turn around the 'thrust of responsibility'. Researchers apparently needed to be given greater rights to protect them-selves against unnecessary infringements or unreasonable demands by the service departments about what could and could not be achieved through human experiments. They also required greater freedom to 'express their views' on which tests should and should not be done, and be given more time to conduct 'fundamental studies', as if this had not previously been possible.[81] These new powers were to be vested in none other than the head of the physiological section—Cullumbine himself. Rather than taking responsibility for the failure to protect servicemen, he was attempting to transform the court of inquiry into a call for greater professional autonomy for Britain's secret science community. The Adrian Committee, which was later tasked with assessing whether tests should resume (see further below), accepted the majority of his recommendations.[82]

In his unpublished autobiography, Cullumbine glossed over Maddison's death entirely. It was not mentioned anywhere. Instead, he rhapsodized about the collegiate atmosphere during Tripartite Conference meetings, and the fun of visiting the United States on a regular basis, when he would be spending the weekend with 'Sam and Virginia Gibbon at their house Jenkintown. A very enjoyable and relaxing interlude.'[83] These were not just scientists on the lookout for more deadly and destructive agents, he wanted his would-be readers to believe, they were family men who enjoyed gardening and the beauty of the Wiltshire countryside. And they were cultured too; he especially liked showing off his knowledge of prehistoric Stonehenge. Agent trials were touched upon, but only those conducted outside Porton to assess the physiological effects of a newly developed 'first-aid treatment for nerve gas poisoning', firstly, in April 1953, with units of the British Army of the Rhine stationed in Germany (for temperate climates), then, at the end of May, in Iraq (for hot and dry climates), and finally in Malaya (for hot and moist climates). His tale resembled an adventure narrative about a group of British explorers amidst the chaos of the Arab and south-east Asian worlds. During the trips he was accompanied by Wing Commander Muir and Major Adrian, the son of the eminent Cambridge scientist Edgar D. Adrian, chair of the Adrian Committee. One can hardly avoid the impression that these men had their minds set somehow on other things. While servicemen were showing serious adverse reactions to nerve gas at the end of April, which, from an ethical perspective, demanded a complete rethink of experimental procedures, the group was about to embark on a 'world tour' to study the agent under different climatic conditions, soaking up different cultures along the way. Any problems requiring their attention at Porton could potentially delay their date of departure.

Stationed at Porton as a medical officer, Major Adrian had attended two similar nerve gas experiments before the incident, and it was his responsibility to monitor the test from outside the gas chamber through a window.[84] Adrian rejected the suggestion that he and his colleagues were 'not particularly disturbed' by Maddison's respiratory collapse. On the contrary, it had been a 'grave emergency', but they had all believed that they would be able to save Maddison's life.[85] These included Thomas W.N. Truckle, senior technician in the physiology laboratory and former employee of the Royal Navy, and his assistant, Herbert W. Lacon.[86] Truckle had fifteen years of experience of human experiments, and had been in charge of the trials on both occasions when servicemen had suffered serious ill-effects: on

27 April, when a soldier had fallen into a coma, and on 6 May, when
Maddison was killed. It raised the possibility that Truckle might have followed a certain routine or perhaps had become careless, even complacent,
in conducting trials with highly toxic agents. In his defence, Truckle maintained that he had told each participant that 'the procedure is a dangerous
one'.[87] Asked by the court whether the soldiers were given any 'written
questions', he replied that they were 'asked if they wanted to ask any questions'.[88] Porton's practice of shifting the responsibility for obtaining information about the experiments to the subjects themselves was later
confirmed by Alan Bangay, who was at Porton at the same time as Maddison,
but did not participate in the same Sarin test.[89] Although a serviceman had
just died in one of his experiments, Truckle felt that, on the whole, the
existing safety arrangements were 'quite adequate', a position which Porton
staff frequently repeated.[90] Leigh Silver, the attending medical officer, who
held a diploma in industrial health, was convinced that everything had
been done to revive Maddison and save his life. In contrast to the case of
Kelly, whose symptoms had been more marked, Leigh Silver had been
surprised when Maddison had 'died suddenly'.[91]

Another witness was the RAF medical officer Adam Muir, who had six
years of experience of nerve agents.[92] Together with Lieutenant Colonel
Cruickshank, Muir had been present during the attempts to save Maddison's
life. From the military perspective, the aim had been to assess the 'potential
danger of liquid nerve gas on the skin', but in the process the scientists had
been astonished by the dosages they had reached. They were fully aware of
the potential risks if they continued to increase the dosages even further:
'We realized that if we went too far it would become too dangerous. On
one or two occasions warning signs were noticed so it was decided to
reduce the amount.'[93] But what they had not anticipated, and perhaps not
fully appreciated, was the possibility that two layers of cloth did not increase
protection, but made Sarin nerve gas more toxic. For the court, it was a
foregone conclusion 'that another Maddison will appear', not so much in
terms of another fatality, but as a person who would be particularly susceptible to nerve gas, and it was Porton's responsibility to prepare for such a
contingency.[94]

Among the last to be interviewed was Lovatt Evans, who happened to be
at Porton when the fatality occurred. Having pursued research into chemical warfare agents since 1916, he had greater knowledge than any of the
other medical experts. He told the court that Porton scientists had 'always

had trouble' applying knowledge obtained from animal tests to human subjects, especially in percutaneous experiments, since the skin of animals could
not easily be compared to that of humans.[95] Like the other witnesses, he
could not explain Maddison's death, but suggested that it might have been
caused by a sudden release of adrenaline which could have triggered a
fibrillation of the heart. Lovatt Evans was so certain about the safety of the
tests that he agreed, in principle, to be subjected to a nerve gas experiment,
but only at 'two thirds of the dosage given to Kelly', which would be the
same amount as that given to Maddison.[96] His ethical perspective—'do not do
to others what you would not do to yourself'—and expert knowledge did not
fail to impress the court.[97] Porton, he argued, was a 'model' establishment
replicated by other nations in which 'there was no real risk at all', a position
seriously called into question in the 2004 inquest proceedings.[98]

Following a visit to the 'scene of the accident', the court acquitted
Porton and its staff of any suggestion of wrongdoing. According to the
panel, the experiment in which Maddison had met his death had apparently been 'a reasonable one', the procedures and conduct of the test had
been 'fully satisfactory', and the dosage as it had been intended; not only
had the subject been perfectly healthy to undertake the test, but the poisoning had been detected early and dealt with in an efficient and professional manner. Indeed, the court was 'impressed by the smoothness of the
working of the organization in dealing with the emergency'.[99] By attrib-
uting Maddison's death to 'a personal idiosyncrasy' which related to either
the way his skin had absorbed the agent, or an 'unusual sensitivity' of his
body to the effects of the substance, or both, the court cleared the way for
a subsequent finding of 'misadventure' by the Coroner. Maddison's death
had apparently been an accident which could not have been prevented.
Since the work of the establishment was of 'such importance', the court
recommended that future tests with nerve agents, in whatever form, should
be 'left to the discretion of the Head of the Establishment', and that the use
of servicemen for gas tests should be continued, but only after their 'terms
of employment' had been carefully studied, and if necessary amended by a
senior lawyer to protect the government against liability. Not only did the
proposal unintentionally lay bare grave procedural shortcomings in Britain's
experimental programme, but it was also based on reckless suggestions by
some of the Porton scientists.[100] According to the court, there were apparently no grounds for imposing a ban on human tests with nerve agents,
since small quantities of the substance, up to 10 mg, could be applied

'without foreseeable danger'.[101] This carefully worded phrase was later taken up by the Treasury Solicitor, H. Woodhouse, who, asked to give legal advice to the Ministry, fulfilled his assignment with the utmost due diligence, so much so that his evidence was not disclosed to Maddison's family or the British public for over fifty years. When it finally did see the light of day, following discovery by the present author at the headquarters of Operation Antler in 2003, it changed the way the case was viewed by the authorities. It was quite literally a 'smoking gun', and the government had had good reason not to publicize or share it.

On 15 May, less than ten days after the incident, Woodhouse came to a conclusion. He had discussed the matter the previous day with his legal counterpart in the MoS, a Mr Griffith-Jones, who had tried to play down matters by suggesting that there had 'never been any fatal accident' at Porton before, except for 'one of the subjects' who had shown 'alarming symptoms' in April—decidedly a gross understatement of the state of affairs in the weeks before Maddison's death. Woodhouse's position was that since servicemen had been misled at Porton, the government should accept full responsibility for Maddison's death and pay compensation to the family. He had realized that there was a significant discrepancy between the procedures Porton was using in recruiting volunteers, including the information provided to them, and the level of risk to which the subjects were exposed. Although the government was not legally liable if it could be demonstrated that Porton staff had not acted negligently, he strongly discouraged the Ministry from taking this approach,

> partly because in dealing with a dangerous but largely unknown substance like G.B. [Sarin] it would be difficult to show that there had been no negligence (a very high degree of care being required in relation to dangerous substances), and partly because the terms of the information to be brought to the notice of personnel to encourage them to volunteer . . . terms indicating that there was not the slightest element of danger, have proved [to be] somewhat misleading.[102]

With regard to future experiments, Woodhouse suggested that the Minister should not adopt a system of indemnities that placed responsibility upon those volunteering for the experiments, but instead pay 'appropriate compensation' where such 'fatal accidents' occurred. He urged the Ministry not to resume tests until Maddison's alleged 'personal idiosyncrasy' had been fully investigated, since other men might have similar conditions, and it was advised to take all reasonable steps to prevent further deaths. If this was not done, and the warning signs not heeded, the government would expose itself to 'serious criticism in the event of any further fatality'. Given that servicemen had received misleading information for tests which included 'a definite element of unknown danger', he also proposed a change of wording in the recruitment notices:

> The sentence: 'Tests are carefully planned to avoid the slightest chance of danger' has proved misleading. Indeed it is difficult to see how it was ever possible to say truthfully that tests with lethal gases did not contain 'the slightest chance of danger'. The true position, I take it, is that the tests are arranged so as to eliminate all foreseeable danger, but that as the tests are designed for the purpose of obtaining further information about substances the properties and performance of which are to some extent unknown, there is always some possibility (even it be exceedingly remote) of a danger being discovered.[103]

Evidence obtained from former staff members portrays a research culture in which some of the scientists were taking unreasonable risks with the lives of subjects. Gradually, ever higher dosages of nerve agents were being applied to push the limits of human endurance. 'There was a terrible urgency to discover the effects of these compounds', recalled one of the scientists, who wanted to remain anonymous: 'In retrospect it was incredibly dangerous as we just didn't know what we were dealing with.'[104] Porton's scientists were quite literally playing with fire, and they knew it. In 2004, Lynch, who had worked in Cullumbine's department, told the inquest that he and his colleagues felt that it was 'very brave' to continue with Sarin tests after one of the subjects had fallen into a coma. Asked whether this was his personal view, he replied:

> I think it was the view generally in the department...We knew we were pushing it. There were very large amounts of GB [Sarin] being used...and because they were human experiments, any of us who knew about them could not help feeling nervous.[105]

By July 1953, officials had introduced most of the Treasury Solicitors' recommendations. Recruitment notices now read: 'The physical discomfort resulting from tests is usually very slight. Tests are arranged so as to eliminate all foreseeable danger, and are under expert medical supervision.'[106] However, instead of providing subjects with more accurate information about the risks involved, officials phrased the invitation in such a way as to provide even less information. The new statement may not have been misleading, at least not to the same extent as the old one, but neither does it appear to have been a fair representation of the nature, purpose, and risk of experiments which were subsequently carried out on human subjects.

Yet the problems highlighted by the fatality extended far beyond mere recruitment notices. There was an unspoken consensus among some senior MoS officials in charge of chemical warfare research that they should tell both the servicemen and the armed services supplying the men to Porton as little as possible about the exact nature of planned nerve agent experiments, largely for security reasons. However, MoS officials soon realized that this could produce additional communication problems between the armed services and their own medical experts, for if the armed services did not know what the tests were about they could hardly follow the advice of the experts from the MoS. About a month after Maddison's death, Cawood, as the MoS's Principal Director of Scientific Research, reflected in a memo to Childs, the MoS's Director of Chemical Defence Research and Development, on the type and quantity of information that needed to be passed to the armed services. Cawood's initial thought had been to suggest that the information given to the armed services 'should cease to be specific as regards the kind of physiological trial we were going to undertake [at Porton]', yet upon thinking the matter through more thoroughly he had come to the conclusion that the approach by the MoS had to be 'somewhat detailed' to avoid undermining the position of the medical services.[107] Assuming wrongly that the MoS required volunteers exclusively for nerve agent tests at Porton, and since these had been temporarily banned by the Minister for the time being anyway, he felt that the best course of action in this matter was to do what civil servants sometimes do when faced with a complex situation: they do nothing except invite further views on the subject, and this he did, from both Childs and Porton. Cawood's correspondence is important as it provides unique insight into the thinking of a senior chemical warfare planner about the level of information that needed to be supplied to the armed services to encourage potential volunteers to go to Porton. There is little or no evidence to suggest that Britain's government agencies and senior warfare officials engaged in a concerted conspiracy intentionally to mislead Britain's soldiers into going to Porton, but there was undoubtedly a certain level of culpability in helping to construct an image and understanding of the tests at Porton that rarely corresponded to the reality the servicemen encountered at the station. It was the responsibility of the MoS to provide all those participating in the human testing programme with the most accurate information possible without endangering national security interests.

The prevailing culture of secrecy that had become firmly established during the war, and which continued long into the postwar period, provides part of the explanation for a surprising lack of information given to those participating in potentially deadly tests. In short, the perceived need for secrecy trumped the need for information. This also meant that changes in the human testing programme or in the toxicity of the agents being used were no longer adequately communicated across the armed services community, and therefore, by implication, no longer reached potential Porton volunteers on the ground.

On 13 July 1953, recognizing some of complex ethical and legal problems raised by Porton's experimental programme, Woodhouse pointed out that the armed services had previously authorized the recruitment of volunteers for the testing of mustard gas, but not for the significantly more dangerous nerve agents:

> It seems... [t]hat the arrangement for service volunteers at Porton were originally made at a time when the experiments related principally if not entirely to mustard gas and that these arrangements have continued over the years without any clear acceptance by the Service Department of the fact that the present experiments involve the use of substances which are more lethal and more uncertain in operation than mustard gas.[108]

Woodhouse had identified the main shortcoming in Porton's experimental procedures. The procedures for recruiting volunteers, for providing them with information about the experiments, and for obtaining their consent, effectively derived from a time when the service departments were principally concerned with the testing of mustard gas. The process of recruiting research subjects at Porton, and for obtaining their consent, had not been updated to take account of the higher degree of risk to which subjects had been exposed since the discovery of German nerve agents.[109] Given this state of affairs, the Treasury Solicitor advised the Ministry on 1 August 1953 that the Crown or the Minister was, in all likelihood, liable for Maddison's death, and that Section 10 of the Crown Proceedings Act 1947, exempting the Crown from legal liability for personal injuries or death sustained by members of the British armed forces, did not apply.[110]

Totally unaware of the political and legal fallout engulfing the government in respect of chemical warfare experiments, John R. Maddison, Maddison's father, an ironworker from Consett in County Durham and a man of modest means who did not possess a telephone, had rather different concerns. Having been informed of his son's death by normal service telegram, he had been brought to Porton by an escort officer to identify the body and given an opportunity to talk to some of the other test subjects, including Newman, who was the only one to become upset. Porton officials made an outward show of supporting a man and his family in this hour of grief, offering him tea and company, together with an unsolicited explanation of how his son had died in a secret experiment; however, they minuted in excruciating detail and in the presence of the Treasury Solicitor the contact Maddison's father had with the institution, and every conversation or general impression which appeared to suggest that he was satisfied with the conduct of the test and the procedures to save his son's life, thereby gathering valuable evidence to quash potential allegations of negligence in future legal proceedings.[111] A poor, but loyal, subject, he believed it to be in the nation's interest to study poison gases with volunteers and agreed to tell the family that Maddison had 'died from an unfortunate accident whilst on duty at Porton', a line which came to represent the government's position for years to come.[112] What he needed, though, were the expenses for the 'loss of work' he had incurred and could not afford to lose, a modest sum of three pounds sterling which, for administrative reasons, was duly paid by the Ministry as part of the funeral expenses. It was this small detail which threatened to unravel a most carefully spun plan to acquit the government from wrongdoing, for this proud man could not accept that this payment should be treated as part of the funeral expenses, which were to be paid by the grandparents. More worryingly for the authorities, he wanted to know more about how his son had died, since he was not satisfied with what he had been told after reading in the press that servicemen were 'acting as guinea pigs' in experiments.[113]

Far from being a model of how to manage the media, Maddison's death initially turned into public relations fiasco for the authorities when a journalist from the Sunday paper *The People*, who had phoned Wiltshire Constabulary, received confirmation that a secret inquest had taken place. Local newspapers immediately ran headlines such as 'Secret Inquest on Soldier who Died at Chemical Depot' and 'Mystery of Dead Airman— Inquest is Kept Secret'. On 25 May, after the *Daily Mail* had reported an MP's probe into the 'death riddle of airman guinea pig', it became apparent that the circumstances surrounding the death had been concealed from the public.[114] Claiming to break down a wall of secrecy, Raymond Stephenson from the *Sunday Dispatch* ran a lead story on a 'guinea pig' soldier who had 'died from suffocation in hush-hush experiment'. Next to images of carefree models competing in Britain's national bathing beauty contest, Stephenson not only revealed Maddison's identity, having gained access to his death certificate, but reported his father's dissatisfaction with Porton's attempts to resuscitate his son.[115] It was all highly embarrassing for the government. Despite attempts to control the release of information, the Ministry's refusal to comment other than that a man had died 'accidentally' about three weeks earlier fuelled further speculations about Britain's secretive warfare establishment.

While pressure on the government was mounting, the Ministry approached Major John G. Morrison, Conservative MP for Salisbury, with a view that he should ask a written question in Parliament, drafted by the Ministry's own officials, to which Duncan Sandys could then issue a carefully worded oral reply.[116] Himself from a long line of immensely rich Wiltshire landowners, educated at Eton and serving in the armed forces, Morrison did as he was told. On 9 June, a week after the Coronation, and in response to Morrison's planted question, Duncan Sandys told the House of Commons in a brief statement that Maddison had 'died from the effects of asphyxia after taking part in a trial with war gas at the Chemical Defence Experimental Establishment, at Porton' and that, in addition to suspending further experiments until further notice, he had launched a 'full technical investigation' into the accident.[117] Months later, in November 1953, the MoD's parliamentary secretary was asked whether he was satisfied that 'when National Service men volunteer their offer of service [they] should be accepted? Would he not agree that, since many of them are under age[118], their status is different from that of a man who is making the Services his career?' In his reply, the official noted: 'The men are volunteers and the nature of the experiment is clearly explained to them and they are then given a chance to withdraw. There has been only one fatal accident since 1922.'[119] Contrary to the Treasury Solicitor's advice suggesting that servicemen had not been adequately informed about the tests, the government maintained that nerve agent experiments had complied with medical morality and professional codes of practice. Its position became increasingly entrenched.[120]

Informed Consent

Existing witness statements obtained by Operation Antler from former servicemen who attended Porton and oral history interviews suggest that many of the servicemen were not properly informed about the risks involved in the experiments.[121] Caution obviously needs to be exercised about any effect the passage of time may have had on their personal recollections, yet the testimonies are, for the most part, credible in their intellectual candour and narrative authenticity. Most of the servicemen not only knew very little, if anything, about Porton before volunteering, but were told that there was no risk involved in the experiments. Tests were apparently 'totally safe'. Although they knew or had heard of mustard gas and other chemical agents, they generally had little or no knowledge of what 'nerve agents' or 'nerve gases' were. Even those who were told that they would be exposed to nerve gas often associated or confused it with mustard gas which they knew from the Second World War or from the experiences of their relatives in the previous conflict. At Porton, they received little if any information about what would happen to them while staying at the facility, although some received an introductory talk, and were lined up and photographed naked. Many just did as they were told.[122] Recalling their visit to Porton in the 1950s, many felt that they would probably have refused to participate in the trials had they known that they would be exposed to nerve agents, been given information about what nerve agents were, and been told of their potential hazards. The news that some fifty years previously they had been exposed to Sarin nerve gas came as a complete shock to some.[123] A few soldiers, admittedly, were told that they would be exposed to nerve agents, but detailed information about the compounds and their potential risks was generally withheld.[124] Indeed, there were some who felt quite strongly they had been placed under considerable pressure and not given any options or say in the experiments, for example to choose the test in which they wanted to participate or to withdraw from a particular test. Evidence from at least one soldier suggests that some form of coercion may have been applied.[125]

Renver Brant, who attended Porton in April 1953, had never heard of the place beforehand, knew nothing about its purpose, and had no knowledge of nerve agents, but he knew about mustard gas and the risks involved in inhaling it. Like others, he thought that because he had volunteered he had also 'consented to take part in the experiments'.[126] Reference to nerve agents would have meant nothing to him.[127] Another veteran, Alan Bangay, had never heard of nerve agents but knew of mustard gas, although the recruitment notices encouraging soldiers to volunteer made 'no reference to either of these substances', something most servicemen confirmed.[128]

Others struggled to understand the medical language of the notices, which meant little to them.[129] At Porton, Bangay and his fellow soldiers were not given any information about the tests. No one asked any questions and they were not given the option to withdraw, 'although I do remember being told to ask questions if I didn't understand any instructions'.[130] Bangay's testimony suggests that the scientists placed the responsibility for obtaining information about the experiments on the shoulders of the experimental subjects. In one set of experiments, Granville Popplewell, who went to Porton in April 1953, was exposed to mustard gas and was told what it was that he would be exposed to. In another test, however, he was exposed to a liquid but was not told what it was, nor was he told about the possible effects of the substance: 'I didn't know what the chemical was. I did, however, trust them.'[131] Porton's investigators seem to have revealed details about experiments with blistering or incapacitating agents, but were reluctant to discuss tests with nerve agents.

Kenneth Earl, who attended Porton at the same time as Maddison and participated in the same kind of Sarin experiment two days earlier, on 4 May 1953, recalled a test inside a heated gas chamber: 'I cannot remember being given any other information in relation to this test and in fact if I had been told (as I know now) what this test involved me coming into contact with, then I would have without doubt have [sic] said "no" to the test' (see Image 25).[132] He was adamant that he had 'no idea' that he would be exposed to nerve gas when he went to Porton. Like many of his peers, he also had no 'knowledge of nerve gas or their effects' before he volunteered.[133] A similar view was expressed by John Newbury, who attended Porton in April and May 1953. If he had known that his visit to Porton involved chemical warfare experiments, he remarked in 2003, he 'would not have volunteered to go'.[134] Upon his arrival, he was told that he would be exposed to 'radioactive nerve gas', which came as a 'complete shock' to him and his group, yet one of the scientists tried to reassure them by emphasizing that the tests were 'totally safe'.[135] He felt that Porton's researchers construed his 'mere presence there as a volunteer ... as consent' and steadfastly maintained that they were never given the choice of withdrawing from the experiment.[136]

Another soldier, James Patrick Kelly, believed that he was participating in a 'Gas Warfare Course' at Porton in April 1953.[137] Rather than attending lectures and training in gas warfare, he took part in a Sarin experiment

Image 25. Kenneth Earl, 1950s
Source: Kenneth Earl, Private Papers, Kent, Image of Kenneth Earl on a Motorbike, 1950s.

without ever being informed about it: 'I had no idea at the time what the liquids were that I was testing. I certainly was not told what the liquids were, or that there would be any short or long term health risks.'[138] Detailed information about the nature and risks of the experiments was generally not forthcoming at Porton:

> In fact when we were at Porton Down the staff did not explain anything about the test that we took part in. No one explained the substances that they were using, or the purpose of the test. We received no formal briefing or explanation about Porton Down, or the work they were doing there. The tester never asked us if we were happy to take part. We were told to take part in a certain test; we had no option to do one test or another.[139]

Kelly subsequently recalled being 'confused' about the entire experience since he did not understand how the experiments related to training in gas warfare, but felt that as a soldier he could not speak up.[140] There were others, though, who received at least some general information. Attending Porton in March 1953, Frederick Moules knew that Porton was a 'Chemical-testing place' and recalled being given 'a briefing that the test was with a nerve agent of some kind'. On exposure, he collapsed and was hospitalized for three days while 'drifting in and out of consciousness'.[141] His visit to Porton was not one of his fondest memories.

Peter de Carle Parker attended Porton at the same time as Maddison and participated in the same Sarin experiment, but was not in the chamber with him on 6 May 1953. He thought that Porton conducted tests with tear gases but 'nothing more than that'.[142] He felt he was misled by the authorities since he consented to being exposed to tear gas and not a nerve gas. The entire process was rather casual and all they were told was that there was 'nothing to worry about'. Parker, like Kenneth Earl and John Newbury, and like Douglas Gray, who attended Porton twice as a Royal Navy participant in 1952 and in 1953, said that he would not have consented to the test had he been told that he would be exposed to a dangerous nerve gas.[143] Gray, on the other hand, said that he *might* have attended, if he had 'just been told it was a nerve agent but not warned of any dangers'.[144]

Whereas Porton veterans expressed concern about the level of consent that had been obtained, most acknowledged that they had not been forced to take part in the experiments: yet there were exceptions to this. In February 1953, Peter Sammons from the Royal Navy, who had never heard of Sarin or other nerve gases, and thought that his father had been exposed to a 'nerve agent' in the First World War, volunteered to go to Porton. He later admitted that he 'really had no idea'.[145] Talking to the Wiltshire police in 2000, he made it clear that at no time had any of the scientists told them 'what it was they were going to test on us'. Like Moules, he was hospitalized for several days after collapsing during a trial, an experience which frightened him to such an extent that he 'informed the scientists that [he] was no longer willing to take part in any other experiments'.[146] Once he had left Porton, he appears to have been 'ordered' to return several times; each time he refused, telling his superiors that he 'didn't want to take part in any more tests'.[147] In August 1953, Sammons finally succumbed to the pressure and returned to Porton, where someone whom he described as the 'head man' tried to persuade him in no uncertain terms to participate in more tests:

> He advised me of how I had let them down by not completing all of the experiments. I was generally made to feel that I had not done everything that was expected of me. I was also told by this 'head man' that I was not to discuss any of my visits to Porton with anyone.[148]

Although the existing witness statements seem to suggest that in general no duress was exercised at Porton, Sammons' statement raises serious issues of coercion and undue persuasion. Porton's scientists, it seems, obtained consent only partially and in a 'roundabout' way. The information they provided to the subjects did not allow them to make an informed decision. Researchers knew that nerve gases were highly toxic in minute quantities and that exposure to them entailed significant risk.[149] They knowingly increased exposure to levels that were dangerous to the subjects.[150] Between 1952 and 1953, six experimental subjects were hospitalized as a result of exposure to nerve agents.[151]

After Maddison's death, research procedures came under scrutiny. In July 1953, the Treasury Solicitor pointed out: 'Misleading statements in an invitation of this sort, even if made in complete innocence, are always apt to give rise to criticism when anything has gone wrong.'[152] Something had indeed gone wrong. According to Cullumbine's handwritten note received at Porton at 3.45 p.m. on 5 May 1953, the day before Maddison's death, and a typed copy of that same note, the object of the experiments was to 'discover the dosage of GB [Sarin], GD [Soman] and GF [Cyclosarin] which when applied to the clothed or bare skin of men would cause incapacitation or death'.[153] A subsequent report of 1954 repeated this objective.[154] So far, no evidence has surfaced that would suggest that any of the experimental subjects, including Maddison, was ever informed about the specific objective of the experiments. Indeed, it is rather unlikely that any man in his right mind would have volunteered for such a trial.[155] The consent that may have been obtained from Maddison would not have qualified as having been 'informed', and was therefore invalid.

The Common Cold

Recent controversy about Britain's chemical warfare programme has centred on allegations, many of them credible, that servicemen were duped into believing they were taking part in research to find a cure for the common cold.[156] Since the mid 1990s, former servicemen have engaged in a campaign to raise awareness about Porton's experiments and, in the hope of gaining political recognition and compensation, have maintained steadfastly that the objective of their trip to Porton appeared to be common cold research rather than experiments into toxic substances, and that the information sent to their units to encourage them to volunteer stated this. In its defence, the government has argued that 'no connection' between Porton and common cold studies could be found.[157] The issues surrounding this aspect of Porton's activity are difficult to reconstruct in retrospect, yet based on the existing evidence some general observations can be made.

Established in 1946 by the MRC on the site of the former Harvard Military Hospital on Harnham Down, Salisbury, which had served as a base for the study of communicable diseases during the war, and which was jointly maintained by the MRC and the MoH, the CCRU conducted research on cold viruses on an estimated 20,000 civilians and soldiers up until 1989.[158] Given their geographical proximity, the site was not only linked to Porton by association—which led to confusion in the minds of many, including soldiers, as to whether Porton and the CCRU were the same—but both facilities and their staff were also connected through jointly organized seminars and the sharing of specialized technology, biological agents, and know-how. In 1952, a discussion forum run by experts from both facilities led to the creation of the South Wiltshire Virology Group. Upon retirement, former Porton staff sometimes continued their work at the CCRU, as in the case of Frank Buckland, who, having been involved in setting up the MRE after the war, moved to the CCRU as a researcher. His contacts allowed CCRU scientists to obtain sampling equipment and stocks of (non-toxic) bacterial spores from Porton for experimental purposes.[159] Suggestions that the CCRU be transferred to Porton for want of better accommodation were however opposed by the MRC for fear that an even closer association would detrimentally affect volunteer recruitment rates.

Recruitment originally concentrated on students and was then expanded, for lack of uptake, to the general public in what developed into a nationwide publicity campaign to enlist civilian and service volunteers. Taking part in common cold trials caught the public imagination. Via newspapers such as *The Daily Telegraph*, *The Guardian*, and *Evening News*, popular magazines such as *Vogue*, *The Lady*, and *Home and Country*—the official mouthpiece of the Women's Institute—and army newsletters, radio broadcasts, and television programmes, throughout Britain the population was asked to come to Salisbury for ten days, preferably in groups of two or three, to study the common cold and influenza in return for healthy walks and good company in the Wiltshire countryside. Posters circulated to libraries in the Greater London boroughs promoted a stay at the CCRU as the 'best package holiday anywhere'.[160] Elsewhere civilians were offered 'ten days free holiday', an opportunity not to be missed by married couples or cash-strapped singles, and were asked to spread the word among their friends. The costs of maintaining the CCRU were balanced against the rising costs of annual cold outbreaks to the national economy. Comprehensive safety precautions guarded against the outbreak of accidental epidemics; wandering off into residential areas or the city of Salisbury was strictly prohibited. Although evidence of military units encouraging soldiers to volunteer is scarce, we know that the services, including the RAF, sought to recruit volunteers from among their staff and family members.[161] By the 1950s, common cold studies had not only benefited scientifically from the growing field of virology and the international onslaught against poliomyelitis in mass immunization trials, but they had become public knowledge, much talked about yet not taken too seriously. A contributing factor to the willingness of servicemen to go to Porton may have been their belief that this was the place where people enjoyed time away from home in the service of science and society.

To anyone looking at the two establishments from the outside, armed only with the limited information available in distant military units, the organizations could easily fuse into one, since recruitment notices were vague: 'There were notices for the Common Cold Unit at Porton Down. Vague notices—volunteers are required', recalled Anderson, Officer Commanding at Ballykelly, where Maddison had been stationed. He and others also remembered that Harnham Down was known as the 'Common Cold Unit at Porton Down' and was referred to as such in SROs. Other SROs apparently referred to 'CDRD, Porton Down' without explaining that chemical warfare tests were being performed at the facility.[162] Anderson may have confused 'CDRD' with Porton's widely used institutional abbreviation 'CDEE' on this occasion, but distinguishing between 'CCRU', the Common Cold Research Unit in Salisbury, and 'CDEE', the Chemical Defence Experimental Establishment in Salisbury, would have required considerable attention to detail. Officers talking about Porton during the 'daily working parade' as if both facilities were one and the same only added to further misunderstanding, thus making it nigh impossible for soldiers to know exactly which one they had actually volunteered for.

A study by Porton's consultant psychologist in 1960/1961 on the 'personality' and 'intelligence' of over 500 service volunteers found two soldiers who had arrived at Porton by 'mistake' because they had 'believed that they were going to the Common Cold Research Unit in Salisbury'.[163] A Porton member of staff later recorded similar instances on a series of card indexes for the period from 1964 to 1977. Although not representative, this provides hard evidence that at least some of the servicemen had come to Porton in the belief they would be assisting in common cold research, or had confused

CDEE (Porton) with the CCRU (the Common Cold Research Unit). Soldiers may not have been intentionally misled by the agencies of the state in an orchestrated conspiracy, but some certainly believed they were volunteering for common cold research when they had in fact signed up for tests with chemical warfare agents.

Another potential source of confusion involved similar patterns of lived experiences at the two facilities. Depending on which research facility servicemen had been to, their experiences and the level of restriction in discussing these freely among peers varied considerably, which led to an asymmetrical, biased flow of information to and from the parent units, and this exacerbated over time the lack of accurate information available to new recruits. Apart from the agents to which subjects were exposed, volunteers experienced remarkably similar environments and a research culture shaped by modern experimental methods; in both cases, they were supplied with a rail pass and arrived at the same railway station before being directed to either CCRU or CDEE; most of them were young servicemen or students in need of some respite from the stresses of adult life; they were housed in similar simple yet comfortable, clean, heated barracks, something not to be sniffed at in austerity Britain; hot food was served, and one was given time off to engage in recreational activities, watching television, or playing table tennis (see Images 26a–b). By April 1953, shortly before Maddison arrived at Porton, over 2,000 volunteers had visited the CCRU.[164] Descriptions of the sites would therefore, in all likelihood, not have diverged significantly, but there were differences as well.

Although volunteers received similar assurances about the harmless nature of the agents prior to the trials, and were asked to undergo a medical examination, the prevailing medical ethics culture seems to have differed remarkably at the two sites. Ever since the MRC had been advised by the Treasury Solicitor about the need to protect itself against legal liability for planned experiments with influenza viruses in the 1930s, the CCRU had aimed to obtain informed consent before any subject underwent tests. This process, however informally it may have been introduced in practice, was largely absent at Porton, where the objectives of toxic trials were rarely explained in any meaningful detail.[165] Informed in writing of the nature of the tests in advance when filling in the 'Volunteer's Application Form', and briefed by members of staff upon arrival, volunteers at the CCRU were given the option to withdraw from the trial at any time.[166] Common cold research was nonetheless subject to ethical scrutiny by a review board and

(a)

(b)

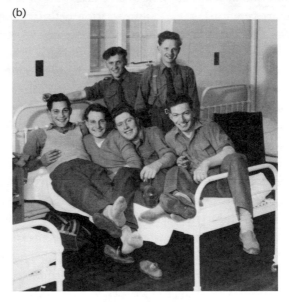

Images 26a–b. Porton Down 'volunteers', 1955
Source: IWM, Photographic Collection, General Conditions for Coming Trial, 18 May 1955.
© Imperial War Museums (F 574/1–2).

occasional criticism from interested groups who saw human testing as 'immoral' and medical scientists as 'heartless'. Local concerns also flared up over proposed plans to allow MRC scientists access to patient cohorts at the district hospital. However, the introduction of an ethical review board was seen, at least in retrospect, as welcome.

Whereas servicemen who had taken part in common cold research could freely talk about their mostly positive experiences, and thus feed their views into their home station's grapevine, those exposed to mustard and tear gas or various types of nerve agents were bound by the Official Secrets Act (OSA) not to disclose anything they had 'seen or heard' at Porton.[167] Moreover, soldiers returning from Porton often had no idea about the type of agents they had been exposed to, and may well have believed that they had taken part in common cold tests. Although not all soldiers signed the OSA upon arrival at or departure from Porton, it was generally understood that they should not talk about individual tests or agents on the grounds of secrecy, which meant that information critical of Porton experiments was rarely made available to members of the subject's Unit or to its officers, either formally or informally, nor did it enter the Unit's grapevine. The fact that Porton was carrying out chemical warfare experiments with nerve agents may therefore scarcely, other than in isolated incidents, have come to the attention of Unit commanders or servicemen. Porton Down seems thus to have become closely associated with common cold research, because the information fed back to soldiers in their units would largely, if not exclusively, have originated from the CCRU or from those left in the belief that they had been tested with common cold viruses while at Porton. There was no formal wrongdoing, only a particular type of negligence. The British authorities never made any serious attempt to correct the confusion which had taken hold among the general public, knowing full well that it allowed secrecy at Porton to be maintained, albeit at a cost to the lives of men. For some, such as Henry J. Newman, who had been with Maddison in the gas chamber, the debate about soldiers being recruited under the pretext of common cold research was of academic interest only, since he and his peers had not really known where or why they were going, except that it was a facility for 'experiments'.[168]

The Adrian Committee

Whereas senior civil servants and politicians were outwardly giving as little attention as possible to Maddison's death by constructing a plausible public narrative, behind the scenes seemingly independent scientific experts were asked to advise the government whether it would be safe to resume human experiments with nerve agents at Porton and, if so, under

Image 27. Edgar Douglas Adrian
Source: Edgar Douglas Adrian (1889–1977) 1st Baron Adrian, Meitner-Graf, Lotte
(1901–1973) / Private Collection / Bridgeman Images.

what conditions. In late June 1953, Edgar D. Adrian at Cambridge, soon to
be elevated to Baron Adrian of Cambridge, President of the Royal Society,
Master of Trinity College, Cambridge, and father of Major Adrian—himself heavily implicated in Maddison's death—was asked by Eric Rideal,
chairman of the Scientific Advisory Council (SAC) at the MoS, to con-
vene a small but 'authoritative expert committee' to advise the government whether to lift the ban on human experiments with nerve agents
that had been imposed by the Minister of Supply after the 'Porton fatality'
(see Image 27).[169] Born into a reasonably prosperous London-based family
with established links to the British civil service—his father, grandfather,
and great-grandfather had all been civil servants—Adrian obtained one of
the highest first-class degrees ever awarded at Trinity College, Cambridge,
shortly before the outbreak of the First World War. His achievements were
so outstanding that his tutor believed that he 'ought to do magnificent
work in scientific medicine'.[170] Destined for an academic career, he began

to conduct experimental work on muscles, nerve cells, and the brain. One of his principal scientific achievements was the 'final demonstration of discrete electrical impulses in single nerve fibres'.[171] In 1932, he and Charles Sherrington were jointly awarded the Nobel Prize in Physiology and Medicine, and five years later he succeeded Joseph Barcroft, by then knighted, as Professor of Physiology at Cambridge, a post which he held until 1951. It was in this high-intensity research environment that Adrian came to meet many of his future friends and colleagues, some of whom were interested in, and had connections to, Britain's developing chemical warfare programme, including Rudolph Peters and Joseph Barcroft. Perhaps not surprisingly, Hodgkin's seventy-three-page biographical account dedicates only about a dozen lines to Adrian's 'work on nerve gases'.[172] To this day, portraits of Adrian and Barcroft hang on either side of one of the main lecture theatres in Cambridge's physiology department, although—according to an unnamed member of staff—students seem to be rather oblivious (they don't 'give a toss') to the context in which some of the research of these elder statesmen of their discipline had originally been conducted.

To provide the committee with sufficient clout, while maintaining a high level of secrecy, Adrian co-opted onto the committee Peters and Cameron, two of his long-time associates. With its immense expertise in the chemical warfare field the Adrian Committee, as it became known, concluded within a month that certain experiments with nerve agents on human subjects should be permitted and could be safely conducted, as long as they were performed within clearly defined parameters.[173] While highlighting the importance of chemical warfare trials with humans generally, the panel used the opportunity to give Porton a clean bill of health by stressing a confidence-inspiring track and safety record. Contrary to the Treasury Solicitor's opinion, which had not been shared with panel members, they believed that the safety precautions were entirely satisfactory. Although nerve agents were highly toxic and fast acting, human experiments needed to continue, they argued, to advance chemical science and develop therapeutic methods for soldiers and civilians. Apart from limiting inhalation experiments to a certain maximum (15 mg·min/m^3), the panel recommended that the dosage to which human subjects could be exposed in percutaneous experiments should not exceed 5 mg, and that tests should in future be conducted only with 'very small doses' of radioactive Sarin—this 'radio labelling' allowing the agent to be tracked in the body.[174]

By recommending that members of the Biology Committee of the CDAB should function as 'authoritative advisers' in all questions related to human experiments, members of the Adrian Committee, who were themselves part of the Biology Committee, not only proposed their own appointment as chief experts, but attempted to gain supervisory control of military trials with humans generally, a move which did not escape the attention of Wansbrough-Jones, the Chief Scientist, who felt that the suggestion that the Biology Committee should 'decide what tests could be conducted without danger' would be unconstitutional.[175] Officials were also uncomfortable with the statement that it 'would be unsafe to make any more experiments in which the safety is determined on the basis of extrapolation of the cholinesterase content of the blood', a criticism, however veiled, of Porton's applied methods and procedures that supported the allegation that Porton had not done everything to ensure the highest level of safety in its experimental programme, and had thus acted negligently in the Maddison case. As a precaution, officials simply deleted the sentence from the draft report before the final version was submitted to, and then endorsed by, the Chief Scientist.[176] At the end of September 1953, after the majority of the recommendations had been accepted by the Ministry and the Army Council, the government authorized the resumption of nerve agent experiments at Porton.[177]

The Adrian Committee undoubtedly consisted of highly distinguished scientists from first-rate academic institutions, whose international reputation in their field was beyond reproach or, as the Chief Scientist put it, could not have been 'superior for this purpose in the world', yet, far from being independent and impartial, their level of self-interestedness and lack of critical detachment from the subject of their inquiry could hardly have been greater. All were an integral part of Britain's chemical warfare establishment, whose professional careers had been shaped by human experiments and depended on them. And as the case touched upon matters of national security, the authorities generally faced little public opposition in conducting one tightly controlled in-house investigation after another, all with well-established, yet fiercely loyal, experts, who dared not challenge the underlying premise of the need to perform nerve agents tests on humans as a precondition to developing Britain's chemical weapon capability during the Cold War.

Moreover, no one in government took much notice of the fact that Edgar D. Adrian in particular had a conflict of interest because of the involvement of his own son Richard in the Maddison case, perhaps because he had been cleared by the earlier court of inquiry. Yet this is not where the many connections between the influential Adrian family and Porton ended. As late as 1994, a year before his death, Richard Adrian corresponded with Porton's then director, Graham Pearson, about how best to manage any media inquiries into Maddison's death after he, Adrian, had been approached on 10 January by the journalist Kim Shillinglaw—currently controller of the BBC Two TV channel—who was researching a film about Porton for Observer Films.[178] The moment the telephone conversation touched upon Maddison, Adrian told Shillinglaw that he was 'unwilling to answer any further questions' since he believed that the case was still covered by the Official Secrets Act. About three weeks later, not sure whether what he had said was true, he wrote to Pearson, asking for advice as to 'what line' he should take if further questions were asked by Shillinglaw or anyone else: 'Unless you advise me that I should make "no comment" on the grounds of the Official Secrets Act, I would be inclined to respond factually...that the division [at Porton] was asked to determine the dose of GB [Sarin] which reduced the serum cholinesterase to 50 per cent.'[179] He wanted to disassociate himself from the case by stressing that he 'had not been involved in planning the trial'.[180] On the whole, he felt that any media investigation into Maddison's death had the potential to cause trouble for Porton and the government, which is why he closed his letter by saying:

> I guess that public anxiety is not going to go away and I would not want to make matters worse by letting cats out of bags. My problem is to know which cats are bagged, so to speak. One could easily create a very shifty impression by refusing to admit to something already known to one's interlocutor.[181]

It would be interesting to know whether Pearson advised him to keep quiet about the Porton case. Whereas his reply to Adrian's letter, if he committed it to writing, has yet to be released, we have a good idea about Porton's institutional response: fearing growing media interest in the Maddison case, which could lead to probing questions by members of parliament or the MoD, Pearson commissioned Graydon Carter, Porton's historical consultant, to conduct an investigation into the existing documentary evidence which could shed light on to how and why Maddison had died.[182] This included accessing the original Coroner's inquest file from 1953 which, as it turned out, was no longer held by the Wiltshire County Council

Archive, but which had recently been retrieved by David Masters, the Coroner for Wiltshire and Swindon, who had likewise been approached by the Observer Film company. Carter's briefing document from March 1994 outlined in great detail the circumstances in which Maddison had met his death and the potential implications of the case for Porton's public image. Although he did not see any objections to the release of selected documents from the original Coroner's inquest file, since 'they contained little that is not now well known and in the public domain', and had also not uncovered any information which, if released, could compromise Britain's defensive capabilities, he had—quite rightly and perceptively—identified two 'residual sensitivities' which had the potential to create public relations and legal liability problems for Porton: a) the fact that volunteers had been 'assured that no danger was involved', and b) that there had been cause for concern only a few days before Maddison's death, i.e. the Kelly incident, which 'had provided a warning that some dangers could readily arise'.[183] The two findings, taken together, raised serious issues of negligence and possible manslaughter as far as the Maddison case was concerned. While not much appeared to be known about the Kelly incident, there was, according to Carter, a chance that the official report about it, written by Cullumbine in May 1953, might be discovered in the Public Record Office, where it had been deposited. This is why Carter, in summing up his findings, was convinced that the 'Maddison fatality', as he called it, 'may still be capable of media exploitation'.[184] For the time being, though, this seemed to be little more than a slightly overambitious investigative journalist making inquiries—until the Maddison case was reopened in 2004.

Much of Britain's chemical warfare programme—the cause of Maddison's death—can be understood only in the context of the Cold War. Recently declassified material seems to suggest that in some cases Britain's national security interests overrode individual human rights and standards of research ethics. During the first ten to fifteen years of the twenty-first century, a similar picture has emerged for US human radiation experiments.[185] The Cold War was, above all, a period of substantial rearmament, arms development, and weapons testing. As the world began to learn the destructive potential of nuclear weapon systems, chemical warfare agents were seen as 'outmoded' and generally ineffective for military use, yet the Second World War had made the British authorities acutely aware that chemical weapons could cause substantial damage and panic among the civilian population.

Britain's threat of retaliation may have prevented Nazi Germany from using chemical weapons. The scale of the German chemical warfare programme became apparent only after the interrogation of German scientists and the discovery of chemical weapon stockpiles. Research to explore the full potentialities of nerve agents in the 1950s and 1960s was not only influenced by the perceived threat that the Soviet Union might use these weapons, but also by the experience of the Second World War. The war had changed the degree of risk scientists were willing to tolerate when conducting experiments on humans, and existing safety precautions, authorized to apply primarily if not exclusively to mustard gas, had not been updated. The Cold War and its perceived threat of mutual destruction provided Porton and other Allied research facilities with the strategic and moral justification for the testing of radiological, chemical, and biological substances on man.[186]

Porton's nerve agent experiments were unique in several respects. They were one of the largest nerve agent trials ever performed by far, involving more than 1,500 subjects.[187] The specific group that was exposed to Sarin, and to which Maddison belonged, included almost 400 subjects.[188] The Porton experiments were also unusual in the magnitude of the risks. An increasing number of subjects were exposed to an increasingly high dosage of the nerve agent Sarin, which was known by the principal investigators to be highly toxic and potentially lethal in minute concentrations.[189] Porton's investigators knew of the great risks involved in the exposure of human subjects to nerve agents.[190] They were also reminded of this fact by the adverse reactions some of the servicemen had to Sarin exposure prior to Maddison's death.[191] From the limited experimental data available, experts calculated in the 1950s that the statistical probability of such a fatality occurring was likely to be one in at least 200, although the frequency was deemed to be significantly less than this.[192] Clearly, the odds against such an event happening were very low indeed. Yet Porton's scientists appear to have carried out on Maddison and other subjects a series of dangerous experiments that demanded, given their nature, the application of the highest degree of safety measures and the most rigorous standards of research ethics known at the time. From the evidence it appears that Maddison's death was an accident waiting to happen, and that it resulted from an inadequate level of disclosure and an understatement of risks, despite the fact that there was widespread consensus that the principles of the Nuremberg Code should govern these types of experiments.

Limited Leverage

Throughout the 1950s, external pressure to make the Porton experimental programme more transparent and accountable increased considerably. Despite the government's permission for the resumption of tests with nerve agents, Britain's service departments were reluctant to assign human volunteers to Porton without additional assurances and medical safeguards. The Army stipulated that the limits laid down by the Adrian Committee should not be exceeded without the prior approval of the Army Council, and the Air Ministry wanted to know that the recommended dosages for inhalation and percutaneous tests would apply to 'all experimental conditions', irrespective of the temperature or duration of exposure of the subject, or whether or not he was engaging in physical exercise. Adrian, as chairman of the committee, was unable to give such a guarantee, since, as noted above, Porton had applied for permission to resume tests, despite his earlier assumption that Porton would not want to conduct experiments under 'conditions which might be expected to increase the toxic effect'.[193] The recommendation of the Adrian Committee applied only to the conditions in which nerve agent experiments had been performed at the time of Maddison's death. They did not sanction experiments where the external conditions 'varied considerably', a fact that did not escape the attention of senior officials in London. For the time being, Porton was restricted to conducting experiments only along the lines laid down by the Adrian Committee. Any plans to diverge from those conditions required prior approval of the Minister and the service departments.[194]

Military representatives also felt that civilians should be considered for Porton's chemical warfare tests. The public, they suggested, disliked the idea of using soldiers for toxic experiments and 'are not comforted by the assurance that the men are volunteers'. Porton's high command rejected this proposal, arguing that such a system was likely to attract 'all sorts of undesirables' and 'publicity seekers'.[195] Another inquiry by the War Office about the number of servicemen subjected to different types of tests, and the payments they received in return, revealed that from July 1950 to May 1954 a total of 2,945 soldiers took part in Porton's experiments.[196] On average, soldiers received 15 shillings per week. Payments were assessed on the 'degree of discomfort suffered and the nature of the test carried out': as a Porton official noted, it would be unfair to pay a man 'holding his hand in a bowl of salt solution for 20 minutes' the same amount as 'a man exposed unprotected to nerve gas'.[197] Whereas four mustard gas burns (two on each forearm) with subsequent treatment would earn soldiers 15 shillings, those exposed to multiple mustard gas burns, atropine injections with exercise, or nerve gas vapour (unprotected) would receive 20 shillings. The highest payments, 30 shillings, were received by servicemen involved in 'climatic atropine trials', which meant being subjected to prolonged periods of 'extreme desert or jungle climate', 'severe exercise' during exposure, continuous urine and sweat collection, 'eight rectal temperature[s]' readings and 'three respiratory tests' per day, 'accommodation in sick quarters', and atropine injections. Given the nature of the tests, soldiers were often subjected to 'severe stress', which necessitated 'their removal from the chamber', an indication of their level of suffering.[198] At a time of economic austerity, however, the War Office probe into Porton's work exposed divisions within the service departments about the method and level of payment for servicemen attending Porton that had been authorized by the Treasury in 1924. Whereas some Whitehall officials argued for greater transparency and equity in the system of payment, others feared that changes to the system might be too restrictive for Porton in offering sufficient inducements to encourage soldiers to volunteer, a view rejected by the War Office and the Air Ministry.[199] If anything, the debate highlighted the fact that Britain's military research with human subjects, propelled by Maddison's death into the public limelight, would in future be more closely monitored than ever before.

VX Testing

While the government sought to contain the political fallout from the Maddison 'fatality', scientists in Britain and the United States were engaged in the development of the next generation of even more toxic nerve gases, code-named 'V'- agents in reference to their 'venomous' nature.[200] At the end of 1952, researchers at the Imperial Chemical Industries (ICI) laboratories, and simultaneously at the international pharmaceutical company Sandoz Ltd, with its headquarters in Germany, discovered a series of organophosphorus compounds intended as potent insecticides but which caught the attention of chemical warfare scientists in Germany, the Soviet Union, Sweden, and Britain. These scientists established that ICI's new product, marketed as a clear, colourless liquid under the trade name 'Amiton', was highly toxic to humans.[201] Allied chemical warfare scientists had previously been reliant on data appropriated from Germany's nerve agent programme, yet now the data obtained from new compounds showed that these had excellent potential as warfare agents, with an initially estimated toxicity fifty times that of Sarin, a viscosity similar to motor oil, a slow rate of evaporation, and an ability to adhere persistently to different surfaces. When inhaled, V-agents were not dissimilar in their mode of action to G-agents, i.e. they were extremely toxic and fast acting in minute concentration, but their main difference—and therefore advantage from a military perspective—was the fact that a much smaller dosage absorbed through the skin could kill more quickly.[202]

Although Britain had begun moving out of its offensive chemical warfare programme in the mid 1950s, the V-agents reawakened military interest in establishing a limited chemical weapons capability with both new and lethal incapacitating agents. First developed in the chemical industry and then reported to the military laboratories, details of a British variant of the substance, known as 'VX', were passed to the United States for mass production, which began at the Newport Chemical Plant in Alabama in 1961 at a rate of approximately 10 tons per day.[203] Over the next decade, the United States produced an estimated 5,000 tons of VX. Porton's technical expertise on V-agents strengthened the British government's negotiating position vis-à-vis the United States over urgently needed nuclear weapons technology. Moreover, since experts had 'every reason to believe that the limit of toxicity and war-like effectiveness of chemical agents' had not yet been achieved, Britain set up a top-secret network in the pharmaceutical and insecticide industry to identify potential new warfare agents.[204] To sustain Britain's bargaining position, and develop effective defensive measures, the military scientists of Porton's Medical Division pressed for an extended programme of human experiments with V-agents (see Image 28). However, ongoing concerns over safety led to a protracted debate and major delays at ministerial level.

In January 1958, Porton proposed to assess the toxicity of V-agents on man by first conducting intravenous tests with Sarin and then, if the results justified it, intravenous injection experiments with V-agents. Ministerial approval for experiments with V-agents first needed to be obtained, however. This was a most complicated process requiring not only lengthy consultations by the SAC, the CDAB, the Biology Committee of the CDAB, and Porton's scientists, but the views of a reconvened and slightly reconstituted Adrian

Image 28. Porton's Medical Division, 19 June 1957

Source: IWM, Photographic Collection. © Imperial War Museums (L 2016).

Committee which had initially, in 1957, been asked to assess Porton's proposal for intravenous nerve agent tests.[205] Rather than authorizing the experiments, Britain's scientific establishment asked for additional reassurances that human subjects would be subjected to the 'most careful clinical examination' before undergoing any tests.

Porton's scientists, though, were reluctant to wait for official approval and went ahead, conducting self-experiments with V-agents, thus breaching the ban on self-testing issued in the wake of Maddison's death.[206] In January, two medical officers exposed their forearms to a microscopic droplet of radioactive VX weighing 50 μg, half the amount then considered to be lethal. The two men, it seems, had become the first humans ever to be involved in a V-agent trial in the Western world. The man in charge was William ('Bill') Ladell (see Image 29), an impatient, energetic researcher with a rather short temper who had succeeded Cullumbine as head of Porton's Medical Division.[207] Born in 1912, Ladell had had a privileged education, attending Aldenham School and later Sidney Sussex College in Cambridge. After a brief stint at Cape Town University and King's College Hospital,

Image 29. William ('Bill') Ladell with members of the Tripartite Conference
Source: IWM, Photographic Collection, no date. © Imperial War Museums (F. 794).
The man standing in the middle is William Ladell.

London, where he pursued his medical studies, he served for ten years as director of the Hot Climate Physiology Research Unit in Lagos, Nigeria, part of the Commonwealth Relations Office that was in existence between 1947 and 1966 to foster Britain's relations with its former colonies. In 1956, Ladell took up a position as assistant director (medical) at Porton with responsibility for advising Porton's director on human experiments.[208] His work soon revolved around the subject of anti-cholinesterase poisoning and different means of treatment.[209] Two years into his job, it seems, Ladell had decided to conduct V-agent experiments and may have been one of the subjects; Bramwell, his colleague, was probably the other.[210] Neither of them apparently experienced any adverse reaction.

In defending the unauthorized test, Ladell argued that Porton staff believed that they were 'at liberty to use their own skin' while permission to use volunteers was sought, an innocent mistake, perhaps, but one which raised serious questions as to whether Porton was actually implementing ministerial instructions in line with established command and communication structures. Worse still, behind closed doors officials began to wonder whether some of Porton's scientists had turned into 'loose cannons', operating, as it were, outside the realm of ministerial control. Responding to such perceived insubordination, Dr Littler from the BJSM, who served the SAC and CDAB as executive officer, told the MoS in January 1958 in a confidential cipher cable that he was 'gravely disturbed by news of skin tests' at Porton: 'No further human tests must be carried out until policy cleared by Adrian Committee.'[211] Although the tests had apparently been 'done in good faith as being free of risk and within authorization', Porton was instructed to halt all experiments until further notice.[212] Over the next fifteen months, tests were strictly confined to pigs. As if this were not enough, there was additional embarrassment in 1962 when it turned out that servicemen had been exposed, again without authorization, to Cyclosarin. Ladell had little difficulty in retrospectively explaining these instances to a newly established medical review committee. The tests had apparently been based on a 'misinterpretation of a previous ruling', he noted.[213]

In total, Porton wanted authorization for three different types of experiments: intravenous injections with Sarin, intravenous injections with V-agents, and percutaneous experiments with V-agents. Although the number of volunteers needed was estimated to be in the 'low hundreds', the subject was believed to be a 'hot potato politically', requiring the utmost sensitivity, legal advice, and foresight.[214] Probing questions into existing safety procedures turned the process of obtaining permission for the tests into a long-drawn-out battle. Lord Evans, having been co-opted onto the Adrian Committee, wanted to know the reasons why this work was needed, the kind of precautions which would be taken, and the first-aid measures available in an emergency, questions which compelled Ladell to produce several memoranda in which he argued that nerve agent injections were one of the safest routes of exposure since diluted solutions could be given slowly and the amount scientifically controlled, and commenting: 'It all gets into the body.'[215] Since animals had previously been 'saved from more than a hundred lethal doses' of Sarin through the use of atropine injections and artificial respiration, it was thought that the same therapeutic measures would be equally applicable to humans. If all else failed, and the subject developed signs of nerve gas poisoning, Porton had instruments and equipment ready and waiting for the 'opening of the chest, defibrillating the heart, and giving cardiac massage for use in the unlikely event of cardiac arrest'.[216] In other words, this was yet another proposal to conduct experiments in an area of the 'scientific unknown', uncharted territory into which man had not yet travelled, and yet the researchers were confident in their ability to manage any potential emergency. Some, though, remained unconvinced. Whereas Ladell regarded intravenous injections of nerve agents as 'toxic experiments', he classified percutaneous nerve agent tests as 'non toxic', prompting a direct response from a seasoned official. In reference to Maddison's death, Eric E. Haddon, DCDRD, and Porton's director in the 1960s, remarked: 'After all, we thought those with GB [Sarin] were in this category until we burnt our fingers.'[217]

In March 1959, once the Adrian Committee had toured Porton to be assured that arrangements had been made 'for every foreseeable emergency', permission was given to conduct experiments with intravenous Sarin injections, and the situation was then to be reviewed to see whether 'to proceed with experiments with other agents'.[218] Since the lodging of the application, however, Porton's research agenda had shifted to skin penetration experiments with 'radio tagged materials' which, yet again, required official approval. Two months later, based on the experience of his V-agent self-experiment, Ladell duly requested permission for 'percutaneous experiments using radio labelled V agents on the intact skin of volunteers'.[219] Concerns over safety issues and legal liability for Porton's experiments made it increasingly difficult for scientists to respond to the latest developments in the chemical warfare field. At the same time, biological and chemical warfare experiments attracted the attention of Parliament, fuelling objections to further experiments with highly dangerous substances. Given the option, some Whitehall officials would have preferred to abandon Porton's programme of human experiments altogether.

Senior officials from the three service arms were particularly alarmed by proposals to conduct experiments with V-agents. Having paid Porton a 'private' visit in September 1959, the chair of the SAC came away a 'little surprised and worried' about the high levels of blood cholinesterase depression requiring clarification found among Porton's test subjects.[220] Meanwhile, the permanent secretary to the Air Ministry, J.F. Mayne, reiterated the concerns raised by the Director General of Medical Services (DGMS) in response to Porton's application for physiological tests. While the information given to soldiers in their units, and the briefing they received at Porton, was seen as 'adequate' for the tests that had hitherto been conducted, the DGMS anticipated the need for amendments in the recruitment notices if the scope of Porton's experiments were to be 'widened to include G. and V. agents'. Although he had no objection to skin tests, in which the risk was estimated to be 'slight', it was felt that there was a 'considerable risk of death if human subjects are used for nerve gas tests of either G. or V. agents by intravenous injections'.[221] Supported by the Admiralty and the War Office, the DGMS, as the Senior Medical Officer of the Air Ministry, felt unable to endorse the experiments or to advise the Minister to accept the new risks unless the entire matter were aired by the relevant experts. This, Mayne cautioned, would also have to include a discussion of how the services could truthfully present the risks to soldiers in the recruitment notices without detrimentally affecting Porton's research programme:

> If we tell them that the experiments could be lethal there would inevitably be a sharp fall off in numbers, and probably a degree of embarrassing publicity. On the other hand, if no more warning of the danger is given than at present, we may be quite rightly accused of deliberate misrepresentation in the future.[222]

A subsequent high-level meeting between top-ranking civil servants, the Chief Scientist, and a Porton representative was meant to assess whether the armed services were prepared to sign up to an expanded experimental programme. Sir Edward Playfair, permanent secretary to the War Office, describing the subject as an 'extremely emotive one in the public eye', was concerned about allegations that the test subjects 'might not all be genuine volunteers', and that some of the soldiers might have volunteered to go to Porton under duress, a situation which at service level had already been addressed by Major General Heyman, Commander-in-Chief, Southern Command, based at Fugglestone Farm near Wilton in Wiltshire, who told his staff that it was of 'utmost importance that all personnel provided [by the Army] are in all respects true volunteers, and that no form of compulsion is used in the provision of volunteers'.[223] Two years earlier, the Royal Navy had issued fleet orders advising volunteers that the tests at Porton were 'carefully planned' to minimize the physical effects of the experiments, and the Army told potential recruits that the research was 'most carefully designed and controlled so that there is no danger to the individual'. According to Defence Council Instructions issued in 1964, and amended in 1967, tests were 'carefully explained' to volunteers, who were under 'no obligation' to participate against their wishes, and could 'withdraw at any time'.[224] Surgeon Commander Burnett from Porton nonetheless tried to defuse any implied criticism about existing recruitment practices. Although all volunteers were 'genuine', he conceded that many 'had no idea of the nature of the physiological tests for which they were volunteering'. Upon arrival, according to Burnett, all soldiers were therefore informed of 'the exact nature of the tests to which they would be subjected and were given an opportunity of refusing to go on with them'.[225] This was a statement which, if not misleading, was not an accurate description of the state of affairs, as revealed in an internal note about recruitment practices: 'Experience has shown that detailed description tends to deter the servicemen and so now very little is said . . . The fewer details the better, but we must not be accused of "insulting the public's intelligence".'[226]

Invited to explain the 'real nature of the risk' in G- and V-agent experiments, Wansbrough-Jones, the Chief Scientist, who had long-established connections to Porton, highlighted two main sources of risk, the possibility of 'human error', which could not be discounted, and 'human idiosyncrasy', which had apparently led to the death of an RAF serviceman from 'a very small dose of gas'. Although Playfair was reassured, and considered the tests 'acceptable', others disagreed. Following a meeting of the permanent secretaries, Whitehall officials, reflecting the views of the service departments, expressed reservations. While they fully recognized the value of the tests for defence purposes, they felt that soldiers needed to know that they were 'not volunteering to go to Porton for just a general experiment'. In their view, a

description of each experiment had to be accompanied by an oral explanation of the known risks so that each serviceman would be 'left in no doubt
of the risk he is agreeing to run'.[227] The Navy's preferred option, rejected by
the War Office as counterproductive from a security and recruitment perspective, envisaged soldiers signing a certificate as evidence of their consent
and understanding of the experiment, suggesting 'no signature, no test'.[228]
On such an 'emotive subject', one official summed up the position, it would
be 'more difficult to convince Ministers about the processes of selecting and
briefing volunteers' than to persuade them about the need for such tests.[229]
In other words, the mandarins of the British establishment, who in their
presumed neutrality rarely appeared above the political parapet, proposed a
major overhaul of Porton's processes and procedures to facilitate the political
process. It was a call, however much couched in diplomatic language, for
major structural reform to prevent, as far as was possible, 'another fatality like
that in 1953', and it would inevitably lead either to the closure of Porton's
human experimental programme or to severe restrictions upon it.[230]

   Whereas Porton's proposals to change the mode of application of known
and hitherto untested nerve agents in human trials made civil servants distinctly nervous, military experts endorsed its programme of research after
the Joint Intelligence Committee (JIC) warned of an increased chemical
warfare threat from the Soviet Union, which was believed to be capable of
mass producing nerve agents, if these were not indeed already in their possession. Research on organophosphorus compounds in the Soviet Union
and among its 'satellites' apparently made the development of 'agents similar
to our V agents' highly likely.[231] British military establishments had been
considering downgrading the strategic significance of biological and chemical weapons in order to protect expenditure in other areas, so the alleged
threat from Soviet attacks with novel types of nerve agents offered a much-
needed reprieve for Porton's scientists, enabling them to pursue for the time
being their experimental activities.[232] Moreover, compared to the 'doubtful
predictability' of biological weapons which, if ever used by an enemy, would
'precipitate nuclear retaliation' with virtual certainty, experts from the
Defence Research Policy Committee (DRPC) envisaged that chemical
weapons might play a tactical role in a future conflict. The West was called
upon actively to pursue chemical weapons research to retaliate in kind if
necessary.[233]

   At the end of 1958, members of the Thirteenth Tripartite Conference,
held in Ottawa and Suffield in Canada, confirmed that there was an 'urgent

need to undertake experiments with human volunteers to determine the toxicity of V agents to man by penetration of the skin'.[234] Although animal tests had demonstrated the enormous level of toxicity of VX under field conditions, corresponding data to estimate the 'degree of hazard to man' had not yet been established. Britain and the United States agreed to 'execute, with the highest priority' a series of such tests to assess the 'military effectiveness' of these compounds.[235] Significant differences in military objectives and approach between the two countries, however, forced Britain to contemplate an independent programme of research with V-agents. The only data available for scientists stemmed from Porton's self-experiments on two volunteers and from intravenous VX tests with similar dosages on some thirty test subjects in the United States and Canada. Britain 'must have its own data', a senior official declared, if only to be in a position to cross-check what the Americans were doing, which, in any event, was going in a different direction: the United States was not only committed to the mass production of VX, and therefore less interested in studying variants of V-agents as a means of developing a defensive capability, but the inconsistent methodology it used to understand the toxicity of these compounds was seen to be irreconcilable with Britain's more systematic approach.[236] Ladell, reporting on a recent visit to Edgewood Arsenal, even went so far as to describe the ad-hoc American approach to VX testing as 'slap dash and dangerous', which Britain's chemical warfare experts would find 'unforgivable'.[237] The American trials were designed to establish the minimum dosage of VX that would cause significant casualties for offensive purposes. 'It follows from this', one official noted, 'that short of killing their subjects, the Americans will continue to try and produce visual proof of the efficacy of their chosen agent (VX)'.[238] Britain, on the other hand, wanted to study the 'marginal effects' and the 'speed and intensity of action' of the compounds in order to develop therapeutic and defensive measures.

Tests with V-agents in the United States started at the end of the 1950s, when Van M. Sim, director of human research at Edgewood Arsenal, performed two not fully authorized self-experiments with VX. His symptoms in the first experiment ranged from headache, sweating, and abdominal cramps to becoming confused and pale, appearing 'out of contact', salivating, and vomiting in the second; observers suggested he had just been 'too frightened to move'.[239] Questioned by the US Senate about the tests in the mid 1970s, he portrayed himself as a selfless scientist interested above all in the health and safety of his subjects, a man unable to 'administer a chemical

unless he ... knew the hazards of the compound himself'.[240] This was followed by an extended programme in which hundreds of research subjects,
most of them servicemen, received intravenous injections, inhaled nerve
agent vapour, drank contaminated water, or tested new therapeutic measures.
Researchers also studied the 'psychological and behavioural effects' on ninety-
three subjects who, having undergone percutaneous VX experiments, experienced anxiety attacks and attention deficits.[241] Accidental exposures were
commonplace, with over two hundred G-agent accidents and twenty cases
involving VX-like substances reported in the 1950s alone.[242]

Evidence about accidents and human experiments with V-agents in
Britain, on the other hand, is mostly circumstantial. According to Alan Care,
the lawyer representing many of the Porton veterans, a Mr J., who at the
time of writing resides in Blackpool, was exposed to various substances at
Porton, including, apparently, VX, which was dropped on his arm while he
sat in a 'gas chamber for some hours'. Mr J. also told the lawyer that nothing
was ever said about VX while he was at Porton.[243] Although investigated by
the Crown Prosecution Service (CPS), the case, as with so many others, was
never taken forward, nor was the VX-agent exposure ever mentioned in the
official documentation, perhaps because of lack of credible evidence.
A somewhat more plausible, but likewise unverifiable, incident with VX
happened to one of Porton's scientists, a Mr R., around the time of the
Cuban Missile Crisis. According to Mr R., who talked to Care on condition
of anonymity, he had accidentally dropped VX onto his own skin, and this
raised concerns at Porton about existing safety measures. Although Mr R.
today suffers from a 'severe disabling neurological condition', this has so far
not been attributed to his alleged exposure to VX.[244] Except, it seems, for
Ladell's self-experiments in the late 1950s and perhaps some minor accidental exposures which may have occurred, few if any subjects were ever
exposed to this most toxic of nerve agents in Britain, and yet the debate
about proposed V-agent experiments was all the more contested.

To persuade departments of the need for tests, Britain's chemical warfare
scientists, who were regularly briefed about developments, engaged in a
concerted lobbying campaign, refuting evidence of the adverse effects of
nerve agent experiments, downplaying any potential risks, and blurring the
boundaries between different types of low-risk and high-risk activities.[245]
'Dangerous signs' observed in Porton's inhalation experiments were apparently 'difficult to believe' since no incident had been reported. The continuation of tests was seen as proof of their alleged safety. Only in one case

Image 30. John Profumo at Porton Down, 1962
Source: IWM, Photographic Collection, John Profumo, Minister for War, Arriving at Porton,
18 May 1962. © Imperial War Museums (F 866/1).

since Maddison's death had a man momentarily lost consciousness, but
whether this had been caused by Sarin gas no one could really tell, experts
suggested.[246] For Jack Gaddum, chair of the Biology Committee, debating
whether V-agents were more or less dangerous than G-agents was futile
since it was 'never possible to be quite certain of anything in this life'. Since
the risk of adverse effects or accident was estimated to be 'negligible', he felt
that Porton's proposed V-agent experiments were broadly comparable with
the risks faced in everyday life: 'Some people are allergic to aspirin and have
been killed by small doses, but no one suggests that aspirin should, therefore,
be forbidden.'[247] Conflating matters further to bounce the armed services
into agreement, he alleged that the risks of not undertaking the tests were
much greater and would compromise national security in case of war, thus
missing the point that reluctance in granting permission originated at the
political level. One official, in an attempt to explain the tests in lay terms,
inquired whether the experiments were 'more or less dangerous than

crossing Whitehall or flying to America'.[248] 'Flying the Atlantic' in a commercial plane apparently involved greater risks than tests with V-agents, another Whitehall mandarin—somewhat disingenuously—replied.[249]

Progress in London remained slow. Whitehall officials dragged their feet on this delicate matter until the minister, having been fully consulted, was willing to take responsibility. Knowing full well the 'public dislike' of experiments on servicemen, John Profumo, the Minister for War—who later resigned over a political scandal in an affair with a call girl linked to an alleged spy—was having none of it (see Image 30). Although willing to authorize the tests in principle, provided the 'risk of untoward effects was very small', he was 'naturally perturbed' about the possibility 'of someone dying as a result of these experiments' since this could permanently jeopardize Porton's work—and his own position in government. In addition to requesting additional safety assurances, he instructed officials to explore the option of casting the 'net for volunteers a little more widely', thinking of civilians, as a way of spreading the risk to other departments if things went wrong. Britain's mandarins were tasked with nothing less than investigating the viability of highly toxic experiments on prisoners, civil servants, civilians, civil defence staff, and members of the Territorial Army, an assignment that, however questionable, was dispatched with stoic efficiency.

Following discussions with the Home Office, the use of prisoner populations, common practice in the United States 'for this sort of thing', was ruled out, not because of difficulties in obtaining a 'plentiful supply of prisoners'—quite the opposite was true—or on the grounds of ethics, but for reasons of secrecy, since prisoners were believed to be 'great gossips' and to attract unwanted media attention.[250] Then there was the option of using regional civil defence personnel, deemed to be reasonably 'discreet', but this, it was thought, could also lead to damaging publicity since the threat of chemical or biological warfare had been played down with the civil defence authorities.[251] Civil servants, on the other hand, were unlikely to be recruited in large numbers 'for the doubtful pleasure of being a guinea pig away from home'. Officials also considered members of the Territorial Army, but were unsure whether they would be looked upon as soldiers or civilians. Although possible in practice as far as 'pay, feeding and accommodation' was concerned, the use of civilians, whether sourced from Porton staff or externally, raised complicated legal issues in case of accident, ill-health, or death.[252] Prior reservations about the use of civilians had ranged from security issues, lack of discipline, and insufficient incentives to the question of how one

could exclude—in words that echoed those of Porton's high command—'publicity seekers and other undesirables'.[253] To make matters worse,
lawyers felt that for legal liability reasons the government would be well
advised to exclude servicemen from V-agent tests as well. What had begun
as an application for permission to perform an extended testing regime at
Porton had now turned in a bureaucratic nightmare.

   In an attempt to break the deadlock, a face-to-face meeting between the
Secretary of State and Ladell from Porton was set up in June 1961, in which
the latter was asked to make his case for V-agent experiments. Rather than
convincing the minister of existing safety precautions, however, Ladell felt
defensive about Porton's experimental programme, so much so that he
'warned' the War Office that the meeting might come to nothing.[254] He was
concerned that the minister, advised by his experts, might be 'shrewd
enough to ask the right questions', which could increase the pressure to
'clamp down' on Porton's inhalation experiments because of their lack of
safety.[255] Ladell also feared that Britain's failure to procure the relevant
experimental data could upset existing tripartite arrangements. For those
working in a highly secretive environment, undisturbed by external scrutiny, the sudden interest in their activities amounted to unwelcome interference. The Secretary of State, on the other hand, was unwilling to authorize
any tests unless officials managed to 'dilute soldier volunteers with civilians'.[256] For Haddon, as DCDRD, Porton appeared to be unable to grasp
either the political implications of its proposal or the fundamental differences between injection and inhalation tests, as he told the Chief Scientist
in strict confidence.[257] Injecting a fast-acting poison, which a nerve agent
effectively was, constituted a 'final and irrevocable step' with unforeseeable
consequences, and no degree of medical supervision could protect against
them, whereas inhalation tests, despite being less accurate and more difficult
to control, allowed for the early withdrawal of test subjects in the event of
adverse reactions. Ladell, by highlighting that he and his staff were 'already
offering themselves for experiments', was also missing the point as far as
widening the circle of volunteers was concerned. This was not a matter of
politics trying to pressure Porton into conducting more self-experiments;
on the contrary, the aim was to have a sophisticated safety regime in place
which would make the real and perceived risks of the experiments acceptable to other departments. This plan, however well conceived, collided with
the realities on the ground where scientists believed that their professional

integrity was being called into question. Science and politics had clearly locked horns.

Another contentious issue concerned the question of compensation for servicemen in the event of serious injury. Whitehall officials, like their colleagues in 1953, clearly understood that Section 10 of the Crown Proceedings Act 1947—which was 'already under fire'—would be applicable to bar a serviceman's claim for compensation only if the person responsible for the test which caused the injury, disability, or death was also a serviceman. In September 1961, a senior official remarked that 'Section 10 would not operate where a civilian was at fault, and in such a case there would be unrestricted access to the Courts by a serviceman claimant'.[258] It was this and other relevant evidence from legal advisers from the 1950s and 1960s which the UK government failed to disclose to the Porton Down veterans and their legal representatives in the 1990s. Any such disclosure would have undermined its policy—by then heavily entrenched—to bar Porton servicemen or their relatives, Maddison's family included, from claiming compensation on the basis that Section 10 of the Crown Proceedings Act 1947 applied—although in actual fact it did not apply, because almost all the scientists conducting the experiments at Porton throughout the Cold War had been civilians.

In early 1962, Whitehall was beginning to take stock. Several years of negotiations had failed to bring the desired result—there seemed to be insurmountable obstacles in the way of gaining future approval. 'What, then, is the risk in relation to new lethal agents?' asked the incoming DCDRD rhetorically, concluding in the double negative that in light of Britain's defensive capability there was 'not now a vital national security risk in not conducting such experiments'.[259] This was one of those exceedingly rare instances where national security considerations were used as an argument to *veto* experiments with toxic substances. After many moons of argument and counter-argument, which senior civil servants believed should at all costs be avoided if such questions ever arose again, Porton was forced to concede defeat in obtaining permission for V-agent tests with volunteers from the armed services. Much less welcome, but tolerated, experiments on Porton's own medical staff continued unabated until 1963.[260] The debate highlighted Porton's inability to communicate highly complex scientific knowledge effectively with policy makers and its failure to recognize the dominant role of health and safety issues within the wider political, medical, and public sphere that influenced the organization in the 1960s.

An Untimely Death

That the concerns raised by civil servants about Porton were not without foundation became apparent when in 1962 the untimely death of the Porton scientist Geoffrey Bacon at the MRE triggered a crisis of confidence that led to sweeping reforms of existing safety procedures, evidenced by a newly established Committee on the Safety of Human Experiments (COSHE), chaired by none other than Ladell himself.[261] Aged forty-four, a moderate pipe smoker, Bacon had for several years been experimenting with a virulent strain of *Pasteurella pestis*—now known as *Yersinia pestis*—to develop a more effective vaccine against plague when, at the end of July 1962, he suddenly began to feel unwell. His local doctor, suspecting a virus infection, advised nothing but bed rest. Three days later, as his condition deteriorated, Bacon was admitted to Odstock Hospital, Salisbury, where he died a day later, on 1 August 1962. Throughout the entire period, Dr H.M. Darlow, Porton's senior safety and hygiene officer remained blissfully unaware that a member of staff was dying of plague, and when he was eventually informed, it was too late. A Board of Inquiry, headed by Charles Dodds, President of the Royal College of Physicians (RCP) and chairman of the Advisory Committee on Scientific Research, and attended by Lord Evans, the Queen's physician, established that the cause of death had been pneumonic plague, the Black Death, which had decimated European populations in the middle ages, and that Bacon had probably become infected either in the laboratory or the animal house, yet its report was deemed too sensitive to be released into the public domain.[262] Since effective communication between the physician, local health authorities, and Porton had been close to non-existent, valuable time to save Bacon's life had been lost. In an attempt to contain the crisis, and prevent further infections, the government responded, as it had done before, in a high-handed manner with little regard for transparency. Wrapped in blankets, the body was immediately encased, and his house and hospital rooms were decontaminated; about thirty contacts, including his wife and two daughters, colleagues, and hospital staff, were given an antibiotic as a precautionary measure and placed under 'voluntary house quarantine'.[263] In the hope that they could 'get away with it', officials were advised to 'refrain from referring to the existence of any report', since this could attract media attention or lead to questions in Parliament. Yet there was no denying that the 'safety system' had failed miserably.[264]

Within days, amidst widespread media coverage, the 'accident' prompted a critical response from concerned citizens and local representatives who, for some time, had 'opposed the work being done at Porton', mainly because of concerns 'over security arrangements'.[265] The Medical Officer of Health for the Salisbury and Wilton rural district, Frederick Lishman, felt that the 'cloak of secrecy thrown over the activities of the Establishment was possibly excessive' and ought to be 'reduced to a minimum compatible with the maintenance of national security'.[266] His appeal to the War Office for more openness to protect the public was echoed by Wiltshire County Council, Salisbury City Council, and the relevant rural district councils, which submitted written representations requesting improvements to Porton safety procedures. This involved keeping local health authorities fully informed about all bacteria and viruses with which Porton was experimenting.[267] Worried by recent radio reports, Christine Robinson from Salisbury took it upon herself to recommend the creation of an isolation ward at Porton where suspected cases of highly infectious diseases could be treated, thus lessening the risk of infection for the general public. The proposal was promptly rejected on grounds of cost.[268] Pamela Edwards, the mother of two baby boys, on the other hand, told the War Office that it had no licence to 'develop these dreadful things' and germ warfare was clearly 'evil'.[269] The incident was rapidly turning into a public relations fiasco.

As fear of secondary plague infections spread among the locals, one Porton scientist told *The Daily Telegraph* that they would 'do everything humanly possible to ensure that this is a once-only incident'.[270] This involved the announcement, widely reported in the press, of a complete overhaul of existing occupational safety procedures, and mechanisms to facilitate communication between doctors and Porton officials.[271] Yet this was easier said than done. Whereas the process of reforming existing safety protocols raised complex 'constitutional and policy factors' requiring time, officials were anxious to address public concerns as soon as possible.[272] It was an acknowledgement that Porton needed to enhance its public image if it wanted to continue to exist in an age of greater public accountability, highlighting, for example, the defensive nature of the work that was directed at developing vaccines against biological weapons. Prime Minister Harold Macmillan, meanwhile, was told the incident would not require Porton's biological warfare research to be curtailed.[273] Four days later, however, Porton was back in the headlines when a pressurized steam sterilizer exploded, triggering a full-scale evacuation of parts of the MRE. As one inquiry was winding down, the next was about to begin.[274]

While Porton provided employment and job security for many in the vicinity, it had traditionally, and through the generations, been viewed with great suspicion. As in the case of Maddison, its cloud of secrecy turned into a ready-made canvas onto which local people projected their most deep-seated existential fears. The tragedy amplified these fears into a collective sense of unease that found vocal expression in media interviews, local council meetings, and detailed petitions to the authorities; here, however, they were read not as justified matters of concern for citizens, but as the machinations of some as yet unknown form of propaganda or communist 'agitation'.[275] At times, senior Whitehall officials showed a form of paranoia reminiscent of their counterparts in Moscow.

For David W. Henderson, the head of the MRE, who took the whole matter 'very much to heart', the fatality was nothing short of a catastrophe. He believed that Porton's image would forever be tarnished in the eyes of the public.[276] It was a stark reminder of how dangerous and unpredictable chemical and biological weapons research was. Yet, far more damaging was the fact that journalists were beginning to link the death with that of Maddison a decade earlier. At the end of August, as was expected, a Coroner's inquest attributed Bacon's death to 'misadventure', but only after the proceedings had been heavily influenced, if not manipulated, by the government.[277] A cover-up was not suspected, but there were certain irregularities during the inquest which were rather 'puzzling'. Having been briefed to avoid, if at all possible, disclosing MRE's safety regulations, or at least to 'forget' to bring them to the inquest, the Assistant Treasury Solicitor thought that it was 'extremely fortunate' for the War Office that the Coroner had not called Dr T.W. Burrows, Porton's senior principal scientific officer, as a key witness, since it was he who had failed to pass on vital information about Bacon's illness to Porton officials, especially to Dr Darlow, the safety and hygiene officer. It also seemed an 'extremely fortunate coincidence' that, just as the inquest was about to open, this witness, who would have had a 'rough time in cross-examination', had embarked on a lengthy trip to Canada.

Worst of all was the realization by the Treasury Solicitor that Porton's staff had acted negligently by not informing the safety and hygiene officer in good time about Bacon's illness, and that therefore, in a civil law suit, the family was likely to win any claims for compensation. Although some costs could be recovered from Bacon's physician, who was deemed equally liable, the government would 'have no alternative but to settle any claim that may be forthcoming on the best terms possible'.[278] Unlike in the Maddison case, the government compensated the family of the deceased out of court to avoid further publicity. Some, however, wanted to talk to the media, including Porton's safety officer, who told journalists that their precautions were 'as near 100 per cent cast-iron as we can devise'. Porton's motto had apparently always been 'You Cannot Be Too Careful'.[279] To those who had suffered from the psychological and physical effects of chemical and biological warfare trials, statements of this kind, highlighting the apparent safety 'precautions' of Britain's nonconventional weapons programme during the Cold War, must have sounded like empty rhetoric.

7
Ethics in the Open Air

Experimental Environments

As an island nation, Britain was widely believed to be particularly vulnerable to large-scale chemical and biological attacks. During the Cold War, research and development activities reached far beyond the identification and testing of ever more toxic chemical compounds in the secure confines of Porton's experimental landscape. With an estimated total of over 750 field trials carried out by Porton between 1946 and 1976, Britain was turned into a large-scale open-air laboratory; her people into an army of unconsenting participants.[1] The size of the trials and the organization, personnel, and costs involved were enormous, and their security classification was top secret. Scholars of popular medical history have nonetheless in the past advanced a rather one-dimensional image of the changing rationalization strategies under-pinning Porton's outdoor weapons trials. According to Porter, 'in a climate of World War and Cold War, it was easy for medical scientists to persuade themselves that their involvement in such un-Hippocratic activities would contribute to medical advance, national survival and the benefit of man-kind'.[2] To capture these 'experimental environments', we need instead to examine not only Britain's evolving defence policy in relation to biological warfare, but to venture into the realm of environmental and medical ethics in order to assess the implications of the tests for British society.[3] Field trials have to be contextualized within the collaborative efforts of Allied military scientists and their attempts to justify an ever-expanding testing programme, yet what was the scientific rationale for using some agents and simulants in and among the public and not others? Debates over the use of toxic compounds had to be resolved through negotiation and compromise. In overseeing the trials, politicians, civil servants, and military experts had to address complex health and safety issues which, in isolated cases, led to the blurring of boundaries between accidents and human experiments. At an institutional level, scientists working in great secrecy needed to become accustomed to a different type of inquiry, one which took place in a visible public space requiring camouflage and subterfuge. Field trials could become a spectacle taking place in a public space without an audience made up of members of the public; but they still required organization and management. Having ventured outside their known, enclosed laboratories, scientists went to great lengths to construct separate identities as a way of preserving the integrity of the work outside Porton's gates. Whereas anonymity was paramount, any use of civilian intermediaries, aimed at detaching Porton from the trials, involved communicating sensitive information which, if released into the public domain, could embarrass the government. Secrecy was maintained through imaginative—but also often clumsy—cover stories designed to appease public anxieties during the Cold War period.

In a climate in which the Chiefs of Staff considered downgrading the risks of major chemical and biological attacks, and civil defence and contingency planning reached new levels of preparedness in the mid to late 1950s, military scientists embarked on a concerted campaign to shape the direction of Britain's warfare policy by conceiving an almost infinite number of national security threats from military strikes by land, air, or sea or from sabotage of Britain's infrastructure. In the quest to formulate a congruence of aims and objectives between Britain's military needs and Porton's postwar plans, no potential warfare scenario, however far-fetched and improbable, was off-limits for Cold War theorists anticipating military Armageddon. In constructing the 'large area coverage' (LAC) principle in the 1950s, which at first was driven by weaponization objectives, and later defined by problems of early warning and defence resulting from the 'dispersal of bacteria from aircraft, guided missiles or sea-borne craft', rather than the identification of compounds on the ground, Porton scientists managed to successfully promote and legitimize continued investment in chemical and biological warfare research. By 1952, following the top-secret report by C.J.M. Aanensen, the head of Porton's meteorological section, on the 'possibility of travel of BW and CW agents across the United Kingdom', experts began to appreciate the 'startling new potential' of the LAC concept for offensive and defensive preparations. Five years later, the LAC concept had become firmly established as a key military theorem which underpinned large-scale open-air trials.[4] It was a period, as Balmer has argued, in which the 'threat had been perpetuated and so had the research programme'.[5] To ensure the rapid allocation of civilian respirators to those most affected by potential LAC attacks, and create a two-hour window to provide protection for at least 85 per cent of the population, research into new detection systems gained military priority. Field trials were seen as an integral part of giving scientists an accurate assessment of the destructive power of nonconventional weapons. Despite mounting political disquiet about rising expenditure, the government funded increased 'activity in this area'.[6]

Threat assessment focused on studying quantitative levels of dissemination and detection of chemical and biological agents in confined and unconfined spaces, in government buildings, unused tunnels, and railway systems. In some cases, potentially harmful chemicals were freely dispersed over vast stretches of open British countryside, over villages, towns, and cities; in others, highly infectious pathogens were released out at sea and on remote islands. For Porton's scientists, these were land- and seascapes without ethical oversight, in which civil and animal rights ranked second to national security considerations, and in which the public was rarely, if ever, informed about the nature and risks involved. Environmental ethics, whether grounded in the individualist deontological or collectivist tradition, almost never played a part in the decision-making, nor was there a systematic assessment of how the trials might affect the sustainability of the ecosystems and local communities concerned.[7] As a consequence of the need to devise means and methods aimed at protecting the British realm from external threats, and to obtain much-needed scientific data, the landscapes in which people walked, lived, and travelled were disrupted. The environment was seen as a resource to satisfy military needs, with no or little value in or of itself.[8]

In Britain, biological warfare was strongly associated with the work of Paul G. Fildes and a new generation of microbiologists, biochemists, and bacterial geneticists from the Biology Department, Porton, which was established during the Second World War (see Image 31), and which became known as the MRE during the Cold War.[9] From its inception, the work was deeply embedded in inter-Allied cooperation and knowledge exchange. In 1942, for instance, Sir Henry Dale, the head of the MRC, attended a top-secret meeting of Canadian biodefence scientists to endorse plans to create a system of 'decentralized laboratories', not unlike in Britain, through contracts with private firms and universities.[10] According to Avery, there is strong evidence of a 'direct relationship' between efforts to develop Allied chemical warfare capabilities during the Second World War and the

Image 31. Senior staff of the Biology Department, Porton Down, October 1943
Source: IWM, Photographic Collection. © Imperial War Museums (HU 102392).

Front (left to right): Dr G.P. Gladstone, Lt W.B. Sarles USN MC, Dr D.W.W. Henderson, Dr Paul
Fildes, Dr J.F.S. Stone, Lt Col A. Nimmo Smith, and Lord Stamp. Back (left to right): Dr D. Herbert,
G.M. Hills (in Home Guard uniform), Lt J.M. Barnes RAMC, Lt J.M. Ledingham RAMC, Dr D.D.
Woods, Lt (jg) C. Howe USN MC, Ensign H.N. Carlisle USN MC, and Lt C.E. Venzke USA VC.

emergence of an active biological weapons programme in Britain, the
United States, and Canada.[11]

Born in London in 1882 into the family of Sir Luke Fildes, a prominent
Victorian artist, Paul G. Fildes researched a new class of synthetic anti-
bacterial compounds before being co-opted, through his links to Edward
Mellanby, the Secretary of the MRC, onto Lord Hankey's committee examining the threat from biological weapons after the outbreak of the Second
World War.[12] Fildes agreed to conduct the necessary experiments, provided
he was given a free hand in his research activities. Although the MRC itself
did not want to be associated with this line of work, it agreed to continue
to pay the salaries of Fildes and his team while they were stationed at Porton.
Among those recruited to his team were Donald Devereux Woods, who
had jointly pioneered with Fildes the idea of chemotherapy, G.P. Gladstone,
L. Packman, Denis Herbert from Cambridge, G.M. Hills from Sheffield,

Norman H. Rydon, who worked as professor of chemistry at Exeter university from 1957 to 1977, Trevor Charles Stamp, subsequently professor of microbiology at the Hammersmith Hospitals' Postgraduate Medical School, and David W. Henderson, who took over as Chief Superintendent of the MRE after the war. In 1964, Henderson was succeeded by Charles E. Gordon Smith who, at the age of only forty, was already a renowned special-ist in the fields of bacteriology, virology, and tropical medicine. As a member of the Colonial Medical Service, Gordon Smith had travelled to Malacca and Kuala Lumpur before being appointed Reader in Virology at the LSHTM.[13] Upon realizing that the future of the MRE was no longer secure in the early 1970s, he returned to civilian science as Dean of the LSHTM and helped up-and-coming MRE scientists to secure temporary teaching positions until biological warfare research offered renewed career prospects.[14]

Experts from the RAMC and the armed services departments joined Fildes and Henderson's rapidly expanding group of biological warfare sci-entists, among them Robert Leishman, Surgeon Lieutenant Commander with the Royal Navy and Royal Marines, who was seconded to Porton to develop biological defence measures during the war.[15] Modelled on CDEE's organizational set-up, the MRE recruited expert scientists from civilian and military backgrounds in equal measure. In 1949, Brigadier Harry T. Findlay, director of pathology of the Middle East Land Forces and former head of the UK's Emergency Vaccine Laboratory, took over as deputy to the Chief Superintendent at the MRE before pursuing a post-retirement career at the PHLS.[16] There were also those whose career paths led from the RAMC, via research and industry, to Porton; the virologist Frank William Sheffield, for example, migrated from the RAMC to work at the Wellcome laboratories under the leadership of John Beale before moving to the MRC and then to MRE Porton with responsibility for vaccine production for the armed forces.[17] Others were persuaded to move sideways from CDEE to MRE, and vice versa, or joined the MRE after retiring from their research or teaching positions; among these was Wilson Smith, a pioneer in the field of virology, veteran of the Great War and former ship's surgeon who in the early 1930s had jointly isolated the virus of epidemic influenza.[18] At University College Hospital, and later at the MRE, he had remained com-mitted to studying various viruses and to training the next generation of expert virologists. Together, researchers advanced the military application of bacteriological science to a level where leading military officials and politicians could be persuaded to invest enormous resources in the field of biodefence and offensive weaponry on both sides of the Atlantic. Throughout the Cold War, Porton certainly offered a viable career path for many up-and-coming biological warfare scientists and their support staff, who enjoyed state-of-the art research and recreational facilities, including a swimming pool, which were part of the newly established MRE building complex (see Image 32).

Large-scale dissemination trials with biological agents and simulants were likewise carried out in and by the United States. Biological weapons research and development, overseen by the Assistant Secretary of Defence (R&D) since 1953, fell into the domain of the Chemical Corps with its decentralized and at times overlapping system of military facilities in Maryland, Arkansas, Utah, and Alabama.[19] Testing sites included coastal areas of Hawaii and California, over the Pacific Ocean, Marshall Islands, Alaska, the Panama Canal, and Florida. Designed at first to develop pathogens with maximum lethality, the US biological weapons programme shifted its attention to 'anti-personnel, anti-animal, and anti-plant agents' to disrupt or destroy the natural environment. For the US military, biological warfare agents had multiple applications: whereas botulinum toxin was classed as

Image 32. MRE swimming pool
Source: University of Sussex, SHIP File, H6.4, Morton Papers, MRE Swimming Pool (no date).

the agent of choice to 'kill many people', *Bacterium tularense* could cause 'protracted disability'. Anthrax spores could produce anthrax disease and prolonged ground contamination; plague bacteria were able to spread deadly epidemics. In addition to the testing of plant pathogens, wheat blight, rusts, defoliants, and soil and water inhibitors, some scientists conducted tests with 'feather bombs' to study crop-destroying agents; others examined the use of mosquitoes, fleas, or ticks as potential carriers of disease. Despite the limitations imposed by the Geneva Protocol, which the United States intended to honour even though they had not ratified it, for Cold War theorists the possibilities for causing mayhem and misery without destroying enemy buildings seemed endless. By 1952, at the height of the Korean War, the Chemical Corps had commissioned 271 projects, many of which involved experiments on animal and human subjects. For twenty years, between 1953 and 1973, scientists conducted hundreds of human trials in Operation Whitecoat at Dugway Proving Ground and Fort Detrick, and among Ohio prison inmates who were exposed to bacterial pathogens: these trials were to assess the effectiveness of biological weapons. Whether in Operation Large Area Coverage of the late 1950s, or 'Project 112' (the large-scale use of aerosols to disseminate chemical and biological agents to cause 'controlled temporary incapacitation' (CTI) from the early 1960s), or Operation SHAD (Shipboard Hazard and Defense) of the 1960s and 1970s (performed to improve naval defence measures against nonconventional weapon attacks), an unsuspecting and unconsenting public often found itself in the midst of major land and sea trials.[20]

Elsewhere in the United States, selected sites provided opportunities for the testing of new weapons technologies, equipment, and materials, and helped in the construction of powerful images for propaganda purposes. In 'Survival City', known as 'Doom Town', two detached Colonial family homes on the Nevada Test Site built with the support of the American Association of Architects were aimed at shoring up popular support for civil contingency measures at the height of the Cold War.[21] Complete with clothed mannequins, food, and period furniture, the houses were modelled on earlier replicas that the military had erected at Dugway Proving Ground to assess the effectiveness of incendiary bombs destined to be dropped on German and Japanese cities during the war. As the nuclear bomb went off, television crews broadcast into American households images of wastelands destroyed by the blast, a national spectacle designed to divert public attention away from top-secret atmospheric trials with atomic, chemical, and biological weapons. Although the bomb on show was anything but a realistic demonstration of thermonuclear destruction, many described it as a 'gripping testimony to the power of atomic weapons'.[22] Revelations and public protests about dangerous radioactive fallout from the tests first shifted experiments underground in the 1960s, and all nuclear tests were subsequently halted. It was a period in which military testing of nuclear, chemical, and biological weapons and training in using them resulted in environmental harm which, though not necessarily intended, was seen as acceptable collateral damage to ensure military preparedness during the Cold War. Environmental warfare—in other words, the systematic destruction of the ecosystem through chemical agents and pesticides, the contamination of rivers, water reservoirs, and agricultural land, or the wanton killing of animals, livestock, and wildlife—formed part of Allied national defence strategies.[23]

Despite being caught between a peculiar affinity for the land and an almost insatiable materialism, large sections of British society have traditionally enjoyed a close relationship with their environment. Reflected in postwar abstract sculptures by artists such as Barbara Hepworth and Henry Moore—who captured in his sketches the stoical spirit of Londoners sheltering from German air raids in the Underground—or in evocative compositions by artists and poets, images of landscapes instilled in the people of Britain a sense of belonging and identity, a well-constructed national heritage many felt ought to be protected long before any 'green' political movement was on the horizon. As early as the 1930s, writers had raised environmental concerns about military testing sites, where 'poison gas tests' and bombing exercises were producing a 'park of death'.[24] Later, in the 1950s and 1960s, Alfred Wainwright, fell-walker and prolific writer of carefully crafted guidebooks, contributed to a growing public awareness about the environmental risks associated with modern society. Large-scale environmental destruction in the Western hemisphere could no longer be ignored. In the United States, chemical industries had polluted lakes and rivers with toxic waste to such an extent that fish could no longer survive, prompting public protests that led the federal government to promulgate environmental protection laws.[25] In Britain, the dumping of nerve agents in the North Sea, reports about ground contamination, and open-air field trials were far from reassuring for a public longing for postwar stability and security. For many, cases of environmental destruction amounted to an attack on the 'public consciousness' for which only the government was to blame.

Despite high levels of secrecy, certain environmental 'experiments' turned into a long-term public relations fiasco for the UK government. During the Second World War, biological warfare trials had been carried out on Gruinard Island (off the north-west coast of Scotland) with anthrax spores which, in addition to killing all sheep, contaminated the island to such an extent—in some areas the level was as high as 45,000 spores per gram of soil—that it was declared unsafe for humans until the late 1980s.[26] Crofters and other members of this close-knit community living on the mainland on the West coast of Scotland may not have known the exact nature of the tests being performed, yet after a series of detonations it was obvious that something untoward was afoot. Most believed it to be 'military exercises'. A local shepherd observing the activities of Porton scientists from afar recalled seeing 'rows of carcasses on the ground', some of which were found washed up on the shore, causing anthrax outbreaks among the resident animal population for which the Admiralty duly paid compensation.[27] The first press reports about Britain's secret wartime research on the island appeared in 1946, yet the work was believed to belong to the field of chemical rather than biological warfare.[28] For Porton the Gruinard field trials set an unwelcome precedent in that, despite the island's remote location, they highlighted long-term hazards that increased public and political sensibilities, especially after officials admitted in 1966 that the 'residual hazard' on the island was linked to anthrax spores.

At a time when Britain was engaged in extensive postwar dumping of chemical stockpiles in the North Sea, media reports about air pollution and land contamination resulting from the storage, incineration, and destruction of tens of thousands of tons of wartime chemical shells raised concerns about public health and safety (see Image 33).[29] Tasked with carrying out any large-scale retaliatory aerial strikes with toxic agents that were ordered, the RAF had encountered major challenges in storing these types of weapons and compounds from the outset, for there were few places left at its disposal after almost all underground storage facilities had been found to show serious structural weaknesses. In outdoor depots such as the one on Bowes Moor in County Durham tons of thin-cased mustard gas weapons were frequently damaged by roaming sheep or natural decay, which caused the containers to leak and the sheep to die. In addition to Britain's postwar legacy of 1,200,000 tons of 'surplus ammunition' and 250,000 tons of 'bombs filled with either high explosives or chemical warfare agents', the Allies had to decommission tens of thousands of tons

Image 33. Mustard gas destruction, 1955
Source: IWM, Photographic Collection, Destruction of Mustard by Burning, 6 March 1955.
© Imperial War Museums (F 566/4).

of German chemical weapons. As Smith and others have shown for the
United States and Canada, the 'health legacy of war was long lasting and
extended to the environment'.[30]

Although tests had shown that stocks of mustard gas could be destroyed
by mixing them with incendiary bombs, the method was deemed to be too
time-consuming.[31] By May 1946, over 57,000 tons of chemical weapons had
simply been thrown overboard into the Irish Sea, and the remainder loaded
onto merchant ships and then scuttled in the deep sea off the Skagerrak,
polluting Norwegian waters for years to come. There was additional negative
publicity when experts raised the alarm about the large-scale incineration
of over 9,000 mustard gas spraying tanks, which covered the area around
Melchbourne Park in Bedfordshire in black smoke for eight months, shock-
ing local residents when their net curtains first became discoloured and
then disintegrated in front of their eyes. Scientists drafted in from Porton
helped in the total destruction of the remaining stockpile at Randle: this
had been transformed from a wartime poison gas factory into a postwar

incineration plant, thus securing additional revenues for ICI, a company now partly owned by the AkzoNobel Corporation, which prides itself on 'managing sustainability' as a way of opening up 'major business opportunities' in a global market. In the past, insatiable human greed drove the engines of industrialism, colonialism, and capitalist expansion across the globe, leaving in their wake politically corrupt regimes under which populations routinely suffered from poverty, malnutrition, and infectious diseases. Green credentials have since turned into a convenient, albeit cynical, smokescreen behind which so-called 'investors' and 'hedgefunds' seek to multiply their fortunes outside any governmental or regulatory framework.[32] Anyone inquiring about the impact of sustainable policies, whether corporate-funded or government-sanctioned, may question the value of environmental policy if it is little more than propaganda for a healthier, wealthier visionary future. The decommissioning activities at Melchbourne Park mentioned above are a case in point. Since the incineration pits had been constructed out of inverted Nissen huts, which of course were completely unsuitable for the safe destruction of the mustard gas spraying tanks, the ground around the area became so heavily contaminated that it was declared unsafe until the late 1980s. Today the site remains fenced off with signs warning the public to keep off the 'poison gas area'.[33] Owned by the MoD, it will be retained by the state in perpetuity.

The decommissioning of all forward filling depots (FFDs) in the 1950s, code-named Operation Pepperpot, led to unexpected public health risks after an explosion in one of the plants at the former Lord's Bridge Air Ammunition Park vaporized over twenty tons of mustard gas in 1955.[34] As the toxic cloud of smoke drifted across the countryside and towards Cambridge, exposed local residents were warned by loudspeaker of possible health risks and advised to undergo medical check-ups, spreading fear across an already weary population affected by postwar austerity. Three years later, as ground contamination reached worrying levels, officials decided to treat the area with bleach paste before selling it to Cambridge University, yet local concerns about ground and water contamination persisted. By the time the filling depots were reopened in 1985 in operation 'Coleman Keg', in reference to the brand of household mustard, experts discovered over 120 damaged containers of mustard gas buried beneath tons of waste, an environmental time-bomb that had been leaking toxic chemicals into the soil for thirty years. Still, in the 1950s and 1960s, in a climate of Cold War *Angst*, localized adverse publicity about chemical accidents or state-sponsored environmental pollution was no obstacle to the government authorizing large-scale sea, air, and land dispersion trials at enormous cost to the taxpayer.

Sea Trials

Collaboration in chemical and biological weapons research between Britain and the United States was particularly close in the 1950s, when visiting military scientists engaged in the sharing of compounds, equipment, and expertise. As Cold War tensions increased, political support for nonconventional weapons remained strong. In July 1953, Sandys, the Minister of Supply, made it plain that Britain needed to be in a position to not only protect civilians, service staff, livestock, and crops against a biological warfare attack, but to 'retaliate offensively and quickly' with such weapons in war.[35] Although the government endorsed Sandys' policy directive, which stipulated that the Allies had to be able to retaliate with chemical and biological weapons 'if this were to their advantage', the rising costs involved in maintaining Britain's capability in this field had not fully been appreciated.[36] In later years, under pressure to drastically reduce expenditure after the relative importance of chemical and biological warfare had been called into question by nuclear weapons, the British government sought even closer cooperation, in which American scientists were invited on joint research programmes in return for financial assistance for Porton.[37] Under threat from closure, military scientists also hoped to exploit alternative funding streams by collaborating with the Colonial Microbiological Institute in Trinidad in the Caribbean, and with other Whitehall departments where research needs could be identified.[38]

Starting in the late 1940s, Britain and her Allies performed five major military operations out at sea to study the warfare capability and behaviour of highly infectious bacterial pathogens, including *Bacillus anthracis* and *Pasteurella pestis*, and of simulants and viral agents.[39] Research was also conducted with *Serratia marcescens*, a bacterial agent which, although thought at the time to be harmless, can cause disease in patients with immunodeficiency. When in 1950 the US authorities released the agent from a ship near the Golden Gate Bridge, San Francisco encountered a number of cases of *S. marcescens* disease and one fatality, leading experts to conclude that the agent was no longer 'a safe biological warfare simulant'.[40] In charge of conceiving many of Britain's sea trials was John D. Morton from MRE Porton, who kept detailed diaries and photographic records of large-scale biological warfare experiments. His material provides rare insight into both the everyday culture and conduct of warfare scientists whilst at work in far-away places such as the Bahamas.[41]

In 1948–1949, in an operation code-named Harness, Porton scientists and their American and Canadian colleagues conducted a total of twenty-two biological weapons trials off the coasts of Antigua and St Kitts with the support of two modified Royal Navy ships, HMS *Narvik* and HMS *Ben Lomond*, to test the effectiveness of spraying and explosive devices for offensive purposes (see Image 34). Some of the tests involved the use of live pathogens such as anthrax and plague.[42] In addition to employing almost 500 scientists, naval officers, and support staff, the operation required considerable expenditure, organization, and security arrangements, for example through an elaborate cover story alluding—in an 'emergency press release'—to chemical weapons and gas-mask tests, with which the public was 'somewhat bored'; trials of this kind were thought to have 'little scare news value'.[43] Since the tests took place on two colonial outposts in the West Indies, thousands of miles away from Britain, few objections were raised to exposing sheep, monkeys, and guinea pigs to bacterial pathogens, two of which, *Bacillus anthracis*, responsible for causing anthrax acute disease, and *Bacillus subtilis*, a disease-producing agent in immuno-deficient patients, which was used as a simulant, were cultured at Porton. Experts from the United States, meanwhile, provided logistical support, a suitable land base, code-named 'Archie's Place', and bombs and bacterial agents to study the travel of infectious clouds a couple of miles offshore. They were, however, shocked to discover that poor planning and communication, malfunctioning equipment, and unreliable data collection led to no or unsatisfactory results in over half the trials, and were greatly concerned about substandard safety protocols, which resulted in a 'considerable risk to personnel'.[44]

Although Porton's assessment of Operation Harness was more positive, it was acknowledged that as a tripartite collaborative experiment it had been too complex and unsafe because of the large number of people involved. Organizational problems aside, the trials highlighted difficulties in balancing the need for secrecy with upholding health and safety. Without elaborate cover stories, the operation constantly risked becoming public knowledge, for example when escaping monkeys prompted questions about animal welfare from anti-vivisectionists and Members of Parliament. Whereas the issue

Image 34. HMS *Ben Lomond*, 1950s
Source: University of Sussex, SHIP File, H6.4, Morton Papers, HMS *Ben Lomond*, 1950s.

of staff contracting venereal diseases on the trip was of little concern, other than as a result of the anticipated 'loss of manpower', those who had become infected with bacteria were placed in isolation wards or flown out to Camp Detrick in Maryland. Even the local communities had to be kept in the dark, as when sharks attacked the dinghies holding the experimental animals, mainly sheep, Rhesus monkeys, and guinea pigs, or when the testing area was moved from the 'safety of the open sea' to an area frequented by small fishing vessels whose crews were in ignorance of the trials. As the operation proceeded under a cloud of secrecy, it generated ever more secrecy to preserve the secrecy of its constituent parts, thus adding pressures to subordinate military medical and environmental ethics to Allied security considerations.

In the early 1950s, in response to an expanded US biological weapons programme, Porton initiated a series of short- and long-range sea trials near the Isle of Lewis (Outer Hebrides) in Operation Cauldron—in reference to the successful wartime commando raid—and Operation Hesperus.[45] Cauldron required 158 members of staff, and Hesperus employed a total of

210 civilian scientists and personnel. Both operations were also visited by dozens of senior scientists and military officials from the United States and Britain who may have been attracted by the thought of a short trip to the west coast of Scotland.[46] Porton's choice of *Pasteurella pestis* as one of the agents to be used turned out to be controversial, however. While some believed that the use of such a lethal agent breached official policy, members of the influential Biological Research Advisory Board (BRAB) saw it as an integral part of Britain's biological armoury that had to be studied for 'political and defensive purposes'.[47]

Following negotiations between the Admiralty and the Scottish Fisheries Office to limit the impact of the operation on the local fishing business, and resolve issues of safety and liability, the Admiralty agreed to issue vessels with sufficient warning notices and 'accept responsibility for any accident arising in the trial area'.[48] Trial preparations involved alterations to the superstructures of the deck of HMS *Ben Lomond*, termed the 'Germ Ship' by Kentish dockyard workers who, despite security precautions, knew of Britain's ongoing warfare trials.[49] Given their sensitivity, London was determined to maintain the utmost secrecy for fear that any revelations about Britain's biological weapons programme could inflame tensions in South East Asia. During the Korean War, the Western Allies accelerated research and development into biological and chemical weapons. North Korea and China alleged that the United States was using biological weapons, and US military officials used this as a pretext to increase preparations for nonconventional warfare. This propaganda war hinted at an apparent requirement that the Allies develop an extended weapons programme so that they could retaliate if necessary. While senior figures from the realms of politics, academia, and religion, including Hewlett Johnson, the 'Red' Dean of Canterbury Cathedral, publicly sided with the North Koreans in the 'germ warfare controversy'—which happened against a backdrop of greater state surveillance of scientists and civil servants suspected of communist sympathies, particularly in the United States and Canada—the allegations about the Allies' development of an extended weapons programme received added credibility thanks to the involvement of left-wing Cambridge sinologist and historian of science Joseph Needham.[50] Asked to investigate the allegations on behalf of the World Peace Council, which had recently awarded the international peace prize to Pablo Picasso and Pablo Neruda, and in the hope of receiving access to rare Chinese books in return, Needham and a small group of pro-communist scientists of the International Scientific

Commission supported the allegations on the basis of evidence which, in at least some instances, turned out to have been fabricated. Needham had a belief in 'Christian socialism' and a political *naïveté* to match that of his colleague J.B.S. Haldane, who believed in the 'humane nature' of chemical warfare, and he had in effect become a pawn in the game of Cold War politics, yet the damage to Britain's top secret research activities was done. In such a charged atmosphere, officials saw the funeral of George VI in February 1952, and Elizabeth II's accession to the throne, scheduled for June 1953, as ideal events to divert public attention away from biological weapons trials. The last thing Whitehall needed was extensive media coverage of a biological warfare accident.[51]

Trials to study the warfare potential of 'virulent plague' and other compounds on the Isle of Lewis in September 1952 were hampered not only by adverse weather conditions, but by an unforeseen incident in which the crew of the trawler *Carella*, eighteen men strong, strayed into a 'toxic cloud' of plague bacteria on the last day of Operation Cauldron.[52] Rather than informing the crew of the grave danger they were in, and treating them with streptomycin as a prophylaxis before placing them under strict medical surveillance, it was decided at a hastily convened emergency meeting in London, attended by Sandys in his capacity as Minister of Supply, Henderson from Porton, and representatives of the Admiralty, to do none of the above but to shadow the trawler on its planned voyage to Icelandic fishing grounds until the incubation period of plague had expired, thus cynically turning what had been an unfortunate accident into an 'experiment of opportunity'.[53] While the crew remained unaware, Whitehall went into overdrive. As a precautionary measure against an outbreak of pneumonic plague, the Admiralty increased stocks of streptomycin along the Scottish coastline and in Iceland, listened in to *Carella*'s radio communication for any signs of a distress call, and swore the medical officer of the ship shadowing the trawler to complete secrecy about the accident: 'The fact that this exposure may have occurred is not at present known to the crew and is on no account to be revealed to them in any casual contact. Should you be called to a case which you suspect [you] ought to diagnose as Plague, it should be referred to as pneumonia.'[54] In an attempt to justify instructions that breached health and safety protocols, if not military medical ethics generally, especially where those responsible for shadowing the trawler were asked to abstain from measures to protect the lives of the crew, the Admiralty made it plain that 'grave political requirements are more important than what may seem best from a strictly medical point of view for individuals'.[55] In cases such as this, the argument ran, national security trumped individual human rights and medical morality. To ensure no traces of the incident remained, except for a single file held by the Admiralty, all involved were told to destroy 'by fire' their top-secret communication, as if it had never taken place.

Scientifically unsatisfactory and politically sensitive, given the need for a concerted cover-up in the wake of the *Carella* incident, the Lewis trials prompted a search, approved by Prime Minister Churchill, for a better and more inconspicuous site in the Bahamas, another former British Crown colony with aspirations to political independence at the time.[56] Following protests by the Cuban government against further trials in the Bahamas, questions were asked as to why the trials could not be conducted on military grounds in the United States or Canada. For British officials the answer was simple: whereas field trials with highly infectious agents were 'absolutely prohibited' in both countries, it was not only possible but perfectly acceptable, ethically and politically, to conduct such tests in the Bahamas 'without restrictions'.[57] For them, it was the best place they 'could find on the surface of the globe'.[58]

In Operation Ozone and Operation Negation, Porton's scientists tested, for the first time, the viral agent Venezuelan Equine Encephalitis (VEE)—a highly infectious, though rarely lethal disease for equine species and humans, causing headaches, high fevers, and weeks of fatigue—and the vaccina virus as a simulant for smallpox.[59] With a mortality rate of below 1 per cent, experts had first contemplated using the VEE virus as a 'nonlethal weapon' in Operation Hesperus but were concerned about exposing British livestock to the potential risk of infection, a risk which they were willing to take on the Bahamas where the political fallout from an epizootic—a sharp rise in the incidence rate of a disease in the general animal population—was thought to be more manageable. Debates about the testing of live viruses for offensive purposes, including the variola virus, the causal agent of smallpox, or the incapacitating influenza, typhus, and Q fever viruses, coincided with an expansion of research in the field of virology which led to the creation of a new virology unit at the MRE and a flourish of activity at the nearby CCRU.

Anyone seeing the classified film footage of Operation Ozone produced to recruit young scientists to Porton might mistake the business of biological warfare research for an extended holiday trip to the Bahamas. Following a film clip of the long flight from the Azores to the Bahamas to the sound of Calypso music, with almost interminable shots tracking the plane's shadow as it approaches the city of Nassau, we see researchers sunbathing bare-chested on the deck of the vessel which is gearing up to release biological agents into the atmosphere.[60] The reality of the operation, however, was remarkably different. Although the use of such pathogens in field trials was welcome from a scientific perspective, Fildes and other experts warned—mostly to little effect, given their limited influence on this multiagency operation—that they could be dangerous to living species, and expose scientists to hitherto unknown risks. The trials in the Bahamas were designed to study the viability of airborne pathogens under realistic conditions, and assess the effects of ultra-violet radiation and humidity on the rate of decay of agents, but they were beset by concerns over animal welfare. The scientists experienced difficulties in concealing from the local community the use and intended destruction of animals during their transfer to the ships, and thus faced adverse media attention when animals suffered from heat exhaustion or prolonged stress. In March 1954, an article by the journalist Chapman Pincher in the *Daily Express* prompted a press release by the Colonial Secretary who, as Acting Governor of the Bahamas, confirmed the trials. Although the *British Medical Journal* tried to play down the risk of the 'germ warfare exercise' by suggesting that it was being performed miles away from shore, the Colonial Secretary's admission nonetheless sparked a public debate about military sea trials, which featured in national newspapers.[61] When in October 1955 the Bahamas *Daily Tribune* ran similar stories about the conduct of the trials, it marked the beginning of the end of Britain's attempt to develop a biological bomb. Changes in Britain's defence policy began to see greater reliance on nuclear weapons as a key deterrent during a period of financial austerity. It was a policy environment within which sea trials were no longer required.[62]

Operation Crusoe

Elsewhere, ongoing combat operations between Malayan government forces and opposition groups allowed Porton to conduct highly secret field trials with persistent tear gas (bromo-benzyl-cyanide, BBC).[63] Aimed at 'sealing off areas against terrorist movement', the trials, code-named Operation Crusoe, were performed in April 1953 on Pulau Tenggoll, a small uninhabited island off the coast of Trengganu that was covered by dense jungle and mountains, to simulate the Malayan terrain in which the gas would be used. The operation was conducted by thirty-three men under the direction of Colonel K. Pennycuick and two scientists from Porton. Half an hour after detonating bombs containing liquid tear gas, which three days later would lead to widespread defoliation, a party of five British, three Malayan, and five Chinese servicemen attempted to overcome the burning sensations in their eyes, throat, and neck as they ran across the contaminated area. Before signing a declaration stating that they were 'volunteers', all the 'guinea pigs', as they were called—who needed to be fit and free from skin diseases—were told that while the trials involved some discomfort they posed 'no danger' and would be of value in combating 'communist troops'.[64] Most of the soldiers agreed that the tear gas had created a 'barrier' which they would not have crossed 'if they had not known that there would be no lasting effects'. Although the number of test subjects was too small to generalize from, military officials believed that they gave an indication of the 'relative toughness' of British soldiers compared to the eight Malayan or Chinese servicemen, who had turned back more readily. Obviously, whether 'Malayan bandits' would turn back was another matter. Officials were confident, though, that the desired effect would be achieved, namely to 'hunt' them out of the jungle, if aeroplanes 'topped up' the existing ground contamination every two days, or even more frequently.[65]

As result of the trials, Gerald Templer, as both High Commissioner of Malaya and Head of Anti-Bandit Operations, decided to request from the British authorities the delivery of 25 tons of persistent tear gas for use against 'Bandit Camps' as a 'delaying agent'; meanwhile, other substances, such as Trioxone, could be used for 'intensive treatment of known Bandit hide out areas' which would force the 'enemy to leave the deep jungle on forage for food'. What concerned British officials most was not the ethics of the trials or any environmental destruction resulting from them, but whether any revelations about the tests could be exploited for propaganda purposes by Malayan opposition forces and their communist allies around the world. Templer thought it advisable for the British to 'tell the truth and shame the devil', if those leakages occurred, but the Foreign Office took a different approach, believing that the best course of action would be to publish the intention to use tear gas in order to counter any 'possible misrepresentation'.[66] If this was not done, officials argued, the 'Communists might be able to persuade a great many people throughout the world that we were using poison gas...[and] might even produce evidence of death.'[67] Templer was unable to accept this, yet he agreed to give the matter 'full publicity' on the day tear gas operations commenced, if he decided to use it.[68] Although the trials occurred thousands of miles away from the British mainland, which meant that they were largely irrelevant to public opinion at home, the debate about their publicity highlights the level of sensitivity military officials and politicians were beginning to attach to the testing and potential use of chemical warfare agents at the height of the Cold War.

Vulnerability Trials

Closer to home, sea trials had been a disappointing affair for Britain's warfare experts trying to confirm the apparent hazards of biological warfare. As the risks from bacterial agents, including virulent plague, had been shown to be lower than originally anticipated, scientists came under pressure to construct alternative arguments for the continuation of Britain's biological weapons programme. Identifying new methods and ways in which an enemy might strike, and testing the relative safety of various structures above and below ground against attacks, helped to address the growing resistance of the service departments to resource-intensive field experiments. Special operations trials to assess the vulnerability of Whitehall's telephone exchange, the Air Ministry Citadel—a large bunker housing various Air Ministry departments and administrative staff during and after the Second World War—and the Treasury building demonstrated that the danger of acts of sabotage with bacterial agents was significant.[69]

Public transport was considered another potential target. Crowded railway carriages in motion posed a particular risk, as biological agents could disperse easily and infect large numbers of people. An initial test in 1953 with an empty train travelling at 40 mph from Salisbury to Exeter revealed that, had there been passengers in the carriages, they all 'would have received an infective dose if the agent had been pathogenic', irrespective of where an individual had been seated.[70] Proposals for further trials using the General Post Office cable network and the London Post Office Railway encountered resistance from the Postmaster General, who restricted the areas to be used. Concerns over adverse publicity for underground warfare tests at a time of a general election raised awareness of health and safety issues for postal staff working beneath the streets of London. For civil contingency planners, the trials confirmed the vulnerability of confined spaces to biological attacks, underground, where different transport and tunnel systems inter-linked, for example at Trafalgar Square, beneath government offices, and above ground, where commuters went about their daily business. In a 1956 report, Henderson described the findings of the trials as 'frightening' and requiring utmost secrecy until further tests had confirmed the results, an assessment echoed by the experts attending the Twelfth Tripartite Conference on Toxicological Warfare, who were gravely 'disturbed at the threat involved'.[71]

Consequently, sabotage trials were proposed to test the effectiveness of spreading non-pathogenic microorganisms through the ventilation system of the London Underground.[72] Given their level of sensitivity, it was another seven years before Porton was given authority to proceed. At the height of the Cold War, senior scientific advisers, including Cawood, felt distinctly uncomfortable about exposing Londoners to living bacteria, however harmless, since even the smallest breach of secrecy could spell political dis-aster for the government, domestically and internationally. Others felt that it was simply impossible to conduct 'large-scale trials in this country with pathogens, and probably not with simulants either'.[73] The imagined threat from various types of attacks simultaneously, however, together with expert assurance that the trials could be performed 'unobtrusively and without public disturbance', using agents whose 'harmlessness' had been verified, seem to have persuaded Whitehall's decision makers.[74] What concerned ministers most was not so much the issue of safety, which could be con-trolled through the use of simulants, or whether a convincing narrative could be constructed, should journalists suspect anything, but the 'public reaction to the tests', if they ever became publicly known.[75] In May 1963, the Secretary of State was informed that 'Ventilation Trials'—the official cover for the tests—would soon commence 'in great secrecy'.[76]

During this unprecedented covert operation, Porton's scientists stayed in the background and allowed others to do the work. On 26 July 1963, under the guise of a 'routine dust-sampling exercise', unsuspecting London Transport staff released 30 g of *Bacillus globigii* spores from a small powder box (see Image 35). Preparations had been taken to considerable lengths. To avoid arousing suspicion, Porton staff had added some of the box's original face powder to the spores to ensure that its mixture would have the right smell. The box was dropped from the window of a moving passenger train on the Northern line south of Waterloo, just as it was travelling north out of Colliers Wood station towards Tooting Broadway. By using the tough and heat resistant *B. globigii* bacteria that they had obtained from Camp Detrick, the scientists were hoping to simulate a potential attack with deadly anthrax spores. Believed to be harmless at the time, *B. globigii* bacteria are today 'considered a pathogen for humans' with the potential to cause food poisoning, eye infections, bacteraemia (the presence of bacteria in the blood), and septicaemia, especially in humans with compromised immune systems.[77]

Image 35. Powder box used in the London Underground ventilation trial, 1963
Source: TNA, WO195/15751, 'Ventilation Trial in the London Underground', MRE Report VT/1, 1964.

The release happened around midday, when most commuters had safely arrived at work, yet unsuspecting passengers, visitors, tourists, those scheduled to come in late for meetings, and workers on late shifts were on board the train that day. Many of them might have heard on the radio about the thousands of people killed in the early hours of that morning in a powerful earthquake which had hit the Yugoslav city of Skopje, the capital of the Republic of Macedonia. It had been a human catastrophe of biblical proportions in which the railway system had been totally destroyed and hospitals were at breaking point. Little would have been further from their mind than that their own city, and the train they were travelling in, had become the stage on which scientists had just launched one of the largest underground dissemination trials ever, to simulate a similar cataclysmic event. Acting as a cloud tracer, the spores were unlikely to have spoilt any of their food, as the test report highlighted. However, without ever having been informed or asked for consent, men, women, and children had all of a sudden become the test subjects in a field trial in which Britain's scientists had turned the London Underground into a large-scale laboratory. The people were neither known to the experimenters, nor were they ever identified or told of the test at a later stage; they are likely to have remained ignorant of it all their lives.

Several days later, trainee engineers, who were probably unaware of the military context of the experiment, measured high concentrations of the spores in the stations where the particles had been released; other samples revealed that contamination had spread 'to a point as far north as Camden Town'.[78] Spores had travelled over 10 miles through the ventilation system. Almost everywhere around London, bacterial spores could be identified, at Charing Cross, Waterloo, Elephant & Castle, Kennington, Bank, Holborn, Oxford Circus, and Tottenham Court Road. They had travelled for miles on the Northern, Bakerloo, Piccadilly, Central, and District lines. Randomly selected coaches on the Northern line were likewise heavily contaminated. A second similar trial was carried out in May 1964—in which B. globigii bacteria and T1 coliphage, a virus simulant, were simultaneously released in the London Underground—and confirmed the previously held belief that 'long distance travel of aerosols was due to transportation within the trains' rather than the air ventilation system.[79]

All those in the know agreed that, had this been an attack with highly toxic bacterial or viral agents, within days infection rates among the people of the London metropolis would have been disproportionately high compared to the average infection rates in the capital around this time of the year, possibly leading to panic amongst large sections of society—and there was little that could be done, other than sealing London Underground's floodgates to prevent further contamination from aerosols. As Carter put it during an interview on BBC Radio 4, in the case of a biological warfare attack the London Underground would have been a 'dangerous place to be'.[80] For the authorities it was clear that Britain's capital and other major cities were vulnerable to this type of warfare, findings which accelerated the approval for similar trials in the United States.[81] In 1965, the Chemical Corps' Special Operations Division (SOD) performed two field experiments with *B. globigii* bacteria in Washington DC. A year later, the New York City underground system became an experimental site for covert tests in which the same agent was dropped 'onto the subway roadbed from a rapidly moving train'.[82] While the trials highlighted far-reaching possibilities of exposing urban populations to diseases, the vast majority of the public remained unaware of the risks, nor were the people ever informed of their involvement. In 1999, an official report concluded that the

> tacit approval for [Britain's] simulant trials where the public might be exposed was strongly influenced by defence security considerations aimed obviously at restricting public knowledge. An important corollary to this was the need to avoid public alarm and disquiet about the vulnerability of the civil population to BW attack.[83]

Zinc Cadmium Sulphide Trials

Many of the field trials performed in the 1950s and 1960s are, to this day, shrouded in secrecy. Among the areas to be investigated were long-range land and sea trials to study the movement of clouds and the dispersion of agents over centres of population. Large-scale dissemination trials over residential areas were first conducted in the early 1950s, when Porton carried out dozens of tests over and around Salisbury, located 7 miles to the south-west. They formed part of the data from which military experts and meteorologists subsequently developed the LAC concept which, in an almost circular argument, required validation through field trials.[84] Between 1953 and 1964, Porton carried out an estimated seventy-six simulated attacks involving the release of about 4,600 kg of zinc cadmium sulphide, an agent with a 'largely unknown toxic potential', from ships, aircraft, and moving lorries, mainly over Cardington, in Bedfordshire, and over the English Channel and the North Sea. Most of the trials corresponded with similar field work undertaken in the United States, Canada, and Scandinavia.[85] Zinc cadmium sulphide, also used for fluorescent paints, had first been employed in the 1930s for fluoroscopic screens in radiology. In the mid 1950s, scientists from Stanford University, contracted by the US Chemical Corps, developed the fluorescent particle tracer technique by using zinc cadmium sulphide for meteorological and military field trials. Although users were advised to handle the material as 'potentially toxic', it was believed that the exposure of populated areas to the agent would pose no safety risk for humans, animals, or the environment.[86] The material used in the trials, cheap and easily produced in large quantities, was mostly imported from the New Jersey Zinc Company and later the US Radium Corporation, though some was also obtained from places such as Nancekuke, Britain's nerve agent manufacturing plant.[87]

In 1957, in one of the first tests, a UK aircraft released 300 pounds of zinc cadmium sulphide over 300 square miles of the North Sea. This demonstrated the enormous warfare potential of infecting up to '28 million people', for example with the bacterial infections tularaemia or Q fever, if the substance used, instead of zinc cadmium sulphide, had been a weaponized biological agent.[88] Two years later, HMS *Blackpool* dispatched fluorescent particles on a nocturnal voyage from Chatham to Londonderry, covering an area of some 14,400 square miles with aerosols. The research required an elaborate system of dozens of stationary sampling sites made available by the MoS, the Meteorological Office, and the US Air Force; Porton, meanwhile, dispatched mobile sampling teams to more remote areas.[89] In 1960, officials estimated that up to 38 million people—over half the population of Britain—had already been exposed, via inhalation or consumption of the agent through the food chain, and this was only the beginning.[90] In a joint venture between Porton and Britain's Atomic Energy Research Establishment, located near Harwell, scientists compared the medium distance release of radio-xenon, a nuclear fission product, with the dispersal of zinc cadmium sulphide particles over the Oxfordshire countryside. The project subsequently set alarm bells ringing among the local population and relatives of scientists with regard to its potential health effects.[91]

In March 1963, after trials over Salisbury were inconclusive, Porton carried out the first in a series of zinc cadmium sulphide dispersion trials over the medium-sized city of Norwich in Norfolk.[92] With the support of the

Meteorological Office, the Home Office, and members of the Norwich Police Force, Porton managed to construct a credible cover story about much-needed 'air pollution tests' which, in truth, were zinc cadmium sulphide releases 20 miles away from the city. It was a truly conspiratorial set up: Porton staff, known only as 'advisers', were instructed to wear overalls, duffel coats, and decontaminated rubber boots to conceal their identity while patrolling the sampling sites in the 'yards adjoining police buildings', the 'gardens of private houses', and Norfolk and Norwich Hospital; anyone asking any questions was immediately referred to the War Office.[93]

Information about the large-scale dissemination of zinc cadmium sulphide over Britain has been in the public domain since the early 1960s, though it appeared to suggest that the trials had been for meteorological rather than warfare purposes. For Porton's scientists, field trials confirmed the 'utility of strategic BW [biological warfare] attacks against Britain', yet they raised widespread alarm about public and environmental safety in the wake of publications addressing the hazards of warfare trials over populated areas in the 1980s.[94] In Norfolk, residents raised concerns about cancer rates, though relating these to Porton's trials proved controversial.[95] According to those involved in setting up the trials, such as R.A. Titt, who headed Porton's munitions research, the trials had posed no risk to the health of the British people: 'I took advice on that. A lot of work had been done on this before I ever touched it. I am not a medical man.'[96] Known since the Second World War to be a poisonous heavy metal, fine dust or fumes of zinc cadmium sulphide particles, which had not been tested for toxicity, were inhaled by those who were outdoors at the time of the trials, and may have contaminated the food consumed by humans, grazing livestock, and wildlife.[97]

There has been considerable controversy among experts as to whether the cadmium sulphide exposure may have been carcinogenic.[98] While some scientists admitted that the failure to assess zinc cadmium sulphide solutions for their toxicity when inhaled could be construed as a 'deficit', they highlighted that the material, which was widely used by the meteorological community, had been 'believed to be safe'. The evidence suggesting any adverse or long-term health effects was apparently circumstantial. A 'retrospective risk assessment' by members of the Academy of Medical Sciences concluded that the release amounted to only 1.2 per cent of the estimated total of cadmium released by industry into the atmosphere in the same period, arguing that the exposure 'should not have' caused any ill-effects among humans.[99] Their reasoning was based on the total dose released in an eleven-year period, but did not take into account the dosage received by individuals over a short period of time, for example at Norwich, nor the specific timing of their exposure, a factor identified in endocrine-disrupting chemicals as having the potential to disrupt hormonal and reproductive systems in animals and humans.[100] Although little has been written about the substance, scientists have observed 'minor local and transitory toxic effects' from exposure to zinc cadmium sulphate, including 'lung and lymph node inflammations, accumulations of foreign bodies in the lung, and altered enzyme, protein, and cell count level'. Cadmium, its principal toxic component, has also been found to be genotoxic, i.e. a chemical substance which damages the genetic information of a cell, resulting in mutations and possible cancer.[101] Be this as it may, while Britain's atmospheric trials may not have posed an immediate health hazard to the public, the government was well aware, as the Chief Scientist warned ominously in 1963, that 'public... knowledge of them by unauthorized persons could be politically embarrassing'.[102] His assessment certainly turned out to be true.

The Cold War threat of mass casualties in the aftermath of a chemical or biological warfare attack on the scale tested, and the total administrative chaos expected to go along with it, encouraged Porton's scientists to propose, and carry out for the next two decades, complex and resource-intensive field trials to study the behaviour of non-pathogenic bacterial clouds travelling long distances over land. Authorized by senior officials and advisory committees, including DCDRD, SAC, CDAB, and DCDEE, the government was kept fully informed of tests in which an unwitting public was, and had been, exposed to various agents.[103] Apart from justifying the trials on military grounds, one of the arguments used then, much as it is now, stressed that the release of microorganisms from industry was on a much higher scale and posed potentially greater health hazards than the strictly controlled trials with non-pathogenic bacteria which replaced 'al fresco' releases of zinc cadmium sulphide during the Cold War.[104]

Lyme Bay Trials

In the notorious Lyme Bay trials carried out between 1963 and 1965, Britain's warfare experts used the experimental trial vessel *Icewhale*, based in Portland, and an RAF Devon aircraft to release *Bacterium aerogenes*, *Bacillus globigii*, and *Escherichia coli*, commonly known as *E. coli*, over Lyme Bay and

Weymouth Bay. The sites had been chosen for their convenient location for the military operation, despite being areas of outstanding natural beauty along the Dorset coast. In each of the trials, between '90 and 488 litres' of bacterial suspension was released into the atmosphere.[105] Prior to this, in collaboration with the National Gas Turbine Establishment and the Balloon Development Establishment (BDE), Cardington, Porton had carried out a series of trials to develop an efficient aircraft delivery system which was later tested by spraying *E. coli* traced with *B. globigii* over Tarrant Rushton airfield in Dorset.[106]

Since large area dispersion trials were carried out in a semi-public environment, near coastal paths and fields frequented by residents and holiday-makers, trial preparations were highly secretive. Working from two mobile laboratories stationed on Crown land at Fleet (Hampshire) and code-named 'Night Fairy' and 'Golden Arrow' (see Image 36), military scientists systematically plotted the path and density of bacterial clouds over parts of Dorset during the dispersion trials. A Porton training film of 1966 not only pictured the complex sampling equipment required for measuring airborne bacteria, but captured the significant moment when Porton scientists left the confines of the laboratories, their 'test sphere', as they called it, to enter new experimental spaces, trial zones for the pro-curement of new knowledge.[107] The Dorset trials suggest a secret spectacle performed for the privileged few, their activities protected by guard dogs, warning signs, and a cover story about 'meteorological and air pollution work'.[108] Although not untrue, it was rather misleading since the people 'polluting' the air with bacterial agents were also those measuring the subsequent 'pollution'.

Here, in a more public sphere, social surveillance and local gossip, as ever, functioned as the glue that made society stick; it kept the community together, but it also meant that secrecy could be compromised. For many locals, it was rather obvious that the black Land Rovers in the Dorset countryside marked the arrival of outsiders, of men and women with learned accents. The need for radio communication with the Porton base posed a security risk, and a word too many over lunch at the Moonfleet Hotel, their daily meeting point, could easily have triggered rumours that something was afoot. Though there may have been talk, the group managed to test, undisturbed by much attention, the viability of getting infectious organisms to reach deep into the lungs of living species. According to an uncensored version of the training film, the trials 'demonstrated,

Image 36. Porton mobile laboratory code-named 'Golden Arrow', 1963
Source: IWM, Photographic Collection, 'Golden Arrow', External Views, 11 September 1963.
© Imperial War Museums (F 936/4).

in a striking way, the feasibility of small-scale biological warfare. An appreciable dose of viable bacteria was achieved over an area greater than 1,000 square miles by the release of only 120 gallons of suspension.'[109] It was a startling admission which, in all likelihood, would not have been made in public. Although venturing out into the open for the duration of the trials, it was not an environment in which Porton scientists felt particularly at ease; their preferred realm, it seems, remained sheltered from the outside world.

Similar measures had been taken by the US Chemical Corps in outdoor biological warfare experiments. In 1951, a group of servicemen and officers camouflaged their top-secret assignment of 'raising diseased wheat for germ warfare' by posing as local farmers dressed in civilian clothes and driving civilian trucks with conventional Idaho number plates, except that what they produced was reported to be 'extremely harmful' to crops grown in the Soviet Union, so much so that none other than John Edgar Hoover himself, head of the Federal Bureau of Investigation (FBI), asked to be kept informed as part of his 'internal security responsibilities'.[110] Without wishing to overstretch the interpretative potential of comparison of the two

Anglo-American 'cover-ups', what is interesting, however, is how the issue of class seems to have mattered more in one case than the other. There was surely agreement among Porton's research corps for the need temporarily to assume another professional identity during the Lyme Bay trials, yet their new identity had to be, if not superior, at least comparable in its academic and social status to their usual one. Whereas the use of highly trained military scientists masquerading as poorly paid and badly treated farm workers trying to make a living in the pounding heat of the Idaho plains conjures up images of John Steinbeck's 1937 novel *Of Mice and Men*, in which the two lead characters travel from ranch to ranch in the hope of a better future, no such downward social movement—albeit only feigned and temporary— would have been acceptable at Porton. In the illusory world of assumed identities in large-scale open-air trials certain class boundaries had to be maintained, partly to ensure that the scientists' educated accents would not give them away, partly to keep intact their own carefully constructed real-life identities, but also to create a certain degree of authority in their dealings with the local population. Downgrading their social status would not have found much support. Moving from an identity as a biological warfare scientist to the impersonation of meteorological scientists in a public sphere, on the other hand, was perfectly respectable.

It is highly improbable that there ever was the intention of infecting humans or livestock with bacterial agents in Britain, or of causing lasting damage to the environment, but the moment documents relating to the tests were placed in the public domain, journalists and Members of Parliament began to raise questions about trials which, according to Carter, had 'led to the gratuitous exposure of large numbers of the population of southern England to these microorganisms'.[111] With miscarriages, chronic ill-health problems, and birth defects among children born in the mid 1960s in evidence, especially around East Lulworth, public concern was understandably high, yet according to the author of an independent review, microbiologist Brian Spratt, the main suspect, strains of *E. coli* bacteria, was not believed to have had 'any significant potential to cause disease in healthy individuals at the doses inhaled in the Dorset Defence Trials', a carefully worded conclusion which did not rule out the possibility of adverse health effects in susceptible individuals.[112]

On closer inspection a more complex picture emerges. Strains of *E. coli* are generally harmless in healthy individuals, where they are present in the intestines and faeces, yet a few, more pathogenic, strains can cause diarrhoea and, in rare cases, acute kidney failure and death. In this instance, we know that the *E. coli* strain widely sprayed over parts of Dorset, MRE 162, was isolated in 1949 by a microbiologist from Porton, not in a state-of-the art laboratory, but from a lavatory seat.[113] Despite some uncertainty about the exact serotype of the *E. coli* strain, there is reason to believe that MRE 162 is probably harmless to humans. However, during the trials *E. coli* bacteria were dispersed in variable particle sizes, which meant that some 'penetrated the lungs [of humans] whereas others will have entered the stomach'. Those entering the lungs could, in a few cases, by gaining access to and multiplying in the blood stream, have led to blood or chest infections.[114] Toxicity tests also showed that in two of the fourteen trials performed in 1963/1964, *E. coli* strains were heavily contaminated but were still used.[115] According to Spratt, it was 'surprising that suspensions with this level of contamination with uncharacteristic bacteria were sprayed across populated areas, as there was a possible risk that the contaminating bacteria had a significant ability to cause disease in humans'.[116] At risk were those undertaking physical activity near the trials and Porton staff exposed to a much higher dosage of bacterial spores, yet neither the death of a thirty-three-year-old Porton microbiologist nor the chronic breathing problems of a crew member of the *Icewhale* could apparently be linked to the trials—although these cases will have to be further investigated as soon as additional source material becomes available.

Ever since Lord Atkin had stipulated in *Donoghue v. Stevenson* (1932) that one 'must take reasonable care to avoid acts or omissions' that are likely to 'injure your neighbour', a person owed a duty of care which made them liable for the losses or injuries of others if these were reasonably foreseeable.[117] Although the Crown and its government have a similar duty of care towards its subjects, it is far from certain whether it can be made liable for acts where the causal link between toxic releases and cases of ill-health cannot be conclusively proved, for example through epidemiological studies, and where it cannot be demonstrated that the alleged injuries were 'reasonably foreseeable'. It seems that the courts are rather reluctant to impose a duty of care unless this causation can firmly be established. As epidemiologists well know, to do this retrospectively on the basis of historical sources is exceedingly difficult, if not impossible. Rather than looking to establish legal liability through negligence, it seems more constructive to draw attention to the government's moral responsibility to protect the British people from potential harm and not to expose individuals and communities to substances, however harmless or innocuous they were believed to be at the time, without their knowledge. For many, Porton's field trials remain morally questionable, at best, and in a few cases irresponsible, in exposing humans, livestock, and the environment to chemical or biological agents during the Cold War.

Defence Policy

Although chemical and biological weapons had been outlawed by the international community, Western governments were willing to fund research into them as a flexible and 'cheap insurance' policy as long as their strategic value was guaranteed. Chemical weapons were able to 'seek out and destroy' enemy forces sheltering from high explosive or nuclear attacks and could achieve a 'lethal coverage' of dozens of square miles with a single aeroplane under variable meteorological conditions. Similarly, via the undetected dispersal of biological agents, it was deemed possible to cover large areas with infectious pathogens, causing widespread incapacitation or death. Alternatively, biological weapons could be used to destroy the enemy's food supplies and disrupt their infrastructure by spreading foot-and-mouth or crop diseases, or to release agents into underground transportation systems.[118] Porton's large area field trials in the 1950s, however, had shown that the use of bacterial agents as a modern attack weapon was rather inefficient. Compared with Britain's nuclear deterrent, chemical and biological weapons also posed considerable problems of delivery and control. While the government regarded the use of the nuclear weapons as 'ethically justifiable', the Geneva Protocol made it difficult, if not impossible, to employ the threat of using the chemical and biological weapons. For Britain it was 'militarily more useful', the DRPC argued, to 'cheat' in any future disarmament treaty aimed at reducing its nuclear arsenal rather than in those that might attempt to reduce its other weapons technologies. The debate was also shaped by financial considerations. Nuclear weapon technology and infrastructure, such as the ROTOR radar detection system, absorbed the majority of Britain's defence budget, leaving few if any resources for conventional or chemical weapons. By relying on US manufacturing and weaponizing capabilities for VX and other agents in case of war, and by abandoning an offensive chemical weapons capability in the 1950s, the government managed to 'both ease the strain on its purse strings and clear its conscience'.[119]

Still, when in 1958 officials considered downgrading the strategic value
of chemical and biological weapons, it was felt that terminating research
into these weapons would be 'unwise' as it could detrimentally affect
intelligence sharing with the United States.[120] Consequently, experimental research continued throughout the 1960s, during which Porton scientists
used the newly developed microthread technique to study the viability
of bacterial pathogens in places such as Southampton, Swindon, and
St Bartholomew's Hospital, London, to examine possible routes of transmission during the 1967/1968 foot-and-mouth disease epidemic, and to
help in the development of—rather ineffective—civil contingency measures. Tests commissioned by the Home Office to see whether Portakabins
could be turned into biological shelters for civilians revealed that the total
dosage inside the cabin 'reached up to 77% of the concentration outside'.[121] It was a finding the public would probably not have found reassuring. Porton also resumed limited sea trials to test the vulnerability of
ships to biological attacks, and performed collaborative field experiments
with the United States in the 1970s and beyond to assess the latest detection systems for biological and chemical warfare agents.[122] In the autumn
of 1975, for example, the people on the Isle of Portland on the south coast
of England were exposed over a three-week period, often several times a
day, to over 2,500 litres of bacterial aerosols, containing a mixture of inac-
tivated *Serratia marcescens* and *B. globigii*, which had the potential to cause
allergic reactions and pose risks to health.[123] Britain's reliance on thermonuclear retaliation remained unchanged, however. In 1970, the Secretary
of State for Defence told Parliament that it was 'inconceivable' that NATO
forces would be attacked with chemical weapons, unless they were used as
part of an invasion, 'in which event more terrible weapons would surely
come into play'.[124]

Environmental Security

Allied warfare trials also had unintended and what some might see as more
benign consequences, particularly when government directives restricting
the activities of people in designated areas helped to prevent the extinction
of certain species and wildlife. In some areas, largely depleted fishing grounds
on the west coast of Scotland recovered to more sustainable levels after local
fishing trawlers were banned from entering specific areas; in others, large

stretches of woodland and farmland became Sites of Special Scientific Interest after lying fallow for decades, as in the case of Porton's downland.[125] These were not spaces untouched by modern civilization, places in which nature had been preserved in a time capsule. On the contrary, they had become military environments in which scientists developed nuclear and nonconventional weapons, landscapes more often than not scarred by toxic waste, death, and destruction. Exceptions to such a state of affairs are few and far between, but they do exist, especially in cases where the military engaged with wider environmental concerns. In Northumberland, it seems, public access restrictions have transformed the Cheviot Hills, a military training ground since 1911, into one of the 'most pristine wildernesses in England', now widely appreciated by ramblers and other nature lovers.[126]

With the end of the Cold War, information about Allied open-air trials began to be released into the public domain, and this raised public concerns about the long-term environmental legacy of these military activities. As tensions between former adversaries eased, discussions about the planned reduction and eventual destruction of nonconventional weapons technology offered startling insight into the lack of health and safety regulations that had led to widespread contamination of military bases and surrounding areas, with estimated clean-up costs of up to 20 billion dollars just for the US Army's Rocky Mountain Arsenal in Colorado, nicknamed the 'most toxic square mile on earth'.[127] Yet we need to recognize that military environmental policy was rarely if ever consistent or aligned with that of other Allied partners. In the 1960s, for example, US biological warfare trials in the Pacific Ocean were governed by stringent safety regulations to prevent the spreading of pathogens by seabirds and ensure the sustainability of marine life.[128] Alert to public opinion, the US government was beginning to respond to growing international concerns about environmental destruction, highlighted in popular books and films such as *The Silent World* (1956) by French oceanographer Jacques-Yves Cousteau, who ran a successful media campaign against the dumping of radioactive waste before becoming the star of his own TV series on underwater expeditions, watched by millions across the globe.[129] Some years later, in 1969, in a complete shift to orthodox policy, the United States unilaterally abandoned its offensive biological weapons programme, thus signalling the start of disarmament negotiations for nonconventional and nuclear weapons systems that resulted in conclusion of the BTWC in 1972. Without differentiating between lethal and nonlethal biological agents, it prohibited the signatories from ever developing, producing, stockpiling, or otherwise acquiring or retaining biological weapons under any circumstances, and compelled them to destroy their existing stockpiles.[130]

According to Van Courtland Moon, a 'sea-change' in American foreign policy had taken place, but had it in reality? In August 1970, in the midst of complex disarmament negotiations, the large-scale deep-sea dumping operation by the United States of gas stockpiles off the coast of the Bahamas and Bermuda, which included over 12,000 rockets filled with nerve agents, and one mine containing VX, caused a level of public outrage that challenged Britain's diplomatic skills to the limits. Paying little more than lip service to the need to protect the 'health and safety of human and marine life' in carefully controlled press releases, while at the same time recognizing the 'strength of the feeling' among the local population and environmentalists, Britain was trying to reconcile its interests in the region without alienating the US government at a critical juncture. In response, the Senate prohibited any future disposal of highly toxic weapons material unless it had been 'rendered harmless'.[131] Since 1991, environmental protection has also become part of a more integrated national security strategy. Western politicians want to be seen to be showing leadership in tackling pressing environmental problems and issues of compliance, not only to ensure their own re-election and to boost their economies, but as part of national defence policy. Cases of environmental damage around military bases and testing sites are seen as having the potential to undermine military preparedness and stability, mainly by turning public opinion against the facilities, and this can have implications for national security, thus reflecting, in a quasi-circular fashion, the overarching themes hitherto employed to justify Allied research into nonconventional weapons.[132]

This may explain why few of those involved in the trials and willing to talk have many regrets in retrospect; theirs was a culture of military deterrence in which peace and stability were believed to be in short supply, and their sense was that the people of Britain were exposed to chemical and biological agents 'for their own good'.[133] While the trials were ostensibly for the 'public good', researchers, at times, expressed a rather patronizing, if not dismissive, attitude towards the people they were meant to be protecting. For Mike Hood, who joined the MRE at the time of Maddison's death and worked at Porton for twenty-five years, the experiments would not have been worth doing if the general public had been consulted: 'The public is so ill-informed, and of course, you would let a potential enemy know what you were doing.'[134] For many, including Porton's former director, Rex Watson, the 'public' remained an unknown entity which had little, if any, bearing on their scientific work, unless democratically elected politicians or senior civil servants felt compelled to respond to perceived public concerns by restricting or limiting research activities on the ground. Porton's know-ledge and awareness of the people of Britain was often indirect, filtered and communicated through the relevant expert and policy channels, rarely immediate, except on those occasions when scientists ventured out into the open to manipulate known and unknown experimental environments. In this, security precautions generally prevented them from engaging or inter-acting with the people inhabiting those landscapes. Except for a few senior officials, Porton's scientists and laboratory technicians generally had relatively little insight into how their work fitted into Britain's evolving military strat-egy, nor were they able to shape policy debates at higher levels. Another scientist stressed that this had not been a matter of 'just popping out' of the laboratory to perform open-air trials: in this he was alluding to the amount of detailed preparations, organization, and team work involved in staging the tests, rather than to careful consideration of military medical ethics. For the latter, external experts, so-called 'top notch' scientists, had apparently been in charge. Few, if any, contemplated taking individual responsibility for the research undertaken at the time, or have spoken publicly about their experiences at Porton since. If anything, former Porton officials continue to be concerned about the release of previously classified information and the resulting public debate which could be exploited by groups or nations hos-tile to Britain.

8

Twilight Threshold

Ethics in Transition

Twilight threshold is the moment when the light becomes faint, when objects and shapes near and far become indistinct, shortly after sunset or before sunrise, the time of day when there is partial darkness and we try to make out what will happen next; it is the 'magic hour when ordinary routines undergo strange transformations', a transitional period situated between decay and renewal, knowing and not knowing, when things are obscure, not yet definite, though somewhere, at a distance, almost invisible, the stage is set on which a prior stimulus is about to show a response; an often quiet, even silent time, it allows pause for thought and constructive reflection; it often is the most creative of times, when we begin to acknowledge and recognize the past, and accept as a challenge the uncertainty which lies before us; the response triggered need not be radical or revolutionary, although we often like to see it as such in retrospect, when we give in to our desire to construct convenient narratives to strengthen fragile identities; it is a process which, once started, cannot easily be stopped, so strong are the historical currents, and it is often gradual and slow, but it can lead to lasting changes in consciousness, in the minds of people, how they think and believe what is right and wrong in their lives, work, and wider society; some may later want us to believe that what has happened was a paradigm shift, whether in science and culture, politics or economics, or they may offer us some other grand-sounding conceptual explanation designed to artificially turn historical experience, undigested and in motion, into an apparently objective, albeit constructed, form of reality that can be neatly stored away, cleared of all the grit and uncertainty that accompanied its original path.[1] In our own story, we can look back on that brief twilight moment, when the future was as yet unclear, and observe carefully what was in transition, when ethics became transformed, and experimental scientists began to show a greater awareness of, and sense of responsibility for, the sanctity of human lives.

Scholars generally tend to agree that in the late 1940s and 1950s, Western research scientists paid little or no attention to modern medical ethics principles as formulated in the Nuremberg Code. A certain cavalier attitude towards human rights in human experimentation was apparently commonplace in both civilian and military science. Capturing this postwar attitude, Jay Katz once remarked that most investigators felt that 'it was a good code for barbarians but an unnecessary code for ordinary physician-scientists'.[2] Alastair MacLean, arguing along similar lines in the Historical Survey, suggested that the Code was inapplicable to most postwar scientists and that 'it had little if any impact on practice'.[3] However, medical ethics were not, it seems, entirely ignored by the prevailing research culture; rather, a complex picture of Cold War science begins to emerge, one which is far from uniform or consistent, and in which generational, social, and ethnic factors, and the specific locality and personalities involved, could shape the response to proposed experimental projects as much as could overriding geopolitical objectives. This period can undoubtedly lay claim to some of the most profound medical ethics violations in the twentieth century, especially in the field of human experimentation; examples range from the notorious Tuskegee Syphilis Study, described by some as a programme of 'controlled genocide', to recent revelations about unethical research in Guatemala.[4] Still, medical ethics and international legal and humanitarian principles— including the Geneva Protocol, the Declaration of Human Rights, the Nuremberg Code, and the Declaration of Helsinki—set in train a reflective process about the ethical legitimacy of existing research practices in both civilian and military facilities. Benefiting from vast investments in medical science and technology, most Anglo-American scientists were inclined to ignore the critical voices calling for caution in the field of human trials, who appeared to them simply to be slowing down the advancement of knowledge designed to protect national interests. Yet as the years rolled on through the 1950s and into the 1960s, their warnings, given informally or in classified committee meetings, began to multiply into an uncomfortable clamour.

In the mid to late 1950s, moreover, the work of military scientists was marked by a noticeable paradigm shift in the chemical warfare field, from developing fast-acting nerve agents for maximum lethality to seeking

compounds causing maximum incapacitation. The objective of incapacitating agents was to produce physiological, psychological, or biological changes
in humans which would prevent them from carrying out their duties yet
without endangering their lives. To make them widely applicable in military and policing operations, their effects had to be predictable, their production, storage, and dissemination reliable, and their symptoms reversible.
Research on these agents raised a series of complex scientific issues relating
to the 'speed of action required, safety margins, the duration of incapacitation and method of delivery', to name but a few.[5] Experts and the media
often referred to such substances as 'riot control agents', 'psychochemicals',
'psychotomimetics', or 'hallucinogens'; the US Army Chemical Corps
called them 'K agents'. At one end of the scale were known, but potentially
lethal, tear gases such as CN (chloracetophenone), first synthesized before
the First World War and then used in chemical warfare training and different
types of riot control. At the other end were nonlethal substances that produced 'profound effects on the physical or mental functioning of the individual'. Some were what the popular press often referred to as 'truth drugs'.[6]

In Britain, experts distinguished between three different types of incapacitants. First, there were those compounds which caused temporary physical disability through sleep, paralysis, weakness, blindness, deafness, or
respiratory problems without the risk of death or permanent injury. Second,
there were agents which produced temporary incapacitation in small doses,
but which involved the risk of death and permanent effects, if larger dosages
were administered. Finally, there was a group of substances which led to
severe mental incapacitation in both animals and humans. All lachrymators
such as CN, DM, or CS gas fell into one of the first two categories, depending on how experts viewed their level of toxicity and legality under international law; whereas CS gas was deemed to be nonlethal by the UK
government, British military and police forces, including those stationed in
Northern Ireland, were prohibited from using the arsenical war gas DM,
also known as 'sickening smoke', since high concentrations were believed to
be 'dangerous' and thus banned under the Geneva Protocol.[7] This had not
always been the case. In the early 1950s, in light of regular 'uprisings' in the
colonies, officials considered the use of DM in combination with tear gas to
'disperse riotous crowds' to be an alternative to 'resorting to rifle fire', and
authorized a series of tear smoke experiments in Nairobi, Trinidad, Zanzibar,
Tanganyika, and Hong Kong. The main argument against more potent and
long-lasting tear gas grenades, as the War Office pointed out, was that the

gas was not only intended for use against 'colonial crowds but also for Europeans and possibly against Englishmen'. The use of really dangerous riot control agents would simply not have been 'tolerated' by the British public, the War Office explained.[8] CS gas, on the other hand, first synthesized and discussed by the American scientists Corson and Stoughton in 1928, and then developed by Porton in the 1950s to replace CN, was taken up by American and Canadian forces as a military and riot control agent.[9]

Nonlethal mental incapacitating agents as a novel form of warfare, however, attracted considerable interest among military scientists and members of the general public, who were gripped by the latest 'science fiction' novel or movie. In 1957, the subject was discussed in secret during the Twelfth Tripartite Toxicological Conference.[10] Two years later, it hit the national headlines after officers of the US Chemical Corps were called upon to testify in front of the US Congressional Committee on Science and Astronautics which, in response to the Soviet Sputnik programme, had been tasked with assessing the status of military science in chemical, biological, and radiological warfare. The same select committee later drafted the relevant legislation for the establishment of the National Aeronautics and Spaces Administration (NASA), instrumental in launching the space age. Amongst other evidence, members of Congress were shown a film clip about an animal experiment, previously aired on national TV, in which a cat drugged with a psychochemical agent could be seen to be 'in great terror of mice ... cowering and leaping about wildly to keep its distance', a highly effective presentation which did not fail to make a lasting impression on both Congress and the American public.[11] Another film demonstrated the 'eccentric' behaviour of servicemen who were under the influence of psychochemical substances. Functioning also as a forum for disseminating Cold War propaganda, the committee disclosed that the Red Army Military Medical Service had shown a 'special interest' in so-called 'psychic poisons' such as mescaline, methedrine, and lysergic acid derivatives. It set the scene for an international arms race to discover the most effective incapacitating agent for use by military or police forces whenever there was a need to regain control in cases of war or public order disruption, but where there was good cause to believe that harming enemy combatants or civilians would be against established political doctrine. Another area of potential use of such agents was thought to lie in secret intelligence operations, and as a way of affecting the 'rationality of important leadership groups', such as members of the Politburo in the Soviet Union, at critical political junctures. As part of the Western alliance, Britain was called upon to meet future challenges by making extensive use of its experimental facilities at Porton.

In 1963, the Macmillan government took the decision—which did not become public knowledge until about the mid 1990s—to launch a top-secret chemical weapons rearmament programme with a new generation of incapacitating agents, only seven years after committing itself to a policy of chemical disarmament which involved abandoning plans for a factory capable of producing 50 tons of nerve gas per week, and disposing of all existing chemical weapons stockpiles. A year earlier, in 1962, following two independent operational assessments, the DRPC had advocated an 'expansion of research on offensive aspects of chemical and biological warfare'. In addition, the Chiefs of Staff had 'identified a possible future need for a chemical warfare capability based on nonlethal psychotomimetic incapacitating agents' and had recommended that 'lethal agents such as Sarin and VX should be available for tactical use in limited war'.[12] On 3 May 1963, the Cabinet Defence Committee, chaired by the Prime Minister, after considering Defence Minister Peter Thorneycroft's memorandum on chemical and biological warfare policy, therefore authorized the MoD to 'proceed with a five year programme of offensively oriented research and limited production of chemical agents'.[13]

Several months later, in August, Porton sought clarification about the kind of incapacitating agents it would be expected—as well as permitted—to develop for different operational requirements. An incapacitating agent, in Porton's view, was defined as 'a substance which can render hostile persons incapable of either aggression or resistance for a limited time without permanently injuring them'.[14] However, in light of the very wide 'range of effects' which could be produced by incapacitating agents, together with the knowledge that the boundaries between lethal and incapacitating agents were blurred, Porton suggested that any attempt to classify these substance into sub-divisions would be both artificial and arbitrary. What was needed, Porton argued, was a clearer idea about the kind of military requirements for which the agents would be used, especially in relation to the 'upper limit of primary lethal causalities that would be acceptable'—i.e. the maximum number of people the substance might kill under certain operational conditions. In a general or limited war it might be deemed acceptable, according to Porton, if 5 per cent of the people exposed to the agent were killed; during counter-insurgency operations, the upper limit of people killed should not exceed 2 per cent, and 0 per cent in riot control situation.[15] In its response, MoD officials drew attention to the fact that Britain was bound by the 1925 Geneva Protocol, which made highly problematic the use of incapacitating agents with an upper 'lethality limit' of 2 or 5 per cent, because the country would be seen to be—and *de facto* would be—in breach of the convention, which could invite retaliation with chemical weapons. The way forward, officials suggested, was to distinguish between two types of incapacitating agents only: those deemed to be safe to use—such as CS— did not breach the Geneva Protocol; those with a 'possible direct lethal effect', on the other hand, could be used only after a potential opponent had used them first. This rather crude distinction between different types of incapacitating agents had important consequences, because it explains why Porton's scientists, in their search for new chemical compounds, showed a particular interest in substances which could cause maximum physical and mental disability for hours or even days after exposure to the agent had ceased, but which were not necessarily also lethal. Once Britain's pro- gramme of research and development into these agents gained momentum in the 1960s, it became apparent that the risk to which participants would be exposed could only increase as the years went by.

In the meantime, the British public was led to believe that the country had given up any ambitions to possess an offensive chemical weapons cap- ability. It was this paradigm shift from developing extremely lethal nerve agents to developing highly potent incapacitating but nonlethal agents which explains why Porton, after initial but limited tests in the 1950s, estab- lished a major testing programme, approved at the highest levels of govern- ment, to study the effects of known and newly synthesized incapacitating agents—including lysergic acid diethylamide, commonly known as LSD, and glycolates—on hundreds of human subjects in the 1960s and 1970s. Porton's experiments with these hitherto untested chemical compounds, performed mostly on servicemen and occasionally on members of staff, often involved exposing participants to a considerable degree of risk.

In attempting to reconstruct the origins of highly secret mind-altering drugs and the debates surrounding them, we can not only detect some of the key ethical dilemmas facing military scientists in their decision-making and begin to see the intricate inter-connectedness between civilian and military scientists—whose professional identities were indistinguishable at times—but also gain a sense of the unease which started to plague seasoned officials when they were asked to grant permission for research into non- lethal chemical weapons. In a way characteristic of Britain, the process by which unease turned into an expression of concern was gradual and slow, and it might never have happened, had it not been for the very visible physical breakdowns and job resignations in some of Porton's scientists who, after testing 'truth drugs' on themselves, changed their mind about their future participation in Britain's chemical warfare programme.

Truth Drugs

The impetus for Britain's exploration of 'truth drugs' in the 1950s seems to have come partly from the United States, especially Harvard anaesthetist and former member of the Office of Strategic Services (OSS) Henry K. Beecher, who is often credited with having exposed medical ethics violations in the mid 1960s.[16] After the Second World War he had been among a group of intelligence experts tasked with verifying the validity of high-altitude and hypothermia experiments carried out by Nazi doctors at Dachau concentration camp. Largely oblivious to ethical implications in respect of their origins, Beecher and his colleagues from naval intelligence concluded that some of the Dachau data could provide an 'important complement to existing knowledge'.[17] Beecher's association with highly secretive military research that circumvented and in some cases flouted standards of medical ethics continued throughout the 1940s and 1950s.[18] For him, the Nuremberg Code's 'rigid rules' were impractical in innovative drug research, yet as someone equally at home within civilian and military contexts, and with considerable influence and connections, he managed to mobilize support for an extended programme experimenting with mind-altering drugs.[19]

In September 1951, Beecher travelled to Europe, representing the US Army's Assistant Chief of Staff, Intelligence Branch, G-2, and the Medical Research and Development Board (MRDB) at the Office of the Surgeon General, to gather information on 'ego-depressant' drugs affecting the central nervous system, including sedatives, hypnotics, antitussives, analgesics, and anaesthetics, and assess their potential as weapons.[20] His assignment was part of a top-secret 'special interrogation programme' of the US intelligence community, code-named Operation Artichoke, initiated by the CIA in March 1951.[21] US military scientists, including Beecher, were eager to develop such substances as 'research tools and as practical instruments for possible use on prisoners (civil and military) if this ever is possible and necessary'. Ostensibly, the aim was to establish whether 'a man of integrity and discretion can be altered without his knowledge so as to lose his integrity and discretion', yet behind the research stood the fear of drugged scientists and diplomats posing a threat to national security by revealing classified information to the enemy.

The army's choice of Beecher, a leading 'authority on anaesthetics and other depressant drugs' who in the late 1940s had been funded by the MRDB to investigate the actions of various 'sedatives', was anything but coincidental. As a long-term project, he had been tasked with developing 'criteria for evaluating sedatives', including their effectiveness, duration, and toxicity, devising rules for the 'sound use' of such compounds, testing newly developed agents on animals and humans, and 'eliminat[ing] certain abuses of agents in this group'.[22] This work went hand in hand with observations on experimental pain he and his colleagues produced in man to assess response variations to powerful analgesic agents.[23] Much of Beecher's research corresponded to CIA and military intelligence objectives. His collaboration with the US intelligence community in Operation Artichoke did not originate from a military–scientific mission under the aegis of the CIA, but from the continuation and expansion of work previously performed under the same agency, the MRDB.

Beecher's trip got off to a difficult start despite being organized in large part by Colonel John Wood, chairman of the MRDB, who, as the man in charge of the medical division at the Army Chemical Center, Edgewood Arsenal, liaised with US civilian scientists and contracted them onto chemical weapon projects. An informal meeting between Beecher and military representatives at the MoD in early September 1951, attended by Brigadier Cheyne, Colonel Artman, Dr Sixsmith, and Dr Gater—the latter a former prisoner of war of the Japanese who had expertise in 'obscure drugs'—at first seemed to suggest that Britain had not pursued this line of work. In spite of, or perhaps because of, their lack of knowledge of ego-depressant drugs, British officials were keen to establish a system of medical intelligence sharing between London and Washington, preferably through the BJSM, a proposal Beecher felt was not quite 'proper' and needed the approval of G-2, the US Army's intelligence branch, and of the CIA. By venturing into the world of military medical interrogation techniques, Beecher opened up new avenues for Britain's intelligence agencies, yet this also meant that inter-Allied collaboration needed to be carefully monitored.

Beecher's caution in discussing US research objectives was mirrored in British attempts to downplay the relevance of the problem. While leading scientists in Oxford, Cambridge, and Edinburgh, including Gaddum and David Whitteridge, seemed unaware of any systematic research and showed little interest, members of the JIC 'expressed polite scepticism as to the importance of work'.[24] He was probably not impressed by their suggestion that the different responses of individuals to questioning after electric shock therapy, leucotomy (a neurosurgical procedure), or anaesthesia should be studied, since US scientists had done this already. Beecher's long-time colleague Sir Henry Dale, President of the Royal Society, on the other hand, remained 'noncommittal' about the risks involved and referred him to the psychiatrist William W. Sargant. The prospects in Britain for Beecher's research looked bleak until his encounter with Sir Frederick Bartlett, professor of experimental psychology at Cambridge, who told him that both the Foreign Office and the RAF had been examining the matter since 1949, after it had transpired that Soviet scientists had tested 'ephedrine-like agents', although he himself, having been consulted, remained 'sceptical of its practical value'.[25] At around the same time, according to unconfirmed reports, tripartite intelligence agencies began holding discussions about possible mind control experiments. Such discussions, if they took place, may have been prompted by yet another show trial in the Eastern bloc reminiscent of Stalin's political purges of the late 1930s, this time against the Hungarian dissident Cardinal Joseph Mindszenty who, after imprisonment in 1949, appeared to have been drugged before confessing in court to crimes he was alleged to have committed.[26] There was however still a general sense that intelligence obtained through drugs could equally be obtained through other means and methods, except perhaps in situations where 'many men are to be interrogated' to gather information quickly. It strengthened Beecher's belief, as he told the Surgeon General, that there was 'hardly anything of significance' going on in Britain.[27]

Another of Beecher's objectives was to identify potential collaborators and junior scientists who could be recruited for secret drug research, provided their 'political loyalty', as one British expert put it, made it possible, from a security perspective, to 'transplant' them to the United States. Although the Cambridge experimental psychologist Derek Russell Davis came highly recommended, it was made clear to Beecher that if he were to enter the field 'the invitation must come from high up' to ensure that responsibility ultimately rested with Britain's military and the government. Though it was more implicit than explicit, experts were well aware that Beecher's proposed line of work posed a series of medico-legal dilemmas, since the use of psycho-pharmaceutical drugs on unsuspecting and non-consenting human subjects for the purpose of intelligence gathering breached traditional norms of ethical medical conduct. How, for example, if at all, would the research subjects be informed of any health hazards? Since the spectrum of medical effects of the drugs in question was very wide, including hallucinations, mania, delirium, convulsions, and psychosis, varying considerably depending on the individuals' psychological and emotional state of mind, it was far from clear how participants could best be selected. Could the subjects be sufficiently protected from sustained or long-term psychological effects, or, even worse, suicidal tendencies? What would happen in case of lasting injury or even death? Who would be legally liable in case something went wrong? Beecher knew that such research, if approved, needed to have strong political and military support.[28]

Travelling on to Belgium, Beecher arrived at the Supreme Headquarters Allied Powers Europe (SHAPE) in Marly-le-Roi on 21 September 1951; there he was met by Colonel Redmond Connelly and Colonel E.B. Nichols, the chiefs of security for SHAPE and Europe respectively. Both believed that the existing security threats from drugs needed to be met through the development of effective countermeasures to 'protect the fighting soldier', irrespective of any ethical considerations. Whereas Cold War intelligence officials expressed little, if any, concern that Beecher and his colleagues were about to embark on a research programme that contravened accepted codes of medical ethics in non-therapeutic research, including the Nuremberg Code, others took matters of ethics more seriously. The Chief Surgeon General from the European Command in Heidelberg, General Guy B. Denit, himself a veteran of the First World War, told Beecher in no uncertain terms that 'as a physician under the Geneva Convention he could have nothing officially to do with the use of drugs for the purposes in mind'.[29] Denit's reservations did not prevent him, however, from introducing Beecher to high-ranking intelligence officials who paved the way for him to gain some first-hand experience of applied interrogation and enhancement techniques at the European Command Interrogation Center (ECIC), the Berlin Military Intelligence Detachment (MID), and the Counter Intelligence Corps (CIC). Upon his return, Beecher told the Surgeon General that there was a need to examine the possibilities of such drugs 'for our own purposes within the Army'.[30] According to Beecher, the military was already in possession of excellent evidence to the effect that

a discreet man of the highest integrity can be made indiscreet and to lose his
integrity, without his knowledge[,] by the secret use of some of the drugs we
are studying... The drugs in question have powers far beyond those of alcohol, and if they are administered without the subjects' knowledge, it is entirely
possible that the subject could be made indiscreet without his knowledge.[31]

On the assumption that Soviet agents were applying drug-induced interrogation techniques, Beecher wanted to return to West Germany, once the
mode of action of the 'newer derivatives of mescaline and lysergic acid' was
better understood, and interview 'high-level refugees and ranking political
figures' who had defected from East Germany. The aim was systematically
to study the 'signs and symptoms' of people who had been drugged without
their knowledge. US military officials were convinced, at this point, that it
was perfectly possible to manipulate the mind of an 'expert physicist at Los
Alamos', by tampering with his food for example, in order that the person
reveal classified information. The reverse was also deemed possible, namely
to use drugs to blur an individual's recollection of events or erase their
memory of unpleasant experiences. Beecher encouraged the US military to
see whether drugs could be used to cover up drug-induced interrogations,
or, as he put it, experts should 'look into the use of amnesia-producing
drugs in blocking out periods of questioning with and without the use of
ego-depressants'.[32] Aware of the potential ethical implications of his proposals, he advised the US Army to increase the security classification for this
type of work to 'top secret', including his own report.

Beecher's recommendations came at a critical juncture in the origins of
Operation Artichoke, which enabled the US Army intelligence branch G-2
to take a leading role in shaping the projects' parameters.[33] Following a
meeting of the Intelligence Advisory Committee on 2 April 1951, an
'exploratory group' had been formed between the US intelligence agencies
of the Army (G-2), Navy (ONI), and Air Force (A-2) and the CIA's Assistant
Director for Scientific Intelligence to avoid duplication of work. It also
emerged that another agency, name unknown, was involved in conducting
a comparative study of 'all polygraphs' and in assessing the biochemistry of
fatigue and nervous stress.[34] G-2, on the other hand, had commissioned
Beecher to examine the whole subject through consultations with scientific
and intelligence experts in Europe, where it was believed that such techniques might already be being employed. After receipt of Beecher's report,
inquiries were made about the progress of the project. In early January 1952,
one official wanted to know whether Beecher would be 'going ahead on

[*sic*] this project?', which agency would be responsible, and whether the whole project, previously called 'Bluebird', now needed a code word in order to request 'clearance in national interest for Dr B.'[35] Attempts at formulating a coordinated approach were at first fraught with disagreement between the CIA and military representatives over who would be responsible. Whereas the CIA proposed the MRDB as the 'appropriate agency', military officials felt that the Joint Medical Intelligence Subcommittee (JMIS) should 'study the problem' and make recommendations to the JIC, yet that it should not be in charge of 'operational and supervisory' issues that might emerge during the research. All the agencies were concerned to assign responsibility to an organization or committee that would allow them to distance themselves if the project were to become public knowledge. At the end of January 1951, the CIA's Deputy Director told the Secretary of Defence:

> I am sure that you will recognize the implications which might be drawn should it become known, generally, that [the] CIA or the Military Intelligence Agencies are directly concerned in this matter, even though this concern stems primarily from the defensive aspect of the problem.[36]

For military intelligence officials, the offensive aspects were at least of equal importance. In mid February 1952, the JIC was asked to authorize a study on 'Special Interrogation Methods' to determine 'whether effective, practical techniques exist whereby an external control can be imposed on the mind and/or will of an individual to cause him to act or react, without his being aware that control has been imposed, in the manner desired by the individual exercising the control'. The CIA was to be 'invited' to take part in the work on a 'consultant basis'.[37] One G-2 official described the objective of Operation Artichoke in rather less bureaucratic terms: 'The problem this paper is designed to solve is the very basic one of whether there is a problem and the defensive and offensive aspects thereof.'[38] For the US military intelligence community, Beecher's fact-finding mission provided additional impetus and scientific credibility to their planned programme of research, which helped them to expedite formal authorization of Operation Artichoke.

In the early 1950s, shocked and partly humiliated by the postwar discovery of German nerve agents, Anglo–American intelligence agencies, including G-2, CIA, and MI6, also known as the Secret Intelligence Service (SIS),[39] prompted and supported by experts such as Beecher, and sanctioned

by the JIC, launched a comprehensive research and development programme into newly synthesized lethal and incapacitating warfare agents,
involving human experiments with hallucinogenic substances such as LSD
and other so-called 'truth sera' at Edgewood Arsenal and Porton Down.[40]
Although some civilian and military investigators expressed concern, often
in private and among trusted colleagues, the majority was as yet unable, and
perhaps unwilling, to identify and expose larger patterns of unethical conduct within the medical community. The tensions between civic, military,
and intelligence duties on the one hand, and their professional obligations
on the other, together with peer pressure, careerism, and various forms of
opportunism, led many to brush off ethical transgressions as an evil necessary to advancing medical knowledge in the climate of the Cold War.

    The literature has made considerable inroads into uncovering Britain's
experimental research with LSD as an incapacitating chemical weapon, a
programme which began in the late 1950s and lasted for over a decade.
However, our knowledge of the more secretive, and probably more sensitive, application of drugs for the purpose of interrogation remains to this
day heavily fragmented. In the light of the alleged involvement of Anglo-
American intelligence agencies in the interrogation of potential terror suspects outside national jurisdictions and in violation of international laws
and conventions, it is unlikely that justified demands for access to classified
sources will be granted in the foreseeable future. The stakes are simply too
high for Western governments to allow greater insight into their psychochemical weapons arsenals.[41] By contextualizing what little there is, we
can begin to see that these were not 'separate' programmes, as some scholars
have suggested, seemingly disconnected from one another, nor did Britain's
intelligence agencies suddenly completely lose interest in the use of psycho-
pharmaceuticals for interrogation and physiological/psychological enhancement techniques in the 1950s. On the contrary, the initial research programme
launched at Porton in the early 1950s to assess the use of LSD as a 'truth
drug' was not only sponsored and conducted by members of MI6 and the
Office of Scientific Intelligence (OSI), a department in the CIA, but was
instrumental in developing the relevant methodologies informing Porton's
research policy on incapacitating agents for years to come.

    LSD had first come to the attention of Porton's scientists after discussion
in the published literature of its effects on 'patients'. In March 1953, prior to
Beecher's visit, the enzyme panel of the CDAB summarized its pharmacological mode of action. Whereas some psychologically stable subjects,

exposed to between 40 and 100 µg of LSD, could experience feelings of euphoria without losing consciousness or the ability for rational judgement, others fell into deep depressions in which their sense of time and space was heavily impaired, so much so that they felt detached from themselves and their own personality. Researchers were particularly interested in assessing the process of 'depersonalization' and, ideally, learning to control it. The effects of LSD generally became more marked after about an hour and lasted for between three and six hours, depending on the dose administered.[42] By 1954, biochemical studies by R.H.S. Thompson, who later served on the Himsworth Committee,[43] gave grounds for suggesting that LSD was a 'relatively powerful inhibitor' of certain enzymes in the human brain, evidence which, if it was shared with MI6, does not seem to have convinced them to reconsider their trials.[44] In total, from what we know, Britain's intelligence agencies used almost forty human participants in LSD 'truth drug' experiments at Porton, none of whom had been psychologically screened before their involvement, or for their physiological suitability for taking part in the trials. In the same year, SIS sponsored a series of LSD self-experiments with an undisclosed number of Porton officials and five service officers, yet the results were apparently so disappointing that 'SIS-sponsored trials involving LSD ceased'.[45]

Among those apparently taking part in Porton's LSD trials was Peter Wright, then employed by MI5, Britain's domestic intelligence service, who recalled in his well-publicized account that he had been 'cooperating with MI6 in a joint programme to investigate how far the hallucinatory drug LSD could be used in interrogations'.[46] It is possible, though there is no evidence to corroborate the suggestion, that Porton's LSD experiments in the early 1950s were a joint venture between MI5 and MI6. It is, however, more likely that, as someone with high security clearance, he would have known about the trials and that he conveniently wrote himself into the events to boost the marketability of his evidently successful book *Spycatcher*.[47] Whether his comment 'I even volunteered as guinea pig on one occasion' reflects a rather casual, perhaps even careless attitude towards LSD trials among members of Britain's intelligence community is perhaps less material than the fact that he made no comment whatsoever about his experience of taking the drug, if indeed he did ever take it. Those who did remembered their LSD trips very vividly in most cases, and rarely positively.

The MoD maintains that none of the servicemen, many of whom received several doses, were placed 'under stress' or suffered any ill-effects.

This contrasts with the recollections of those who did take part. Nineteen-year-old Eric Gow, a Royal Navy radio operator, was amongst those service-men who went to Porton in the belief that their stay would help to find a cure for the common cold. He experienced 'vivid hallucinations' after being drugged with LSD without his knowledge.[48] This was achieved surrepti-tiously by administration of the substance from a sherry glass in a convivial social environment, which gave him a false sense of security. None of the subjects, including Gow, were informed or 'warned' of any adverse effects, nor were they medically supervised during their 'trip'. In the mid 1960s, as Porton was trialling various incapacitating agents, Ladell admitted that pre-vious LSD experiments had been 'tentative and inadequately controlled'.[49] In retrospect, many of those able to recall their Porton experiences consider the tests to have been highly 'irresponsible' and 'reckless', a sentiment shared by Don Webb, then a nineteen-year-old RAF servicemen, who after being fed LSD twice in one week experienced a psychological nightmare: 'walls melting, cracks appearing in people's faces, you could see their skulls, eyes would run down cheeks, Salvador Dali-type faces, all in broad daylight'.[50] Years of flashbacks without any form of medical follow-up turned him into an outspoken campaigner for the Porton veterans. Others expressed their anger at having been 'drugged and duped', as Gow told *The Guardian* news-paper in 2002: 'To use your own as guinea pigs and put them in harm's way at all is not really on, is it?'[51]

Three years later, in an unprecedented step to contain more damage to the reputation of Britain's security services and prevent further disclosure of top-secret but heavily redacted documents to the lawyer representing Gow, Webb, and Brian Hughes, another participant in the non-therapeutic LSD trials of the 1950s, the Foreign and Commonwealth Office (FCO), as the ministry responsible for MI6, agreed an 'out-of-court' settlement worth thousands of pounds. It prevented the men or their lawyers from disclosing the exact amount of compensation, or passing on any evidence to interested parties. However, this attempt to control the free exchange of information on such a sensitive subject in an age of instant mass communication had inadvertently done untold damage. News about the compensation, believed to be the first ever personal injury (PI) claim accepted by MI6 in its history, spread within days around the globe, with over 144,000 website hits on the subject of 'MI6/LSD' on the internet search engine Google alone.[52] It was a public relations blunder of monumental proportions. If ever the British secret service had wanted to publicize its past ethical shortcomings, by paying out what their lawyer described as a 'modest sum', it had not only spectacularly exceeded expectations, but had fuelled a wave of internet-based conspiracy theories alleging the systematic involvement of Britain's state agencies in criminal acts against its citizens.[53]

It also turned out that the scientist in charge of the fateful nerve gas experiment on Maddison in 1953, Harry Cullumbine, had been involved in Porton's LSD experiments at the behest of the SIS. In his unpublished autobiography, he recalled that Porton had stopped further trials 'when it was reported that in a few people it might produce suicidal tendencies'.[54] Assuming that Cullumbine's recollections are correct, and there are no obvious reasons to doubt them, and assuming further that they refer to the 1953 and 1954 experiments, rather than the later ones, then the rationale for temporarily suspending LSD trials at Porton may not lie only in the seemingly poor results obtained from LSD for interrogation purposes, even if the data was disappointing. The impetus for halting all further tests may in fact have been the fear among Porton scientists that their entire experimental programme could be called into question if just one of the subjects drugged by LSD suffered serious harm or committed suicide. Following Maddison's death in May 1953, Porton had come under immense pressure to explain its existing safety protocols. The death of another serviceman not much later would have spelled disaster for the organization, especially if it had become public knowledge that the person had been drugged with a psychologically incapacitating agent without consent. If anything, the SIS-sponsored trials highlighted the need for screening tests to eliminate as far as possible the possibility of selecting servicemen whose mental constitution would make them susceptible to LSD's potentially life-threatening effects.

The gradual introduction of greater ethical oversight and improved safety standards in one of Britain's most secretive Cold War research facilities did not happen because of greater regard among Porton's scientists for international medical law and human rights as codified in the principles of the Nuremberg Code, nor for the welfare and well-being of research participants. It happened as a result of a collapse in authority and trust between Porton and its political masters, who responded to Maddison's death, for reasons of national security, by instigating a complex cover-up which breached established principles of democratic accountability. In the eyes of some senior officials, Porton had irrevocably and permanently lost its 'innocence'. At the same time, it made Porton scientists realize, perhaps for the first time, that their operational independence, established and consolidated in the interwar period, could be challenged by greater centralized control unless more formalized safety procedures were implemented. Maddison's death not only made changes in Porton's military medical ethics culture possible, it made them a priority. It had been a game changer.

Screening Humans

As part of the intelligence agencies' drive to screen hundreds of new compounds for their incapacitating and chemical weapons potential, Porton's interest in LSD continued throughout the 1950s despite the difficult circumstances surrounding the initial test series.[55] In 1956, the DRPC authorized a preliminary programme of research to test the potential of LSD as an incapacitating agent against 'individuals, key groups or perhaps in controlling hostile crowds'.[56] Another five years elapsed until, in 1961, Porton's human tests with LSD commenced in earnest in the form of laboratory experiments and three major field trials, called 'Moneybags', 'Recount', and 'Small Change', to study the effects of hallucinogenic drugs on group dynamics, rather than on individuals, since soldiers in the field generally operated in teams.[57] It is in this transitionary period that we begin to see the emergence of some form of human subject protection regime at Porton, still in an embryonic form, but visible, in negotiations over screening tests, or in controversies over how best to balance the need for the safety of human participants with the demands for greater progress in this field of work.

One of the most significant procedural changes introduced at Porton to reduce the risk of injury from LSD exposure was a battery of psychiatric and psychological screening tests of all potential participants. This was done in tandem with assessing the deleterious effects of new compounds to reduce even further any potential risk.[58] Concerned that some of the tests might 'set in train some irreversible effect', the CDAB proposed to study the family history of human participants and exclude all those exhibiting signs of mental instability or, as Ladell put it in less diplomatic terms, to 'eliminate all psychopaths and schizophrenics'.[59] In addition to consulting expert psychiatrists and psychologists from the Maudsley Hospital, South London (Sir Aubrey Lewis), the Royal Victoria Hospital, Netley (Major Stephens), the MRC Unit of Applied Psychology at Cambridge, and the Director of Army Psychiatry, Brigadier John McGhie, who believed that irreversible effects from carefully controlled LSD tests were 'unlikely', Porton managed to enlist the support of Army psychiatrists in carrying out the interviews.[60] Yet despite elaborate precautions, senior representatives from the Royal Naval and Army Medical Services and various other 'quarters' expressed 'slight misgivings'—which was code for grave anxieties—about administering 'psychotomimetic' drugs to service volunteers. It put Ladell and others at Porton on notice to implement such a programme, if at all, with great caution.

Screening tests were a practical expression of Porton's desire to manage risk, but they also provided researchers with additional tools to learn more about the psychological and sociological make-up of the service population that had signed up for tests, their age profile, rank, social background, mental stability, personality, intelligence, and motivation and reasons for volunteering. Although the tests were ostensibly designed to gather information about subjects' suitability for tests with incapacitants, Porton's consultant psychiatrists and psychologists quickly realized that in-depth studies of different cohorts of servicemen offered a research opportunity which should not be missed. In constructing seemingly objective criteria for the selection of servicemen to test the effects of psychochemicals, the assessors turned themselves into researchers who performed psychological tests on experimental subjects not yet selected. Thus, a serviceman who had gone to Porton for a fortnight to leave the boredom of service life behind, at least momentarily, could easily find himself, without his knowledge, the object of an elaborate assessment programme before the tests he believed he had volunteered for actually began. If his experience of those tests was different from what he had anticipated, if accurate information about the nature and purpose of the trial was withheld, or if informed consent was not obtained, he may have realized, in retrospect at least, that he had been misled not just once or twice, but three, four, five, or six times: whenever a member of Porton's staff had used him in one of their many overlapping human studies.

For physical incapacitants such as riot control agents, Porton used a multiple-choice questionnaire to assess the level of motivation of test subjects. Based on the assumption that rioters were 'highly motivated people', the idea was to test physical incapacitants on at least equally motivated participants. In order to achieve this, the degree of motivation among soldiers needed to be established and, if necessary, increased. Soldiers might be motivated to endure harassing agents for longer, Porton hoped, through financial incentives, though the hypothesis could not be substantiated. A study performed in the mid 1960s to assess the 'social values' of servicemen seemed to suggest that both Porton's service volunteers and the general service populations had a 'greater interest in money and a lesser interest in aesthetics and ethical matters' compared to the Porton laboratory staff and US college students who had formerly taken the test. Since the majority of national servicemen came from the lower and lower middle classes—so that their educational and professional backgrounds might have exposed them less frequently to questions of ethics or aesthetics—the result may not altogether surprising, perhaps even less so considering the range of mundane incentives which motivated many to volunteer—a free railway ticket home to see family and (girl)friends, time off from tedious military service, or some additional pocket money for a good night out; yet a closer look reveals quite an ambiguous picture.[61] To see 'how much discomfort and danger a man was prepared to face for money', soldiers were given additional financial rewards depending on how long they stayed in the gas chamber, yet the amount offered appeared to be an 'inadequate bait' to enhance endurance. It led scientists to conclude that it was 'doubtful' the motivation of service personnel could be improved through 'cash rewards'.[62] Money may have played some role—previous studies had shown it was not a predominant one—in servicemen's decisions to go to Porton, but the amounts offered were clearly too little to entice them, once they were there, to take part in more prolonged tests with harassing agents.

Psychological screening tests, which lasted several days, included the Maudsley Personality Inventory to gauge 'emotionality and extraversion' of potential participants; an extended interview by an expert military psychiatrist, who recorded any family history of mental disease, injuries, or unusual personal habits; the Raven's Progressive Matrix test to estimate general intelligence by answering sixty problems from a 'test book'; the Archimedes Spiral test to 'measure' different levels of anxiety; the controversial Sedation Threshold test, in which participants had to perform simple arithmetic tasks under increasing sedation to see whether they suffered from psychosis; and a final interview by a medical officer. In theory, it was only at the last stage that participants with a 'normal mentality' would be selected to take part in tests with psychological incapacitants.[63]

Data compiled by Porton's consultant psychologist Kenneth H. Kemp in 1960/1961 on over 500 servicemen suggested that those who had agreed to take part in trials were disproportionately more 'extravert' and much more 'neurotic' compared to the general and service population; that they also seemed to be more intelligent was seen as unremarkable since the 'least intelligent' men were apparently rejected by the services, while the 'most intelligent' ones would be 'skimmed off for commission'. Between the Royal Navy and the Army there were no discernible differences, though a high number of 'very intelligent' men apparently came from the RAF.[64] As far as the overall evaluation of the Porton volunteers was concerned, their 'intelligence' and 'personality' were regarded as 'abnormal'—i.e. not repre-sentative—when compared to those of British civilians and servicemen generally. Even more illuminating were the reasons why soldiers went to Porton. Only two men arrived with their friends. From a total of 379 men questioned, more than three-quarters chose to go to Porton for one of two reasons: 47 per cent wanted to experience a 'change' of scenery, at least on their first visit, though less so on their second, while 32 per cent came to Porton out of 'interest' or 'curiosity', findings which confirmed earlier work done by Porton's consultant psychologist Basil Clarke, RAMC, who in 1953 had carried out an 'exploratory study' into the 'Psychological Effects of a G-Agent on Men'.[65] There were some who wanted to avoid certain indi-viduals, duties, or situations. Few of the men had apparently come for the 'money', to have a 'rest', or be 'near home'. While more recent testimonies suggest that these motives played a role in volunteering, these may say more about the construction of retrospective justifications than about the variety of reasons why men decided to go to Porton.[66]

The findings broadly confirmed the results of an earlier study by R.J. Shephard, Porton's consultant psychiatrist, in which 117 servicemen completed a modified medical questionnaire originally designed to assess patients with mental conditions; soldiers attending courses at Winterbourne Gunner had served as a control group. According to the assessors, who were conscious of a 'biased experimental population', there were generally 'two types of individuals' putting themselves forward for tests: those with a 'hys-teric and neurotic' personality seeking recognition from 'secret tests', and a smaller group of those wanting to serve their country as good citizens. Although the sample was smaller, the motives for volunteering were similar; most men simply seemed to be 'bored' with their day-to-day work. Again, the longing for change rather than shortage of money was the deciding factor in volunteering. Both studies appeared to suggest that Porton's 'vol-unteer population' was made up of a disproportionately large number of 'neurotic' and 'introverted' men.[67] How this related to, or impacted upon, their ability to serve as test subjects was less clear, except that many of them seem to have been excluded on those grounds from participating in trials with incapacitants.

Porton's screening programme quickly ran into trouble in the early 1960s when it became apparent that only one-third, and in some cases fewer than one-fifth, of all participants were deemed eligible for the tests, thus strengthening the perception that progress in LSD research was disproportionately slow. The problem was further compounded by the realization that the number of available servicemen had dropped by about 50 per cent, from an average of 627 in the 1950s to 340 in the early 1960s, and with predictions suggesting a further downward trend. Indeed, in the three years between 1964 and 1966 Porton had access to an average of only 147 service volunteers. Smaller sample sizes obviously created additional methodological problems in obtaining representative results.[68] To artificially increase the 'volunteer population' through inducements, on the other hand, for example through payments or the provision of more comfort, raised the 'ethical question of removing "voluntary consent" from the recruitment process'.[69] Alarmed by these figures, expert advisers nonetheless began watering down the existing screening procedure by questioning the rationale for the large number of tests; others proposed a more flexible system, introducing variable screening tests depending on the doses to be studied. Procedures were also influenced by the introduction of new tests and the modification or removal of old ones.[70] The revised arrangement resembled, in modern parlance, a form of 'personalized screening system', to ensure an increase in the number of eligible test subjects. Overall, there was a tendency to relax the screening process. This was done against the advice of Porton's director, who feared that that 'a single accident would put a stop to future tests'. In 1967, in response to being seen by some as 'over-cautious', Porton permitted participation in LSD trials by subjects who had been classed as 'borderline'.[71] Whether the changes to the selection process exposed British servicemen to greater risks is difficult to tell in retrospect, given that human psychology is not an exact science, but what seems certain is that the tension between ensuring the safety of human participants on the one hand and the advancement of chemical warfare knowledge on the other was decided in favour of the latter.

However, such a system could only legitimately be maintained as long as lives were not put at risk. Porton may have been exempt from public scrutiny, but it was not above the law of the land. By the mid 1960s, as evidence of serious ill-effects among staff members and service personnel involved in tests could no longer be ignored, Porton's Senior Medical Officer was faced with a stark choice: to resist the demands of expert advisers to study the threshold dosages of psychological and physically incapacitating agents, and risk potential consequences to his career, or to continue with the experimental programme with the risk of being accused of manslaughter later. Whereas the security of the British realm had previously trumped almost any other argument in contentious debates about chemical warfare, the role of medical ethics suddenly moved to the forefront of Porton's deliberations, so much so that tests with incapacitants were temporarily suspended in 1965. Non-therapeutic experiments classed as 'dangerous', Porton's medical experts argued, were simply unethical and could not legitimately be conducted in peacetime, irrespective of the ongoing Cold War. To understand how Porton's experiments had developed to the point where those in charge of the safety of the tests were no longer willing to accept responsibility on the grounds of ethics, we need to historicize Porton's work with different types of incapacitating agents.

Incapacitating Humans

From early on, medical experts in the United States and Britain expressed concerns that the use of incapacitants involved unpredictable dangers. Marijuana, for example, was believed to have the ability to cause 'pathological changes' in individuals that would make the testing of such compounds on service volunteers a risky enterprise. LSD, on the other hand, discovered during the Second World War and then used for years in the treatment of patients with mental conditions, was being criticized in the mid 1950s for its potentially harmful effects; those under the influence of LSD, experts warned in the British *Lancet*, could be a 'danger to themselves' or suffer from 'profound mental disturbance'. The substance could also exacerbate 'psychotic illness', which made it unsuitable in the treatment of people with underlying mental problems.[72]

Such information did not go unnoticed. In the United States, Van M. Sim, in charge of human experiments at Edgewood Arsenal, who had spearheaded clinical trials into VX, warned his colleagues against 'immediate large-scale experiments' with psychological incapacitants. Although the BJSM, based in Washington DC, was doubtful about reports suggesting a 'small margin of safety' in trialling LSD, experts on the Chemistry Committee of the CDAB, who shared much the same sentiment as their US colleagues, made their support for Porton's LSD tests conditional upon the level of risk involved. In March 1959, Gaddum was asked whether he could reassure the committee that the adverse effect of LSD would always be 'temporary and entirely reversible'.[73] He could not. According to Gaddum, 'the effects of a few doses was [sic] usually reversible but if repeated doses were given, an irreversible effect might be produced'.[74] To avert criticism of Porton's safety standards, Ladell agreed that 'volunteers would not be given more than one dose of any compound being tested', yet over the next five years staff and servicemen were regularly exposed to multiple doses of the same or varying agents, a situation which, over time, created an ever greater sense of unease among members of staff about the existing test programme. Most scientists, including Ladell, were less concerned about exposing humans to highly potent nerve gases, including Sarin and VX, than about administering psychochemicals to unsuspecting subjects because, unlike the former, their mode of action was neither fully understood nor predictable with any degree of certainty. Their concerns were not entirely unjustified.

According to official figures, Porton carried out a total of 136 human tests with LSD, though some servicemen had multiple exposures.[75] Porton's staff members also carried out a series of self-experiments. Seemingly excited about psychological incapacitants as 'safe and humanitarian' weapons, and rarely shy about expressing themselves, however half-baked or risky their ideas, some of the scientists used their LSD induced trips to explore their innermost artistic potential in drawings that apparently represented feelings of 'transcendental truth'.[76] By testing the drugs on themselves, so the justification ran, they would obtain additional 'moral authority' in conducting LSD tests on servicemen since they would know what they might experience. This would help them to organize the trials more effectively. It is not difficult to see why they neither argued for, nor applied, such a system in mustard gas or nerve agent tests, although it would have been warranted, since those compounds could only harm, but in that case the scientists would have had nothing whatsoever to gain. With LSD the situation was different. The main aim of their elaborate, albeit hardly convincing, rationale for self-experimentation was to have an LSD trip on the cheap. Not all of the scientists were convinced it had been a good idea. In late 1961, four staff members took 50 µg of LSD intravenously under 'psychiatric supervision' to assess its effect, which meant being placed in a darkened room with a tape recorder; one of them disliked the 'unpleasant experience' so much that he was reluctant to discuss it years later.[77]

From December 1961 until January 1965, when further tests were stopped, Porton carried out a total of fifty-nine LSD experiments on forty-seven servicemen in an experimental unit specially constructed next to the hospital, in case something went wrong.[78] Secrecy, in order to avoid potentially adverse publicity, was paramount: the fear that local workmen refurbishing the hospital complex might witness humans under the influence of LSD and report to the media was sufficient to postpone the start of the tests until the building work had been completed; any breach of secrecy could have spelled disaster.[79] Of twenty participants involved in a first tranche of tests with 50 μg of LSD in 1961/1962, about 50 per cent experienced 'mood changes and disturbances of perception'; others served as controls or were given sedatives as a potential antidote.[80] Test subjects who received an increased dosage of 200 μg LSD a year later experienced feelings of 'depression' coupled with a lack of concentration for two days after the trial.

More worrying were the results of Porton's first large-scale field trial, carried out at the end of 1964 and code-named 'Moneybags', in which sixteen servicemen from 41 Commando Royal Marines recruited through one of Porton's open days, which had been introduced to enhance Porton's public image, received 200 μg of LSD. The seventeenth participant, deemed unsuitable for such a high dose, was given 75 μg. The three-day field trial was meant to resemble recent military operations the men had experienced in places such as Borneo and Cyprus and involved an imaginary attack by 'rebels' who, having been 'repulsed', needed to be captured. Other than that they would receive a drug of some sort, none of the men knew or were informed of the nature of the trial or the possible effects of LSD, an omission the scientists tried to justify by alluding to the drug's association with the hippie movement. They were perhaps concerned that unsuspecting national servicemen who believed they were serving their country might refuse to take part in trials with a known 'hippie drug', yet such a scenario is rather far-fetched. It is more probable that Porton simply did not reveal the nature of the drug on grounds of secrecy.

After drinking water spiked with LSD on the second day, the group became 'progressively disorganized, ill-disciplined and incapable of taking orders'. Communication between the commanding officer and his men was increasingly erratic and chaotic. As military discipline deteriorated, the soldiers wandered aimlessly around in the open in full view of potential enemy

fire, feeding 'imaginary birds', climbing, or chopping down a tree or point-
ing the rocket launcher at their own comrades. After about half an hour, the
commanding officer had completely lost control of his troops; unable to
issue further instructions, he declared, 'I am wiped out as an attacking force.'
Laughing, giggling, and not in their right minds, his troops refused to board
the ambulance after the conclusion of the exercise. For all concerned it was
clear that the platoon would have been 'annihilated by modest enemy
action' after sixty minutes. Although most of the men quickly recovered,
one man had to be hospitalized, having suffered a 'temporary breakdown',
severe depression, and feelings of paranoia for up to five hours after exposure. The trial was recorded on film for study, and we see a gentle young
man pacing up and down the hospital ward constantly muttering to himself:
'I am dying—it can't go on.'[81] The man remained disturbed for several
hours, but had reportedly recovered the day after. When in 1965 the film
was first screened to the newly established Applied Biology Committee, one
expert criticized Porton for not having provided adequate psychological
treatment to the soldier worst affected. Other than being 'watched' by the
army psychiatrist, Major Ronald J. Wawman, he had received no further
therapy. The officer commanding was also reported to have been disturbed
upon seeing the film, though most of his men were either amused or
remained unmoved.[82] Others thought that there should be no interference
in the independent recovery of men thus drugged.[83] Meanwhile, reports of
possible 'chromosome damage' from LSD fuelled speculation about possible
long-term health hazards of incapacitants.

Meanwhile, alarm bells were beginning to ring over a parallel series of
tests with anticholinergic glycolates, especially with the long-acting BZ
(3-quinuclidinyl benzilate), which had been first synthesized by Hoffmann-La
Roche Inc. in 1951 as part of research into antispasmodic agents.[84] In the late
1950s, US warfare scientists based at Edgewood Arsenal became interested in
investigating the drug under the name EA 2277. Unofficially, the agent
became known as 'Buzz' because it causes severe forms of 'mental aberra-
tions'.[85] Following the onset of symptoms, evidenced by feelings of euphoria,
muscle twitching, and slurred speech, those under the influence of glycolates
could experience total disassociation from their environment. They would
run around, tired, restless, and disoriented; constantly muttering, and out of
their mind, they no longer felt any need to eat, drink, or sleep. Compared to
those drugged with LSD, who generally retained some level of mental and
physical control, the subjects could no longer communicate or perform any

tasks. Instead of remembering brightly coloured forms, as those drugged with LSD would often do, they would recall 'objects, animals, and people', followed by amnesia. The effects of BZ could be severe and prolonged. Two subjects in the United States, after receiving 8 μg of BZ, 'became delirious and noisy, had hallucinations and kept moving around continuously for a week'.[86] After evidence suggested that the compound could have a direct effect on the heart, US scientists temporarily suspended their BZ tests on humans and warned Porton to conduct human studies only with 'full medical and psychological cover', since otherwise, as one official put it bluntly, the 'subjects become zombies'.[87]

Over a two-year period, from August 1962 to August 1964, Porton carried out a total of about twenty human exposures to BZ under the leadership of Surgeon Lieutenant Commander W.M. Hollyhock, Royal Navy, who also took responsibility for the screening programme.[88] While most of the symptoms observed were not unexpected, the effects of the drug on some subjects raised great concern. In one man a paranoid state of mind lasted for three days. Nine hours after receiving 7.5 μg of BZ, the person was found in a 'completely confused and psychotic' state and suffering from severe auditory and visual hallucinations, disorientation, and aggressive behaviour. It took more than three days for him to regain some form of rationality. Although they had anticipated such symptoms at this level of intoxication, the scientists were disturbed to detect unusually high blood pressure for over thirty hours. It had placed the subject in real danger for his life. Compared to the US tests, in which the subjects experienced complete amnesia, one of the soldiers recalled that he displayed 'violent reactions' and he 'was difficult to reassure'.[89] Researchers also felt that the Porton's experimental unit was unsuitable for subjects intoxicated with BZ. Crowded together among other drugged subjects, they had no space to run around, felt monitored, and put others in harm's way during violent fits in which they destroyed anything around them, a form of excessive aggressive behaviour the scientists euphemistically called 'exploratory activity'.[90] In reviewing the tests, Porton concluded that two of the subjects had suffered from 'severe toxic delirium' for prolonged periods of time and that further BZ trials should no longer be considered safe. Although tests were briefly resumed in 1967, BZ experiments were discontinued thereafter as the researchers shifted their attention to 'new' glycolates.[91]

As if this were not enough, human tests with newly synthesized physical incapacitating substances made Porton scientists realize that they were approaching dangerous threshold levels that put lives at risk. In February 1961, while visiting one of its 'commercial liaison sources', probably the pharmaceutical company J.F. Macfarlan & Co. Ltd in Edinburgh, Porton learned of the existence of a powerful new synthetic analgesic made from oripavine. Its derivatives were similar in their mode of action to morphine, only between 1,000 and 10,000 times more powerful. In low dosages they could lead to 'euphoria, nausea, and vomiting', though animal tests had already suggested that death could occur from 'respiratory depression'.[92] Drug samples were obtained from both J.F. Macfarlan & Co. Ltd and Reckitt & Sons Ltd in Hull. This enabled Porton to test four of the five oripavine derivatives in a total of 135 human experiments over the next two years, involving five members of staff and 107 servicemen.[93] A series of controlled tests with TL2636 began after a Porton researcher who had accidentally come into contact with the substance suffered from disorientation, light-headedness, vertigo, nausea, and severe vomiting. Before increasingly higher doses of the substance were tested on servicemen, four members of Porton's medical staff performed eleven pilot trials, the effects of which were similar to those produced by the accident. Yet during their attempt to assess the 'safety of higher doses', one participant, who had been given 10 μg/kg of body mass of TL2636 orally, suffered not only from the usual symptoms of nausea and dizziness but from a worrying fall in blood pressure, apparently because he had 'decided' not to vomit; this, the records laconically state, '[might] have been his undoing' had his blood pressure remained low. Fortunately, the man made a 'complete and spontaneous recovery'. Porton had, yet again, taken another high-risk gamble with the life of a serviceman. In assessing the finding, Porton scientists, while speculating about the possibility of inducing 'a cataleptic state in man' with high dosages, recognized the inherent dangers involved. For them, the experience of seeing a man almost die was sufficiently concerning to temporarily suspend human tests with TL2636 because of its 'low safety ratio'—i.e. the small margin of safety between lethal and incapacitating dose—but they then resumed the tests five years later under laboratory and field conditions.[94]

Tests also continued with TL2833, a short-acting oripavine derivative which has a 'rapid knock down' effect when injected subcutaneously. Although it is not entirely clear whether this effect had first been observed in animal studies, there is some evidence to suggest that humans were involved in the testing of the substance from early on. In March 1964, one serviceman, name unknown, injected with 100 μg of TL2833, suffered cat-atonic tremors for several minutes. As an antidote, he was immediately given nalorphine. Two further subjects also suffered dangerous depressions of their cardiovascular system. By the end of 1964, the number of serious ill-effects observed among servicemen and staff drugged with incapacitants had reached such an alarming level that Porton's medical experts considered it to be only a matter of time before a test subject suffered serious injury or death. At this point, arguably not before time, those medically trained among Porton's staff began to raise issues of medical ethics that had hitherto been of secondary importance, and to express serious doubts about the experi-mental programme as a whole. As was to be expected, Porton's research programme began to show signs of systemic failure; these allow us to gain insight into contentious debates about the need to improve medical ethics standards.

Crisis Management

In January 1965, the situation finally came to a head when a senior member of staff, most probably Hollyhock, was suddenly admitted to hospital with depression. Doctors were concerned that he might have become addicted to LSD 25, which he had self-administered on multiple occasions.[95] Although he recovered, he never returned to work at Porton. Two members of Porton's Medical Division had already resigned, in November and December 1964, and there was the possibility that a third member, Hollyhock's assistant, might resign in the near future because he felt 'very near breaking point'.[96] He left a few weeks later.[97] Just as the death of a scientist from plague in 1962 had triggered a crisis of confidence in Porton's biological research at the MRE, events in 1964 did not bode well for the chemical warfare section. Faced with a situation in which several members of his staff had become seriously ill or resigned in short order, Ladell, as the chief medical adviser to Porton's director, convened a meeting of COSHE on 2 February 1965 to review Porton's experimental programme.[98] All instances in which human subjects had recently suffered serious adverse effects were discussed. In the case of psychological incapacitants, Ladell and what remained of his team were worried about the depersonalizing effect of LSD, 'a frightening fea-ture' of the drug with unknown consequences for those involved. Likewise, the three-day toxic delirium observed in subjects under the influence of BZ gave reason to believe that the substance could cause 'irreversible changes in cortical function and personality'.[99] None of the scientists was as yet in a position to say what the long-term implications of such a delirium, its sub-conscious memories, or indeed the experience of reliving these memories might be for a person's behaviour. It remained an unexplored field. Physical incapacitants, on the other hand, were in a class of their own. Tests with TL2636 seemed to suggest that while it might be acceptable to allow sub-jects to suffer from a 5 per cent drop in organ function, for example in the liver or the kidney, it was seen as an 'unacceptable risk' to perform tests that could lead to a 'permanent fall-off in brain function'.[100] Finally, the short-acting drug TL2833 had led to such a dramatic depression of the cardiovas-cular system that Porton's medical staff believed that there was a 'real danger' that research subjects could suffer permanent brain damage if starved of oxygen in what is termed cerebral hypoxia. The situation was obviously grave. Although incapacitant agents were believed by the scientific commu-nity to be relatively 'safe', there were 'strong reasons', according to Ladell, why this assessment could no longer be upheld: 'If tests were dangerous, even if the effects appeared to be innocuous, it was considered unethical and unjustified to conduct human tests with these agents in peace-time.'[101] Before the COSHE meeting was adjourned, its members agreed to con-sider whether any further clinical trials with these types of agents should be carried out on humans in the future.

The COSHE meeting in February 1965 brought to a head ethical con-cerns that had been building up for years. Just as a magnifying glass concen-trates rays of light to create ignition, the meeting sparked off a comprehensive re-evaluation of existing safety procedures at Porton. For most medical sci-entists serious ill-effects in individual subjects were insufficient cause for concern, since this had become the 'norm' in Porton's research culture; this was perceived as 'normal' experimental practice in such a sensitive, highly classified, military environment in which the objective was, in most cases, to establish the threshold dosage at which humans became seriously affected by a certain agent. The object of the experiments was to produce these effects artificially, but without irreversibly or intentionally harming partici-pants. Neither was the repeated experience of observing serious ill-effects among servicemen and staff seen as sufficient cause to raise the alarm, nor was the knowledge that some of the subjects had cheated death by a small margin. Things radically changed, however, when all of a sudden Porton's scientists were themselves affected, when their health and professional lives became part of the equation; it was only then, when they became ill or had to resign because they could not take it any longer—the stress, the responsibility, the feeling of being 'near breaking point'—that immediate action was called for to preserve their physical and psychological well-being, and safeguard their professional status within Porton's institutional setting. At this moment Porton's medical experts began to accept ethical responsibility. Remarkably, the core of their reasoning was that dangerous tests are unethical and unjustified in peacetime. The surprising new factor appears in a simple word: 'peacetime'. For years, in every conceivable controversy over the allocation of resources or human tests, Porton's scientists had raised the spectre of the Cold War—apparently about to develop into an armed conflict of monumental proportions with the potential to annihilate Western civilization, if not humanity as a whole—and yet now, when their own interests were at stake, and under pressure to rationalize their action, they applied a description of their external political and social reality which stood in complete opposition to the Cold War: peacetime. It was a description as vague and misleading as the references to military necessity, national security, or any other higher ideal that had previously served to sanction their secretive work. If anything, it reflected their desire and ability to survive.

On 12 February 1965, ten days after the COSHE meeting, and after discussing the matter with Sir Aubrey Lewis from Maudsley Hospital, who advised Porton on its screening programme, Ladell banned all human experiments with hallucinogenic drugs until further notice.[102] Although nominal responsibility for Porton's medical research division fell to the Senior Medical Officer (Research), Francis W. Beswick, a qualified physician who had previously lectured at the University of Wales, Ladell had gradually appropriated considerable responsibility for almost all aspects of human experiments. As the chair of COSHE, he was in a powerful position to temporarily ban, in theory, all human trials.[103] Banning tests with hallucinogenic drugs was a bold step, one he had not taken lightly, he told the University of Edinburgh Medical School, but he could not see 'any justification whatsoever for putting a healthy man in even remote danger of permanent damage either to body or mind'.[104] Weeks later, he extended the ban to include all oripavine derivatives.[105]

Although Ladell's decision was probably the only one possible under the circumstances to avoid making himself liable for injury or death suffered by any of the subjects, it was not welcomed at higher levels. Haddon, as Porton's director, was furious that Ladell's blanket ban, which the latter termed a 'question of medical conscience', had 'caused considerable embarrassment to senior officials in London', particularly for the SAC chairman, the Chief Scientist (Army) and his deputy, whose support was believed to be vital to Porton's continued existence.[106] He knew that if Whitehall's scientific civil servants lost patience with Porton as a viable military facility, or failed to make the necessary representations in political circles, the future of Porton could be at stake. In explaining the crisis to the Deputy Secretary of State for Defence—though not until it had been resolved—the Chief Scientist (Army) noted that Ladell had had 'some doubt about the propriety from the medical ethical point of view' of intentionally exposing healthy participants to chemical compounds that would cause 'temporary physical or psychological malfunctioning'.[107] To avert a public unravelling of Porton's experimental programme, Haddon, with the agreement of the Chief Scientist, approached John M. Barnes, chairman of the Biology Committee of the SAC, who arranged an emergency SAC meeting of 'eminent people in the medical world'.[108] What qualified these men to take a view on the ethics of Porton's research culture?

As head of the MRC's Toxicology Research Unit, Barnes had been associated with Porton for over twenty years: he had first been head of the MRC's Burns Research Unit in Oxford and, as a member of RAMC, had conducted toxicity tests at Porton during the war; later he had held an advisory role for the MoD. His postwar work had focused on the toxicology of various organophosphorus compounds, including nerve agents, as well as on beryllium, organotin compounds, and carbon disulphide.[109] The MRC's Toxicology Research Unit had been founded at Porton in 1947 under his leadership with only a few members of staff, including W. Norman Aldridge, a former assistant to Lovatt Evans, and the experimental pathologist Frank A. Denz, a New Zealander. The Unit moved to civilian premises at Carshalton, Surrey, in 1950 where it flourished and developed into a major research centre advising governments and international health organizations about the potential hazards of environmental pollutants and toxic agents.[110] In 1953, for instance, the WHO commissioned Barnes to report on the 'Toxic Hazards of Certain Pesticides to Man', a task that helped the Unit to become recognized as an essential reference centre for the evaluation and testing of insecticides.[111] Together with leading wartime chemical warfare scientists, he also belonged to a newly established advisory committee that assisted the MRC on the toxicology of industrial hazards.[112] Barnes' expertise in the mode of action of toxic chemicals on the central nervous system, together with his interest in formulating innovative safety regulations for dealing with hazardous materials, meant that he was well placed to assess the risks involved in Porton's incapacitating experiments.

Barnes was joined by Sir Aubrey Lewis of the Maudsley Hospital, born in 1900 in Adelaide in South Australia, who was a leading figure in postwar British psychiatry and a senior consultant to Porton's psychochemical warfare screening programme—an obvious choice. Max L. Rosenheim, born in London in 1908, emeritus professor of medicine at University College Hospital and a member of the RAMC, had served as consultant physician to the Allied Forces in South East Asia with the rank of brigadier. He was known for his work on renal disease and hypertension and was about to become President of the Royal College of Physicians. Born in 1915 in Kingston, Surrey, John R. Squire was professor of experimental pathology at Birmingham University, honorary Major in the RAMC and director general of the MRC's Clinical Research Centre at Northwick Park Hospital, Harrow. Andrew Wilson, born in 1909, a professor of pharmacology at Liverpool University, had, as explained earlier (see Chapter 5 above), advised the MoS after the war on the effects of organophosphorus compounds such as PF-3 which, to the embarrassment of some expert scientists, had previously been dismissed as a chemical warfare agent.[113] His work appeared to suggest that some insecticides damaged the myelin sheaths of nerve fibres. As an expert on the effects of drugs on the central nervous and cardiovascular system, he had conducted clinical trials with LSD and Ritalin, and had responded to the Thalidomide scandal with proposals on how to improve clinical trial procedures.[114]

All those present at the meeting were senior scientists, born between 1900 and 1915, with extensive expertise in psychology, pharmacology, toxicology, biochemistry, and experimental pathology, and all had served on various advisory committees in the past. What distinguished them from others equally qualified was their intricate web of connections to Porton. Some had worked there in the past or had acted as expert advisers; others had used Porton's laboratory facilities as a platform to launch their own research institutes in the postwar period. Almost all had served as members of the CDAB and its subcommittees, and thus possessed the necessary security clearance. What qualified them was not so much their knowledge and interest in questions of medical ethics, but their scientific expertise, professional standing, and loyalty to Britain's chemical warfare corps.

Finally, there was Robert H.S. Thompson, a leading biochemist and head
of the Courtauld Institute of Biochemistry, who during the Second World
War had been involved in developing defensive measures against gas warfare
before serving as a major in the RAMC. Born in Croydon in 1912 into a
family of medical practitioners, he was probably the most experienced of
those attending the emergency SAC meeting as far as chemical warfare
experiments on human subjects were concerned. He had just moved from
Guy's Hospital, where he had held the chair in chemical pathology, to
become professor of biochemistry and director of the Courtauld Institute.
As a member of the Biology Committee of the CDAB since 1948, a member of the MRC from 1958 to 1962, and a trustee of the Wellcome Trust
since 1963, Thompson occupied one of the most senior positions bridging
civilian and military research in Britain. Three years later, in 1968, he took
over the chairmanship of the SAC, which he held until 1975. His biography
is testament to the profound continuities which run deep within Britain's
chemical warfare community, from Barcroft in the First World War and his
assistant Peters, to the latter's laboratory in the Second World War and
his assistant: this very Thompson, who proceeded to shape and direct
Britain's chemical warfare work during much of the Cold War.[115]

Before the start of the SAC meeting, Ladell had been asked to report on
the problems which had plagued Porton.[116] The aim was to define the level
of incapacitation which could be ethically justified, and reassure Ladell and
other concerned researchers that Porton's experiments with incapacitating
agents would not go beyond what 'our medical colleagues outside Porton
would consider justifiable'.[117] If ever there was a moment in which Porton's
senior scientists and Whitehall officials reflected critically about the ethical
boundaries of non-therapeutic military research, it was now, in the recognition that Porton's work, albeit in the service of the state, could not depart
from, or violate, medical ethics standards which had evolved in, and been
codified by, the medical community since the end of the war.

The SAC meeting took place in early August 1965 at University
College Hospital in London. Much of the discussion focused on the question of whether Porton's medical staff was acting with permission when
'deliberately dosing healthy men with drugs specifically designed to
induce some malfunction, either physiological or psychological'.[118] For
most experts present this seemed ethically justifiable, as long as the intention was that Porton would as a result 'develop therapies' against agents
that enemy powers might employ against British armed forces. However,

as Ladell had to admit, this was actually not the case: 'I had to therefore disclose after warning those present that this was a highly secret matter that we were in fact looking for an agent which we could use under certain circumstances.'[119] Or, to put it differently, Porton was seeking to develop an incapacitating nonlethal chemical warfare agent for offensive purposes. Most of those present at the SAC meeting probably knew very little, if anything, about a top-secret research and development programme into incapacitating and lethal agents which had been authorized by the Macmillan government two years earlier.[120] It was a revelation which, according to the records, 'changed the complexion [of the meeting] very considerably'.[121]

Some members of Britain's most senior scientific advisory committee, disturbed by what they had heard, felt that Porton staff were tasked with research objectives which 'went far beyond the Medical Research Council rules for human experiments'. For them, the MRC statement of 1962/1963 provided the most authoritative medical ethics standard against which the ethicacy of Porton's research needed to be measured. Other more practically minded colleagues disagreed. In trying to show Porton a way out of its present dilemma, and rather ironically, they sought refuge in the utilitarian argument to which the Nuremberg Code refers in its Principle 2. As long as Porton's experiments with incapacitants 'yield[ed] fruitful results for the good of society', they argued, the tests could apparently be ethically justified. In a complete reversal of previous criticisms of the Code, which had been viewed by many as detrimental to the advancement of science, British medical experts now used the Code's general reference to the 'good of society' as leverage to sanction the resumption of Porton's experiments. Incidentally, the authors of the Code had included the phrase 'for the good of society' as a guideline against 'arbitrary' experiments, such as those performed in Nazi Germany, but not as a justification for disproportionately 'dangerous' tests, as were proposed here. Medical ethics rules such as the Code, it seems, were cited if they served a particular purpose, criticized if they did not, and interpreted as lending support to multiple arguments at a given time. If circumstances changed, as in this case, senior scientists had few moral qualms in changing their interpretative ethical framework. In addition to reassuring Ladell and his team that the experiments they were doing, and intended to do, were not only necessary and important but 'acceptable to medical colleagues outside' Porton, a criterion which apparently served as a yardstick for their ethicacy, the SAC experts discussed the creation of an

Applied Biology Committee (ABC) which, in future, would function as a 'father confessor' to Porton's medical scientists.[122]

Apart from recommencing trials as soon as possible, the aim of the ABC was to avoid another experimental ban by establishing an 'advisory machinery' that would 'guide and support' Porton's medical staff in deciding whether to study new chemical agents using human beings. It was also meant to function as a forum in which ethical concerns and issues of conscience could be aired.[123] Rather than addressing the profound ethical problems of Porton's experiments with incapacitants, or its programme with human subjects as a whole, the majority of those attending the emergency SAC meeting viewed those who disagreed with the conduct of Porton's experiments as themselves somewhat disagreeable. At the same time, in the tradition of 'naming and shaming', the ABC's task was to 'damn the proposals [for experiments] of those who were trying to go too far and too fast'.[124]

The very act of holding a semi-public debate on Porton's military medical ethics standards among trusted colleagues with high security clearance—an unprecedented act in itself—and the creation of an external supervisory committee were however testament to the growing recognition among Whitehall officials and Porton's leadership that a gradual reform of safety procedures was, in the long term, inevitable if Porton was to be brought into line with accepted research standards in the civilian world.[125] Whether the authorities liked it or not, the inertia with which they had resisted procedural changes in research governance had been overcome, and there was no going back. Porton had forever changed.

One immediate effect of the crisis was the reduced availability of staff in Porton's medical department. The problem of the resignation of four medically qualified officers was overcome only when the armed services agreed to supply further personnel. By January 1966, the RAF's medical representative, Squadron Leader D. Price, had been replaced by Wing Commander Robert J. Moylan-Jones, who had just returned from secondment on a three-year MRC research project into 'traveller's diarrhoea' in the Middle East, which he had jointly conducted with Lieutenant Colonel J. Barnes.[126] As the 'longest serving military medical officer' at Porton, Moylan-Jones, known to his peers as Peter, came to play an influential role in its research programme until his retirement.[127] The Navy, meanwhile, appointed Surgeon Commander K.J. Martin to fill the post formerly held by Hollyhock. With the appointment of Beswick as new medical superintendent for research and vice-chairman of COSHE,[128] it had also been possible to fill

one of the three vacant civilian research positions.[129] There is some suggestion that Ladell's own health was beginning to break down, possibly owing
to the stress of being responsible for such a sensitive but questionable testing
programme. He certainly suffered from ill-health for some time thereafter
and died five years later.[130] As someone with a confrontational personality,
who often made his views heard, he may have antagonized some of his
peers during the crisis. Yet there were more significant changes afoot.
Any form of self-experimentation with chemical agents or drugs was no
longer permitted.[131] Following the resumption of tests, servicemen and staff
received only one dose per person of incapacitating agent, or received a
lower dosage altogether, as in Operation Recount.[132] For external observers,
unaccustomed to Porton's research culture, this might seem an unremarkable achievement, but it reduced the risk of harm for thousands of human
subjects in the years to come.

Ethics Transformed

Although working in great secrecy, Porton did not operate in a social and
political vacuum. Substantial effort has in the past been expended by the
British authorities to ensure the contours of Porton's research activities
remain, if not secret, at least opaque and undefined; this strategy has sometimes benefited, if unintentionally, from politically motivated if poorly
informed news reporting and public debate.[133] Porton was anything but a
self-contained system. Its intellectual boundaries, meant to keep civilian life
at bay, were far too permeable. It had relied on external expert advice from
outside the armed forces ever since its establishment in the First World War.
This was its *raison d'être*, the foundation on which it had thrived in the interwar period, but it meant that paradigm shifts in civilian medical ethics, or
public controversy about atomic, chemical, and biological weapons, could
influence Porton's self-perception and the conduct of its research. The
internal debates about Porton's research ethics, and those within the multi-
layered system of external advisory committees monitoring the organization's research activities, developed their most powerful dynamic at around
the time when the international medical community proclaimed the dawn
of a new era in research governance. To dismiss this as mere chronological
coincidence would be to overlook the range of informal links between
Britain's military research establishment and world-class science. If one was

about to change tack, the other would follow suit, sooner rather than later; it would keep to its own terms and stay within the confines of conducting secret science, but it would reform.

Even before medical organizations such as the RCP began contemplating the introduction of Research Ethics Committees (RECs) in the late 1960s—a 'form of practical machinery' to reassure the public, preserve clinical autonomy, protect medical institutions from legal liability, and ensure that scientists were eligible for research grants in the United States—Britain established an independent agency to 'review and advise on problems in applied biology . . . arising in the field of chemical warfare'.[134] Reporting to the CDAB, the ABC became the responsible body, and first point of call, for authorizing human experiments at Porton. In addition, 'all new departures' in the testing of chemical agents were referred to it for approval. Its civilian membership was made up of John Barnes, John Squire, and Robert Thompson—all of whom had attended the ad hoc SAC meeting in August 1965—Otto Edholm, born in 1909 and head of the division of human physiology at the MRC's National Institute of Medical Research in Hampstead, North London, Cyril A. Keele, born in 1905 and attached to the department of pharmacology at Middlesex Hospital Medical School, and Malcolm D. Milne, born in 1915 and attached to Westminster Hospital. It also included representatives of the medical directors general of each of the three armed service departments.[135]

The ABC had the power, as its chairman Thompson noted, to veto individual experiments, in which case the decision would be final and not subject to appeal. A telephone call from the ABC's chairman, or his representative, was sufficient to halt the start of a trial.[136] Lines of communication were informal, which had the advantage of not producing a paper trail that could place scientists in a potentially embarrassing situation. The ABC did not curtail the power or influence of the MoD, which had the power to 'ban any particular experiment on political grounds', nor that of COSHE, Porton's internal committee on human safety, whose chairman reserved the right to prohibit specific tests. All COSHE proceedings were regularly submitted to the ABC to keep it informed of human testing (see Figure 3). The aim of adding yet another layer of expertise to existing oversight structures was to ensure a thorough ethical review process of Porton's planned experiments in order to ensure that the risk of harm to servicemen was almost negligible. This may, however, have reduced the degree to which the scientists felt responsible for human trials.

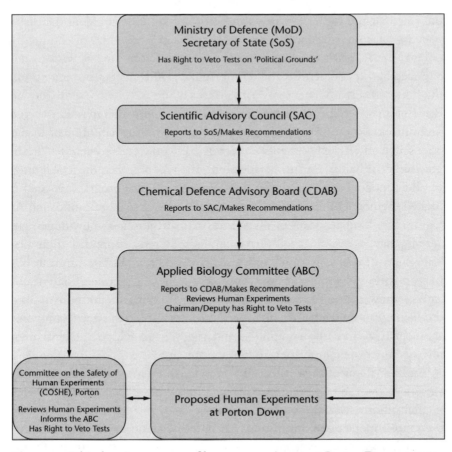

Figure 3. Ethical review process of human experiments at Porton Down, *c.* 1965
Source: TNA, WO 195/16273; ACSRTD, Applied Biology Committee, 6 July 1966.

The ABC originated from a profound crisis of confidence among Porton's staff over the ethical legitimacy and safety of its tests. Attempts by some Porton scientists to downplay events in retrospect were meant to facilitate changes in research governance, and to manage the transition from LSD experiments to higher priority tests with glycolates.[137] Once testing with incapacitants resumed, officials had little appetite for raking over Porton's history of medical ethics transgressions. Both the chairman of the Biology Committee of the SAC and the Chief Scientist (Army) acknowledged that work on incapacitants had gone 'very far into the realms of the unknown' in terms of the accurate assessment of the safety of experiments.[138] It was an 'uncharted field' requiring careful monitoring. Above all, there was the fear that the use of newly synthesized compounds could, as had happened previously, risk 'another serious accident at Porton'.[139]

At the ABC's first meeting in November 1965, convened at Porton, and attended by expert scientists and senior military officers alike—among them the future Director General of Army Medical Services, Lieutenant General R.P. Bradshaw—there was general consensus that non-therapeutic research on humans carried a degree of risk, however remote, that could be managed effectively only if experiments were not to go beyond accepted medical practice.[140] Whereas Porton's leadership was anxious that the committee should function as a 'watchdog' for its experimental programme, Ladell invited members of the ABC to provide scientific and ethical guidance. At a grassroots level, his team of researchers had already begun to implement certain changes in research governance that required a more thorough ethical review of trial procedures and, if needed, 'additional safety measures'.[141] In its discussion, members of the ABC raised a whole series of contentious issues, ranging from insufficient information supplied to the services and servicemen about the nature and purpose of the tests, to the need to appoint a psychiatrist onto the committee and the way in which the system of rewards functioned in relation to 'unpleasant' tests.

Another focus of their discussions was Porton's latest recruitment strategies to boost the number of participants through the use of staff and regimental officers, who would function as de facto recruitment officers, and the employment of colourful propaganda posters and a specially commissioned film 'showing volunteers at work and play'.[142] Whereas the film is hardly an impartial and accurate representation of life at Porton which can be used as credible evidence to demonstrate the 'consent and voluntariness of the volunteers', it nonetheless offers insight into how the authorities wanted to portray the organization in the mid 1960s.[143] In the film, produced in 1966, servicemen arriving at Porton can be seen listening to an introductory talk by the RAF's adviser on defence pharmacology, Moylan-Jones, who gives them a chance to withdraw from each of the trials; a highly constructed scene, yet one which, according to some veterans, seems to have gradually become reality at Porton, certainly by the early 1970s.[144] An advocate of Christian moral values genuinely committed to the Anglican Church, as evidenced by his being a 'lay reader in four local parishes' for seventeen years, Moylan-Jones may well have believed in respecting the autonomy of individuals to withdraw from an experiment at any given time if they so wished, as depicted in the 1966 film. In his obituary, written in 1985, former colleagues also spoke highly about his moral outlook and standing in the community, comparing him with the ideal of a gentleman 'who never inflicts pain', a man guided by charitable beliefs who apparently deserved 'credit for the exemplary safety of the research programme'. However, this statement, if not misleading, was rather economical with the truth as far as the effective protection of research subjects at Porton was concerned.[145] There is little evidence to corroborate what seems to have been a retrospective projection, of an idealized image of a scientist grounded in equal measure in scientific and religious beliefs, on to one of Porton's leading officers in charge of recruitment. Although there were doubts as to whether the volunteers were 'representative of the service population at large', since many were deemed to be poor soldiers, Porton was reluctant to widen its recruitment base to include members of the police or civil defence force, nor was it prepared to accept, seemingly because of 'administrative difficulties', prisoners or university students as test subjects. Women were likewise excluded.

From the perspective of the armed services, there was 'no objection to any tests, provided the servicemen returned to duty without residual damage'. As long as no immediate or long-term harm was done to the soldiers, Porton continued to be, more or less, free to do what it liked within the limits of the law, and as long as all members of COSHE agreed about the need for certain experiments. As it turned out, however, this was not always the case. Indeed, there was some controversy about the justification for recommencing LSD inhalation trials 'until more was known of the persistence of mood effects'. Since 'iron curtain countries' allegedly showed a peculiar interest in these substances, there seemed to be a political rationale for the trials, yet some experts remained concerned about possible side-effects and forms of addiction, as widely reported by the media, and requested additional reassurances to protect the 'unpredictable, hypersensitive minority'.[146] Ladell, surprisingly, despite regarding LSD 25 as a 'dangerous drug', supported the tests, arguing that the potential effects on British servicemen as a whole 'might [just] be a few more mental breakdowns and suicides'. In his view, 'LSD 25 did not itself induce suicidal tendencies, it just stimulates introspection'.[147] In trying to reassure the ABC, he may have wanted to strengthen his position as Porton's medical supremo, yet his comments revealed, more than anything, a paradigm shift in international research, which became increasingly risk-averse in order to avoid issues of legal liability. As long as chemical or biological agents could not be linked directly to specific injuries or diseases, or 'induce' abnormal psychological tendencies, it remained scientifically extremely difficult, if not outright impossible, to hold those agents responsible, and thus the institution legally accountable, for any harm subjects might suffer in connection with them. Indeed, his comments were a reflection of wider changes that had been affecting medical research ethics since the beginning of the 1960s.

9

Ethics within Limits

Ethics Exposed

Although some of Porton's research activities may appear in retrospect 'Ethically Impossible'—in the words of the title of a recent US government report into ethical wrongdoing of US scientists in the 1940s—there is little evidence to suggest that staff suspected, or sensed, any major shortcomings in their work for most of the time, nor do they seem to have been well informed about cases of unethical practice occurring elsewhere.[1] Given that few external organizations were able to give any meaningful advice regarding Britain's military research culture, staff at Porton relied heavily on what they believed to be best practice in such an environment. According to MRC officials theorizing about the 'unusual position' of servicemen as test subjects in 1969, there was always 'a certain element of risk', which apparently was an 'acceptable part of service life'.[2] The lines of demarcation between what was done voluntarily by soldiers and what could be classed as duty were believed to be blurred. MRC officials remained convinced, however, that the MRC's 'recommendations on ethics', particularly those outlined in its statement 'Responsibility in Investigations on Human Subjects' in 1962/1963, had been 'accepted nationally' and were applicable to all research participants, including servicemen.[3] Indeed, in July 1964, a month after the promulgation of the Declaration of Helsinki, *The Lancet* informed Britain's medical community about the MRC's new policy on human experiments, stipulating that all subjects enrolled in non-therapeutic experiments should 'explicitly consent'; researchers were also advised to obtain 'consent verbally in front of a witness'.[4] The MRC's assumption that their principles were valid for all types of research subjects may have been based in part on reports it had received in which the Director of Army Operational Science and Research had stated that the MRC statement applied to all service personnel. If there was a 'special relationship', say between the investigator and subject, military lawyers had argued, then 'more than normal care must be taken to ensure that the subject's consent is a true consent and not assumed or obtained by undue influence'.[5] MRC scientists using soldiers as test subjects were required to apply the 'same high standards' as they would do with civilians, but whether Porton agreed with this position was an entirely different matter. Still, without monitoring the implementation of its policy, the MRC thought that those monitoring the trials at Porton MRE were 'sufficiently sensitive to outside opinion that great care is taken to ensure that subjects are true consenting volunteers and that full ethical standards are preserved'.[6] Given the level of secrecy in Porton's warfare research, however, no outside agency had been tasked with verifying compliance with the MRC's or any other ethics standards within inter-Allied military facilities, nor did such an assignment fall within the remit of advisory bodies such as the ABC; for most of the time, ethical conduct could only be assumed, sometimes incorrectly. In 2003, the CPS concluded that there was sufficient evidence indicating 'that the fully informed consent of the observers was not obtained' in Porton's experiments with certain incapacitants.[7] Ethics transgressions were surely widespread and ignorance about them not confined to Porton.

In the United States, meanwhile, for a considerable time the unethical medical experiments performed on thousands of inmates in federal penitentiaries, asylums, orphanages, and military facilities were neither widely reported nor visible to the public eye. In 1962, as the first draft of the Declaration of Helsinki was published, the Tuskegee Syphilis Study, which had begun in the 1930s, and in which medical treatment was withheld from hundreds of African Americans, was still ongoing. The men from Macon County, Alabama, were never told that they were taking part in a long-term medical study or that they were suffering from treatable syphilis. It was another decade before the gross violations of patient rights perpetrated by scientists of the US Public Health Service (PHS) over a forty-year period were publicly exposed, ushering in a period of major regulatory change that saw the introduction of Institutional Review Boards (IRBs).[8] The study still ranks among one of the greatest medical ethics scandals in the history of the United States. For some, it was a 'programme of controlled genocide'; others called it 'America's Nuremberg'.[9] Yet the knowledge that US scientists had not deliberately infected the men with syphilis gave many grounds to believe that human and civil rights had not been violated. Recent discoveries demonstrating that US scientists, funded by the then newly established National Institutes of Health (NIH), intentionally and through deception infected hundreds of impoverished and vulnerable men and women with syphilis in Guatemala between 1946 and 1948, while American lawyers were passing judgement on Nazi doctors at Nuremberg, not only challenge this assumption, but seem to substantiate what Lederer has termed the insatiable drive of Western scientists to conduct 'research without borders'.[10]

Many of those seeing themselves at the cutting edge of science quite literally no longer knew any formal bounds, neither geographically in terms of respecting national boundaries, local customs, or cultural identities, nor legally, ethically, or scientifically, since those who pursued their research most aggressively reaped the greatest professional and financial rewards. As the Cold War heated up, Western governments were determined to exploit not only established political traditions and belief in the market economy as evidence of Western cultural superiority, but advancements in medical science and technology. It was a climate of unrelenting, unscrupulous optimism. Yet by making enormous investments in medicine, science, and technology, state agencies had created a situation in which the available resources appeared to be greater 'than the supply of responsible investigators'.[11] Although precise figures of research spending by public, private, and non-profit organizations are difficult to obtain, it is possible to identify certain patterns. Funding by the NIH, for example, increased from about 2.8 million dollars in 1945 to 81 million dollars in 1955 and to a total of 959 million dollars ten years later, evidence of the enormous excitement felt in the research community after the development of an effective polio vaccine had demonstrated the power of medical science. Yet, at the same time, we need to recognize that the resulting NIH budget increases were levelling off in the early 1960s, an indication that the initial hope for rapid discoveries had turned into a greater sense of realism about the need for long-term investments. The establishment of Medicare and Medicaid in the early 1960s, together with an expanding US space flight programme, was also temporarily shifting resources into other priority areas.[12] The overall upward trend nonetheless continued, especially after President Nixon declared 'war on cancer', so that by 1975 the NIH was spending over 2 billion dollars on medical and health research (see Figure 4).[13] In Canada gross expenditure on research by the Department of National Health and Welfare increased from 150,000 Canadian dollars in 1948/1949 to about 3.3 million dollars in 1960/1961, partly as an incentive to prevent researchers from emigrating to

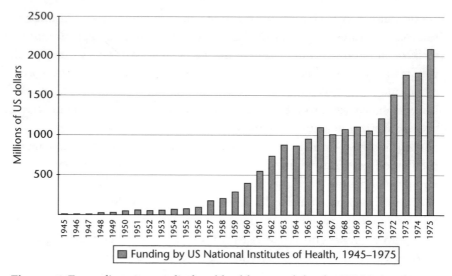

Figure 4. Expenditure on medical and health research by the US National
Institutes of Health, 1945–1975
Source: NIH, Office of the Director, NIH Almanac 2002, NIH Publication No. 02–5,
December 2002, Data for the years 1945–1975.

the United States. The Canadian health authorities boosted the work of
major research organizations by spending over 15 million dollars on general
public and mental health in the preceding decade, i.e. from 1950 to 1960.[14]
The argument that projects had to be 'held off' for lack of funds was no
longer valid. In Britain, meanwhile, the total volume of research funding
was much lower than in the United States but it also increased significantly
in the postwar period. The MRC's grant-in-aid, for example, rose from
195,000 pounds sterling in 1939 to 295,000 pounds sterling in 1945, to
770,000 pounds sterling in 1948 and to over 1 million pounds sterling in
1949. Through a sharp rise in the number of MRC research institutes from
sixteen in 1939 to forty in 1948, often staffed with former Porton scientists,
it also saw a marked extension of its research activities in the fields of public
and industrial health.[15]

It may have seemed a Golden Age for young, ambitious, often unscrupulous investigators. They exposed pregnant women to the dangers of radioactive isotopes at Vanderbilt University; initiated hepatitis experiments on
severely disabled children and adolescents at the Willowbrook School in
New York; injected patients with 'live cancer cells' at the Jewish Chronic
Disease Hospital in Brooklyn in New York without obtaining their consent;

conducted experiments on hundreds of inmates of Holmesburg Prison to test facial creams and perfumes. Theirs was a generation of scientists wanting to push the boundaries of knowledge, a world in which medical progress was seemingly dependent on human sacrifice.[16] What made their work problematic was not so much the frequency with which it breached medical ethics, or the publicity it attracted when it was exposed, but the issue of its legality. Senior officials in major research organizations came to realize that by allowing unethical research work to continue, they were running the risk of inviting a wave of legal claims that could not only tarnish their reputation but also reduce access to important streams of revenue.

Given the primacy of national security considerations, tensions erupted between military scientists and legal experts over the contentious issue of informed consent. US officials, at least, secretly voiced concern about the country's lack of preparedness if it had to launch chemical or biological warfare, arguing that there was a 'serious need for increased testing of these weapons, in particular, experiments involving humans'.[17] Senior legal advisers cautioned that clinical trials on humans could be conducted only according to the principles of the Nuremberg Code since these 'already had international juridical sanction'.[18] Yet researchers, while they were prepared to accept a set of general ethical rules, demanded that the Code's restrictive principles be softened to align them with the 'capabilities of the average investigator'.[19] Medical ethics guidelines, in other words, could be accepted as long as they did not curtail the work of the investigator. The threat of legal liability and public embarrassment, however, made such a position untenable in the long term.

In Britain, the MRC advised investigators to use written consent forms for specific projects, and accepted the principles of the Code as setting out 'adequately the requirements which should be satisfied before the consent could be termed full'.[20] Scientists were asked to 'err on the side of punctiliousness' in abiding by the Code, since British research interests would be at stake 'if any clinical investigator was publicly or even privately criticized for lack of care'.[21] Scientists nonetheless expressed reservations in applying the consent principle to all healthy subjects, especially in potentially therapeutic trials. The use of placebos, for one, had come to play an integral part in the testing of new drugs and innovative therapies, and this conflicted with the need to inform participants about the nature and risk of certain trials.[22] This difference in opinion resulted from far-reaching changes in the organization and conduct of randomized clinical trials within the postwar National

Health Service (NHS), a reform process in which the MRC attempted to centralize and coordinate university-based medical research more efficiently.[23] Given the increased dependence on external funding from government agencies and charitable organizations, together with mounting pressure to bring scientists in line with standardized best practice, the medical profession felt compelled to seek greater clarity in the field of clinical research.

Whereas some began to detect an 'ethical wilderness', others criticized the Code for not providing scientists with 'a secure legal backstop'.[24] No wonder then that the subject of human experimentation became one of the central foci of the National Conference on the Legal Environment of Medicine at the University of Chicago in 1959. Although the 150 delegates publicly signed up to the principles of the Code as the 'guidepost to the ethics of clinical research in the western world', disagreements about their feasibility continued to inform the discussion.[25] American scientists were faced with the prospect of greater state and judicial interference through more formal ethics regulations; Beecher, for whom human experiments were a 'social necessity', was among those who expressed grave concerns. In the same year, Beecher reiterated his view that 'potentially dangerous experiments without the subject's knowledge and consent' were all but 'unethical and immoral', yet he also maintained that informed consent was sometimes unobtainable, given that researchers were often unable to know of all the potential risks involved, and could not communicate these to lay subjects.[26] A similar sentiment was mirrored across the Atlantic by Sir Austin Bradford Hill, a biostatistician, who remained unconvinced of the need for informed consent in controlled trials.[27] For Beecher and other investigators any codified rules were seen to be detrimental to the advancement of medical science: 'It is not my view that many rules can be laid down to govern experimentation in man. In most cases, these are more likely to do harm than good.'[28]

Only two years later, in 1961, Harvard's medical community, in which Beecher played a leading role, found itself on a direct collision course with the US Army, one of its major funding bodies, after it began to include in its research contracts a near copy of the Code, with the added requirement of *written* consent.[29] One of the most outspoken opponents of the Code was Harvard's Assistant Dean of the Medical School, Joseph W. Gardella, who expressed the views of senior scientists when he said that the principles of the Code were 'not necessarily pertinent to or adequate for the conduct of

medical research in the United States'.[30] By forcefully claiming that potentially beneficial experiments with unhealthy patients were outside the moral
framework of the Code, and by criticizing the 'legal overtones and implications' of the Army's regulations, especially its requirement for 'written consent', he offered a distinct interpretative reading that helped researchers to
challenge the Code's universal applicability and influenced, albeit indirectly,
the debate over the formulation of the Declaration of Helsinki, which distinguished between therapeutic and non-therapeutic research on man.[31]
Beecher likewise stressed that 'rigid rules' on human experimentation were
likely to endanger American medical research.[32] As an advocate of American
research interests, he kept up the pressure on the international medical
community, urging them to address the alleged shortcomings of the Code
and to seek a unified approach to regulating human experimentation, which
he saw as a 'world problem'. In March 1960, publishing in the *World Medical
Journal*, Beecher called for the creation of a 'general code' by an international body such as the WMA that would 'serve the best interests of science
and mankind in the realm of human experimentation'.[33]

The Limits to Helsinki

Although our understanding of the history that shaped the formation of an
international medical ethics code by the WMA is limited at best, newly
discovered material which complements existing scholarship by Susan
Lederer and others allows us to see some of the contours of certain policy
debates that drove, held back, and at times accelerated the drafting process.
One of the more important factors responsible for the creation of the
Declaration of Helsinki in 1964 was a specific tension between, on the one
side, international health and legal organizations that desired to draft and
ideally implement international medical law in the postwar period and, on
the other, the newly established WMA as the body tasked with protecting
the interests of the medical profession. These interests often went hand in
hand with those of pharmaceutical and other companies sponsoring the
organization in its first decade, which is why by the mid 1950s the WMA
saw itself as 'the only protection for industry', including the tobacco industry.[34] The process of defining the limits to Helsinki, the conceptual bound-
ary between what is deemed to be ethically and legally permissible in
human experiments, is thrown into stark relief by looking at the political

controversies and negotiated compromises on the subject of medical ethics. What becomes apparent, more than anything, is the determination with which the WMA, in its first decade, was fighting for its independent status in the world, against international organizations, political interference, and even the rule of international law.

Following the postwar condemnation of Nazi medical war crimes, the WMA not only reaffirmed its broad support for Hippocratic medical ideals and paternalistic values in the 1948 Declaration of Geneva, but issued an International Code of medical ethics a year later that amounted to little more than a repetition of basic ethical principles relating to confidentiality, beneficence, and non-maleficence (to do no harm); doctors around the world were encouraged to display a framed copy of the International Code in their offices.[35] By 1951, the year West German physicians were admitted to the organization, WMA delegates rejected a proposal to turn the International Code into a more authoritative document through the inclusion of principles dealing with human experimentation. They were adamant that the International Code needed to remain a 'broad statement of ethical principles' which could be reinforced, if necessary, by national laws and regulations. Under no circumstances was the Code's 'brevity and simplicity' to be altered, they argued; and indeed recently, some have claimed that a revised version of the Declaration of Helsinki has to 'remain readable within fifteen minutes'.[36] To be acceptable to doctors around the world, the argument seems to imply—then as now—the document needs to be brief and simple, otherwise it will either not be read or it will be rejected.

In continental Europe, medical war crimes trials held since the end of hostilities in the Allied zones of occupation had contributed to a climate in which public debate about the role of research ethics became increasingly inevitable; experts remained broadly divided over the question whether the conduct of human experiments should in future be left solely to physicians and research scientists. In the wake of the revelation of ever more atrocities in postwar trials, however, national medical organizations, funding bodies, and other non-state actors rushed to disassociate themselves from Nazi medicine. The prosecution and stiff sentencing of German chemical warfare scientists during the Struthof Medical Trials in Metz and Lyon in the early 1950s, for instance, prompted the French National Academy of Medicine and the Medico-Juridical Commission (MJC) of Monaco—which had a mixed membership comprising not only military and civilian physicians but also lawyers—to take a firm stand on medical misconduct in the field of clinical research.[37] Yet by trying to salvage what was left of the reputation and moral integrity of the medical profession through the creation of clearer rules and regulations, interest groups such as the MJC found themselves on a collision course with the WMA.

In 1952, the WMA responded furiously to reports that the MJC was planning to promulgate an international code of medical ethics as a means to inform the future creation of international medical laws. The battle-lines between the WMA, which, as the body representing the interests of the medical community, was fiercely opposed to greater state and legal regulation, and the MJC, whose membership represented international medical jurisprudence, were clearly drawn. During its Sixth General Assembly, held in Athens, the WMA adopted a resolution, simultaneously transmitted to leading international organizations, that made it clear that the MJC had 'no competence in the matter of medical ethics and medical law'. In a not-so-veiled threat, the WMA also declared that 'if this Commission persists in drafting such a code, this code will not be accepted by the medical profession of the world'.[38] A couple of years later, in another rearguard action to prevent medical lawyers, legislators, and physicians attending the first International Congress on Medical Ethics, funded by the French Ordre des Médecins, from issuing internationally binding medical ethics guidelines, the WMA not only refused to send a representative, but reiterated its position that it was the 'function of the medical doctors of the world to formulate any code of international medical law'.[39]

The strategy temporarily averted external encroachment on what the WMA regarded as its area of competence, yet by insisting that it was the only legitimate organization with the moral authority and expertise to draft such a document the WMA found itself under pressure to produce a more authoritative text. Some delegates even had close family connections to those whose postwar mission it had been to bring Nazi perpetrators to account and to prevent a repetition of medical atrocities through the formulation of more stringent ethical guidelines. The future president of the WMA, Lambert A. Hulst, who had been actively involved in the Dutch resistance movement, and whose wife Helene Hulst, née Alexander, was the sister of the Jewish émigré psychiatrist Leo Alexander, one of the architects of the Nuremberg Code, began to raise awareness about the steady increase in the use of experimental subjects.[40] Apart from introducing a conceptual distinction between therapeutic and non-therapeutic research in all but name, Hulst, speaking for a majority of delegates, condemned as 'criminal acts' the Nazi physicians' use of test subjects under compulsion. Experiments had to be voluntary, he noted, and were permissible only if the participant was informed about his or her right to 'consent or refuse'.[41] Hulst called upon the WMA to define more clearly the boundaries within which research could legitimately be performed. Adopted by the WMA in 1954, the Resolution on the Principle of Human Experimentation stressed, among other 'scientific and moral' dimensions of experimentation, the conditions under which healthy and unhealthy subjects could take part, and required full disclosure of the nature, purpose, and risks of the experiment.[42] In the United States, meanwhile, the newly established Clinical Center of the NIH, founded in 1953, introduced a form of group review of all intramural research projects that 'deviated from acceptable medical practice or involved unusual hazard'.[43] For NIH research projects some, but not all, research protocols had to be reviewed by external reviewers. Some hoped that the Clinical Research Committees (CRCs) of the NIH, precursors of the IRBs, would be replicated in the US research community, but as they had no applicability outside the NIH, this did not happen.

Though they informed discussion on clinical research ethics, these documents fell far short of satisfying the international community. The ICRC, the ICMMP, and the WHO were all pressing ahead with drafting international medical laws that would be applicable to doctors in both peace and wartime. This required them to define the jurisdiction of ethics codes in times of war. Under threat of marginalization on the world stage, the WMA reluctantly agreed to cooperate with these bodies in formulating what became known as the 1957 'Regulations in Time of Armed Conflict'. Apart from reiterating the obligations of physicians, the Regulations made it clear, under Point 3, that 'medical ethics in times of armed conflict is identical with medical ethics in times of peace'. By strictly prohibiting experimental research on 'all persons deprived of their liberty', they also excluded all civilian and military prisoners and the civilian population of occupied territories from human tests, a ban which came to haunt the WMA during its negotiations over the exact wording of the Declaration of Helsinki.[44]

While ostensibly being opposed to political or other interference in the conduct of its business, most WMA representatives and delegates to its General Assembly, as well as their wives and, less frequently, their husbands, enjoyed official travel to distant countries, a golden opportunity, in times of general austerity and postwar gloom, to see the world. A particular highlight of these trips remained the official reception by the head of state. This could be a democratically elected prime minister or president, as in 1956, when Konrad Adenauer welcomed WMA Council members in his residence; a constitutional monarch, when Her Royal Majesty Juliana, Queen of the Netherlands, received the WMA Council in her summer palace in 1953; or indeed the occasional dictator. These visits, however, also enabled politicians and unelected dignitaries of the Church to impress upon the WMA what was expected in the field of medical ethics. In 1954, Pope Pius XII invited the participants in the WMA's Eighth General Assembly to his summer residence in Castel Gandolfo. He is the subject of continuing historical controversy: during the war he had been kept well informed about medical atrocities committed by German doctors in the name of racial science, and was heavily criticized for his collusion with the regime and his unexplained silence on the subject. The ageing Pope, a life-long anti-communist, gave the delegates a rather unexpected lecture about their duties as doctors in time of war, and discussed human experimentation and the 'general foundation of medical ethics'.[45] It had at least the desired effect of boosting the WMA's international reputation. By the late 1950s, as the WMA's resistance to undue influence was gradually replaced by greater political realism and willingness to compromise, medical experts felt more confident in embracing a revision of the existing ethics regime.

The acceptance by the WMA that non-therapeutic research was being done not to benefit human beings, but to 'obtain information', and that it therefore fell into the realm of the law, fundamentally changed the parameters of the debate.[46] By the end of the 1950s, when work on a WMA code governing human experiments began in earnest, most of the medical and legal discussions centred around certain types of tests, some of which were conducted at Porton. Of particular concern were experiments to assess the effectiveness of drugs and mind-altering tests affecting the personality of participants, large-scale inoculation studies with control groups to study the efficacy of vaccines, tests which bore no relation to the condition for which the person had been admitted to hospitals and, last but not least, controlled trials on 'captive groups' such as asylum and prison inmates.[47] By 1960, as a way of overcoming conceptual difficulties, it was agreed to produce two codes in one by having distinct sections dealing with experiments on healthy and unhealthy persons. The dividing line between the two sections was whether the experiment was performed 'for the benefit of the patient' or whether it was conducted 'solely for the acquisition of knowledge'.[48] We need to recognize that the process of revising the WMA's international medical ethics code began from the moment of its inception in 1949. From the perspective of the WMA, each stage constituted a more authoritative document, yet for most legal experts this was still insufficient in protecting research subjects from potential harm, which is why various professional groups and international organizations were determined to bring the medical ethics field into line with international humanitarian law.[49]

In the decade after the promulgation of the Nuremberg Code, the ethics of Western research culture underwent a process of transformation in which ongoing human and civil rights violations in modern medicine went hand in hand with a grudging realization by some of the self-appointed leaders in the field, including Beecher, that further resistance against public and political demands for change could only lead to incalculable damage to the profession. By the beginning of the 1960s, in the light of ever more frequent revelations of unethical research on disadvantaged and vulnerable populations, and after the widely criticized Thalidomide tragedy prompted further calls for greater state regulation in 1961/1962, it was becoming increasingly difficult to oppose the reform of existing research practices; the political, legal, and financial stakes had simply become too high for the medical community.[50] If fundamental change to research governance could no longer be delayed, senior scientists hoped to take the lead in appropriating and controlling the argument, and perhaps even to publicize carefully managed adjustments in research ethics as an apparent reflection of greater transparency and public accountability in medical science.

In 1961, while American medical scientists continued to hold informal discussions about the ethics of clinical trials, the medical ethics committee of the WMA, chaired by Hugh Clegg, editor of the *BMJ*, produced a 'Draft Code of Ethics on Human Experimentation' which, after discussion at the WMA General Assembly, was published by the *BMJ* in October 1962.[51] The other two members of the drafting committee included A.P. Mittra from India and Antonio Spinelli from Italy, President of the WMA from 1954 to 1955. While there is some debate about whether the Nuremberg Code left its hallmark on the Declaration of Helsinki, we can be more certain in the case of the Draft Code. The ten general principles listed under Section II (B) of the Draft Code are almost identical, if not in wording at least in meaning, to those set out in the Nuremberg Code.[52] The dominant role of the informed voluntary consent principle, which in the Nuremberg Code is deemed to be 'absolutely essential', is also reflected in the Draft Code. Permissible human tests require that the 'nature, the reasons, and the risk of the experiment are fully explained to the subject'. The participant must have 'complete freedom to decide whether or not he wishes to take part in the experiment'.[53] Significantly, the authors of the Draft Code went to great lengths to try to provide sufficient protection for children involved in human research; this concerned the way in which proxy consent had to be obtained from their legal guardians and the prohibition on using institutionalized children and those not under the care of relatives. In addition, the most stringent safeguards applied to tests that did not solely benefit the participants, irrespective of whether they were healthy or unhealthy. Doctors and medical scientists were advised not to conduct experiments on those who stood in a 'dependent relationship' to themselves, and never to subject to experiments prisoners and other captive groups 'deprived' of their freedom.[54] This served as a reminder that research should be pursued on humans, if at all, only under considerable caution, and then only on those persons capable of making free and informed decisions; it also raised the spectre of restricting certain research practices, particularly those on children and prisoners.

A year later, in 1963, a fierce controversy over the Draft Code engulfed the WMA, in which the views of American physicians, as represented in the AMA, played a key role. Moreover, NASA had begun to monitor the work of the WMA to ensure that its programme of manned space flight, which involved de facto non-beneficial experiments on humans, complied with international standards of medical ethics, for instance by dispatching its acting Director of Space Medicine, George Knauf, to the WMA meeting that same year.[55] Cold War politics was never far away. During the state of heightened diplomatic tension between the United States and the Soviet Union in the wake of the Cuban Missile Crisis, the WMA occasionally functioned as a clearing house for supplying the AMA with information about colleagues in communist-controlled regimes. Intelligence received from the Finnish Medical Association about Cuban doctors registering for the Helsinki General Assembly was swiftly forwarded to the AMA.[56]

Membership of the medical ethics committee now consisted of Gerald D. Dorman, President of the AMA, Ole K. Harlem, Editor of the *Norwegian Medical Journal*, Jean Maystre, the long-standing liaison officer of international organizations based in Geneva with an interest in medical affairs, Urpo Siirala, President of the Finnish Otolaryngological Society and organizer of the Eighteenth General Assembly, and Antonio Spinelli from Italy, who served as chairman. As members of the WMA Council, Dorman,

Harlem, Siirala, and Spinelli were able to exercise particular influence over the Draft Code's exact wording. Matters requiring clarification, as pointed out by Maystre, and recorded in the minutes, centred on the protection of prisoners of war, and on the extent to which the new WMA ethics principles conformed to the Nuremberg Code.[57] It was also unclear whether the rules, as formulated, would apply to all scientists involved in research work with humans, including those 'who are not doctors', an issue which was particularly pertinent to Porton's research corps. The most controversial problem needing to be resolved, however, related to the question whether experiments on institutionalized children and prisoners should be permissible.

The extent to which these issues divided opinion among member associations, which had been invited to comment and, if necessary, amend the relevant sections, was highlighted by the fact that there was still no agreed consensus by the time the Eighteenth General Assembly opened in Helsinki on 13 June to adopt the WMA's new ethics code. On Sunday 14 June, at 10.00 a.m., twenty-four hours before the start of the plenary sessions, and only hours before the inauguration ceremonies were due to begin in the presence of Urho K. Kekkonen, President of Finland, the WMA Council, under the chairmanship of Filip Worré from Luxembourg, decided to change the name of the WMA ethics code from 'Ethical Principles Guiding Research Workers in Clinical Medicine' to 'Recommendations Guiding Doctors in Clinical Research', thus shifting the emphasis from ethical standards informing the work of research scientists in modern medicine to those guiding the work of doctors who are also conducting research: a small, but far-reaching last-minute linguistic amendment.[58] It allowed biomedical and chemical scientists, who were not doctors but were involved in human experimentation, including those at Edgewood Arsenal or Porton Down, to claim that the actual terms of the Declaration did not apply to them. At the stroke of a pen, the work of several years of discussion about how best to protect the human rights of patients and experimental subjects in modern research had received a major setback; the group to whom the principles effectively applied was all of a sudden limited to those with a medical degree, and none other. It was a smart and effective way of eliminating, for the time being, the possibility that the WMA ethics code could be used as a point of reference in arguing against research scientists in a court of law, in the United States or anywhere else. Clearly, the lawyers advising the AMA, such as A. Leslie Hodson from Chicago, a shrewd business lawyer who in the mid

1950s had defended US corporations against the charge of conspiring against anti-trust legislation, had done their homework.[59]

On the same day, the WMA Council took another key decision, namely to delete Clause III 3c of the Draft Code, which stated that 'no clinical research should be undertaken when the subject is in a dependent relationship to the investigator', and to replace it with an addition to Clause III 4a: 'The investigator must respect the right of each individual to safeguard his personal integrity, especially if the subject is in a dependent relationship to the investigator' (*surtout si l'individu est en état de dépendance vis à vis de lui*).[60] Within less than two hours, the character of the WMA's ethics code had fundamentally changed. Experimental research on institutionalized children, asylum inmates, psychologically and/or physically handicapped, or the elderly, while requiring due care and special attention, was no longer ruled out. Ironically, four days later the General Assembly closed its proceedings with a discussion forum dealing with 'factors affecting the development of children'.[61] The final version was also conspicuously silent on the subject of prisoners and other vulnerable populations. For the time being, research scientists could carry on as if nothing had changed.

In June 1964, after years of debate, the WMA finally adopted parts of the Draft Code during its Eighteenth General Assembly in the Finnish capital. The document became known as the Declaration of Helsinki.[62] As we have seen, however, important provisions of the Draft Code such as the prohibition on conducting human experiments on prisoners of war, whether military or civilian, or on persons confined to prisons and mental institutions, had been deleted from the Declaration.[63] American scientists, in particular, having made extensive use of prison inmates in clinical trials during the Second World War, were concerned that additional safeguards for these populations could hamper US-led drug research conducted in US penitentiaries, and, as historical research has begun to reveal, across the globe.[64] British scientists, on the other hand, felt that 'American influence' might have weakened the Declaration.[65] Given the WMA's 'advertised financial crisis', overcome only after the AMA and the WMA's United States Committee had pledged to fund the organization with a grant of 500,000 dollars over five years, it is difficult to avoid the impression that financial considerations may have played a part, albeit indirect, in allowing the representatives of the AMA to succeed in substantially watering down the original Draft Code of 1962.[66] In the summary of its activities for the year 1964, the WMA gave fewer than three lines to a document that it now considers to be one of its most successful declarations.[67] It certainly did not anticipate the impact the document would have on biomedical research ethics over the next fifty years.[68]

In promulgating the Declaration, the medical community had succeeded in supplanting the Nuremberg Code with research guidelines that strengthened the position of physician-scientists. For American scientists and stakeholders, especially the pharmaceutical industry, the Declaration constituted a significant breakthrough as part of a negotiated response in order to neutralize as best they could any potential legal challenges originating from the Code. Endorsed by the AMA, the American Society for Clinical Investigation, and the American Federation for Clinical Research, the Declaration promoted an important shift in the quality of international ethical codes, from the rights of patients and the protection of human subjects in clinical trials, as expressed in the Code, to the protection of patient welfare through physicians' responsibility. From its early conception, the Declaration was more aligned to the current research culture, yet it also shifted attention away from the central importance of informed consent, and introduced a more paternalistic value system that emphasized the traditional physician–patient relationship. The authors of the Declaration effectively moved away from a language of rights and legal liability in clinical trials to a protective system emphasizing patient health and welfare. What mattered in research, yet again, was the duty and responsibility of the scientist, rather than some abstract concept such as informed consent, which many believed was unobtainable even in the most enlightened of participants. Succumbing to pressure from US scientists, who wanted to protect lucrative drug research, the WMA's negotiated compromise meant that the Declaration prohibited the use in clinical trials neither of prisoners of war, whether civilian or military, nor of inmates in mental institutions and penitentiaries. The Declaration, for all its shortcomings, nonetheless marked a major sea-change in research ethics. The fact that British experts had played a decisive role in drafting the document, together with its international and public visibility, meant that the process of ethical reform in civilian research, once it was under way, began to influence military science as well.

While the debate about human experimentation defined the period leading up the Declaration, and to some extent thereafter, it fell short of acting as a catalyst in launching a similar discourse within the military. Instead, what seems to have resonated with Porton scientists was that the Declaration itself constituted a powerful expression of intent by the world

medical community to protect the health and well-being of research participants through a reaffirmation of Hippocratic medical ideals, in particular
the undertaking not to do any harm. As much, if not most, of Porton's work
was to assess the threshold dosage at which chemical agents had a harassing,
incapacitating, or even lethal effect, military scientists began to reflect about
the impact that a new international ethics regime, to which the world medical community had committed itself, might have on their work. It was the
international and symbolic status of the Declaration that Porton could not
ignore, even if it wanted to. For an interdisciplinary, inter-Allied military
facility there was increasing pressure to conform to existing best practice.
When interviewed by Operation Antler in the 1990s, senior Porton scientists who had been involved in human experiments in the 1960s and 1970s
made it plain that Porton had full knowledge of, and wanted to abide by, the
international medical ethics standards as laid down in the Declaration.[69] It is
difficult to tell, though, whether their stated claim to ethical propriety was
genuine or just a convenient act of personal legitimization in the face of
anticipated court proceedings.

Public Relations

Central discussions about the role of research ethics coincided with fundamental social and political change in Western societies, a period defined not
only by the Cuban Missile Crisis, which brought mankind to the brink of
the abyss, but also by gender conflicts, improvements in social mobility, and
greater demands for human and civil rights. It was a world divided ideologically between West and East, in which the postwar sense of uncertainty and
desire for more stability in an age of austerity was gradually replaced by a
generation full of energy and hope. Young people wanted to take charge of
their future lives. Middle-class men and women growing up in Britain, anxious to break with established tradition, saw the world as full of injustice, but
they also perceived opportunities, whether these concerned calls for the end
of private education and class privilege, for the dissolution of the monarchy,
for the reform of the established Anglican Church, or for the abolition of
the country's nuclear weapons arsenal; a group of Sussex students drawing
up the constitution of their debating society in 1962 held these to be perfectly
reasonable demands, not unrealistic, unattainable utopian visions.[70] It was
a society in transition in which international humanitarian, environmental,

and peace movements increasingly influenced public opinion about Britain's nonconventional weapons capability.

At a cultural level, the symbolically rich postwar work of artists such as Pablo Picasso highlighted people's longing for 'peace and freedom on both sides of the Iron Curtain', a desire to develop an artistic and literary genre which would transcend ideological and aesthetic divides, particularly between the more abstract, conceptual Western art of the likes of Rothko, Pollock, and Beuys on the one hand, and Socialist Realism in the East on the other. Picasso's ambitious history paintings—*The Charnel House* (1944–1945), *Massacre in Korea* (1951), *War and Peace* (1951–1958), *Women of Algiers* (1954–1955), *Las Meninas* (1957), and *Rape of the Sabine Women* (1962–1963)—were informed by contemporary political and military crises: the Korean War, the Algerian war of independence, and the global threat from atomic, chemical, and biological weapons.[71] Much of his work in the 1940s and early 1950s maintained his opposition to the conduct of war as politics by other means, which he had expressed most vividly in his iconic painting *Guernica* (1937). These works of art were testament to the timeless horrors of war, which indiscriminately killed and maimed women, children, and the elderly, a visual depiction of human suffering that had found artistic representations ever since the advent of modern warfare. This far from obedient member of the French Communist Party, who was refused entry to the United States but permitted to attend the Sheffield World Peace Congress in November 1950, provided the international peace movement with a powerful canvas for the dissemination of its critique of the Cold War military machine, and simultaneously for a call for freedom, human, and civil rights, in a way that reached mass audiences around the world. The World Peace Congress, banned by the Attlee government after the outbreak of the Korean War, was widely publicized on French- and English-language posters with one of Picasso's doves of peace.[72] Liberal-minded intellectuals and scientists, some of whom had experienced gas warfare, helped to galvanize 'global efforts for peace, equality, and human rights' that found their material expression in exhibitions such as *World without War* at the Galleries of the Royal Society of British Artists (RBA) in London. The International Committee of the Red Cross, religious and political leaders, as well as leading nuclear and theoretical physicists, including Albert Einstein, called for an international ban on atomic weapons. In Britain, the peace movement received additional public support through the Campaign for Nuclear Disarmament

(CND), which became a leading force in staging local protests against chemical and 'germ' warfare outside Porton's gates.

Among members of the CND was the New Zealand-born physicist and molecular biologist Maurice Wilkins, who in 1962 was jointly awarded the Nobel Prize together with Crick and Watson for discovering the double helical structure of DNA.[73] At the outbreak of war, Wilkins had been an anti-war activist and member of the communist party, but had then joined the Manhattan project to develop the atom bomb at Los Alamos, a decision about which he seems to have had, in retrospect, 'mixed feelings'. The enormous civilian suffering and devastation caused by the bombing of Hiroshima and Nagasaki persuaded him to leave the field of physics and campaign for nuclear disarmament, which is why MI5 placed him under surveillance for a while for fear that he might leak nuclear secrets to the Soviet Union; no incriminating evidence was ever found.[74] Wilkins, together with other prominent scientists, promoted greater social responsibility and ethical conduct in science—for example through the British Society for Social Responsibility in Science, which he helped to establish—and highlighted the role of science in the development of chemical and biological weapons in Vietnam in the late 1960s; Wilkins could not easily be discredited for alleged left-wing sympathies, and he and his peers provided CND campaigners with much-needed legitimacy and public visibility to raise awareness about weapons of mass destruction.[75]

Debates about disarmament provided Porton with a temporary lifeline for its activities, since a potential reduction in nuclear arms increased the relative significance of chemical and biological weapons, but it also meant that Porton was inadvertently drawn into politically charged controversies about Britain's nonconventional weapons arsenal. By the late 1950s, the tide of public opinion in both Britain and the United States had firmly turned against chemical and biological weapons as legitimate means of waging war. By linking nuclear disarmament with weapons of mass destruction in vocal demonstrations outside Porton's fenced perimeters, or in the small town of Salisbury, members of CND and other campaign groups, including the Committee of 100—a civil disobedience group against nuclear weapons set up with 100 public signatories by Bertrand Russell and others—the 'Porton Action Group' and the Women's International League for Peace and Freedom managed to attract public attention to Britain's secret weapons programme. Citizens were shocked to learn that the UK government had violated public trust by exposing citizens, in total secrecy, to chemical and bacterial agents without their knowledge. Trials of this nature had been deemed possible in a communist dictatorship, but for most they had been unthinkable in a modern democracy in which civil and human rights were believed to be upheld by the rule of law. For the government, on the other hand, there had apparently been 'no option beyond secrecy' to protect the British realm during the Cold War.

Eager to learn what was going on behind the barbed wire, the British media had shown a keen interest in Porton's activities ever since its creation during the Great War; the development of modern weapons of mass destruction had imbued the place with an imagined sense of military power that was, to many, fascinating and horrifying in equal measure. For local residents living in the vicinity, Porton's existence could be worrying, yet in general it was seen as providing regional employment and stability, and this went hand in hand with a sense of loyalty; protesters travelling to or marching in Salisbury could easily be seen as threats to peace and tranquillity and as foreign elements undermining the local community, irrespective of the political message they wanted to convey. In March 1953, two months before Maddison's death, the 'Non-Violent Resistance Group', a small group of pacifist campaigners, called upon Porton's staff to boycott working in what it deemed to be a 'germ factory'.[76] Their protest, and the resulting hostile response from some of the locals, was duly reported by the media alongside a photograph identifying members of the twenty-three strong group.

In order to respond to small-scale, localized incidents the intelligence agencies required little more than prior warning, and sometimes the involvement of the military police and limited media management. It was profoundly more difficult to control shifting international debates about the value or risks of chemical and biological warfare. The greater sophistication and increasingly rapid dissemination of news through modern media also made the management of secret science all the more difficult for national governments. Officials often had to weigh up whether it was in the public interest to correct ill-informed press reporting, or better simply to abstain from drawing attention to places such as Aldermaston, Porton, and Nancekuke that were associated with Britain's secret weapons programmes. For some scientists, chemical and biological weapons had become outdated because of the destructive power of thermonuclear weapons; others, such as radar pioneer Sir Robert Watson-Watt, propelled Porton's MRE into the media spotlight after drawing attention to the existence of botulinum toxin, one of the most toxic substances known to man, which apparently had the power to wipe out all living beings on the planet. His comments, made in 1959, reiterated those of Brock Chisholm, Director General of the WHO and former Director of Medical Services of the Canadian Army, who a decade earlier had warned ominously that 'some seven ounces of a certain biological [compound]... would be sufficient to kill all the people of the world'.[77] Within days, after Britain's deadly chemical and biological weapon stockpiles had received front-line news coverage, an increasingly hostile debate focused its attention on Porton after the Rural District Councillor for Amesbury, Austin Underwood, publicly labelled the facility as an 'animal Belsen', thus linking Britain military science with the horrors of Nazi concentration camps. Research conducted there was apparently the work of the 'Devil's disciple for the destruction of mankind', Watson–Watt argued, a line quickly taken up by several newspaper editors and politicians who jumped on the publicity bandwagon. The relentlessness of these attacks on Porton's public image was unprecedented. Rather than allaying public anxieties, the government's attempt to defend Porton's record and reputation in the House of Commons only drew unintended attention to the ethics of warfare experimentation with both animals and humans. The refusal to allow a group of visiting MPs to see Porton's animal cages, together with unsubstantiated reports about 'pets', 'cats', and 'drugged animals' apparently being used in deadly experiments, further fuelled the public debate about animal rights that had plagued the institution since the 1920s. The *Sunday Pictorial*, for example, ran the headline 'Stop it! Terror in the Animals' Belsen'.[78] As if this were not enough, Porton was forced to deal with an evolving news story of what US papers termed 'a germ-war test monkey' which had escaped in transit.

Meanwhile, popular and scientific commentators focused on the ethics and secrecy of Porton's work. While the *BMJ* addressed the ethics of biological warfare, the journal *Nature* discussed the implications resulting from a public and professional 'War on Chemical and BW [Biological Warfare]'. US university campuses had recently seen a wave of protest against Fort Detrick's biological weapons programme, resulting not only from the refusal of molecular biologists to attend its twenty-fifth anniversary conference, but also from the unexplained death of large numbers of sheep in the state of Utah from what seems to have been nerve gas poisoning. In Britain, Nobel-prize-winning scientists asked the government to provide 'tangible proof' that its interest in chemical and biological weapons was purely defensive by transferring both establishments, CDEE and MRE, to the MoH. While buying into the idea that Britain's 'comparatively small research programme' was aimed at ensuring Britain's defensive capability, the *Nature* authors recognized the need to anticipate developments in offensive weapons technology that any 'prudent' government needed to keep secret. Asking the UK government to abandon 'secrecy' and declassify all of the work of Porton was therefore unrealistic.[79] As an interesting aside, the article compared the position of the UK government on chemical and biological weapons with that of the Indian government on nuclear arms; both professed to harbour no offensive military intentions but were actively engaged in weapons research to ensure the availability of military options, if ever these were necessary. The key for both governments was to 'make the good intentions credible'. Porton, for example, was well advised to engage in 'informed public discussion' by publishing, on a regular basis, general reports about its otherwise classified work. Some, like Underwood, also launched a broad offensive against the perceived exploitation of medicine and science in the development of nonconventional arms technology.[80] Although doctors working at Porton were not necessarily trained physicians, but doctors of philosophy or of applied sciences, some felt compelled to warn the British medical profession about the 'prostitution of medical knowledge' for offensive purposes, which stood 'in direct breach of their Hippocratic oath'.[81]

The year 1959 saw Porton's previously opaque existence, officially neither confirmed nor denied by the UK authorities, thrown into the limelight during a gathering of twenty-six eminent scientists in the small town of Pugwash in Nova Scotia, Canada, to discuss the subject of biological and chemical warfare.[82] The objective of what became known as the Pugwash Conferences on Science and World Affairs, established in 1957 in response to the Russell–Einstein Manifesto, was to encourage 'world peace' by addressing the threat to global security and stability from nuclear, chemical, and biological weapons.[83] International support from senior officials of the WHO prior to and during the meeting was particularly noticeable.[84] Attendees included the Polish émigré physicist Joseph (Józef) Rotblat, Pugwash's first secretary-general, whose wife had perished in the Holocaust, the WHO's former Director General Brock Chisholm, who believed that man's worst enemy was not disease but man himself, the WHO's chief veterinary public health officer Martin M. Kaplan, the Danish virologist and WHO adviser Preben von Magnus, the French microbiologist André Michel Lwoff, the Russian chemist Mikhail Dubinin—who discussed quite openly, and a year later wrote about, the chemical formulae and effects of nerve agents and other toxic compounds—the British climatologist Gordon Manley, the American biostatistician Hugo Muench, the American nuclear physicist Eugene Rabinowitch, the American biophysicist Alexander Rich, and the British radar scientist Watson-Watt.[85] It was in this informal environment that the dangers from toxins and microbiological and novel hallucinating agents were highlighted by comparing them with 'certain types of atomic weapons'. The suggestion that these weapons might constitute a more 'humane' form of warfare, a recurring feature since the 1920s, was strongly contested. Whilst acknowledging the greater destructive power of hydrogen bombs, the participants expressed grave concerns about the difficulties in controlling these types of chemical and biological weapons through an international system of inspection, and called upon all nations to disclose their scientific and technical knowledge about the agents as a way of prohibiting their future use: a theme which, back in Britain, led certain media outlets to claim that Porton's MRE had become a 'peace-time danger to public health'.[86] The death of one of Porton's scientists from plague in 1963, discussed earlier, the disappearance and death under mysterious circumstances of a young female Porton researcher about ten years later, and the accidental though fortunately not fatal infection of another Porton scientist with the Ebola virus in 1976 helped little in dispersing public concerns; on the contrary, the call for improved safety precautions in laboratory and experimental procedures grew increasingly louder, and with it the pressure to reform military research practices.[87]

The tide in international public opinion about weapons of mass destruction was clearly shifting. Only months before the Pugwash meeting Chisholm had launched a blistering attack in the *Bulletin of the Atomic Scientists* on some of the most secretive research facilities on earth, Porton included, for trying to hide from the citizens of the world the 'facts' about the destructive potential of chemical and biological weapons.[88] 'We, the people of the world, are not children', he told his audience, who would just keep quiet about the indefensible policies of national governments that had brought the world to the brink of disaster. Rather than keeping it continually in the dark, warfare scientists and their political masters were called upon to inform the global community about the 'potential threats to our lives or our welfare'.[89] Yet Chisholm's passionate plea did not stop there. He wanted there to be far more drastic action if national governments were unable or unwilling to work towards lasting peace and security. His was more than a 'demand for answers': it was a call to arms to change the social

and political system, if necessary. Showing certain similarities to H.G.Wells'
thirty-year campaign to establish a quasi-socialist 'global government', what
was needed, Chisholm argued, was 'some kind of world federation of governments' which would police the proliferation of nonconventional weapons as a precondition for lasting peace.[90] Interventions by public figures
such as Chisholm marked the beginning of a sea-change in the political
environment in which Porton would from now on have to operate, one
which was far more hostile than anything the organization had experienced
in the decades before.

The mid 1960s, marked by intense political debates and confrontations
between the generations, were characterized by a re-emergence of violent
protests and personal attacks on Porton scientists, especially after Cold War
tensions, fuelled by the Cuban Missile Crisis, had led to the Cabinet's decision to establish regional seats of government, or 'deep defence shelters', as a
defensive measure against nuclear attacks. When two protesters belonging to
the Committee of 100 forced their way into the compound at Porton, and
thus breached security, the government responded with a raid by a special
intelligence unit of the police (Special Branch) on the headquarters of the
campaign group and enhanced security measures. Drafted in to protect the
establishment, members of the Royal Scots and the Royal Ulster Rifles army
units, apparently unarmed, duly arrested the majority of protesters gathering
at Porton in 1963. Although the employment of troops and other similar
heavy-handed methods of riot control helped to contain the level of violence at anti-Porton demonstrations, officials recognized the need to 'manage openness and secrecy' more proactively.[91] Reports about royal visits, for
example by Prince Philip, Duke of Edinburgh, who side-stepped a small
group of protesters by arriving by helicopter for Porton's fiftieth anniversary
in May 1966, and the organization of open days in the 1960s and 1970s, were
intended to improve Porton's battered public image (see Images 37a–b).[92]

Porton MRE first opened its doors to the press in 1962; two years later,
Porton CDEE followed suit. Added to scheduled open days came the coordinated release of previously sensitive information which included the disclosure of the 'general formulae for VX' during a 'teach-in' event at
Edinburgh, as well as interviews given to the media by the directors of
CDEE and MRE. Whitehall officials more often intervened in, and on
occasion criticized, what they considered to be biased reporting by radio
and television programmes. In spite of all this, the year 1968 became Porton's
'year of the barricades' (see Images 38 and 39).[93]

Images 37a–b. Prince Philip, Duke of Edinburgh, visiting Porton Down, 27 May 1966

Source: IWM, Photographic Collection. © Imperial War Museums (Prince Philip 1 and 2)

Image 38. Anti-Porton Down demonstration at Porton, 1963
Source: IWM, Photographic Collection, Porton Demonstration, 3 July 1963. © Imperial War
Museums (F 923/5).

Among those responsible for managing Porton's response to public protests was Gordon Smith, the MRE's Chief Superintendent and future Dean
of the LSHTM. Although his obituary, written in 1991, tried to present him
as someone who had transformed the MRE 'from an object of suspicion
visited by protest marches to an open and scientifically respected laboratory', the reality in the mid 1960s looked less rosy.[94] Political demands for
more openness, coupled with repeated calls to transfer authority for Porton's
microbiological research to civilian control, as requested by Tam Dalyell,
MP for West Lothian at the time, or to the United Nations, as suggested by
Michael G. Jones, Bishop of St Albans, received support from the editor of
the *New Scientist*, who not only saw the need for a new 'code of conduct',
but criticized Porton scientists as 'warmongers who can corrupt the harvest
of science'.[95] He believed that scientists would be less likely to participate in
chemical and biological warfare research if such work were not recognized
by the academic community, yet he seems to have been unaware that the

Image 39. Anti-Porton Down march in London, 1968
Source: TNA, Fotolibra, Anti-Porton Down March, London, July 1968, Image ID: FOT135635

contributions of some of Britain's most celebrated scientists had often been made in collaboration with colleagues at Porton, who were themselves advising the authorities about chemical and biological weapons. Dalyell was reprimanded by Parliament for the unauthorized release of privileged information, first published by *The Observer* in May 1968 under the headline 'Biological Warfare: Dons Named', which suggested that Britain possessed no chemical weapon stockpiles; the article had however shown the extent to which British universities were collaborating with the military establishment in developing outlawed weapon technologies.[96] A subsequent press report published under the headline 'Technology Gone Mad—Who Cares?' suggested that at least twenty-two universities were involved in 'defence-related work for Porton', among them King's College London; St Andrews, Edinburgh, Oxford, and Manchester universities; Middlesex Hospital

Medical School; and Queen's University, Belfast.[97] While officials accepted
the need to strike a balance between national security and accountability,
large sections of British society were beginning to support a campaign,
shored up by none other than the *Sun* newspaper, to lift the veil of secrecy
hanging over Porton, especially after the BBC had screened the television
programme 'A Plague on Your Children' to the 'overwhelming horror and
revulsion' of the general public.[98]

As the flood gates suddenly opened, a powerful current of public disquiet
threatened to engulf the existence of Porton's carefully constructed empire.
Internationally, the WHO's report on 'Health Aspects of Chemical and
Biological Weapons', published in 1970 by a group of expert consultants
who included Kaplan, Lwoff, Julian Perry Robinson, and Matthew Meselson,
informed member states about the health effects of nonconventional weapons on civilian populations as possible targets in a future war.[99] Moreover,
by the late 1960s, ever more victims of alleged accidents with toxic chemicals at Porton and its manufacturing facility at Nancekuke were coming
forward to claim compensation; others demanded an apology for the kind
of treatment they had received at the hands of the state.[100] For example, two
employees from Nancekuke, known as 'toxic fitters', reported accidental
exposure to deadly nerve agents in laboratories and from huge condensers
captured in Germany's chemical warfare plants during the last war. Both
had fallen seriously ill: one of these was Trevor Martin, accidentally exposed
to Sarin nerve gas in 1961.[101] Experiencing violent convulsions and chest
pain over the Christmas period, Martin consulted the plant's medical officer,
a Dr Burnell, who, at the age of seventy-five was already well past retirement age, refused to see the patient, telling him that his symptoms were
unrelated to his employment at Nancekuke. Martin and the other victims
did not receive much better treatment from the NHS system: some were
transferred from one department to another, in one case to a geriatric ward,
in another to a psychiatric clinic. No one seemed to believe that their health
and mental problems were linked to occupational hazards at their former
workplace which, in some cases, had turned them into 'nervous wrecks'. In
November 1969, the government officially denied allegations which linked
the deaths of two men and the illnesses of three others, all of whom had
worked at Nancekuke, to the work they had been carrying out at the facility.[102] In an attempt to construct a 'blanket of secrecy', it banned Martin
from disclosing to his doctor the nature of the compounds with which he
had been working by reminding him of his 'obligations and liabilities under

the Official Secrets Act', a statement the minister responsible later 'regretted' had been made.[103]

Other reports were more difficult to dismiss. In 1953, the former RAF officer William Cockayne was accidentally exposed to what the authorities described as a 'mild dose of nerve gas' during a field exercise to study the vulnerability of tanks to toxic agents. His exposure, resulting from a mal-functioning respirator, was sufficient for him to collapse and be transferred to Porton's hospital. Though his memory was vague, he recalled feeling enormous pain in his chest and head before he was transferred to a psychi-atric ward at RAF Hospital Halton. He resigned from the services shortly thereafter, and he and his family led a miserable life for fifteen years, marked by unemployment, financial difficulties, anger, and frustration, and occupy-ing a flat for 'problem families' in Lewisham, South London. At one point, in complete despair, Cockayne tried to kill himself. Then, in June 1968, the unexpected happened; after watching the BBC documentary 'A Plague on Your Children', he understood the connection between his health prob-lems—'violent convulsion, nausea and giddiness'—and his accident with nerve gas at Porton. Although the local MP supported Cockayne's case, the Department of Health and Social Security (DHSS) at first refused to grant him a pension. By presiding over secret research facilities, and by failing to provide adequate medical treatment for those injured there, concerned staff and citizens argued, the government had acted negligently in their duty of care towards employees.[104] The debate was gaining momentum at grassroots level. There was a concerted campaign by the Anti-Biological Warfare group, headed by Elizabeth Compton, a housewife and mother of six children, and environmentalists who suspected a link between the unexplained deaths of grey seals along the Cornish coast and work undertaken at Nancekuke.[105] Ten years later, in 1980, after remarrying and changing her name to Elizabeth Sigmund, she published *Rage against the Dying*, the book which chronicled her grassroots campaign against chemical and biological warfare.[106] MPs tried to appease members of their constituencies by raising the matter with their ministerial colleagues. As calls for an all-party inquiry into rates of death and illnesses at Porton and Nancekuke grew ever more strident, it became clear that the government's safety record in these and other secret facilities was coming under public scrutiny. Attention needed to be diverted through measured concessions, for example by raising the prospect of a pension in certain cases.[107] In a remarkable U-turn, the MoD also commis-sioned a statistical survey to see whether the rates of death and disease among the employees at Nancekuke were higher than those in the general population, only to dismiss the suggestion a year later.[108] The MoD's approach in stonewalling potential claims for compensation, and making concessions only if absolutely necessary, was remarkably similar to the way in which the Ministry responded to the claims by Porton veterans some twenty-five years later. Although individual cases were looked upon more favourably, the authorities generally refused to pay compensation for accidental injuries that were linked to either Porton or Nancekuke. Summarizing the feelings of many, Compton told the readers of *Peace News*:

> What I cannot understand is why I, with little education and no political experience, position or advantages, have had to fight for these defenceless sick men. They were used by our society, they did nothing but obey the orders that were given them in our name, and when they became sick were not accorded the care or kindness given to criminals.[109]

A few years later, in 1976, after a campaign lasting eighteen years, the MoD sent Tom Griffiths a cheque for 1.75 pounds sterling (roughly equivalent to two hours' work at the current minimum wage) for the injuries he had sustained at Nancekuke from nerve gas exposure.[110] It not only added insult to injury at an individual level, but fuelled public anger at what some saw as 'a peculiar type of official inhumanity to the victims—a combination of irresponsibility, meanness, secrecy, and dishonesty', a forceful criticism which questioned the government's ability to manage its relationship with the public effectively whenever questions of national security were involved.[111] No wonder then that political activists and music artists such as the singer-songwriter Peter Hammill began to aim their fire at the facility; his rock song 'Porton Down', released as part of his solo album *pH7* in 1979, skilfully tuned into the nihilist atmosphere of the Cold War. In typically dramatic fashion, his lyrics portrayed Porton as a frightening hub of bacteria and disease which threatened the world with extinction, the 'final violence' which would erase mankind from the face of the earth.[112]

Power Politics

Porton's public image was further undermined by the political and legal controversy surrounding the use of CS gas in Northern Ireland.[113] Showing distinct similarities with the debate on chemical warfare in the 1920s, the arguments used by those who supported the use of CS gas in the late 1960s followed the same lines as J.B.S. Haldane had done earlier, who had suggested putting 'people to sleep for a few hours' as an effective method of riot control.[114] CS gas—discovered in the late 1920s by the US chemists Ben Corson and Roger Stoughton[115]—was developed by Porton in collaboration with the Colonial Office, Hong Kong's Commissioner of Police, and the US Army after the Second World War to replace certain lethal characteristics of tear gas which, with time, can solidify and turn into small projectiles. In 1956, as part of this collaboration, Porton had started a systematic research programme, involving gas chamber tests with human participants, to find an agent for riot control which fulfilled the following criteria: it had to incapacitate quickly and ideally affect more than just the eyes; its use had to be legal within the terms of current international law; it had to be nontoxic, even to children and the elderly, stable in extreme climates, and cheap and easy to manufacture. The irritant properties of CS gas had been recognized by Porton as early as 1934, yet trials had shown that its value as a chemical warfare agent was limited.[116] Critics of CS gas stressed, however, that the gas could produce painful skin injuries. It reportedly also had the disadvantage of producing concentrations of cyanide in the body which, although sublethal, could cause brain damage.[117]

Sustained reports of the use of chemical weapons by Egyptian forces in Yemen since 1962, alleged to include blistering and nerve agents, propelled the subject of chemical weapons on to the international headlines, thus intensifying political pressure on national governments to achieve measurable progress in the field of nonconventional arms control. British politicians in particular found themselves treading a fine line, condemning the use of such weapons without lending tacit support to those who criticized the United States for attacking the Vietcong with tear gas and Agent Orange.[118] In the United States, the authorities tried to justify the use of CS gas in Vietnam on 'humanitarian grounds', yet the argument that it reduced casualty numbers among all combatants lacked credibility in light of overwhelming evidence that showed women and young children being 'flushed out' from their protective natural cover only to be killed by helicopter gunfire. It was setting people up 'for the kill', opponents of CS claimed. By hardening the attitude of the Vietcong, it seemed to have escalated the conflict. Its use as 'riot control' agents on the campuses of American universities, and during the civil disturbances in Paris during the summer of 1968, was likewise met with public criticism. Although it had been made available to about half of all police forces in Britain to 'flush' out dangerous criminals from their hideouts—which seemed to increase, rather than decrease, casualty figures—officials still found themselves obliged to refute allegations about its potentially lethal effects in confined spaces. A concerted media campaign instead suggested that reports about injuries or deaths from CS gas were grossly exaggerated or simply untrue. Besides, whilst the export of CS 'equipment' around the world, except to France, the United States, and South Africa, was publicly acknowledged, it was widely pointed out that the agent had never been used for 'riot control purposes' on the British mainland.[119] This did not prevent CND campaigners, much to the annoyance of the Wiltshire local community, from staging yet another public demonstration in Salisbury in June, this time under the headline 'Porton Gas in Vietnam'.[120]

Following the use of CS gas by the Royal Ulster Constabulary (RUC) during the Londonderry riots in August 1969, which raised the issue of possible adverse medical effects on exposed civilians, the government appointed a small expert committee, chaired by Sir Harold Himsworth, a leading British scientist known for his work on diabetes, to examine the matter scientifically.[121] Despite initially finding no causal link between CS and illnesses in healthy individuals, the committee proceeded to examine the long-term adverse effects of CS gas, and susceptibility to it, among different generational groups, including the young, the elderly, and those with underlying health problems. At the request of the Himsworth Committee, Porton was tasked with exploring, through animal experiments, the toxicology and pathology of CS, especially whether exposure to it could lead to physical deformities in foetuses.[122] Although the committee's interim report was inconclusive, since evidence about the toxicity of CS gas was believed to be 'too scanty', the authorities came under increasing pressure to explain why the use of CS gas, officially claimed to be not a 'tear or poison gas', but a non-toxic 'screening smoke', was thought to be outside the terms of the Geneva Protocol—and therefore acceptable for use in riot-control situations—especially after President Nixon had announced in November that the United States would unilaterally abandon its biological weapons capability. Twenty-four hours later, Solly Zuckerman, the government's chief scientific adviser, and a keen advocate of nuclear, chemical, and biological non-proliferation, informed the Prime Minister that the Himsworth Committee's statement had 'profoundly changed' the context of Britain's policy on CS, and that the legality of riot control agents now needed to be reconsidered.[123] At first, the government tried to hold the line.

One of the key questions concerned the level of toxicity of CS gas. The official position, as stated in Parliament in February 1970, was that CS gas was not harmful to humans 'in other than wholly exceptional circumstances' and that it was therefore believed to be outside the scope of the Geneva Protocol.[124] To exclude CS from the Protocol, lawyers advising the government had applied the *ejusdem generis* rule, which meant that the gas had to be 'significantly harmful' to be banned, since oxygen for airline pilots would otherwise also have been prohibited. It also defined that the harm done to a person had to occur over a substantial period of time. On the basis of these rather stringent criteria, CS was considered not harmful except in 'very exceptional circumstances'. The beauty of the phrase, as one ministerial aide remarked, was its simplicity and general applicability for dissemination of the official position to the general public: 'Almost anything, from peanuts to departmental minutes, do lasting harm to the human constitution if taken in excess.'[125] No one seriously suggested that peanuts were dangerous to health when consumed in moderation. Excessive exposure to CS gas might well cause blisters, but so would excessive exposure to certain soaps and detergents. On such a politically sensitive subject as CS gas the government was determined to win if not hearts, then at least minds. This, as it turned out, was easier said than done.

Isolated protests against Britain's position were propelled into the media spotlight after two CS gas grenades were thrown into one of the chambers of Parliament.[126] In April 1970, the *Sunday Times* published a feature-length article containing vivid images of CS gas blistering that further fuelled public debate and put the government on the defensive; senior officials had simply been unaware of the Edgewood Arsenal human experiments with CS gas on which the article was based.[127] Weeks later, it became apparent that Members of Parliament were getting impatient for the government to publish Porton's research findings. Rumours that the results were being suppressed were not true, but officials were also not forthcoming with the findings since the Prime Minister was reluctant to raise the issue in the run-up to the general election; publication of Porton's report was simply postponed for political reasons.[128] The Church of Scotland, meanwhile, wanted to adopt a resolution condemning Britain's policy on CS gas. Experts and the public were eventually left confused, if not outright shocked, when a Porton spokesperson, as yet unaccustomed to public relations management, referred to CS gas as being 'no more than bonfire smoke'.[129] Against a backdrop in which many wondered how Labour MPs could square their support for the government with their belief in socialism, and in which toxicologists argued that CS gas was not only 'more poisonous than chlorine', but that its toxicity also depended on particle size and air intake by the lungs—as highlighted by Julian Perry Robinson in his submission to the British Pugwash Group in April 1970—it is hardly surprising that the controversy caused further damage to Porton's already bruised reputation.[130]

At a political and military level, after the June 1970 general election had put into power the Conservative Party under the leadership of Edward Heath, the subject of CS gas exposed inter-departmental divisions between the FCO, the MoD, and the Attorney General over the correct interpretation of the Geneva Protocol. Three months later, in September, the incoming Foreign and Commonwealth Secretary invited the MoD to give its opinion, a development which, according to *The Times*, suggested the government was 'reconsidering' its policy on CS.[131] The MoD, however, felt that CS gas provided the military with an effective means for 'riot control' in Northern Ireland, averting, as it were, the need for lethal firearms—and anyway its use apparently did not fall within the remit of the Geneva Protocol. It belonged to one of many 'valuable options' the military could employ in 'internal security or counter-insurgency operations'. The military, in other words, wanted to retain the option of using CS gas both in peacetime and in wartime, irrespective of the 1969 UN resolution to work towards the 'prohibition of chemical and biological weapons in international armed conflicts'.[132] A reversal of UK policy on this matter, the MoD argued, could potentially undermine the US government, and thus strain inter-Allied relations. Even more politically sensitive were the ongoing complex negotiations about the Biological and Toxin Weapons Convention, where a change of UK policy was seen as having the potential to weaken Britain's 'international standing' and thereby play into the hand of the Warsaw Pact and other countries seemingly opposed to the agreement.[133] Above all, the MoD was concerned about how the government could explain a sudden U-turn after having seemingly studied the problem so comprehensively, unless it were to admit that the expert advice previously received by the authorities 'had been at fault'. To do this, officials knew, would have seriously undermined the scientific community in the service of the British military, including Porton. On balance, the Secretary of Defence was therefore 'very strongly in favour of leaving things as they are'.[134] When pressed on the matter by the FCO, the Law Officers informally indicated that there was 'very little doubt that CS was covered by the prohibition in the 1925 Geneva Protocol'.[135] This could have placed the government in a precarious legal position as far as its continued use of CS gas in Northern Ireland was concerned. In April 1971, the FCO finally made it plain that it had 'certain doubts' about the wisdom of the decision to exclude CS from the Geneva Protocol, a position which, on the basis of the law, could no longer be sustained. What was at stake, the FCO argued, was the 'interpretation of an international agreement to which the UK is party'.[136]

An international ban on CS gas was anything but the most pressing of problems for the MoD. Negotiations over arms control placed it in an extremely difficult position in terms of maintaining, and possibly even expanding, Britain's retaliatory chemical warfare capability. In a rapidly changing security environment, an active US chemical weapons capability in Europe could not be taken for granted any longer, the Chiefs of Staffs warned, but it was also unrealistic to seek public and political support for a nonconventional rearmament programme in the midst of disarmament talks; most people would simply view such a proposal as coming at a 'remarkably strange and inopportune time'. The Minister was therefore advised to leave the subject in abeyance unless 'circumstances change markedly'.[137]

Meanwhile, Porton's scientists were becoming weary of being subjected to public and professional attacks by CND and other, mostly peaceful, campaign groups. In July 1968, in light of the 'publicity' the issue of CS gas had attracted, a high-ranking delegation, led by Secretary of Defence Denis Healey, visited Porton to discuss its research and development programme as well as experiments on animals and humans (see Image 40).[138] Arriving by helicopter, Healey and the Army's Chief Scientist were met by the directors of CDEE and MRE, G. Neville Gadsby and Charles E. Gordon Smith respectively, before being whisked away to see the laboratories and listen to a series of lectures dealing with chemical warfare agents. Records of the preparations for the visit yield additional biographical details about a representative cross-section of staff from CDEE and MRE in the late 1960s, a chronological snap-shot illustrative of wider trends in Porton's recruiting practices. Most of the men were trained chemists, chemical engineers, physicists, biochemists, and microbiologists, or career officers with a degree in one or more of these fields of study. Almost all had served in the military. The deputy directors of the CDEE and the MRE were both chemists with considerable overseas experience; T.F. Watkins of the CDEE had done military service in India and Canada, while Major L.H. Kent had been assigned to the Mobile Anti-Gas Laboratory in France and the Middle East during

Image 40. Secretary of Defence Denis Healey visiting Porton Down, 1968
Source: University of Sussex, SHIP File, H6.4, Morton Papers, Secretary of Defence
Denis Healey Visiting Porton Down, 16 July 1968.
Left to right: Charles E. Gordon Smith, Denis Healey, G. Neville Gadsby. A note on the back of the
photograph says: 'Denis Healey surrounded by hot air, looking for the elephant up to its knees etc.'
It was probably written by John D. Morton, a staff member at MRE Porton.

the war before transferring from CDEE to MRE. Responsibility for the
development of defensive measures rested with M. Ainsworth, the
Superintendent of the Protection Research Division, a specialist in biophys-
ics with an interest in the 'properties of skin'. He had joined CDEE from
Leeds University to design new protective garments. P.H. Schwabe, the
Senior Scientific Officer of the Engineering and Respiratory Division,
worked at Porton on the latest air filtration systems for tanks, submarines,
and buildings. Both had joined CDEE in the 1950s. Offensive work, on the
other hand, was carried out by the Chemistry Research Division, headed by
A. Bebbington, which was tasked with studying and developing new types
of chemical warfare agents.[139] Also in attendance that day was a group of
senior military officials, among them Commodore A.C. Simmonds, Royal
Navy, Wing Commander D.R. Levinson, RAF, Lieutenant Colonel J.F.
Fitzgerald-Smith, British Army, and Lieutenant Colonel N.C. Burnett, a
trained microbiologist who served as liaison officer with the US Chemical
Corps.[140]

In charge of human experimentation were Beswick as the Senior Medical Officer (Research) and Ladell as Assistant Director (Medical). Pharmacology was covered by R.W. Brimblecombe, the Principal Scientific Officer at CDEE, who had previously worked at a Bristol psychiatric hospital and for the MRC. Operational assessments and weapons development fell into the realm of K.F. Sawyer, a trained physicist with experience of locust control in East Africa, who had joined CDEE in 1940. He was supported by R.A. Titt, Superintendent of the Munitions Research Division, himself a long-serving member at CDEE with overseas experience in India, Canada, and the United States. He was responsible for developing riot control devices, for example for the police forces in Hong Kong, so his work was of particular interest to Healey. The head of the Process Research Division at Nancekuke, L.W.J. Warner, on the other hand, a trained chemical engineer, had been assigned to managing public relations with the local authorities in Cornwall over the contentious issue of CS gas. Responding to public pressure for greater transparency, and informed by the briefings given to him, Healey was able to tell a group of waiting journalists that aspects of Porton's work had to remain secret to safeguard Britain's defensive capability.[141] He also agreed to discuss concerns about the government's public relations strategy with MRE representatives on the National Joint Industrial Council, known as the Whitley Council, who pointed out that MRE staff had been subjected to 'personal attacks' in the media without being allowed to respond. It was not government policy or the institution that was being criticized, they argued, but they themselves. Officials had simply done too little to 'defend their character and careers'.[142] As Britain began to assess the policy implications resulting from disarmament negotiations in the field of chemical and biological warfare, industrial relations between the MRE and its employer, the MoD, were reaching a new low.

For Porton, already on the defensive to safeguard its fragile existence, revelations about medical ethics violations in experimental research could not have come at a worse time. At the beginning of 1970, Britain's armed forces became the subject of intense media speculation after a Catholic priest, Monsignor John Barry, alleged that the MoD was secretly conducting human experiments on 'elderly people' before disposing of them in an act of 'euthanasia'.[143] The allegations were at first dismissed as 'preposterous', and the MoD's Special Investigation Branch launched a thorough inquiry to contain the political fallout. MPs such as Dalyell and David Steel, the future leader of the Liberal Party, raised the issue in Parliament

after receiving confidential letters from members of their constituencies.
On 10 February, Prime Minister Harold Wilson was forced to respond to
the allegations in the House of Commons. Although the evidence turned
out to have been fabricated by someone who seemed to be a mentally
unstable non-commissioned officer from Glasgow, who had 'imagined' the
details of the tests, the political damage was done.[144] Whether informally
among senior Whitehall officials or among seasoned commentators, questions were being asked: might there have been a kernel of truth in the
affair? Some even suggested a connection with Porton's increasingly
unpopular microbiological work.[145] Prior to taking over as head of MRE,
Gordon Smith had been trialling new cancer therapies that involved treating elderly people suffering from the disease with a specific virus. Officials
were quick to point out that the work had been done to 'save human life',
and which had 'no connection whatsoever' with the MoD.

Thirty years later, the story again hit the headlines in the wake of
Operation Antler, the police investigation into claims that soldiers were
duped into taking part in toxic experiments. Blissfully unaware of the true
facts of the case, a *Daily Express* journalist jumped the gun, comparing the
alleged experiments with Nazi medical war crimes, a deeply flawed but also
meaningless comparison: German scientists involved in Nazi medical experiments showed a much greater degree of criminal intent and recklessness,
and also a greater willingness to harm individual human lives for an assumed
greater good in times of national crisis, than did Allied researchers during
and after the Second World War.[146] Given the close correlation between the
start of a major police inquiry into Porton's affairs and the 'reappearance' of
what sources close to the MoD knew was a red herring, a more sinister
reading of these facts is also possible. Assuming the MoD or a related agency,
possibly Porton itself, had leaked the information to the media—an unlikely
but not impossible scenario—this would have strengthened the suggestion
that the government was circulating knowingly false allegations among the
public that could be disproved, if necessary, at any time on the basis of hard
evidence; by implication, this would undermine the credibility of closely
related allegations the Wiltshire police were examining as part of Operation
Antler. Although this is somewhat speculative, it allows for the possibility
that senior defence sources may have learned their lesson by trying to divert
public attention from Porton through an aggressive media and propaganda
campaign. At around the same time, MPs who raised concerns about
Porton's work were told by senior colleagues that they were 'taking a risk'
in asking awkward questions, a reminder of the affair about privileged

information that had led to Dalyell's removal from the Select Committee on Science and Technology in 1968, coupled with a not-so-veiled threat to their future career prospects in British politics.[147]

Back in Wiltshire, there was no denying any longer that Britain's biological warfare programme was infinitely unpopular with the general public. The government's swift disassociation with Porton was understood to form part of a comprehensive review to assess the possible risks and benefits of transferring the MRE from military to civilian control, affecting approximately 400 members of staff, including 125 researchers. Nearly a third of its annual running costs, about 1 million pounds, were being paid by the civilian sector, in particular the DHSS and the MRC, and there were not only fiscal pressures to make greater savings in the defence budget but also mounting political arguments for the transfer of all biological defence work to civilian agencies as a precondition to prevent offensive research. The government was therefore yet again, as it had been in the 1920s, called upon to seek a negotiated solution that would satisfy evolving public sentiment at an international level while simultaneously ensuring Britain's defence needs.[148] Another contributing factor concerned the unilateral decision by the United States to abandon its offensive biological weapons programme. This included the destruction of its existing biological stockpiles and plans to transfer the authority of Fort Detrick from the military to the Department of Health, Education, and Welfare. Convinced that biological weapons research would continue in other US facilities, at Edgewood and Dugway especially, British officials were under no illusion that the well-managed propaganda campaign in the United States was likely to have repercussions on how Britain would be perceived at home and abroad.[149] Although a decision was made to review the matter in five years' time, many understood that the writing was on the wall. Only months later, in January 1971, Gordon Smith returned to London to take up the position of Dean of the LSHTM.[150] Given what seemed to be an imminent ban on the production and stockpiling of biological weapons, he knew full well that the MRE, and Porton as it had been conceived during much of the Cold War, was unlikely to survive if the security environment, especially the threat from chemical and biological attack, were to change substantially.[151]

For seasoned military experts, however, trials had to go on regardless. Changes in military research ethics convinced many of the need to reassess some of the underlying principles and theories of incapacitation that had shaped the field over the last two decades. In contrast to work conducted after the Second World War, which focused on lethality, there was now a

much greater emphasis on agents that caused 'reversible incapacitation'. As
early as 1947, Adolph H. Corwin, professor of organic chemistry at Johns
Hopkins, had proposed to the US Chemical Corps the application of a
series of 'incapacitation concepts' that would underpin research into ways
of attacking the enzyme system, and the use of agents for the production of
'mass hallucinations and uncontrollable hysteria'.[152] By studying cases of
'naturally occurring incapacitation', resulting, in most cases, from respiratory, gastro-intestinal, or psychological problems at the workplace or from
toxic hazards in industry such as carcinogenic metals; by re-examining the
effects of previously discarded chemical agents, which might have been
tested for their lethal powers alone; by looking more closely at how enzyme
systems could be responsible for 'body inhibition'; and by reviewing different modes of incapacitation resulting from human diseases, Porton scientists
wanted to develop innovative methodologies which they hoped would help
them in their quest for 'an ideal CW incapacitant'.[153] Both physical and
mental incapacitants had been shown to have quite specific effects, but
also to involve risks and levels of unpredictability, which Porton wanted to
overcome through the testing of various combinations of agents. Agents
stimulating certain sensory nerve endings, on the other hand, showed
greater predictability in affecting the human brain and respiratory system.
Unfortunately, the researchers remarked, these substances involved the 'danger of permanent effect or even death'. For the time being, the Holy Grail
remained an equivalent to nerve agents in the lethal field, most probably an
agent that would inhibit a vital enzyme of the central nervous system, that
would cause serious, yet reversible, incapacitation. For a select few, though,
it became painfully apparent that these objectives were not just 'science
fiction'; for them, the memory of their experience at Porton was as surreal
as it was life-changing, though not in any positive sense of the term.

Talking to the Dead

In assessing the narrative structures among Porton veterans, one might easily be struck by profound similarities in the spatial, temporal, and emotional
experience of men recruited as test subjects at Porton during the Cold War.
Implementing newly formulated ethics standards was, if anything, an excruciatingly slow process. In mid 1972, almost twenty years after Maddison had
embarked from Northern Ireland on his fateful journey to Porton, a young

man named Richard B.M. Skinner, born in February 1953, and his friend Philip Coughlan, both stationed at RAF Buchan near Peterhead in Aberdeenshire, decided, as had many in the preceding decades, to travel to Porton to take part in physiological tests to develop protective equipment. After one of their superiors had told them that 'it was an easy touch to earn some extra money', and since both were 'skint', they did not think twice about what became, quite literally, a life-changing experience. Nothing had been said about the use of chemical weapons and both were totally unaware of what Porton had in store for them after their arrival. Following a short introductory talk by an RAF officer, believed to be the Squadron Leader, probably Moylan-Jones, the participants were given a chance to withdraw from the experiments.[154] Each test would be fully explained, they were told, yet, to their surprise, this was not the case. Most medical scientists told them as little as possible and for anyone asking any questions, the staff had a series of 'stock answers'. Discipline seemed lax; as long as they turned up for certain tests at the right time 'nobody seemed to care'. Upon realizing that both men possessed the 'desired height, weight and lung capacity', the scientists 'latched onto' them in a frantic effort to persuade them to take part in a 'special test' worth a 'considerable amount of money'. Skinner later recalled he had been 'groomed for these particular experiments from the first day'.[155] Considerable psychological pressure was also applied. It was either both or neither of them, they were told, but they had to make up their minds quickly, preferably before lunchtime. Once they had agreed, they were informed of certain stages of the experiment and were given another opportunity to withdraw, provided they 'never reveal[ed]' what they had been told. 'As we didn't seem to have been told much this seemed a bit odd', Skinner recalled.[156]

On 7 June 1972, following a series of prior assessments, Skinner was the first to be exposed to the newly developed psychological incapacitant T3436, also known as MPIPG (N-methyl-4-piperidyl isopropyl phenyl glycolate), at a dose of 8 μg per kilogram of body weight, the highest dose of the glycolate ever to be given to a human at Porton. In total, Porton exposed twenty-one servicemen to T3436 in inhalation tests between June 1971 and July 1972, with dosages ranging from 2 μg/kg to 8 μg/kg.[157] These were part of a wider series of experiments, carried out between 1967 and 1972, in which over 120 soldiers received T3436 either orally or through inhalation.[158] Some thirty years later, Skinner's memory of what happened next remains 'very hazy'. Except for certain memorable fragments—an 'arithmetic test' he felt incapable of

doing, food he threw on the floor, or orders being shouted at him—his recollections are vague: 'I do not recall responding to any of these orders and I
believe I became abusive and uncooperative towards the staff.'[159] It is quite
possible that Porton's researchers wanted to assess how a severely drugged
person responded to 'provocation' by 'shouting orders' at him. A Porton
report about the effects of glycolates in man noted: 'Outbursts of aggression
and violence occur which might be due to a paranoid state which sometimes
becomes spontaneously apparent or following provocation on the part of an
attendant.'[160] His time on the medical ward appears to have been erased from
his memory, despite a scene he will never forget: he vividly remembers 'talking to someone who was dead. I was convinced a boy called Martin, who died
while I was at school, was in the room and I had a lengthy talk with him.'[161]
As it turned out, for four and a half hours Skinner had sat in front of, and
talked to, a fire extinguisher. For him, the red-coloured metal canister had
become the material realization of a young life snuffed out too early. It not
only signified life's transience and fragility, but offered a dream-like passage
into another world in which the dead interacted with the living, yet it had
been a trip he had never agreed to nor wanted to undertake. At no point was
he informed of the likely effects that inhalation of the substance would have
on him, nor given any guidance about the level of incapacitation, dissociation,
hallucination, or personality change he would experience. Given what had
been known for over a decade about glycolate intoxication, whether administered orally or inhaled, the omission by the scientists to provide Skinner and
his colleague with at least the bare minimum of information about the possible consequences of the test on which they were about to embark was tanta-
mount to gross negligence. When he woke up, the attending psychiatrist asked
him how he felt and whether he remembered anything:

> I told him of the arithmetic test and then of the 'dream about Martin' as
> I called it. He made notes on a single sheet of paper. He said that explained a
> lot and showed me a clip of videotape of me sitting in a corner apparently
> talking to a fire extinguisher. Although my mouth was opening and closing as
> if talking no sound was coming out. A second clip that I was shown showed
> me bouncing on the beds and swinging on the rails like a chimp or monkey.
> He asked if I remembered that but I didn't. Until this point I didn't realize
> that my entire time in the ward had been videoed [sic]. At this point he again
> asked me how I felt and I said I felt confused and a bit upset. He said that
> [was] understandable and that I just needed a rest and would be fine in a day
> or so. He reminded me that this was 'higher than Top Secret' and that I was to
> say absolutely nothing to anybody. He especially warned me that I was to say

nothing to SAC Coughlan, as it would compromise the test. He was worried that I would say something, as we were 'such good friends'.[162]

Skinner heeded his warning, not knowing that he would witness his friend having similarly upsetting near-death experiences coupled with suicidal urges. When Coughlan did not return from his test the following Tuesday, Skinner, upon inquiring, was told that 'they were keeping him an extra night'. When he asked why, the chief technician simply responded 'bigger bloke, bigger dose' and refused to engage in conversation about the matter. Later that night, at 11.00 p.m., as Skinner was watching TV, a Porton official took him to one side, explaining 'that there were a few problems and could I go up to the Medical Centre with him. He said SAC Coughlan was not responding as expected and a friendly face might help.'[163] At the Medical Centre, Porton's psychiatrist informed him that 'SAC Coughlan was emotionally disturbed and they thought he might attempt to harm himself'. Asked whether he was willing to spend the night with Coughlan, he agreed, but only after he had been assured that he 'would not be in any danger and would be rescued if attacked'.[164] Moments later, upon entering the ward, he witnessed the other man's fragile mental state:

> When I entered the ward SAC Coughlan was at one of the windows, which were high up in the walls, and hammering on the window frame with his fists. I started to talk to him and managed to get him down and sitting on a bed. After a short while he became very agitated and was back at the window. He kept repeating 'They're coming, they're coming, they're coming to see me', and 'I've got to go with them.' At one stage he mentioned the name of one of 'them' as Dougie Grubb, which was strange because he had been in training with us and had died, Phil [Coughlan] was not very friendly with him and did not really like him. I looked out the window and saw nothing except some streetlights and a few trees. I asked him who 'they' were but he became even more upset. At last he calmed down and we just sat in silence for a while before he said, 'They're all dead.' I asked who and he pointed to the window and said 'Them, they're dead and they want me', and then he burst into tears. Shortly after this he cried himself to sleep. I remained awake but there were no more problems.[165]

This was not a terminally ill patient wishing to die through either passive or active measures, nor had a suicidal tendency been a characteristic feature of his personality; rather, it had been induced artificially by a powerfully acting drug at a British military facility. For Skinner, the Porton experience had a profound and lasting effect. He still endures sleepless nights and frequent

nightmares, often a repetition of what he calls the 'talking to Martin experience', an unintended, involuntary sense of being dragged into the past—in
which the dead control the lives of the living. Since that time at Porton, he
has had an inability to conform, an 'anti-authority streak' perhaps, as he likes
to see it, which seems more a conscious or subconscious attempt to prevent
a repetition of the traumatic event the MoD euphemistically recorded as a
case of 'incapacitation'. Convinced the test had led to 'a change in personality', he still struggles to come to terms with the level and type of information he was given at the time, when they were told that they would receive
a 'mild dose of an anaesthetic', words he remembers clearly to this day:
'Both Philip [Coughlan] and I thought there was no problem with just a
mild dose of anaesthetic.'[166]

It raises the question as to why military scientists intentionally, it seems,
misinformed human participants in specific tests, seven years after procedural reforms were meant to signal the dawn of a new area of military
medical ethics. Their conduct flew in the face of every conceivable ethics
declaration, the Nuremberg Code of 1947, the MRC ethics statement of
1962/1963, the Helsinki Declaration of 1964, and the RCP ethics guidelines of 1967, documents which had received considerable public and
political airing, and indeed government acceptance, from the early 1960s.
This was an unreconstructed research culture. Military science, seemingly
transparent and repackaged, was now accountable to external experts who
remained detached from the reality of the traumatic experiences suffered
by soldiers. The fresh inquest into Maddison's death in 2004 provided the
Porton veterans with probably their only chance to have their case heard
in open court, and thus overcome the government's claim to Crown
immunity. The Skinner case furnished the contextual backdrop that
helped to achieve a mediated settlement between the MoD and the
Porton Down Veterans Support Group (PDVSG). Both served as powerful
imageries with which experts and the public could identify.

Who were the researchers performing the trials? What was their motivation? Moylan-Jones and Peter Holland were directly involved in glycolates
experiments for which Beswick, as the head of the Medical Division (see
Image 41), was ultimately responsible. The person in charge of screening the
servicemen was Kenneth H. Kemp, who worked with Wawman, the army
psychiatrist. They all, in their own way, played a part in experiments with
incapacitants, yet our attention needs to focus on Holland, since it was he
who conducted most of the tests with glycolates. According to the CPS,
Holland 'was a newly qualified medical practitioner with less than one year's

Image 41. Medical Division, Porton Down, 1975–1976

Source: IWM, Photographic Collection, CDEE, Group Photographs, Medical Division, 1975–1976. © Imperial War Museums (Medical Division 1975).

The members of staff pictured—in order of seniority—are as follows: 1. Maj J.A. Tanner; 2. Dr B. Ballantyne; 3. Dr J. Hill; 4. Gp Capt R.J. Moylan-Jones; 5. Dr F. Beswick; 6. Dr P. Holland; 7. Dr D. Gall; 8. Mr K.[H.] Kemp; 9. Lt Col R. Scott; 10. Mrs J. Harfield; 11. Mrs J. Moxham; 12. Mrs S. Sambrook; 13. Mrs A. Ramsden; 14. Miss P. Tudge; 15. Miss H. Thornton; 16. Mrs E. Duxbury; 17. Miss P. Fletcher; 18. Mrs M. Scaife; 19. H. Colgrave; 20. V. Foster; 21. W. Ponting; 22. D. Parkes; 23. P. Cole; 24. P. Williams; 25. T. Webber; 26. P. Baker; 27. W. Wells; 28. J. Randles; 29. WO II MacDonald; 30. C. Long; 31. F. Aldous; 32. Sgt S. Worth; 33. P. Parker; 34. R. White; 35. J. Edginton.

service at Porton Down' in June 1967. When interviewed by the police 'under caution' in May 2000, he stated that 'he always went into a fairly detailed description of what the observers could expect during an experiment as he was giving them the option not to do it'.[167] When asked by officers from Operation Antler whether there were 'any tests considered sufficiently sensitive that volunteers could not be given that level of information', Holland cited trials with glycolate BZ, a central nervous system drug that affected the brain. According to Holland, volunteers were told that the drug would make them feel 'not quite right' but that they would quickly recover. Other than that, research subjects were told 'little else'. Holland then made the following frank admission, which he later retracted, to the police officers from Operation Antler:

> *Holland*: If you said to a volunteer, look you, you might go suicidal, you might go psychotic, you might go this, you might go that, forget it.
> *Operation Antler*: Forget what?
> *Holland*: Forget the study.
> *Operation Antler*: Why?
> *Holland*: You wouldn't get any volunteers would you?[168]

In experiments considered to be 'a little bit dicey', military scientists intentionally and knowingly downplayed the risks to ensure that human subjects would agree to take part. They knew that it was highly unlikely that any man in his right mind would consent to such a trial. They themselves would not have. Misleading participants, they believed, was an integral part of the study, since only it made the study possible. More significantly, his statement provides insight into the intricate—though rarely admitted—relationship between the level of information scientists felt they were required to supply and the potential risk to which participants would be subjected. The lower the risk of possible harm, it seems, the greater was their willingness to disclose all known adverse effects. Conversely, an increase in risk seems to have led to a corresponding reduction in information they supplied about possible side-effects or nasty reactions.

This raises a question: at what point did military scientists decide, either in their own mind or collectively and informally—since anything else might have exposed them to disciplinary action—when a specific trial was too dangerous to warrant full and frank disclosure of all risks, as the trial would otherwise, so they believed, not take place? Attempting to rationalize, and indeed historicize, highly subjective decision-making processes among scientists in one of the most secretive facilities in Britain, which effectively took place outside any meaningful external supervisory control, without a representative paper trail, obviously poses complex methodological problems. Holland's specific revelations, however, may offer certain clues about lines of demarcation which, albeit heavily blurred, helped scientists to distinguish between different types of trials. If he had been aware of, or suspected, any *long-term* health problems resulting from the experiment, he told the CPS, he 'simply' would not have done it: 'It was against his ethics and it was his duty to see that the observers did not come to any harm, as required by the Declaration of Helsinki.'[169] It is difficult to know whether Holland's ethical awareness, which he so vividly expressed on this occasion, stemmed from the late 1960s or whether he used it to portray himself more favourably later. Porton, according to Holland, seems to have had neither a specific 'policy' on informed consent, nor consent forms, though the Declaration itself seems to have been 'written' into official Porton policy. Researchers wanting to conduct human experiments since about the mid to late 1970s had to demonstrate that the 'study was carried out in accordance with the provisions of the Declaration of Helsinki', and would have been aware of the need to abide by it.[170] If we are to believe Holland, and there is no reason to question his credibility in his first interview with Operation Antler, then the factors dividing ethical from unethical tests were not so much the short-term psychological or physical effects that certain compounds might have on the bodies of soldiers—though these were taken into account if they were of a lethal or sublethal nature—but the long-term health consequences. Since little was, and is still, known about the potential long-term health effects of chemical warfare and incapacitating agents, and since these effects are epidemiologically difficult to assess, because of all the environmental and life-style factors affecting human health, the scientists saw little need to concern themselves with them. In other words, if the scientist concluded in his own mind that no long-term health complications were to be expected, which in most cases he could, if he wanted to, then he believed it did not really matter whether full informed consent was obtained and ethics standards were being violated, as long as the test could be performed. In 2003, the CPS concluded that there was 'evidence available to the effect that an explanation of the more uncomfortable aspects of the likely effects of the test [with the glycolate BZ] was deliberately omitted by Dr Holland'.[171] The irrevocable violation of thousands of servicemen's trust in the authorities, and in man himself, through deliberate deception, continues to be among perhaps the most disconcerting aspects of Porton's Cold War legacy.

10

The Politics of Medical Memory

Mnemogogues

In his early short story 'I Mnemagoghi', Primo Levi coined this term
(translated into English as 'The Mnemogogues') to refer to the 'arousers of
memories'. To construct powerful narratives of suffering and victimhood,
these self-appointed and often state-controlled agents in charge of memory
production require a contextual framework within which commemoration
can take place for a group of psychologically harmed or persecuted people.
The victims of the Holocaust are a case in point, as are the tens of thousands
of damaged lives of those belonging to ethnic minorities, those living under
modern dictatorships, apartheid, or civil war, and those suffering from
disease. The literary and documented narratives of survivors of collective
injustices committed by former governments and criminal regimes may be
substantiated by empirical evidence, but it is more important that they
should be appropriated into a collective national story. This is just as true for
the struggle to obtain freedom for African Americans as it is for the deported,
falsely imprisoned, and often forgotten minorities of major military conflicts. In Britain, the 'memory boom' of the late 1990s was fuelled by quite
specific political, economic, and cultural preconditions in which greater
affluence and government investment coincided with a recognition in society about the importance of 'traumatic memory'. It was realized that family
members had returned home from the battlefields of the First and Second
World Wars, as prisoners of war, or as persecuted minorities, in the words
of Walter Benjamin, 'not richer but poorer in communicable experience'.[1]
Silence turned into a popular subject of examination.[2] For many who had
suffered in some way, the emotional experience of the event was too
overwhelming to talk about, and their painful memories were channelled

into a desire to rebuild shattered lives. Through story-telling, exhibitions, reading groups, witness seminars, and public lectures across the country, sections of society apparently began to reconnect with repressed landscapes of the past, a form of collective catharsis aimed at strengthening a sense of national belonging and identity. Eligibility for individuals and groups of people to participate in, and benefit from, such state-sanctioned processes of commemoration was largely dependent upon their officially recognized status as victims of injustice. It offered those who 'qualified' an opportunity to tell their tale, as seemingly independent producers of newly constructed national narratives, yet those denied official recognition, including the chemical and nuclear war veterans, were forced to keep silence. It was a period during which the English, as Tony Judt put it, further cultivated their unique ability to 'feel genuine nostalgia for a fake heritage' as a means of denying a more uncomfortable past. The 'memory boom', conceived and promoted by a new generation of cultural historians under the tutelage of their master prophet Jay Winter, who today have usurped for themselves the position of comptroller of state-sanctioned—and state-funded—'historical knowledge', has produced little more than a 'countrywide bowdlerization of memory', an inauthentic heritage industry for an inauthentic land.[3] At the same time, the link between Porton's historical origins in the First World War and Britain's evolving culture of remembrance, highly visible ever since the 'invention' of Armistice Day, in effect encouraged the Porton veterans to fight for justice: the communicators of historical knowledge in the form of mass media and museums sought to appropriate their experiences and incorporate them into a revisionist perspective conflicting with the official narrative. Without that direct connection with the shared experience of Europe's most devastating military conflicts, public understanding and support for the Porton veterans might well have been less forthcoming.

Mnemogogues of medical rather than traumatic memories, perhaps deemed unsuitable for national identity creation or popular consumption because of their underlying critical commentary on Britain's military activities, faced another, more profound dilemma: much of the evidence underpinning the case of the Porton veterans for recognition was, at first, based on witness testimony, and thus subject to external scrutiny about its veracity. Few, if any, of the Porton veterans intentionally constructed false testimonies, yet their narratives rarely provided either access to the traumatic event itself or a deeper understanding of it. Inaccuracies, inconsistencies, and gaps in witness testimonies do not come as a surprise to scholars, especially where traumatic events are being recalled, as in Holocaust survivor testimony. When the character of a witness is called into question, however, their testimony is prevented from entering into the national narrative, and this happened in the case of the Porton veterans. The words of these victims were likely to fall on deaf ears, even, if not especially, in a society where the processes of commemoration and remembrance are closely tied to national identity formation and the celebration of wartime heroism. Although the victim of trauma was unable to produce a verifiable and officially sanctioned memory of the event, since he might not have been 'fully conscious during the [event] itself' and seemed to come away psychologically unharmed, any testimony put forward by a Porton veteran in newspapers and other media outlets functioned as a constant 'reminder of the event'.[4] Whatever the UK government did to discredit the veterans' case, whether in public, in Parliament, or in the courts, their individual life stories, told with genuine conviction to anyone who cared to listen, created a counter-narrative which began to call into question Britain's glorified national identity and public image.

A British 'Erin Brockovich'

To understand the politics of medical memory for the Porton veterans we need to look at ways in which individuals, interest groups, and organizations managed to pursue a joint strategy through small incremental steps and negotiated compromises. It was a process so painfully slow that it required not only an unreasonable level of personal commitment from those involved but also a major sea-change in international debate about the long-term health effects of Cold War testing programmes involving nonconventional weapons. Similar concerns were being raised by individuals and action groups elsewhere, most notably in United States, Australia, and Canada, so Porton veterans managed to attract, quite early on, significant public attention. However, given the enormous scientific and legal complexities of the case, and the likelihood that it could take years to reach an out-of-court settlement, there were few lawyers prepared to work on such cases on a no-win-no-fee basis. The veterans, on the other hand, lacked the means to finance a court case independently. For the British government, the stakes were too high to allow these cases to be aired in open court, in terms of both national security and potential political embarrassment; officials therefore resisted an amicable settlement which they knew could be construed as a precedent for future legal claims by the Porton or any other veteran group. As a result, veterans were frequently denied access to their medical files and reports on spurious grounds, and when access was granted, the information provided was often incomplete.

In the United States, veterans made major headway for their cause by launching a concerted campaign against alleged 'injustices' committed by US federal agencies during the Cold War and the First Gulf War. In articles and published studies such as *Veterans at Risk* (1993), which looked at chemical warfare experiments during the Second World War, the public learned that soldiers had 'risked their health and safety to help develop better means of protection against chemical warfare'.[5] It was a period in which major ethics scandals followed one another in quick succession. In 1994, Eileen Welsome received the Pulitzer Prize for exposing US pluto-nium experiments in the *Albuquerque Tribune*.[6] In the same year, a former US serviceman was awarded 400,000 dollars in damages for LSD experi-ments after a private Senate Bill was passed.[7] Reporting on the question of whether military research was hazardous to veterans, including the Gulf War veterans, the US Senate committee on veterans' affairs, chaired by John D. Rockefeller, concluded that for most Americans, experiments intended to harm 'unwitting guinea pigs', even if only temporarily, were unethical, irrespective of whether the tests might have pursued higher goals; because it had failed to comply with accepted ethical standards, the US military was charged with having 'put hundreds of thousands of US service members at risk, and [having possibly] caused lasting harm to many individuals'.[8] The US Department of Defense was singled out for having repeatedly misrepresented the risks of different types of 'military expo-sures'. Congress was called upon to establish a centralized database of all federally funded human experiments, initiate a nationwide declassification process of test-related documents, and re-establish a National Commission for the Protection of Human Subjects. The government was now on notice to take decisive action in a matter of national concern.

By the time the United States Advisory Committee for Human Radiation Experiments was created to 'uncover the history of human radiation exper-iments and intentional environmental releases of radiation; to identify the ethical and scientific standards for evaluating these events; and to make rec-ommendations to ensure that whatever wrongdoing may have occurred in the past cannot be repeated'—which also involved proposals to compensate thousands of servicemen exposed to toxic agents—it began to dawn on Porton veterans that their case would not be resolved anytime soon.[9] As late as 1987, Porton officials had defended nerve gas experiments on humans in the *New Scientist*, despite such tests having been 'banned' in the United States for over a decade for fear that they might cause changes in human 'body chemistry'.[10] The British Medical Association (BMA) echoed the WMA's planned policy declaration prohibiting physicians from participating in offensive chemical and biological warfare research, but this helped little in softening the government's position.[11] Bridget Goodwin's award-winning documentary film 'Keen as Mustard' (1989) detailing Britain's involvement in chemical warfare experiments in Australia during the Second World War likewise received a muted response.[12] The UK government was not prepared to appoint a group of independent experts to investigate the veterans' claims about long-term health effects along the US model, as was proposed by the Labour Shadow Defence Minister, Derek Fatchett, who hoped to position the Labour Party within the ex-servicemen community in the run-up to the next election, nor was it willing to set up an official inquiry into Porton's experimental programme.[13] Such an enquiry was believed to be impractical, too costly, and politically too sensitive. Despite some of the attention-seeking actions of individual veterans and the occasional support from journalists and MPs, including Ken Livingstone, the future Mayor of London, according to officials no wrong had been committed. The screening of an hour-long ITV documentary 'The Secrets of Porton Down' (1994), which investigated the ethics of Britain's chemical warfare experiments, did little to persuade the authorities to reconsider their position, yet it parachuted Porton into the public and political spotlight.[14] Interviewed as part of the programme, Porton's director, Graham Pearson, gave a sorry account of himself and the institution he was supposed to lead, arguing dogmatically that since the mid 1950s Porton had been 'wholly concerned with saving lives', only then to retract his statement in a letter to Parliament. Feigning historical ignorance was no longer an option to paper over past ethical wrongdoing.

The response by Britain's warfare experts to such reporting was one of widespread indignation against what some believed to be unfair criticism made with 'perfect hindsight'. Porton could not be held responsible for any ethical transgressions, countered Hugh Dudley, chairman of Porton's ethics committee. The fact that 'other' research facilities, including civilian ones, had likewise conducted research now deemed to be 'unethical' was put forward as proof that Porton had been no different from anyone else, which is why no 'blame' should be apportioned to Porton's 'scientific predecessors'. According to Dudley, there was no a priori evidence suggesting any short- or long-term effects from nerve agent experiments, a view much welcomed by Whitehall's civil servants, but the quality of its ethical evaluation and record-keeping system was apparently such that it would allow Porton to 'trace every subject for follow-up', if ever that were necessary.[15] In retrospect, it makes it all the more surprising that a systematic in-house monitoring programme was never set up, even at this late stage, to gain insight into the health, mental, and social effects of toxic experiments. At a time when Britain was actively engaging in international disarmament and arms control negotiations in the run-up to the CWC, seen as integral to the country's national security, her political and chemical warfare establishment was closing ranks in order to defend long-term professional and national interests.

This is where the story might have ended, as it did for other veteran groups, had it not been for the mind-numbing stubbornness and perseverance of individuals such as Alan Care, a fifty-something, chain-smoking, no-nonsense personal injury lawyer with links to the trade unions who had specialized in chemical poisoning claims, a 'sort of male, slightly older, British Erin Brockovitch [sic]'—a reference to the US environmental activist who helped to bring a case against the Pacific Gas and Electric Company.[16] Fearless and determined like no other, for over fifteen years he represented most of the Porton veterans. His interest in Porton coincided with the dawn of a new era in which chemical weapons were meant to be banned once and for all. On the way to business meetings or holidays in the West Country, Care recalled, he had often driven past Porton, noticing the barbed wire fencing, the red flags, and the warning signs to unwanted visitors: 'MoD Property—Keep Out'.[17] It had intrigued him, as it had many people over the years who had wondered what went on behind Porton's forbidding gates. One of the most outspoken campaigners against the effects of chemical and biological agents, Elizabeth Sigmund, known among her admirers as the 'toxic avenger', referred Care to Michael Roche, founder of the Porton Down Volunteers Association (the precursor to the PDVSG), who had gone on hunger strike to obtain his medical records about the tests he had taken part in.[18] It did not take Care long to realize that the government's insistence on Section 10 of the 1947 Crown Proceedings Act (CPA), which gives the Crown immunity from legal liability for personal injuries or death sustained by members of the British armed forces, was preventing Roche and other Porton veterans from suing the MoD.[19] In August 1995, the conservative politician Peter Lilley, the then Secretary of State for Social Services, who three years earlier had vowed to 'close down the something for nothing society' by ridiculing the lives of people on benefit—displaying a sense of humour that is surely not to everyone's taste in today's austerity Britain—issued a Section 10 Certificate to Roche's legal team, thus making it impossible to pursue the case any further in the UK.[20] It was a draconian measure which, according to Care, allowed the MoD to stop any of the Porton cases in their tracks before they reached the law courts. Colleagues told Care the 'prospects of success were zero'.[21]

Although the 1987 Crown Proceedings (Armed Forces) Act repealed Section 10 of the 1947 CPA, the law did not permit soldiers to sue the government for any damages incurred prior to the new act coming into force. Any 'incidents or injuries before 1987' were not covered, the Minister for the Armed Services, Nicholas Soames, told Parliament in 1996 in response to a veterans' claim that they had been duped into participating in dangerous tests at Porton. There was no viable legal avenue, it seemed, that allowed the Porton veterans to bring their case to court. Besides having a weak legal case, a non-existent medical case, and no proven moral case, the group, which had so far registered their concerns with the War Pensions Agency, was embarrassingly small, not exceeding about forty at this stage. Of more than 21,000 veterans, fewer than a hundred former servicemen had requested their medical records from Porton.

Given the large number of servicemen who had gone to Porton during the Second World War and the postwar period, most of the complaints related to the late 1940, 1950s, and 1960s, but this made it extremely difficult, if not impossible, to distinguish epidemiologically between age- or life-style related illnesses on the one hand, and ill-health resulting from participation in Porton trials on the other. Statistics published by the MoD suggested that the number of servicemen who had attended Porton had gradually decreased, although officials had taken into account neither the prewar figures nor the sudden rise in the number of experimental subjects required during the Second World War (see Figure 5). The data also said little about the type of experiments, their short- and long-term health effects, or how they were experienced at an individual level.

For many, the Porton veterans seemed to have no case. Porton's former director, Graham Pearson, told the *Sunday Herald* in a somewhat patronizing

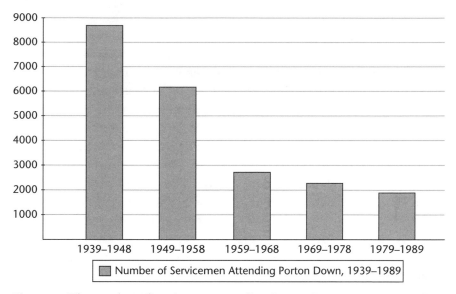

Figure 5. The number of servicemen attending Porton Down, 1939–1989
Source: Historical Survey 2006, p. xi (Table 1).

manner that Maddison's death was 'deeply regretted' but that the experiments had been conducted 'in accordance with the ethics of the day'.[22] He portrayed Porton scientists as 'responsible, careful individuals' who worked within the framework of the Cold War, and called for caution in judging the trials in hindsight, a strategy frequently employed to censure investigation into controversial state affairs. Others felt emboldened by the government's power to stonewall any future claims for damages. Soames not only praised Porton for improving the equipment worn by British forces during the Gulf War, but stressed that the principles laid down in the Nuremberg Code had 'governed all the work relating to human subjects at Porton Down', a statement which came to haunt the MoD for years to come.[23] For the time being though, any evidence that challenged Porton's seemingly impeccable ethical record during the twentieth century was barred from being reviewed in court.

Operation Antler

Although a first attempt at an amicable settlement between the MoD and the Porton veterans had failed, pressure on the government mounted after the Wiltshire Constabulary launched an unprecedented criminal investigation in 1999 into allegations made by former servicemen that they had been 'duped' into taking part in potentially lethal chemical warfare experiments at Porton. Determined to pursue their investigation 'wherever the evidence would take them', the officers eventually uncovered a major government conspiracy which they presented to the Coroner, who felt that the entire Maddison inquest needed to be re-examined as a matter of 'public interest'. The undertaking cost the British taxpayer a total sum of 2.4 million pounds sterling.[24] Rumour has it that when asked about the name of the operation, Detective Superintendent Gerry Luckett, the man in charge, spotted an old typewriter in his office called 'Antler'. Thus was born Operation Antler. Luckett's dedicated team of some thirty officers and staff now began the herculean task of tracing former witnesses, recording the testimony of servicemen, locating often highly classified documents, and liaising with HM Coroner for Wiltshire and Swindon, David Masters, who showed a keen interest in the Maddison case, which fell into his area of responsibility. Operation Antler generated hundreds of thousands of documents believed to be invaluable for any potential civil action the veterans might want to bring against the MoD. It was perhaps only a start, but the police inquiry raised at least the theoretical possibility that the CPS might initiate criminal proceedings against individual Porton scientists. Possible charges ranged from 'administering noxious substances' contrary to the 1861 Offences against the Persons Act, assault, grievous bodily harm (GBH), actual bodily harm (ABH), or criminal manslaughter, provided, of course, that sufficient evidence of wrongdoing could be uncovered against those few who were still alive and fit enough to stand trial. Even if this was not possible, any evidence that criminal offences had been committed was likely to strengthen the veterans' claim for exemplary damages for what was alleged to have been 'oppressive and arbitrary action by the state'.[25] Since many veterans had been exposed to toxic agents in a gas chamber without their consent, there was even a suggestion that they might claim 'false imprisonment', however far-fetched such a charge might have sounded. For the lawyers representing Maddison's family and over 400 Porton veterans, organized from 2000 in the PDVSG, the police investigation was a step in the right direction. Above all, they wanted to know who the 'directing mind' had been behind the experimental programme—a simplistic understanding of how the business of collective governance works in a parliamentarian democracy, but no less effective in raising the stakes still further.

Additional pressure originated from a concerted media campaign about the plight of Britain's chemical veterans; feature-length articles and news bulletins published by the legal team and sympathetic journalists in mainstream newspapers displayed eye-catching headlines such as 'Poisoned by their own people', prompting the chairman of the Commons Defence Committee to admit that Porton was 'too big' an institution for parliamentarians to be fully informed about all the 'things happening there'.[26] In an attempt to jump on the bandwagon after Operation Antler had been launched, and exploit public concerns for the benefit of their constituencies, some MPs asked probing question in Parliament about the long-term health consequences resulting from other, formerly secret, military establishments. The Labour MP for the Cornish constituency of Falmouth and Camborne, Candy Atherton, for example, called on the government to initiate a 'totally new inquiry' into the Nancekuke base, but her request was met with a response almost identical to the one used to put off the Porton veterans for years, namely that there was 'no evidence' that staff had suffered any adverse health effects from working there. That a total of forty-one employees had died within a space of nineteen years, between 1950 and 1969, in an organization numbering barely 150 members of staff, appeared to be of little concern to the MoD.[27]

Meanwhile, unease about Porton experiments was growing in certain quarters of the science community. In October 1999, the expert toxicologist Alastair Hay from Leeds University went on record in the BBC documentary 'A Death at Porton Down' to claim that Porton scientists had risked harming human subjects: 'They were exposing people to concentrations which in the event only killed one man but weren't far off perhaps killing a number of others.'[28] Following the publication of Evans' book *Gassed* in 2000, Hay described Britain's nerve gas tests as 'ethically questionable and scientifically flawed' because scientists had 'failed to properly assess the risks'. The veterans had been treated 'disgracefully', he said.[29] In the same year, Frontline Scotland's *Trial and Error* broadcast a radio programme linking the experience and alleged suffering of the Porton veterans with Remembrance Day. The programme not only highlighted the veterans' treatment by the authorities but threw into stark relief complex methodological and legal issues. Porton's flippant assertion that records had apparently not been particularly well kept prompted a furious response from Hay, who told listeners that if this turned out to be true it was nothing short of a 'disgrace': 'If the agency that was doing these tests can't keep decent records, then I find it difficult to see how the individuals can a) prove their case, or, perhaps more importantly, how Porton can deny these people have a claim.'[30] If anything, the broadcast underscored the value—and potential media impact—of connecting with a carefully choreographed annual process of remembering those who had served and died for their country. In 2001, Porton veterans marched through Whitehall on Remembrance Day with banners displaying slogans such as 'Ignored and Forgotten' or 'This is How your Country Treats Servicemen', this time attracting even greater public attention, their stories sometimes featuring next to narratives about national sacrifice and heroism.[31] Care and his legal team, it seemed, were winning over politicians and the public through a combination of expert debate, moral blackmail, and carefully constructed propaganda targeted at a cross-section of British society.

It also turned out that Wiltshire police were about to ask the CPS to 'charge up to five retired scientists with criminal offences' in relation to chemical warfare trials. For Care, the news, which had inadvertently come to light in an MoD briefing document, 'vindicates everything we have been saying for the last seven years'.[32] The mere prospect of holding Porton scientists or even the responsible Minister to account over Britain's warfare programme made Whitehall's civil service corps distinctly nervous. Most of the ministers in question either declined to comment, such as Lord Carrington, or suffered a convenient bout of amnesia; Lord Gilmore, Defence Minister in 1974, 'could not remember' whether he was ever briefed about Porton's experiments, while Lord Healey, Defence Minister between 1964 and 1970, had apparently told officials that he 'did not want to know all secrets at the MoD'.[33] For some, it seemed as if Britain's governing class was uninterested in the type of military research their country was involved in. It was a strategy of plausible deniability which allowed them to claim ignorance later.

Although in 1997 the incoming Labour government at first refused to set up a long-term health study of the veterans on ground of practicability, it agreed to establish a 'Porton Down Helpline'. In specially designed information leaflets, Porton veterans were assured that the trials had always been performed with the 'utmost regard for the safety, health and well-being of volunteers'; anyone concerned about ill-health was advised to contact the Helpline, which would be able to supply information about compensation, so long as the MoD had 'a legal obligation' to provide it.[34] What they did not know, however, was that their conversations with the Helpline were being secretly tape-recorded as potential evidence to be used against them in a future court case. The revelation, made during the Maddison inquest, added to a long list of public relations blunders by the MoD. It also gave the ministry a good idea of the size and allegations of the group which, in theory, if all else failed, needed to be compensated. At one point, the MoD used the information to ask why only about 1,000 veterans had come forward, suggesting that just 5 per cent of all veterans claimed that their health had been impaired by Porton's experiments, 'a very small proportion', as one MP pointed out.[35]

Steady progress was being made nonetheless. In November 2000, as a way of responding to growing public concern, the Department of Health announced the establishment of a Medical Assessment Programme (MAP) for all Porton veterans at St Thomas' Hospital in London, and appointed Sir Ian Kennedy, a highly respected medical ethicist known for having chaired the public inquiry into the Alder Hey Children's Hospital organs scandal, to review the ethics of Porton's human experiments.[36] There were good reasons for taking a more conciliatory approach: two weeks after the publication of the Alder Hey report, Salisbury NHS District Hospital admitted having sold to Porton the skin from plastic surgery patients for chemical weapons tests for an annual fee of 17,000 pounds sterling, a practice which had started in 1995. On their consent form, patients allowed the skin to be used for 'medical research', a convenient euphemism for de facto weapons experiments.[37]

In another move to shift attention away from a judicial inquiry, epidemiologists from Oxford University, funded by the MoD under the auspices of the MRC, launched a survey into the long-term health effects of Porton's experiments, the findings of which, when they were published in 2009, were as disappointing for the Porton veterans' group as they were predictable. By looking at the death certificates and cancer records of 18,276 male Porton veterans followed up over a period of forty years, from 1941 to 2004, and by comparing them with 17,600 veterans who had not undergone experiments and served as a control group, the epidemiologists found only a 'small increase in overall death rates' among the Porton veterans compared to other veterans but 'no increase in overall cancer rates'.[38] Mental health issues were not included in the study. Given that these had not been recorded centrally over the several decades that had passed, it might have been logistically too complicated and time-consuming for the researchers to include them in their analysis. A lack of information about smoking, overseas service, and other factors affecting people's health and illness also made it impossible to establish whether the small increase in mortality rate could be linked to chemical exposure at Porton. All in all, the study said more about certain methodological limitations and inherent biases of epidemiological work generally than about the complex kaleidoscope of health experiences and medical memories among Porton veterans.

Behind the scenes, news was equally disappointing. According to Care, the whole case could have been resolved many years earlier, and no later than 2002, when the head of claims for the MoD, Jef Mitchell, who had previously turned down any claims for compensation, responded constructively to a proposed settlement scheme. At this point, the cost of the claim, including legal fees, was estimated at around 200,000 pounds sterling, a mere 2 per cent of the total the compensation scheme would eventually cost the British taxpayer. At the eleventh hour, however, the MoD introduced a new policy adviser, Chris Baker, to the negotiations and he constantly repeated that there was no clinical evidence linking ill-health with participation in Porton's human experiments. Described by Care as the 'coldest fish I have yet to meet', Baker seemed to have absolutely no time for the veterans' case, so much so that Care temporarily lost his otherwise unshakable composure, telling Baker: 'You cannot just sit there repeating that long term health phrase like a [expletive] parrot, for I am coming at you like a [expletive] steam train and I will never give up.'[39] This signalled the end of negotiations, and threw into relief the sheer determination of those who had taken up the mantle of legal representation for the veterans. For Care, Porton had turned into a crusade. But this also meant he was now far from impartial when assessing newly discovered evidence. His media presentation suggesting that Maddison was exposed to a V-agent instead of a G-agent, Sarin, turned out to be a red herring, since it was based on recollections by G. Neville Gadsby, Porton's director from 1968 to 1972, who had no first-hand knowledge of the incident (see Image 40). Gadsby's tape-recorded interview lacked credibility, but it provided Care with a much-needed opportunity to keep the story in the public limelight.[40] Admittedly, he was by now clutching at straws.

A year later, in 2003, the CPS decided that there was insufficient evidence to prosecute any of the sixty-six 'development' cases—i.e. cases which they had initially taken forward to see whether a prosecution might stand a chance of success—relating to Porton scientists involved in human experiments, a bombshell which threw the veterans' campaign into disarray. The decision had been taken against the advice of the Wiltshire police, who recommended prosecutions against three scientists.[41] After four years of painstaking police work, in which over 2,000 former servicemen were interviewed, and over 2 million pounds spent, it all had come to nothing. The level of frustration was accordingly high. For Kenneth Earl (see Image 25), the public face of the PDVSG, who had been exposed to Sarin at Porton only two days before Maddison's death, the CPS decision was totally incomprehensible.[42] Having received prior warning about the decision from Sean Rayment, the defence correspondent of the *Sunday Telegraph* who happened to have a reliable source inside the CPS, Care called it 'madness', since the forthcoming Maddison inquest was likely to unearth further evidence. The government had got 'off the hook', remarked Liberal Democrat politician Matthew Taylor, MP for the Cornish constituency of Truro, who had supported the veterans' campaign; additional insights about the risks involved and the number of victims no longer appeared possible, he noted: 'This ruling keeps the genie firmly in the bottle.'[43] Prior to this, the Criminal Injuries Compensation Authority had indicated that it had no discretion in making awards for injuries incurred before the year 1964, a cut-off point that excluded the majority of veterans. Barred from bringing a civil action against the MoD on grounds of Crown immunity, and with criminal proceedings now no longer an option, the Porton veterans had reached the end of the road as far as seeking justice in a UK court of law was concerned. One of the few remaining legal avenues for seeking redress involved an application to the European Court of Human Rights (ECHR) for breaching Article 3 of the Convention for the Protection of Human Rights—'no one shall be subjected to torture or degrading treatment or punishment'— an expensive and time-consuming undertaking. Time was a commodity that most veterans were running out of.

Meanwhile, records uncovered by Operation Antler were starting to contradict the officially sanctioned government position. Whereas MoD officials, including the Under-Secretary of State for Defence, were insistent that there was no evidence demonstrating that LSD experiments had taken place prior to 1961, the police discovered information which appeared to suggest otherwise. As a matter of course, the police had also conducted a thorough examination of the inquest into the death of Ronald Maddison, which Rob Evans from *The Guardian* called 'one of the biggest cover ups of the Cold War'. It was this evidence which led the Wiltshire Constabulary and the Coroner to ask the Attorney General for permission to apply to the

High Court for a fresh inquest, which was granted in April 2002; such permission, they knew, was granted only under 'exceptional circumstances'.[44] Maddison had been a member of the armed forces and his death had occurred at the hand of the state, which is why the then Coroner had been under a particular obligation to investigate his death fully. What concerned senior legal experts was the fact that the inquest had been held in camera because it had seemed convenient for one of the parties—the state—which had allegedly been responsible for Maddison's death, and that key pieces of evidence had not been placed before the Coroner. Reflecting the growing public interest, the BBC and other news outlets now regularly reported about the case, especially after the MoD had indicated that it would not oppose the Coroner's application for a fresh inquest in the High Court.[45] In November 2002, Lord Woolf, the Lord Chief Justice, when he quashed the original verdict of misadventure, pointed out:

> That death should occur in such a situation is a matter of real public concern. There can be no doubt in this case that the concerns which existed as to how Mr Maddison should have been put in a position where he was subject to an experiment which risked his life are still alive today and still matters of public interest.[46]

He also made it plain that the then Coroner had not been given a 'full account of the circumstances of an experiment' that had preceded the one in which Maddison had died, a reference to the Kelly incident, and that Maddison's family had been 'kept in total ignorance as to what happened' for half a century.[47] In ordering a fresh inquest, Woolf, sitting with Mrs Justice Hallett, noted that in the interest of justice the whole affair had to be properly investigated.[48]

Few legal experts were under any illusion that holding a fresh inquest some fifty years after the death of a man posed extraordinary methodological, conceptual, and judicial problems: evidence before the Coroner at the time might no longer be available; witnesses might be difficult to trace, no longer be alive or, through the passage of time, unable to recall events with any degree of accuracy. What status ought the court give to the testimony of those who might remember what had happened to them? How likely was it that veterans would be able to distinguish between, on the one hand, what they had read and seen in many of the newspapers, internet sites, blogs, and TV programmes covering the story since the 1990s, and, on the other, their own personal, often fragmented recollection about their decision to volunteer for physiological tests at Porton? Would interested parties be permitted, through cross-examination for example, to test the truthfulness of conflicting witness testimony? Conversely, was it fair to expect ageing research scientists to remember how they had conducted human experiments half a century earlier? Could their written statements or oral testimony be used against them, if the CPS decided, after all, to launch criminal proceedings? How and by whom would the available documentary evidence be evaluated? Could the absence of evidence, for example of informed consent forms, be construed as evidence of ethical wrongdoing, especially if the use of informed consent forms was not deemed to have been generally accepted practice at the time?

Given the endless list of legal and procedural problems, it was not surprising that almost all interested parties sought refuge in the role of experts. For the Coroner, the written submissions and cross-examination of expert scientists, forensic pathologists, toxicologists, and medical historians—including the present author—became a central plank in providing the jury with essential guidance so that they could judge the merits of the case before them. That there seemed to be a case to answer became apparent when Dr Alexander T. Proudfoot, the toxicologist appointed by the MoD, reported that the enormous experience Porton scientists had accumulated over the years 'did not justify believing that they were not exposing at least some of their subjects to serious risk', especially after several men had shown cholinesterase inhibitions of over 80 per cent.[49] According to Proudfoot, the scientists had failed to appreciate the 'serious nature of the adverse effects' they had induced in several test subjects. Although this 'ought to have set alarm bells ringing', they had continued with experiments which went way beyond 80 per cent ChE inhibition, behaviour which Proudfoot felt had been reckless. He also thought that the method by which the agent had been applied to the arms of the men, a simple pipette with a rubber bulb, had been inefficient and subject to 'errors in the dose applied'.[50] After more than eight years' campaigning, the representatives of the Porton veterans had finally—in the Ronald Maddison case—found some degree of legal leverage to force the government to listen. The decision by the Canadian government to recognize the claims of veterans exposed to chemical agents during the Second World War through a multi-million dollar settlement scheme came as an unexpected morale boost to the British veterans,[51] but before long the atmosphere turned sour again. On 23 April 2004, just weeks before the opening of the Maddison inquest, the MoD released

a press statement about 'clinical findings in III ex-Porton Down volunteers', a two-year study which made it plain that there was no evidence to
suggest that 'participation in the Porton Down trials produced any long-
term adverse health effects or unusual patterns of disease compared to
those of the general population of the same age'.[52] Although Care's team
of experts had heard the phrase many times before, it signalled the start of
an acrimonious legal battle in which the issue of informed consent became
of utmost importance for veterans to uphold the claim that Britain's chemical warfare scientists had been, if not legally, at least morally responsible for
exposing them to highly toxic agents. The stage was set for high drama in
one of the longest inquests in UK legal history, less than a year after the
inquest into the death of the chemical weapons expert David Kelly in 2003
had been adjourned indefinitely—only to be replaced with a non-statutory
public inquiry by Lord Hutton—and international observers started to take
note of the Porton Down case.[53]

The Inquest

On Wednesday 5 May 2004, in the Victorian town hall in Trowbridge,
Wiltshire, presiding judge David Masters, a man of considerable experience
and seniority, impressive in his dark-blue gown, reopened the inquest into
the death of Ronald Maddison, which had taken place almost fifty-one
years to the day. This was undoubtedly a 'unique' inquest, he told the ten
members of the jury: 'No Coroner or jury has been required before today
to investigate a death which took place as long ago as this one.'[54] The
inquest would have to take them back to the Britain of the 1950s, he said,
when wartime rations had just ended and television was a 'novelty', a world
divided ideologically between Western capitalism and Eastern communism,
in which two superpowers and their allies were engulfed in a desperate race
to develop the most destructive weapons capability.[55] The boundaries of the
inquest were unusually wide, he noted; the jury would hear testimony from
over fifty witnesses and see written statements from another forty-three;
two of the witnesses had actually been with Maddison in the gas chamber
at the time of the fatal experiment, though none of the scientists involved
would attend, since they had all since died. The jury would be able to con-
sult, for the first time, the Coroner's handwritten notes of the original
inquest, which suggested that at least one scientist thought that the levels

of Sarin exposure used in the Maddison test were 'well above the normal limits'; they would hear from many of the servicemen who had gone to Porton believing they were taking part in tests to find a cure for the common cold. The court would examine whether Maddison had given informed consent and interrogate a range of independent experts to establish whether the scientists knew of the potentially lethal consequences of the test.[56] Most importantly, all interested parties would be given ample opportunity to state their case to the jury.

Present on behalf of the MoD was Leigh-Ann Mulcahy, a London-based barrister with experience in professional negligence cases who had been instructed by the Treasury Solicitor; although the Porton Down Litigation, as it was officially called, was not to be her finest hour, it helped her climb the professional ladder to become a QC.[57] In 2012, acting again as the representative of the MoD, she 'succeeded', as her curriculum vitae proudly states, in persuading the Supreme Court to turn down the appeal by the British nuclear test veterans to have their cases heard in open court, a judgement with which three out of seven senior judges dissented.[58]

Representing Maddison's family, on the other hand, was Gerwyn Samuel, QC, a barrister with a razor-sharp mind and sanguine temperament from Doughty Street Chambers, and his assistant Nicholas Brown, both of whom had been instructed by the law firm Thomson Snell & Passmore. In addition to Kenneth Earl and Eric Gow, who appeared on behalf of the PDVSG, relatives and interested parties attended for two of Porton's medical officers who had been present at the time of Maddison's death and had tried to save his life, Wing Commander Adam Muir and Major Richard H. Adrian: these were John Muir (Adam Muir's son) and Dr Lucy Adrian (widow of Richard Adrian and daughter-in-law of Lord Adrian).[59] The Chief Constable of Wiltshire was represented by Simon McKay, an expert in covert policing and criminal law. Their 'day in court' is what Care had promised the Porton veterans sitting three rows deep on wooden benches, perhaps not in the way they had hoped for, but an opportunity to tell their tale in public nonetheless. Outside the courthouse, Maddison's sister, Lillias Craik, holding a picture in her hands of her brother Ronald, told a group of journalists after the first hearing: 'My family has never known the truth and why he had to die so young.'[60]

In stark contrast to the original inquest, which had been held in camera, the Coroner had gone to great lengths to ensure that this would be a public event (see Image 42), one in which the case would be heard in front of a jury

Image 42. Maddison inquest, Trowbridge, 2004

Source: Inquest by David Masters, HM Coroner for Wiltshire and Swindon, into the Death of Ronald Maddison, 2004. I am grateful to Terry Alderson for granting me permission to use the image in the book.

made up of civilians, and which journalists and the general public would be permitted to attend, unless the material under discussion were to be too sensitive or still classified, as in the case of certain documents from the United States. Those instances, the Coroner assured the assembled crowd, would be kept to a minimum. Compared to the British and Canadian authorities, who had agreed to release into the public domain most of the relevant information, the US Department of Defense had been less 'flexible in its approach'.[61] Having travelled to see officials at the US Pentagon, the Coroner had managed to obtain almost all relevant sources, except for about five documents, on condition that the sensitive sections would be redacted, that is, blacked out. For US officials it was paramount that none of the material disclosed could 'encourage use of chemical and biological weapons by terrorists'.[62]

In summarizing the facts of the case, David Masters compared the present inquest to a 'pictorial canvas' of enormous size, which made it difficult for members of the jury to keep an overview among the many detailed features, unless they stood back and examined the 'vast picture' systematically in its totality. He was not necessarily thinking of the old masters, of Rembrandt's 1632 oil painting *The Anatomy Lesson of Dr Nicolaes Tulp* or Velázquez's 1656 *Las Meninas*, for example, though both are of considerably complexity, but more of a constructed reality as represented in Andreas Gursky's sizeable 1993 digital photograph *Paris, Montparnasse*, a 'giant patchwork block of an apartment building' in which the viewer, able to identify the interiors and private urban lives in the French capital, is nonetheless faced with the 'impossible task of reading each detail as though it were a clue to the meaning of the whole'.[63] As the 'sole arbiter of the facts', the jury had to decide who the deceased was, and how, when, and where the deceased had died, but it had to be done without pre-determining any issues of criminal or civil liability. From the start of the trial, all were aware of the limitations and methodological difficulties of different types of evidence. Masters reminded the jury of the problems of prejudice against the MoD, given the passage of time. Although medical memories could be 'jogged', there was the problem of reconciling conflicting or inaccurate memories with written contemporaneous sources. On the whole, though, he was confident that the members of the jury had been similarly 'impressed' by the 'transparent honesty' that was conveyed 'loud and clear' in the testimony of the Porton veterans (see Image 43). Then there was the issue of textual records. Though surprisingly numerous, they likewise contained inaccuracies and omissions; following the restructuring of the MoS in 1960, records had been shredded or lost, which meant that the 'absence of evidence' could not be construed as 'evidence of absence', he reminded the jury. Still, in assessing the evidence it was important to pay attention to 'contemporaneous documents' since these would provide them with a deeper understanding of the thinking at the time; whether they were considering the ethics of non-therapeutic human experimentation or the existing knowledge among those designing the trials about the possible and likely effects of nerve agents on the body, they had to integrate the pieces of evidence into a coherent whole. Most importantly, the inquest had to answer the question of *how* Maddison had been put into a position 'where he was subject to an experiment which risked his life'.[64]

According to the Coroner, there were three possible verdicts open to the jury: unlawful killing, misadventure, and an open verdict. In considering an 'unlawful killing' verdict, the jury needed to differentiate between 'unlawful act manslaughter' and 'gross negligence manslaughter', and in both cases—since they implied criminal wrongdoing—the standard of proof needed to

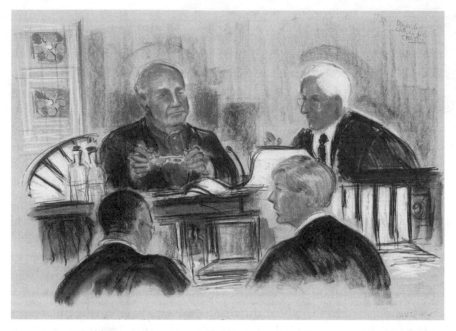

Image 43. Maddison inquest, Trowbridge, evidence by Porton veteran Granville Popplewell, 20 May 2004

Source: Inquest by David Masters, HM Coroner for Wiltshire and Swindon, into the Death of Ronald Maddison, 2004. I am grateful to Terry Alderson for granting me permission to use the image in the book.

be 'beyond reasonable doubt', which meant they had to be 'sure'. For an act to be classed an 'unlawful act manslaughter', a person had to have 'intentionally committed an unlawful and dangerous act which inadvertently caused the death' of another person. It had to be an act which did not consist of mere negligence. The person committing the act did not have to know or realize that the act was dangerous or illegal; what sufficed was that the person had acted with intent. There was general agreement, the Coroner remarked, that the application of a nerve agent 'would be unlawful if there is no valid consent given by the deceased'. However, if the person did consent and understood the essential nature and risks of the act, which was the 'application of a chemical warfare [nerve] agent in a non-therapeutic experiment', then this would not constitute an unlawful act of manslaughter.[65] In directing the jury, the Coroner argued that Porton's series of non-therapeutic experiments were justified by the political and military imperative of the Cold War; they had been 'carried out for good reason in the public interest'. The essential thrust of what the Coroner was saying related to the question of consent. If the jury concluded that Maddison had not consented to the application of Sarin nerve gas, then a verdict of unlawful killing would be a distinct possibility, but they had to be 'sure' that he had not given consent. If, however, the person responsible for, and committing the act, the Porton scientist, genuinely believed that Maddison had consented to the experiment, then a case of 'unlawful act manslaughter' could not be upheld. The unlawful and dangerous act, in other words, had to be committed with intent. It was therefore critical to establish what the responsible scientist, even if he did not perform the experiment himself, thought about the trial. So the jury needed to ascertain Cullumbine's views in this regard, as he was the scientist in charge of the experiments who had taken the decision to continue the tests after the Kelly incident.[66]

For 'gross negligence manslaughter', on the other hand, the parameters were different. In this case, the person committing the act had to owe a 'duty of care' to the victim; this duty of care had to have been breached and this breach had to have contributed significantly to, but did not have to have been the sole or principal cause of, the death of Maddison. The aforementioned breach of duty had to be 'grossly negligent' in order to qualify as a crime and deserve punishment. The 'duty of care' each of Porton's scientists owed to the servicemen involved exercising the 'skill and care of a reasonably competent research scientist performing non-therapeutic experiments on human volunteer subjects in 1953'. This meant that the scientists had to plan and carry out the test with necessary caution, inform the participants of the risks associated with the experiment, and obtain their consent. The Coroner also highlighted the difference between 'duty of care' and 'standard of care', two interrelated but distinct concepts; whereas the former referred to the duty which someone owed to another person, the latter 'informs or qualifies' that duty. In the case of Porton, there was no doubt in the Coroner's mind that the general standard of care servicemen could reasonably expect 'was to be the very highest'.[67]

Having briefly considered the position of the *dramatis personae* and their respective responsibilities, foremost among them Porton's lead scientists and medical officers—Mumford, Perren, Cullumbine, Truckle, Lacon, Adrian, Muir, Leigh Silver, Rutland, Ainsworth, Callaway, Cruickshank, Lovatt Evans, and Cross—the Coroner advised the jury to consider carefully the following aspects: the socio-political and military climate which necessitated experiments with warfare agents during the Cold War; the purpose, planning, and execution of a series of experiments involving Sarin nerve agent; the knowledge Maddison himself had about these specific experiments—so as to come to a conclusion about the issue of consent; what the scientists knew before embarking on the tests, in terms of understanding the physiological effects of the agent; what they knew in terms of whether they believed that Maddison had consented to the test; and the actual circumstances surrounding the test on the day he died. More generally, they had to look at non-therapeutic experimental practices at the time, and decide whether Porton's practices were comparable with, or fell short of, accepted clinical research ethics elsewhere. Finally, and most importantly, they had to take a considered view on 'whether or not this experiment [which cost Maddison his life] should have been carried out', and if so, 'whether or not it should have been carried out in the way that it was'.[68] The Coroner's summary of the issues now awaiting examination by the jury was a shining example of how to explain, 'without fear or favour', to a group of randomly selected lay members of the public the most complex legal, political, and scientific matters in a lucid and accessible fashion, a testament to his scholarly and legal integrity.

The alleged failure to obtain prior informed consent may have been of central concern to the majority of veterans, who used their 'fighting fund' to have a constant presence at the inquest, but for the court, interested in the more narrow questions of how and why Maddison had died, issues of human susceptibility, toxicology, and risk were of at least equal, if not greater importance, especially after the initial inquiry had attributed his death to a 'personal idiosyncrasy'.[69] Evidence uncovered during the police investigation appeared to suggest that Porton's scientists knew of the enormous variability with which humans responded to nerve agents and other organophosphorus compounds. It raised one of the most central questions of the inquest: were the scientists able to distinguish between high susceptibility in humans and the adverse physiological reactions a person of normal susceptibility would show following exposure to nerve gas? The establishment of the level of understanding about this relationship was central in assessing the degree of risk to which Maddison had been exposed.

According to a contemporary memorandum on the 'Probability of Extreme Susceptibility in Humans', written by the Porton scientist and statistician S. Callaway, if any given population received exactly the same dosage of nerve gas under exactly the same conditions, about 2.5 per cent of that population 'would react to a dosage below twice the standard deviation of the population distribution of tolerance dosages from the average

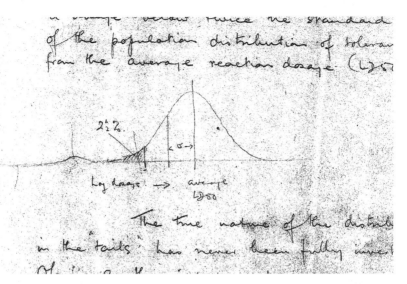

Image 44. Probability of extreme susceptibility in humans
Source: MI, Folder 2B, Exhibit JJH/187/2, Callaway, Handwritten note 'Probability of Extreme Susceptibility in Humans', no date (*c.* 1953), pp. 207–8.

reaction dosage (LD50)', i.e. the dose required to kill half the members of a tested population after a specified test duration (see Image 44).[70] In lay terms, it meant that the bodies of the 2.5 per cent who were particularly susceptible to a certain agent responded in such a way that when the data was visualized on a bell curve graphic, they were located on its edges, or what scientists called the 'tails'. He noted in the memorandum that the 'true nature' of the population distribution in the 'tails' had never been fully examined. In addition, available data from human experiments did not allow any predictions about whether it was probable or improbable that an individual would be susceptible to a certain agent.

For nerve agent experiments, this meant the following: the majority of research subjects never even got close to the 'lethal range', and of those few who showed a high cholinesterase inhibition, fewer still showed marked physiological symptoms. It was because of this rather crude balance of probability that Porton scientists believed, wrongly as we now know, that it was most unlikely that there would be lethal effects at the dosages used in the experiments. Maddison belonged to the group considered to be particularly susceptible to nerve gas. His degree of susceptibility to nerve agents would have been located on the 'outer edges of the cohort', i.e. the 'tails' of the bell curve graphic, which is why one of the inquest toxicologists, Professor Forrest, in evidence, commented that the 'devil is in the detail', a fitting pun in otherwise tragic circumstances.[71] For legal experts such as Care, the answer to the whole case could be found in the *tails*: in those areas of the population distribution least understood by the scientists and in which the risks were consequently 'known unknowns'. By knowingly venturing into such uncharted territory, they had acted recklessly and grossly negligently, according to Care. Callaway had also made it plain that he and his colleagues had no way of knowing whether the symptoms shown by a person resulted from the reaction to the agent itself or from a particular susceptibility a person might have:

> Unfortunately the conditions under which percutaneous penetration occurs are so variable and the factors governing the amount absorbed so little understood that in any given instance it is almost impossible to dissociate intrinsic high susceptibility from normal reaction to high absolute dose.[72]

In addition to the uncertainty resulting from general susceptibility to chemical agents there was clear awareness among senior warfare scientists of the extreme variability of humans to cholinesterase inhibition. It added yet another layer of uncertainty to the experiments. In other words, as far as certainty about the risk of serious harm or death was concerned, Porton scientists were working completely in the dark.[73] They were unable to measure, quantify, and thus control the risk, and they knew it.

Among those recognizing the dangers involved in the experiments was none other than Cullumbine himself. He had summarized his findings about the 'percutaneous toxicity' of nerve agents in a seven-page memorandum handwritten the day before Maddison died, and in a typed version of 8 May, which not only formed the basis of Porton Technical Paper (PTP) 399, but served as a critical piece of evidence in the 2004 inquest. He had decided, for reasons unknown, to omit from this memorandum the aforementioned discussion about the 'Probability of Extreme Susceptibility in Humans', which was among the reports available to him.[74] He seems to have come to realize that the risk of harm could potentially be significant for humans with a particular but undetectable susceptibility to nerve agents. Yet instead of drawing attention to what might have appeared to him to be more of a theoretical problem, given that on the balance of probability such a case appeared to be extremely unlikely ever to occur in practice, he remarked in the top left hand corner of the paper on extreme susceptibility: 'Not used.'[75] The words stand testament to the fact that any semi-official acknowledgement by Porton's scientists about the enormous risks and uncertainties involved in its nerve agent programme, even within its secret science community, would have been seen as weakening their case for future resources. It seems likely that Cullumbine did not share the findings of Callaway's memorandum with his colleagues, since it would have required a review and possibly a suspension of the experiments; along the line of 'let sleeping dogs lie', the issue was simply dropped.

So what then was the state of knowledge among Porton scientists as far as the risk of the experiment was concerned shortly before Maddison went into the gas chamber? Did they know, or could they have known, that the experiment posed a significant risk to the lives of the participants? According to Cullumbine, the object of Porton's experiments was to 'discover the dosage of GB [Sarin], GD [Soman] and GF [Cyclosarin], which when applied to the clothed or bare skin of men would cause incapacitation or death'.[76] The aim of the experiment was not to kill a human being; researchers wanted rather to establish more reliable estimates about incapacitating and lethal dosages of different types of nerve agents through extrapolation from animal and human data. However, as early as February 1953, senior scientists had argued that the idea of extrapolating 'lethal dosages' from 'nonlethal effects' in humans was not very promising because 'the decline in cholinesterase level [was] not ... sufficiently predictable'.[77] This fact had not escaped the notice of Cullumbine. The day before Maddison's death, he acknowledged that the 'most striking' feature of the existing data so far was the 'great variation in response of different individuals to the same degree of contamination'.[78] Plotted onto a single graph (see Figure 6), the available data about the ChE inhibition of all known servicemen exposed to varying dosages of nerve gas between 19 January 1953 and 6 May 1953 suggests that there was no, or at the very least no reliable, correlation between ChE inhibition and nerve agent poisoning and its associated clinical symptoms. Yes, there are the occasional 'spikes' into the realm of above 80 per cent ChE inhibition, a total of fourteen cases, to be precise (see Figure 2), and we can also see that the number of 'spikes', i.e. servicemen showing in excess of 80 per cent ChE inhibition, steadily increased as time went by (the servicemen's 'blood numbers' were allocated in chronological order up to 6 May 1953, the end point of the graph), which suggests that ever greater risks were being taken by altering the composition and number of layers of cloth.[79] In other

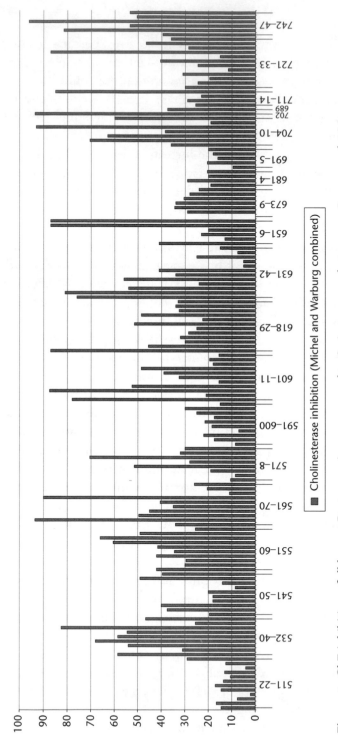

Figure 6. ChE inhibition of all known Porton servicemen exposed to Sarin nerve gas between 19 January and 6 May 1953

Source: MI, Folder 2B, Exhibit MNJ/30, PTP 399, 'Percutaneous Toxicity of G-Compounds', 11 January 1954, pp. 267–318; MI, Folder 2H, Wiltshire Constabulary; Operation Antler; Data to Show ChE % Inhibitions, Symptoms, and Other Relevant Information on Volunteers during GB Tests between 19 January 1953 and 6 May 1953. Prepared by DC Goundry for HM Coroner of Swindon and Wiltshire Mr D Masters.

ChE inhibition levels are shown for each serviceman's 'Blood Number' (x axis). Sequences of Blood Numbers, including omissions and errors, follow the data as recorded in the Observers' Chamber Tests Book.

■ Cholinesterase inhibition (Michel and Warburg combined)

words, the scientists had great difficulty in establishing a reliable pattern or relationship between cholinesterase inhibition and clinical symptoms. In order, therefore, to obtain information about a mean response in humans to nerve gas a relatively large group of test participants was needed for each contamination level. Based on the assumption that a 100 per cent cholinesterase inhibition would be fatal, Cullumbine remarked: 'We have never produced this condition, but we have been near it.'[80] A fatal dose of nerve gas poisoning, he stated, was likely to be produced with 600 mg of Sarin on bare skin or with one layer of serge, which is why a dose of 300 mg or 200 mg was believed to be comparatively safe. Tests with two layers of clothing were in progress.

Unable to explain why different individuals showed such great variation in inhibition levels after being exposed to the same dosage under exactly the same conditions, Cullumbine had recognized that there was a fine line between serious adverse reactions and actual death: 'The margin between ChE [cholinesterase] inhibition necessary to cause severe symptoms and that for death is probably extremely small.'[81] For Forrest, one of the inquest toxicologists, it constituted 'the most important sentence' of the entire evidence, for if anyone exploring 'a dangerous region . . . known to be potentially dangerous' goes a little further then there is real chance of entering a 'fatal region', and at Porton the scientists had been in that region with their work for some time.[82] Proudfoot, the other inquest toxicologist, on the other hand, thought that it provided 'unique insight' into Cullumbine's mindset. The experiments were a 'step into the unknown' which, at the very least, required careful and constant monitoring.[83] Forrest agreed. With mean inhibition levels on the rise, it was incomprehensible why the 'controlling minds' had not fully reviewed the experiments, knowing that 'they needed to be very, very careful. Knowledge was incomplete.'[84] This became especially apparent after they had recorded, on 4 May, a mean inhibition level of 87 per cent for Mr Slater, one of Porton's research subjects, who showed no clinical symptoms. From this moment onwards it was clear, beyond any reasonable doubt, assuming the data was available to the scientists, that inhibition level could not necessarily be associated with different levels of nerve gas poisoning. The results obtained from the experiment, in other words, were unreliable and the methodology was flawed. A Porton scientist confirmed, after looking at the statistical data as part of Operation Antler, that he had the 'strong feeling' that the experiments 'had gone out of control', that the experimental design had changed, the dosage, the purity of the

Sarin—just 'something' which increased the level of nerve gas poisoning among participants.[85] By failing to 'pause for reflection', Britain's warfare scientists had been pushing 'the experimental envelope', Forrest argued, and as they were entering into dangerous territory, that area into which they should not have dared to go, they were ignoring all relevant warning signs.[86] Instead of initiating a full review, and putting further tests on hold, the scientists took unacceptable risks by changing two things at the same time, the dosage and the layers of clothing: 'You do not do two things at once, there are risks', Forrest remarked. He considered the continuation of the experiments to be 'thoughtless' once inhibition levels above 80 per cent had been produced, and the possible use of an ordinary pipette, rather than a calibrated one for added precision, as 'reckless'; the Porton scientists' lack of regard for the possible consequences of their actions bordered on the 'incomprehensible', he noted.[87] A responsible group of competent scientists would not have proceeded with the tests. 'The experiment to which Mr Maddison was subjected should not have occurred, full stop', Forrest told the jury; it was negligent.[88] One day after Cullumbine had written his memorandum, Maddison died with a cholinesterase inhibition of 99 per cent, according to one type of measurement.[89] The merely theoretical possibility of exposing to nerve gas a serviceman with a high susceptibility to the agent, or who absorbed disproportionately large amounts of it through his skin, or a combination of both, had all of a sudden become a stark reality.

In the mid 1950s, reflecting on his postwar work, Cullumbine wrote a detailed report for Porton about the medical aspects of nerve gas poisoning in which he indicated, quoting Francis Bacon, what he deemed to be his scientific motto: 'Read not to contradict and confute, nor to believe and take for granted, nor to find talk and discourse, but to weigh and consider.'[90] Later observers might wonder whether Maddison's death would not have occurred if Cullumbine had considered and acted upon the guiding principles he held in such high esteem.

At a more philosophical level the inquest engaged with the relationship between 'scientific purpose and intuition', highlighting the extent to which proper scientific methodology underpinned the accuracy and credibility of new knowledge. Researchers failing to apply sound scientific methodology laid themselves open to allegations of professional misconduct, especially in the field of human experimentation, where there was always a remote risk, however small, of harming participants. The debate, the

Coroner reminded the jury, threw into relief the fundamental importance of proper safeguards: 'Safety of subjects is paramount.'[91] Although Proudfoot and Forrest agreed that the 'proper study of mankind is man', they were adamant that nerve agent tests had to be performed in 'an environment of perfect safety'. The two experts agreed that the duty of care the scientists owed to their participants was an 'exceptionally high one'. In ethical terms, exposing human subjects to lethal nerve agents in a non-therapeutic experiment propelled that duty to the 'top of the scale'. Only the 'highest' standard of care could likewise be expected. Proudfoot felt that the methodology ought to have been more clearly defined since it might have prevented the experiments from gaining a 'momentum' of their own that increased the risks. This lack of definition about the nature and purpose of the experiments was a 'significant failure' for which the scientists were responsible, a form of 'negligence worthy of being publicly explored'.[92]

In view of such undiluted criticism from expert toxicologists about the conduct of Porton's scientists, the MoD tried to raise a greater degree of 'doubt' in the minds of the jury members, particularly through the testimony of Dr Paul Rice, senior Porton scientist and MoD military adviser, a highly intelligent but also somewhat 'shady' Porton character who, behind the scenes, seems to have drafted many of the MoD's uncompromising position statements. He introduced the plausible hypothesis, not yet disproved, that the rise in mean inhibition levels at the end of April and beginning of May, when something was obviously 'not going right', might have been due to a phenomenon known as T2121, in which Sarin nerve gas, contaminated by water vapour, became more toxic. However, if the theory was correct, experts wondered, why did the T2121 phenomenon not affect any of the other servicemen undergoing the same test? Most accepted, on balance, that it could have been a 'contributory factor', but not much more. Rice also raised the possibility that factors such as the height of the drops, the degree of their spread and thus the level of evaporation, the tightness of the cloth, and the distance between cloth and human skin could all have affected the experiments. For most observers it was little more than a skilled but failed attempt by the MoD to introduce 'late in the race', as the Coroner put it, more uncertainty into the proceedings, since the jury ultimately had to judge whether the evidence warranted an unlawful killing verdict 'beyond reasonable doubt'. They had to be sure.

Although even-handed throughout his deliberations, on a few occasions the Coroner could barely conceal his criticism of Porton's past conduct. Evidence revealed in the course of the proceedings showed that Porton, despite having been instructed after Maddison's death to ensure strict compliance with the ministerial ban on 'tests of all kinds', had continued to conduct nerve agent tests in a mobile gas chamber in July and August 1953, a most unfortunate breakdown in professional discipline. None of the inquest experts could 'condone' such 'irresponsible' behaviour, arguing that 'all exposures to [Sarin] should have stopped'.[93] Although the tests had been deemed to be of low risk, the experts were astounded that any 'risk to well-being' had been taken at all, given that a man had just died. Shocked to learn afterwards that they had been exposed to nerve gas, those taking part in the tests recalled being told by the attending Sergeant: 'That is why you weren't told.'[94] By suggesting to the jury that the 'involvement of human volunteers in this way should not have taken place under any circumstances', the Coroner highlighted grave shortcomings in the process of obtaining informed consent from human volunteers. Porton's 'approach to providing information' could not be justified, he remarked. For him, the act of violating the ministerial ban, and of performing nerve agent tests without informing participants of any risks involved, mattered more than words; it undermined the credibility of contemporary witness statements made during the court of inquiry in 1953, and it nullified Porton's claim about the ethicacy of its experiments. How could one trust what the scientists had said during the court of inquiry about the level of information given to servicemen if, only weeks later, they conducted unethical, if not illegal, trials in blatant breach of ministerial orders? The revelations profoundly weakened Porton's moral position, since its scientists could no longer be trusted: an implied, though no less damning indictment. It undermined any defence maintaining that the scientists had honestly and genuinely believed that Maddison had given consent, and thus strengthened the case for a verdict of unlawful act manslaughter.[95]

There was more bad news for the MoD when Robert Lynch, Porton's experimental officer in Cullumbine's physiological department, testified at length. As a Royal Air Force serviceman with experience of the Middle East, he had been posted to Porton from 1948 to 1953 before embarking on a career as a civilian scientist there, quickly rising through the ranks and eventually retiring as a Principal Scientific Officer. Having had access to top-secret Tripartite reports in a department of some thirty people, he possessed detailed knowledge of experimental procedures, inter-Allied modes of communication, and internal ethical debates. 'It was a very small group', he noted, not a 'Cistercian monastery', a group in which everyone talked to everyone and knew what others were doing, and in which medical officers were seen and could act as 'absolute masters in their own right', a view which tallied with the way senior medical experts exercised 'ascribed power' in the 1960s.[96] Their power was based less on tradition or high office, although hierarchies mattered greatly at Porton, but on the power which others attributed to those in possession of medical and physiological knowledge. Rightly or wrongly, Cullumbine, as head of department, had the 'absolute authority' to sanction or prohibit any human experiment.[97] Once staff had realized that the toxicity of Sarin nerve gas increased with clothing, they had tried, unsuccessfully, it seems, to persuade Cullumbine 'to go carefully', as one of them recalled.[98]

Lynch's testimony offered compelling evidence that staff had acknowledged and expressed their concerns about the risks after the Kelly incident: 'They [the scientists conducting human tests] were very brave to carry on. The general view was, we were pushing it.'[99] He disagreed with those who described Cullumbine as 'ruthless', but conceded that Porton's scientists were 'under pressure' to deliver the required data to Tripartite Conference members. At times, the atmosphere must have resembled a pressure-cooker in which small teams, huddled together over cups of tea, made far-reaching week-to-week decisions about human experiments, an informal, intense environment conducive to the efficient exchange of knowledge and the occasional gossip.[100] Most seem to have been fully aware of the methodological and ethical problems affecting the tests:

> So most of us then thought that we were going into very dangerous areas. It was well known that there were massive problems with variability and response, both animal and human. I knew, as most of us did, that there were untoward reactions, but there was no point in putting such small amounts on anybody that nothing would happen, but we weren't trying to kill, obviously.[101]

Lynch's evidence was the closest the inquest came to reconstructing Porton's research culture and ethical worldview in the run-up to Maddison's death. International ethical debates had apparently been irrelevant to Porton scientists, at least according to the MoD, yet Lynch confirmed his knowledge of the Nuremberg Code in 1953. Lynch acknowledged that the experts at Porton had taken note of the Code's ten ethical principles for non–therapeutic experiments, although he had never witnessed 'any form of written consent'.[102] Members of the jury were astonished by this, as they were also to hear that he and his scientific colleagues were not in the business of producing certainties but 'standard errors' and probabilities. There is no certainty, he told them, 'not in this trade'.[103] All knowledge is admittedly relative, and a known fact can turn out to be wrong or can change owing to circumstances. However, for most observers, including the Coroner, this excursus into the philosophy of science was rather unexpected. Lynch seemed unaware that concepts such as 'certainty' and 'uncertainty', quite apart from their applied meaning in laboratories and other spaces where science operates, carried considerable ethical and legal weight in the context of the case at hand, especially if it could be shown that Porton scientists had knowingly exposed participants to undue risk. Lynch made it plain that he and others in the department 'knew what the statistics' meant, that the uncertainties surrounding risk were considerable. By admitting that he had been aware that 'sooner or later there was a real risk that somebody [might] die' as a result of certain tests, Lynch seemed, the Wiltshire Constabulary realized, unintentionally to have incriminated himself.[104]

For a brief moment in June 2004, the inquest had to be adjourned and the case referred to the CPS casework directorate in London to see whether criminal charges should be brought against Lynch. The original brief for Operation Antler, set up under the auspices of the Wiltshire Constabulary, had been to examine whether there had been any criminal wrongdoing by Porton scientists. Prior to the inquest the CPS had taken the view not to prosecute the 'development' cases submitted by Operation Antler but there was still a remote possibility that they might initiate criminal proceedings if new evidence came to light, and now it had.[105] Having been called as a 'witness of fact', at the age of eighty and in fragile health, Lynch faced the real possibility of becoming a defendant in a trial based on evidence he had just given. His testimony could not be undone, the Coroner remarked. Once it was put on the record, it was there for all to see, and the police were under an obligation to act. All of a sudden, the inquest was hanging in the balance, and with it the carefully reconstructed national memories of the veterans community, since a prosecution of Lynch would have led to a prolonged postponement, if not a cancellation, of the inquest proceedings. For Britain's chemical warfare veterans, this would have quashed all hopes of coming to terms with their past, and been the end of the road in seeking justice through the legal process. In the event, the CPS ruled that a prosecution against Lynch was not in the public interest. There was a metaphorical heartfelt sigh of relief from the bench: Lynch's testimony could continue, and so too the inquest into Maddison's death. The Wiltshire Coroner could resume the task of making sure that Porton's medical memories were not to become buried deep beneath an impenetrable legal and political system.

Next came questions of ethics, which the Coroner saw as the 'last top coat' on this vast canvas the jury was looking at; experts, the present author included, were tasked with assessing the ethical principles underpinning non-therapeutic experiments at Porton, and in Britain more generally, and the extent to which these principles were applied in practice. A senior physician and former chairman of the Department of Medicine at Hammersmith Hospital in the mid 1960s, Sir Christopher Booth, painted a picture of research practices allegedly governed by trust rather than accountability, and in which verbal rather than written consent was obtained by giving subjects a 'moderate amount of information'. Patients were hardly ever informed about potential risks or the exact nature and purpose of untested diagnostic and treatment regimes. Grounded in the Hippocratic medical tradition, researchers made no distinction between therapeutic and non-therapeutic experiments. He believed that moral decision-making and the conscience of the scientists functioned as appropriate safeguards to protect participants; scientists at the Hammersmith did not feel bound by, or take much notice of, ethical principles laid down in the Nuremberg Code—widely believed to be applicable to German doctors only—or the Declaration of Helsinki: 'We did not discuss ethics. We knew what we were doing.'[106] The Code's collectivist notion 'for the good of society' had a 'Hitlerian ring' to it, he told the jury, which is why, perhaps, he and his colleagues never discussed it, nor was it believed to be in any way relevant to their work, a fact which had not escaped medical professionals such as Maurice Pappworth who in the 1960s publicly condemned the hospital's track record.[107] Booth was adamant that 'the matter of consent was not uppermost in the minds of physicians or experimenters until the mid 1960s', when public and political controversy about the ethics of human experimentation compelled the British medical profession to review its guidelines.[108] Still, he would not have expected any medical scientist to have performed an experiment that was known or likely to cause serious or lasting harm to a participant, since this would have been breached the person's professional responsibilities.[109] He entirely agreed with the assertion, made by the Coroner, that 'the safety of service volunteers should not be put at risk'.[110] Put simply, if there was a risk of 'serious injury' the experiment should not have gone ahead. More fundamentally, if the scientific methodology was flawed, he told the jury, then the work was not ethical either and should not be carried out: 'Bad science is bad ethics.' Although providing helpful context coloured by his personal recollections of aspects of Britain's research culture in the 1950s and 1960s, Booth had little to say about military research ethics as understood and practised at Porton and other secret Allied establishments. 'He did not know what was going on', the Coroner advised the jury.[111]

As a distinguished authority in the field of medical ethics and law, and external adviser on MoD committees, Sir Ian Kennedy was called upon at the inquest to assess whether Porton's scientists had behaved 'in a way which right-minded others would think at the time was ethically appropriate and justified, taking due account of prevailing values and circumstance'.[112] In his written submission to the MoD's 2006 Historical Survey, he suggested that 'until at least the middle of the 1970s, paternalism tended to hold sway in practice in the conduct of research. It was reflected in the proposition that the volunteer need not be concerned about details which he might well not understand, and that his safety and welfare could safely be left in the hands of the researchers'.[113] As an expert tasked in 2001 with examining and commenting on the material, covering a period of over half a century, presented in the Historical Survey, he felt hurt when he was criticized—by the inquest toxicologists—for not reviewing all the documentary evidence the jury had seen in recent weeks. In his testimony, he carefully resisted the temptation to comment on specific aspects of the case that required greater knowledge of the sources, yet for some observers it was still unclear why, following his appointment to contribute to the Historical Survey, he had not researched or asked to see additional documents. He had entirely, if somewhat naively, relied on the material supplied by the MoD in producing his 'ethical assessment'.[114] In his defence during the inquest, he made it plain that he felt misled by the MoD, since he had believed that he was dealing with, and commenting on, a rigorously researched expert report: 'I was not going to sign up for something which was really an exercise in exploring an "Idiot's Guide" to what happened in Porton Down', he told Leigh-Ann Mulcahy, acting as Counsel for the MoD, in a blistering exchange.[115] He also expressed disappointment that the MoD had excluded the views and experiences of Porton scientists from the Survey.[116] His conclusions were nonetheless valid, he said, until and unless other material contradicting or correcting him was placed before him.

Porton's scientists had taken a 'great deal of care' in conducting human experiments, he noted. Their manner of work had been 'thorough, painstaking, careful and often ingenious', and while there was no evidence to conclude that the 'conduct of the trials at any point went beyond the limits of what should ever be contemplated, far less tolerated, in a civilized society', he had been persuaded that on a few occasions the scientists had been 'operating at the edges of their knowledge', and, as a result, had not met the required ethical standards. Performing toxic experiments with the knowledge that one is 'at the edges of danger' meant that the line between the ethical and the unethical had been crossed.[117] The test on Maddison, in particular, had constituted a 'serious departure' from what responsible scientists should have done.[118] He was also concerned about the pace at which the experiments had been proceeding. They lacked reflection and proper analysis. The Nuremberg Code was 'a good start', he told the jury, in defining the ethical principles by which non-therapeutic experiments at Porton should be judged. Since the tests had been performed on healthy subjects, and not on patients who were ill, the scientists had had an ethical obligation to gain an understanding of the 'range of risks' from prior animal experimentation. Importantly, the subjects had had to consent to the trials, a most 'complicated notion', as Kennedy pointed out, since one needed to distinguish between their general consent—'did people know what they were signing up for?'—and their specific consent to individual tests once they had arrived at Porton. The quantity and quality of the information given to the subjects prior to their consent also mattered as an indicator as to whether one was dealing with 'people who are properly volunteers'.[119]

Departing from the basis that the safety of human participants 'should not ordinarily be put at risk', Kennedy moved on to assess different degrees of risk, distinguishing, as it were, between a likely and an unlikely risk on the one hand, and the nature of the risk on the other. Would something that might well happen be quite trivial, for example a slight headache, or would there be a risk of serious mental or physical injury or even of killing the subject?[120] If a risk of serious bodily harm or death were likely, he argued, then that was a risk the subject 'should never be exposed to'; it should cause scientists to pursue their tests no further, whatever the rationale for the experiments may have been. This is where the ethical threshold should be imposed.[121] For Mulcahy these were mostly retrospective judgements with little bearing on the case, since what mattered were the ethics of the day. She resorted to generalizations to create more uncertainty in the minds of jury members and, without citing specific examples, claimed that there was apparently a body of literature suggesting that if scientists were prepared to conduct tests on themselves, then these tests were 'ethical in terms of harm and risk'.[122] Kennedy disagreed. He conceded that some scientists might well have taken this line of argument in the 1950s, but he questioned whether it was representative of the scientific community as a whole. Good science could clearly be unethical if participants were exposed to unjustifiable risks or if they had not given their consent: 'I think the argument was bad then and I think the argument remains bad now', he said, citing views on self-experimentation held by some health lawyers and expert scientists in the 1950s.[123] He also could not accept Mulcahy's proposition that ethics was 'really left to the researcher' to decide. It was the application of ethical principles that mattered; evidence of scientists objecting or refusing to conduct certain types of research, and instances of supervisory bodies giving specific guidance—'you cannot do that, it is too dangerous' or 'it is inappropriate ethically'—demonstrated that Porton researchers were aware of ongoing ethical debates and, in all likelihood, discussed them. Why would Porton have introduced a range of 'precautionary measures' to safeguard participants from the 1930s, he asked rhetorically, unless it felt a need to observe certain 'fundamental ethical principles' in their work? Although questions of ethics may have been articulated and nuanced to a lesser degree than is the norm today, there was no doubt in his mind that researchers showed an awareness of complex issues relating to risk and safety.

In light of the principle that one does not expose human subjects to risk one cannot control, it was essential for the Porton researchers to be aware of all possible risks involved, to understand their relative importance and relationship to each other, and to see whether they might have been eliminated or controlled. Since no one had as yet explained how Maddison had died, Kennedy suggested that one possible contributory factor which 'may be significant', as he cautiously put it, might have been the lack of skin fat on his arm, as this could have resulted in faster penetration and greater absorption of nerve gas into his body. Indeed, in reviewing wide variations in nerve agent response on 5 May 1953, Cullumbine had acknowledged that the physiological factors affecting skin absorption might 'be important' in understanding individual reactions. Writing in the present tense, he then made the all-important comment that 'fat content of different skins *is* [emphasis added] being studied'.[124] In fact, a post-mortem examination performed on Maddison's body revealed that his subsurface skin fat was 'practically absent'; while that of James Patrick Kelly, who took part in a nerve gas trial a week before Maddison, and who became unconscious with cholinesterase inhibition levels of 94 and 98 percent, had been below average.[125] Apart from examining different types of cloth, Porton had been concerned with various factors relating to nerve agents, including cholinesterase inhibition levels and skin fat. The issue at stake was not so much whether skin fat makes any measurable difference to nerve gas absorption, but whether the scientists of the day had assumed that the factor was of any importance. This was not something Porton scientists planned to examine in some distant future as a matter of general curiosity; yet it was already deemed to be of real significance at the time of Maddison's death.

Since there was compelling evidence to suggest general concerns at Porton about absorption, and about the absorption of skin fat in particular, which could have explained wide variations in toxicity, it was vital to know whether a procedure existed to measure skin fat, and whether such a method could have been developed. By failing to measure skin fat despite knowing or suspecting its potential significance, and by failing to conduct further work to assess its true importance, Kennedy's argument ran, the researchers had exposed Maddison to an 'uncontrollable danger of serious harm or death'.[126] Their method of experimentation had turned into one of 'let's try this, [let's] try that'; rather than being systematic, conscientious, and methodical, it had become 'experiential'. The experiment, which cost Maddison his life, should not have been performed since it posed a serious risk of harm; it went 'beyond what was ethically permissible'.[127] Porton scientists had been under an ethical obligation to conduct further basic studies in order better to understand the risk and to be able to control it. Any other course of action, Kennedy told the Coroner, was unethical:

> [T]he uncertainties surrounding the penetration of the skin or the absorption of it in relation to GB [Sarin] were so great, the uncertainties were so great, that before proceeding to further research [on humans] they should have been appropriately tested, analysed, with a view to controlling them, otherwise one is in the territory of an uncontrollable danger, and ethically, one should not be in that territory in terms of exposing volunteers to it. It is wrong to do so.[128]

Attempts to detect variations in agent response, which resulted in small safety margins and thus greater risks to experimental subjects, and the study of methodological uncertainties more generally, had been made both before and after Maddison's death. Seen from a certain perspective, these activities had been part of the general level of care: the scientists had wanted to avoid taking unreasonable risks with the lives of human participants. These had constituted their 'safety check'; yet their responses had differed markedly over time. In looking at the findings of unauthorized nerve agent experiments with Cyclosarin in 1962, Ladell had uncovered 'considerable variation' in the subjects' reactions. Partly due to normal human variance, this had partly also been because of certain 'intrinsic faults' in experimental procedures; and these had decreased the general safety of the tests.[129] Whereas little could be done about human variability, unless specific participants were selected, trial procedures could and should have been improved, yet in some cases even this was insufficient justification for continuing the trials. In concluding his review of early exploratory experiments with BZ, another Porton scientist had identified a 'considerable variation in the susceptibility of individuals to the compound'.[130] In this case, it had not been possible to detect a correlation between the administered dose of the agent and the degree to which the subjects had exhibited hallucinatory and other psychological effects. Some subjects had even shown more intense effects at a lower dosage. Such findings were worrying, to say the least, since they made it impossible for researchers accurately to assess the level of risk involved in the tests. Further trials, it had been believed, would be unsafe, and they had therefore been stopped. What was striking in the Maddison case, in comparison, was the sheer determination and pace with which Cullumbine's team had pursued its programme of nerve agent tests, irrespective of the existing warning signs that they had been approaching potentially lethal exposure levels, and in the light of the enormous uncertainties surrounding the risk of the trials. They had seen themselves as 'medical intelligence agents for defence', secret scientists striving to ensure—through human experiments—that no enemy would ever be able to attack the British realm with toxic agents which were unknown to British scientists or against which the nation had no defence.[131] In pursuing this overriding objective it had been deemed acceptable to take certain, albeit limited, risks with the lives of humans. A more detached, critical reflection about the methodological problems involved would have shown that the trials were no longer safe.

On 15 November 2004, after sitting for sixty-four days—the longest inquest in UK legal history prior to the 2007–2008 inquest into the death of Princess Diana—and more than six hours of deliberation, the jury ruled that Maddison had been 'killed unlawfully', and that the cause of death had been the 'application of a chemical warfare nerve agent in a non-therapeutic experiment'.[132] The atmosphere outside the courthouse was one of triumphant jubilation. Media interest had been understandably high, and in the after-math of the inquest verdict the story hit the headlines on all major news channels, national newspapers, and internet blogs.[133] The *Daily Mirror*, true to form, called Porton's warfare experiments 'Sheer Poison' which had killed an 'unwitting guinea pig'; the MoD's reluctance to compensate hundreds of veterans was in itself 'scandalously cruel and unjust', and while these men had apparently been 'abused' at Porton, the evidence uncovered as part of the Maddison inquest demonstrated, in an almost circular fashion, how the government cared little 'for the men who serve their country'.[134] Some papers clearly could not resist the temptation of the familiar nation-alist rhetoric—that the UK must be in a position to defend itself against any type of foreign aggression—but what caught people's imagination in the majority of news reporting was the personal and emotional identification with a man who had died a tragic death at the hands of an all-powerful state, coupled with the ongoing suffering of servicemen who wasted little time in telling their tale to journalists up and down the country. The story started to focus people's minds: a grave injustice needed to be rectified. Legal experts, meanwhile, believed the inquest to be a turning point in UK legal history with profound consequences for all servicemen exposed to chem-ical and other toxic agents during and before the Cold War, including Gulf War veterans. No Coroner had ever been required to investigate a death that had taken place so long ago, and there had been considerable obstacles to overcome, yet the ethical, legal, and symbolic implications of the inquest seemed largely undisputed. On issues of statutory legislation, the Coroner promised to recommend to the Home Office a review of the law on non-therapeutic human experimentation.[135] The legacy of this 'momentous inquest', as he called it, in terms of scope, duration, and cost to the taxpayer, at first seemed to offer fresh impetus for initiating legislative reform to ensure greater protection for future research participants. More broadly, it was seen as a legal milestone that might help Britain to come to terms with her contested Cold War past. Fresh calls for a public inquiry into Porton's experiments, however, remained unanswered.[136]

Mediation

If the Porton veterans had hoped to see a mediated settlement emerge from the inquest without additional efforts to overcome the government's intransigence, they were badly mistaken. The inquest had brought into the public domain an alternative Cold War story that undermined, or at least questioned, the officially sanctioned and heavily funded edifice of national memories about Britain's alleged superior moral and political position that had been important in keeping Britain's heritage industry afloat, but the authorities were in fact far more concerned about the practical, long-term financial considerations flowing from the verdict. By making powerful representations at the High Court, which went hand in hand with allegations about the conduct of the Coroner's court, the government was flexing its legal and political muscles. While much of the post-inquest debate revolved around the question of whether Whitehall would accede to the veterans' demands for a public inquiry or engage in negotiations over compensation, it was the Coroner's ruling to leave it open to the jury to decide an unlawful killing verdict—on the basis of either unlawful act manslaughter or gross negligent manslaughter—that caused the greatest degree of legal argument.

The response by the MoD to the verdict was swift and uncompromising. On Tuesday 21 December 2004, on the House of Commons' last session before its Christmas recess, the Under-Secretary of State for Defence, Ivor Caplin, told Parliament in a carefully worded statement that the MoD had 'apologized' to the Maddison family for the fact that Porton had 'proceeded' with an experiment that led to his death, although an identical test two days earlier had shown an 'adverse blood test result in one serviceman'.[137] To the uninformed observer it all sounded, yet again, like an unfortunate incident, an accident in which scientists had not taken sufficient note of a simple blood test before embarking on a routine experiment that ended in death. Caplin's statement in effect belittled the ethical gravity and legal complexity of the case. He did concede, though, that the MoD would look favourably on any claim for compensation from the family as long as it was based on the type of negligence he had outlined. Negligence of any other kind was ruled out. As if this were not enough as an opening gambit, he then told Parliament that the MoD would challenge the inquest verdict of unlawful killing through a judicial review. The battle-lines were drawn in what quickly descended into a complex legal dispute at the High Court.

In considering whether to grant the MoD permission to bring a judicial review, a High Court judge made it clear in April 2005 that the court would have to consider whether the Coroner ought to have been 'entitled' to leave it open to the jury to return a manslaughter verdict at all, since the evidence presented in the case was deemed to be, on the whole—at least according to the MoD—insufficient to justify any form of manslaughter verdict, except perhaps for a case of gross negligence. But even such a case could not include, MoD lawyers argued, 'alleged negligence in relation to whether the consent was regarded as true consent or whether the deceased had been misinformed as to the true nature of the experiments with which he was involved'.[138] The Coroner now found himself in the unenviable position of defending individual rulings and the conduct of his proceedings, including the pejorative 'tone of voice' in which he had apparently given certain directions to the jury. By granting the MoD the right to request the release of the tapes of the hearing, a move which some saw as an underhand tactic to gain information against Masters, the High Court only increased the pressure on an already beleaguered Coroner.

For the MoD, there was apparently insufficient evidence to demonstrate beyond reasonable doubt, the standard of proof required for a manslaughter verdict, that Maddison had not fully consented to the experiment. Since a manslaughter verdict implied criminal wrongdoing, the burden of proof was on the family of the deceased to show that the MoD had not obtained the consent from Maddison. Given the passage of time and lack of documents, this was near impossible. The MoD, with its superior financial and legal resources compared to other interested parties, made it plain that it would consider a gross negligent manslaughter verdict only if it related to the 'conduct and planning' of the experiment, but not if it implied that Maddison had not given informed consent. Such an implication could spell disaster for the MoD. Since the group of servicemen who took part in experiments at Porton and other military facilities across Britain and her former colonies numbered in the tens of thousands, it was of paramount importance for the MoD to have the inquest verdict of unlawful killing overturned. The suggestion of criminal wrongdoing in the way non-therapeutic experiments had been carried out in those places for more than half a century, given the theoretically very high number of potential claimants who might argue that they had not consented to a certain experiment, could involve incalculable costs. For the MoD, the verdict was a time-bomb that needed to be defused by all means possible.[139]

This was the position when Lord Justice Richards and Mr Justice David Clarke opened the judicial review proceedings at the High Court of Justice on 13 February 2006, expecting to hear legal argument and counter-argument for a period of ten days. Few had anticipated however, least of all the Coroner, that behind-the-scenes negotiations between the lawyers representing the family and the MoD had produced an agreed compromise, a 'pragmatic proposal', as Care later liked to call it, in which the family accepted, or at least would not challenge, the MoD's position that there was insufficient evidence for the Coroner to have left to the jury 'the verdict of unlawful act manslaughter and the verdict of gross negligence manslaughter in relation to the obtaining of consent', and in return the MoD would no longer attempt to quash the unlawful killing verdict. Provided all interested parties agreed, the inquest verdict would be amended accordingly, namely to state that Maddison had been unlawfully killed 'by reason of gross negligence manslaughter relating to the conduct and planning of the experiment on the Deceased'.[140] Knowing full well that an unlawful killing verdict, if it were to stand and not be overturned in the High Court, would substantially increase the level of compensation awarded to Maddison's family, the lawyers acting on their behalf had decided not to argue the case in court, probably because they feared the MoD's challenge would succeed, but had instead traded in the issue of whether Maddison had ever consented to the experiment, and thus, by implication, undermined the conduct and integrity of the Coroner's inquest proceedings. No wonder then that the Coroner, upon hearing of the proposal, is said to have expressed his serious displeasure in no uncertain terms. Less than twelve weeks later, the MoD settled the claim for compensation with Maddison's family for 100,000 pounds sterling.[141] The Treasury Solicitor had recommended in 1953 that compensation be paid in this and similar cases, and that the authorities should not 'throw the responsibility upon the persons volunteering for the tests'; it had taken the government fifty-three years to heed his initial advice.[142] The family's legal representatives, foremost among them Alan Care, had achieved what they had set out to do, but where did this leave the veterans? Whereas some expressed a sense of disappointment, others recognized that neither the family nor the veterans would ever have had any chance of receiving compensation if the unlawful killing verdict had been overturned by the High Court. What concerned them most was whether they would now be able to pursue their claim further. Their call for justice was certainly not lacking in political momentum.

Public pressure on the government to consider the veterans' case on moral rather than legal or strictly medical grounds had been steadily building since the inquest verdict; widespread media reports about servicemen having been 'duped' and 'misled' into taking part in experiments without their consent were starting to haunt the authorities. Evidence was mounting that the self-reported quality of life of veterans was 'consistently lower' than those of citizens of the same or similar age and social background, with complaints about headaches, memory loss, depression, heart disease, hypertension, skin problems, infertility, and a significantly higher incidence of fatigue symptoms, and while 'no clear pattern of specific morbidities' could be detected, experts did not rule out a possible link between chemical exposures at Porton and subsequent ill-health.[143] 'Statistically there's not a lot left of us, there's not a lot', is how the Porton veteran Terry Alderson put it, which was why, in his view, the case had to be 'settled quickly'.[144] Legal representatives now called on Prime Minister Tony Blair to get involved, arguing that the Porton experiments were like a 'cankerous sore' which would continue to fester unless his government put right the wrongs that had been committed. The revelations of the inquest were such that only a public inquiry could command sufficient authority to examine the merits of the case, and not the MoD, as it had done in the past, since the 'fox [would otherwise] be left to guard the chicken house'.[145] Members of the PDVSG, meanwhile, by now representing over 550 veterans, launched a concerted campaign to rally support from their local MPs in the run-up to the general election, scheduled for May 2005, a strategy which had the desired effect. In January, the conservative MP for Poole, Robert Syms, raised the issue of Porton Down on behalf of one of his constituents in a fifteen-minute late-night Adjournment debate in the House of Commons. In his response, however, Caplin, the Under-Secretary of State for Defence, failed to deal with the contentious issue of consent which, according to one MP, appeared to have been 'null and void' in most cases.[146]

At the same time, important behind-the-scenes concessions were being made. At the end of January, the MoD decided—after apparently believing for over fifty years that it was 'arguable in law' that the nerve agent which had been used in the experiments could be classed as 'supplies', and that therefore Section 10(2) of the Crown Proceedings Act 1947 applied—that it would no longer rely on Section 10(2) as a defence against claims made by Porton veterans.[147] The move was coordinated with the FCO which now no longer applied the CPA 1947 as a defence against claims at the ECHR.[148] This meant, in a nutshell, that one of the most potent legal obstacles standing in the way of a political settlement had been removed, and marked a policy change, brought about by irrefutable evidence that had come to light during the Maddison inquest, which would have implications that were far-reaching, albeit hardly aired or debated in public.

A month later, MPs from across the political spectrum, responding to an initiative by Patrick Hall, Labour MP for Bedford, engaged in a bipartisan debate about Porton Down in the House of Commons.[149] Speaking on behalf of his constituent Peter Parker, who had undergone the same experiment as Maddison only two day earlier, Hall highlighted the need for an independent public inquiry into whether former servicemen had been deceived into undergoing toxic trials. The existing historical evidence advising soldiers that there was not 'the slightest chance of danger', 'no foreseeable danger', or 'no danger' at all, raised serious questions about the quality of the consent obtained and constituted, in Hall's view, a 'prima facie case of volunteers not being told the truth' in contravention of the principles of the Nuremberg Code, irrespective of whether this had been incorporated into UK domestic law.[150] The government was criticized for sending 'mixed messages' by commissioning a long-term health study into effects of nerve gas exposure and, at the same time, attempting to quash the unanimous inquest verdict of unlawful killing by way of a judicial review, at substantial cost to the taxpayer. Hall skilfully framed the debate within the wider context and public discourse about the memorialization of the Second World War, especially in relation to the upcoming sixtieth anniversary of Victory in Europe Day, which brought to mind powerful imageries of liberated concentration camp inmates, some of whom had been forced by the Nazis into taking part in human experiments in breach of international law. He concluded his speech with a passionate plea for the 'full story' to be told about Porton Down. By linking the case of the Porton veterans with the history of British veterans generally, he had constructed a contextual framework that elevated the alleged suffering of individuals to a group of psychologically wounded and badly treated national servicemen, and MPs were ready to rise to the occasion. In the oak-panelled confines of the Grand Committee Room just off Westminster Hall, a group of backbenchers engaged in the construction and reconstruction of national memories, however painful these might be for the national conscience, mnemogogues in the truest meaning of Levi's word. Would the government listen to them?

Ann Widdecombe, MP for Maidstone and the Weald, well known for her outspoken ways, called the matter an 'appalling story of an arrogant state and innocent young people'. It was a story, she said, in which the state had found it acceptable to conduct experiments on its own citizens without obtaining consent, a 'story of utter innocence and trust'.[151] By citing the personal recollections of her constituent Kenneth Earl, co-founder of the PDVSG, she added a sense of poignancy to a narrative heavily pregnant with emotive imagery, of soldiers being 'betrayed' by their country, a 'disgraceful episode' in Britain's recent past. These men were at an advanced age, and few remained to tell their tale, she argued, which is why it was time for the government to say that 'wrong was done'. Widdecombe's figures of speech appealed to a conservative audience with a traditional value system, in which 'common courtesy' and a 'sense of fairness', for which Britain had once been renowned, mattered more than financial or legal considerations. Others, such as the Labour MP for Mitcham and Morden, Siobhain McDonagh, or the Conservative MP for Bournemouth East, David Atkinson, who had spoken on behalf of a Porton veteran as early as 1996, joined the call for a full and frank inquiry without delay. The idea that the veterans had simply been 'confusing' Porton's recruitment notices with those aimed at attracting volunteers to the Common Cold Unit at Harnham Down simply did 'not wash'; according to Atkinson, it was a 'national scandal' that required redress. The Father of the House, Tam Dalyell, the serving MP for Linlithgow, who in the late 1960s had been reprimanded for leaking privileged information about Porton to *The Observer*, likewise supported the plea for a 'public inquiry and for justice'.[152]

Up until now it had been an otherwise reasoned debate until Robert Key, MP for Salisbury and member of the Defence Select Committee, rose from his seat. He abstained from opposing a public inquiry, which he believed was more suitable than an inquest by a Coroner's court, but he also could not resist giving MPs a tutorial about Porton's activities since the First World War, repeating for the most part what he had told the BBC four years earlier.[153] Essential to the defence of the British realm, the work there was 'world class', he said, its spin-offs instrumental in developing vaccines and treatment regimes against major infectious diseases. By drawing attention to the fact that Porton's ethics committee was fully compliant with the 1964 Declaration of Helsinki, he wanted to highlight how far the organization had changed since the 1950s, yet he seemed to have been unaware that the Declaration had since then been revised many times. After he had delivered another round of jargon-laden comments suggesting that Porton scientists were working at the 'cutting edge of blue skies research' in which 'industrial innovation and clinical application' found a happy marriage, one MP questioned whether Key was little more than the MoD's stooge ('Who wrote all that?'). Key's support of Porton just sounded too good to be true, but Key was having none of it. He now went straight into the attack. People should 'snap out of it', he told the House, 'get real and move into the 21st century'. He angrily rejected the way the facility and its 'highly motivated' staff was portrayed in the national press, yet by juxtaposing its popular media image with the day-to-day reality, he unintentionally revealed some of the underlying tensions that had plagued the place for almost a century: 'It is not some secret, behind-the-wire, white-coated colony of aliens. They are real families who shop at Tesco, sing in our choirs, join our sport and leisure activities and bring to our local schools a high profile for science education.'[154] The speech provided the perfect prelude for the Thatcherite politician Gerald Howarth, MP for Aldershot—who became the MoD's Under-Secretary of State under the Coalition government in 2010, and at the time of writing serves as chairman for the conservative think tank 'Conservative Way Forward'—to raise the spectre of the 'free world' being threatened by nonconventional weaponry. Although he praised Porton's work, it had apparently exposed veterans to 'uncontrollable danger' in the past, which is why the government was called upon to side with the estimated 1,000 veterans, who claimed that their health had been affected, 'rather than with the Treasury', a position he seems to have abandoned following his party's entry into government.[155]

In his reply, Caplin, speaking for the MoD, tried to hold the government's line by repeating the well-rehearsed narrative about British armed forces requiring protection from chemical and biological weapons.[156] He alluded to existing and alleged threats from nonconventional weapons in the Middle East and 'closer to home', a reference to attempted acts of terrorism on the British mainland, and portrayed Porton as the UK's 'scientific response to terrorism', thus elevating the organization to a pillar of homeland defence. In retrospect, Caplin's words have a certain sense of foreboding. Four months later, on 7 July 2005, Britain suffered its worst ever terrorist attack, when a series of coordinated bomb blasts wrought havoc on the streets of London, killing fifty-two civilians and injuring another seven hundred. The threats were all of a sudden only too real. By conflating questions about the ethicacy of Porton's research conduct with the need for Britain's defensive capabilities against chemical and biological weapons by state and non-state actors, and by linking all of this with Britain's 'war on terror', the government had framed the debate in such a way that calls for a public inquiry no longer seemed to have priority.

Compensating Maddison's family and the worst excesses of Porton's experimental activities, including three of five 'mind control' studies with

LSD conducted by Britain's foreign intelligence service SIS/MI6 at Porton in the 1950s, may have contained the immediate fallout from the inquest, but it did not resolve the broader issue of the Porton veterans, which continued to 'fester', as Care had warned it would, until it threatened to damage the government's public image. The publication of the much-anticipated but largely disappointing Historical Survey in 2006 only added to a sense of frustration among legal experts and commentators, who despaired of seeing the veterans' case being resolved any time soon. Compared to the detailed report published by the US President's Advisory Committee for Human Radiation Experiments in 1995, the British survey was anything but impartial; rather than being researched by a team of independent experts, it was written by a group of anonymous authors from the MoD who were not specialist historians, nor did they seem to have the necessary knowledge to contextualize the material. Despite having had access to rare and previously unpublished sources about Britain's military research culture in the twentieth century, the MoD made it plain that it would 'devote no effort... to release these documents, either in whole or in sanitized form, to the public domain'.[157] Scholars trying to verify important aspects of the Historical Survey, for instance in relation to 'psychological incapacitating agents', quickly reached a dead end with their enquiries.[158] The US authorities aimed for maximum transparency and accountability with their final report by publishing almost all the documents on the internet. The MoD's web link to the Historical Survey, in contrast, is no longer active at the time of writing. Students and scholars wanting to study the survey now have to go to considerable lengths to find a copy in a British or overseas library. The two reports highlight significant national and cultural differences in addressing complex issues of reconciliation and understanding of moral wrongdoing by past governments. In Britain there was clearly no appetite for a full public inquiry into Porton's human experiments, because it was deemed to be too expensive, would have lasted too long, and would perhaps even be too embarrassing, and so the government begrudgingly edged towards a negotiated settlement.

At the end of 2006, Mark Townsend from *The Guardian* speculated that the Porton 'guinea pigs' would receive 6 million pounds sterling, a hugely inflated and unrealistic sum at this point.[159] Additional representations stressing the ongoing plight of the veterans to Ann Abraham, the UK Parliamentary and Health Service Ombudsman, received a muted response, in so far as her remit appeared to be insufficiently broad to allow her to

get involved.[160] In March 2007, the Porton Down veterans, now represented by the legal firms Thomson Snell & Passmore and Leigh Day & Co,
submitted their multi-party action (MPA) to the MoD, but by the autumn
almost all avenues for the exercise of any meaningful pressure on the government to reconsider its position seemed to be exhausted. Prior to a
meeting with the Canadian Ombudsman in London, one of the inquest
experts told Care informally that the case had taken up the best part of
seven years, suggesting that it was time to call it a day unless a resolution
could be found. Asked whether those representing the chemical warfare
veterans in the UK could do more to persuade the government to right
the wrong that had been committed, the Ombudsman replied that there
was nothing else that could be done, except wait for the government to
become politically weak, since this had helped to secure ex gratia payments for the Canadian veterans a year earlier. Shortly thereafter, Prime
Minister Gordon Brown contemplated calling an election, but then fate-
fully back-tracked, which resulted in a barrage of public criticism for his
government. The ongoing 'Porton saga' was suddenly seen as an unnecessary distraction for a government in the run-up to the election, now
expected to be in May 2008. The MoD all of a sudden indicated that it
was interested in a settlement by way of mediation.

Following two highly confidential mediation meetings on 21 December
2007 and 11 January 2008, the MoD and the PDVSG reached an amicable
settlement for 359 veterans claiming to have suffered ill-health as a result of
Cold War experiments, which some may have been 'duped' to take part in,
the risks involved having possibly not been properly explained to them.
Although long-term health effects could not be demonstrated, given the
way the government-funded epidemiological studies about the health and
well-being of the Porton veterans had been framed within a surprisingly
limited body of literature, the settlement was an official recognition that the
veterans had sustained short-term and acute injuries; those who had not
thus suffered would not qualify for personal injury compensation under its
terms. Failure to obtain consent was insufficient to qualify.[161] The speed
with which a solution had been found caught everyone by surprise. News
about a settlement of 8,300 pounds sterling for each claimant was first
reported in mid January, leading the blogosphere run by serving and former servicemen to go into overdrive: some called the experiments 'crimes
against humanity' which had to be tried by the International Criminal
Court (ICC), while others made the age-old reference to Nazi and Japanese

medical atrocities. Elsewhere in the electronic universe, conspiracy theo-rists saw their self-fulfilling anti-government prejudices corroborated. There was a general sense among veterans that it was too little too late; still others felt it was a step in the right direction, with one blogger asking: 'Will the Nuclear vets be next?'[162]

On 31 January 2008, the Parliamentary Under-Secretary of State for Defence, Derek Twigg, announced the payment of a global sum of 3 mil-lion pounds sterling as a 'full and final settlement' for the Porton veterans without an admission of liability by the government, and offered a public apology in the House of Commons: 'The Government accept that there were aspects of the trials where there may have been shortcomings and where, in particular, the life or health of participants may have been put at risk. The Government sincerely apologize to those who may have been affected.'[163] The government was attempting to draw a line under the mat-ter without admitting legal liability which, it was believed, could 'open a can of worms' as far as other veterans' groups were concerned, especially the nuclear war veterans, who had a case pending. Trying to do this at the same time as ensuring that justice was done and seen to be done, the government had punctuated its statement with so many caveats that its apology had become almost meaningless. Some veterans regarded it as a grudging apology, but an apology it was nonetheless. It marked a central milestone in the decade-long campaign by the PDVSG to prove that the non-therapeutic human trials in which they had taken part had been unethical, and that they warranted an apology and financial compensa-tion, which is why the story was given extensive media coverage. 'Today makes it all worthwhile', Eric Gow, one of the veterans, commented: 'I am just so very sorry and angry that many of our comrades had to die before we reached this point—but I am sure they will be looking down on us today with some degree of satisfaction.'[164] Between 2008 and 2010, the British government paid over 10 million pounds sterling in compensation, including legal costs, to about 670 Porton Down veterans, a costly resolu-tion to an unfortunate Cold War affair.[165]

Remembering the Living

How has Porton itself been remembered? Have the staff, those thousands of scientific experts, military officials, and civil servants working at and for Porton over the last hundred years, been commemorated, decorated, or celebrated? Have any memorials been erected in their name, or any commemorative plates or objects been produced? Have any paintings been commissioned? In short, has there been an attempt to construct a life-long bond between the men and women working in Britain's chemical and biological warfare community through a sense of institutional loyalty and military tradition? All of these questions can be answered in the affirmative. Ever since the end of the First World War, when the 'Old Portonians'—a self-selecting group of some fifty 'officers' of the British army who had served in the war—formed an elitist little society that met up at the Trocadero Restaurant in London's Piccadilly Circus and at other venues for their annual dinner, initially in the presence of Porton's first commandant Colonel A. W. Crossley, Porton as an institution and as an idea has fostered a closely knit community of experts tasked with providing Britain, if necessary, with a credible chemical and biological warfare capability and the means for its defence. Crossley had always reminded his men that he wanted Porton to be 'the best and most powerful of its kind'. Those not attending the annual 'Chemical Warfare Reunion Dinner', which in April 1926 (see Image 45), for example, was held at the Hotel Cecil in London—the first headquarters of the Royal Air Force—were reprimanded in no uncertain terms as being 'absent from duty'.[166] Absentees were told that Porton had been a joint effort and those who took part in it 'must help to commemorate it'.[167]

Given the initial perception of chemical warfare as the 'Cinderella Arm' of Britain's armed services, Crossley's determination to create a certain *esprit de corps* has been integral to Porton's mission and tradition ever since, as a way of strengthening the organization's self-confidence to fight what senior staff regarded as 'unwarranted prejudices', based on 'abysmal ignorance and false sentimentality', against this type of warfare.[168] Occasional visits by men wielding considerable influence in political, military, and royal circles offered additional support; they included Lord Mountbatten, Chief of the Defence Staff until 1965 and uncle of Prince Philip, Duke of Edinburgh, Viscount Montgomery, Commander-in-Chief of the BAOR in post-war Germany and then Chief of the Imperial General Staff, Sir Arthur Tedder, Deputy Supreme Commander at SHAEF and subsequently Chief of the Air Staff, Emanuel Shinwell, Minister of War, and Duncan Sandys, Minister of Defence. Throughout the decades, the oil painting of Crossley, commissioned a year after his death in 1928, has hung in the office of whoever is in charge of the organization, as a tribute to the perceived heroism of the past

Image 45. Chemical warfare reunion dinner, Hotel Cecil, London, 30 April 1926
Source: IWM, Photographic Collection. © Imperial War Museums (Chemical Warfare Dinner 1926).

and a reminder of future expectations. Constructing historical continuity has been achieved through all sorts of means, from newsletters, photographs, and films to brass plates, engraved objects, and memorials.[169] Many of Porton's senior figures became Fellows of the Royal Society, others were knighted. Belonging to the British establishment, or being seen to belong, was what mattered to them. Throughout its complex history, Porton's personal and professional network of expertise and influence has reached deep into British society and the agencies of the state, from the political and military sphere and the civil service corps to cutting-edge science laboratories and academia, the chemical and pharmaceutical industries, civil contingency agencies, public health services, and the meteorological office, to name but a few. Since the early 1990s, there has been a steady stream of publications highlighting the apparently 'defensive' nature of Britain's chemical and biological warfare programme. In 2016, as a way of marking the centenary of its creation, Porton will undoubtedly celebrate its past 'achievements' in making Britain a safer place. It is likely to be a self-serving exercise in which the individual life experiences of tens of thousands of servicemen who underwent toxic tests for the good of their country will hardly figure at all.

Yet what has happened to the remaining 21,000 or so veterans who took part in Porton tests but were not, for whatever reason, members of the PDVSG, did not claim any damage to their physical and mental health, or simply passed away before any settlement was agreed? Have their services been sufficiently recognized by the authorities? Did the government approach them and their families, and incorporate their memories into a more nuanced, critical narrative of Britain's experimental programme? How are they being remembered? More broadly, has their story changed the government's approach in dealing with Britain's veteran community, those still alive and claiming recognition and compensation? Has it transformed the 'negative attitude' at the MoD, as one MP once poignantly put it? Far from it. Porton veterans querying why they had not been approached before the June 2008 deadline expired were told that the MoD was under no obligation to contact 'each and every one of the tens of thousands of veterans who attended Porton Down over the years'.[170] Others were treated no differently. Gulf War veterans requesting information about a testing programme with a combined anthrax and pertussis (whooping cough) vaccine were first told by the MoD that it had been conducted with the soldiers' 'confirmed consent', which apparently showed that the programme had not been an 'experiment', though there was a subsequent admission that 'consent forms were not used in the Gulf in 1990/1991'. Secrecy had apparently restricted 'the flow of information', including the information needed to give informed consent to the vaccine tests.[171] As if no lessons had been learned, it was then the turn of Britain's atomic veterans to reach the end of the road for their legal challenge. In 2012, the Supreme Court turned down the appeal to have their cases heard in open court. With three out of seven senior judges dissenting, this was hardly a unanimous judgement. For some, it was a major human rights scandal, for others just another case of Britain's continuing inability to come to terms with her Cold War past. The lawyer acting on behalf of the MoD was none other than Leigh-Ann Mulcahy. Few experts seem as yet to have realized that the Porton Down Litigation served as a fitting 'training exercise' for those representing the MoD and enabled them to defeat potential claims for compensation by the atomic veterans a couple of years later.[172]

Some twenty years ago, the authors of a major survey into the health effects of mustard gas and lewisite exposure sustained by US servicemen during the Second World War, one of the first of its kind, noted that the story about veterans being exposed to toxic agents in highly secret wartime research facilities was rather 'unusual' in its nature; it was a story, they hoped, that would 'never have to be told again'.[173] The present study must come as a deep disappointment to them, in so far as it echoes many of their disturbing findings about a 'well-ingrained pattern of abuse and neglect' experienced by Allied servicemen. With collaborative arrangements forming the basis of Allied intelligence networks in the field of nonconventional weapons programmes, it is not altogether surprising that the story uncovered in the United States in the early 1990s was a mirror image of Britain's human volunteer programme, the other side of the same coin, yet the research conducted and initiated by Britain was also influenced by political, legal, and cultural traditions resulting from its former position as an imperial power with long-standing links to Canada, India, and Australia, all of which governed the science and ethics of military experiments under its control in the twentieth century. It is this contextual heritage which explains why the approach by successive British governments to the contentious subject of secret military experiments has differed so remarkably in comparison to most countries in the Western world.

Veterans in Britain, including the Porton veterans, have never been afforded the sanctuary of a truly independent expert committee examining their claims; funds have never been made available for a full public inquiry to document and make available their medical memories; there has never been a proper public hearing at which they could freely tell their tale without being placed under pressure from lawyers waiting to challenge their testimony. No government resources have ever been made available to create a research or educational centre for future generations, one in which the country's national heritage is not misrepresented. History, if it has a purpose, requires balanced perspectives and impartial analysis rather than self-serving national narratives. Britain, in short, has never seen the likes of a President's Advisory Committee for Human Radiation Experiments, which examined the veterans' claims in an impartial and transparent but also generous fashion. Rather than starting from a position where their testimony was deemed to be potentially unreliable, misleading, or downright false, and therefore inadmissible in any legal proceedings, as has been the case in Britain, public hearings in the United States with veterans, their spouses, and relatives have allowed experts to gain valuable insight into experimental conditions, the culture of research ethics, and a wide range of diseases from which the veterans were suffering, including different types of mental illnesses. The remit of the UK government-funded so-called 'independent' scientific studies, on the other hand, has been, with few exceptions, exceedingly narrow, and the results have accordingly been predictable, suggesting that there is no evidence demonstrating that any of the claimants had sustained any long-term or serious injury. This is why almost each and every one of the veterans' cases had to be fought in the law courts. As a result, many of the cases never progressed for want of resources, lack of evidence, or qualifying legal argument; often cases never even reached the point where they were heard in court at all. Since taking a firm line with regard to an avalanche of pension claims in the aftermath of the First World War, the UK government seems to have engaged in a massive and prolonged cost-saving exercise; paying compensation to any of the veterans' groups is seen as a last resort and only when all other avenues have been exhausted, but almost never as a recognition for the services and loyalty these men and women have shown their country.

Britain has one of the most flourishing and lucrative commemorative cultures in the world, its scholars are world leading in the social and cultural history of memory, its heritage industry is second to none and is an integral part of the country's long-awaited economic recovery, yet all of this somehow seems to be unconnected to those in society who, while still alive, take issue with the government's past conduct. There seems to be an uncomfortable relationship between Britain's culture of commemorating armed conflicts of the past on the one hand, and, on the other, the government's handling of veterans' affairs in the present. Not unlike a marriage in crisis, it is a relationship in considerable disharmony, one which may require a period of reflection to ensure greater sensitivity and understanding between the parties involved. For the time being, it seems to be a culture in which government recognition is earned only after death. This study has taken a distinctly different approach, one in which space has been given for the evidence, as it has unfolded, to be critically explored without fear or favour, and which has hopefully awarded the voices and experiences of those claiming justice today their rightful place in history; perhaps one day Britain will be a country in which the services of the living will be remembered in equal measure with those of the departed.

Epilogue
The Truth Lies in Fragmented Tales

For the present study, it has proven fruitful to turn on its head the debate about whether research conducted in great secrecy can also be ethical and transparent, by exploring the origins and development of regulatory systems within military research facilities. One way of doing this was to study a range of representative incidents that resulted in sudden or gradual changes in research behaviour and ethical outlook among scientists working under conditions of great secrecy. How did Porton, the military, central government agencies, and their advisers respond to such incidents and subsequent political and public demands for reform? By studying the 'cracks' in the system that arise when military research departs from the expected pattern, when the normal becomes abnormal, and military scientists and senior civil servants start exchanging notes, arranging meetings, talking informally, on or off the record, negotiating, or blaming others in order to preserve their professional interests, when administrative structures are 'stress tested' and advisory committees are called upon to justify their existence, we can begin to see how military medical science operates and adapts to unforeseen challenges. It is at these moments that military experts and civil servants sometimes throw linguistic caution to the wind, not in order to breach secrecy, but to make robust representations and stake their position. By looking at certain game-changing military medical ethics crises, while simultaneously exercising caution in not misinterpreting the 'extraordinary' as the 'ordinary', it has been possible to gain insight into the culture of communication in secret science environments. This approach has allowed us to explore how groups of researchers talked to their political and civil service masters, to chart trends in scientific modes of thinking, and to reconstruct emerging plans to improve existing systems of research governance.

Rather than offering evidence for high levels of consistency behind Porton's fenced perimeters, we have instead detected a significant, albeit unexpected, diversity of research and communication cultures. In some instances, lines of command and control could at times be strictly hierarchical and efficient, like a well-oiled military machine, and researchers managed, through informal day-to-day conversations, to cross disciplinary boundaries in order to facilitate knowledge exchange and creative thinking. In other instances, work could be undertaken in a haphazard, inconsistent, and compartmentalized manner, scientists isolated and ignorant of each others' findings with sometimes serious implications for the accurate assessment of risk. Often only a selected few possessed access to, or knowledge of, the bigger picture and were thus able to integrate Porton's human volunteer programme into inter-Allied strategic decision-making about the potential use of chemical weapons technology.

This book thus raises a series of important but also exceedingly difficult questions in relation to the historiography and methodology of medical ethics. How best to write a history of modern medical ethics in the twentieth and twenty-first centuries? Which is the methodological approach most appropriate to do justice to both the history and the memory of those involved in human experimentation? What kind of lessons can we learn from other subject areas and historiographical debates to construct a more sophisticated and multi-dimensional narrative of modern medical ethics? How can historians serious about the subject make a valuable contribution to narrative discourses which continue, more often than not, to be dominated by medical scientists, health lawyers, philosophers, and bioethicists? At the most general level it seems fruitful to bridge the artificial separation between the writing of history and memory proposed by Broszat and recently and convincingly challenged in the Holocaust historiography by Friedländer in his two-volume magnum opus *Nazi Germany and the Jews* and *The Years of Extermination*.[1] At the core of these very contentious debates has been the issue of historicization and the method of *Alltagsgeschichte* (the history of everyday life) which, it was suspected by some, might lead to 'normalizing' and 'apologetic' tendencies, yet Friedländer has shown that historicization which 'preserves the Holocaust as the centrepiece of the Third Reich' is possible. History writing on highly emotive and politically sensitive subjects, as Stone has pointed out, would be 'sterile' and 'morally problematic' if it were to exclude a critical engagement with memory, and I hope to have demonstrated that this applies equally to the historical

controversies surrounding the issue of human experimentation.[2] Yet
whereas Friedländer first developed a theoretical framework over many
years which he then tested, by all accounts successfully, in an alternative
historiography of the Holocaust which seems to have overcome the risk of
'neutralizing the past', the present study has gone in the opposite direction
for the field of medical ethics by writing a history which consciously incor-
porates elements of narrative structure, multivocality, and critical commentary with witness testimony and the memories of participants and bystanders,
whether as patient-subjects, physician-scientists, or civil servants. In contrast
to the sources underpinning the history of the Holocaust, which nowadays
are relatively easily accessible, the secrecy surrounding the history of military research not only made access to relevant material particularly challenging but also shaped an important part of the structure of the book. At
every turn, the secretive nature of the sources had to be consciously borne
in mind as their explanatory potential for the history of human research
ethics generally was gauged. The approach to this book—and the writing of
medical ethics generally—has been a journey outwards from the contextualized and critically examined sources, however fragmented these may have
been, to the development of principles broadly applicable to medical ethics
history. Friedländer, on the other hand, has taken the opposite route, gradually moving inwards from a clearly defined theoretical paradigm. Although
we have approached two different but equally contentious and morally
complex topics from two opposing directions, we have arrived at similar
conclusions as far as the historicization of the material is concerned. Key to
our historical enterprise has been the role of contextualization. I therefore
agree with Friedländer's dictum that historicization can be achieved only if
the work is 'entirely integrated within a complex historical context'.[3] This
book has aimed to present a significantly revised history of medical ethics,
one that looks at civilian and military medical ethics as two sides of the
same coin, one that examines continuity and change in ethical debates and
practices at various levels of society, and that does so using a comparative
and international perspective. If it has succeeded, this is due to the realization that contextualization is of fundamental importance, and that without
it, nuanced historicization remains simply an aspiration.

Can we identify certain subject areas historians of medical ethics ought
to examine to ensure that a piece of work has a coherent narrative structure and sufficient intellectual depth? Or, to put it differently, what are the
philosophical and historiographical concepts that need to be addressed in

writing a history of modern medical ethics? Over the last forty-odd years bioethicists have established themselves as a powerful professional force in most Western societies, yet the history of their discipline has barely been studied or understood. In 1968, at a time when Britain's chemical and biological warfare community, and Porton in particular, were faced with a barrage of public criticism, a group of experts from the medical sciences, philosophy, law, public health, history, sociology, and anthropology—what some today might class as the 'medical humanities'—came together under the chairmanship of Paul A. Freund, Harvard law professor and former President of the US Academy of Arts and Sciences, to discuss contemporary 'Ethical Aspects of Experimentation with Human Subjects'.[4] Contributors to the discourse included the perceived 'pioneers' of the bioethics movement, such as Henry K. Beecher and Jay Katz, who looked at existing guidance and regulatory frameworks in medical experimentation. Their arguments, reflected in this study, highlighted a range of conceptual issues that ought to underpin the study and writing of the history of medical ethics.

Foremost among the issues identified was the concept of informed consent. Almost all agreed that a non-therapeutic experiment involving a high degree of risk should not only not be performed but also not be 'put to the patient for consent'.[5] Equally, it was acknowledged that consent in and by itself would 'not protect a badly designed or negligently conducted experiment'.[6] For the historian of medical ethics the study of consent serves a broader, more symbolic function since it offers a historical reference point against which varying degrees of 'respect for individual integrity' among scientists and officials can be assessed. It can provide a valuable pathway into the reflective process among scientists about the nature, design, and purpose of the experiments, and about internal and external concerns about the risks involved. The 'best safeguard for the protection of research subjects', Katz argued, was scientists who were fully committed to the principle of 'voluntary consent', as formulated in Principle 1 of the Nuremberg Code; it is thus the job of the medical ethics historian to examine, as best he can, not only different but changing levels of commitment to the consent principle among various research communities, including those operating under conditions of great secrecy.[7]

For the émigré-philosopher Hans Jonas, a contemporary and friend of Hannah Arendt, who fled from Nazi Germany in 1933, and whose mother perished in the Holocaust, there was 'something sacrificial...involved in the selective abrogation of personal inviolability and the ritualized exposure to gratuitous risk of health and life, justified by a presumed greater, social good'.[8] In this sense, any serious scholarly inquiry has to have, as its conceptual starting point, an examination of the values and principles that in the past have been used to justify the infringement of a person's right to remain physically and psychologically unharmed. Jonas was adamant that those wanting to conduct experiments on human beings 'must justify the infringement of a primary inviolability, which needs no justification itself; and the justification of its infringement must be by values and needs of a dignity commensurate with those to be sacrificed'.[9] Condensed as this statement may be, it is well worth reading again since it provides us with a 'roadmap' for examining the history of twentieth-century human research ethics, highlighting, as Böhme put it, that arguments based on ethics, instead of protecting participants and vulnerable groups from harm, seem to have been part of the problem that made unethical research possible in the first place, the case of Viktor von Weizsäcker being a case in point.[10] Key bio-ethical principles of individual autonomy (principle of respect for persons), beneficence (to do good), non-maleficence (to avoid doing harm), and justice (fair distribution of goods and services, including medical goods and services), developed by Beauchamp and Childress a decade later, were already central to Jonas' argumentation.[11] According to Jonas, the right of humans to remain bodily unharmed needs no 'justification itself', but any kind of action on, or interference with the body, however small, has to be fully justified. For scholars, this means the following: in order to determine what an acceptable justification for the 'infringement of personal inviolability' for experimental subjects could be, whether historically or contemporaneously, we first need to examine the inherent tension between the individual good and the common good, not by resorting to the language of 'interests' or 'numbers', but by distinguishing between a 'moral appeal' to a certain cause that encourages an individual to volunteer, and an enforceable 'right' by some higher authority that demands full compliance. A free and open society, as advocated by Karl Popper and others, may have a 'moral claim' to conduct certain experiments on humans—and this claim may or may not be met by the individual—but it does not have a right to perform them.[12] While scientists and other creative minds have at all times sacrificed themselves on the 'altar of their vocation . . . no one, not even society, has the shred of a right to expect and ask these things [i.e. 'true sacrifice from highest devotion']. They come to the rest of us as *gratia gratis data*.'[13] This is why the whole process of volunteering—in all its stages and complexity—is of such fundamental importance, since it offers us an indication of whether the volunteered act was genuinely voluntary. If the act of volunteering was genuine, we can safely progress to examine the moral claim itself to see whether the value of it was of the same order as, or of a higher order than, that being sacrificed. If it was not, and if the subject did not volunteer, then the moral claim, whatever its value or importance to society, is insufficient to justify the act. In other words, a moral claim cannot transform an involuntary act into a voluntary one. An experiment is ethical or unethical at its inception; it cannot become ethical retrospectively by linking it to a moral or societal claim, however important that claim may be. As the prosecution in the Nuremberg Doctors' Trial pointed out:

> It is the most fundamental tenet of medical ethics and human decency that the subjects volunteer for the experiment after being informed of its nature and hazards. This is the clear dividing line between criminal and what may be non-criminal. If the experimental subjects cannot be said to have volunteered, then the inquiry need proceed no further.[14]

Thus, by studying the shifting rationalization and justification strategies of scientists trying to gain access to vast state resources for experiments on humans, both civilians and service personnel, and by investigating the processes and procedures by which those experiments were implemented, we may be able to determine whether the experiments can be considered as having been ethical and legitimate under the conditions of the time.

War puts the issue under yet another light. Does not war, or a national emergency, which permits the state to call upon its citizens to make certain sacrifices, temporarily suspend the universal applicability of these principles? It does, but only to a certain extent. Sending armies of young soldiers into battle to fight or die for the survival of their nation or community, as has been the case throughout history, does not require their consent; they are conscripted 'according to law' and 'sacrificed' for the survival of the many. In a democratic and non-totalitarian system of society the powers of the state are naturally curtailed and kept in check by representatives of the people; we do not tolerate 'forced labour', nor do we accept 'forced risk, injury, and indignity' in medical research, yet it is also broadly accepted, and has been demonstrated in this study, that in time of war, even if it is only a 'cold' war, the carefully constructed balance between the individual and the common good can shift heavily towards the latter.[15] Human experiments are rarely applicable to extreme situations in which the survival of the national community is at stake, nor are the risks and sacrifices in any way comparable to those experienced by combat soldiers. Still, human experiments count among the 'extraordinary' rather than the 'ordinary' ways of contributing to society, and where the aim is to enhance individual or public health, the societal claim is even weaker.

While most would agree that the scientific community is best placed to make the call for research participants, it is also the group where historically we can detect the greatest number of conflicts of interest. Participants are generally needed to advance the scientists' knowledge and career, which is why independent monitoring is needed. Research governance frameworks and ethics codes can mitigate but not resolve this problem. The ideal—to recruit all participants from within the research community—would be neither practical nor scientifically useful. However, in an inversion of normal 'market' behaviour, the principles applying to scientists as test subjects can equally apply to other research participants: they should be persons 'where a maximum of identification, understanding, and spontaneity can be expected', and should be selected, in descending order, from 'among the most highly motivated, the most highly educated, and the least "captive" members of the community'.[16] Yet why should the standard be so high? Why should research participants be afforded greater protection and consideration than, for example, soldiers serving their nation in time of war? Here, finally, is the crux of the matter. The essential problem with experimental research, compared to other 'services' society can demand from individuals, especially in a national emergency, is that it requires the human subject to be turned into a passive token object, a thing on which a token action is performed. Whatever the circumstances of his or her recruitment, and risks faced on the battlefield, a soldier still has the capacity to act as a person in a real world scenario; he or she is 'not a token and not a thing'.[17] At the heart of human experimentation lies an inherent process of depersonalization, objectification, and at times, as we have seen, dehumanization. According to Jonas, this means that the 'surrender of one's body to medical experimentation is entirely outside the enforceable "social contract"'.[18] Historians are thus called upon to reconstruct the depersonalized context in which medical science operates in order as far as possible to restore the personhood of participants. This task is made particularly challenging in the field of military medicine and state-controlled science, where the work is all too often shrouded in secrecy, and where secrecy itself often becomes a powerful epistemic tool for the creation of new realities.[19]

To understand what motivates humans to take part in experiments, it is not sufficient to focus exclusively on public rights and duties towards society. We need to learn more about people's sense of moral obligation and moral conscience. A person's inner 'calling' to undertake medical experiments may be based on their 'compassion with human suffering, zeal for humanity, reverence for the Golden Rule, enthusiasm for progress, homage to the cause of knowledge' or any other worthy cause.[20] The research community needs reminding from time to time not to exploit this 'sacred source'. Even if the motives are more mundane, as in the case of the Porton veterans, most of whom longed for little more than a change of scenery, extra pocket money, or a free rail pass to spend time with family and friends, what matters is that the human being is able to act and decide in an autonomous and informed fashion. In debating what society can and cannot afford, Jonas was adamant 'that society would indeed be threatened by the erosion of those moral values whose loss, possibly caused by too ruthless a pursuit of scientific progress, would make its most dazzling triumphs not worth having'.[21]

This is where we can employ another conceptual lever to assess the ethics of research practices in past societies and different research settings, not by entering into the opaque world of human and collective morality, which is difficult to understand at the best of times, but by applying the principle of 'reasonableness'. To what extent was the intended action, in our case an experiment or a series of experiments on human subjects, 'reasonable', as the scientists may have believed them to be? Unless serious doubt can be cast on the sincerity of the researchers planning and executing the experiments—not an easy thing to demonstrate on the basis of the historical material alone, and without talking to the scientists themselves—the intended action, in this case the research, can be measured only against existing rules and regulations governing, informing, or guiding the conduct of medical science, for example the Nuremberg Code. Was it 'reasonable' to justify, sanction, promote, enable, or conduct the experiment under the conditions of the time? Were the risks involved 'proportionate' to the expected outcomes? What was known about the risks involved prior to the start of the tests? Did what was known about the risks encompass everything that could have been known by the scientists? What were the unknown risks at the time and how much was known about them? If more could have been known about the risks, existing or potential methodological flaws, or other 'known unknowns', as opposed to 'unknown unknowns', why had that knowledge not been obtained by, or communicated to, those responsible for the design of the experiment? Was the information given to participants to encourage them to volunteer, and obtain their consent, partial and incomplete and, if so, was this intentional? The principle of reasonableness allows us to look at what can be a highly elusive interface between actions deemed to be permissible and those deemed impermissible. This marginal space is key to whether research could be, or in the past has been, pushed over the ethical threshold into legal territory concerned with issues of negligence, bodily harm, or criminal manslaughter.

The book has given much prominence to the role of memory. It has documented and brought to life largely forgotten 'medical memories' of servicemen involved in military experiments, a concept which has evolved from the idea of 'traumatic memory'. Whereas the latter has been more widely applied in debates about the Holocaust and other large-scale injustices, the concept of 'medical memories' relates more specifically to the circumstances of those who experienced past events and environments of a medical or experimental nature, but where the potential for psychological scarring may have been proportionally less severe. Medical memories can incorporate an element of trauma, nevertheless, especially where research participants have been exposed to different types of psychological agents. Most people, it appears, are less likely to suppress 'medical memories' to the realm of the subconscious than they are to suppress severe or prolonged trauma, and they are often able and willing to express their experiences clearly and coherently. The concept of 'medical memories', then, refers to the totality of medical and health-related societal recollections and traditions relating to personal and collective well-being, including those which provide us with an understanding of how different medical ethics cultures developed in civilian and military research environments. Such memorialization is not restricted to textual or oral witness testimony, but can find expression in material artefacts, instruments, and visual representations. Through an analysis of medical memories, this study has aimed to enhance our understanding of people's lives at the time of the events described, their motivations and aspirations; to explain the reasons and justification strategies used by scientists who conducted thousands of toxic tests on human beings; and to see how people came to agree to take part in tests, sometimes with serious consequences for their health and well-being. It may serve to inform those wishing to take part in human trials, not as a warning from history, but as a way of improving their conditions and making them aware of their rights to full disclosure. It has been an attempt to write a history of modern medical ethics from a social and political perspective, one in which the history of secret science has been comprehensively contextualized within the medical memories of the twentieth and twenty-first centuries.

The type of research described in this book affected the personal and working lives of human beings, and resulted in ill-health, uncertainty, and suffering. The book has looked at the tension between expertise and experience in the secret laboratories of the past. The complex tapestry presented here of often forgotten memories, some about large-scale outdoor experiments and some about laboratory experiments, form an integral part of a lived experience so frequently overlooked in official military histories. For some, such as the French political scientist Pierre Nora, any reference to narrated memory is inextricably linked to the Shoah, the systematic extermination of European Jewry during the Second World War; for others, debates about memory are a mirror image of national politics, a process closely interconnected with identity formation. For Primo Levi, a trained chemist and Auschwitz survivor, who after the war experienced the sensation that he was living 'without being alive', both aspects of narrated memory happened to be true. By bringing his Holocaust experience to life, by bearing witness to what seemed so incomprehensible, not during or shortly after the event like the diarist Victor Klemperer, but in retrospect, from memory, first through public story-telling whilst travelling on crowded trains between Turin and Milan—a cathartic, self-absorbed process to rediscover hidden fragments of the past and of himself—and then in poems and powerful personal narratives such as *Se questo è un uomo* (*If this is a Man*), Levi tried to capture the essence of what it meant to be a human being.[22] Trying to overcome feelings of guilt at having survived the camps, he began a semi-spiritual journey to understand those who had shown no sense of compassion for their fellow men; for him, story-telling turned into a vehicle to explain what seemed so completely inexplicable.

It is through the generation of time, chronopoiesis, that Levi wanted to convey the enormity of human suffering in the camps, but this brought him face to face with the painful paradox that those who had witnessed events and were able to narrate them to others after the war were not the true witnesses; the true witnesses were the *sommersi*, the drowned rather than the saved, those whose physical and spiritual existence had been eradicated from the face of the earth, extinguished, as if they had never existed in the first place. By consciously creating and manipulating time, Levi produced an artificial world in which readers could relive the human experience of the camps. For him, the loss of time in the narrative became a powerful metaphor for the extent to which human beings associated with the camps had lost their humanity and human dignity. No one had any time any longer, he wrote: 'For us, history has stopped.' The victims, those who were intimidated, traumatized, and violated on a daily basis no longer possessed any history, any prospect of telling a story in order to create meaning for what seemed so utterly meaningless. What defined their existence was the unbearable present, which is why important sections of *If this is a Man* were written in the present tense, not as a literary device to bring readers closer to the action, but as a reflection of human despair. The notion that humans might have a future, have hope, is linked to temporality and narrative depth, as Levi makes plain at the end of the book by returning to the past tense, the language of historical narrative. Understanding and explaining human relations, their interaction, and forms of communication through story-telling is a central theme of Levi's literary oeuvre.

The same is true for the present study. It has been, by any measure, a 'moderately paced story' from a temporal perspective. It has incorporated the multi-layered textures, inter-personal connections, and constantly evolving contours of modern research ethics in different institutional and national settings as a way of highlighting ambiguity and inconsistency, rather than following an undisturbed linear progression. In this sense, the approach of the book resembles in many respects Paul Klee's painting *Hauptweg und Nebenwege* ('Highway and Byways') from 1929, the year the world became engulfed in a global economic crisis, when existing capitalist orthodoxies lost their currency and plunged Western democracies into a prolonged crisis. Klee's painting invites the viewer to undertake a journey away from the main road on byways full of colour and surprise. The present narrative has likewise consciously resisted being hurried along the 'highway'; it has taken its time, so to speak, to provide temporal space for the sources to be explored; it has been history and memory in the making. 'Speed destroys space, and it erases temporal distance', Huyssen points out in his analysis of today's memorial culture, in which the distinction between fact and fiction, reality and perception has not only become blurred, but replaced with simultaneity, simulation, and postmodern imagination, a process as intellectually dissatisfying as channel-flicking or prolonged internet browsing.[23] For a subject as sensitive and contentious as this one, on the other hand, temporal distance is required whenever the aim is true understanding rather than spectacle or 'infotainment'. So this book has not been about memory as a vehicle of forgetting, bringing the suffering of research participants into the present before 'flicking' to another subject and thus legitimizing historical amnesia. It has also not been about the 'imagination' or 'normalization' of an uncomfortable reality in order to construct a more 'usable past' for different stakeholders. Instead it has been concerned with how we remember the past, and how we can arrive at a representation of the past which is as much attuned to subjectivity and historical empathy as it is to temporal distance as a precondition for a dispassionate and critical analysis. For Levi, the Third Reich engaged in a relentless 'war against memory, an Orwellian falsification of memory, falsification of reality, negation of reality'.[24] The aim throughout this book has been to resist the flight from reality, the negation of historical truth, however unfashionable or uncomfortable it may appear to some.

Before being accepted into the Chemical Kommando at Auschwitz, which presented an opportunity to secure his survival, Levi was interrogated by the German engineer Wilhelm Pannwitz, tall, blond, without any sense of empathy.[25] It was the experience of being observed, scientifically, seemingly objectively, yet coldly, as a thing that might 'contain some utilizable element', which intrigued but also deeply troubled him. He asked himself how Pannwitz 'really functioned as a man; how he filled his time, outside of the Polymerization and the Indo-Germanic conscience'. He thought about the time when he would walk again as a free man, hoping to 'meet him again, not from a spirit of revenge, but merely from a personal curiosity about the human soul'. Indeed, Levi tried to find Pannwitz after the war, only to discover that he had died of a brain tumour. It was that look between them which had etched itself on his mind, since it was not one between two men: 'If I had known how completely to explain the nature of that look, which came as if across the glass window of an aquarium between two beings who live in different worlds, I would also have explained the essence of the great insanity of the third Germany.'[26] It is in the objectification of human beings, their reduction into things, that Levi detected explanatory potential for the Holocaust. The Polymerization Department became a fitting metaphor for Auschwitz as one 'giant laboratory experiment designed to transform the substance of mankind'.[27] In *If this is a Man*, Levi does not see himself as a conscientious archivist tasked with documenting human encounters, but as a literary scholar weaving together a range of artistic influences into a powerful tapestry of human existence.[28] It is through a combination of real encounters, relived memory, and literary invention that Levi has merged historical documentation with autobiography to construct Dantesque landscapes of human experience.

For historical story-telling, however, as in the case of this book, caution needs to be exercised to avoid its wandering off into the realm of literary fiction. The material in this account, however powerful in its emotional significance and relevant to writing a history of medical ethics, had to be anchored within the political and military history of Britain's nonconventional weapons programme. What a book of this nature could do was to examine a broad range of contemporary sources in conjunction with the retrospective recollections of veterans, scientists, and civil servants, and their memoirs and witness testimonies, in order not only to reconstruct how experiments were experienced, or remembered in retrospect, but to gain greater insight into the relationship between secret scientists and test subjects. To avoid any misunderstanding, this has not been an attempt to pitch Allied against Nazi scientists by highlighting similarities in professional mentalities, as a way of rationalizing the enormity of the crime, or worse, to relativize the degree of culpability of Nazi scientists for medical atrocities. Not unlike Levi's oeuvre, though, this book has looked at how Allied scientists in charge of human trials functioned as human beings, away from the immediacy of their laboratories, in negotiations over policy, status, and resources, how they viewed the servicemen destined for field experiments, and explained changing patterns of ethical decision-making. How did they make sense of the world around them, their secret science environment, how did they explain and justify to themselves, their colleagues, friends, and relatives the work they were undertaking week by week, year by year? A nuanced, albeit often fragmented historical narrative, in which the past contains multiple alternatives, can enhance our understanding of the development of military medical ethics as a precondition for measured reform. Progress, however contested a term that may be, Ignatieff argues, can be achieved through the realization that 'Pannwitz was wrong: our species is one, and each of the individuals who compose it is entitled to equal moral consideration.'[29] This, we have argued here, holds equally true for ethical progress that defines the relationship between physician-scientists and patient-subjects, independently of the context in which the two happen to meet.

At the same time, the evidence presented has highlighted how painfully slow, uncoordinated, and protracted such a process has been in the past. According to Ignatieff, a human rights regime in which human agency is sufficiently guaranteed serves as a way of protecting human beings against abuse, degradation, and oppression. This ideal typical model has rarely corresponded to the historical realities in human subject research during the twentieth century, despite being reflected in Article 7 of the International Covenant on Civil and Political Rights and other human rights treaties since 1945.[30] We need to recognize that the proliferation of human rights in medicine and science has historically been inconsistent, nationally and culturally diverse and often ineffectively implemented, even more so in research environments operating under conditions of great secrecy.

International biomedical research ethics has recently become the focus of the Presidential Commission for the Study of Bioethical Issues, which investigated unethical research practices by US scientists in Guatemala in the 1940s.[31] Military medical ethics, however, has largely been outside the purview of the Commission,[32] which has been tasked to assure the US government that 'current rules for research participants protect people from harm or unethical treatment'. It remains to be seen whether this will become more than simply an aspiration within tightly controlled military research environments.[33] As Amy Gutmann, chair of the commission, puts it,

> we must look to and learn from the past so that we can assure the public that scientific and medical research today is conducted in an ethical manner. Research with human subjects is a sacred trust. Without public confidence, participation will decline and critical research will be stopped. It is imperative that we get this right.[34]

Such statements of intent require international and cross-disciplinary collaboration, political compromise, and resources to ensure the monitoring of sufficiently robust safety standards in military medicine. In the long term, a greater knowledge and understanding of the work undertaken in top-secret military research facilities, such as offered in the present study, may help scholars to recommend, through medical ethics training and education, constructive changes that are acceptable to military scientists and the authorities alike.[35] These communities need to realize that research performed in an ethically responsible manner neither lacks in quality nor undermines national security; rather, it has the added virtue of being seen as 'clean' and thus enjoying broad political support, once scholars are

permitted to discuss the work more openly, thereby protecting governments from legal liability and public embarrassment in an environment in
which financial prudence and stability is going to have a high priority.

In a world in which access to almost any conceivable information is
apparently readily available on the internet, and in which members of the
public are led to believe that democratic participation can be achieved by
texting, blogging, or Skyping their views into virtual online fora, any revelation or 'rediscovery' of past state secrets, however unsubstantiated, will not
only attract large audiences—measured in the number of comments or
website hits—but probably also fuel existing or emerging conspiracy theories. Under the leadership of Sir Richard Evans and other senior scholars,
Cambridge University launched in 2012 a research project on the interrela-
tionship between conspiracy, democracy, and the internet that goes against
the grain of constructing glorified, yet narrowly focused narratives of past
national achievements. The present study has similarly taken its own direction, one which neither vilifies nor unjustifiably idealizes or apologizes.
Balanced history writing that knows neither fear nor favour may not make
a great impact in periods of sustained austerity, but it is needed if we, as
society, wish to continue to strive towards greater understanding. It is what
makes scholarship relevant.

The year 2014, as I write, has seen the start of four years of stage-managed
collective remembrance and national catharsis about the First World War—
one in which children and youth are to be enrolled in ever larger numbers
as a way of constructing powerful imageries of generational continuity. We
are not only set to become the unintended witnesses in the sentimental
outpourings of people's emotions, but will have to endure the products of
consumer kitsch, including 'chocolate helmets' and 'Passchendaele Beer', on
an unprecedented scale. In short, public and political debates about the tools
and ethics underpinning the modern machinery of war are likely to be
sentimentally rather than historically informed. Already in the late 1920s,
critics of an emerging 'war tourism' such as Stefan Zweig warned of the risk
of trivializing the suffering of millions through 'must-see' visits to the battlefields of Flanders. Ypres, the 'tragically famous town' flourishing on little
more than its cemeteries, had become a place of pilgrimage for tens of
thousands of members of the British Empire; yet Zweig also praised the
process of remembrance and drew attention to the great responsibility that
recent history had placed upon the shoulders of the European people and
their leaders: 'only when we face up to it with strength and full awareness

will we do justice to our painful past, and hence to our future'.[36] The sheer number of names of those killed by high explosives, gas warfare, and other methods of destruction was so overwhelming that 'language turned into ornament', Zweig noted.[37] Memorials dedicated to the First World War had turned into monuments opposing war as a rational means of conflict resolution. Rather than idealizing notions of heroism and self-sacrifice in literary accounts of the 'Great War', large sections of postwar European societies were longing for a period of political stability, economic prosperity, and peaceful collaboration between nations, a longing with which many in the financially unstable, conflict-ridden global community of the twenty-first century are likely to sympathize.

Endnotes

CHAPTER I

1. MI, Transcript, Day 1; see also Schmidt 2006; Schmidt 2007b.
2. MI, Transcript, Day 1, p. 103.
3. MI, Folder 2A, Exhibit MNJ/20/1, Ministry of Supply (MoS), 'Report of a Court of Inquiry into Death of Maddison', May 1953, pp. 84–142, here p. 107. 'Observer' was the term used by the military to refer to human experimental subjects: see Chapter 2.
4. MI, Folder 1A, Witness Statement Alfred Thomas Thornhill, 25 July 2003.
5. MI, Transcript, Day 1, pp. 99f.; also pp. 108ff.
6. Barnett 2003; also McCamley 2006, p. 145; see also MI, Folder 1A, Witness Statement Alfred Thomas Thornhill, 25 July 2003.
7. A report, written in 1984, suggested that 'too vigorous dosing with atropine' may have contributed to Maddison's death, yet this was not a line of inquiry the 2004 inquest felt worth pursuing. CDE Technical Note No. 605, R.J. Moylan-Jones, 'Experience in Man with Nerve Agents with Reference to Generalised Symptoms—A Review and Proposals for Further Experiment', April 1984. I am indebted to Alan Care for supplying this document; for the use of atropine as a poison and as an antidote see Emsley 2008, pp. 46–67.
8. MI, Transcript, Day 1, pp. 43ff.; also MI, Folder 2D, Exhibit MPG/36, Extracts from Observers Chamber Tests Book, 20 December 1950–31 May 1954, p. 14; MI, Folder 2D, Exhibit MPG/45, Extracts from Observers Summary Book, 14 July 1950–23 August 1959, pp. 17–36, here p. 33.
9. Cholinesterase inhibition refers to inhibition of the acetylcholinesterase enzyme, which is of fundamental importance for the functioning of the peripheral and central nervous systems.
10. The book is the result of a project, funded by the Wellcome Trust, on 'Cold War at Porton Down: Medical Ethics and the Legal Dimension of Britain's Biological and Chemical Warfare Programme, 1945–1989'. I am grateful to the Wellcome Trust for their generous support.
11. Historical Survey of the Porton Down Volunteer Programme (London, MoD, unpublished manuscript, 2006), hereafter Historical Survey 2006, p. xi (Table 1); see also Figure 5 in Chapter 10.
12. University of Kent (UoK), Porton Archive, A105.11.2, Maddison, MoD Correspondence, Bolton (MoD) to author, 15 May 2001.

13. UoK, Porton Archive, A105.11.2, Maddison, MoD Correspondence, Bolton (MoD) to author, 15 May 2001.
14. Historical Survey 2006.
15. Hammond, Carter 2002, p. 212. The argument looked remarkably similar to the official line taken by the UK government over half a century earlier to justify carefully managed media reporting about non-conventional weapons research; Balmer 2002.
16. Suskind 2004; see also Chomsky 2012, epigraph; Gray 2012.
17. Senate Select Committee on Intelligence 2014; also Ackerman et al. 2014; for the involvement of health professionals in CIA torture practices see Physicians for Human Rights 2014.
18. Chivers 2014.
19. Quoted from 'Exchange between Hagel and Congress on Chemical Weapons Exposures in Iraq', *The New York Times*, 6 November 2014.
20. Sharp 2006, p. 632.
21. Sharp 2006, p. 631.
22. Proctor 1992, p. 24.
23. Moreno 1999, p. 16.
24. Moreno 2007.
25. Levidow 1990; Balmer 2004.
26. Moreno 2007; Gross 2013; Moreno 1999; Moreno 2006; Moreno 2011; Schmidt 2012b.
27. Lederer 1995; Elkeles 1996; Tröhler, Reiter-Theil 1998; Roelcke, Maio 2004; Eckart 2006; Schmidt 2007a; Schmidt, Frewer 2007; Frewer, Schmidt 2014.
28. Annas, Grodin 1992; Katz 1996; Katz 1997; Tröhler, Reiter-Theil 1998; Frewer, Wiesemann 1999; Frewer 2000; Roelcke, Maio 2004; Schmidt 2004; Eckart 2006; Goodman et al. 2003; LaFleur et al. 2007; Schmidt 2007a; Schmidt 2007b; Schmidt 2007c; Schmidt, Frewer 2007; Schmidt 2009a, Schmidt 2009b; Frewer 2010; Frewer, Rothhaar 2010; Frewer, Schmidt 2014.
29. Nie et al. 2010; also Felton 2012; Williams, Wallace 1989.
30. These issues recently stood at the forefront of discussions to mark the fiftieth anniversary of the Declaration of Helsinki at an international conference on 'Research within Bounds: Protecting Human Participants in Modern Medicine and the Declaration of Helsinki', organized by U. Schmidt, A. Frewer, D. Sprumont, and S. Fluss, Brocher Foundation, Hermance, 12/13 September 2013. See Schmidt, Frewer 2007; Schmidt, Frewer 2014a; Schmidt, Frewer 2014b; Frewer, Schmidt 2014. An edited collection of articles about the history of the Declaration of Helsinki, to be published by Oxford University Press, is currently in preparation.
31. Gross 2006, pp. 245-86, here p. 246.
32. See Guillemin 2005; Rappert 2006; Rappert 2007; Rappert 2009; L.I. Lutwick, S.M. Lutwick 2009; Moreno 2013; Avery 2013.
33. See, for example, Spiers 1986; Balmer 2001; Coleman 2005; Tucker 2006; Wheelis, Lajos, Dando 2006; Spiers 2010.

34. See Müller 1980; Groehler 1989; Geissler 1999; Houghton 2004; Schmaltz 2005; Vilensky 2005; Vivian 2009.

35. Bryden 1989; Pechura, Rall 1993; United States Advisory Committee on Human Radiation Experiments 1995.

36. Goodwin 1998; Evans, R. 2000a; see also Plunkett 2007.

37. Welsome 1999; Moreno 1999; also Goliszek 2003; Smith 2008; Lindee 2011; Smith 2011; Lederer 2011; Reagan 2011; Masterson 2014.

38. Elliot et al. 2002.

39. Stockholm International Peace Research Institute (SIPRI) 1971–1975; for a history of Britain's disarmament see Walker 2012; see also Brian Balmer and Catriona McLeish's AHRC-funded project 'Understanding Biological Disarmament: The Historical Context of the Biological Weapons Convention (BWC)'.

40. Harris, Paxman 1982.

41. Cole 1988.

42. TNA, WO188/802, 'A History of Porton' (1960); WO188/785, 'A Brief History of the Chemical Defence Experimental Establishment Porton', March 1961. Its appendix includes 'The Early History of Porton' by J.F.S. Stone, a Porton scientist and amateur archaeologist, who died in 1957.

43. Carter 2000; also Carter 1991b; Carter, Pearson 1996b; Carter, Pearson 1999; Carter, Balmer 1999.

44. Hammond, Carter 2002.

45. Avery 2013; also Avery 2006; Avery 1998.

46. Zuckerman 1966; Craughwell 2010.

47. Parker 1996.

48. Edgerton 2011, p. 241.

49. Edgerton 2006; also Eisner 2000.

50. One such exception is Susan Lindee's work, which looks at the intricate relationship between science and different forms of violence; Lindee 2011.

51. McCamley 2006.

52. Balmer 2012.

53. Historical Survey 2006, pp. 111–27, pp. 140f.

54. National Archives and Records Administration (NARA), RG175, Chemical Warfare Service (1917–1963); RG544, US Army Materiel Command (1941–1973); also Balmer 2006a, pp. 716f.; Ede 2011.

55. Workshop on 'Cold War Science', German Historical Institute, Moscow, 29 November 2012.

56. Workshop on 'Cold War Science', German Historical Institute, Moscow, 29 November 2012.

57. Balmer 2006a, p. 692; for the nature and use of secret intelligence see Butler Review 2004, pp. 7ff.; also UoK, taped interview with Lord Butler of Brockwell, chairman of the Committee of Privy Counsellors who reviewed the intelligence on Iraq's weapons of mass destruction in 2004, 15 February 2008; taped interview with Dr David Langley, former Porton member of staff and senior

government science and policy adviser on chemical and biological warfare (CBW) matters, 8 January 2008; taped presentation by David Langley, 5 November 2008.

58. Chulov et al. 2013; Beaumont, Sample 2013.
59. Withnall 2013; also Tucker 2001; Rappert 2006, pp. 82ff.
60. Hammond, Carter 2002, pp. 211ff.
61. 'Whitehall' is shorthand for the part of the British civil service that is involved in government.
62. In 2004, the author was appointed historical expert to HM Coroner for Wiltshire and Swindon at the inquest looking into the death of Ronald Maddison (Maddison Inquest, abbreviated to MI). Unless stated otherwise, the material presented derives from the 'Exhibits' that were supplied to the interested parties and from the Inquest 'Transcript'; Schmidt 2006; Schmidt 2007b; Schmidt 2012a.
63. See, for instance, MI, Folders 2A–2G.
64. Carter 1995.
65. Balmer 2002.
66. Balmer 2002.
67. For recent debates on military medical ethics see Gross, Carrick 2013.
68. Balmer 2006a.
69. Edgerton 2002
70. Schmidt 2004, p. 280.
71. Weiss 2010, p. 173.

CHAPTER 2

1. For some of the scholarship on the history of biological and chemical warfare since the First World War see SIPRI 1971; Harris, Paxman 1982; Haber 1986; Richter 1994; Evans, R. 2000a; Balmer 2001; Hammond, Carter 2002; Wheelis et al. 2006; Tucker 2006; Schmidt 2006; Schmidt 2007b; Schmidt, Frewer 2007; Spiers 2010. For the use of chlorine in 1915 see also Cowell et al. 2007. A shorter version of this chapter has previously been published as Schmidt 2012a.
2. IWM, private papers J.D. Keddie (998), Keddie to his mother, 4 May 1915; also MacDonald 1993, p. 194. For a survey of soldiers and civilians who witnessed the first gas attack in modern history see Dendooven 2005.
3. Szöllösi-Janze 1998, p. 318; Piet Chielens from the Flanders Fields Museum, Ypres, Belgium, has recently suggested that the number of 'casualties' of the German gas attack near the Belgian town of Ypres in April 1915 was significantly lower than previously assumed; Chielens 2014; also Corrigan 2003, pp. 164–5.
4. Buffetaut 2008.
5. Harris, Paxman 1982, p. 10.
6. Haber 1924, pp. 25–41, here p. 35. In the epigraph to the first edition of their book *A Higher Form of Killing*, published in 1982 by Chatto & Windus Ltd,

Harris and Paxman suggest that Haber referred to the use of poison gas in war as 'a higher form of killing' in his acceptance speech for the Nobel Prize for Chemistry in 1919. His Nobel Lecture, however, delivered in June 1920, focuses almost exclusively on 'the synthesis of ammonia from its elements' and does not contain the German equivalent of the phrase, i.e. *eine höhere Form des Tötens*. In the second edition of the book, published in 2002 by Arrow Books, the authors changed the wording of the epigraph's reference, which now said: 'Professor Fritz Haber, winner of the Nobel Prize for Chemistry, inventor of chemical warfare, 1923'. However, Haber's lectures of that year, especially on 'Chemistry in War' and 'On the History of Gas Warfare', likewise do not contain the phrase. Since no documented evidence has so far come to light suggesting that Haber used the phrase, at least not in public, and since the phrase appears to have become common currency in debates over chemical and biological warfare only *after* Harris and Paxman published the book with that title, the two authors, one of whom is a known writer of fiction, may well have 'invented' it at the time of publishing the first edition as a fitting shorthand for the so-called 'inventor' of modern chemical warfare, i.e. Haber, and then failed to retract it because of its widespread use in the literature and by the mass media; see Harris, Paxman 1982; Harris, Paxman 2002; Haber 1924, pp. 25–41 and 76–92. Haber's biographer, Prof Margit Szöllösi-Janze, was likewise unable to attribute the phrase to Haber, which is why she did not use it in her book; see Szöllösi-Janze 1998.

7. For Haber's biography see Szöllösi-Janze 1998; Stolzenberg 2004; Charles 2005; see also the account by his son Lutz F. Haber in Haber 1986.
8. See Welch, Fox 2012.
9. Harrison 2010, pp. 106–9.
10. Jones et al. 2008, p. 1420.
11. Shephard 2000, p. 64.
12. Shephard 2000, p. 64.
13. Shephard 2000, p. 64; for the debate about 'hysteria' see Lerner 2003, pp. 61–85.
14. Wellcome Trust Library (WL), Archives and Manuscripts, RAMC/739/6, 'Diary: At Bailleul with No. 8 Casualty Clearing Station', 17 June 1916, frame 148f.; also Wittmann 2005.
15. I am grateful to Dominiek Dendooven for sharing this source with me; In Flanders Fields Museum, Documentation Centre, Toudy papers; also Dendooven 2005.
16. Roberts 2001, pp. 220ff.
17. Buffetaut 2008, pp. 18ff.; Tucker 2006, p. 11; Terraine 1992, pp. 155ff.; Foulkes 1934, p. 31.
18. Hobbs et al. 2007, pp. 256–61.
19. Tucker 2006, p. 13.
20. Convention (II) with Respect to the Laws and Custom of War on Land and its Annex: Regulations Concerning the Laws and Customs of War on Land. The Hague, 29 July 1899.

21. Tucker 2006, pp. 10f.
22. Harris, Paxman 1982, p. 5.
23. SIPRI 1971, p. 231.
24. Buffetaut 2008, p. 20.
25. Foulkes 1934, p. 19; also Carter 2000, p. 2, who misquotes French in this instance.
26. Foulkes 1934, pp. 19f.; Harris, Paxman 1982, p. 5; Hobbs et al. 2007, pp. 260; also TNA, WO142/241, correspondence between Sir John French and Lord Kitchener, 23–24 April 1915.
27. For John S. Haldane see Douglas 1936; Sturdy 1987; Goodman 2008; Sturdy 2011; see also Haldane 1925, p. 63, who recounts how his father was sent to France to identify the gas which the Germans had used.
28. Sturdy 1998.
29. Thorpe 1936, p. 525; also Foulkes 1934, p. 37.
30. TNA, WO188/802, p. 1.
31. TNA, WO188/802, p. 1.
32. Hobbs et al. 2007, p. 260; TNA, CAB 37/127/40, Asquith to George V, 26 April 1915.
33. SIPRI 1971, pp. 231ff.
34. *The Times*, 29 April 1915, p. 9; also UoK, Porton Archive, A201, WWI CW Media Articles.
35. *Daily Mirror*, 29 April 1915.
36. The *Frankfurter Zeitung*, 26 April 1915; quoted from SIPRI 1971, p. 232.
37. See also Spiers 2010, p. 40.
38. Graves 1919, p. 34.
39. IWM, private papers N. Noble (854), Chance to Noble, 9 May 1915.
40. For Foulkes see Hobbs et al. 2007, pp. 271–5; Harris, Paxman 1982, pp. 7–22; Foulkes 1934, p. 17.
41. Foulkes 1934, pp. 39f.; see also SIPRI 1971, p. 233.
42. Harris, Paxman 1982, p. 21.
43. Van Bergen 2012.
44. Quoted from Hobbs et al. 2007, p. 261.
45. See Lloyd 2006.
46. Hobbs et al. 2007, pp. 260f.; also Spiers 1986, p. 24.
47. SIPRI 1971, pp. 234f.
48. Sturdy 1998.
49. See, for example, WL, PP/CLE/A.9, Jodrell Chair; PP/CLE/A.11.
50. Green 1948.
51. For Lovatt-Evans see WL, PP/CLE/A.11, Service at Porton Experimental Station, Wiltshire, during the Second World War; for J.A. Sadd, who worked at Porton Down up until the early 1950s, see Carter 2000, p. 14; see also Sturdy 1998, pp. 67ff.; Dudley later became Chairman of Porton's Ethics Committee.
52. 'The German gas attack against the Allies . . . resulted in a rapid decision by the Allies to retaliate. This necessitated the British finding and establishing a trial

ground on which possible methods of gas attack could be studied, and methods of defence investigated. So was Porton born';TNA,WO188/802, p. 1.

53. TNA,WO142/264, Lt Col A.W. Crossley RE, 'The Royal Engineers Experimental Station, Porton' (1919); also TNA,WO188/802, p. 1; Carter 2000, p. 3.

54. TNA, WO142/264, Lt Col A.W. Crossley RE, 'The Royal Engineers Experimental Station, Porton' (1919), pp. 3f. Work at the Station is believed to have commenced on 7 March 1916 when the first officer from the Royal Engineers reported for permanent duty.

55. During the war, Porton was divided into four departments: the Commandant, the Division Officer Royal Engineers, the Works Department, and the Experimental Department. While the Division Officer Royal Engineers was responsible for the general upkeep of the facility, the Works Department, line-managed by the Superintendent of Experimental Grounds, carried out the construction work through civilian labourers. By 1918, the Experimental Department was divided into six sections: the Chemical Laboratory, the Anti-Gas Department, the Physiology Laboratory, the Meteorological Station, the Experimental Battery RA, and the Experimental Company RE; TNA, WO188/802, p. 3, pp. 10f.; for Crossley see TNA, WO142/264, Lt Col A.W. Crossley RE, 'The Royal Engineers Experimental Station, Porton' (1919).

56. TNA,WO188/802, p. 10; McCamley 2006, p. 97.

57. TNA,WO188/802, p. 20.

58. Harris, Paxman 1982, p. 22.

59. Mustard gas, or dichlorodiethyl sulphide, was code-named 'H' or 'HS'. Lewisite, or chlorovinyl dichloroarsine, was code-named 'L'. The other main chemical warfare agents tested during the war by Porton were code-named 'HT' or 'T724', 'HQ' or 'T1792', various nitrogen mustard agents ('HN-1'; 'HN-2' or 'S', 'T1024'; and 'HN-3' or 'T773'), 'ED' or Ethyl Dick, 'MD' or Methyl Dick and 'PD' or 'MA'. For the exact chemical names of the code-named warfare agents see Historical Survey 2006, p. 209.

60. For the properties of phosgene as a chemical warfare agent see Marrs et al. 1996, pp. 185–202.

61. Klee 1997, p. 269.

62. TNA,WO188/802, p. 3; see also Roughton 1949, p. 320.

63. McCamley 2006, p. 97.

64. TNA,WO188/802, p. 8.

65. Carter 2000, pp. 15f.

66. 'Oxbridge' is shorthand for the universities of Oxford and Cambridge (United Kingdom).

67. For the 'Old Portonians' see Carter 1995; Evans, R. 2000a, p. 30.

68. After suffering a stroke in 1968, Charles Lovatt Evans, who lived in the village of Winterslow, near Porton, moved into the Officers' Mess; De Burgh Daly, Gregory 1970, p. 248.

69. Carter 2000, p. 16; also TNA,WO188/802, pp. 149f.

70. Sturdy 1998.

71. During earlier work in the mining industry, Haldane developed respirators to protect miners and emergency personnel from the effects of toxic gases; see Douglas 1936, pp. 117ff.; Sturdy 1998.

72. TNA, WO188/802, pp. 14f.; also Carter 2000, p. 14. 'Hypo solution' refers to a crystalline substance, sodium hyposulphite, also known as sodium thiosulphate, which protects against chlorine.

73. Carter 2000, p. 14; see also TNA, WO188/802, pp. 7f., 14, 20.

74. Sulphur mustard (mustard gas) was first synthesized in the mid nineteenth century and developed as a chemical warfare agent during the First World War. For the chemical properties of sulphur mustard see Marrs et al. 1996, pp. 139–73.

75. Tucker 2006, p. 19; Klee 1997, p. 269; Groehler 1989, p. 72.

76. See also Sturdy 2011.

77. *BMJ*, Obituary, Charles Lovatt Evans, 3 (1968), 5619, pp. 684–5.

78. De Burgh Daly, Gregory 1970, p. 233, p. 246.

79. De Burgh Daly, Gregory 1970, p. 235.

80. De Burgh Daly, Gregory 1970, p. 236.

81. CHF, Archive Collection, GB98.09, Williams–Miles Reprint Collection, William Williams, Notebook: US Gas School, 1918.

82. On 16 September 1918, King George V visited Porton in recognition of the establishment's work during the Great War. Lovatt Evans remembered the visit to have taken place in late 1917 when 'King George V came on a visit to Porton, and I well remember a scrum in the mess that night, when I had a rib broken.' De Burgh Daly, Gregory 1970, p. 237; Carter 2000, p. 23.

83. Roughton 1949, pp. 322ff.

84. Roughton 1949, p. 333.

85. Garner 2003, p. 139.

86. Roughton 1949, p. 320; see also TNA, WO188/802, p. 17.

87. The decision was taken by the Chemical Advisory Committee under Barcroft's leadership: TNA, WO142/264, Lt Col A.W. Crossley RE, 'The Royal Engineers Experimental Station, Porton' (1919), pp. 11ff.; also TNA, WO188/802, p. 7; Sturdy 1998, p. 70.

88. During the First World War, Rudolph Peters worked as the medical officer under A.E. Kent, who was in charge of offensive chemical warfare on sections of the front controlled by the British First Army, and who later made the first attempt at writing an official history of Porton; others included A.E. Boycott, J. Saw-Dunn, Capt Hunt and Harold Hartley, who later joined the War Office; TNA, WO188/802, p. 7.

89. Thompson, Ogston 1983, p. 499.

90. Garner 2003, p. 138.

91. TNA, WO188/802, p. 15; see also Gibson 1941, pp. 321f.; for Pope see also IWM, Photographic Collection, Portrait W.J. Pope (1870–1939).

92. For a history of lewisite see Vilensky 2005.

93. Garner 2003, pp. 139f.

94. WL, M:QV662 1916G78m, 'Memorandum on Gas Poisoning in Warfare with Notes on its Pathology and Treatment', 20 July 1916; also GC/42/11/1, 'Memorandum on Gas Poisoning in Warfare with Notes on its Pathology and Treatment', 1 April 1918; Harrison 2010, pp. 106–9.

95. TNA, WO188/802, p. 16.

96. TNA, WO188/802, p. 15; for the testing of various toxic substances on human subjects in the 1920s see WO188/373, 'Experimental Station, Porton'. Section IV. 'Physiological & Medical Research. Quarterly Reports for the Years 1926 to 1928'.

97. Garner 2003, p. 141.

98. For Lovatt Evans' subsequent professional career see WL, PP/CLE/A.9, Jodrell Chair; PP/CLE/A.11, Service at Porton Experimental Station, Wiltshire, during the Second World War. Miscellaneous Correspondence re. Secondment and Service. For Barcroft's postwar career as a Reader in Physiology at Cambridge University see Roughton 1949. During the early 1920s, Peters worked with F.G. Hopkins, Malcolm Dixon, and J.B.S. Haldane at the Balfour Laboratory at Cambridge University; see Peters 1959.

99. Lt (later Maj) J.A. Sadd continued work as a senior civilian scientist at Porton until the 1950s. Lt Col W.A. Salt, Lt Col A.E. Kent, Capt S.J. Steadman, and Lt A.C. Peacock all worked at Porton Down after the Great War.

100. Spiers 2010, pp. 40f.

101. Michalski 2003, p. 122.

102. *Poems of the Great War, 1914–1918* (1998), pp. 30f.; see also Van Bergen 2012 for the poem 'Gas', written by the Belgian soldier Daan Boens.

103. Spiers 2010, p. 41.

104. Michalski 2003.

105. Silver 2010, pp. 15–51, here pp. 18ff.; Michalski 2003, pp. 53–69; also Crockett 1999, pp. 96–7; Presler 1992, pp. 94ff.

106. Silver 2010, pp. 18f; p. 174; see also Cotter 2010, p. C7.

107. Silver 2010, pp. 18f.; Presler 1992, pp. 94f.

108. Silver 2010, pp. 18f.

109. See also Spiers 2010, pp. 47–68.

110. Kershaw 1998, p. 136.

111. 'The use of asphyxiating, poisonous or other gases and all analogous liquids, materials or devices being prohibited, their manufacture and importation are strictly forbidden in Germany'; Treaty of Versailles, Article 171; Tucker 2006, p. 21; Hobbs et al. 2007, pp. 278f. Britain's proposal during the Versailles Treaty negotiations for full disclosure of Germany's wartime manufacturing processes was seen as an attempt at economic espionage, and rejected by the United States; see also SIPRI 1971, pp. 235f.

112. See SIPRI 1971, pp. 231–67, Chapter 3: 'Popular Attitudes towards CBW', 1919–39.

113. *The Times*, 29 November 1918, p. 6.

490 ENDNOTES TO PAGES 45–47

114. See Van Bergen 2012.
115. CHF, Archive Collection, GB98.09, Williams—Miles Reprint Collection, William Williams, Notebook: US Gas School, 1918.
116. CHF, The Edgewood Arsenal, Special Edition of *Chemical Warfare*, vol. 1, no. 5 (March 1919); for the origins of the CWS see Brophy, Fisher 1959; Ede 2011.
117. SIPRI 1971, pp. 239–42; Hobbs et al. 2007, p. 280; Van Bergen 2012.
118. SIPRI 1971, pp. 242ff.
119. Article 5 of the Washington Agreement stated: 'The use in war of asphyxiating, poisonous or other gases, and all analogous liquids, or materials, of devices, having been justly condemned by the general opinion of the civilized world, and a prohibition of such use having been declared in treaties to which a majority of the civilized powers are parties; now to the end that this prohibition shall be universally accepted as a part of international law, binding alike the conscience and practice of nations, the signatory powers declare their assent to such prohibition, agree to be bound thereby between themselves, and invite all other civilized nations to adhere thereto.'
120. Whereas the British representative pointed out that it is 'impossible to prevent a nation bent upon Chemical Warfare from making preparations in peacetime, no matter what the rules of war may be', the French Government reserved the right 'to act in accordance with the circumstances' if an enemy refused to give a guarantee not 'to use poison gas'; TNA, WO188/802, p. 48; Tucker 2006, p. 21; Hobbs et al. 2007, p. 280.
121. Subordinated to the Chemical Warfare Department, Porton shared responsibility for chemical warfare research with a number of supervisory committees and organizations, including the Chemical Warfare Committee and university research facilities.
122. Hansard, HC Debate, vol. 122 c60W, Experimental Ground, Porton, 1 December 1919.
123. For the total cost of Porton Down between 1919 and 1924 see Hansard, HC Debate, vol. 181 c1108, Chemical Warfare Research Department, 10 March 1925.
124. Hansard, HC Debate, vol. 130 c1063, Chemical Experimental Ground, 15 June 1920.
125. Hansard, HC Debate, vol. 152 c984W, Asphyxiating Gas (Washington Treaty), 27 March 1922.
126. UoK, Porton Archive, A207, 'Report of the Committee on Chemical Warfare Organization', 7 July 1919, p. 5; also TNA, WO188/802, p. 30. The Holland Committee was chaired by Lt Gen A.E.A. Holland and included Maj Gen W. Napier, Maj Gen H.F. Thuillier, Maj Gen Sir H.S. Jeudwine, Brig Gen C.H. Foulkes, Brig Gen H. Hartley, Brig Gen O.F. Philips, Lt Col J.D. Lavarack, Lt E.A. Hepburn, Capt A.L. Rossiter, Lt Col J.M. Prower (Canadian Forces), Cdr J.W. Scott, Lt Cdr R. Butcher, Cdr A.S. Langley, Sir William Pope, Prof A. Smithells, and J. Barcroft.

127. Subordinating field trials to the military requirements of war had, according to some, slowed down, if not inhibited, Britain's chemical warfare programme during the Great War; UoK, Porton Archive, A207, 'Report of the Committee on Chemical Warfare Organization', 7 July 1919, pp. 3ff.; TNA, WO188/802, p. 13, p. 17.

128. UoK, Porton Archive, A207, 'Report of the Committee on Chemical Warfare Organization', 7 July 1919, p. 5.

129. UoK, Porton Archive, A207, 'Report of the Committee on Chemical Warfare Organization', 7 July 1919, p. 5; TNA, WO188/802, pp. 30f.

130. UoK, Porton Archive, A207, 'Report of the Committee on Chemical Warfare Organization', 7 July 1919, p. 10; also TNA, WO188/802, pp. 30f.

131. In 1920, members of the Chemical Warfare Committee included: Joseph Barcroft (professor of physiology, Cambridge University), A.W. Crossley (former Commandant Porton and Director of the Cotton Industry Research Association), C.G. Douglas (physiologist, Oxford), Harold Hartley (chemist, Oxford), H. Levinstein (representative of Levinstein Limited, chemical manufacturers), Sir William Pope (professor of chemistry, Cambridge University), Jocelyn F. Thorpe (professor of organic chemistry at Imperial College and representative of the Department of Scientific and Industrial Research), A.M. Tyndall (professor of physics, Bristol University); see TNA, WO188/802, pp. 32ff.

132. See Carter, Pearson 1996b, pp. 60f.; Carter 2000, pp. 52f.

133. Historical Survey 2006.

134. See also French 1975; Rupke 1987; for animal experiments by the CWS see Ede 2011, p. 31.

135. See also Carter 2000, p. 10.

136. *BMJ*, 26 May 1923, p. 909.

137. 1924 was also the year in which ninety-two animals were used for a single experiment, the largest number involved in any one experiment during the interwar period; Hansard, HC Debate, vol. 181 cc1144–5W, Experimental Station, Porton, 10 March 1925; also vol. 237 c633W, Chemical Warfare (Experiments on Animals), 27 March 1930; vol. 251 c1466W, Chemical Warfare (Experiments on Animals), 28 April 1931.

138. House of Commons Parliamentary Papers Online, Cruelty to Animals Bill, 1876.

139. See IWM, Photographic Collection, Porton Down, c. 1916–1970s, which contains a number of images of experiments conducted on dogs.

140. See Hansard, HC Debate, vol. 199 cc897–8W, Chemical Warfare (Research and Experiments), 9 November 1926; vol. 210 c1154W, Chemical Warfare (Experiments), 17 November 1927; vol. 216 cc377–8W, Poison Gas (Experiments, Living Animals), 19 April 1928; vol. 244 cc486–7W, Animals (Experiments), 3 November 1930; vol. 244 cc652–3, Animals (Experiments), 4 November 1930; vol. 244 c1480W, Animals (Experiments), 11 November 1930;

vol. 265 c817W, Poison Gas Experiments, 2 May 1932; vol. 285 c965, Chemical Defence Experiments, 6 February 1934; vol. 351 cc1837–8W, Experiments on Living Animals (Poison Gas), 3 October 1939.

141. Hansard, HC Debate, vol. 199 cc897–8W, Chemical Warfare (Research and Experiments), 9 November 1926.

142. Hansard, HC Debate, vol. 244 cc486–7W, Animals (Experiments), 3 November 1930; vol. 244 cc652–3, Animals (Experiments), 4 November 1930.

143. See Woolf 1995; Wilkie, Penman 1995; Woolf 2010.

144. Hansard, HC Debate, vol. 252 cc213–14W, Research Experiments (Living Animals), 5 May 1931.

145. From 1921 to 1937, Porton performed a total of 2,927 experiments with rabbits, of which 1,672 were killed, 2,059 experiments with guinea pigs, of which 1,665 were killed, 1,233 experiments with mice, of which 1,027 were killed, and 782 tests with rats, of which 523 were killed; see Hansard, HC Debate, vol. 237 cc633W, 634–5W, Chemical Warfare (Experiments on Animals), 27 March 1930; vol. 303 cc171–3, Chemical Defence Experiments, 18 June 1935; vol. 342 cc50–1W, Chemical Warfare (Experiments on Animals), 28 November 1938.

146. Hansard, HC Debate, vol. 210 c1154W, Chemical Warfare (Experiments), 17 November 1927; also vol. 244 cc486–7W, Animals (Experiments), 3 November 1930; vol. 245 cc2414–15W, Experiments on Animals, Porton, 4 December 1930.

147. Hansard, HC Debate, vol. 210 c1154W, Chemical Warfare (Experiments), 17 November 1927.

148. Hansard, HC Debate, vol. 241 cc1483–4W, Poison Gas (Experiments on Animals), 17 July 1930.

149. Hansard, HC Debate, vol. 249 cc1007–74, 10 March 1931.

150. Carter 2000, p. 12.

151. Charcot 1889.

152. Foulkes 1934, pp. 272f.

153. TNA, WO188/802, p. 14 and p. 23; also TNA, WO142/264, Lt Col A.W. Crossley RE, 'The Royal Engineers Experimental Station, Porton' (1919), p. 82.

154. TNA, WO188/802, pp. 18f.

155. Foulkes 1934, pp. 272f.

156. TNA, WO188/802, pp. 57.

157. MI, Folder 2A/I, Exhibit MNJ/20/2, 'Memorandum on the Exposure to Gas of Personnel of the Chemical Warfare Experimental Station', 4 January 1924, pp. 130–3.

158. MI, Folder 2A/I, Exhibit MNJ/20/2, 'Memorandum on the Exposure to Gas of Personnel of the Chemical Warfare Experimental Station', 4 January 1924, pp. 130–3, here p. 133.

159. MI, Folder 2A/I, Exhibit MNJ/20/2, 'Memorandum on the Exposure to Gas of Personnel of the Chemical Warfare Experimental Station', 4 January 1924, pp. 130–3.

160. MI, Folder 2A/I, Exhibit MNJ/20/2, Extract from 'Third Annual Report of Chemical Defence Research Department (CDRD), March 1923, Exposure of Personnel to Gas for Experimental Purposes', p. 129.

161. MI, Folder 2A/I, Exhibit MNJ/20/2, 'Memorandum on the Exposure to Gas of Personnel of the Chemical Warfare Experimental Station', 4 January 1924, pp. 130-3.

162. MI, Folder 2A/I, Exhibit MNJ/20/2, 'Notes of Meeting held in Room 240 Lansdowne House at 11.00 a.m. on Tuesday 8 March 1955 to Discuss the Question of Remuneration of Service Volunteers Taking Part in Certain Tests at the Chemical Defence Experimental Establishment Porton' (and further correspondence), pp. 70-80; MI, Folder 2A/I, Exhibit MNJ/20/2, 'Fatality at Porton', 7 May 1953, p. 297. The extra pay service personnel received was as follows in 1924: 1s (approximately £1.50 at 2015 values) for each physiological test, 6d (approximately £0.75) for every breathing test, and 6d in cases where the volunteer was asked to grow a beard and be confined to barracks to test 'the effect of face-pieces'; see TNA, T162/507, War Office to Treasury, 2 January 1924; Treasury to War Office, 19 June 1924; Admiralty to Treasury, 8 August 1932; War Office to Treasury, 20 January 1939; War Office to Treasury, 15 April 1939; UoK, Porton Archive, A206, GB Pre-Cold War; Tests–Vets.

163. From 1927, all civilian employees working at Porton and Sutton Oak who suffered from disabilities due to gas poisoning had a right to be admitted to military hospitals free of charge, and be paid compensation if the injury arose as a result of their employment. This included those cases in which staff volunteered for tests involving toxic agents. TNA, T164/72/10 and T164/71/28; UoK, Porton Archive, A204, Porton Experimental History WWI to WWII; also MI, Folder 2A/I, Exhibit MNJ/20/2, 'Compensation for Injury or Death through Gas Poisoning on Duty' (and further correspondence), c. 1930/1931, pp. 139-41.

164. TNA, WO188/802, p. 61.

165. UoK, Porton Archive, A204, Porton Experimental History WWI to WWII.

166. TNA, WO286/11, War Office to General Officer, Commander-in-Chief, Southern Command, Salisbury, 30 July 1925.

167. TNA, WO286/11, Parliamentary Question, Poison Gas Experiments, 18 December 1930.

168. TNA, WO286/11, Parliamentary Question, Poison Gas Experiments, 18 December 1930.

169. UoK, Porton Archive, A204, Porton Experimental History WWI to WWII. 'Station (routine) orders' (SROs), normally displayed on mess notice boards, governed servicemen's daily lives.

170. UoK, Porton Archive, A204, Porton Experimental History WWI to WWII.

171. MI, Folder 2A/I, Exhibit MNJ/20/2, Col R.F. Look, Commandant, Experimental Station Porton, to the Chief Superintendent, CDRD, War Office, 24 January 1931 (and further correspondence), pp. 142-3.

172. Hansard, HC Debate, vol. 181 c1108, Chemical Warfare Research Establishment, 10 March 1925.

173. Hansard, HC Debate, vol. 245 cc1079–80, Chemical Warfare (Experiments), 25 November 1930.

174. Historical Survey 2006.

175. Hansard, HC Debate, vol. 245 cc1079–80, Chemical Warfare (Experiments), 25 November 1930.

176. See, for example, Hansard, HC Debate, vol. 272 cc811–12, Chemical Warfare, 30 November 1932; vol. 284 cc1469–70, Chemical Warfare (Defensive Measures), 21 December 1933; also SIPRI 1971, pp. 269.

177. TNA, WO188/802, p. 59.

178. TNA, WO188/802, p. 11.

179. Chemical Corps Association 1948, pp. 14ff.

180. UoK, Porton Archive, A205, Porton Experiments 1920s, Atkisson to Chief of CWS, Washington, 15 July 1924.

181. UoK, Porton Archive, A205, Porton Experiments 1920s, Atkisson to Chief of CWS, Washington, 15 July 1924.

182. UoK, Porton Archive, A205, Porton Experiments 1920s, Atkisson to Chief of CWS, Washington, 15 July 1924.

183. TNA, WO188/802, pp. 86–90.

184. TNA, WO188/802, pp. 86ff.

185. TNA, WO188/802, p. 88; see also Evans, R. 2007.

186. A pamphlet published by the League of Nations noted that 'everywhere except Germany, experiments in Chemical Warfare openly proceed ... It will not necessarily inflict more pain than high explosive, but will tend to aggravate the burden of war upon the civilian population'; TNA, WO188/802, p. 49.

187. Hobbs et al. 2007, pp. 261–5; for the debate in the Netherlands see Van Bergen 2012.

188. Balmer 2012, p. 32; Balmer 2002.

189. Harris, Paxman 1982, pp. 33f.

190. Tucker 2006, pp. 20f.

191. Hobbs et al. 2007, pp. 263f.

192. SIPRI 1971, pp. 234f.

193. Haldane 1925; Callinicus was the architect of Heliopolis, who discovered a 'burning liquid', named 'Greek fire', used by the Byzantine Greeks in naval warfare. Haldane referred to Callinicus as 'He who conquers in a noble or beautiful manner'; for J.B.S. Haldane see Clark 1984; Adams 2000; also Hobbs et al. 2007, pp. 268–71.

194. Haldane 1925, pp. 45f.

195. Haldane 1925, p. 7.

196. Haldane 1925, p. 82; Haldane's line of argument seems to have had a lasting legacy among some scholars of bioethics who have argued that the use of chemical or biological agents developed with the help of medical experts to

cause illness is 'not qualitatively different' from using high explosives to inflict injury; as long as neither of them causes 'unnecessary suffering', these weapons of war apparently do not violate the 'laws of humanity'. Scientists and doctors should therefore 'be free to develop both' unless chemical or biological weapons have the capability of causing mass destruction. Gross 2006, p. 256.

197. Haldane 1927, p. 190; also Haldane 1925, p. 27; also Hobbs et al. 2007, p. 271.

198. Haldane 1925, p. 82.

199. Hobbs et al. 2007, pp. 255–95, here pp. 286f.; for the use of tear gas in dealing with civil disturbances in the United States see SIPRI 1971, p. 270.

200. In 1991, the United Kingdom withdrew Part (2) of the reservations; see Sims 1992, p. 477.

201. See Schmidt 2006, pp. 366–80; also Schmidt 2007b.

202. Schmidt 2007b, pp. 288f.

203. Schmidt 2007, pp. 288f.

204. MI, Folder 2A/I, Exhibit MNJ/20/2, Expanded Statement (B), 19 November 1930, pp. 136–8.

205. TNA, WO286/11, Parliamentary Question No. 170, 18 December 1930.

206. MI, Folder 2A/I, Exhibit MNJ/20/2, Col R.F. Look, Commandant, Experimental Station Porton, to the Chief Superintendent, CDRD, War Office, 24 January 1931 (and further correspondence), pp. 142–3.

207. TNA, WO188/802, p. 44.

208. The title of the conference was 'Conference for the Reduction and Limitation of Armaments'.

209. TNA, WO188/802, p. 49; see also the debate in parliament about Britain's 'offensive' and 'defensive' chemical warfare capability; Hansard, HC Debate, vol. 272 cc811–12, Chemical Warfare, 30 November 1932.

210. MI, Folder 2A/I, Exhibit MNJ/20/2, Memorandum by the War Committee, 'Employment of Observers from the Services on Physiological Tests involving Exposure to Sternutators', 23 April 1940, pp. 146–7.

211. SIPRI 1971, p. 247; Hobbs et al. 2007, pp. 287ff.

212. SIPRI 1971, pp. 265f.

213. Hobbs et al. 2007, pp. 288f.; also TNA, PRO30/69/1273, 'Some Questions on the Geneva Protocol' (1925).

214. TNA, WO188/802, p. 51; Grayzel 2012, pp. 181f.

215. TNA, WO188/802, p. 89.

216. SIPRI 1971, pp. 258ff.; Balfour 2002, pp. 123–56.

217. In 1936, following reports suggesting German and Russian biological warfare research with anthrax spores, foot and mouth disease, and crop-destroying germs, the British government commissioned a report to assess the 'practicability of employing biological warfare and to recommend counter measures'; TNA, WO188/802, p. 51; see also Balmer 2001.

218. SIPRI 1971, p. 260; Hansard, HC Debate, vol. 272 cc811–12, Chemical Warfare, 30 November 1932; vol. 284 cc1469–70, Chemical Warfare (Defensive

Measures), 21 December 1933; also Air Raid Precautions Handbook, Personal Protection Against Gas (1938, 1942, 1944).

219. '"Gas"-Masks for Peace no Less than War: Protection from Fumes and Noxious Dust', *The Illustrated London News*, 24 December 1932, p. 1005.

220. Sisson 1938; IWM, Film and Video Archive, 'Your Book' (1938), HOY 81; Grayzel 2012, p. 221.

221. WL, QV662 1941 G78e, 'Enemy Gas Attacks: Notes Prepared for the Minister of Health and the Secretary of State for Scotland on the Diagnosis and Treatment of Casualties', *c.* 1941.

222. Grayzel 2012, pp. 224–50.

223. Grayzel 2012, pp. 235ff.

224. For a discussion of the trials see Grayzel 2012, pp. 238–45.

225. IWM, Photographic Collection, MH 6713.

226. TNA, CAB4/24, Committee of Imperial Defence, 'Policy with Regard to the Possible Use of Gas as a Retaliatory Measure in War', 8 July 1936; also Historical Survey 2006, p. 209.

227. TNA, WO188/802, p. 89.

228. Grayzel 2012, p. 250; also Harris, Paxman 1982, pp. 107f.

229. UoK, Porton Archive, CDE, Porton Down, Technical Note No. 1058, 'Asbestos in World War II Respirator Canisters', October 1989. I am grateful to Alan Care for drawing my attention to this document; see also TNA, WO188/429; WO188/2443 and WO189/4426.

230. UoK, Porton Archive, CDE, Porton Down, Technical Note No. 1058, 'Asbestos in World War II Respirator Canisters', October 1989.

231. TNA, WO188/2443, 'Production of Asbestos Bearing Filters': includes correspondence on exposure to asbestos of women working in factories producing respirators during the Second World War, and subsequent high rates of occurrence of mesothelioma, 1951–1977.

232. TNA, WO188/802, p. 44.

233. TNA, WO188/802, p. 44.

234. That smoke could be used as an effective weapon of war had been recognized as early as April 1915, days before Germany's first gas attack, when Winston Churchill as the First Lord of the Admiralty had commissioned a number of 'wonderful smoke-making experiments'; Churchill 1923, pp. 84f.; also Carter 2000, pp. 53f.

235. TNA, WO188/802, pp. 53–66.

236. Whereas the scientific staff had risen from twenty-three to fifty-one between 1922 and 1925, it had more than doubled to 120 by 1936/37. By 1938, Porton had a total of 152 researchers working on all aspects of defensive and offensive chemical warfare. The annual 'Dominion Day' event, for example, organized by Porton between 1937 and 1942, offered visitors insight into Porton's research and development programme; TNA, WO188/802, pp. 41, 89.

237. McCamley 2006, p. 100.

238. Hansard, HL Debate, vol. 98 cc749–73, Precautions against Air Raids, 23 July 1935; also Edgerton 2011, pp. 36f.
239. Haldane 1937; see also Haldane 1940, pp. 161–5; Avery 2013, p. 18.
240. Grayzel 2012, pp. 118f.
241. Haldane 1937; Haldane 1938; Proctor 1988, p. 343.
242. Jacobs 1996, pp. 46–8; see also Connelly, Goebel (2016, forthcoming).
243. Quoted from Scholem 1992, p. 267; and Evers 2014, p. 279; also Benjamin 1972–89, p. 473.

CHAPTER 3

1. Combined Intelligence Objectives Sub-Committee (CIOS), Report, Item No. 80, 'A New Group of War Gases', 23 April 1945. A shorter version of this chapter has previously been published as Schmidt 2013.
2. Schmaltz 2005, pp. 452–5; Klee 1997, p. 274; Tucker 2006, pp. 45ff. For the directorship of Dyhernfurth see IWM, Nuremberg Documents, NI-9772, Affidavit Albert Palm, 24 July 1947.
3. British Intelligence Objectives Sub-Committee (BIOS), Final Report, No. 782 (Interrogation Report No. 291), Item No. 8, 'Interrogation of Prof Ferdinand Flury and Dr Wolfgang Wirth on the Toxicology of Chemical Warfare Agents' (no date).
4. CIOS, Item No. 8, 'Chemical Warfare Installations in the Munsterlager Area', 23 April–3 June [1945], 5.
5. CIOS, Item No. 8, 'Chemical Warfare Installations in the Munsterlager Area', 23 April–3 June [1945], 3.
6. Balmer 2004, p. 201; Balmer 2012, p. 39.
7. Balmer 2004, p. 220.
8. Harris, Paxman 1982, pp. 53–67 (Chapter 3: 'Hitler's Secret Weapon').
9. See Tucker 2006, pp. 42–63.
10. Gellermann 1986, p. 211; Tucker 2006, p. 44.
11. Brown 1968; Gellermann 1986, p. 211.
12. IMT 1971, pp. 527f.
13. Schmaltz 2005, p. 24; also NARA, RG338, Entry 6C, Box 96, US Chemical Warfare Project, Bericht über Produktion und Einsatz von K-Stoffen, Raumexplosionen und Raumbränden, bearbeitet von Hermann Ochsner, P-004a.
14. Ebbinghaus 1999, pp. 190f.; Müller 1999, pp. 705–10; Schmaltz 2005, pp. 24f.
15. For an analysis of the informal, personalized, largely oral and detached system of communication see Schmidt 2007a, pp. 207–53.
16. Schmaltz 2005, Schmaltz 2006a; Schmaltz 2006b, Schmaltz 2006c; Tucker 2006, pp. 30ff.
17. Schmaltz 2005, pp. 192–356.
18. Schmaltz 2005, pp. 357–432; 480.

19. Klee 1997, p. 272; Tucker 2006: 30ff.; also IWM, CIOS, 'Investigation of Chemical Warfare Installations in the Munsterlager Area, including Raubkammer', APO 413.
20. For the discovery of nerve agents see SIPRI 1971, pp. 71f.; Harris, Paxman 1982, pp. 53–67; Schmaltz 2005, pp. 433–79; BIOS, Final Report, No. 714, Gerhard Schrader, 'The Development of New Insecticides'; presented by S.A. Mumford and E.A. Perren, MoS, 1945; BIOS, Final Report, No. 542, Item No. 8, 'Interrogation of Certain German Personalities Connected with Chemical Warfare', 1946. For Schrader's biography see TNA, FO1031/105, curriculum vitae Gerhard Schrader, 30 August 1945; see also TNA, FO1031/239, 'Gerhard Schrader, No. 13—Arbeiten aus der Tabun-, Sarin- und Somanreihe, Dustbin', 8 October 1945, p. 7; NARA, RG319, Entry IRR, Box 200, Gerhard Schrader, 'The Development of New Insecticides', part 2: 'Organophosphorus Compounds', 30 October 1945, p. 4.
21. Harris, Paxman 1982, pp. 53f.; Schmaltz 2005, pp. 435f.; also BIOS, Final Report, No. 138, Item No. 8, 'Interrogation of German CW Medical Personnel', August/September 1945.
22. Tucker 2006, p. 28.
23. Tucker 2006, pp. 29f.
24. Schmaltz 2005, pp. 438f.
25. Schmaltz 2005, p. 441.
26. Quoted from Schmaltz 2005, p. 441.
27. Tucker 2006, pp. 34f.
28. For the discovery of Sarin see Schmaltz 2005, pp. 446ff.; Harris, Paxman 1982, p. 54, and Tucker 2006, p. 40 erroneously list Col Rüdiger instead of Ritter as one of the individuals involved in the development of Sarin; BIOS, Final Report, No. 44, Item No. 8, 'Examination of Various German Scientists', 29 August–1 September 1945; BIOS, Final Report, No. 542, Item No. 8, 'Interrogation of Certain German Personalities Connected with Chemical Warfare', 1946. For Ambros see IWM, Nuremberg Documents, NI-6788, Affidavit Otto Ambros, 1 May 1947.
29. Schmaltz 2005, p. 450.
30. Schmaltz 2005, p. 452.
31. CIOS, Report, Item No. 80, 'A New Group of War Gases', 23 April 1945.
32. Schmaltz 2005, pp. 455f.
33. CIOS, Item No. 8, 'Chemical Warfare Installations in the Munsterlager Area', 23 April–3 June [1945], p. 6; also BIOS, Final Report, No. 138, Item No. 8, 'Interrogation of German CW Medical Personnel', August/September 1945.
34. It is not entirely clear, though, whether Britain introduced its safety procedures before, during, or after the Second World War; see MI, Folder 2A/I, Exhibit MNJ/20/2; 'Procedure in Connection with Reporting Accidents to Headquarters', December 1952, pp. 281–4.
35. BIOS, Final Report, No. 782 (Interrogation Report No. 291), Item No. 8, 'Interrogation of Prof Ferdinand Flury and Dr Wolfgang Wirth on the

Toxicology of Chemical Warfare Agents' (no date); also BIOS, Final Report, No. 41, Item No. 8, 'Interrogation of German CW Personnel at Heidelberg and Frankfurt' (no date); also Klee 1997, p. 277.

36. CIOS, Report No. 30, 'Chemical Warfare—IG Farbenindustrie AG, Frankfurt/Main', c. April 1945; also Harris, Paxman 1982, p. 57.

37. CIOS, Item No. 8, 'Chemical Warfare Installations in the Munsterlager Area', 23 April–3 June [1945], p. 6; Harris, Paxman 1982, p. 57; also Tucker 2006, p. 48.

38. CIOS, Item No. 8, 'Chemical Warfare Installations in the Munsterlager Area', 23 April–3 June [1945], p. 7; also Tucker 2006, p. 48.

39. Schmaltz 2005, p. 456; Sprenger 1996, p. 242; Groehler 1989, p. 246.

40. Schmaltz 2005, p. 456.

41. BIOS, Final Report, No. 782 (Interrogation Report No. 291), Item No. 8, 'Interrogation of Prof Ferdinand Flury and Dr Wolfgang Wirth on the Toxicology of Chemical Warfare Agents' (no date); also Schmaltz 2005, pp. 455ff.

42. The quote was written in English and has not been edited. CIOS, Report No. 30, 'Chemical Warfare—IG Farbenindustrie AG, Frankfurt/Main', c. April 1945; also Harris, Paxman 1982, p. 57.

43. Schmidt 2007a, pp. 117–72.

44. BIOS, Final Report, No. 542, Item No. 8, 'Interrogation of Certain German Personalities Connected with Chemical Warfare', 1946, p. 24; also Schmidt 2007a, pp. 291f.

45. BIOS, Final Report, No. 138, Item No. 8, 'Interrogation of German CW Medical Personnel', August/September 1945; CIOS, Item No. 8, 'Chemical Warfare Installations in the Munsterlager Area', 23 April–3 June [1945], p. 6.

46. CIOS, Item No. 8, 'Chemical Warfare Installations in the Munsterlager Area', 23 April–3 June [1945], p. 1.

47. BIOS, Final Report, No. 138, Item No. 8, 'Interrogation of German CW Medical Personnel', August/September 1945.

48. CIOS, Item No. 8, 'Chemical Warfare Installations in the Munsterlager Area', 23 April–3 June [1945], p. 4.

49. CIOS, Item No. 8, 'Chemical Warfare Installations in the Munsterlager Area', 23 April–3 June [1945], p. 6.

50. CIOS, Item No. 8, 'Chemical Warfare Installations in the Munsterlager Area', 23 April–3 June [1945], p. 9. Harris and Paxman have taken the quote out of context by deleting the last sentence, which suggests that Allied investigators felt that there was not sufficient evidence to back up the claim that political prisoners had been used in the experiments; Harris, Paxman 1982, p. 60.

51. Klee 1997, pp. 274f.

52. BIOS, Final Report, No. 138, Item No. 8, 'Interrogation of German CW Medical Personnel', August/September 1945; also Tucker 2006, pp. 36ff.

53. Schmaltz 2005, p. 457.

54. Klee 1997, pp. 270f.; according to Wirth, the tests involved small quantities of Tabun ($0.1–1.0$ mg/m^3), yet in the absence of other evidence it is difficult know whether his postwar recollections are accurate; Schmaltz 2005, p. 457.

55. Schmaltz 2005, pp. 459–79.

56. Klee 1997, pp. 274f.

57. Klee 1997, pp. 272ff.; in 1995, Gebhard Schultz organized the 'Sperrgebiet Zitadelle' exhibition. 'Sperrgebiet Zitadelle' refers to the Spandau Citadel, a fortress in Berlin, Germany, which during the war was generally 'off limits' to civilians. The exhibition also addressed the subject of human experiments conducted at the Spandau Citadel.

58. Schmaltz 2005, pp. 456f.

59. CIOS, Item No. 8, 'Chemical Warfare Installations in the Munsterlager Area', 23 April–3 June [1945], p. 6.

60. Field Information Agency, Technical (FIAT), Control Commission for Germany, British Element (CCG, BE), 'Report on Chemical Warfare, Based on Interrogation and Written Reports of Jürgen E. von Klenck, Speer, and Dr E. Mohrhardt', 6 December 1945, p. 21; also Schmidt 2007a, p. 290.

61. Klee 1997, pp. 275f.; also Bundesarchiv-Militärarchiv (BA-MA), RHD 43/56, Kampfstoffverletzungen. Bildsammlung zur Klinik und Pathologie der Verletzungen durch chemische Kampfstoffe und durch andere militärisch wichtige Stoffe.

62. CIOS, Item No. 8, 'Chemical Warfare Installations in the Munsterlager Area', 23 April–3 June [1945], p. 3.

63. CIOS, Item No. 8, 'Chemical Warfare Installations in the Munsterlager Area', 23 April–3 June [1945], pp. 2ff.; also Harris, Paxman 1982, pp. 57f.

64. Sass 1983; Grodin 1992, pp. 130ff.

65. I am grateful to Prof Christian Bonah for sharing his information about the intended 'target group' of the 1931 Regulations.

66. Annas, Grodin 1992, pp. 83f.; Schmidt 2007a, pp. 255–96.

67. Schmidt 2004; Schmidt 2007a.

68. BIOS, Final Report, No. 782 (Interrogation Report No. 291), Item No. 8, 'Interrogation of Prof Ferdinand Flury and Dr Wolfgang Wirth on the Toxicology of Chemical Warfare Agents' (no date).

69. BIOS, Final Report, No. 138, Item No. 8, 'Interrogation of German CW Medical Personnel', August/September 1945.

70. BIOS, Final Report, No. 138, Item No. 8, 'Interrogation of German CW Medical Personnel', August/September 1945.

71. BIOS, Final Report, No. 138, Item No. 8, 'Interrogation of German CW Medical Personnel', August/September 1945.

72. Harris and Paxman allege that nerve agents 'were almost certainly tested on the inmates of concentration camps' but do not provide any evidence to back up their claim; Harris, Paxman 1982, p. 61.

73. Nuremberg Doctors' Trial (NDT) Documents, frame 3/2641; also Schmidt 2007a, pp. 284–96.

74. NDT Documents, frame 4/2058; BAK, Allgemeine Prozesse, hereafter All. Proz. 2/FC 6069 P, Vernehmung Karl Brandt, 1 March 1947; also Schmidt 2007a, p. 287.

75. Schmidt 2007a, pp. 293–5.
76. Klee 1997, pp. 361f.
77. Klee 1997, pp. 364f.
78. NDT Documents, frames 3/2914f.; also frames 3/1094–7; Klee 1997, p. 366; Schmidt 2007a, p. 293. Other sources suggest a total number of approximately 150 experimental subjects of whom about forty died; also Mitscherlich, Mielke 1962, pp. 170f.
79. NDT Documents, frames 3/1094–7; Mitscherlich, Mielke 1962, p. 170.
80. NDT Documents, frame 3/2991.
81. CIOS, Item No. 8, 'Chemical Warfare Installations in the Munsterlager Area', 23 April–3 June [1945], 7f.; NDT Documents, frames 3/2460–1.
82. Klee 1997, p. 366; Mitscherlich, Mielke 1962, pp. 168f.
83. NDT Documents, frame 3/1095.
84. CIOS, Item No. 8, 'Chemical Warfare Installations in the Munsterlager Area', 23 April–3 June [1945], p. 8.
85. NDT Documents, frame 2/2690.
86. Klee 1997, pp. 382f.
87. NDT Documents, frames 3/2110–30, here frame 3/2128.
88. NDT Documents, frame 3/1836; see also Mitscherlich, Mielke 1962, pp. 171f.
89. Klee 1997, pp. 177–9.
90. NDT Documents, frame 3/2088, frame 3/3114, frame 4/2060; BAK, All. Proz. 2/FC 6069 P, Vernehmung Karl Brandt, 5 November 1946; see also Woelk 2003; Kopke, Schultz 2006; Schmidt 2007a, pp. 295f.
91. NDT Documents, frame 3/2088.
92. NDT Documents, frame 4/2058; BAK, All. Proz. 2/FC 6069 P, Vernehmung Karl Brandt, 1 March 1947; also Schmidt 2007a, p. 287.
93. Harris, Paxman 1982, pp. 119–23; Gellermann 1986, pp. 160–5; Arvidson 1994; Müller 1999, p. 712; Schmaltz 2005, pp. 28f.
94. CIOS, Item No. 8, 'Chemical Warfare Installations in the Munsterlager Area', 23 April–3 June [1945], p. 3.
95. BIOS, Final Report, No. 542, Item No. 8, 'Interrogation of Certain German Personalities Connected with Chemical Warfare', 1946, p. 21.
96. NDT Documents, frame 2/2410.
97. NDT Documents, frame 4/2058.
98. NDT Documents, frame 4/2058. Brandt's figures differ slightly; see BIOS, Final Report, No. 542, Item No. 8, 'Interrogation of Certain German Personalities Connected with Chemical Warfare', 1946, p. 22; also Schmidt 2007a, p. 287.
99. FIAT, CCG, BE, 'Report on Chemical Warfare, Based on Interrogation and Written Reports of Jürgen E. von Klenck, Speer, and Dr E. Mohrhardt', 6 December 1945, p. 20; Schmaltz 2005, p. 29; Tucker argues that Brandt was charged with the production of 45 million 'people's gas masks'; Tucker 2006, pp. 62f.

100. Kehrl 1973, pp. 415ff. In 1949, Kehrl was sentenced to fifteen years imprisonment at one of the Nuremberg trials for his involvement in the exploitation of the occupied territories for Germany's war effort.

101. Fröhlich 1993–96, part 2, vol. 11, p. 548, 25 March 1944.

102. BAK, All. Proz. 2/FC 6069 P, Vernehmung Karl Brandt, 1 March 1947.

103. Friedrich 2002, p. 115.

104. FIAT, CCG, BE, 'Report on Chemical Warfare, Based on Interrogation and Written Reports of Jürgen E. von Klenck, Speer, and Dr E. Mohrhardt', 6 December 1945, p. 20.

105. FIAT, CCG, BE, 'Report on Chemical Warfare, Based on Interrogation and Written Reports of Jürgen E. von Klenck, Speer, and Dr E. Mohrhardt', 6 December 1945, p. 8.

106. For the history of the discovery of Soman see Schmaltz 2005, pp. 480–93; Tucker 2006, pp. 51–4; pp. 62f.; Schmidt 2007a, pp. 291f.

107. BIOS, Final Report, No. 542, Item No. 8, 'Interrogation of Certain German Personalities Connected with Chemical Warfare', 1946, pp. 6f.

108. See also BIOS, Final Report, No. 542, Item No. 8, 'Interrogation of Certain German Personalities Connected with Chemical Warfare', 1946, p. 29.

109. Tucker 2006, pp. 68f.; IMT, Speer Testimony, 21 June 1946, pp. 527–30; see also NARA, RG338, Entry 6C, Box 96, US Chemical Warfare Project, Bericht über Produktion und Einsatz von K-Stoffen, Raumexplosionen und Raumbränden, bearbeitet von Hermann Ochsner, P-004a, in Brauch, Müller 1985, pp. 217–36 (Document 69).

110. Schmaltz 2005, p. 29; also Tucker 2006, pp. 66f.

111. Schmaltz 2005, p. 29; also Bundesarchiv Berlin, R3/1734, fol. 1, Speer to Keitel, 10 October 1944, in: Brauch, Müller 1985, p. 191 (Document 53); also Gellermann 1986, p. 173; Tucker overlooks, or ignores, the fact that Keitel actually turned down Speer's request; Tucker 2006, pp. 68f.

112. Tucker 2006, p. 69; 'Aktenvermerk über die K-Stoff-Besprechung beim Amtschef des Rüstungslieferungsamtes, Staatsrat Dr Walther Schieber, 2 November 1944', in Brauch, Müller 1985, pp. 192–5 (Document 54).

113. Brandt had been concerned about the security precautions, 'a double or triple, partly electrified fence', which had apparently led to unnecessary delays in the manufacture of chemical weapons, perhaps because prisoners had been killed; Schmidt 2007a, pp. 292f.; also NDT Documents, frame 3/1089.

114. BIOS, Final Report, No. 542, Item No. 8, 'Interrogation of Certain German Personalities Connected with Chemical Warfare', 1946, p. 25; for Brandt's postwar tendency to be somewhat economical with the truth see Schmidt 2007a, pp. 325–83.

115. FIAT, CCG, BE, 'Report on Chemical Warfare, Based on Interrogation and Written Reports of Jürgen E. von Klenck, Speer, and Dr E. Mohrhardt', 6 December 1945, pp. 10ff.; pp. 23–35; Harris, Paxman 1982, p. 138; Schmaltz 2005, pp 29f.; Tucker 2006, p. 69–82.

116. Harris, Paxman 1982, p. 67.

CHAPTER 4

1. Evans, R. 2000a, pp. 105f.; p. 188.
2. Spiers, for instance, suggests that 'lack of preparedness was a principal reason for non-use of chemical or biological weapons between the major belligerents in the Second World War'; Spiers 2010, p. 57.
3. TNA, AIR2/5117, Note by the Air Staff, 8 October 1940.
4. Harris, Paxman 1982, pp. 107–36; Spiers 2010, pp. 57ff.
5. Harris, Paxman 1982, p. 83, p. 107.
6. Harris, Paxman 1982, pp. 109ff.
7. Harris, Paxman 1982, p. 110.
8. Harris, Paxman 1982, p. 110; also Parker 1996, p. 49.
9. Harris, Paxman 1982, pp. 111ff.
10. Harris, Paxman 1982, pp. 112f.
11. Evans, R. 2000a, p. 81; Sinclair 1989, p. 84; see also TNA, AVIA22/1218; see also IWM, Duxford, Photographic Collection, Portrait G.L. Watkinson (Commandant, 17 February 1941 to 23 August 1942).
12. TNA, WO188/802, p. 97; see also p. 100.
13. TNA, WO188/802, pp. 97–100.
14. TNA, WO188/802, pp. 113f.
15. Edgerton 2006, pp. 162ff.
16. Carter 2000, p. 49.
17. WL, PP/CLE/A.11, Lovatt Evans papers.
18. *BMJ*, 'The Substance Called "BAL"', 1 (1946), 4441, pp. 240–1; Ord, Stocken 2005; Campbell, Stocken 1998; Vilensky 2005, pp. 78–85; Irvine 2009.
19. Although Douglas' contributions to Britain's gas defences ought to be acknowledged, the claim that his work actually 'prevented Hitler from using gas warfare' is rather wide of the mark; *BMJ*, Book Reviews, Distinguished Fellows, 1 May 1965, pp. 1178f.
20. Cameron 1948.
21. *BMJ*, Obituary, Sir Roy Cameron, 2 (1966), 5519, pp. 955–6. In his postwar career, Cameron took an active part in shaping the field of pathology and wielded considerable influence as a member of the MRC, the Agricultural Research Council (ARC), the Imperial Cancer Research Council (ICRC), and the Beit Memorial Research Council (BMRC). Cameron was also director of the Graham Research Laboratories.
22. Roughton 1949, pp. 322ff.; Sutton 1951, pp. 495f.; Feldberg 1967, pp. 62f.; Oakley 1968, pp. 89ff.; Sinclair 1989, p. 85; Thompson, Ogston 1983, pp. 503ff.; Evans, R. 2000a, p. 188; Bevington, Gowenlock 2002, pp. 293f. Other scientists working at Porton during the war were H.M. Carleton, C.G. Douglas, and J.M. Barnes.
23. *BMJ*, Obituary, Col E.C. Linton, 1 (1970), 5693, p. 438. Linton later became deputy assistant director of pathology and hygiene in Malta.
24. *BMJ*, Obituary, Lt Col J.D. Cruickshank, 1 (1956), 4959, pp. 174–5.
25. *BMJ*, Obituary, Gp Capt Thomas Montgomery, 1 (1966), 5500, p. 1428.

26. *BMJ*, Obituary, Leopold Thomas Poole, 1 (1965), 5445, p. 1316.

27. *BMJ*, Cathcart Chair of Biochemistry, 1 (1966), 5486, pp. 555–6.

28. *BMJ*, Obituary, Walter Somerville, 331 (2005), 7517, p. 639.

29. *BMJ*, Obituary, Henry Matthew Adam, 329 (2004), 7466, p. 628.

30. *BMJ*, Obituary, Sir James Kilpatrick, 1 (1960), 5180, pp. 1211–12. Kilpatrick received an OBE (Officer of the Most Excellent Order of the British Empire) in 1946, a CB (Companion of the Most Honourable Order of the Bath) in 1952, and was knighted in 1953. He became Honorary Physician to the King in 1951 and to the Queen in 1952.

31. *BMJ*, Obituary, Joseph Henry Cranston Walker, 1 (1964), 5390, p. 1123.

32. *BMJ*, Obituary, Sydney Curwen, 2 (1977), 6096, p. 1228.

33. *BMJ*, New Professors in the University of London, 283 (1981), 6283, p. 70.

34. Hazelgrove 2002; Schmidt 2012b.

35. *BMJ*, Obituary, Trevor Charles Stamp, 295 (1987), 6612, p. 1572; Hazelgrove 2002.

36. *BMJ*, Obituary, C. Wally Crane, 300 (1990), 6734, p. 1269.

37. *BMJ*, Obituary, Maj Gen Robert Scott, 302 (1991), 6790, p. 1459.

38. *BMJ*, Obituary, Gp Capt Gerald Struan Marshall, 1 (1968), 5586, p. 256.

39. *BMJ*, Obituary, Archibald Fairley, 2 (1957), 5045, pp. 647–8.

40. Oakley 1968, p. 90; Gladstone, Knight, Wilson 1973, pp. 336–8.

41. Edgerton 2006, pp. 162ff.

42. *BMJ*, Obituary, Claude Gordon Douglas, 1 (1963), 5334, p. 890; *BMJ*, Obituary, Paul Fildes, 1 (1971), 5746, p. 463; *BMJ*, Obituary, Sir Roy Cameron, 2 (1966), 5519, pp. 955–6; *BMJ*, Obituary, Gp Capt Gerald Struan Marshall, 1 (1968), 5586, p. 256; *BMJ*, Obituary, Wilson Smith, 2 (1965), 5455, p. 240; *BMJ*, Obituary, Donald Devereux Woods, 2 (1964), 5420, p. 1337; for Edgar D. Adrian, Baron Adrian of Cambridge, see Hodgkin 1979; for Charles Lovatt Evans, see De Burgh Daly, Gregory 1970; for Neil Kensington Adam, see Carrington et al. 1974; for Kenneth Bailey, see Chibnall 1964; for David W.W. Henderson, see Kent, Morgan 1970; for Richard H. Adrian, Second Baron Adrian of Cambridge, see Huxley 1997.

43. TNA, WO188/802, p. 106.

44. WL, PP/CLE/A.11, Lovatt Evans papers, Lovatt Evans to Davidson Pratt, 6 August 1941.

45. WL, PP/CLE/A.11, Lovatt Evans papers, Davidson Pratt to Lovatt Evans, 7 August 1941.

46. WL, PP/CLE/A.11, Lovatt Evans papers, Watkinson to Lovatt Evans, 20 August 1941.

47. See, for example, Campbell, Stocken 1998.

48. WL, PP/CLE/A.11, Lovatt Evans papers, Hill to Lovatt Evans, 24 April 1944; Hill to Grigg, 24 April 1944; Lovatt Evans to Hill, 27 April 1944.

49. WL, PP/CLE/A.11, Lovatt Evans papers, Hill to Lovatt Evans, 24 April 1944.

50. WL, PP/CLE/A.11, Lovatt Evans papers, Lovatt Evans to Watkinson, 14 September 1942.

51. WL, PP/CLE/A.11, Lovatt Evans papers, Air Cdre RAF [G. Combe] to Lovatt Evans, 16 September 1942.
52. WL, PP/CLE/A.11, Lovatt Evans papers, Lovatt Evans to Air Cdre RAF [G. Combe], 19 September 1942.
53. WL, PP/CLE/A.11, Lovatt Evans papers, Crawford to Davidson Pratt, 8 October 1941.
54. TNA, AIR2/5117, Minutes of a Meeting held at the Air Ministry, 27 June 1940; also Carter 2000, pp. 47ff.
55. TNA, WO188/802, p. 108.
56. TNA, WO188/802, p. 110.
57. TNA, WO188/802, p. 96.
58. McCamley 2006, pp. 103–25; Edgerton 2011, pp. 201f.
59. Agency factories were run by Imperial Chemical Industries on behalf of the MoS to manufacture chemical warfare agents if and when these were needed by the state.
60. McCamley 2006, pp. 101f., p. 109.
61. Carter 2000, pp. 52f.; Carter, Pearson 1996b, pp. 60f.
62. Wachtel 1941, pp. 62–111.
63. Defence Evaluation and Research Agency (DERA) 1999, p. 13; for the use of ricin in chemical warfare see also Emsley 2008, pp. 4ff.
64. TNA, WO188/802, p. 103.
65. TNA, WO188/802, p. 101; see also Evans, R. 2000a, p. 105.
66. Evans, R. 2000a, p. 81; Sinclair 1989, pp. 84f.; *BMJ*, Obituary, Archibald Fairley, 2 (1957), 5045, pp. 647–8.
67. TNA, WO188/802, pp. 111f.
68. Evans, R. 2000a, p. 81; see also TNA, WO188/624, 'Porton Priority Programme of Research: Brief Review', 12 July 1940.
69. TNA, WO188/802, p. 106.
70. See also Evans, R. 2000a, pp. 106f.
71. Evans, R. 2000a, p. 89.
72. Evans, R. 2000a, pp. 89f.
73. MI, Folder 2A/I, Memorandum by the War Committee, 'Employment of Observers from the Services on Physiological Tests Involving Exposure to Sternutators', 23 April 1940, pp. 146–7.
74. MI, Folder 2A/I, Memorandum by the War Committee, 'Employment of Observers from the Services on Physiological Tests Involving Exposure to Sternutators', 23 April 1940, pp. 146–7.
75. Evans, R. 2000a, p. 82; also TNA, WO195/14846, Porton Note No. 119, 'History of the Service Volunteer Observer Scheme at Porton Down', November 1959.
76. Evans, R. 2000a, p. 82; also TNA, WO195/14846, Porton Note No. 119, 'History of the Service Volunteer Observer Scheme at Porton Down', November 1959.
77. WL, PP/CLE/A.11, Lovatt Evans papers, 'Dermatitis Due to Respirator Facepiece'; see also Davidson Pratt to Lovatt Evans, 25 November 1943.

78. Historical Survey 2006, p. 211; Evans, R. 2000a, p. 82; also Historical Survey 2006, Experimental Log MPG 144.

79. In June 1940, six staff members were exposed to a low concentration of lewisite to see whether the agent could be detected by smell, and in 1942, 'manual workers and clerks' took part in a trial to assess the relative sensitivity to mustard gas of the skin at different sites of the body; Historical Survey 2006, p. 211; p. 214; also Experimental Log MPG 31.

80. Institution of Royal Engineers c. 2005; Napier 2005. At Porton, the Royal Engineers stood under the command of Maj Houston during the war; Sinclair 1989, p. 87.

81. Evans, R. 2000a, pp. 82f.

82. Quoted from Evans, R. 2000a, p. 83; p. 85.

83. Quoted from Evans, R. 2000a, p. 83.

84. MI, Folder 2A/I, Exhibit MNJ/20/2, 'Volunteer Observers for CDES, Porton', 24 March 1941, p. 148.

85. Evans, R. 2000a, p. 87.

86. Historical Survey 2006, pp. 209–32; also Experimental Log MPG 24.

87. TNA, WO188/802, p. 100.

88. Historical Survey 2006, pp. 211f.; also Porton Report No. 2429, 'The Relative Insensitivity to Mustard Gas of the Skin of the Hand', 21 September 1942.

89. Historical Survey 2006, p. 212, here especially Lewisite Hypersensitivity. Phys.S/1273/44, 22 June 1944.

90. Historical Survey 2006, p. 212; Table 17.3: Summary of Vesicant Power Tests with H and L Variants.

91. Historical Survey 2006, pp. 212f.; also Experimental Log MPG 58.

92. Historical Survey 2006, p. 209; Carter 2000, p. 53; Evans, R. 2000a, p. 109.

93. The subsequent discovery of patent specifications seems to confirm that IG Farben was indeed conducting research with nitrogen mustard; Historical Survey 2006, p. 213; also Porton Memorandum No. 22, 'Comprehensive Report on S', 5 March 1943.

94. Historical Survey 2006, pp. 213f.; Table 17.4: Summary of Vesicant Power Tests with Nitrogen Mustards. The figures do not seem to include a trial in January 1942 with twenty-four servicemen who were exposed to nitrogen mustard (HN-3), and a trial in March 1943 with fifty-five servicemen, known to be hypersensitive to mustard gas, to compare the effects of mustard gas and nitrogen mustard.

95. In 1943, for example, thirty-five servicemen were 'presented in the laboratory with the smells of HN-2 [nitrogen mustard], H [mustard gas] and L [lewisite]', yet only sixteen of the participants could recognize the odour of lewisite, leading Porton to conclude that 'untrained soldiers would not reliably be able to detect L [lewisite] by smell'; Historical Survey 2006, pp. 214f.; here also especially Lewisite smelling trial, 5 April 1943, PhysSR41/43/LE, 6 April 1943.

96. Evans, R. 2000a, p. 83.

97. Evans, R. 2000a, p. 84.

98. Historical Survey 2006, p. 214.

99. Historical Survey 2006, p. 214; also Experimental Log MPG 49 and 50; Porton Report No. 2553, 'The Effect of Lewisite Vapour on Small Animals and on Man', 29 October 1943.

100. Historical Survey 2006, p. 217; Porton Memorandum No. 22, 'Comprehensive Report on S', 5 March 1943.

101. Historical Survey 2006, p. 217; also Porton Report No. 2563, 'The Effects of HN-2 Vapour on Human and Rabbit Eyes', 18 November 1943.

102. Historical Survey 2006, pp. 217–20.

103. In the rangefinder task, subjects were asked to look down a tube at a photograph of an aircraft and attempt to correct the refraction of the image which was brought about by a rotating glass mechanism. Subjects performing the pegboard task had to push wooden, numbered pegs into numbered hole in a board; Historical Survey 2006, pp. 221f.; Evans, R. 2000a, pp. 83f.; also Porton Report No. 2370, 'A Psychological Test for the Harassing Effects of Lachrymators on Vision', 3 June 1942.

104. Historical Survey 2006, p. 221; also Porton Memorandum No. 12, 'The Effects of Arsenical Particulate Clouds on Soldiers and Civil Population Equipped with Respirators', 13 August 1941.

105. Historical Survey 2006, p. 221; see also Porton Memorandum No. 12, 'The Effects of Arsenical Particulate Clouds on Soldiers and Civil Population Equipped with Respirators', 13 August 1941.

106. Porton's scientists also performed ground emission trials and training exercises with mustard gas on the field range and in other parts of the country; TNA, WO188/802, p. 98.

107. Conversation with Mary Pilcher, Canterbury, who lived in Devizes during the Second World War, 8 March 2013.

108. Historical Survey 2006, p. 226; also Porton Report No. 2313, 'Trial to Determine the Casualty Producing Value of "Initial Clouds" of Mustard Gas', 16 December 1941.

109. Historical Survey 2006, p. 226; also Porton Report No. 2313, 'Trial to Determine the Casualty Producing Value of "Initial Clouds" of Mustard Gas', 16 December 1941.

110. Historical Survey 2006, p. 227; also Porton Report No. 2377, 'Development of Vesicant Thermal Generator', 10 June 1942.

111. Historical Survey 2006, p. 227; also Porton Report No. 2377, 'Development of Vesicant Thermal Generator', 10 June 1942.

112. Historical Survey 2006, p. 227; also Porton Report No. 2356, 'The Comparative Casualty Producing Powers of Viscous and Gel Mustard Chargings in Air-Burst Shell Used for Direct Contamination of Personnel', 7 February 1942.

113. Historical Survey 2006, p. 227; also Porton Report No. 2343, 'Medical Report on Casualties Produced by Airburst Mustard Gas Shell', 10 March 1942.

114. Historical Survey 2006, p. 227; also Porton Report No. 2387, 'The Casualty Producing Value of Mustard Gas Spray from BE Shell Charged HBv', 28 July 1942.

115. WL, PP/CLE/A.11, Lovatt Evans papers, Lovatt Evans to Watkinson, 18 December 1941; Watkinson to Lovatt Evans, [n.d.] December 1941.

116. Historical Survey 2006, pp. 215f.; pp. 227f.; pp. 292f.; see also Porton Report No. 2522, 'The Treatment of Mustard Gas Blisters', 20 July 1943.

117. Evans, R. 2000a, pp. 87f.

118. TNA, WO188/802, pp. 109f.

119. Quoted from Goodwin 1998, p. 63; also Sinclair 1989, p. 86.

120. Cullumbine 1946.

121. Historical Survey 2006, pp. 229f.; see also Court of Inquiry Proceedings and Inquest by the Coroner of the City of New Sarum (Salisbury), 5 January 1944; also Experimental Diary of Field Trials 1941 to 1944.

122. Historical Survey 2006, pp. 231f.; also Porton Report No. 2303, 'The Effects of Mustard Gas on Railways—Report on Preliminary Trial Carried out by the LMS Railway 15 and 16 October 1941', 24 November 1941.

123. Historical Survey 2006, pp. 215ff.; see also pp. 279–96 (Chapter 20: Skin Protection).

124. Historical Survey 2006, p. 215; also Experimental Log MPG 54 and 55.

125. Historical Survey 2006, p. 215; also Porton Memorandum No. 22, 'Comprehensive Report on S', 5 March 1943.

126. Evans, R. 2000a, pp. 84f.

127. Evans, R. 2000a, p. 84.

128. TNA, WO286/11, Childs to Baum, 18 August 1944.

129. TNA, WO286/11, Childs to Baum, 18 August 1944.

130. TNA, WO286/11, Childs to Baum, 18 August 1944.

131. TNA, WO286/11, Baum to Childs, 18 November 1944.

132. Historical Survey 2006, pp. 279–85; also Carter 2000, pp. 54f.

133. Evans, R. 2000a, pp. 86f.

134. Historical Survey 2006, pp. 281f.; also Porton Report No. 2374, 'The Protection of Vulnerable Areas of the Body against H Vapour in Hot Climates', 22 May 1942.

135. Historical Survey 2006, pp. 282–4; Experimental Log MPG 49; TNA, WO189/3242; CDRE(I), Report No. 254, 'Protection of the Scrotal Area against Vesicant Gases', 28 May 1943.

136. Historical Survey 2006, p. 283; also Experimental Log MPG 50–8.

137. TNA, WO188/802, p. 100; Historical Survey 2006, pp. 279–96, here p. 288; also Ord, Stocken 2005.

138. Pepper had responded to a recruitment notice which referred to mustard gas and lewisite; Evans, R. 2000a, p. 86.

139. Carter 2000, p. 50.

140. Evans, R. 2000a, pp. 88f.; Carter 2000, pp. 50f.

141. WL, Archives and Manuscripts, SA/SRL/M.1/2/1, CDRD, Reports 1939–1950; also SA/SRL/M.1/2/2, CDRD, Reports and Papers, *c.* 1940s, Honor B. Fell, Appendix. Unpublished Chemical Warfare Research, *c.* 1944.

142. Campbell, Stocken 1998, p. 423; Ord, Stocken 2005, p. 141; also Vilensky 2005, pp. 78–85; Quirke 2007; Edgerton 2011, p. 255.

143. WL, Archives and Manuscripts, SA/SRL/M.1/4, Box 31, G.R. Cameron, F. Burgess, V.S. Trenwith, Porton Report No. 2673, 'The Possibility of Toxic Effects from BAL in Conditions of Impaired Renal or Hepatic Function', 10 March 1945; for the toxic effects of BAL see also Vilensky 2005, p. 82.

144. Ord, Stocken 2005, p. 141; also TNA, WO32/20606, AMD7, D. Path. (Beyd) to DSWV (G.H.C. Pennycook), 17 May 1946.

145. Historical Survey 2006, pp. 285–9; also Porton Report No. 2518, 'The Prevention of Vesication', 20 July 1943; Porton Report No. 2631, 'New Active Constituents for Anti-gas Ointments, part 1: Competitors: With a Note on the Numerical Assessment of Mustard Gas Burns', 20 July 1944; Porton Report No. 2637, 'New Active Constituents for Anti-gas Ointments, part 2: p-Alkoxy-Derivatives of Chloramine B', 21 July 1944; also Carter 2000, pp. 54f.

146. Historical Survey 2006, p. 291; also Porton Report No. 2638, 'Anti-gas Ointments for Use in the Tropics, part 1: Exploratory Experiments', 14 August 1944.

147. Historical Survey 2006, p. 292; also Porton Report No. 2522, 'The Treatment of Mustard Gas Blisters', 20 July 1943.

148. Historical Survey 2006, p. 293; also Porton Report No. 2560, 'Some Further Studies on the Treatment of Mustard Gas Blisters and a Comparison of the Healing of Mustard Gas and Lewisite Burns', 10 November 1943.

149. Historical Survey 2006, p. 296; also Experimental Log MPG 54; Harris, Paxman 1982, p. 84.

150. Historical Survey 2006, p. 296; also Experimental Log MPG 49–52, 54, 56–8.

151. Carter 2000, p. 57.

152. TNA, AIR20/8731, Porton Note (Ptn.) 1230/2 (T.4855), 'Attack on Cities with Gas', 12 April 1943.

153. TNA, AIR20/8731, Ptn. 1230/2 (T.4855), 'Attack on Cities with Gas', 12 April 1943, pp. 1ff.

154. TNA, AIR20/8731, Ptn. 1230/2 (T.4855), 'Attack on Cities with Gas', 12 April 1943, pp. 3ff.

155. TNA, AIR20/8731, Ptn. 1230/2 (T.4855), 'Attack on Cities with Gas', 12 April 1943, p. 5.

156. Hayward 2001, pp. 93f.

157. Hayward 2001, pp. 90–4.

158. Schmidt 2007a, pp. 231ff.; pp. 276ff.; Friedrich 2002, pp. 113ff.

159. Freeman 1991, pp. 31ff.

160. Carter 2000, pp. 51f.

161. Carter 2000, p. 52. Barrett 1948; Ombudsman for National Defence and Canadian Forces (NDCF), redacted extract of a soldier remembering his time at Suffield, pp. 1234–42; also pp. 1229–31. H.M. Barrett from the University of Toronto became Head of Research, and Maj J.C. Paterson from the Royal Canadian Army Medical Corps led the physiological and pathological department; also Smith, Mawdsley 2011; Avery 2013, pp. 20ff.

162. For example, Ombudsman (NDCF), Field Experiment 124, Trial 1, Preliminary Trial with 'H' Thermal Generator, 2 December 1943.

163. TNA, WO188/802, p. 94. Tests were also conducted at the Chemical Warfare Laboratories in Ottawa.

164. Because research subjects were assigned 'physiological observer numbers' sequentially, it has been assumed that there were about 2,500 participants. Ombudsman (NDCF), Briefing Note, Complaints Concerning Chemical Agent Tests at Suffield during World War II, 18 December 2003; Ombudsman for NDCF 2004; also Clement Laforce to Suzanne Belson, 29 July 2003. An estimated 900 soldiers also participated in experiments at the Chemical Warfare Laboratories in Ottawa; Pugliese 2003.

165. Ombudsman (NDCF), Briefing Note, Complaints Concerning Chemical Agent Tests at Suffield during World War II, 18 December 2003; Ombudsman for NDCF 2004.

166. Ombudsman (NDCF), Regulations Governing the Use of Volunteers for Physiological Tests, 5 August 1942, pp. 909–11.

167. Ombudsman (NDCF), Information for Prospective Subjects for Physiological Tests (ES Suffield), 5 August 1942, p. 908.

168. Handschuh 2004.

169. Ombudsman (NDCF), Letter (anonymized), 21 January 2004, p. 703.

170. Ombudsman (NDCF), Regulations Governing the Use of Volunteers for Physiological Tests, 5 August 1942, pp. 909–11.

171. Ombudsman (NDCF), Security. Document in Personnel Jacket of R76998, LAC Cockroft, Stanley Philips, National Archives, 00–42687, R100, Microfilm Ref. WSB 804–8, p. 923; also Security of Military Information Following Discharge, pp. 1004f.

172. Ombudsman (NDCF), Suffield Gas Veterans Group, WWII, Anonymized, December 1942, p. 694.

173. Ombudsman (NDCF), Suffield Gas Veterans Group, WWII, Anonymized, no date, p. 750.

174. Ombudsman (NDCF), Suffield Report on Expt No. 36, Notes for CEO, 1942; also Suffield Gas Veterans Group, WWII, RCAF, Unanimous, 1941–1943, p. 698.

175. Ombudsman (NDCF), Field Experiment No. 275, part 2, Ground Contamination Shoot with [Redacted] 4.2. Inch CM Shell Charged Mustard Gas, 18 July 1945; correspondence between Suzanne Belson and Clement Laforce, 23/24 February 2004; numerous soldiers later reported that they had

been exposed to mustard gas during decontamination work; Suffield Gas Veterans Group, WWII, p. 735, p. 746.

176. Ombudsman (NDCF), Interim Report on Field Experiment No. 36, The Casualty Producing Power of High Spray from Air Craft, 9 September 1942.

177. Ombudsman (NDCF), Field Experiment No. 52, 18 August 1942.

178. Ombudsman (NDCF), Interim Report on Field Experiment No. 36, The Casualty Producing Power of High Spray from Air Craft, 9 September 1942; also Field Experiment 234, Ground Contamination with [Redacted] Mortar Bombs Charged [with] Mustard Gas, 18 October 1944.

179. *BMJ*, Obituary, Walter Somerville, 331 (2005), 7517, p. 639.

180. Ombudsman (NDCF), Suffield Report No. 81, 'The Effect of the Lesions Produced by Mustard Spray on the Performance of Troops Engaged in a Field Exercise', 17 August 1943. Around the same time, two trials with twenty servicemen each produced injuries of 'casualty severity' in two men, the other in five men. Someone later crossed out the word 'five', replacing it with the word 'two'; see Physiology Section Report of Field Experiment 142, Trial I, 12 June 1943; Physiology Section Report, Field Experiment No. 158, 13 November 1943.

181. Ombudsman (NDCF), Physiology Section Report on Field Experiment 141, Trial I, held 16 July 1943, Vapour Danger from Grass Mustard Gas Contamination, 28 July 1943.

182. Ombudsman (NDCF), Field Experiment 215 Trial VI, The Physiological Effect of Mustard Vapour at Low Temperature, 3 April 1945.

183. Chemical Corps Association 1948, pp. 18–21; for research and development at Edgewood Arsenal see Brophy, Miles, Cochrane 1959, pp. 28–48, here pp. 32–6; also Brophy, Fisher 1959; Klever, Birdsell 1966.

184. Brophy, Miles, Cochrane 1959, pp. 36ff.

185. CHF, Chalmer G. Kirkbride, Transcript of an Interview conducted by James J. Bohning in Washington, DC, 15 July 1993, pp. 20ff.

186. Kirby 2007, pp. 11–36.

187. Chemical Warfare Service 1948, pp. 20–32; Office of Civilian Defense 1941.

188. McKusick 2000.

189. McKusick 2000, p. 89. By developing quantitative methods to examine the 'physiology and pharmacology of neuromuscular transmission', McGehee Harvey advanced the study of organophosphorus compounds that were 'capable of destroying cholinesterase and thereby disrupting the orderly sequence of synthesis, release, and destruction of acetylcholine at the neuromuscular junction'.

190. MI, Folder 2E, Exhibit MPG/231, Chemical Corps Advisory Council, Medical and Related Problems Committee Meeting, Army Chemical Center, Maryland, 20–21 March 1953, pp. 88–115. The meeting was chaired by Dr Abner McGehee Harvey.

191. TNA, WO188/802, pp. 117f.

192. Brophy, Miles, Cochrane 1959, p. 45; Carter, Pearson 1996a, pp. 78ff.

193. Pechura, Rall 1993, pp. 67f.; Freeman 1991, p. 34.

194. Pechura, Rall 1993, pp. 65ff.

195. Pechura, Rall 1993, p. 67.

196. Pechura, Rall 1993, p. 66.

197. Pechura, Rall 1993, p. 66.

198. Freeman 1991, pp. 33f.; also Smith 2008.

199. TNA, WO188/802, pp. 118f.; also Evans, R. 2000a, pp. 104f.; Freeman 1991, p. 33.

200. TNA, WO188/802, pp. 118f.

201. Freeman 1991, p. 35.

202. TNA, WO188/802, pp. 118f.

203. Carter, Pearson 1996a, pp. 83–97.

204. TNA, WO188/802, p. 88, pp. 116f.; Carter 2000, pp. 58f.; also Evans, R. 2007. In 1941, one of Porton's Technical Officers was dispatched to India to support research at the CDRE; a year later, Porton's reconstituted Anti-Gas Laboratory No. 1 was sent to Singapore, but was diverted to India after the fall of Singapore to support the Ninth Army during the Burma campaign.

205. Quoted from Evans, R. 2000a, p. 98.

206. In the experiment, a total of 590 British and Indian servicemen were exposed to blistering agents in particularly hot weather conditions; quoted from Evans, R. 2000a, pp. 98ff.

207. TNA, WO189/3330; CDRE(I), Note No. 18/1942, 'The Treatment of Mustard Gas Burns with Special Reference to the Use of Amyl Salicylate'; see also TNA, WO189/3238; CDRE(I), Report No. 247, 'The Casualty-Producing Power of Small Drops of Vesicants under Tropical Conditions', 22 January 1943; also Evans, R. 2000a, pp. 99f.; Evans, R. 2007.

208. Evans, R. 2000a, p. 100; also Evans, R. 2007.

209. TNA, WO189/3238; CDRE(I), Report No. 247, 'The Casualty-Producing Power of Small Drops of Vesicants under Tropical Conditions', 22 January 1943.

210. Research carried out at CDRE(I) suggested marked differences in the effectiveness of mustard gas and lewisite under warm and humid conditions. In 1945, the US CWS commissioned human experiments on an 'ad hoc' basis; these showed that lewisite was a 'relatively ineffective' and unsuitable blistering agent in tropical climates; TNA, WO189/3364; CDRE(I), Report No. 76, 'Some Experiments on the Skin-Burning Power of Lewisite Vapour in a Warm Humid Climate', 19 April 1946.

211. TNA, WO189/3238; CDRE(I), Report No. 247, 'The Casualty-Producing Power of Small Drops of Vesicants under Tropical Condition's, 22 January 1943; TNA, WO189/3293; CDRE(I), Report No. 310, 'The Protective Value of Un-impregnated Anklets Web [= gaiters] and Puttees against Liquid Vesicants when Worn [with] Un-Dubbined Boots, Impregnated Trousers and Sock[s] in Tropical Conditions', 1 October 1945.

212. TNA, WO189/3242; CDRE(I), Report No. 254, 'Protection of the Scrotal Area against Vesicant Gases', 28 May 1943.

213. TNA, WO188/802, p. 104; Carter 2000, p. 56; see also the papers in the Wellcome Trust library which are concerned with malaria research; Lovatt Evans papers.

214. *BMJ*, 'The Toxicity of 2,2-bis (p-chlorphenyl) 1,1,1-trichlorethane (DDT)', 1 (1945), 4407, pp. 865–71, here p. 868; for a summary of Porton's entomological research see TNA, WO188/802, pp. 145ff.

215. For other collaborative projects between Porton and the WHO see Carter, Balmer 1999, p. 328.

216. TNA, WO189/3269; CDRE(I), Report No. 286, 'Progress Summary No. 1', 9 December 1944; also TNA, WO188/802, p. 116; WO189/3364; CDRE(I), Report No. 76, 'Some Experiments on the Skin-Burning Power of Lewisite Vapour in a Warm Humid Climate', 19 April 1946.

217. TNA, WO189/3276; CDRE(I), Report No. 290, 'The Protective Value and Irritancy of CC2 Impregnated Clothing during Wear under Tropical Conditions', 7 April 1945; also Evans, R. 2007; tests were also carried out with British and Indian subjects who wore impregnated gloves to protect them from mustard gas and lewisite exposure; TNA, WO189/3295; CDRE(I), Report No. 312, 'The Protective Value against Vesicant Liquid Contamination and the Serviceability of an Experimental Impregnated Glove', 7 October 1945; TNA, WO189/3297; CDRE(I), Report No. 314, 'Protection of the Hands from Various Liquid Contaminations', 26 November 1945 (signed A.S.G. Hill, Offg. Controller).

218. TNA, WO189/3276; CDRE(I), Report No. 290, 'The Protective Value and Irritancy of CC2 Impregnated Clothing during Wear under Tropical Conditions', 7 April 1945; Evans, R. 2000a, pp. 99f.; also Evans, R. 2007.

219. Evans, R. 2000a, p. 99; also Evans, R. 2007.

220. UoK, Porton Archive, A208, War Cabinet, Chiefs of Staff Committee, 6 March 1941, p. 2; also Carter 2000, pp. 58f.

221. See also Evans, R. 2000a, pp. 104–10.

222. TNA, WO188/802, p. 118.

223. Evans, R. 2000a, p. 104.

224. *BMJ*, Obituary, F.S. Gorrill, 1 (1975), 5955, p. 462. After the war, Gorrill became the curator of the Hunterian Museum of the Royal College of Surgeons and took over as director of Glaxo. For the history of chemical warfare research in Australia see also Plunkett 2007.

225. Rhodes 1990; Sinclair 1989, p. 98; Carter 2000, p. 58; Freeman 1991, p. 32.

226. Evans, R. 2000a, pp. 90f.

227. Goodwin 1998, pp. 114f.; see also Goodwin's documentary film 'Keen as Mustard' (1989).

228. Sinclair 1948, p. 290; Sinclair 1949, p. 476.

229. Evans, R. 2000a, pp. 91f.

230. Evans, R. 2000a, p. 92.
231. Evans, R. 2000a, p. 105.
232. Freeman 1991, p. 32; see also Cochrane 1947.
233. Evans, R. 2000a, p. 94.
234. Freeman 1991, p. 32.
235. Evans, R. 2000a, p. 94.
236. Goodwin 1998, pp. 127–49; Evans, R. 2000a, pp. 96–8; Bolton 2004, pp. 54–79.
237. See also Bolton 2004, pp. 54–79. The trials, which were recorded in the film 'Brook Island Trial' (1944), were supported by Davidson Pratt from the MoS, Cornelius Rhoads, head of the CWS, and Phillip Weldon, secretary of the Australian Chemical Defence Board; Goodwin 1998, p. 127.
238. Goodwin 1998, p. 132, p. 148.
239. Evans, R. 2000a, pp. 96ff.; TNA, WO106/4594A, Maj Gen J.S. Lethbridge, General Staff Commander, Chemical Warfare Interim Report 23, 29 November 1943.
240. Freeman 1991, p. 37.
241. WL, PP/CLE/A.11, Lovatt Evans papers, Hill to Lovatt Evans, 24 April 1944.
242. WL, PP/CLE/A.11, Lovatt Evans papers, Lovatt Evans to Hill, 27 April 1944.
243. At the end of 1944, Lovatt Evans was invited to become a member of the Chemical Board, its Physiological and Medical Sub-Committees, and of the Informal Conferences of Chairmen; WL, PP/CLE/A.11, Lovatt Evans papers, Lovatt Evans to Pratt, 22 April 1944; Pratt to Lovatt Evans, 26 April 1944; Sellar to Lovatt Evans, 29 December 1944; Pratt to Lovatt Evans, 1 February 1945; Lovatt Evans to Pratt, 6 February 1945.
244. WL, PP/CLE/A.11, Lovatt Evans papers, Wilson to Lovatt Evans, 1 May 1944.
245. WL, PP/CLE/A.11, Lovatt Evans papers, unidentified author to Lovatt Evans, 23 April 1944.
246. TNA, WO188/802, p. 112.
247. DERA 1999, p. 54.
248. TNA, PREM3/65, Brown to Churchill, 27 January 1944 (Most Secret).
249. DERA 1999, p. 54; Parker 1996, pp. 64–8.
250. Harris, Paxman 1982, pp. 68–106; Parker 1996, pp. 61ff.; DERA 1999, pp. 13f.; another biological warfare option under consideration was the use of the Brucella bacteria, code-named 'US'. Known as brucellosis, the disease can lead to fevers, headaches, night sweats, and fatigue in humans and can be transmitted by consuming unpasteurized milk or exposure to livestock such as cattle, sheep, and pigs; TNA, DEFE2/1251, Appendix, P. Fildes, 12 November 1945.
251. TNA, PREM3/65, Cherwell to Churchill, 25 February 1944 (Most Secret).
252. TNA, PREM3/89, Personal Minute Churchill to Ismay, 6 July 1944; also Harris, Paxman 1982, pp. 127ff.
253. TNA, PREM3/89, Personal Minute Churchill to Ismay, 6 July 1944; also Harris, Paxman 1982, pp. 127ff.

254. TNA, PREM3/89, 'Military Considerations Affecting the Initiation of Chemical and Other Special Forms of Warfare'; Harris, Paxman 1982, pp. 130ff.

255. TNA, PREM3/89, 'Military Considerations Affecting the Initiation of Chemical and Other Special Forms of Warfare'.

256. Carter 2000, p. 53.

257. TNA, PREM3/89, 'Military Considerations Affecting the Initiation of Chemical and Other Special Forms of Warfare'.

258. TNA, PREM3/89, 'Military Considerations Affecting the Initiation of Chemical and Other Special Forms of Warfare'.

259. TNA, PREM3/89, 'Military Considerations Affecting the Initiation of Chemical and Other Special Forms of Warfare'; Harris, Paxman 1982, p. 132.

260. TNA, PREM3/89, 'Military Considerations Affecting the Initiation of Chemical and Other Special Forms of Warfare'.

261. TNA, PREM3/89, Personal Minute, Ismay to Churchill, 28 July 1944.

262. TNA, PREM3/89, Personal Minute, Churchill to Ismay, 29 July 1944.

263. TNA, PREM3/89, War Cabinet, Joint Intelligence Subcommittee, 'Use of Chemical Warfare by the Germans', 23 April 1945.

CHAPTER 5

1. Breitman 1999, pp. 207ff.

2. Ministry of Home Security 1943, p. 23.

3. TNA, WO32/21200, 'Disposal of Enemy Gas Samples Overseas', 15 November 1944.

4. TNA, WO32/21200, 'German Gas Shell', 16 April 1945.

5. TNA, WO32/21200, Bolkin (DSWV) to Davidson Pratt (CCDD), 'Capture of German Gas Bomb Dumps', 28 April 1945.

6. TNA, WO32/21200, 'Report on Enemy Shell from Chief Superintendent, Chemical Defence Experimental Station, Porton, Top Secret, to CCDD, MoS', 10 April 1945.

7. 'Nitrile' is the correct term used in the source. It is not 'nitrite'.

8. TNA, WO32/21200, 'Report on Enemy Shell from Chief Superintendent, Chemical Defence Experimental Station, Porton, Top Secret, to CCDD, MoS', 10 April 1945.

9. TNA, WO32/21200, 'Report on Enemy Shell from Chief Superintendent, Chemical Defence Experimental Station, Porton, Top Secret, to CCDD, MoS', 10 April 1945.

10. TNA, WO32/21200, 'Progress Report No. 1—Enemy Gas Shell', Top Secret, 11 April 1945.

11. TNA, WO32/21200, 'Second Progress Report on German Shell Filling', Top Secret, 12 April 1945.

12. TNA, WO32/21200, 'Second Progress Report on German Shell Filling', Top Secret, 12 April 1945.

13. In 1989/90, Feldberg's research practices on animals—which involved the 'burning' of rabbits and surgical operations without proper anaesthesia—were exposed by an animal rights group which led to a Medical Research Council inquiry and the withdrawal of his Home Office Project License.

14. Adrian et al. 1946; see also Adrian et al. 1947; SIPRI 1971, p. 65 on the history of carbamates (a class of ChE inhibiting agents); also Saunders 1957.

15. Adrian et al. 1946; also E.D. Adrian, W. Feldberg, B.A. Kilby, and M. Kilby, 'Report XZ71 on Dimethyl Fluorophosphonates to the MoS', 8 October 1941; A.A. Barrett, W. Feldberg, B.A. Kilby, and M. Kilby, 'Report XZII1 on Physiological Examination of Di*iso*propyl Fluorophosphonates to the MoS', 10 November 1942; both reports in Adrian et al. 1946.

16. M. Dixon, and J.F. Mackworth, Report No. 13, 'Mode of Action of Fluorophosphonate Esters', to the MoS, 23 April 1942; M. Dixon and E.C. Webb, Report No. 27, 'The Potency of Fluorophosphonate Esters and Related Compounds as Inhibitors of Cholinesterase', to the MoS, 18 May 1944; both reports in Adrian et al. 1946.

17. University of Liverpool (UoL), Special Collection and Archives, D106/2/13, Porton Report No. 2632, E. Boyland and F.F. McDonald, 'The Toxicity and Stability of PF-3 and T 2002', 17 July 1944. Correspondence of Prof Wilson, whilst at University College Hospital Medical School, London, with the MoS (Porton Experimental Station) regarding his PF-3 research (1946–1951).

18. UoL, Special Collection and Archives, D106/2/13, Porton Report No. 2632, E. Boyland and F.F. McDonald, 'The Toxicity and Stability of PF-3 and T 2002', 17 July 1944.

19. TNA, WO32/21200, Brunswick (DSWV) to Assistant Chief of the Imperial General Staff ACIGS (W), 14 April 1945.

20. TNA, WO32/21200, 'Second Progress Report on German Shell Filling', Top Secret, 12 April 1945.

21. TNA, WO32/21200, Main HQ 21 Army Group, 'German Grünring 3 Shell', 16 April 1945. In this context, the term 'charging' refers to the active content inside a chemical weapon, i.e. 'payload', specifically to the newly discovered nerve agents.

22. TNA, WO32/21200, Invitation to Meeting at Savoy Hill House, 13 April 1945.

23. TNA, WO32/21200, Brunswick (DSWV) to ACIGS(W), 14 April 1945.

24. The cipher telegram included ACIGS, the Directors of Military Operations (DMO), Military Intelligence (DMI), Military Training (DMT), and Royal Artillery (DRA), the Director General of Army Medical Services (DGAMS), the Military Liaison Officers (MLO) for Australia, South Africa and New Zealand and the war staff in the India Office; TNA, WO32/21200, Cipher Telegram, 16 April 1945.

25. TNA, WO32/21200, 'German Gas Shell', 17 April 1945.

26. TNA, WO32/21200, 'German Gas Shell', 17 April 1945.

27. Haldane 1940, p. 163.

28. For an analysis of rumours as an instrument of propaganda see Fox 2013.

29. TNA, WO193/723, CSDIC, 'Report of German Chemical Weapons Research Based on Interview with an Unidentified Prisoner of War', 7 March 1943; Tucker 2006, p. 55.

30. TNA, WO32/21200, Brunswick (DSWV) to ACIGS(W), 14 April 1945.

31. TNA, WO32/21200, War Office to BAS Washington, 18 May 1945.

32. TNA, WO32/21200, Air Ministry, Special Signals Office (AMSSO) to the British Joint Services Mission in Washington (BJSM Washington), Top Secret Cipher Telegram, Dispatched by OTP (one-time pad, an uncrackable encryption technique), 19 June 1945.

33. TNA, WO32/21200, Admiralty, Naval Staff, Tactical, Torpedo and Staff Duties Division to War Office, DSWV, 29 June 1945.

34. TNA, WO32/21200, Maj Gen Brunskill (DSWV) to Headquarters, 21 Army Group, 16 April 1945.

35. TNA, WO32/21200, Davidson Pratt (CCDD) to War Office, 26 April 1945.

36. TNA, WO32/21200, Bolkin (DSWV) to Davidson Pratt (CCDD), 'Capture of German Gas Bomb Dumps', 28 April 1945.

37. TNA, WO32/21200, 'Examination of CW Samples', 22 April 1945.

38. TNA, WO32/21200, Bolkin (DSWV) to Davidson Pratt (CCDD), 'Capture of German Gas Bomb Dumps', 28 April 1945.

39. A US Chemical Warfare Officer, for example, discovered two new types of chemical bombs in southern Germany, one marked with a yellow nose, green ring, and green cross, and one with a yellow nose, green ring, and red cross; TNA, WO32/21200, Wansbrough-Jones (DSWV) to CCDD, 30 April 1945.

40. TNA, WO32/21200, Wansbrough-Jones (DSWV) to 21 Army Group, 29 April 1945.

41. TNA, WO32/21200, 'Appreciation of the Information of the Sarin Type Compounds Available to the USSR', 24 October 1945.

42. TNA, WO32/21200, 'Appreciation of the Information of the Sarin Type Compounds Available to the USSR', 24 October 1945; see also TNA, WO32/21200, Jürgen E. von Klenck, 'History of the Seewerk', no date.

43. TNA, WO32/21200, Ptn. 4240 (V. 3956), 'Substance T. 2104, Interim Report', 26 April 1945.

44. TNA, WO32/21200, Ptn. 4240 (V. 3956), 'Substance T. 2104, Interim Report', 26 April 1945.

45. Schmidt 2004, p. 129.

46. TNA, WO32/21200, Signals Message, Secret, BM 5267, 19 May 1945. For Welchman and Davidson Pratt see also Images 7 and 13.

47. TNA, FO371/46914.

48. TNA, WO32/21200, Minutes of the Meeting held in the Oak Room, Metropole Building, War Office, on 25 May 1945 to discuss the Employment of Raubkammer.

49. TNA, WO32/21200, Ptn./1516/1, Porton Group, 'Trials at Raubkammer–Summer 1945', 4 June 1945.

50. TNA, WO32/21200, Ptn./1516/1, Porton Group, 'Trials at Raubkammer–Summer 1945', 4 June 1945.

51. TNA, WO32/21200, S.J. Notley to CS Porton, Press Reporters Visit to Raubkammer, 20 July 1945; War Office (Brunskill) to 21 Army Group (Brig T & CW), 23 July 1945.

52. TNA, WO32/21200, 'First Interim Review of the Work at Raubkammer of No. 1 Porton Group', 30 July 1945.

53. TNA, WO32/21200, No. 1 Porton Group, BLA (British Liberation Army), 'Some Notes on German CW Air Weapons and Reputed Performances', 15 August 1945. The report was signed by Lt Col H. Cullumbine (RAMC), Sqn Ldr R. Hartigan, Maj Irving P. Graef (MC, AUS) and Dean (CWS, USSTAF).

54. TNA, WO32/21200, 'Interrogation of German Personnel', 27 July 1945; 'Interrogation of German Personnel at Dustbin and Ashcan', 8 August, 1945.

55. TNA, WO32/21200, GS01, Handwritten note (22 July 1945).

56. TNA, WO32/21200, 'Arrangements for BIOS Interrogation of Hermann Ochsner', c. November 1945.

57. TNA, WO32/21200, 'Questionnaire and Aide-Memoire for Interrogation of German Personnel at Dustbin', no date. For the history of the Nuremberg Doctors' Trial see Schmidt 2006.

58. TNA, WO32/21200, 'Reports of Interrogations on CW of von Rundstedt, Halder, and Blumentritt', September 1945; see also Schmidt 2004, pp. 73–104.

59. TNA, WO32/21200, 'Interrogation of German General Officers on CW Policy', 20 September 1945.

60. TNA, WO32/21200, Top Secret Cipher Telegram about the disposal of stocks of German CW material, 19 August 1945; also McCamley 2006, pp. 135ff.

61. TNA, WO32/21200, 'Disposal of Stocks of German Nerve Gases', February 1946.

62. TNA, WO32/21200, War Office to Cabinet Offices, 26 February 1946.

63. TNA, WO32/21200, 'Disposal of Stocks of German Nerve Gases', February 1946.

64. TNA, WO32/21200, 'Disposal of Stocks of German Nerve Gases', February 1946.

65. McCamley 2006, pp. 136–40.

66. TNA, WO32/21200, 'Disposal of Raubkammer', HQ BAOR to Under Secretary of State, War Office, 18 February 1946.

67. TNA, WO32/20606, Draft notes on 'Special Informal Conference of Chairman of Sub-Committee of the Chemical Board, Held on 22 October 45 to Discuss General Staff Policy on Chemical Warfare', 31 October 1945; see also Image 17. Many of those who attended the meeting in October 1945 can be seen in the photograph, including Childs, Hartley, Lovatt Evans, and Wansbrough-Jones.

68. TNA, WO32/20606, Brunswick (DSWV) to Controller, Chemical Defence Development (CCDD), October 1945.

69. TNA, WO32/20606, 'Organisation and Weapons Policy Committee. Chemical Warfare: General Staff Policy'. Appendix 'A', 14 February 1946.

70. SIPRI 1971, pp. 84f.

71. SIPRI 1971, p. 85.

72. SIPRI 1971, p. 85.

73. Dubinin 1960, p. 250.

74. MI, Folder 2A/I, Exhibit MNJ/20/2, 'Physiological Observers for Porton', DSWV (G. Brunskill) to D[irector] of O[perations], 28 May 1945, p. 149; also Schmidt 2006; Schmidt 2007a.

75. MI, Folder 2A/I, Exhibit MNJ/20/2, 'Physiological Observers for Porton', DSWV (G. Brunskill) to D[irector] of O[perations], 28 May 1945, p. 149.

76. MI, Folder 2A/I, Exhibit MNJ/20/2, 'Physiological Observers for Porton', DSWV (G. Brunskill) to D[irector] of O[perations], 28 May 1945, p. 149.

77. MI, Folder 2A/I, Exhibit MNJ/20/2, 'Physiological Observers for Porton', DSWV (G. Brunskill) to D[irector] of O[perations], 28 May 1945, p. 149. See note 714 above for the term 'charging'.

78. MI, Folder 2A/I, Exhibit MNJ/20/2, 'Instructions for Special Attachment of a Platoon to the CDES, Porton', 16 July 1945, pp. 150f.

79. TNA, WO188/802, pp. 131f.

80. TNA, WO32/20606, 'Policy for the Appointment of Chief Superintendents at the CDES, Porton', no date.

81. TNA, WO32/20606, DSWV (G.H.C. Pennycook) to AMD7, D. Path. (Beyd), 14 May 1946; AMD7, D. Path. (Beyd) to DSWV (G.H.C. Pennycook), 17 May 1946.

82. TNA, WO195/9103, MoS, CDAB, 'Resume of Work on Nerve Gases', 24 July 1946.

83. TNA, WO195/9103, MoS, CDAB, 'Resume of Work on Nerve Gases', 24 July 1946, p. 3.

84. Malcolm Dixon had worked with Rudolph Peters and J.B.S. Haldane in the former Balfour Biological Laboratory for Women in Cambridge during the early 1920s; Peters 1959, p. 4.

85. TNA, WO195/9103, MoS, CDAB, 'Resume of Work on Nerve Gases', 24 July 1946, pp. 5f. The following experts contributed to the 1947 symposium: M. Dixon; A.G. Ogston; J.C. Boursnell; D.M. Needham, R.H.S. Thompson; E.C. Webb; E. Boyland, R.A. Peters; see Williams 1948. For Krebs' experiments on conscientious objectors see Pemberton 2006.

86. UoL, Special Collection and Archives, D106/2/13, Correspondence of Prof Wilson, whilst at University College Hospital Medical School, London, with the MoS (Porton Experimental Station) regarding his PF-3 research (1946–1951).

87. UoL, Special Collection and Archives, D106/2/13, Edson to Wilson, 7 May 1946; Wilson to Edson, 11 May 1946.

88. Pemberton 2006.

89. UoL, Special Collection and Archives, D106/2/13, Uffelmann to Wilson, 14 June 1946.

90. UoL, Special Collection and Archives, D106/2/13, Edson to Wilson, 8 July 1946; Edson to Wilson, 17 September 1946.

91. UoL, Special Collection and Archives, D106/2/13, Edson to Wilson, 8 July 1946.

92. UoL, Special Collection and Archives, D106/2/13, Edson to Wilson, 9 September 1946.

93. UoL, Special Collection and Archives, D106/2/13, Edson to Wilson, 9 September 1946.

94. UoL, Special Collection and Archives, D106/2/13, Edson Memorandum, 5 October 1946.

95. UoL, Special Collection and Archives, D106/2/13, Wilson to Edson, 23 January 1947.

96. *BMJ*, Medical News, Appointments at Birmingham University, 2 (1964), 5419, p. 1275; *BMJ*, Universities and Colleges, 287 (1983), 6391, p. 566; *BMJ*, Medical News, New Professors, University of London, 2 (1979), 6181, p. 56.

97. *BMJ*, New Director General of Army Medical Services, 1 (1977), 6065, p. 912; also TNA, WO195/16136, Porton Note No. 119, Annexure A of Addendum, 'Administrative Instructions for the Attachment of Army Personnel to the Chemical Defence Experimental Establishment as Volunteers for Tests', December 1963 (Lt Col R.P. Bradshaw) and Annexure C of Addendum, 'Notice Board Leaflet', 1964 (Lt Col R.P. Bradshaw).

98. *BMJ*, Obituary, T. Simpson, 287 (1983), 6386, p. 223.

99. *BMJ*, Obituary, R.J. Moylan-Jones, 291 (1985), 6496, p. 681; and 291 (1985), 6498, p. 830.

100. NARA, RG319, Entry 47-A, Box 13, File 383.4–600.IT, John Edgar Hoover (FBI) to Assistant Chief of Staff-G-2, Department of the Army, 23 September 1952.

101. Hansard, HC Debate, vol. 342 cc818–22, Nancekuke Base, 18 January 2000.

102. NARA, RG319, Entry 47-A, Box 13, File 470.6 (1949), DCDRD (UK) to Chief Chemical Officer, Department of the Army, 4 January 1952.

103. TNA, WO32/20606, BJSM, Washington, to MoD, London, 20 April 1953; Cabinet Defence Committee, 'Policy for Chemical Warfare', 8 February 1954.

104. MI, Folder 2B, Exhibit RCL/41, Porton Report No. 2747, 'Preliminary Report on the Potential Value of Nerve Gases as CW Agents', 18 January 1947, p. 1.

105. TNA, WO32/21200, 'Second Progress Report on German Shell Filling', Top Secret, 12 April 1945.

106. MI, Folder 2B, Exhibit RCL/41, Porton Report No. 2747, 'Preliminary Report on the Potential Value of Nerve Gases as CW Agents', 18 January 1947, p. 1.

107. MI, Folder 2B, Exhibit RCL/41, Porton Report No. 2747, 'Preliminary Report on the Potential Value of Nerve Gases as CW Agents', 18 January 1947, pp. 5f.

108. MI, Folder 2D, Exhibit CR/6, Pamphlet entitled 'Defence against Gas (Navy). Nerve Gases', 1947, pp. 782–8; MI, Folder 2D, Exhibit CR/7, 'Home Office Civil Defence Manual of Basic Training', vol. 2: Pamphlet No. 1 1949, pp. 789–93; MI, Folder 2D, Exhibit CR/5, VHS Video entitled 'Nerve Gas' (Air Ministry Training Film 1952), in envelope at front of file; see also the TV documentary 'The Secrets of Porton Down' (Observer Films, 1994).

109. MoS 1952a; MoS 1952b.

110. MoS, Minutes of Biology Committee of the CDAB, 9 February 1951.

111. Carter, Balmer 1999, p. 303; Harris, Paxman 1982, p. 177.

112. WO188/2307, Progress Reports from Sobo Field Trials Area, Obanakoro, Nigeria, 1949–1951; WO188/2201, Field Trials at Benin Obanakoro Plain, Nigeria, of Weapons, Equipment, Stores and Clothing under Tropical Conditions, April to June 1951; WO188/2309, Investigation of Possible Field Trials Area at Sobo, Obanakoro, Nigeria, 1950–1952; WO189/1400, Report on 1951–1952 Expedition to Obanakoro, Nigeria, 1953; WO195/12220; Offensive Equipment Committee: Report on Expedition to Obanakoro Nigeria, 1953; WO189/1403; Report on Fourth Expedition to Obanakoro, Nigeria, 1954–1955.

113. *BMJ*, Obituary, W.S.S. Ladell, 4 (1970), 5737, pp. 751–2; TNA, DEFE13/1055, Chemical Warfare, 'Biographical Notes of People to be Met at CDEE and MRE', 12 July 1968.

114. TNA, WO188/802, pp. 133f.

115. The IWM, Duxford, holds a collection of an estimated one hundred images of one of Porton's 'expeditions' to Sobo, Obanakoro, Nigeria in January and February 1952. The images were shot in four batches on 13 January 1952, 16 January 1952, [?] January 1952, and 5 February 1952. However, since these images exist as negatives only, a full assessment of the material will have to wait until it is more readily accessible in either printed or digitized format. IWM, Photographic Collection, Folder Leica Index LE, SoBo, West Africa Trial, *c.* 1952.

116. MI, Folder 2B, Exhibit RCL/41, Porton Report No. 2747, 'Preliminary Report on the Potential Value of Nerve Gases as CW Agents', 18 January 1947, p. 1.

117. MI, Folder 2B, Exhibit MNJ/39, Porton Memorandum No. 34, 'Appreciation of the Potential CW Value of Nerve Gases Based on Information Available up to 30.6.49', 30 June 1949, pp. 29–38, here p. 31, p. 37.

118. For the history of the Nuremberg Doctors' Trial see Schmidt 2004; see also Schmidt 2007a and Schmidt 2007c. The organization declared criminal by the IMT was Himmler's SS (*Schutzstaffel*).

119. TNA, WO195/9678, CDAB, 'German CW Experiments on Human Beings', Maj D.C. Evans, 12 January 1948.

120. TNA, WO195/9678, CDAB, 'German CW Experiments on Human Beings', Maj D.C. Evans, 12 January 1948.

121. TNA, WO195/9678, CDAB, 'German CW Experiments on Human Beings', Maj D.C. Evans, 12 January 1948.

122. TNA, WO195/9678, CDAB, 'German CW Experiments on Human Beings', Maj D.C. Evans, 12 January 1948.
123. TNA, WO195/9678, CDAB, 'German CW Experiments on Human Beings', Maj D.C. Evans, 12 January 1948.
124. TNA, WO195/9678, CDAB, 'German CW Experiments on Human Beings', Maj D.C. Evans, 12 January 1948.
125. For debates about the origin and authorship of the Nuremberg Code see, for example, Grodin 1992; Shuster 1997; Shuster 1998; Shevell 1998; Schmidt 2001; Schmidt 2004, Schmidt 2007c.
126. Schmidt 2004, pp. 256f.; also Dörner, Ebbinghaus 1999, pp. 11,374–5.
127. Schmidt 2004, pp. 256f.; also Dörner, Ebbinghaus 1999, pp. 11,374–5.
128. Pulvertaft 1952, p. 840.
129. Pulvertaft 1952, p. 840.
130. Shimkin 1953, p. 206.
131. Shimkin 1953, p. 206.
132. Klee 1997, pp. 173–6; also TNA, WO195/9678, CDAB, 'German CW Experiments on Human Beings', Maj D.C. Evans, 12 January 1948.
133. TNA, WO32/20606, Scientific Adviser to the Army Council to Brig G.H.C. Pennycook, DSWV, War Office, 19 August 1947.
134. TNA, WO32/20606, Scientific Adviser to the Army Council to Brig G.H.C. Pennycook, DSWV, War Office, 19 August 1947.
135. TNA, WO32/20606, Handwritten notes on 'Toxic Fragments', 22 August 1947.
136. TNA, WO32/20606, Handwritten notes on 'Toxic Fragments', 22 August 1947.
137. TNA, WO195/10813, Biology Committee of the CDAB, W.H.E. McKee and B. Woolcott, PTP 143, 'Report on Exposures of Unprotected Men and Rabbits to Low Concentrations of Nerve Gas Vapour', 22 December 1949.
138. MI, Folder 2B, Exhibit RCL/41, Porton Report No. 2747, 'Preliminary Report on the Potential Value of Nerve Gases as CW Agents', 18 January 1947, p. 1.
139. See UoK, Porton Archive, B311/US CW/Use of Volunteers, The Inspector General, Department of the Army, 'Use of Volunteers in Chemical Agent Research', 10 March 1976.
140. Schmidt 2012b, pp. 5ff.
141. Moreno 1999, p. 161.
142. Moreno 1999, p. 167.
143. Moreno 1999, p. 168.
144. Moreno 1999, p. 169.
145. United States Advisory Committee on Human Radiation Experiments 1995, pp. 56–63.
146. Moreno 1999, pp. 169f.
147. UoK, Hot Docs Alan Folder, Evans to Mumford, 23 January 1953.
148. UoK, Hot Docs Alan Folder, Evans to Mumford, 23 January 1953.

149. UoK, Hot Docs Alan Folder, Mumford and Perren to Evans, 11 February 1953.

150. UoK, Hot Docs Alan Folder, Mumford and Perren to Evans, 11 February 1953; Appendix 'A' to War Office Memorandum 112/Misc/5860/AG1(A) dated 6 November 1950.

151. The Chemical Corps Medical Laboratories were represented by Col M.W. Bayliss, Col G.L. Orth, Lt Col H.K. Greer, Lt J.F. Gammill, G.L. Bushey, J.B. Dill, T.W. Green, J.E. Robinson, S.D. Silver, H.J. Stubblefield, A.G. Wedum, A.S. Marrazzi. Maj S.E. Lifton and David Grob attended as guests. MI, Folder 2E, Exhibit MPG/231, Medical and Related Problems Committee Meeting of the Chemical Corps Advisory Council, Army Chemical Center, 20–21 March 1953, pp. 88–115, here p. 91.

152. MI, Folder 2E, Exhibit MPG/231, Medical and Related Problems Committee Meeting of the Chemical Corps Advisory Council, Army Chemical Center, 20–21 March 1953, pp. 88–115, here p. 113.

153. For McGehee Harvey see McKusick 2000; also McGehee Harvey 1981.

154. For the Nuremberg Doctors' Trial see Schmidt 2004.

155. MI, Folder 2E, Exhibit MPG/231, Medical and Related Problems Committee Meeting of the Chemical Corps Advisory Council, Army Chemical Center, 20–21 March 1953, pp. 88–115, here p. 105. For Grob's research work on nerve agents at Johns Hopkins see Marrs et al. 1996, p. 118.

156. MI, Folder 2E, Exhibit MPG/231, Medical and Related Problems Committee Meeting of the Chemical Corps Advisory Council, Army Chemical Center, 20–21 March 1953, pp. 88–115, here pp. 110–13.

157. MI, Folder 2E, Exhibit MPG/231, Medical and Related Problems Committee Meeting of the Chemical Corps Advisory Council, Army Chemical Center, 20–21 March 1953, pp. 88–115, here pp. 110–13.

158. MI, Folder 2E, Exhibit MPG/231, Medical and Related Problems Committee Meeting of the Chemical Corps Advisory Council, Army Chemical Center, 20–21 March 1953, pp. 88–115, here p. 113.

159. MI, Folder 2E, Exhibit MPG/231, Medical and Related Problems Committee Meeting of the Chemical Corps Advisory Council, Army Chemical Center, 20–21 March 1953, pp. 88–115, here p. 113.

160. Moreno 1999, pp. 172ff.

161. MI, Folder 2B, Exhibit MNJ/39, Porton Memorandum No. 34, 'Appreciation of the Potential CW Value of Nerve Gases Based on Information Available up to 30.6.49', 30 June 1949, pp. 29–38, here p. 31; MI, Transcript, Day 60, p. 88.

162. MI, Folder 2B, Exhibit RCL/41, Porton Report No. 2747, 'Preliminary Report on the Potential Value of Nerve Gases as CW Agents', 18 January 1947, p. 5; MI, Folder 2B, Exhibit MNJ/39, Porton Memorandum No. 34, 'Appreciation of the Potential CW Value of Nerve Gases Based on Information Available up to 30.6.49', 30 June 1949, pp. 29–38, here p. 31; pp. 36f.

163. MI, Folder 2B, Exhibit JJH/49, PTP 134, 'Penetration of Clothing by Liquid GB and GF', 3 March 1950, pp. 76–90; MI, Folder 2B, Exhibit RCL/26, PTP 172, 'Absorption of GB Vapour through the Skin of Rabbits', 8 March 1950, pp. 91–108; MI, Transcript, Day 60, p. 95.

164. See also MI, Folder 2B, Exhibit RCL/75, PTP 215, 'A Comparison between Depilated and Clipped Skin on the Percutaneous Toxicity of Nerve Gases to Rabbits', c. January 1951, pp. 126–34.

165. MI, Transcript, Day 60, p. 93.

166. MI, Folder 2B, Exhibit MNJ/39, Porton Memorandum No. 34, 'Appreciation of the Potential CW Value of Nerve Gases Based on Information Available up to 30.6.49', 30 June 1949, pp. 29–38, here p. 38.

167. Carter, Pearson 1996a, pp. 83–97.

168. MI, Folder 2E, Exhibit MPG/197/A, Fourth Tripartite Co-ordination Meeting, 5–16 September 1949, pp. 1–2.

169. MI, Folder 2E, Exhibit MPG/198, Fifth Tripartite Co-ordination Meeting on Chemical and Biological Warfare, 4–13 October 1950, pp. 3–9, here p. 5; 'Report of Subcommittee on Percutaneous Toxicity of Nerve Gas'; also Suffield Experimental Station, Alberta, 'Minutes of Second Meeting to Discuss Dispersion of Agents CW, Smoke and Flame', 10 October 1950.

170. MI, Folder 2B, Exhibit MNJ/30, PTP 399, 'Percutaneous Toxicity of G-Compounds', 11 January 1954, pp. 267–318, here p. 273; MI, Transcript, Day 60, p. 102.

171. MI, Folder 2E, Exhibit MPG/198, Fifth Tripartite Co-ordination Meeting on Chemical and Biological Warfare, 4–13 October 1950, pp. 3–9.

172. MI, Folder 2E, Exhibit MPG/184, 'Suffield Experimental Station, A Brief Review of the Activities at Suffield during 1951', 12 September 1951, pp. 16–21.

173. MI, Folder 2E, Exhibit MPG/198, Fifth Tripartite Co-ordination Meeting on Chemical and Biological Warfare, 4–13 October 1950, pp. 3–9, here p. 7.

174. MI, Transcript, Day 60, p. 105; also MI, Folder 2E, Exhibit MPG/197/A, Sixth Tripartite Meeting, 17–28 September 1951, pp. 22–4.

175. TNA, WO188/719, 'CDEE Progress of CW Items of Service Interest', Twelfth Meeting, 28 November 1952; TNA, WO195/12139, Biology Committee of the CDAB, 7 January 1953.

176. Porton staff attending the meeting included M. Ainsworth, J.D. Cruikshank, H. Cullumbine, D.R. Davis, R. Holmes, A. Muir, E.A. Perren, A.L. Leigh Silver, and K.E.V. Spencer. J.A. Clements, and H.O. Michel from the United States were working at Porton on secondment. E.E. Haddon represented the CDRD. P.G. Wright attended on behalf of University College London.

177. TNA, WO195/12139, Biology Committee of the CDAB, 7 January 1953.

178. TNA, WO188/719, 'CDEE Progress of CW Items of Service Interest', Twelfth Meeting, 28 November 1952.

179. MI, Folder 2B, Exhibit RCL/27, PTP 135, 'Cholinesterase as an Aid to the Early Diagnosis of Nerve Gas Poisoning', part 1: 'Variations in the Cholinesterase

in the Blood of Humans', 26 September 1949, pp. 39–49; MI, Folder 2B, Exhibit RCL/28/A, PTP 136, 'Cholinesterase as an Aid to the Early Diagnosis of Nerve Gas Poisoning', part 2: 'The Variation of Blood Cholinesterase in Man before and after the Administration of Very Small Quantities of G Vapour by Inhalation', 27 September 1949, pp. 50–69; MI, Folder 2B, Exhibit RCL/29/A, PTP 236, 'Cholinesterase as an Aid to the Early Diagnosis of Nerve Gas Poisoning', part 3: 'The Variation of Plasma and Red Blood Cell Cholinesterase in Healthy Adults', 25 April 1951, pp. 109–25; TNA, WO195/12139, Biology Committee of the CDAB, 7 January 1953.

180. Callaway et al. 1951; Barnes, Davies 1951; Aldridge, Davies 1952; Lucas, Miles 1955; Davies, Nicholls 1955.

181. MI, Folder 2B, Exhibit MNJ/134, CDAB, 5 February 1953, pp. 173–82. The meeting was attended by E.D. Adrian, S. Barratt, A.E. Childs, H.J. Emeleus, P. Fildes, J.H. Gaddum, G.N. Gadsby, J.M. Holford, E.E.H. Jones, J.W. Martin, S.A. Mumford, J.W.C. Phillips, R.H.S. Thompson, F.L. Dawney, G.A.A. Moir, E.E. Bateman, A.C. Peacock, E.A. Perren, J.A. Sadd, E.E. Haddon, and J. McAulay.

182. Galbraith 2000, pp. 104f.

183. MI, Folder 2B, Exhibit MNJ/134, CDAB, 5 February 1953, pp. 173–82, here p. 178; MI, Transcript, Day 27, pp. 51f.

184. MI, Folder 2B, Exhibit MNJ/134, CDAB, 5 February 1953, pp. 173–82.

185. MI, Folder 2E, Exhibit MPG/197/A, Seventh Tripartite Conference, 15–26 September 1952, pp. 84–5; MI, Transcript, Day 60, pp. 106f.

186. UoK, Hot Docs Alan Folder, MoS to Porton, 10 June 1952.

187. UoK, Hot Docs Alan Folder, Porton to MoS, 20 June 1952; MoS to Evans, 26 June 1952.

188. MI, Folder 2E, Exhibit MPG/200, Franklin to Cullumbine, 22 October 1952, pp. 116–21, p. 117; also MI, Folder 2A, Exhibit MNJ/20/1, MoS, 'Report of a Court of Inquiry into Death of Maddison', May 1953, pp. 84–142, Testimony Harry Cullumbine, pp. 91–7.

189. MI, Folder 2E, Exhibit MPG/200, Muir to Franklin, 29 October 1952, pp. 116–21, here p. 118.

190. MI, Folder 2B, Exhibit CEB/16/2, Cullumbine, Handwritten note 'The Percutaneous Toxicity of the G-Compounds', 5 May 1953, pp. 186–92, here p. 187; also MI, Transcript, Day 59, pp. 73ff.

191. MI, Folder 2D, Exhibit MPG/36, Extracts from Observers Chamber Tests Book, 20 December 1950–31 May 1954, pp. 10f.

192. MI, Folder 2B, Exhibit CEB/16/2, Cullumbine, Handwritten note 'The Percutaneous Toxicity of the G-Compounds', 5 May 1953, pp. 186–92, here p. 187; MI, Folder 2B, Exhibit JJH/187/5, Cullumbine, Typed note 'The Percutaneous Toxicity of the G-Compounds', 8 May 1953, pp. 204–6, here p. 204; also MI, Transcript, Day 59, pp. 73ff.

193. MI, Transcript, Day 59, pp. 73ff.

194. MI, Transcript, Day 59, p. 78; MI, Folder 2B, Exhibit MNJ/134, CDAB, 5 February 1953, pp. 173–82.

195. MI, Transcript, Day 59, p. 84.

196. MI, Folder 2E, Exhibit MPG/197/A, Evans to Cullumbine, 10 March 1953, pp. 86–7.

197. MI, Folder 2E, Exhibit MPG/200, Cullumbine to Evans, 30 March 1953, pp. 116–21, here p. 120; the three men to whom Cullumbine referred were Mr Sammons (volunteer no. 562), Mr Perry (no. 567) and Mr Moules (no. 603); MI, Transcript, Day 60, pp. 61f.

198. MI, Folder 2E, Exhibit MPG/200, Cullumbine to Evans, 30 March 1953, pp. 116–21, here p. 120.

199. MI, Transcript, Day 60, pp. 60–2.

200. TNA, WO195/12304, Biology Committee of the CDAB, 'Case Report of a Severe Human Poisoning by GB', December 1952, pp. 1–8; see MI, Ulf Schmidt, 'Report on Informed Consent' (unpublished, 2003).

201. TNA, WO195/12304, Biology Committee of the CDAB, 'Case Report of a Severe Human Poisoning by GB', December 1952, pp. 1ff.

202. TNA, WO195/12304, Biology Committee of the CDAB, 'Case Report of a Severe Human Poisoning by GB', December 1952, pp. 3f.

CHAPTER 6

1. TNA, WO32/20843, DGAMS to A.C.W. Drew (DUS (A)), 13 July 1960.

2. MI, Folder 1A, Witness Statement Leslie John Anderson, 22 January 2001, 31 January 2001; MI, Folder 2C, Exhibit LJA/1, Written Narrative L.J. Anderson, 22 January 2001, pp. 450–2.

3. MI, Folder 1A, Witness Statement Leslie John Anderson, 22 January 2001, 31 January 2001; MI, Folder 2C, Exhibit LJA/1, Written Narrative L.J. Anderson, 22 January 2001, pp. 450–2.

4. In July 1999, the Wiltshire Constabulary began to investigate allegations made by a former serviceman, who stated that during his National Service he took part in research into finding a cure for the Common Cold at Porton. As a result of this and other allegations the Constabulary initiated a major enquiry, called 'Operation Antler'. The purpose of the investigation was to examine the role of the Service Volunteer Programme at Porton Down in relation to chemical and biological warfare experiments during the period 1939–1989.

5. MI, Folder 1A, Witness Statement Leslie John Anderson, 22 January 2001, 31 January 2001; MI, Folder 2C, Exhibit LJA/1, Written Narrative L.J. Anderson, 22 January 2001, pp. 450–2.

6. MI, Transcript, Day 61, pp. 99f.

7. MI, Folder 2C, Exhibit MBC/5/A, Air Ministry Orders Re: Porton Down 'Volunteers for Physiological Experiments', 12 February 1953, p. 506; MI, Transcript, Day 59, pp. 94ff.; MI, Folder 2A, Exhibit MNJ/20/1, MoS, 'Report of a Court of Inquiry into Death of Maddison', May 1953, pp. 84–142, here p. 137.

8. MI, Transcript, Day 59, pp. 94ff.; MI, Folder 2A, Exhibit MNJ/20/1, MoS, 'Report of a Court of Inquiry into Death of Maddison', May 1953, pp. 84–142, here p. 137.

9. Equivalent to three hours' work at the current minimum wage.

10. MI, Folder 2B, Exhibit MNJ/30, PTP 399, 'Percutaneous Toxicity of G-Compounds', 11 January 1954, pp. 267–318, here p. 272. MI, Transcript, Day 60, p. 65 lists Sammons' ChE level as 95 and 92 respectively, depending on whether the Warburg or Michel method of measurement was used. Whereas the Coroner used the data recorded in the chamber books, PTP 399 used the mean cholinesterase inhibition level.

11. MI, Folder 2B, Exhibit MNJ/17, PTP 373, 'A Fatal Case of Poisoning with GB', 9 September 1953, pp. 234–50, here p. 245; see also MI, Transcript, Day 60, pp. 63ff.

12. MI, Folder 2B, Exhibit MNJ/30, PTP 399, 'Percutaneous Toxicity of G-Compounds', 11 January 1954, pp. 267–318, here p. 283; MI, Transcript, Day 60, p. 66.

13. MI, Folder 2D, Exhibit MPG/36, Extracts from Observers Chamber Tests Book, 20 December 1950–31 May 1954, p. 12; MI, Folder 2B, Exhibit MNJ/30, PTP 399, 'Percutaneous Toxicity of G-Compounds', 11 January 1954, pp. 267–318, here p. 283; MI, Transcript, Day 60, pp. 66f.

14. MI, Folder 2B, Exhibit MNJ/30, PTP 399, 'Percutaneous Toxicity of G-Compounds', 11 January 1954, pp. 267–318, here p. 283; MI, Transcript, Day 60, pp. 68f.

15. The ChE level of subject number 714, Mr Allan, increased from a mean 85 per cent to 92 per cent some twenty-six hours after contamination. MI, Transcript, Day 60, p. 75.

16. A week after the experiment, still 'mildly confused' as a result of his near-death experience, Kelly was asked by Basil Clarke to undertake a series of psychological tests to assess his 'intellectual efficiency', 'spatial' and 'temporal orientation', 'immediate and recent memory', and 'comprehension'. MI, Folder 2B, Exhibit MNJ/18, PTP 361, 'A Case of Severe GB Poisoning in Man', 21 May 1953, Appendix II, 'Psychological State A Week after Exposure', by Basil Clarke, pp. 222–3.

17. MI, Transcript, Day 60, p. 76.

18. MI, Transcript, Day 60, pp. 72ff.

19. MI, Transcript, Day 61, p. 42.

20. MI, Folder 2D, Exhibit MPG/36, Extracts from Observers Chamber Tests Book, 20 December 1950–31 May 1954, p. 14; MI, Folder 2B, Exhibit MNJ/30, PTP 399, 'Percutaneous Toxicity of G-Compounds', 11 January 1954, pp. 267–318, here p. 284; see especially PTP 361.

21. MI, Folder 2B, Exhibit JJH/187/3, Memorandum by S.A. Mumford on 'Percutaneous Toxicity of Nerve Gas', 29 April 1953, p. 185; MI, Transcript, Day 1; MI, Transcript, Day 60, pp. 79ff.; MI, Folder 1A, Witness Statement Robert Desmond Lynch, 11 February 2004; also Schmidt 2006; Schmidt 2007b.

22. MI, Folder 2B, Exhibit JJH/187/3, Memorandum by S.A. Mumford on 'Percutaneous Toxicity of Nerve Gas', 29 April 1953, p. 185.
23. MI, Transcript, Day 63, p. 68.
24. MI, Folder 2B, Exhibit CEB/16/2, Cullumbine, Handwritten note 'The Percutaneous Toxicity of the G-Compounds', 5 May 1953, pp. 186–192, here pp. 191f.; MI, Folder 2B, Exhibit JJH/187/5, Cullumbine, Typed note 'The Percutaneous Toxicity of the G-Compounds', 8 May 1953, pp. 204–6, here p. 206.
25. MI, Transcript, Day 53, pp. 167f.; MI, Transcript, Day 63, pp. 36f.; Kennedy 2006, pp. 403–34.
26. MI, Folder 2B, Exhibit MNJ/17, PTP 373, 'A Fatal Case of Poisoning with GB', 9 September 1953, pp. 234–50, here p. 244; see also Porton's continued investigation into, and debate about, the 'skin of man' in MI, Folder 2B, Exhibit MNJ/30, PTP 399, 'Percutaneous Toxicity of G-Compounds', 11 January 1954, pp. 267–318, here p. 279.
27. MI, Transcript, Day 61, pp. 42f.; MI, Folder 2B, Exhibit CEB/16/2, Cullumbine, Handwritten note 'The Percutaneous Toxicity of the G-Compounds', 5 May 1953, pp. 186–92, here pp. 189f.
28. WL, Archives and Manuscripts, SA/SRL/M.1/4, Box 31, Lt Col H. Cullumbine, RAMC, 'The Burning Power of White Phosphorus', Addendum I to Porton Report No. 2604, 1 October 1944.
29. MI, Transcript, Day 53, pp. 23f.; MI, Transcript, Day 63, pp. 23f.
30. MI, Transcript, Day 60, pp. 80f.
31. MI, Folder 1A, Witness Statement Henry John Newman, 27 April 2000; also MI, Folder 2D, Exhibit JAM/16, RAF Service Record Ronald Maddison, pp. 144–5; Laville 2004a.
32. MI, Folder 2A, Exhibit MNJ/20/1, MoS, 'Report of a Court of Inquiry into Death of Maddison', May 1953, pp. 84–142, here p. 131; MI, Folder 2D, Exhibit RCL/67/1, PTP 378, 'Psychological Effects of a G-Agent on Men', 14 September 1953, pp. 151–5; TNA, WO195/15638, PTP 857, 'A Study of Personality and Intelligence of Service Volunteers at CDEE', 10 June 1963.
33. MI, Folder 1A, Witness Statement Arthur Derek Ian Ashton, 19 January 2004; John Patrick Greenwood, 26 March 2003; William John Milliken, 8 January 2001.
34. MI, Folder 1A, Witness Statement Henry John Newman, 27 April 2000.
35. MI, Folder 1A, Witness Statement Henry John Newman, 27 April 2000; also MI, Folder 2A/1, Exhibit MNJ/20/2, Statement by M.B. Cox, 8 May 1953, p. 243.
36. MI, Transcript, Day 1; see also Schmidt 2006; Schmidt 2007b.
37. MI, Transcript, Day 1, p. 103.
38. MI, Folder 1A, Witness Statement Alfred Thomas Thornhill, 25 July 2003.
39. MI, Folder 1A, Witness Statement Alfred Thomas Thornhill, 25 July 2003.
40. MI, Transcript, Day 1, pp. 43ff.; also MI, Folder 2D, Exhibit MPG/36, Extracts from Observers Chamber Tests Book, 20 December 1950–31 May 1954, p. 14;

MI, Folder 2D, Exhibit MPG/45, Extracts from Observers Summary Book, 14 July 1950–23 August 1959, p. 33.

41. MI, Folder 2A/I, Exhibit MNJ/20/2, 'Procedure in Connection with Reporting Accidents to Headquarters', December 1952, pp. 281–4.

42. MI, Folder 2A, Exhibit GWL/1/A, Coroner's File re Maddison, 16 May 1953, pp. 1–83, here pp. 47–9.

43. MI, Folder 2A/I, Exhibit MNJ/20/2, Notification to Coroner, Statements by Dr Leigh Silver and Dr Cullumbine, 27 May 1953, p. 215.

44. MI, Folder 2A/I, Exhibit MNJ/20/2, Notification to Coroner, Statements by Dr Leigh Silver and Dr Cullumbine, 27 May 1953, p. 215; MI, Folder 2A, Exhibit GWL/1/A, Coroner's File re Maddison, 16 May 1953, pp. 1–83, here pp. 31–3.

45. MI, Folder 2A, Exhibit GWL/1/A, Coroner's File re Maddison, 16 May 1953, pp. 1–83, here p. 54.

46. McCamley 2006, p. 144.

47. MI, Folder 2A, Exhibit GWL/1/A, Coroner's File re Maddison, 16 May 1953, pp. 1–83, here p. 59. In his 1994 compilation of the then available evidence 'The Maddison Death at CDEE Porton: 1953', Porton's historical consultant, Graydon Carter, concluded that the Coroner had been 'consulted' by the Home Office. However, this does not correspond to the available archival evidence; see MI, Folder 2A/I, Exhibit MNJ/20/2, 'The Maddison Death at CDEE Porton: 1953', 30 March 1994, pp. 314–20, here p. 315. From a contemporary perspective, the Home Office instructions, in essence the telephone call from the Home Office, constituted the equivalent of a Public Interest Immunity Certificate. This meant that the Home Office, in consultation with the MoD, would have to authorize the release of the Coroner's inquest file fifty years later; MI, Folder 2A/I, Exhibit MNJ/20/2, 'The Maddison Death at CDEE Porton: 1953', 30 March 1994, pp. 314–20, here p. 320.

48. MI, Folder 2A, Exhibit GWL/1/A, Coroner's File re Maddison, 16 May 1953, pp. 1–83, here p. 61.

49. MI, Folder 2A/I, Exhibit MNJ/20/2, 'The Maddison Death at CDEE Porton: 1953', 30 March 1994, pp. 314–20, here p. 316.

50. MI, Folder 2A/I, Exhibit MNJ/20/2, 'The Maddison Death at CDEE Porton: 1953', 30 March 1994, pp. 314–20.

51. Maddison's death was officially registered on 19 May 1953 at Salisbury District; MI, Folder 2D, Exhibit CW/1, Certified Copy of Death Certificate of Ronald George Maddison, p. 150.

52. MI, Folder 2A/I, Exhibit MNJ/20/2, Duncan Sandys to Prime Minister Churchill, 7 May 1953, pp. 226–7.

53. MI, Folder 2A/I, Exhibit MNJ/20/2, Duncan Sandys to Prime Minister Churchill, 7 May 1953, pp. 226–7.

54. MI, Folder 2A/I, Exhibit MNJ/20/2, Duncan Sandys to Prime Minister Churchill, 7 May 1953, pp. 226–7.

55. MI, Folder 2A/I, Exhibit MNJ/20/2, Duncan Sandys to Prime Minister Churchill, 7 May 1953, pp. 226–7.

56. MI, Folder 2A/I, Exhibit MNJ/20/2, MoS to Chief Superintendent, Porton, 8 May 1953, p. 301; MI, Folder 2D, Exhibit JJH/187/4, Typed memorandum, Chief Superintendent, Porton, to Head of Physiology Section, 8 May 1953, p. 149.

57. MI, Folder 2A/I, Exhibit MNJ/20/2, 'Fatal Accident at the Chemical Defence Experimental Establishment, Porton, near Salisbury, on 6 May 1953', Statement by the MoS, pp. 196–8.

58. MI, Folder 2A/I, Exhibit MNJ/20/2, 'Nerve Gas Test—6 May 1953', Statements by M.B. Cox, F. Verallo, H.J. Newman, W. Jenkins, M.L. Grady, 8 May 1953, pp. 243–7.

59. MI, Folder 2A, Exhibit GWL/1/A, Coroner's File re Maddison, 16 May 1953, pp. 1–83, here p. 25; also Laville 2004a.

60. TNA, WO286/11, 'Death of LAC Maddison', H. Woodhouse (for the Treasury Solicitor), to Legal 1 (Mr Griffith-Jones), MoS, 15 May 1953; MI, Folder 2A/I, Exhibit MNJ/20/2, 'Death of LAC Maddison', H. Woodhouse (for the Treasury Solicitor), to Legal 1 (Mr Griffith-Jones), MoS, 15 May 1953, pp. 188–189, here p. 189.

61. MI, Folder 2A, Exhibit GWL/1/A, Coroner's File re Maddison, 16 May 1953, pp. 1–83, here pp. 62f.

62. MI, Folder 2A, Exhibit MNJ/20/1, MoS, 'Report of a Court of Inquiry into Death of Maddison', May 1953, pp. 84–142; also MI, Transcript, Day 61, pp. 35ff.

63. Members of the Court of Inquiry included A.E. Childs, DCDRD, D.W. Henderson, Chief Superintendent Microbiological Research Department, B.A. Weston, Deputy Chief Safety Officer, M.P. Griffith-Jones, Legal 1, J.H. Chambers, Principal Medical Officer, R&D Estabs., R.D. Max, RAF, and J.M. Barnes, MRC; MI, Folder 2A, Exhibit MNJ/20/1, MoS, 'Report of a Court of Inquiry into Death of Maddison', May 1953, pp. 84–142, here p. 86.

64. MI, Folder 2A, Exhibit MNJ/20/1, MoS, 'Report of a Court of Inquiry into Death of Maddison', May 1953, pp. 84–142, here pp. 91–129.

65. MI, Folder 2A, Exhibit MNJ/20/1, MoS, 'Report of a Court of Inquiry into Death of Maddison', May 1953, pp. 84–142, here p. 127; MI, Transcript, Day 61, pp. 105f.

66. MI, Folder 2A, Exhibit MNJ/20/1, MoS, 'Report of a Court of Inquiry into Death of Maddison', May 1953, pp. 84–142, here p. 125.

67. MI, Folder 2A, Exhibit MNJ/20/1, MoS, 'Report of a Court of Inquiry into Death of Maddison', May 1953, pp. 84–142, into p. 127.

68. MI, Folder 2A, Exhibit MNJ/20/1, MoS, 'Report of a Court of Inquiry into Death of Maddison', May 1953, pp. 84–142, here p. 128.

69. MI, Folder 2A, Exhibit MNJ/20/1, MoS, 'Report of a Court of Inquiry into Death of Maddison', May 1953, pp. 84–142, here pp. 127f.

70. MI, Folder 2A, Exhibit MNJ/20/1, MoS, 'Report of a Court of Inquiry into Death of Maddison', May 1953, pp. 84–142, here p. 129.

71. MI, Folder 2A, Exhibit MNJ/20/1, MoS, 'Report of a Court of Inquiry into Death of Maddison', May 1953, pp. 84–142, Testimony Harry Cullumbine, pp. 91–7; MI, Folder 2A/I, Exhibit MNJ/20/2, Statement by Harry Cullumbine, no date, pp. 285–6.

72. MI, Folder 2D (Version 2), Exhibit MPG/11/A/2, M. Ainsworth, paragraph concerning author's recollection of Harry Cullumbine from typed document 'Some Recollections of CDE', 6 May 1976, p. 794.

73. MI, Folder 2D (Version 2), Exhibit MPG/11/A/3, M. Ainsworth, paragraph entitled 'The Fatal Accident 1953', extracted from a copy of a typed document 'Some Recollections of CDE', 6 May 1976, p. 795; MI, Transcript, Day 62, pp. 20f.; see also MI, Folder 2B, Exhibit JJH/187/3, Memorandum by S.A. Mumford on 'Percutaneous Toxicity of Nerve Gas', 29 April 1953, p. 185; MI, Transcript, Day 1; MI, Transcript, Day 60, pp. 79ff.

74. Cullumbine 1946; Cullumbine, Box 1946; Pattle, Cullumbine 1956.

75. Cullumbine 1946, p. 576.

76. Cullumbine 1946, p. 576.

77. MI, Folder 2A, Exhibit MNJ/20/1, MoS, 'Report of a Court of Inquiry into Death of Maddison', May 1953, pp. 84–142, Testimony Harry Cullumbine, pp. 95f.

78. MI, Folder 2A, Exhibit MNJ/20/1, MoS, 'Report of a Court of Inquiry into Death of Maddison', May 1953, pp. 84–142, Testimony Harry Cullumbine, pp. 95f.; TNA, WO286/11, 'Death of LAC Maddison', H. Woodhouse (for the Treasury Solicitor), to Legal 1 (Mr Griffith-Jones), MoS, 13 July 1953.

79. MI, Folder 2A, Exhibit MNJ/20/1, MoS, 'Report of a Court of Inquiry into Death of Maddison', May 1953, pp. 84–142, Testimony Harry Cullumbine, pp. 95f.; also MI, Transcript, Day 61, pp. 53f.

80. MI, Folder 2A, Exhibit MNJ/20/1, MoS, 'Report of a Court of Inquiry into Death of Maddison', May 1953, pp. 84–142, Testimony Harry Cullumbine, p. 96.

81. Mumford confirmed Porton's autonomy, stating that the establishment was free to decide the types of tests to be undertaken with all necessary safeguards; MI, Transcript, Day 61, pp. 99f.

82. MI, Folder 2A/I, Exhibit MNJ/20/2, Report by E.D. Adrian to E. Rideal, 12 August 1953, pp. 115–16, here p. 116; MI, Transcript, Day 62, pp. 10ff.

83. MI, Folder 2D, Exhibit MPG/199/1, Cullumbine, unpublished autobiography, 1980s, pp. 226–7.

84. MI, Folder 2A, Exhibit MNJ/20/1, MoS, 'Report of a Court of Inquiry into Death of Maddison', May 1953, pp. 84–142, here pp. 98–100.

85. MI, Folder 2A, Exhibit MNJ/20/1, MoS, 'Report of a Court of Inquiry into Death of Maddison', May 1953, pp. 84–142, here p. 100.

86. MI, Folder 2A, Exhibit MNJ/20/1, MoS, 'Report of a Court of Inquiry into Death of Maddison', May 1953, pp. 84–142, here pp. 101–3; pp. 104–6.

87. MI, Folder 2A, Exhibit MNJ/20/1, MoS, 'Report of a Court of Inquiry into Death of Maddison', May 1953, pp. 84–142, here pp. 104ff.; MI, Folder 2A/I, Exhibit MNJ/20/2, Statements by Richard H. Adrian, Herbert W. Lacon and Thomas W.N. Truckle, no date, pp. 287–90.

88. MI, Folder 2A, Exhibit MNJ/20/1, MoS, 'Report of a Court of Inquiry into Death of Maddison', May 1953, pp. 84–142, here p. 106.

89. MI, Folder 1A, Witness Statement Alan Bangay, 4 May 2000.

90. MI, Folder 2A, Exhibit MNJ/20/1, MoS, 'Report of a Court of Inquiry into Death of Maddison', May 1953, pp. 84–142, here p. 106.

91. MI, Folder 2A, Exhibit MNJ/20/1, MoS, 'Report of a Court of Inquiry into Death of Maddison', May 1953, pp. 84–142, here pp. 107–9; MI, Folder 2A/I, Exhibit MNJ/20/2, Statement by Alfred L. Leigh Silver, no date, pp. 291–2.

92. MI, Folder 2A, Exhibit MNJ/20/1, MoS, 'Report of a Court of Inquiry into Death of Maddison', May 1953, pp. 84–142, here pp. 113–18.

93. MI, Folder 2A, Exhibit MNJ/20/1, MoS, 'Report of a Court of Inquiry into Death of Maddison', May 1953, pp. 84–142, here p. 114.

94. MI, Folder 2A, Exhibit MNJ/20/1, MoS, 'Report of a Court of Inquiry into Death of Maddison', May 1953, pp. 84–142, here p. 118.

95. MI, Folder 2A, Exhibit MNJ/20/1, MoS, 'Report of a Court of Inquiry into Death of Maddison', May 1953, pp. 84–142, here pp. 119–22.

96. MI, Folder 2A, Exhibit MNJ/20/1, MoS, 'Report of a Court of Inquiry into Death of Maddison', May 1953, pp. 84–142, here p. 122.

97. MI, Transcript, Day 61, pp. 94ff.

98. MI, Folder 2A, Exhibit MNJ/20/1, MoS, 'Report of a Court of Inquiry into Death of Maddison', May 1953, pp. 84–142, here p. 122.

99. MI, Folder 2A, p. 89.

100. MI, Folder 2A, pp. 89f.; also Interview (under caution) with Robert Lynch of Porton's physiological department in 1953, 18 February 2002, pp. 1ff., 20, 28–30.

101. MI, Folder 2A, p. 90.

102. TNA, WO286/11, 'Death of LAC Maddison', H. Woodhouse (for the Treasury Solicitor), to Legal 1 (Mr Griffith-Jones), MoS, 15 May 1953; also MI, Folder 2A/I, Exhibit MNJ/20/2, 'Death of LAC Maddison', H. Woodhouse (for the Treasury Solicitor), to Legal 1 (Mr Griffith-Jones), MoS, 15 May 1953, pp. 188–9, here p. 188.

103. TNA, WO286/11, 'Death of LAC Maddison', H. Woodhouse (for the Treasury Solicitor), to Legal 1 (Mr Griffith-Jones), MoS, 15 May 1953; MI, Folder 2A/I, Exhibit MNJ/20/2, 'Death of LAC Maddison', H. Woodhouse (for the Treasury Solicitor), to Legal 1 (Mr Griffith-Jones), MoS, 15 May 1953, pp. 188–9, here p. 189.

104. BBC documentary 'Cold War Dirty Science' (2005), Rob Evans, tape-recorded interview with Porton scientist. Evans subsequently confirmed that the scientist was Kenneth H. Kemp, who died in 2003.

105. MI, Transcript, Day 18, p. 94; also MI, Folder 1A, Witness Statement Robert Desmond Lynch, 11 February 2004.

106. TNA, WO286/11, 'Death of LAC Maddison', Appendix 'A' to 86/Chemical/899(SW1), dated 9 July 1953.

107. MI, Folder 2A/I, Exhibit MNJ/20/2/21, Cawood, PDSR(D) to Childs, DCDRD, 'Volunteers for Physiological Tests at CDEE Porton', 16 June 1953.

108. TNA, WO286/11, 'Death of LAC Maddison', H. Woodhouse (for the Treasury Solicitor), to Legal 1 (Mr Griffith-Jones), MoS, 13 July 1953.

109. See MI, Folder 2A, Exhibit MNJ/20/1, MoS, 'Report of a Court of Inquiry into Death of Maddison', May 1953, pp. 84–142, here p. 95.

110. TNA, WO286/11, 'Death of LAC Maddison', H. Woodhouse (for the Treasury Solicitor), to Legal 1 (Mr Griffith-Jones), MoS, 1 August 1953. The author discovered this correspondence on 17 October 2003 at the headquarters of Operation Antler in Devizes, Wiltshire. As a result, the UK MoD decided in 2005 not to rely on Section 10(2) of the Crown Proceedings Act 1947 as a defence in cases involving nerve agents.

111. MI, Folder 2A/I, Exhibit MNJ/20/2, 'Death of LAC Maddison—Notes on Information given to Father' (and further correspondence), May 1953, pp. 203–14.

112. MI, Folder 2A/I, Exhibit MNJ/20/2, 'Details of Contact between Mr Maddison and CDEE, Porton', 27 May 1953; Statement by Wing Commander Cross, 27 May 1953, pp. 209–11; Carrell 2002, p. 18.

113. MI, Folder 2A/I, Exhibit MNJ/20/2, J.R. Maddison to Chief Superintendent Porton, no date, c. May 1953, p. 222.

114. MI, Folder 2A, Exhibit GWL/1/A, Coroner's File re Maddison, 16 May 1953, pp. 1–83, here p. 78.

115. MI, Folder 2A, Exhibit GWL/1/A, Coroner's File re Maddison, 16 May 1953, pp. 1–83, here p. 79.

116. MI, Folder 2A/I, Exhibit MNJ/20/2, A.R.W. Low (MoS) to Maj John G. Morrison, 27 May 1953, p. 201.

117. MI, Folder 2A/I, Exhibit MNJ/20/2, Extract from Hansard, vol. 516, no. 116, cc5–6, Chemical Defence Establishment, Porton (Fatality), p. 186; also MI, Folder 2A, Exhibit MNJ/20/1, MoS, 'Report of a Court of Inquiry into Death of Maddison', May 1953, pp. 84–142, here p. 85.

118. Age of majority at the time was twenty-one.

119. TNA, WO286/11, 'Death of LAC Maddison', House of Commons, Official Report 17 November 1953, Cols. 1567/8, Experimental Work (Service Volunteers).

120. See MI, Folder 2A, Exhibit MNJ/20/1, MoS, 'Report of a Court of Inquiry into Death of Maddison', May 1953, pp. 84–142, here p. 86 and p. 93.

121. Schmidt 2007b, pp. 300–6; also Lee et al. 2004, p. 19.

122. Statements of Geoffrey Mervin Thorne, 13 January 2003; John Dudley Shepherd, 13 July 2000.

123. MI, Folder 1A, Witness Statement Geoffrey Mervin Thorne, 13 January 2003.
124. MI, Folder 1A, Witness Statement John Dudley Shepherd, 13 July 2000.
125. Schmidt 2007b, pp. 300–6.
126. MI, Folder 1A, Witness Statement Renver Charles Brant, 23 October 2002; Granville Popplewell, 20 December 2000; also John Leonard Newbury, 22 March 2000; 29 April 2003.
127. Statements of Renver Charles Brant, 23 October 2002; Derek Melbourne Johns, 21 January 2003.
128. MI, Folder 1A, Witness Statement Alan Bangay, 4 May 2000; Granville Popplewell, 20 December 2000; Derrick Henry Johnson, 6 February 2003. Peter Sammons remembered that the notice included the word 'nerve gas' but it did not mean anything to him; Statement of Peter John Sammons, 2 May 2003.
129. MI, Folder 1A, Witness Statement Derrick Henry Johnson, 6 February 2003. Johnson may have been referring to the word 'physiological', which appears to have been on the notices asking for research subjects.
130. MI, Folder 1A, Witness Statement Alan Bangay, 4 May 2000.
131. MI, Folder 1A, Witness Statement Granville Popplewell, 20 December 2000.
132. MI, Folder 1A, Witness Statement Kenneth Earl, 15 May 2000; also UoK, Porton Archive, video-taped interview with Kenneth Earl, 17 June 2005.
133. MI, Folder 1A, Witness Statement Kenneth Earl, 16 November 2000, James Patrick Kelly, 2 May 2003.
134. MI, Folder 1A, Witness Statement John Leonard Newbury, 29 April 2003.
135. MI, Folder 1A, Witness Statement John Leonard Newbury, 22 March 2000; also Statement of John Dudley Shepherd, 13 July 2000, who was told that Porton was 'investigating [the] side effects of a very low dose of a nerve gas of some type by using [a] radioactive tracer label'.
136. MI, Folder 1A, Witness Statement John Leonard Newbury, 22 March 2000; 29 April 2003.
137. MI, Folder 1A, Witness Statement James Patrick Kelly, 2 May 2003.
138. MI, Folder 1A, Witness Statement James Patrick Kelly, 18 November 1999.
139. MI, Folder 1A, Witness Statement James Patrick Kelly, 2 May 2003.
140. MI, Folder 1A, Witness Statement James Patrick Kelly, 2 May 2003.
141. MI, Folder 1A, Witness Statement Frederick Henry John Moules, 5 June 2000.
142. MI, Folder 1A, Witness Statement Peter George de Carle Parker, 7 June 2000.
143. MI, Folder 1A, Witness Statement Peter George de Carle Parker, 13 December 2001; Kenneth Earl, 15 May 2000; John Leonard Newbury, 29 April 2003; Douglas Michael Gray, 17 February 2003.
144. MI, Folder 1A, Witness Statement Douglas Michael Gray, 17 February 2003.
145. MI, Folder 1A, Witness Statement Peter John Sammons, 2 May 2003.
146. MI, Folder 1A, Witness Statement Peter John Sammons, 7 December 2000.
147. 'Although I was recalled to Porton, I was determined not to take part in any further tests. My experiences had scared me to death. I was so frightened by

it that I was able to refuse requests by senior officers who wanted me to take part in further tests. I would not ordinarily have refused a senior officer's requests': MI, Folder 1A, Witness Statement Peter John Sammons, 2 May 2003.

148. MI, Folder 1A, Witness Statement Peter John Sammons, 7 December 2000.

149. See MI, Folder 2B, Exhibit MNJ/39, Porton Memorandum No. 34, 'Appreciation of the Potential CW Value of Nerve Gases Based on Information Available up to 30.6.49', 30 June 1949, pp. 29–38, and MI, Folder 2D, Exhibit MNJ/19, Porton Memorandum No. 39, 'Physiological Assessment of the Nerve Gases', 2 August 1950, pp. 74–97.

150. See MI, Folder 2A, Exhibit GWL/1/A, Coroner's File re Maddison, 16 May 1953, pp. 1–86, here p. 74.

151. MI, Folder 2B, Exhibit MNJ/17, PTP 373, 'A Fatal Case of Poisoning with GB', 9 September 1953, pp. 234–50, here p. 245.

152. TNA, WO286/11, 'Death of LAC Maddison', H. Woodhouse (for the Treasury Solicitor), to Legal 1 (Mr Griffith-Jones), MoS, 13 July 1953.

153. MI, Folder 2B, Exhibit CEB/16/2, Cullumbine, Handwritten note 'The Percutaneous Toxicity of the G-Compounds', 5 May 1953, pp. 186–92; MI, Folder 2B, Exhibit JJH/187/5, Cullumbine, Typed note 'The Percutaneous Toxicity of the G-Compounds', 8 May 1953, pp. 204–6.

154. MI, Folder 2B, Exhibit MNJ/30, PTP 399, 'Percutaneous Toxicity of G-Compounds', 11 January 1954, pp. 267–318.

155. See also Witness Statement F.J. Verallo, 17 March 2000.

156. Tyrrell, Fielder 2002; Historical Survey 2006, pp. 35–48; also Hammond, Carter 2002.

157. Historical Survey 2006, pp. 35–48, here p. 42.

158. Tyrrell, Fielder 2002; Historical Survey 2006, pp. 35–48; Green 1948, p. 463.

159. Tyrrell, Fielder 2002, pp. 188f.

160. Historical Survey 2006, pp. 35–48.

161. Historical Survey 2006, pp. 40f.

162. MI, Transcript, Day 7, Leslie John Anderson, pp. 72ff.

163. TNA, WO195/15638, PTP 857, 'A Study of Personality and Intelligence of Service Volunteers at CDEE', 10 June 1963.

164. Tyrrell, Fielder 2002, pp. 78f.

165. Tyrrell, Fielder 2002, pp. 154f.; also Schmidt 2007b.

166. MI, Folder 2G, Exhibit DGK/22, 'Volunteer's Application Form for Common Cold Research Unit, Salisbury', pp. 211–12.

167. See IWM, Film and Video Archive, DED 46A, 'The Chemical Defence Experimental Establishment Porton Down, Volunteers for Porton', 1966.

168. MI, Transcript, Day 17, Witness Testimony Henry John Newman, p. 89.

169. MI, Folder 2A/I, Exhibit MNJ/20/2, Dr W. Cawood, PDSR(D) to E. Rideal, 26 June 1953, p. 124; for Edgar D. Adrian, Baron Adrian of Cambridge, see Hodgkin 1979.

170. Hodgkin 1979, p. 6.

171. Hodgkin 1979, p. 11.

172. Hodgkin 1979, p. 44.

173. MI, Folder 2A/I, Exhibit MNJ/20/2, Report by E.D. Adrian to E. Rideal, 12 August 1953, pp. 115–16.

174. MI, Folder 2A/I, Exhibit MNJ/20/2, Report by E.D. Adrian to E. Rideal, 12 August 1953, pp. 115–116.

175. MI, Folder 2A/I, Exhibit MNJ/20/2, O.H. Wansbrough-Jones (Chief Scientist) to Duncan Sandys (MoS), 20 August 1953, p. 114.

176. MI, Folder 2A/I, Exhibit MNJ/20/2, Draft Report by E.D. Adrian to E. Rideal, 1 August 1953, pp. 118–21.

177. MI, Folder 2A/I, Exhibit MNJ/20/2, Under Secretary (Research), MoS, to Under Secretary of State, War Office, 30 September 1953, pp. 105–6.

178. MI, Folder 2D (Version 2), Exhibit DGK/15, Handwritten letter by Lord Adrian to Dr Pearson, 30 January 1994, pp. 1046A–1046D; MI, Transcript, Day 27, pp. 68f.; also Bill Lyons et al., 'The Secrets of Porton Down' (Observer Films, 1994).

179. MI, Folder 2D (Version 2), Exhibit DGK/15, Handwritten letter by Lord Adrian to Dr Pearson, 30 January 1994, pp. 1046A–1046D, here p. 1046B.

180. MI, Folder 2D (Version 2), Exhibit DGK/15, Handwritten letter by Lord Adrian to Dr Pearson, 30 January 1994, pp. 1046A–1046D, here p. 1046B.

181. MI, Folder 2D (Version 2), Exhibit DGK/15, Handwritten letter by Lord Adrian to Dr Pearson, 30 January 1994, pp. 1046A–1046D, here p. 1046D.

182. MI, Folder 2A/I, Exhibit MNJ/20/2, 'The Maddison Death at CDEE Porton: 1953', 30 March 1994, pp. 314–20.

183. MI, Folder 2A/I, Exhibit MNJ/20/2, 'The Maddison Death at CDEE Porton: 1953', 30 March 1994, pp. 314–20, here p. 320.

184. MI, Folder 2A/I, Exhibit MNJ/20/2, 'The Maddison Death at CDEE Porton: 1953', 30 March 1994, pp. 314–20, here p. 320.

185. United States Advisory Committee on Human Radiation Experiments 1995; Moreno 1999.

186. For the United States see United States Advisory Committee on Human Radiation Experiments 1995; also Pechura, Rall 1993; Lederer 1995; Vilensky 2005. For the United Kingdom see Harris, Paxman 1982, reprint 2002; Carter 1992; Goodwin 1998; Bud, Gummett 1999; Carter 2000; Care 2002a; Care 2002b; Evans, R. 2000a; Balmer 2001; Hammond, Carter 2002; Schmidt 2004.

187. H. Cullumbine, Head of the Physiology Section at Porton, stated in May 1953 that 'in all, some 1,726 subjects have been tested' with nerve gases (see MI, Folder 2A, Exhibit MNJ/20/1, MoS, 'Report of a Court of Inquiry into Death of Maddison', May 1953, pp. 84–142, here p. 91). An internal Porton statistic, Note No. 119, on the 'History of the Service Volunteer Observer Scheme at CDEE', gives the following figures: thirty-four (1945/1946); 242 (1948/1949); 159 (1949/1950); 234 (1950/1951); 384 (1951/1952); 531 (1952/1953). This makes a total of 1,584 subjects who were exposed to nerve gas.

188. A total of 396 men were contaminated with varying doses of liquid GB. MI, Folder 2B, Exhibit MNJ/17, PTP 373, 'A Fatal Case of Poisoning with GB', 9 September 1953, pp. 234–50; MI, Folder 2B, Exhibit MNJ/30, PTP 399, 'Percutaneous Toxicity of G-Compounds', 11 January 1954, pp. 267–318. In total, 254 servicemen were exposed to liquid nerve agents applied to their skin either directly or through various layers of clothing; MI, Folder 2A/I, Exhibit MNJ/20/2, 'Fatality at Porton', 7 May 1953, p. 297; also MI, Folder 2A/I, Exhibit MNJ/20/2, 'The Maddison Death at CDEE Porton: 1953', 30 March 1994, pp. 314–20, here, p. 314.

189. See MI, Folder 2A, Exhibit MNJ/20/1, MoS, 'Report of a Court of Inquiry into Death of Maddison', May 1953, pp. 84–142, here pp. 114f.

190. MoS 1952a; MoS 1952b.

191. MI, Folder 2B, Exhibit MNJ/17, PTP 373, 'A Fatal Case of Poisoning with GB', 9 September 1953, pp. 234–50, here p. 245.

192. MI, Folder 2A/I, Exhibit MNJ/20/2, 'Probability of Occurrence of Sensitive Individuals', 10 June 1953, p. 256.

193. MI, Folder 2A/I, Exhibit MNJ/20/2, War Office to Under Secretary (Research), MoS, 29 December 1953 (and further correspondence), pp. 86–90; MI, Folder 2A/I, Exhibit MNJ/20/2, E.D. Adrian to A.E. Childs about 'Volunteer Observers at Porton' (and further correspondence), 12 December 1953, pp. 94–5.

194. MI, Folder 2A/I, Exhibit MNJ/20/2, 'Employment of Volunteers for Physiological Tests with GB', 13 February 1954, pp. 84–95.

195. MI, Folder 2A/I, Exhibit MNJ/20/2, 'Volunteers for Physiological Tests at Porton', 11 January 1954 (and further correspondence), pp. 91–3.

196. MI, Folder 2A/I, Exhibit MNJ/20/2, 'Volunteer Service Observers', 21 May 1954, pp. 80–3.

197. MI, Folder 2A/I, Exhibit MNJ/20/2, 'Volunteer Service Observers', 21 May 1954, pp. 80–3, here p. 82.

198. MI, Folder 2A/I, Exhibit MNJ/20/2, 'Volunteer Service Observers', 21 May 1954, pp. 80–3, here pp. 82f.

199. MI, Folder 2A/I, Exhibit MNJ/20/2, 'Notes of Meeting held in Room 240 Lansdowne House at 11.00 a.m. on Tuesday 8 March 1955 to Discuss the Question of Remuneration of Service Volunteers Taking Part in Certain Tests at the Chemical Defence Experimental Establishment Porton' (and further correspondence), pp. 70–80.

200. For a history of V-agents see, for example, Tucker 2006, pp. 158–89.

201. McCamley 2006, pp. 134ff.

202. SIPRI 1971, p. 85.

203. TNA, WO32/20843, 'Tests with V-Agents and G-Agents on Human Volunteers' (Memorandum by the Secretary of State, no date).

204. TNA, WO286/78, Defence Research Policy Committee, 15 April 1958.

205. MI, Folder 2A/I, Exhibit MNJ/20/2, 'Percutaneous Experiments with V', 7 May 1959 (and further correspondence), pp. 10–27 and pp. 46–51; also MI,

Folder 2A/I, Exhibit MNJ/20/2, 'Proposal to Administer Anticholinesterase Agents by Intravenous Injection to Man' (Ptn./IT. 4203/2714/57), 24 June 1957, pp. 53–9. The reconstituted Adrian Committee consisted of Lord Adrian, Lord Evans, Sir Charles Dodds, and Sir Rudolph Peters. See also TNA, WO32/20843, 'List of Members of Biology Committee (CDAB)': J.H. Gaddum, P.R. Allison, E. Boyland, F. Dickens, Lord Evans, Charles Lovatt Evans, Howard Florey, W.D.M Paton, George Pickering, M.L. Rosenheim, R.H.S. Thompson, A. Wilson, H.J. Emeleus.

206. Evans, R. 2000a, p. 190.

207. TNA, WO188/802, p. 159.

208. *BMJ*, Obituary, W.S.S. Ladell, 4 (1970), 5737, pp. 751–2; TNA, DEFE13/1055, Chemical Warfare, 'Biographical Notes of People to be Met at CDEE and MRE', 12 July 1968.

209. Ladell 1958.

210. TNA, WO32/20843, Ladell to Haddon, 12 May 1961; see also Evans, R. 2000a, pp. 184f.

211. MI, Folder 2A/I, Exhibit MNJ/20/2, BJSM to MoS, 7 January 1958, p. 44.

212. MI, Folder 2A/I, Exhibit MNJ/20/2, MoS to BJSM, 9 January 1958, p. 44.

213. WO195/16227, 'Report on the Human Safety Committee', *c.* March 1966.

214. TNA, WO32/20843, 'Note of a Meeting, War Office, 21 December 1959, to Discuss Chemical Tests on Service Volunteers at CDEE Porton', 6 January 1960.

215. MI, Folder 2A/I, Exhibit MNJ/20/2, 'Human Experiments with Anticholinesterase Agents' (no date), pp. 32–4, here p. 33.

216. MI, Folder 2A/I, Exhibit MNJ/20/2, 'Human Experiments with Anticholinesterase Agents', 22 April 1959, pp. 18–20, here p. 19.

217. MI, Folder 2A/I, Exhibit MNJ/20/2, Haddon to Ladell, 28 April 1959, pp. 13f.

218. MI, Folder 2A/I, Exhibit MNJ/20/2, Report by Adrian Committee, 25 March 1959, p. 23.

219. MI, Folder 2A/I, Exhibit MNJ/20/2, 'Percutaneous Experiments with V', 7 May 1959, p. 10.

220. TNA, WO32/20843, Visser to Haddon, 14 August 1959; Ladell to Morrison, 31 August 1959; Ladell to Gaddum, 1 September 1959; Haddon to Emeleus, 7 September 1959.

221. TNA, AIR20/10719, Loose Minute by J.F. Mayne, Permanent Secretary to Secretary of State for Air, 15 September 1959 (B257 Porton Volunteer Recruitment).

222. TNA, AIR20/10719, Loose Minute by J.F. Mayne, Permanent Secretary to Secretary of State for Air, 15 September 1959 (B257 Porton Volunteer Recruitment).

223. TNA, AIR20/10719, 'Note of a Meeting on 23 September 1959 to Discuss Nerve Gas Tests on Human Observers', 2 October 1959 (B257 Porton Volunteer Recruitment); Orders by Maj Gen G.D.G. Heyman, Commanding-

in-Chief, Southern Command, February 1959. I am grateful to Alan Care for supplying the above document.

224. MI, Folder 2C, Exhibit JJH/412/A, Admiralty Fleet Order 2088 Ratings. 'Volunteers for Physiological Tests at Porton Down', 16 August 1957, p. 578; MI, Folder 2C, Exhibit JJH/413/A, Defence Council Instructions (Army). Chemical Warfare.'Volunteers for Tests at the Chemical Defence Experimental Establishment, Porton Down', 29 April 1964, pp. 579–81. See also TNA, WO195/16136, Porton Note No. 119, Annexure A of Addendum, 'Administrative Instructions for the Attachment of Army Personnel to the Chemical Defence Experimental Establishment as Volunteers for Tests', December 1963 (Lt Col R.P. Bradshaw) and Annexure C of Addendum, 'Notice Board Leaflet', 1964 (Lt Col R.P. Bradshaw); Historical Survey 2006, p. 319.

225. TNA, AIR20/10719, 'Note of a Meeting on 23 September 1959 to Discuss Nerve Gas Tests on Human Observers', 2 October 1959 (B257 Porton Volunteer Recruitment).

226. TNA, WO32/20843, Haddon (Porton) to Gale (Assistant Secretary), 17 August 1961; also Evans, R. 2000a, p. 176.

227. TNA, AIR20/10719, Note by N.K. Reeve, Private Secretary to the Permanent Secretary, 7 October 1959 (B257 Porton Volunteer Recruitment); WO32/20843, J.A. Drew (MoD) to A.C.W. Drew (War Office), 29 November 1960; also Evans, R. 2000a, p. 167.

228. TNA, WO32/20843, TNA, WO32/20843, 'Note of a Meeting, War Office, 21 December 1959, to Discuss Chemical Tests on Service Volunteers at CDEE Porton', 6 January 1960; Ormond (Admiralty) to A.C.W. Drew (War Office), 2 December 1960; Ormond (Admiralty) to A.C.W. Drew (War Office), 25 January 1961; Evans, R. 2000a, p. 189.

229. TNA, WO32/20843, J.A. Drew (MoD) to A.C.W. Drew (War Office), 29 November 1960.

230. TNA, WO32/20843, 'Note of a Meeting, War Office, 21 December 1959, to Discuss Chemical Tests on Service Volunteers at CDEE Porton', 6 January 1960.

231. TNA, WO32/20843, Montgomery (MoD) to Key (War Office), 14 January 1960, includes excerpt of Section 10 of JIC (59) 29 (Final), 'Soviet Research and Development up to the End of 1958'.

232. Balmer 2001, pp. 162–7.

233. TNA, WO286/78, 'Summary of Report by DRPC Working Party on BW and CW', 18 April 1958.

234. MI, Folder 2A/I, Exhibit MNJ/20/2, E.A. Perren (D/CDEE) to R. Peters, and a copy to J.H. Gaddum, c. 1958, p. 27; also TNA, WO195/14473, CDAB, 9 October 1958 (UoK, Porton Archive, B211, GB CW, CDAB).

235. MI, Folder 2A/I, Exhibit MNJ/20/2, Conclusions and Recommendations of Thirteenth Tripartite Conference, c. 1958, p. 28.

236. TNA, WO32/20843, Haddon to AUS (B), 1 November 1960.

237. TNA, WO32/20843, Ladell to Haddon, 11 May 1961; also 'Minute of War Office Meeting Held on 9 May 1960 to Discuss the Subject of Human Tests with G- and V-agents', 10 May 1960.

238. TNA, WO32/20843, AUS (B) to DUS (A), 14 December 1960.

239. Marrs et al. 1996, pp. 115–37, here p. 127; Evans, R. 2000a, p. 192.

240. Evans, R. 2000a, p. 192.

241. Marrs et al. 1996, p. 131.

242. Marrs et al. 1996, pp. 132f.

243. Alan Care to author, 17 September 2012; also UoK, Porton Archive, A105.4.1, Maddison Case, CPS Development Cases.

244. Alan Care to author, 17 September 2012.

245. TNA, WO32/20843, Haddon to Emeleus, 7 September 1959.

246. TNA, WO32/20843, 'Memorandum on Percutaneous and Intravenous Tests on Men with G and V agents', 19 February 1960.

247. TNA, WO32/20843, Note by J.H. Gaddum, 'Human Experiments with Nerve Gases'. February 1960.

248. TNA, WO32/20843, A.C.W. Drew (DUS (A)) to DGAMS, 11 July 1960.

249. TNA, WO32/20843, DGAMS to A.C.W. Drew (DUS (A)), 13 July 1960.

250. TNA, WO32/20843, A.C.W. Drew (DUS (A)) to Allan (Home Office), 28 July 1961; A.C.W. Drew (DUS (A)) to DCS (B), 11 August 1961.

251. TNA, WO32/20843, A.C.W. Drew (DUS (A)) to Allen (Home Office), 9 October 1961; Allen (Home Office) to A.C.W. Drew (DUS (A)), 23 November 1961.

252. TNA, WO32/20843, Haddon (Porton) to Gale (Assistant Secretary), 17 August 1961.

253. TNA, WO32/20843, Moore (DWD), Reference Minute 138 and 144, 19 January 1954.

254. TNA, WO32/20843, Ladell to Haddon, 12 May 1961; Haddon to Cawood, 16 May 1961.

255. TNA, WO32/20843, Ladell to Haddon, 12 May 1961; also Evans, R. 2000a, p. 187.

256. TNA, WO32/20843, AUS to DUS (A), 28 November 1961.

257. TNA, WO32/20843, Haddon to Cawood, 16 May 1961.

258. TNA, WO32/20843, DC of C to Assistant Secretary, 22 September 1961 (B257.1 Conditions for Experiments).

259. TNA, WO32/20843, DCDRD to Chief Scientist, 2 February 1962.

260. Evans, R. 2000a, pp. 193–6.

261. For the death of Geoffrey Bacon see TNA, WO32/19633, 20162, 20403, 21372; TNA, DEFE68/202; also Hersh 1970, pp. 291ff.

262. Members of the Board of Inquiry also included W.B. Littler, War Office Deputy Chief Scientist, W.A. Bailey, War Office Director of Safety Services, A.M. Critchley, War Office Principal Medical Officer, E.T. Conybeare, Ministry of Health, Lord Evans, Consulting Physician, Graham Wilson,

Director of Public Health Laboratory Service, H.E. Wade, Non-industrial Staff Representative, and A.R. Blake, Industrial Staff Representative; TNA, WO32/20403, 'Report of Board of Inquiry' (1962), p. 3.

263. TNA, WO32/20403, 'Report of Board of Inquiry' (1962), p. 12.

264. TNA, WO32/20403, 'Safety System Failed for Plague Victim', *Daily Telegraph*, 25 August 1962.

265. TNA, WO32/19633, 'Germ Warfare Scientist Dies', *Daily Telegraph*, 3 August 1962; for some of the media coverage see Hammond, Carter 2002, p. 224 and footnotes 159–67.

266. TNA, WO32/21372, 'Extra-Ordinary Meeting of the Amesbury Rural District Council', 14 September 1962.

267. TNA, DEFE62/202, 'Death Germs Secrets Banned to Doctors', *Daily Mail*, 26 November 1962.

268. TNA, WO32/21372, Christine Robinson to War Office, 31 August 1962.

269. TNA, WO32/21372, Pamela Edwards to War Office, 21 August 1962.

270. TNA, WO32/19633, '"Black Death" Inquest Postponed 24 Hours', *Daily Telegraph*, 4 August 1962.

271. TNA, WO32/20403, 'Report of Board of Inquiry' (1962), p. 7; 'The Plague Death Centre Gets New Safety Rules', *Evening Standard*, 25 August 1962; 'New Safety Measures to be Enforced at Germ Warfare Centre', *Sunday Times*, 26 August 1962; 'Health Security at Porton Tightened', *Sunday Telegraph*, 26 August, 1962; 'New Precautions at Porton', *The Times*, 27 August 1962; WO32/19633, 'Porton Safety Rules Revised', *Daily Telegraph*, 24 August 1962; see also DEFE68/202, Director of Safety Services at the War Office to DPBR, 4 December 1962.

272. TNA, WO32/19633, 'Porton Down—Board of Inquiry', 16 August 1962.

273. TNA, WO32/20403, Secretary of State for War to Prime Minister, Porton MRE, 22 August 1962.

274. TNA, WO32/20403, 'Steriliser Explosion at MRE Porton', 28 August 1962.

275. TNA, WO32/21372.

276. For Henderson's biography see Balmer 2001, p. 202 (footnote 34).

277. TNA, WO32/20403, 'Safety System Failed for Plague Victim', *Daily Telegraph*, 25 August 1962; 'Plague Man's Faith', *Daily Express*, 25 August 1962; 'Germ Scientist's Sick Note Was not Alarming', *Daily Post*, 25 August 1962.

278. TNA, WO32/20403, Assistant Treasury Solicitor (R.L. Allen) to War Office, Inquest on Geoffrey Arthur Bacon, 27 August 1962.

279. TNA, DEFE68/202, 'Scientist Worked on Bubonic Plague', *Evening Standard*, 3 August 1962.

CHAPTER 7

1. I am grateful to Mike Kenner for supplying me with his data, collected over a fifteen-year period, of known open-air biological warfare trials between 1949 and 1976; also Barnett 2002.

2. Porter 1997, p. 650.
3. For the history of biological weapons programmes in the United States, Canada, France, the Soviet Union, Non-Soviet Warsaw Pact Countries, Iraq, and South Africa see Wheelis et al. 2006.
4. DERA 2000, pp. 13f.; the DERA report also references two Porton Notes about the origins of the LAC principle: Ptn./TU1208/268A/5, C.J.M. Aanensen, 'A Note on the Possibility of Travel of BW and CW Agents across the United Kingdom', 13 June 1952; and Ptn./TU1208/2129/57, 'Study of the Possible Attack of Large Areas with BW Agents', 1 February 1957.
5. Balmer 2001, pp. 175–83, here p. 183.
6. Balmer 2001, pp. 176f.
7. For the literature on environmental and ecological ethics see, for example, Palmer 1998, Botzler, Armstrong 1998; Curry 2006.
8. Palmer 1997; Palmer 1998; Walker 2000.
9. Oakley 1968, p. 90; Gladstone, Knight, Wilson 1973, pp. 336–8.
10. Avery 2013, p. 24.
11. Avery 2013, pp. 14–55.
12. For Fildes see Gladstone, Knight, Wilson 1973.
13. Gladstone, Knight, Wilson 1973, pp. 336–8; *BMJ*, Obituary, Donald Devereux Woods, 2 (1964), 5420, p. 1337; *BMJ*, Obituary, Trevor Charles Stamp, 295 (1987), 6612, p. 1572.
14. *BMJ*, Medical News, New Director of Research at Porton, 2 (1964), 5401, p. 132; *BMJ*, Medical News, New Dean, 3 (1970), 5713, p. 54; *BMJ*, Universities and Colleges, 287 (1983), 6391, p. 566.
15. *BMJ*, Obituary, Robert Leishman, 1 (1979), 6180, p. 1790.
16. *BMJ*, Obituary, Harry Taylor Findlay, 1 (1975), 5950, p. 158.
17. *BMJ*, Obituary, Frank William Sheffield, 332 (2006), 7539, p. 493; also *BMJ*, Obituary, John Beale, 332 (2006), 7534, p. 181.
18. *BMJ*, Obituary, Wilson Smith, 2 (1965), 5455, p. 240; for staff who joined the MRE after having previously worked at CDEE see TNA, DEFE13/1055, Chemical Warfare, 'Biographical Notes of People to be Met at CDEE and MRE', July 1968.
19. Van Courtland Moon 2006.
20. Van Courtland Moon 2006, pp. 24ff.
21. Vanderbilt 2002.
22. Lucas 1998.
23. Floyd 2010, pp. 82f.
24. Edgerton 2011, p. 28.
25. DeFur 1999, pp. 339f.
26. Simmons 2001, pp. 283f.; DERA 1999, pp. 13f.
27. Parker 1996, pp. 61–4.
28. Hammond, Carter 2002, p. 214.

29. McCamley 2006, pp. 158–72; for the postwar dumping of mustard gas and other toxic agents into the Atlantic Ocean by the United States and Canada see Smith 2011.
30. Smith 2011, p. 35; also Vilensky 2005, pp. 108ff.
31. McCamley 2006, p. 164.
32. ZDF zoom (German state TV programme), 'Mister Karstadt. Der rätzelhafte Nicolaus Berggruen', 14 March 2012; Gassmann 2013.
33. I am grateful to the Airfield Exchange Network for their research on this subject.
34. McCamley 2006, pp. 167ff.
35. TNA, DEFE13/287, 'Biological Warfare Research and Development, Draft Directive by Minister of Supply', 13 July 1953.
36. TNA, DEFE13/287, 'Biological Warfare Policy', September 1953.
37. TNA, DEFE13/287, 'Biological Warfare. Research and Development', c. 1953.
38. TNA, WO286/78, MoS to Colonial Office, 23 August 1957.
39. Balmer 2001, pp. 104–27; also Willis 2003.
40. Evans, R. 2000a, p. 359; Independent Review 1999, p. 4.
41. University of Sussex, SHIP File, H6.4, Morton Papers.
42. Balmer 2006b, p. 56; Hammond and Carter mention twenty-seven trials; Hammond, Carter 2002, p. 25; DERA 1999, pp. 15–17; Avery 2013, pp. 76ff.
43. Balmer 2001, p. 105.
44. Hammond, Carter 2002, pp. 25f.
45. Van Courtland Moon 2006; see also IWM, instructional film 'Operation Cauldron' (1952); as well as Matt Fletcher and Jolyon Jenkins, BBC Radio 4 programme 'Operation Cauldron', 22 September 2005 (<https://archive.org/details/OperationCauldron>).
46. DERA 1999, pp. 17–23.
47. Balmer 2001, p. 114.
48. Balmer 2004, p. 206.
49. Hammond, Carter 2002, pp. 27–32; DERA 1999, p. 25.
50. Avery 2013, pp. 86f.; Furmanski, Wheelis 2006.
51. TNA, WO188/666, BW Subcommittee. 'Field Trials with BW Agents', 12 February 1952; also Balmer 2001, p. 114.
52. Willis 2003; Balmer 2004; also Matt Fletcher and Jolyon Jenkins, BBC Radio 4 programme 'Operation Cauldron', 22 September 2005 (<https://archive.org/details/OperationCauldron>).
53. Moreno 1999, pp. 219–26; also Schmidt 2013.
54. Balmer 2004, p. 215.
55. Balmer 2004, p. 217.
56. Hammond, Carter 2002, pp. 32–9.
57. TNA, WO286/78, 'Germ Warfare Trials in Bahamian Waters', 13 August 1954; also 'Requirement for Further BW Sea Trials in 1957/58', 24 August 1956, p. 2.
58. DERA 1999, p. 23.

59. TNA, DEFE13/287, 'Biological Warfare. Research and Development, Summary of Report on Operations Hesperus, 1953, and Ozone, 1954'.

60. IWM, Film and Video Archive, DED 87, 'Operation Ozone 1954. A Footnote to the Cauldron Film', made by John Morton, MRD, Porton.

61. DERA 1999, p. 25; *BMJ*, 'Germ Warfare Exercise', 1 (1954), 4863, p. 714.

62. DERA 1999, p. 30.

63. TNA, AIR23/8593, 'Operational Research Unit Far East, Operation Crusoe', 1953; 'Trials with BBC in Malaya', 4 March 1953; 'BBC Gas Trials', 6 March 1953.

64. TNA, AIR23/8593, 'BBC Gas Trials', 25 March 1953.

65. TNA, AIR23/8593, 'Operational Research Unit Far East, Operation Crusoe', 1953.

66. TNA, AIR23/8593, 'BBC Publicity', November 1953.

67. TNA, AIR23/8593, 'BBC Publicity', November 1953.

68. TNA, AIR23/8593, 'BBC Publicity', November 1953.

69. DERA 1999, pp. 31–3.

70. DERA 1999, pp. 31f.; Hammond, Carter 2002, pp. 113–17.

71. TNA, WO286/78, Chief Scientists to Minister, 10 December 1956; WO286/78, Defence Research Policy Committee, 15 April 1958.

72. DERA 1999, pp. 32f.; Balmer 2001, pp. 180–3; Parker 1996, pp. 116f.; TNA, WO195/15751, BRAB, 'Ventilation Trial in the London Underground', MRE Report VT/1, 1964.

73. TNA, WO195/14405, Forty-first Meeting of BRAB, July 1958; also Evans, R. 2000a, p. 357.

74. Balmer 2001, pp. 180f.

75. Balmer 2001, p. 181.

76. UoK, Porton Archive, B207, Public Tests UK, Chief Scientist to Secretary of State, 30 May 1963.

77. Page et al. 2007, p. 74.

78. TNA, WO195/15751, BRAB, 'Ventilation Trial in the London Underground', MRE Report VT/1, 1964; Hammond, Carter 2002, p. 117.

79. TNA, WO195/15751, BRAB, 'Ventilation Trial in the London Underground', MRE Report VT/1, 1964; also DEFE55/166, 'Exploratory Ventilation Trial in the London Underground Railways', 1965.

80. Mike Thompson and Jane Ray, BBC Radio 4 programme 'The Secrets of the Icewhale', 12 September 2002 (<https://archive.org/details/Document TheSecretsOfTheIcewhale>). Graydon Carter was Porton's historical adviser.

81. Independent Review 1999, p. 10; also DERA 1999, p. 11.

82. Van Courtland Moon 2006, pp. 27f.

83. DERA 1999, p. 11.

84. DERA 2000, pp. 13f.

85. DERA 2000, pp. 11ff.; for a list of Porton's field trials with zinc cadmium sulphide see DERA 2000, pp. 16–23; Evans, R. 2000a, pp. 355ff.; Elliot et al. 2002.

86. Leighton 1955.

87. DERA 2000, pp. 4–9.

88. Evans, R. 2000a, p. 353; Balmer 2001, pp. 161ff.; also TNA, WO286/78, Defence Research Policy Committee, 15 April 1958; also DERA 1999, p. 34.

89. For sampling techniques see, for example, UoK, Porton Archive, B207, Public Tests UK, Porton Note No. 188, 'The Long Distance Travel of Particulate Clouds'.

90. TNA, WO195/14995, Forty-eighth Meeting of BRAB, July 1960; Evans, R. 2000a, p. 465 (footnote 14).

91. TNA, WO189/1105, N. Thompson, 'A Comparison of Radio-Xenon and Zinc-Cadmium Sulphide Particle Tracers over Medium Distances of Travel', PTP, No. 794; Mike Thompson and Jane Ray, BBC Radio 4 programme 'The Secrets of the Icewhale', 12 September 2002 (<https://archive.org/details/DocumentTheSecretsOfTheIcewhale>).

92. UoK, Porton Archive, B207, Public Tests UK, Porton Field Trial Report No. 610, 'The Penetration of Built-Up Areas by Aerosols at Night', 7 May 1964; also DERA 2000, pp. 21f.

93. UoK, Porton Archive, B207, Public Tests UK, Chief Scientist to Secretary of State, 30 May 1963.

94. Harris, Paxman 1982; Cole 1988.

95. BBC News, Inquiry into Spray Cancer Claims, 7 December 2005.

96. Quoted from Evans, R. 2000a, p. 356.

97. BBC Inside Out, 'Clouds of Secrecy' (2006); National Research Council 1997; also Academy of Medical Sciences 1999.

98. Hammond, Carter 2002, pp. 41f.; whereas the US National Research Council cautiously suggested that the substances were 'probably harmless' and have 'probably caused no human illness', the UK Academy of Medical Sciences concluded that there was 'no danger to health' for the British population. The Cambridge immunologist Peter Lachmann, founding President of the Academy of Medical Sciences, later admitted that the panel he had chaired had neither seen nor looked for all the evidence; BBC Inside Out Documentary series, 'Clouds of Secrecy' (2006).

99. Elliot et al. 2002, pp. 13–17.

100. DeFur 1999.

101. Page et al. 2007, pp. 97f.

102. UoK, Porton Archive, B207, Public Tests UK, Chief Scientist to Secretary of State, 30 May 1963.

103. See also DERA 1999, pp. 11f.

104. UoK, Porton Archive, B207, Public Tests UK, Chief Scientist to Secretary of State, 30 May 1963.

105. DERA 1999, p. 39; also Mike Thompson and Jane Ray, BBC Radio 4 programme 'The Secrets of the Icewhale', 12 September 2002 (<https://archive.org/details/DocumentTheSecretsOfTheIcewhale>).

106. DERA 1999, pp. 35f.
107. IWM, Film and Video Archive, 'The Lyme Bay Trials' (1966).
108. DERA 1999, pp. 11f.; pp. 38–41.
109. IWM, Film and Video Archive, 'The Lyme Bay Trials' (1966). I am grateful to Mike Kenner for supplying me with a copy of the film; see also IMW, Film and Video Archive, 'The Lyme Bay Trials' (1968, censored version).
110. NARA, RG319, Entry 47-A, Box 11, File 381–400.112 Research, John Edgar Hoover to Assistant Chief of Staff, G-2, Department of the Army, 15 November 1951.
111. Hammond, Carter 2002, p. 241, note 36.
112. Independent Review 1999, p. 20; also Hammond, Carter 2002, p. 55.
113. Independent Report 1999, p. 7.
114. Independent Report 1999, p. 7.
115. UoK, Porton Archive, B207, Public Tests UK, K.P. Norris, MRE Field Trial Report No. 3, 'Concentration, Viability and Immunological Properties of Airborne Bacteria Released from a Massive Line Source', January 1966, Table 5–1, Pre-Trial Tests of *E. coli* Suspension.
116. Independent Report 1999, p. 12.
117. *Donoghue v. Stevenson* [1931] UKHL 3, 1932 SC (HL) 31, [1932] AC 562 (26 May 1931).
118. TNA, WO286/78, Defence Research Policy Committee, 15 April 1958.
119. McCamley 2006, p. 171.
120. TNA, WO286/78, Defence Research Policy Committee, 15 April 1958; also Balmer 2001, pp. 162–7.
121. DERA 1999, p. 51.
122. DERA 1999, pp. 42–53; Evans, R. 2000a, pp. 358ff.
123. I am grateful to Mike Kenner for supplying me with a declassified report about the trials; see US Army Research and Development Command, Chemical System Laboratory, Aberdeen Proving Ground, Trials, Procedures, and Details of the Biological Challenges, July 1977.
124. McCamley 2006, pp. 172.
125. Hammond, Carter 2002, pp. 1ff.; also Wells et al. 1976.
126. *Country Walking*, June 2013, p. 33.
127. Floyd 2010, pp. 82f.
128. Van Courtland Moon 2006, p. 27.
129. See also Smith 2011 for an analysis of Rachel Carson's popular book *The Sea around Us* (1951).
130. Van Courtland Moon 2006, pp. 9f.; Biological Weapons Convention 1972 (Article 1); for a recent study of Britain's policy of disarmament since the mid 1950s see Walker 2012; see also Sims 1986; Sims 2001; Sims 2009.
131. TNA, DEFE13/1055, Chemical Warfare, 'Report on Disposal of US Gas Stocks', 13 August 1970; also Hammond, Carter 2002, p. 231.
132. See also Floyd 2010, pp. 65f.

133. Evans, R. 2000a, p. 363.
134. Quoted from Evans, R. 2000a, p. 362.

CHAPTER 8

1. For scholars and artists who in the past have engaged with the subject of 'twilight' see, for example, Huyssen 1995; Crewdson 2002.
2. Katz 1992, p. 228; Katz 1996, p. 1663; also Rothman 1991, pp. 62f.
3. MacLean 2006, p. 395.
4. Reverby 2011.
5. Walker 2012, pp. 13–30; here p. 13.
6. TNA, DEFE10/382, 'MoD, Defence Research Policy Staff, Incapacitating Agents, UK Eyes Only', c. 1959 (UoK, Porton Archive, B209).
7. TNA, CAB537/2711, 'Riot Control', 7 October 1948 (UoK, Porton Archive, B209).
8. TNA, CAB537/2711, 'Report on Use of 92 Type Tear Smoke Grenade in Hong Kong', 31 December 1947; CAB537/5346, 'Tests of No. 91 Tear Smoke Grenade', 14 January 1950; CAB537/5346, Governor of Uganda, 'Tear Smoke Equipment', 8 September 1950; CAB537/5346, War Office to Colonial Office, 26 October 1950; War Office to Colonial Office, 30 November 1950; Governor of Nairobi, 'Tear Smoke Equipment', 31 October 1950; also 'DM Gas Report'; December 1950 (UoK, Porton Archive, B209).
9. TNA, WO195/16840, 'Irritant Agents', Statement by DBCD, 2 January 1969; for the development of CS see TNA, CAB537/2711, 'Lachrymatory Devices, Notes of a Meeting Held at Porton on 17 March 1948 to Discuss Anti-Riot Weapon Requirements' (UoK, Porton Archive, B209).
10. TNA, DEFE10/283, British Joint Staff Mission, 18 February 1958.
11. TNA, DEFE10/382, 'MoD, Defence Research Policy Staff, Incapacitating Agents', c. 1959, includes extract from 'Report of US House Committee on Science and Astronautics, Chemical, Biological, and Radiological Warfare Agents: Hearings before the Committee on Science and Astronautics', Eighty-sixth Congress, First session, June 1959 (UoK, Porton Archive, B209); also Kirby 2006.
12. Carter, Pearson 1996b.
13. Carter, Pearson 1996b, p. 65; TNA, CAB131/28, Minister of Defence, Memorandum to the Cabinet Defence Committee, 'Biological and Chemical Warfare Policy', D(63), 16 April 1963.
14. Walker 2012, pp. 18f.; also TNA, WO32/20163, M.A.P. Hogg, 'The Operational Use of Chemical Incapacitating Agents', CDEE Porton Down, 29 August 1963.
15. Walker 2012, p. 19; TNA, WO32/20163, M.A.P. Hogg, 'The Operational Use of Chemical Incapacitating Agents', CDEE Porton Down, 29 August 1963.
16. Beecher 1966a; Beecher 1969; Beecher 1970.

17. Schmidt 2004, pp. 109f.

18. E.R. Koch, 'Folterexperten—Die geheimen Methoden der CIA' (Documentary Film, SWR, released on 9 July 2007); McCoy 2007.

19. Moreno 1999, p. 240.

20. NARA, RG319, Entry 47-A, Box 13, File 400.112, Beecher to Surgeon General, Col John R. Wood, 21 October 1951; I am grateful to Egmont R. Koch for drawing my attention to this document.

21. NARA, RG319, Entry 47-A, Box 13, File 400.112, Walter Smith, Director CIA, to Chairman, Research and Development Board, Request for Technical Assistance, 5 March 1952; H. Marshall Chadwell, Assistant Director, Scientific Intelligence, to Assistant Chief of Staff, G-2, Department of the Army, 6 March 1952; see also Goliszek 2003, pp. 151ff.

22. NARA, RG319, Box 219, Assistant Chief of Staff (G-2), Intelligence ('P') Files, 1946–1951, Army Medical Research and Development Board, Office of the Surgeon General, Investigation on Sedatives, Progress Reports 1 October–31 December 1947; 1 January–31 March 1948; 1 July–30 September 1948. The Army also funded a series of experimental studies by Curt P. Richter at Johns Hopkins University on 'peripheral nerve injuries', mostly on patients with mental conditions and injured soldiers suffering from some type of peripheral vascular disease; Progress Report 1 October–31 December 1948.

23. Beecher 1966b.

24. NARA, RG319, Entry 47-A, Box 13, File 400.112, Beecher to Surgeon General, Col John R. Wood, 21 October 1951.

25. NARA, RG319, Entry 47-A, Box 13, File 400.112, Beecher to Surgeon General, Col John R. Wood, 21 October 1951.

26. Evans, R. 2000a, pp. 252f.

27. NARA, RG319, Entry 47-A, Box 13, File 400.112, Beecher to Surgeon General, Col John R. Wood, 21 October 1951.

28. NARA, RG319, Entry 47-A, Box 13, File 400.112, Beecher to Surgeon General, Col John R. Wood, 21 October 1951.

29. NARA, RG319, Entry 47-A, Box 13, File 400.112, Beecher to Surgeon General, Col John R. Wood, 21 October 1951; for the history of the Geneva Declaration see Frewer 2010; also McCoy 2007, p. 411.

30. NARA, RG319, Entry 47-A, Box 13, File 400.112, Beecher to Surgeon General, Col John R. Wood, 21 October 1951.

31. NARA, RG319, Entry 47-A, Box 13, File 400.112, Beecher to Surgeon General, Col John R. Wood, 21 October 1951.

32. NARA, RG319, Entry 47-A, Box 13, File 400.112, Beecher to Surgeon General, Col John R. Wood, 21 October 1951.

33. NARA, RG319, Entry 47-A, Box 13, File 400.112, CIA, Memorandum, Special Interrogation Program, 19 March 1951.

34. NARA, RG319, Entry 47-A, Box 13, File 400.112, CIA, Artichoke Project, 28 August 1951.

35. NARA, RG319, Entry 47-A, Box 13, File 400.112, Handwritten note about phone conversation with Maj Lund with regard to Dr Beecher, 5 January 1952.

36. NARA, RG319, Entry 47-A, Box 13, File 400.112, Deputy Director for Central Intelligence to Secretary of Defence, Evaluation of Certain Scientific Techniques of Possible Concern to National Security, 28 January 1952.

37. NARA, RG319, Entry 47-A, Box 13, File 400.112, Note by the Secretaries to the Joint Intelligence Committee on Special Interrogation Methods, JIC 604, 14 February 1952.

38. NARA, RG319, Entry 47-A, Box 13, File 400.112, Handwritten note by G-2 official, 30 January 1952.

39. The terms 'MI6' and 'SIS' are used interchangeably.

40. For unknown reasons, some sources refer to LSD as T3456; see TNA, WO195/16427, 'Progress Report on Work with T3456', 13 March 1967.

41. Of all the sources listed in the MoD's historical survey in relation to 'psychological incapacitating agents', for example, approximately 80 per cent are not in the public domain and can therefore not be verified; Historical Survey 2006, pp. 111–27, pp. 140f.

42. Historical Survey 2006, pp. 112f.

43. The Himsworth Committee was appointed by the British government to examine possible adverse medical effects of CS gas on civilians during riots in Londonderry (Northern Ireland) in August 1969; see Chapter 9 below.

44. TNA, WO195/2778, Advisory Council on Scientific Research and Technical Development (ACSRTD), Enzyme Panel and Biology Committee of the CDAB, 'Studies with Lysergic Acid Diethylamide', 1 May 1954.

45. Historical Survey 2006, pp. 112f.

46. Wright, Greengrass 1987, p. 160; also Evans, R. 2000a, p. 249.

47. Wright, Greengrass 1987.

48. Evans, R. 2005; Evans, R. 2002.

49. Evans, R. 2003.

50. Evans, R. 2002; Evans, R. 2003; Evans, R. 2005.

51. Evans, R. 2002.

52. A. Care, The MI6/SIS (Secret Intelligence Service)/MoD LSD 1950s Experiments. Government Disclosure. A Retrospective (unpublished article).

53. Evans, R. 2006a.

54. Evans, R. 2005.

55. Between 1961 and 1963, for example, the number of compounds tested in animal screening tests increased from sixty-seven to 150; Historical Survey 2006, p. 111.

56. Historical Survey 2006, p. 113.

57. For the literature about Porton's LSD field trials see, for example, Evans, R. 2000a, Bolton 2004; also IWM, Film and Video Archive, 'Moneybags'. For 'Small Change' see TNA, WO189/122, Technical Note No. 53, 'Small Change. A Brief Preliminary Report' (UoK, Porton Archive, B209).

58. TNA, WO189/1078, PTP 765; WO189/1079, PTP 766 and PTP 793.

59. TNA, WO195/15381, 'Human Testing of Behaviour Affecting Drugs'. Oral Statement to Biology Committee, c. 1962.

60. Historical Survey 2006, p. 111. Most of the interviews were carried out by Surgeon Lt Cdr W.M. Hollyhock, RN, responsible for the screening and testing programme, and K.H. Kemp, a psychology graduate from UCL; TNA, WO195/15381, 'Human Testing of Behaviour Affecting Drugs'. Oral Statement to Biology Committee, c. 1962.

61. TNA, WO189/167, PTP 950. K.H. Kemp and R.J. Shephard, 'Further Studies of the Service Volunteer at CDEE', 23 March 1966; see also a somewhat misleading interpretation of the findings of the study in Historical Survey 2006, p. 462.

62. TNA, WO189/167, PTP 950. K.H. Kemp and R.J. Shephard, 'Further Studies of the Service Volunteer at CDEE', 23 March 1966.

63. TNA, WO195/15026, Porton Note No. 166, 'Screening Tests Prior to Administration of Psychotomimetic Drugs in Human Subjects', c. 1959/1960.

64. TNA, WO195/15638, PTP 857, 'A Study of Personality and Intelligence of Service Volunteers at CDEE', 10 June 1963; also WO189/377; Historical Survey 2006, pp. 457f.

65. TNA, WO195/15638, PTP 857, 'A Study of Personality and Intelligence of Service Volunteers at CDEE', 10 June 1963; TNA, WO195/12218, PTP 322, 'Psychological Effects of a G-Agent on Men. Preliminary Report', 4 March 1953; TNA, WO195/12493, PTP 378, 'Psychological Effects of a G-Agent on Men', 14 September 1953.

66. See MI, Folder 1A, Witness Statements.

67. TNA, WO195/15070, Porton Note No. 173, 'The "Volunteer" Personality. Responses to a Modified Cornell Medical Index Health Questionnaire', November 1960.

68. Historical Survey 2006, p. 112.

69. TNA, WO195/15070, Porton Note No. 173, 'The "Volunteer" Personality. Responses to a Modified Cornell Medical Index Health Questionnaire', November 1960.

70. Historical Survey 2006, p. 458.

71. TNA, WO195/16462, Applied Biology Committee, Fourth Meeting, 26 April 1967.

72. Evans, R. 2000a, p. 234; The Lancet, vol. 268, 2 April 1955, p. 719.

73. TNA, DEFE10/283, BJSM, 18 February 1958; WO195/15026, Porton Note No. 166, 'Screening Tests Prior to Administration of Psychotomimetic Drugs in Human Subjects', c. 1959/1960.

74. Quoted from Evans, R. 2000a, p. 235; Historical Survey 2006, p. 115.

75. Evans, R. 2000a, p. 249.

76. Evans, R. 2000a, p. 235.

77. TNA, WO195/16213, 'Summary of Work on Lysergic Acid Diethylamide at Porton in the Last Five Years', c. 1966 (UoK, Porton Archive, B209); also Historical Survey 2006, p. 113.

78. TNA, WO195/16427, 'Progress Report on Work with T3456', 13 March 1967 (UoK, Porton Archive, B209).
79. TNA, WO195/15381, 'Human Testing of Behaviour Affecting Drugs. Oral Statement to Biology Committee', c. 1962.
80. Historical Survey 2006, pp. 114f.
81. IWM, Film and Video Archive, DED 82 and DED 77. Porton's film on Operation Moneybags was distributed in three different lengths, depending on whether the film would be watched by experts or a general audience. The longest version lasted twenty-five minutes; see also Gatton 2000.
82. TNA, WO195/16161; ACSRTD, Applied Biology Committee, 14 January 1966.
83. TNA, WO195/16273; ACSRTD, Applied Biology Committee, 6 July 1966.
84. Historical Survey 2006, pp. 120–7; Carter, Balmer 1999, pp. 306f.; Kirby 2006, p. 2.
85. Kirby 2006, p. 2.
86. Historical Survey 2006, p. 120.
87. Historical Survey 2006, p. 120; see also TNA, WO195/16462; ACSRTD, Applied Biology Committee, 25 May 1967.
88. Other records suggest that there were only nineteen human exposures, involving seventeen subjects; TNA, WO195/16428, 'Early Exploratory Work with BZ in the UK', 10 March 1967; for a discussion of the unresolved discrepancy see Historical Survey 2006, p. 121.
89. Historical Survey 2006, p. 122.
90. Historical Survey 2006, p. 122.
91. TNA, WO195/16428, 'Early Exploratory Work with BZ in the UK', 10 March 1967; Historical Survey 2006, pp. 122f.
92. TNA, WO189/357, PTP 835, 'An Oripavine Derivative (TL2636) as a Potential Incapacitating Agent', 9 January 1963 (UoK, Porton Archive, B209); Historical Survey 2006, pp. 129–35.
93. TNA, WO189/357, PTP 835, 'An Oripavine Derivative (TL2636) as a Potential Incapacitating Agent', 9 January 1963 (UoK, Porton Archive, B209).
94. During Operation Small Change, another field trial into the effects of LSD on troop behaviour, several men were given TL2636 with the result that one man had to be immediately hospitalized; Historical Survey 2006, pp. 132f.; also TNA, WO195/16691, 'The Effects of Small Doses of TL2636 on Human Subjects at Rest and Exercising in the Laboratory and in the Field', c. 1968 (UoK, Porton Archive, B209).
95. TNA, WO195/16273; ACSRTD, Applied Biology Committee, 6 July 1966. In reporting the incident to the Deputy Secretary of State for Defence, the Chief Scientist (Army) referred to the person having resigned as a 'Naval officer'. Since Hollyhock was the only naval officer with responsibilities for both the screening and testing programme with incapacitating agents, it is highly probable that he was the officer who resigned in January 1965 on grounds of ill-health. His name does not appear in any of the subsequent Porton reports; TNA, DEFE13/846, Chemical Warfare, Chief Scientist (Army) to Deputy Secretary of State for Defence and Minister of Defence for the Army, 30 November 1965.

96. Historical Survey 2006, p. 138; Ladell to University of Edinburgh Medical School, 8 and 12 February 1965.
97. Historical Survey 2006, p. 138; Deputy Chief Scientist (Army) to University of Edinburgh Medical School, 17 February 1965.
98. Historical Survey 2006, pp. 138f.; Twelfth COSHE meeting, 2 February 1965.
99. Historical Survey 2006, p. 138.
100. Historical Survey 2006, p. 138.
101. Historical Survey 2006, p. 138.
102. Historical Survey 2006, p. 138; COSHE Proceedings, 12 February 1965.
103. TNA, DEFE13/1055, Chemical Warfare, 'Biographical Notes of People to be Met at CDEE and MRE', 12 July 1968.
104. Historical Survey 2006, p. 138; Ladell to University of Edinburgh Medical School, 8 and 12 February 1965.
105. Historical Survey 2006, p. 138; Thirteenth COSHE meeting, 19 March 1965.
106. Historical Survey 2006, p. 138; Ladell to Director Porton and Deputy Chief Scientist, 17 February 1965; see also Ladell to Director Porton, 19 February 1965.
107. TNA, DEFE13/846, Chemical Warfare, Chief Scientist (Army) to Deputy Secretary of State for Defence and Minister of Defence for the Army, 30 November 1965.
108. TNA, DEFE13/846, Chemical Warfare, Chief Scientist (Army) to Deputy Secretary of State for Defence and Minister of Defence for the Army, 30 November 1965.
109. BMJ, Obituary, John M. Barnes, 4 (1975), 5989, p. 170; Thomson 1975, p. 299; Oakley 1968, pp. 90f.
110. For the history and work of the MRC Toxicology Research Unit see TNA, FD1/279; FD1/280; FD9/592; FD11/25, FD23/381; FD23/383; see also FD23/1431; also Johnson 2001; BMJ, Obituaries, Frank Anton Denz, 1 (1960), 5188, p. 1817.
111. Barnes 1953; Thomson 1975, pp. 100f.
112. The MRC advisory committee included G.R. Cameron, J.H. Gaddum, D. Hunter, F.C. MacIntosh, E.R.A. Merewether, R.A. Peters, J. Davidson Pratt, J.R. Squire, J. Walker, and J.M. Barnes as secretary; BMJ, 'Toxicological Research', 2 (1947), 4531, p. 739; Green 1948.
113. UoL, Special Collection and Archives, D106/2/13. Correspondence of Prof Wilson, whilst at University College Hospital Medical School, London, with the MoS (Porton Experimental Station) regarding his PF-3 research (1946–51).
114. UoL, Special Collection and Archives, D106/2/13, Correspondence of Prof Wilson, whilst at University College Hospital Medical School, London, with the MoS (Porton Experimental Station) regarding his PF-3 research (1946–51); D106/2/29, Distaval Clinical Trials (correspondence, completed questionnaires, and summaries), and correspondence regarding LSD and Ritalin (1958–62);

D106/2/29/7, four journal articles on the nature and control of clinical trials, specifically those involving Thalidomide, and 'A Proposal for the Improvement of Clinical Trial Procedure' (1959–62); D106/4/1/2, Poisoning by Drugs, Local Anaesthetics, Antagonists of ACh, Diuretics, Histamine and Anti Histamines, Action of Drugs on CNS [Central Nervous System], and Therapy of Allergic Disease, 1950–56 and n.d. (1950–56); D106/4/1/5, Cardiovascular System, Action of Drugs on CVS, Drugs Acting on the Heart, Respiratory Failure, Pharmacology of Respiratory System, Applied Pharmacology, 1960–71 and n.d. (1960–71); Historical Survey 2006, p. 88.

115. Royal College of Physicians, Munk's Rolls, Robert Henry Stewart Thompson (1912–98); <http://munksroll.rcplondon.ac.uk/Biography/Details/5495> (accessed January 2015).

116. Historical Survey 2006, p. 138; Director Porton to Chairman of SAC, 3 March 1965.

117. Historical Survey 2006, p. 138; see also Ladell to Director Porton, 19 February 1965.

118. Historical Survey 2006, p. 139; COSHE Proceedings. Ad Hoc Meeting on Human Experiments. Ladell to Porton Director, 11 August 1965.

119. Historical Survey 2006, p. 139; COSHE Proceedings. Ad Hoc Meeting on Human Experiments. Ladell to Porton Director, 11 August 1965.

120. Carter, Pearson 1996b, p. 65.

121. Historical Survey 2006, p. 139; COSHE Proceedings. Ad Hoc Meeting on Human Experiments. Ladell to Porton Director, 11 August 1965.

122. Historical Survey 2006, p. 139; SAC Chairman to Chief Scientist (Army), 10 August 1965; COSHE Proceedings. Ad Hoc Meeting on Human Experiments. Ladell to Porton Director, 11 August 1965; TNA, WO195/16161, First Meeting of ABC, November 1965; also WO195/16131, report by the Chairman of COSHE, November 1965.

123. Historical Survey 2006, p. 139; SAC Chairman to Chief Scientist (Army), 10 August 1965.

124. Historical Survey 2006, p. 139; COSHE Proceedings. Ad Hoc Meeting on Human Experiments. Ladell to Porton Director, 11 August 1965.

125. For the establishment of the ABC see TNA, WO195/16134, 'Terms of Reference of the ABC', 4 November 1965; see also Historical Survey 2006, p. 139; Director Porton to Chief Scientist (Army), 25 October 1965.

126. TNA, FD23/1431, 'Research Work on Traveller's Diarrhoea: Report by Lt Col J. Barnes and Wg Cdr R.J. Moylan-Jones', June 1966.

127. BMJ, Obituary, R.J. Moylan-Jones, 291 (1985), 6496, p. 681; and 291 (1985), 6498, p. 830.

128. For some of Beswick's research work see Ballantyne, Beswick 1972, pp. 121–8.

129. TNA, DEFE13/846, Chemical Warfare, Chief Scientist (Army) to Deputy Secretary of State for Defence and Minister of Defence for the Army,

30 November 1965; WO195/16161; ACSRTD, Applied Biology Committee, 14 January 1966; WO195/16227, 'Report on the Human Safety Committee', c. March 1966.

130. Evans, R. 2000a, p. 419, footnote 71; *BMJ*, Obituary, W.S.S. Ladell, 4 (1970), 5737, pp. 751–2.

131. TNA, WO195/16161; ACSRTD, Applied Biology Committee, 14 January 1966; WO195/16371; ACSRTD, Applied Biology Committee, 2 December 1966.

132. TNA, WO195/16371; ACSRTD, Applied Biology Committee, 2 December 1966; Item 5 (c), 'Field Experiments—"Exercise Recount"—Preliminary Report of a Field Experiment by CDEE'; Item 6 (c), 'The Present Situation on First Aid and Therapy in Poisoning by Lysergic Acid Diethylamide' (UoK, Porton Archive, B209).

133. Hammond, Carter 2002, pp. 211–35.

134. TNA, WO195/16161; ACSRTD, Applied Biology Committee, 14 January 1966; see also Hedgecoe 2009, pp. 335 ff.

135. TNA, DEFE13/846, Chemical Warfare, Chief Scientist (Army) to Deputy Secretary of State for Defence and Minister of Defence for the Army, 30 November 1965.

136. TNA, WO195/16273; ACSRTD, Applied Biology Committee, 6 July 1966.

137. TNA, WO195/16273; ACSRTD, Applied Biology Committee, 6 July 1966.

138. TNA, DEFE13/846, Chemical Warfare, Chief Scientist (Army) to Deputy Secretary of State for Defence and Minister of Defence for the Army, 30 November 1965; also Historical Survey 2006, p. 139.

139. TNA, WO195/16161; ACSRTD, Applied Biology Committee, 14 January 1966. Little more than a year later, Haddon indirectly referred to the death of Ronald Maddison: 'Mr Haddon said that the 1953 ruling on GB tests, following an accident at CDEE and the subsequent findings of the committee presided over by Lord Adrian, was that G tests with human subjects must be confined to GB. That had since been extended to include tests with VX'; see TNA, WO195/16462; ACSRTD, Applied Biology Committee, 25 May 1967.

140. Present were Prof R.H.S. Thompson (Chairman), Dr J.M. Barnes, Dr O.G. Edholm, Surgeon Capt J. Glass (M.D.G. (N)), Mr Haddon (D/CDEE), Prof C.A. Keele, Col R.P. Leake (A.M.D.8), Prof M.D. Milne, Prof A. Wilson, Air Cdre R.O. Yerbury (D.M.R. (RAF)), and Mr F.M.D. Yeo (Secretary). The following also attended: Mr K.W. Jones (AD/CD), Lt Col R.P. Bradshaw, Mr R.W. Brimblecombe, Prof Sir Lovatt Evans, Mr K.H. Kemp, Dr W.S.S. Ladell, Dr J. Mackay, Wg Cdr R.J. Moylan-Jones, all of CDEE. Apologies for absence were received from Prof R.B. Fisher, Mr G.N. Gadsby (DBCD) and Prof J.R. Squire; TNA, WO195/16161; ACSRTD, Applied Biology Committee, 14 January 1966; *BMJ*, New Director General of Army Medical Services, 1 (1977), 6065, p. 912.

141. TNA, WO195/16227, 'Report on the Human Safety Committee', *c.* March 1966.
142. IWM, Film and Video Archive, DED 46A, 'The Chemical Defence Experimental Establishment Porton Down, Volunteers for Porton', 1966.
143. Historical Survey 2006, p. 421.
144. IWM, Film and Video Archive, DED 46A, 'The Chemical Defence Experimental Establishment Porton Down, Volunteers for Porton', 1966. The film was apparently shown to service officers and NCOs at the Defence Nuclear, Biological, and Chemical School at Winterbourne Gunner and at army units through the Army Kinema Corporation and 'Astra' cinemas; Operation Antler, Witness Statement Richard B.M. Skinner, 9 January 2001.
145. *BMJ*, Obituary, R.J. Moylan-Jones, 291 (1985), 6496, p. 681; and 291 (1985), 6498, p. 830.
146. TNA, WO195/16161; ACSRTD, Applied Biology Committee, 14 January 1966; WO195/16273; ACSRTD, Applied Biology Committee, 6 July 1966; also WO195/16214, ACSRTD, Applied Biology Committee, Item 6 (b), Proposals for Future Work on LSD 25 in Medical Research Division, part 1: Animal Work.
147. TNA, WO195/16161; ACSRTD, Applied Biology Committee, 14 January 1966; see also TNA, WO195/16427, 'Progress Report on Work with T3456', 13 March 1967 (UoK, Porton Archive, B209).

CHAPTER 9

1. See Presidential Commission for the Study of Bioethical Issues 2011.
2. TNA, FD9/3940; Internal MRC Note for file, 14 August 1969.
3. TNA, FD9/3940; Internal MRC Note for file, 14 August 1969.
4. MI, Folder 2C, Exhibit CCB/3, 'Medical Research', *The Lancet*, 18 July 1964, pp. 459–60.
5. TNA, FD9/3940; Col R.S. Marshall, Legal staff, ALS 2, to Director of Army Operational Science and Research, 3 March 1967.
6. TNA, FD9/3940; Internal MRC Note for file, 14 August 1969.
7. UoK, Porton Archive, Porton Down MPA, CPS letter to Mr J. Stubbs, 12 December 2003, para. 13.17.
8. Jones 1981, pp. 188–205; Schmidt 2004, pp. 284f.
9. Jones 1981, p. 216; Reverby 2011, p. 8.
10. Reverby 2011; Spector-Bagdady and Lombardo 2013; Lederer 2004; Lederer 2007; Presidential Commission for the Study of Bioethical Issues 2011.
11. Beecher 1966a, p. 1355; also Schmidt 2004, pp. 284ff.
12. I am grateful to Prof Robert Field, Drexel University, for drawing my attention to these issues; see Field 2007, p. 347; also Starr 1982.
13. NIH, Office of the Director, NIH Almanac 2002, NIH Publication No. 02–5, December 2002; see <http://www.nih.gov/about/almanac/appropriations/part2.htm> (accessed July 2012); also Schmidt 2004, pp. 284ff.

14. WMA Archive, Department of National Health and Welfare, Ottawa, Canada, National Health Grants, 1948–1961 (January 1962), pp. 26–35, p. 29.
15. Green 1948.
16. Hornblum 1998; Moreno 1999, pp. 246ff.; Schmidt 2004.
17. Moreno 1999, p. 161; also Moreno 1997.
18. Moreno 1999, p. 167.
19. Moreno 1999, p. 168.
20. TNA, FD9/855, Draft—Council memorandum 'Experiments on Man: Conditions for Conduct', including statement on the 'Condition on which Experiments can be Conducted on Man', 2 January 1956; also MRC's statement on 'Responsibility in Investigations on Human Subjects' from 1962/1963; for the history of research ethics in postwar Britain see Hazelgrove 2002; Valier, Timmermann 2008; Hedgecoe 2009, pp. 333f.
21. TNA, FD9/855, Draft—Council memorandum 'Experiments on Man: Conditions for Conduct', including statement on the 'Condition on which experiments can be conducted on man', 2 January 1956.
22. Beecher 1955; Lederer 2004, p. 203; Valier, Timmermann 2008, pp. 499ff.
23. Valier, Timmermann 2008, p. 497.
24. Guttentag 1964; Langer 1964.
25. United States Advisory Committee on Human Radiation Experiments 1995, pp. 88f.
26. Beecher 1959, p. 473.
27. Perley et al. 1992, p. 156.
28. Beecher 1959, p. 471.
29. Annas, Grodin 1992, pp. 343–5; United States Advisory Committee on Human Radiation Experiments 1995, pp. 90f.
30. United States Advisory Committee on Human Radiation Experiments 1995, p. 90.
31. WMA Archive, Summary of Activities of the WMA, Inc., 1958–1971 (1960/1961), p. 13, p. 18.
32. United States Advisory Committee on Human Radiation Experiments 1995, p. 91.
33. Beecher 1960, p. 80; also Beecher 1959.
34. WMA Archive, Minutes of Ninth Annual Meeting, 16 April 1956; also Summary of Activities of the WMA, Inc., 1958–1971 (1967), p. 59.
35. WMA Archive, First Decade Report of the WMA, 1947–1957, unpublished manuscript, c. 1957, Chapter 4, pp. 2–3; for the Declaration of Geneva see Frewer 2010.
36. WMA Archive, First Decade Report of the WMA, 1947–1957, unpublished manuscript, c. 1957, Chapter 4, pp. 7; Urban Wiesing, The Future of the Declaration of Helsinki. Introduction—Remarks about the Next Revision. Presentation delivered at Rotterdam, 26 June 2012.

37. Christian Bonah and Florian Schmaltz, 'From Nuremberg to Helsinki: The Prosecution of Medical War Crimes at the Struthof Medical Trials, France, 1952–1954', paper presented at the expert conference 'Research within Bounds: Protecting Human Participants in Modern Medicine and the Declaration of Helsinki, 1964–2014', Brocher Foundation, September 2013. The paper is currently being prepared for publication; also Maio 2004.

38. The resolution was transmitted to the MJC, the WHO, the ICRC, the International Committee on Military Medicine and Pharmacy (ICMMP) and the International Labour Organization (ILO); WMA Archive, First Decade Report of the WMA, 1947–1957, unpublished manuscript, c. 1957, Chapter 4, p. 4.

39. WMA Archive, First Decade Report of the WMA, 1947–57, unpublished manuscript, c. 1957, Chapter 4, p. 9.

40. For Hulst and his connections to the Alexander family see Schmidt 2004.

41. WMA Archive, Pol, DoH, Adopted Versions, 1953 onwards.

42. WMA Archive, First Decade Report of the WMA, 1947–57, unpublished manuscript, c. 1957, Chapter 4, pp. 5f.; also Chapter 10; see also 'Principles for Those in Research and Experimentation', The General Assembly of the World Medical Association, 1954, *World Medical Journal* (1955), No. 2, pp. 14–15.

43. NIH, Memorandum approved by the Director NIH, 'Group Consideration of Clinical Research Procedures Deviating from Accepted Medical Practice or Involving Unusual Hazards' (1953), quoted in Fletcher 2002, pp. B-10f.; also Jastone 2006, pp. 17f.

44. WMA Archive, Report of the International Liaison and Medical Ethics Committees. Regulations in Time of Armed Conflict, 24 May 1957.

45. WMA Archive, First Decade Report of the WMA, 1947–1957, unpublished manuscript, c. 1957, Chapter 18, p. 3.

46. WMA Archive, Summary of Activities of the WMA, Inc., 1958–71 (1958), p. 1.

47. WMA Archive, Summary of Activities of the WMA, Inc., 1958–71 (1959), p. 7.

48. WMA Archive, Summary of Activities of the WMA, Inc., 1958–71 (1960/1961), p. 13, p. 18.

49. WMA Archive, Report of the International Liaison Committee, Symposium on International Humanitarian Law in the World Today, 28 January 1964; Tenth Meeting on International Medical Law, Working Group of IRCC, ICMMP, WMA, WHO, Monaco, 11–12 May 1964.

50. Schmidt 2004, pp. 264–97.

51. 'Draft Code of Ethics on Human Experimentation', *BMJ*, 27 October 1962.

52. WMA Archive, Pol, DoH, Adopted Versions, 1953 onwards; Medical Ethics Committee 1962; Fluss 1999, p. 19.

53. WMA Archive, Pol, DoH, Adopted Versions, 1953 onwards.

54. WMA Archive, Pol, DoH, Adopted Versions, 1953 onwards.

55. WMA Archive, Biographies and Photos of Programme Participants, WMA 1963 Meeting.

56. WMA Archive, Gear (WMA) to Annis (AMA), 19 May 1964.

57. Among matters to be resolved, the minutes note: 'Conformity with the Neurenbourg [sic] Rules'; WMA Archive, Minutes, Medical Ethics Committee, Forty-ninth Council Session, 21 October 1963.

58. The meeting was attended by the following WMA council members: F. Worré (Luxembourg), M. Ali (Pakistan), E.R. Annis (United States), D.M. Cardoso (Brazil), G.D. Dorman (United States), E. Fromm (Germany), O.K. Harlem (Norway), A.P. Mittra (India), J.R. Nicholson-Lailey, U. Siirala (Finland), A. Spinelli (Italy), G.V. Tamesis (Philippines), and A.H. Tonkin (South Africa). The following attended as officials, observers, and WMA committee members: H.S. Gear (United States), S.S.B. Gilder (Great Britain), J.-R. Gosset (France), E. Grey-Turner (Great Britain), J.G. Hunter (Australia), K.E.U. Jäämeri, C. Jacobsen (Denmark), P.M. Kaul (Assistant Director General, WHO, Switzerland), J. Maystre (Official Liaison Officer, Switzerland), M. Poumailoux (France), R. Schlögell (Germany), and D.P. Stevenson (Great Britain); WMA Archive, Minutes of Fifty-first Council Session, Helsinki, Finland, 13–14 June 1964.

59. For Hodson see WMA Archive, First Decade Report of the WMA, 1947–57, unpublished manuscript, c. 1957, Chapter 17, p. 6; also *United States v. Standard Ultramarine & Color Co.*, 137 F. Supp. 167 (1955).

60. WMA Archive, Minutes of Fifty-first Council Session, Helsinki, Finland, 13–14 June 1964.

61. WMA Archive, Eighteenth World Medical Assembly, Helsinki, Finland, 13–20 June 1964, Programme.

62. Schmidt, Frewer 2007; Schmidt 2012b; Schmidt, Frewer 2014a; Schmidt, Frewer 2014b; Frewer, Schmidt 2014.

63. Katz 1992, p. 233.

64. Lederer 2004, p. 210; Reverby 2011.

65. Lederer 2004, p. 210.

66. WMA Archive, Summary of Activities of the WMA, Inc., 1958–71 (1959), p. 37.

67. WMA Archive, Summary of Activities of the WMA, Inc., 1958–71 (1959), p. 36.

68. See also Schmidt 2012b.

69. UoK, Porton Archive, Porton Down MPA, CPS letter to Mr J. Stubbs, 12 December 2003, para. 12.19, vii) b.

70. Hare 2012, p. 2.

71. Morris, Grunenberg 2010.

72. Morris 2010, p. 61.

73. Arnott et al. 2006; see also King's College London Archive, K/PP178/11/6/2, Papers of M.H.F. Wilkins, papers relating to a campaign to end secrecy at Porton Down, June to July 1968.

74. Travis 2010.
75. Arnott et al. 2006, pp. 473–5.
76. Hammond, Carter 2002, pp. 217f.
77. Avery 2013, p. 79.
78. Hammond, Carter 2002, footnote 154; 'Stop it! Terror in the Animals' Belsen', *Sunday Pictorial*, 23 December 1960.
79. 'War on Chemical and BW', *Nature*, vol. 218 (1968), pp. 905–6.
80. Hammond, Carter 2002, pp. 221f.; 'Ethics and BW', *BMJ*, 8 June 1968; 'War on Chemical and BW', *Nature*, vol. 218 (1968), pp. 905–6.
81. Hammond, Carter 2002, p. 221.
82. For the role of Pugwash in the debates over chemical and biological weapons see Perry Robinson 1998.
83. Rabinowitch 1957.
84. Chisholm 1959.
85. The 1959 Pugwash conference was attended by Dr M.L. Ahuja (India), Sir Frederick Bawden (UK), Dr Brock Chisholm (Canada), Prof Claude E. Dolman (Canada), Acad. M. Dubinin (Russia), Prof Sven Gard (Sweden); Prof H. Bentley Glass (USA), Dr Charles C. Higgins (USA), Acad. Alexandre A. Imshenetzky (Russia), Dr Martin M. Kaplan (USA/Switzerland), Prof Donald Kerr (Canada), Prof Chauncey D. Leake (USA), Dr Patricia J. Lindop (UK), Prof André Lwoff (France), Dr Preben von Magnus (Denmark), Prof Gordon Manley (UK), Prof Hugo Muench (USA), Dr Vladimir P. Pavlichenko (Russia), Prof Eugene Rabinowitch (USA), Prof Alexander Rich (USA), Dr Theodor Rosebury (USA), Prof Joseph Rotblat (UK), Prof A.A. Smorodintsev (Russia), Prof M.G.P. Stoker (UK), Prof Pierre Thibault (France), and Sir Robert Watson-Watt (UK); 'On Biological and Chemical Warfare', *Bulletin of the Atomic Scientists*, vol. 15 (October 1959), no. 8, pp. 337–9; 'Biological and Chemical Warfare. An International Symposium', *Bulletin of the Atomic Scientists*, vol. 16 (June 1960), no. 6, pp. 226–7; Dubinin 1960.
86. Hammond, Carter 2002, p. 223; 'Microbiological Weapons Research and the Public Health', *County Councils Gazette*, 54 (February 1961).
87. Hammond, Carter 2002, pp. 231f.; 'Woman Scientist from Germ Base Vanishes', *Daily Telegraph*, 22 February 1974; 'Laughing Happy Girl Who Vanished', *Salisbury Journal*, 28 February 1974; 'Riddle of Woman Scientist', *Daily Telegraph*, 31 March 1974; 'Porton Woman's Death Unsolved', *Daily Telegraph*, 13 July 1974.
88. Chisholm 1959.
89. Chisholm 1959, p. 211.
90. Chisholm 1959, p. 211; Adams 2000, p. 472.
91. See also Balmer 2012, p. 113; Hammond, Carter 2002, pp. 224f.
92. Hammond, Carter 2002, pp. 224f.; the Science Museum, London, has a collection of posters of Porton's open days. I am grateful to Robert Bud for this information. See also IWM, Film and Video Archive, The Microbiological Research Establishment at Porton.

93. Balmer 2012, pp. 91–114; Balmer 2006a, pp. 702f.

94. *BMJ*, Obituary, C.E.G. Smith, 303 (1991), 6811, p. 1197.

95. Hammond, Carter 2002, pp. 226ff.

96. See also Dalyell's gloss on why he 'was nearly expelled' from the House of Commons in 1968 after he had leaked privileged information about Porton; Hansard (Westminster Hall), vol. 431 cc32–53WH, Porton Down (here c43WH), 22 February 2005.

97. Hammond, Carter 2002, p. 230; Galbraith 2000, p. 108; 'Technology Gone Mad—Who Cares?', *Wessex News*, March 1970.

98. Balmer 2012, pp. 100ff.; see also Cookson, Nottingham 1969.

99. WHO Group of Consultants 1970; see also the substantially revised second edition of the report, entitled WHO Guidance 2004.

100. 'Nerve Gas Death Claim Rejected', *Daily Telegraph*, 21 November 1969, p. 3; 'Ministry Inquiry on "Gas" Deaths', *The Times*, 22 November 1969; John Owen, 'Accidents at Secret Nerve Gas Factory', *Daily Telegraph*, 22 November 1969; 'Service at Nancekuke', *The Times*, 26 November 1969; 'Nerve Gas Man Reveals How He was Crippled', *The Times*, 7 December 1969.

101. 'Nerve Gas Man Reveals How He was Crippled', *The Times*, 7 December 1969; also Parker 1996, pp. 102f.; see also Sigmund 1980.

102. 'Nerve Gas Death Claim Rejected', *Daily Telegraph*, 21 November 1969.

103. 'Nancekuke: Secrets Order Regretted', *Birmingham Post*, 5 December 1969.

104. 'RAF Man "Victim of Porton Nerve Gas"', *The Observer*, 11 August 1968, p. 3; M. Steinberg, 'Nerve Gas Mystery', *The Times*, 23 February 1969, p. 10; 'Evidence to be Called on Nerve Gas', *The Guardian*, 8 September 1969, p. 16; P. Wright, H. Stanhope, 'Ex-Officer Tells of Nerve Gas Test', *The Times*, 8 September 1969, p. 1; 'New Look at Nerve Gas Case', *The Observer*, 14 September 1969, p. 3; 'Nerve Gas Plea Fails', *The Sunday Times*, 5 April 1970, p. 3 (UoK, Porton Archive, A105.7).

105. 'One Housewife's Fight for CBW Victims', *Peace News*, 6 March 1970. In 1970, Elizabeth Sigmund, née Tillotson, was married to the writer David Compton, which is why the article published in *Peace News* refers to her as Elizabeth Compton; see also Sigmund 1980; Picardie 1995.

106. Sigmund 1980.

107. 'Calls for Nerve Gas Inquiry', *The Times*, 26 November 1969; 'New Help for Nancekuke Man in 8-Year Fight?', *Birmingham Post*, 2 December 1969; 'Nerve Gas Pledge by Minister', *Daily Telegraph*, 3 December 1969; 'Promise on Nerve Gas', *The Times*, 3 December 1969; 'Nancekuke: Secrets Order Regretted', *Birmingham Post*, 5 December 1969; 'Death Inquiry at Nerve Gas Factory', *Daily Telegraph*, 5 December 1969; Pearce Wright, 'Gas Victim May Get Pension', *The Times*, 6 December 1969 (UoK, Porton Archive, A105.7).

108. 'Death Risks no Higher for Staff at Nancekuke', *The Times*, 3 November 1970; also Hansard, HC Debate, vol. 342 cc818–22, Nancekuke Base, 18 January 2000.

109. 'One Housewife's Fight for CBW Victims', *Peace News*, 6 March 1970.
110. Dennis Barker, '£1.75 Payout for Nerve Gas Victim', *The Guardian*, 16 February 1976; almost twenty-five years later, Griffiths' case stood at the centre of a parliamentary debate about the Nancekuke plant; Hansard, HC Debate, vol. 342 cc818–22, Nancekuke Base, 18 January 2000.
111. 'One Housewife's Fight for CBW Victims', *Peace News*, 6 March 1970.
112. See Peter Hammill's official website: <http://www.sofasound.com/phcds/ph7lyrics.htm#3>.
113. Jones 1971.
114. TNA, WO195/16840, 'Irritant Agents', Statement by DBCD, 2 January 1969 (UoK, Porton Archive, B209).
115. See Corson, Stoughton 1928.
116. IWM, Film and Video Archive, DED 31, 'An Improved Tear Gas for Riot Control'; also DED 27, 'Filmed Record of Trials Carried out with Troops to Compare the Effectiveness of CS and CN as Riot Control Agents'. The trials involved 160 soldiers.
117. TNA, CAB537/2711, 'Lachrymatory Devices, Notes of a Meeting held at Porton on 17 March 1948 to Discuss Anti-Riot Weapon Requirements'; also Secret Telegram by the Secretary of State for the Colonies about 'Tear Smoke Equipment', 11 May 1948 (UoK, Porton Archive, B209).
118. Tucker 2006, pp. 190–202.
119. TNA, WO195/16840, 'Irritant Agents, Statement by Directorate of Biological and Chemical Defence (DBCD)', 2 January 1969; TNA, DEFE13/705, 'CDE Paper on Toxicology etc. of CS. Possible Questions and Proposed Answers'; also 'Brief for Defence Debate March 1970' (UoK, Porton Archive, B209).
120. Hammond, Carter 2002, pp. 226f.
121. For Himsworth see Black, Gray 1995.
122. The other members of the Himsworth Committee were Robert H.S. Thompson, Professor of Chemical Pathology, Guy's Hospital Medical School, University of London, and A.C. Dornhorst, Professor of Medicine, St George's Hospital Medical School. The Committee subsequently also included Prof A. Neuberger, Prof W.D.M. Paton, Prof D.A.K. Black, Prof T. Crawford, and Dr J.C. Gilson. TNA, DEFE13/705, 'Brief for Defence Debate', March 1970; also Report by Chief Scientist (Army), 'Medical Effects of CS Smoke', 18 May 1970 (UoK, Porton Archive, B209); Hansard, HC Debate, vol. 806 cc243–4W, CS, 12 November 1970.
123. TNA CAB164/789, Solly Zuckerman (Chief Scientific Adviser) to Prime Minister, 26 November 1969 (UoK, Porton Archive, B209).
124. Hansard, HC Debate, vol. 795 cc17–18W, Disarmament, 2 February 1970; TNA, DEFE13/705, 'Brief for Defence Debate', March 1970 (UoK, Porton Archive, B209).
125. TNA, DEFE13/705, 'Note on CS Gas', *c.* 1970 (UoK, Porton Archive, B209).

126. Jones 1971, p. 690.

127. TNA, DEFE13/705, Alexander Mitchell, 'Grim Evidence on CS Gas', *The Sunday Times*, 5 April 1970; the Edgewood Arsenal report was entitled 'The Effects of Thermally Generated CS Aerosols on Human Skin' (January 1967); also TNA, DEFE13/705, W.F. Mumford, Head of DS22, to Whiteford, Deputy Chaplain General, 8 May 1970.

128. TNA, DEFE13/705, Jaffray, MoD, to Private Secretary to Foreign and Commonwealth Secretary, Home Secretary, and Chief Scientific Adviser, 13 May 1970.

129. Jones 1971, p. 690.

130. Jones 1971, p. 691.

131. TNA, DEFE13/1055, Chemical Warfare, 'Review of CS Decision: Chronology', c. March/April 1971.

132. TNA, DEFE13/1055, Chemical Warfare, Permanent Secretary to the Secretary of Defence to Foreign and Commonwealth Office, 6 October 1970.

133. For some discussions about the BTWC see TNA, DEFE13/705, Minister of State, FCO, to Prime Minister, 21 April 1970.

134. TNA, DEFE13/1055, Chemical Warfare, Permanent Secretary to the Secretary of Defence to Foreign and Commonwealth Office, 6 October 1970.

135. TNA, DEFE13/1055, Chemical Warfare, 'Review of CS Decision': Chronology (1970–71), 19 March 1971 (Flag F).

136. TNA, DEFE13/1055, Chemical Warfare, Foreign and Commonwealth Secretary, Denis Greenhill, to MoD, Sir James Dunnett, 28 April 1971.

137. TNA, DEFE13/705, Chiefs of Staffs Committee to Assistant Private Secretary/Secretary of State, 18 February 1970 (UoK, Porton Archive, B209).

138. TNA, DEFE13/1055, Chemical Warfare, Porton to MoD, 11 July 1968. The staff attending the Secretary's visit were as follows: G.N. Gadsby, C.E. Gordon Smith, T.F. Watkins, Maj L.H. Kent, Wg Cdr D.H. Levinson, W.S.S. Ladell, K.F. Sawyer, I.H. Silver, Cdr A.C. Simmonds, Lt Col J.P. Fitzgerald-Smith, Lt Col N.C. Burnett (US), E.A. Martin, F.W. Beswick, R.A. Titt, R.W. Brimblecombe, L.W.J. Warner, M. Ainsworth, P.H. Schwabe, A. Bebbington, R.G. Picknett, F. Belton, H.M. Darlow, H.A. Drueit, S. Peacock, G.J. Harper.

139. TNA, DEFE13/1055, Chemical Warfare, Porton to MoD, 11 July 1968.

140. TNA, DEFE13/1055, Chemical Warfare, Porton to MoD, 11 July 1968.

141. Hammond, Carter 2002, p. 227.

142. TNA, DEFE13/1055, Chemical Warfare, 'Points to be Raised by Whitley', 12 July 1968.

143. TNA, DEFE13/1055, Chemical Warfare, Press Clippings, 1970; also Pearse 2000.

144. TNA, DEFE13/1055, Chemical Warfare, 'Allegations about Experiments by MoD on Old People', 17 June 1970. The file contains a wealth of material, including copies of the letters containing the allegations.

145. Hammond, Carter 2002, pp. 226–35.

146. Rees, Dixon 2000; Pearse 2000; Comment: 'Official Secrets Act Must Never Cover Horrific Abuse', *Daily Express*, 20 November 2000.

147. Galbraith 2000, pp. 113–19, here p. 117; Hansard, HC Debate, vol. 342 cc818–22, Nancekuke Base, 18 January 2000.

148. TNA, DEFE13/1055, Chemical Warfare, 'Report of the Working Party on the Future of the Microbiological Research Establishment, Porton', October 1970; also DEFE13/846, 'Chemical Warfare and Biological Warfare—Future of MRE and CDEE', Porton, 29 August 1967; 'Future of MRE Porton', 14 November 1967.

149. TNA, DEFE13/1055, Chemical Warfare, 'Working Party on the Future of the Microbiological Research Establishment, Porton', October 1970.

150. *BMJ*, Medical News, New Dean, C.E. Gordon Smith, 3 (1970), 5713, p. 54.

151. See also Hammond, Carter 2002, pp. 231f.

152. TNA, WO195/16429, Applied Biology Committee, Item 4, 'A Review of Some Concepts of Incapacitation', 22 December 1966 (UoK, Porton Archive, B209).

153. TNA, WO195/16429, Applied Biology Committee, Item 4, 'A Review of Some Concepts of Incapacitation', 22 December 1966 (UoK, Porton Archive, B209).

154. Operation Antler, Witness Statement Richard B.M. Skinner, 9 January 2001.

155. Thomson Snell & Passmore, Witness Statement Richard B.M. Skinner, 25 January 2006.

156. Operation Antler, Witness Statement Richard B.M. Skinner, 9 January 2001.

157. Historical Survey 2006, pp. 122–4, here p. 124; Table 11.6.

158. For some of the earliest tests with T3436 see TNA, WO195/16529, Applied Biology Committee, 'Progress Report on Laboratory Experiments with T3436', 19 October 1967 (UoK, Porton Archive, B209).

159. Operation Antler, Witness Statement Richard B.M. Skinner, 9 January 2001.

160. TNA, WO195/16804, P. Holland, 'The Behavioural Effects of Drugs on Man as Illustrated by the Glycollates [*sic*]', 4 December 1968.

161. Operation Antler, Witness Statement Richard B.M. Skinner, 9 January 2001.

162. Operation Antler, Witness Statement Richard B.M. Skinner, 9 January 2001.

163. Operation Antler, Witness Statement Richard B.M. Skinner, 9 January 2001.

164. Operation Antler, Witness Statement Richard B.M. Skinner, 9 January 2001.

165. Operation Antler, Witness Statement Richard B.M. Skinner, 9 January 2001.

166. Thomson Snell & Passmore, Witness Statement Richard B.M. Skinner, 25 January 2006.

167. UoK, Porton Archive, Porton Down MPA, CPS letter to Mr J. Stubbs, 12 December 2003, para. 12.15.

168. UoK, Porton Archive, Porton Down MPA, CPS letter to Mr J. Stubbs, 12 December 2003, para. 12.15.

169. UoK, Porton Archive, Porton Down MPA, CPS letter to Mr J. Stubbs, 12 December 2003, para. 12.16.

170. Historical Survey (2006), pp. 338f.
171. UoK, Porton Archive, Porton Down MPA, CPS letter to Mr J. Stubbs, 12 December 2003, para. 13.8.

CHAPTER 10

1. 'The Storyteller', in Benjamin 1996–2003, vol. 3, pp. 143–66, here p. 144. See also Winter 2000, pp. 69–92; also Winter 1995; see also Ashplant et al. 2004.
2. Gregory 1994; Echternkamp, Martens 2010.
3. Judt 2009, pp. 224ff.
4. Bernard-Donals 2000, pp. 573f.; Caruth 1996.
5. Pechura, Rall 1993, p. viii.
6. Welsome 1999.
7. US case law report, *US v. James Stanley*, 483 US 669 (1987).
8. US Senate, 103rd Congress, Second Session, 'Is Military Research Hazardous to Veterans' Health? Lessons Spanning Half a Century', a Staff Report Prepared for the Committee on Veterans Affairs, 8 December 1994.
9. United States Advisory Committee on Human Radiation Experiments 1995; also Welsh 2009.
10. 'Porton Defends Nerve-Gas Tests on Humans', *New Scientist*, 16 July 1987; see also Syal 2002.
11. WMA Declaration on Chemical and Biological Weapons, Adopted by the Forty-second World Medical Assembly, Rancho Mirage, CA, USA, October 1990, and rescinded at the WMA General Assembly, Santiago 2005.
12. See Bridget Goodwin's TV documentary 'Keen as Mustard' (1989).
13. Care 2002b, p. 16; Care 2008, p. 23; Derek Fatchett, 'Labour Highlights Human Experiments at Porton Down', press release, 25 April 1995; Hansard (Westminster Hall), vol. 431 cc32–53WH, Porton Down (here c42WH), 22 February 2005.
14. Ken Livingstone, Press Conference in the House of Commons regarding the creation of the Porton Down Volunteers Association, 1994; see also the TV documentary by Bill Lyons et al., 'The Secrets of Porton Down' (Observer Films, 1994).
15. Dudley 1994.
16. Alan Care, Memorandum Re Porton Down, 1 February 2008 (includes feed-back from friends of Care's son after the UK government had agreed to a compensation scheme for the Porton Down veterans).
17. Care 2008; also UoK, Porton Archive, video-taped interview with Alan Care, 3 May 2005.
18. Elizabeth Sigmund headed the Anti-Biological Warfare group in the 1970s, when her name was Elizabeth Compton; see Chapter 9. For Sigmund see also Picardie 1995; also Sigmund 1980; for Roche see Parker 1996, pp. 105ff.
19. Care 2000; North 1994.

20. Alan Care Archive, Section 10 Certificate issued by Minister of State DSS (Re Michael Roche), August 1995 (until then the only one ever issued by the government). Referred to Liberty UK, Roche's case was eventually heard by the ECHR, which ruled that the UK government had violated his human rights under Article 8 of the Convention. In particular, the UK had 'not fulfilled the positive obligation to provide an effective and accessible procedure enabling the applicant to have access to all relevant and appropriate information that would allow him to assess any risk to which he had been exposed during his participation in the tests'; see Liberty UK press release, 'Government Withheld Vital Information from Poisoned Serviceman, says European Court', 19 October 2005; ECHR, Grand Chamber, Case of Roche v. The United Kingdom (Application no. 32555/96), Judgement, Strasbourg, 19 October 2005, p. 53; also Oliver 2005.

21. Care 2008, p. 24.

22. Edwards 2000b.

23. Hansard, HC Debate, vol. 282 cc785–93, Mr Michael Paynter, 16 October 1996; also Baroness Cumberledge, who argued along similar lines in response to a Parliamentary Question, 27 October 1994.

24. Hansard (Westminster Hall), vol. 431 cc32–53 WH, Porton Down, 22 February 2005.

25. Care 2002b, p. 17.

26. Care 2000; Evans, R. 2000b; 'UK Chemical Base "Too Big", says MP', BBC News, 20 August 1999.

27. Hansard, HC Debate, vol. 342 cc818–22, Nancekuke Base, 18 January 2000.

28. Davison 1999.

29. Edwards 2000a; Edwards 2000b.

30. UoK, Porton Archive, A105.7, Maddison Media, Frontline Scotland: 'Transcript: Trial and Error', BBC News, 7 March 2000.

31. Wightwick 2000; also Alan Care, 'Porton Down Veterans Will March on Whitehall on Remembrance Day 2001', Press Release.

32. Carrell 2001, p. 4.

33. Syal, Bisset 2000; UoK, Porton Archive, A105.7, Maddison Media.

34. Leaflet about Porton Down Volunteers Helpline, c. 1998.

35. Hansard, HC Debate, vol. 429 c136, Mr Douglas Shave, 10 January 2005; Hansard (Westminster Hall), cc32–53 WH, Porton Down, 22 February 2005.

36. UoK, Porton Archive, A105.7, Maddison Media, DoH, 'Porton Down Volunteers: Medical Assessment Programme', 21 November 2000.

37. Vasagar 2001.

38. Venables et al. 2009; Carpenter et al. 2009; for an assessment of the long-term health effects resulting from chemical agent tests at Edgewood Arsenal see Page 2003, pp. 239–45; also Hansard (Westminster Hall), vol. 431 cc32–53 WH, Porton Down, 22 February 2005, Mr Patrick Hall (Bedford, Lab): cc32 WH–37 WH.

39. UoK, Porton Archive, video-taped interview with Alan Care, 3 May 2005; see also Care 2008, where the expletives are omitted.

40. Alan Care, 'Porton Down Death—New Evidence—Did a V Nerve Agent Kill Ronald Maddison?', Press Release, 7 November 2002; also Care 2000.
41. Rayment 2003. Following a case review in 2006, the CPS upheld its decision not to prosecute any of the Porton scientists; CPS, Special Crime Division, Kate Leonard to Alan Care, 9 June 2006.
42. Hedges 2003; also Boggan 2003.
43. Rayment 2003.
44. UoK, Porton Archive, A105.8, Post Inquest Developments, Royal Courts of Justice, The Lord Chief Justice of England and Wales, The Lord Woolf of Barnes and Mrs Justice Hallett, 18 November 2002.
45. 'Porton Down Inquest May Re-Open', BBC News, 19 December 2000; 'New Inquest on Porton Down Victim', BBC News, 22 April 2002; 'MoD "Will not Oppose" New Inquest', BBC News, 29 July 2002; 'Nerve Gas Inquest to be Re-Opened', BBC News, 18 November 2002.
46. UoK, Porton Archive, A105.8, Post Inquest Developments, Royal Courts of Justice, The Lord Chief Justice of England and Wales, The Lord Woolf of Barnes and Mrs Justice Hallett, 18 November 2002; also Schmidt 2007b, p. 307.
47. UoK, Porton Archive, A105.8, Post Inquest Developments, Royal Courts of Justice, The Lord Chief Justice of England and Wales, The Lord Woolf of Barnes and Mrs Justice Hallett, 18 November 2002; Bowcott 2002, p. 6.
48. Evans, R. 2003, p. 9; Rosenberg, Britten 2002.
49. MI, Report by Dr Proudfoot, para. 17.8., p. 36.
50. MI, Report by Dr Proudfoot, para. 17.16, p. 38.
51. Ombudsman for NDCF 2004.
52. Lee et al. 2004.
53. Goslett, Rentoul 2013.
54. MI, Transcript, Day 1, p. 7; also Laville 2004a, p. 8; Milmo 2004a.
55. De Bruxelles 2004, p. 10.
56. Laville 2004a.
57. See <http://www.4newsquare.com/barristers/88/Leigh-Ann-b-Mulcahy-b-QC/cv>.
58. *MoD (Respondent) v. AB and others (Appellants)* [2012] UKSC 9; on appeal from [2010] EWCA Civ 1317; Justices: Lord Phillips (President); Lord Walker; Lady Hale; Lord Brown; Lord Mance; Lord Kerr; Lord Wilson.
59. MI, Transcript, Day 1, p. 25.
60. Pook 2004a, p. 8.
61. MI, Transcript, Day 1, p. 33.
62. Pook 2004a.
63. Stallabrass 1995, pp. 16f.
64. MI, Transcript, Day 1, p. 22.
65. MI, Transcript, Day 59, p. 33.
66. MI, Transcript, Day 63, pp. 68f.
67. MI, Transcript, Day 59, p. 40.

68. MI, Transcript, Day 59, pp. 57f.
69. Care 2002b, p. 17.
70. MI, Folder 2B, Exhibit JJH/187/2, Callaway, Handwritten note 'Probability of Extreme Susceptibility in Humans', no date (c. 1953), pp. 207–8; see also MI, Transcript, Day 29, pp. 4–13, on the issue of 'standard deviation'. For Callaway's scientific work see also Callaway et al. 1951.
71. MI, Transcript, Day 32, pp. 81ff.
72. MI, Folder 2B, Exhibit JJH/187/2, Callaway, Handwritten note 'Probability of Extreme Susceptibility in Humans', no date (c. 1953), p. 208.
73. MI, Folder 2B, Exhibit JJH/187/2, Callaway, Handwritten note 'Probability of Extreme Susceptibility in Humans', no date (c. 1953), p. 208.
74. MI, Folder 2B, Exhibit CEB/16/2, Cullumbine, Handwritten note 'The Percutaneous Toxicity of the G-Compounds', 5 May 1953, pp. 186–92; MI, Folder 2B, Exhibit JJH/187/5, Cullumbine, Typed note 'The Percutaneous Toxicity of the G-Compounds', 8 May 1953, pp. 204–6; MI, Folder 2B, Exhibit MNJ/30, PTP 399, 'Percutaneous Toxicity of G-Compounds', 11 January 1954, pp. 267–318; also MI, Transcript, Day 61, pp. 4ff.
75. MI, Folder 2B, Exhibit JJH/187/2, Callaway, Handwritten note 'Probability of Extreme Susceptibility in Humans', no date (c. 1953), p. 207. Since Callaway's paper was found among the research material which Cullumbine used to write his own memorandum on 'The Percutaneous Toxicity of the G-Compounds', he (Cullumbine) is more likely than anyone else to have written the brief annotation 'Not Used' in the top left hand corner of the paper.
76. MI, Folder 2B, Exhibit CEB/16/2, Cullumbine, Handwritten note 'The Percutaneous Toxicity of the G-Compounds', 5 May 1953, pp. 186–92, here p. 186; MI, Folder 2B, Exhibit JJH/187/5, Cullumbine, Typed note 'The Percutaneous Toxicity of the G-Compounds', 8 May 1953, pp. 204–6, here p. 204; also MI, Transcript, Day 61, pp. 4ff.
77. MI, Folder 2B, Exhibit MNJ/134, CDAB, 5 February 1953, pp. 173–82; MI, Transcript, Day 27, pp. 51f.
78. MI, Folder 2B, Exhibit CEB/16/2, Cullumbine, Handwritten note 'The Percutaneous Toxicity of the G-Compounds', 5 May 1953, pp. 186–92, here p. 189.
79. See also MI, Transcript, Day 31, pp. 12f.
80. MI, Folder 2B, Exhibit CEB/16/2, Cullumbine, Handwritten note 'The Percutaneous Toxicity of the G-Compounds', 5 May 1953, pp. 186–92, here p. 190.
81. Cullumbine reiterated the point during the Court of Inquiry; see MI, Transcript, Day 61, pp. 44f.
82. MI, Transcript, Day 30, pp. 47f.
83. MI, Transcript, Day 31, p. 18.
84. MI, Transcript, Day 62, pp. 50ff.; MI, Transcript, Day 31, p. 14.
85. MI, Folder 1A, Witness Statement Robert Desmond Lynch, 11 February 2004.

86. MI, Transcript, Day 28, pp. 109ff.
87. MI, Transcript, Day 62, pp. 52ff. If an inappropriate pipette was used, Proudfoot concurred, then this constituted another significant shortcoming: 'You do not cut corners.'
88. MI, Transcript, Day 28, p. 110.
89. MI, Transcript, Day 61, pp. 88f.
90. H. Cullumbine, 'The Medical Aspects of Nerve Gas Poisoning', CDEE Report, Porton, March 1956.
91. MI, Transcript, Day 62, pp. 44.
92. MI, Transcript, Day 62, pp. 44f.
93. MI, Transcript, Day 62, pp. 4ff.
94. MI, Transcript, Day 62, pp. 7ff.
95. MI, Transcript, Day 63, pp. 50f.
96. For 'ascribed power' see Overy 2004.
97. MI, Transcript, Day 18, pp. 106ff.
98. MI, Transcript, Day 18, pp. 93f.
99. MI, Transcript, Day 62, pp. 20ff.; also MI, Transcript, Day 18, p. 94.
100. MI, Transcript, Day 18, p. 121.
101. MI, Transcript, Day 62, p. 22. The quote seems to have been compiled by the Coroner from Robert Lynch's written and oral testimony; MI, Transcript, Day 18, p. 139; Day 22, p. 148; MI, Folder 1A, Witness Statement Robert Desmond Lynch, 11 February 2004.
102. MI, Transcript, Day 62, pp. 23f.
103. MI, Transcript, Day 18, pp. 134f.
104. MI, Transcript, Day 19, pp. 8ff.
105. See also 'No Charges over Porton Down Tests', BBC News Channel, 12 June 2006.
106. MI, Transcript, Day 62, p. 114.
107. See Schmidt 2012b; also MI, Transcript, Day 62, pp. 118f.
108. MI, Transcript, Day 62, p. 106.
109. MI, Transcript, Day 62, p. 106.
110. MI, Transcript, Day 62, p. 109.
111. MI, Transcript, Day 62, p. 122.
112. Kennedy 2006, p. 403; also Sharp 2006, p. 631.
113. Kennedy 2006, p. 416.
114. MI, Transcript, Day 53, pp. 32ff.; see Kennedy 2006; also Weindling 2006.
115. MI, Transcript, Day 53, pp. 102f.
116. Sharp 2006, p. 631.
117. MI, Transcript, Day 53, pp. 19f.; pp. 25ff.; Kennedy 2006, p. 432; Evans, M. 2006; Evans, R. 2006c.
118. MI, Transcript, Day 53, p. 27.
119. MI, Transcript, Day 53, pp. 16f.
120. MI, Transcript, Day 53, p. 18; MI, Transcript, Day 63, p. 22.

121. MI, Transcript, Day 53, p. 18.
122. MI, Transcript, Day 53, p. 155.
123. MI, Transcript, Day 53, p. 155; see Kidd 1953.
124. MI, Folder 2B, Exhibit CEB/16/2, Cullumbine, Handwritten note 'The Percutaneous Toxicity of the G-Compounds', 5 May 1953, pp. 186–92, here pp. 191f.; MI, Folder 2B, Exhibit JJH/187/5, Cullumbine, Typed note 'The Percutaneous Toxicity of the G-Compounds', 8 May 1953, pp. 204–6, here p. 206; see also MI, Folder 2B, Exhibit MNJ/30, PTP 399, 'Percutaneous Toxicity of G-Compounds', 11 January 1954, pp. 267–318, here p. 279.
125. MI, Transcript, Day 53, pp. 22f.; see Chapter 6 for details of the 'Kelly incident'.
126. MI, Transcript, Day 53, pp. 23f.; MI, Transcript, Day 63, pp. 23f. Somewhat conspiratorially, and without checking basic facts, the defence editor of *The Times*, Michael Evans, wrongly claimed that the MoD had withheld Kennedy's report in 1953(!), yet the report had been produced almost fifty years later as part of the MoD's Historical Survey; Evans, M. 2004a, p. 8.
127. MI, Transcript, Day 53, p. 24; MI, Transcript, Day 63, p. 26.
128. MI, Transcript, Day 53, pp. 167f.; MI, Transcript, Day 63, pp. 36f.
129. TNA, WO195/16227, 'Report on the Human Safety Committee', *c*. March 1966.
130. TNA, WO195/16428, 'Early Exploratory Work with BZ in the UK', 10 March 1967.
131. MI, Folder 2A, Exhibit MNJ/20/1, MoS, 'Report of a Court of Inquiry into Death of Maddison', May 1953, pp. 84–142, Testimony Harry Cullumbine, p. 96; MI, Transcript, Day 61, p. 56.
132. MI, Transcript, Day 64, pp. 15f.
133. See, for example, Evans, Laville 2004; Evans, M. 2004b; Pook 2004b; Milmo 2004b; Laville 2004b; Jenkins 2004.
134. 'Sheer Poison', *Daily Mirror*, 16 November 2004.
135. MI, Transcript, Day 64, p. 30.
136. Hansard (Westminster Hall), vol. 431 cc32–53WH, Porton Down, 22 February 2005. See also Care 2005; Evans, Laville 2004; Evans, M. 2004b; Jenkins 2004; Robins 2005.
137. Hansard Written Ministerial Statements, c167WS, Ronald Maddison, 21 December 2004.
138. *R (on the application of MoD) v Wiltshire and Swindon Coroner (Craik and others, interested parties)*, All England Law Reports 2005, vol. 4, pp. 44–51. [2005] EWHC 889 (Admin). Queen's Bench Division (Administrative Court); also 'MoD Can Challenge Porton Case', BBC News, 19 April 2005.
139. The centrality of the informed consent issue in the Maddison case also explains, in retrospect, why the MoD had been categorically opposed to allowing the inquest jury to see the 'Report on Informed Consent' that the author of this study had been asked to submit to the Coroner in October

2003. In the report, I came to the following conclusion: 'It is my opinion, having considered the historical evidence available at this stage, that judged against the "standards of the day", and against medical morality more generally, the Porton Down experiment on Maddison may appear reckless and irresponsible, and lacking appropriate caution and attention to the issue of informed consent.' MI, Ulf Schmidt, 'Report on Informed Consent' (unpublished, 2003), p. 52.

140. Joint Press Release between Thomson Snell & Passmore and the MoD, 13 February 2006.

141. Evans, R. 2006b.

142. TNA, WO286/11, 'Death of LAC Maddison', H. Woodhouse (for the Treasury Solicitor), to Legal 1 (Mr Griffith-Jones), MoS, 15 May 1953; MI, Folder 2A/I, Exhibit MNJ/20/2, 'Death of LAC Maddison', H. Woodhouse (for the Treasury Solicitor), to Legal 1 (Mr Griffith-Jones), MoS, 15 May 1953, pp. 188–9, here p. 189.

143. Allender et al. 2006; also Page 2003.

144. UoK, Porton Archive, A104.1, Interview Transcript Terry Alderson, 20 September 2006.

145. UoK, Porton Archive, A105.8, Post Inquest Developments, Care to Prime Minister, 17 November 2004; Care to Prime Minister, 25 November 2004.

146. Hansard, HC Debate, vol. 429 c136, Mr Douglas Shave, 10 January 2005.

147. UoK, Porton Archive, A105.8, Post Inquest Developments, Vennai to Care, 27 January 2005.

148. ECHR, Grand Chamber, Case of Roche v. The United Kingdom (Application no. 32555/96), Judgement, Strasbourg, 19 October 2005, p. 40.

149. Hansard (Westminster Hall), vol. 431 cc32–53 WH, Porton Down, 22 February 2005.

150. Hansard (Westminster Hall), vol. 431 cc32–53 WH, Porton Down, 22 February 2005, Mr Patrick Hall (Bedford, Lab): cc32WH–37WH.

151. Hansard (Westminster Hall), vol. 431 cc32–53 WH, Porton Down, 22 February 2005, Miss Ann Widdecombe (Maidstone and The Weald, Con): cc37WH–40WH.

152. Hansard (Westminster Hall), vol. 431 cc32–53 WH, Porton Down, 22 February 2005, Mr Tam Dalyell (Linlithgow, Lab): cc43WH–44WH; Galbraith 2000, pp. 101–19.

153. Hansard (Westminster Hall), vol. 431 cc32–53 WH, Porton Down, 22 February 2005, Mr Robert Key (Salisbury, Con): cc44WH–47WH; 'MP Defends Porton Down', BBC News, 8 November 2000.

154. Hansard (Westminster Hall), vol. 431 cc32–53 WH, Porton Down, 22 February 2005, Mr Robert Key (Salisbury, Con): cc44WH–47WH (here c46WH).

155. Hansard (Westminster Hall), vol. 431 cc32–53 WH, Porton Down, 22 February 2005, Mr Gerald Howarth (Aldershot, Con): cc48WH–50WH (here c50WH).

156. Hansard (Westminster Hall), vol. 431 cc32–53 WH, Porton Down, 22 February 2005, Mr Ivor Caplin (Parliamentary Under-Secretary of State for Defence): cc50WH–53WH.

157. Historical Survey (2006), p. viii.
158. Historical Survey 2006, pp. 111–27, pp. 140f.
159. Mark Townsend, 'Porton Down "Guinea Pigs" set for £6m', *The Guardian*, 17 December 2006.
160. UoK, Porton Archive, A109.1, UK Ombudsman, Schmidt to Ann Abraham, 25 September 2007; Ann Abraham to Schmidt, 29 September 2007.
161. Care 2008, pp. 23f.
162. BBC News, 'Porton Down Veterans Offered £3m', 17 January 2008; Laura Clout, 'Porton Down Veterans "To Get Compensation"', *The Telegraph*, 17 January 2008; Michael Evans, 'Porton Down Guinea Pigs Get Apology', The Times Online, 18 January 2008; Jon Robinson, 'Ex-Soldier Still Bitter over Gas Test "Con Trick"', *Nottingham Evening Post*, 18 January 2008; also 'The Army Rumour Service' (Blog), 17 January 2008.
163. Hansard Written Ministerial Statements, c26WS, Porton Down Veterans, 31 January 2008.
164. Robins 2008.
165. In 2007/2008, the MoD settled a total of 360 Porton claims at a total cost of 4.7 million pounds sterling, including legal costs. In 2008/2009, the MoD settled a first tranche of 130 claims at a total cost of 3.87 million pounds sterling, including legal costs. In 2009/2010, the MoD settled a second tranche of 141 claims at a total cost of 1.39 million pounds sterling, including legal costs. In 2010/2011, the MoD settled a third tranche of eighteen claims at a total cost of 165,661 pounds sterling, including legal costs. Of seventeen new Porton claims received in 2010/2011, the MoD settled all it had received; MoD, Claims, Annual Reports, 2008–2011.
166. Carter 1995, p. 165.
167. Carter 1995, p. 165.
168. TNA, WO188/802, pp. 137–9.
169. Carter 1995, p. 166.
170. MoD to Francis Brown, 24 September 2009; <https://www.whatdotheyknow.com/request/contact_of_porton_down_veterans>.
171. MoD to Alvin Pritchard, 25 May 2012; <https://www.whatdotheyknow.com/request/porton_down_monitoring_1st_gulf#comment-28014>.
172. *MoD (Respondent) v AB and others (Appellants)* [2012] UKSC 9; on appeal from [2010] EWCA Civ 1317; Justices: Lord Phillips (President); Lord Walker; Lady Hale; Lord Brown; Lord Mance; Lord Kerr; Lord Wilson.
173. Pechura, Rall 1993, p. x.

EPILOGUE

1. Broszat 1990, pp. 77–87; Broszat, Friedländer 1990, pp. 102–34; Friedländer 1997; Friedländer 2007.
2. Stone 2013, pp. 37–48.
3. Quoted from Friedländer 1990, p. 99; see also Stone 2013, p. 37; Berger, Niven 2014.

4. American Academy of Arts and Sciences 1969.
5. Freund 1969, p. x.
6. Freund 1969, p. xii
7. Katz 1996, p. 1666.
8. Jonas 1969, p. 224; see also LaFleur 2007.
9. Jonas 1969, p. 220.
10. Böhme 2007.
11. Beauchamp, Childress 1979.
12. See, for example, Popper 1994.
13. Jonas 1969, p. 222.
14. NDT Documents, frames 2/10920ff.; see also Shuster 1998, p. 974.
15. Jonas 1969, p. 226.
16. Jonas 1969, p. 235; LaFleur 2007, p. 241.
17. Jonas 1969, p. 235.
18. Jonas 1969, p. 231.
19. Balmer 2012, p. 116; Balmer 2006a, p. 692.
20. Jonas 1969, pp. 236, 232.
21. Jonas 1969, p. 245.
22. Levi 2001a.
23. Huyssen 1995, pp. 249–60.
24. Levi 1989, p. 18.
25. Angier 2003, pp. 324–7.
26. Levi 2001a, pp. 111f; see also Levi 2001b.
27. Thomson 2012, p. 14.
28. Thomson 2012, p. 14.
29. Ignatieff 2001, pp. 3ff.
30. Gutmann 2001.
31. Presidential Commission for the Study of Bioethical Issues 2011.
32. Reverby 2011; Schmidt 2012b; Findings from a CDC Report 2010.
33. Presidential Commission for the Study of Bioethical Issues 2011.
34. Presidential Commission for the Study of Bioethical Issues, Sixth Meeting, 29–30 August 2011; <http://bioethics.gov/node/280>.
35. Carrick 2008; Carrick et al. 2009; Gross 2013.
36. Stefan Zweig, 'Ypern', *Berliner Tageblatt*, 16 September 1928; also Zweig 2004, pp. 267–76.
37. Schwarz 2008.

Bibliography

ARCHIVE MATERIAL

The author of the present study is greatly indebted to the Bundesarchiv Berlin, Koblenz and Freiburg, the Chemical Heritage Foundation, King's College London, the Imperial War Museum, the National Archives and Records Administration, Washington DC, the Ombudsman for National Defence and Canadian Forces, the University of Sussex (Science Policy Research Unit), the National Archive, the Wellcome Trust Library, the World Medical Association, and numerous individuals for granting access to, and providing copies of, relevant source material. The files and amalgamated collections listed under University of Kent (UoK), Porton Archive were of particular use for the present study.

Allied Intelligence Reports
British Intelligence Objectives Sub-Committee (BIOS) Reports
BIOS, Final Report, No. 41, Item No. 8, 'Interrogation of German CW Personnel at Heidelberg and Frankfurt' (no date)

BIOS, Final Report, No. 44, Item No. 8, 'Examination of Various German Scientists', 29 August–1 September 1945

BIOS, Final Report, No. 138, Item No. 8, 'Interrogation of German CW Medical Personnel', August/September 1945

BIOS, Final Report No. 542, Item No. 8, 'Interrogation of Certain German Personalities Connected with Chemical Warfare', 1946

BIOS Final Report 714, Gerhard Schrader, 'The Development of New Insecticides'; presented by S.A. Mumford and E.A. Perren, MoS, 1945

BIOS, Final Report, No. 782 (Interrogation Report No. 291), Item No. 8, 'Interrogation of Professor Ferdinand Flury and Dr Wolfgang Wirth on the Toxicology of Chemical Warfare Agents' (no date)

Combined Intelligence Objectives Sub-Committee (CIOS) Reports
CIOS, Report, Item No. 80, 'A New Group of War Gases', 23 April 1945

CIOS, Report No. 30, 'Chemical Warfare—IG Farbenindustrie AG, Frankfurt/Main', c. April 1945

CIOS, Item No. 8, 'Chemical Warfare Installations in the Munsterlager Area', 23 April–3 June [1945]

CIOS, 'Investigation of Chemical Warfare Installations in the Munsterlager Area, including Raubkammer', APO 413

Field Information Agency, Technical (FIAT) Reports

FIAT, Control Commission for Germany (BE), 'Report on Chemical Warfare, based on Interrogation and Written Reports of Jürgen E. von Klenck, Speer, and Dr E. Mohrhardt', 6 December 1945

Bundesarchiv-Berlin (BAB), Bundesarchiv-Koblenz (BAK), and Bundesarchiv-Militärarchiv (BA-MA)

BAB, R3/1734, fol. 1, Speer to Keitel, 10 October 1944

BAK, All. Proz. 2/FC 6069 P, Vernehmung Karl Brandt, 5 November 1946 and 1 March 1947

BA-MA, RHD 43/56, Kampfstoffverletzungen. Bildsammlung zur Klinik und Pathologie der Verletzungen durch chemische Kampfstoffe und durch andere militärisch wichtige Stoffe

Chemical Heritage Foundation (CHF), Archive Collection

Chalmer G. Kirkbride, Transcript of an Interview conducted by James J. Bohning in Washington, DC, 15 July 1993

GB98.09, Williams–Miles Reprint Collection, William Williams, Notebook: US Gas School, 1918

The Edgewood Arsenal, Special Edition of *Chemical Warfare*, vol. 1, no. 5 (March 1919)

Hansard

HC Debate, vol. 122 c60W, Experimental Ground, Porton, 1 December 1919

HC Debate, vol. 130 c1063, Chemical Experimental Ground, 15 June 1920

HC Debate, vol. 152 c984W, Asphyxiating Gas (Washington Treaty), 27 March 1922

HC Debate, vol. 181 c1108, Chemical Warfare Research Department, 10 March 1925

HC Debate, vol. 181 cc1144–5W, Experimental Station, Porton, 10 March 1925

HC Debate, vol. 199 cc897–8W, Chemical Warfare (Research and Experiments), 9 November 1926

HC Debate, vol. 210 c1154W, Chemical Warfare (Experiments), 17 November 1927

HC Debate, vol. 216 cc377–8W, Poison Gas (Experiments, Living Animals), 19 April 1928

HC Debate, vol. 237 cc633W, 634–5W, Chemical Warfare (Experiments on Animals), 27 March 1930

HC Debate, vol. 241 cc1483–4W, Poison Gas (Experiments on Animals), 17 July 1930

HC Debate, vol. 244 cc486–7W, Animals (Experiments), 3 November 1930

HC Debate, vol. 244 cc652–3, Animals (Experiments), 4 November 1930

HC Debate, vol. 244 c1480W, Animals (Experiments), 11 November 1930

HC Debate, vol. 245 cc1079–80, Chemical Warfare (Experiments), 25 November 1930

HC Debate, vol. 245 cc2414–15W, Experiments on Animals, Porton, 4 December 1930

HC Debate, vol. 249 cc1007–74, Mr Short's Statement, 10 March 1931

HC Debate, vol. 251 c1466W, Chemical Warfare (Experiments on Animals), 28 April 1931

HC Debate, vol. 252 cc213–14W, Research Experiments (Living Animals), 5 May 1931

HC Debate, vol. 284 cc1469–70, Chemical Warfare (Defensive Measures), 21 December 1933

HC Debate, vol. 265 c817W, Poison Gas Experiments, 2 May 1932

HC Debate, vol. 272 cc811–12, Chemical Warfare, 30 November 1932

HC Debate, vol. 285 c965, Chemical Defence Experiments, 6 February 1934

HC Debate, vol. 303 cc171–3, Chemical Defence Experiments, 18 June 1935

HC Debate, vol. 342 cc50–1W, Chemical Warfare (Experiments on Animals), 28 November 1938

HC Debate, vol. 351 cc1837–8W, Experiments on Living Animals (Poison Gas), 3 October 1939

HC Debate, vol. 795 cc17–18W, Disarmament, 2 February 1970

HC Debate, vol. 806 cc243–4W, CS, 12 November 1970

HC Debate, vol. 282 cc785–93, Mr Michael Paynter, 16 October 1996

HC Debate, vol. 342 cc818–22, Nancekuke Base, 18 January 2000

HC Debate, vol. 429 c136, Mr Douglas Shave, 10 January 2005

HL Debate, vol. 98 cc749–73, Precautions against Air Raids, 23 July 1935

Written Ministerial Statements, c167WS, Ronald Maddison, 21 December 2004

Written Ministerial Statements, c26WS, Porton Down Veterans, 31 January 2008

(Westminster Hall), vol. 431 cc32–53WH, Porton Down, 22 February 2005

Imperial War Museum, Duxford

Photographic Collection, Porton Down, *c.* 1916–70s

Imperial War Museum, London

Documents

International Military Tribunal (IMT), Speer Testimony, 21 June 1946

Nuremberg Documents, NI-6788, Affidavit Otto Ambros, 1 May 1947

Nuremberg Documents, NI-9772, Affidavit Albert Palm, 24 July 1947

Film and Video Archive

DED 27, 'Filmed Record of Trials Carried out with Troops to Compare the Effectiveness of CS and CN as Riot Control Agents' (no date)

DED 31, 'An Improved Tear Gas for Riot Control' (no date)

DED 46A, 'The Chemical Defence Experimental Establishment Porton Down, Volunteers for Porton' (1966)

DED 77, DED 82, 'Operation Moneybags' (1964)

DED 87, 'Operation Ozone. A Footnote to the Cauldron Film' (1954)

HOY 81, 'Your Book' (1938)

'Operation Cauldron' (1952)

'The Lyme Bay Trials' (1966)

Private Papers
J.D. Keddie (998)
N. Noble (854)

In Flanders Fields Museum, Ypres, Documentation Centre
Private Papers
Toudy Papers

King's College London, Liddell Hart Centre for Military Archives
'Gassed' Collection (Rob Evans)
A, Former Public Record Office (PRO) papers relating to the recruitment of volunteers; award of war pensions for poison gas disabilities after the First World War
B, Former PRO papers relating to the Advisory Council on Scientific Research and Technical Development (ACSRTD), and the Chemical Defence Advisory Board of the ACSRTD, 1947 to 1966
C, Former PRO papers relating to the Biology Committee and the Applied Biology Committee of the Chemical Defence Advisory Board of the ACSRTD, 1947 to 1968
D, Former PRO papers relating to the Chemistry Committee of the Chemical Defence Advisory Board of the ACSRTD, 1947 to 1961, and related material
E and F, Former PRO papers relating to the testing of LSD and other incapacitants on human subjects at Porton Down, 1960s
G, Former PRO papers relating to the exchange of information on CBW between Britain and the United States between 1948 and 1964
H, Former PRO papers relating to the search at Porton Down for new chemical agents, *c.*1920 to *c.*1960
I, Porton Down Annual Reports
J, Articles and notes on the use of poison gas in the First World War
K, Former PRO papers relating to the testing of V–agents on human subjects at Porton Down, 1961 to 1964
L, Chemical Weapons Convention Bulletin and other publications
M, Former PRO papers relating to annual reports of chemical warfare research at Porton Down, 1921 to 1965
N, Former PRO papers relating to the testing of various chemicals on humans at Porton Down between the First and Second World War
O, Former PRO paper about the development, testing, and use of CS tear gas from the 1930s to the present
P, Former PRO papers relating to the testing of chemical weapons on humans by Porton scientists in India between 1920 and 1945
Q, Collection of papers relating to the testing of chemical weapons on service personnel in Australia during the Second World War by Australian and British scientists
R, Collection of papers relating to chemical warfare in the Second World War

S, Collection of correspondence, parliamentary answers, press articles, etc.

T, Former PRO papers relating to the testing of nerve gas on human subjects at Porton Down, 1945 to 1956

U, Collection of parliamentary answers, press articles, official documents, Porton technical papers

V, Collection of official documents, press cuttings

W, Collection of papers relating to the death of Ronald Maddison, 1953 and the re-opened inquest, 2004

X, Former PRO papers relating to large-scale BW trials by Porton Down in public places, 1953 to 1977

King's College London Archive
Maurice Wilkins papers

National Archives and Records Administration (NARA), Washington, DC
RG175, Chemical Warfare Service (1917–63)

RG319, Box 219, Assistant Chief of Staff (G-2), Intelligence ('P') Files, 1946–51, Army Medical Research and Development Board, Office of the Surgeon General, Investigation on Sedatives, Progress Reports 1 October–31 December 1947; 1 January–31 March 1948; 1 July–30 September 1948

RG319, Entry 47-A, Box 11, File 381–400.112 Research, John Edgar Hoover to Assistant Chief of Staff, G-2, Department of the Army, 15 November 1951

RG319, Entry 47-A, Box 13, File 383.4–600.IT, John Edgar Hoover (FBI) to Assistant Chief of Staff-G-2, Department of the Army, 23 September 1952

RG319, Entry 47-A, Box 13, File 400.112, CIA, Artichoke Project, 28 August 1951

RG319, Entry 47-A, Box 13, File 400.112, Beecher to Surgeon General, Colonel John R. Wood, 21 October 1951

RG319, Entry 47-A, Box 13, File 400.112, CIA, Memorandum, Special Interrogation Program, 19 March 1951

RG319, Entry 47-A, Box 13, File 400.112, Deputy Director for Central Intelligence to Secretary of Defence, Evaluation of Certain Scientific Techniques of Possible Concern to National Security, 28 January 1952

RG319, Entry 47-A, Box 13, File 400.112, Handwritten note by G-2 official, 30 January 1952

RG319, Entry 47-A, Box 13, File 400.112, Handwritten note about phone conversation with Major Lund with regard to Dr Beecher, 5 January 1952

RG319, Entry 47-A, Box 13, File 400.112, Note by the Secretaries to the Joint Intelligence Committee on Special Interrogation Methods, JIC. 604, 14 February 1952

RG319, Entry 47-A, Box 13, File 400.112, Walter Smith, Director CIA, to Chairman, Research and Development Board, Request for Technical Assistance, 5 March 1952; H. Marshall Chadwell, Assistant Director, Scientific Intelligence, to Assistant Chief of Staff, G-2, Department of the Army, 6 March 1952

RG319, Entry 47-A, Box 13, File 470.6 (1949), Director CDRD (UK) to Chief Chemical Officer, Department of the Army, 4 January 1952

RG319, Entry IRR, Box 200, Gerhard Schrader, The Development of New Insecticides, part 2: Organophosphorus Compounds, 30 October 1945, p. 4

RG338, Entry 6C, Box 96, US Chemical Warfare Project, Bericht über Produktion und Einsatz von K-Stoffen, Raumexplosionen und Raumbränden, bearbeitet von Hermann Ochsner, P-004a

RG544, US Army Materiel Command (1941–73)

Ombudsman for National Defence and Canadian Forces (NDCF)

Briefing Note, Complaints Concerning Chemical Agent Tests at Suffield during World War II, 18 December 2003

Correspondence between Suzanne Belson and Clement Laforce, 23/24 February 2004

Field Experiment No. 52, 18 August 1942

Field Experiment 124, Trial 1, Preliminary Trial with 'H' Thermal Generator, 2 December 1943

Field Experiment 215 Trial VI, The Physiological Effect of Mustard Vapour at Low Temperature, 3 April 1945

Field Experiment 234, Ground Contamination with [Redacted] Mortar Bombs Charged Mustard Gas, 18 October 1944

Field Experiment No. 275, part 2, Ground Contamination Shoot with [Redacted] 4.2. Inch CM Shell Charged Mustard Gas, 18 July 1945

Final Report: Complaints Concerning Chemical Agent Testing during World War II, February 2004

Information for Prospective Subjects for Physiological Tests (ES Suffield), 5 August 1942, p. 908

Interim Report on Field Experiment No. 36, The Casualty Producing Power of High Spray from Aircraft, 9 September 1942

Letter (Anonymized), 21 January 2004, p. 703

Physiology Report of Field Experiment 142, Trial I, 12 June 1943

Physiology Report on Field Experiment 141, Trial I, held 16 July 1943, Vapour Danger from Grass Mustard Gas Contamination, 28 July 1943

Physiology Section Report, Field Experiment No. 158, 13 November 1943

Regulations Governing the Use of Volunteers for Physiological Tests, 5 August 1942, pp. 909–11

Redacted Extract of a Soldier Remembering his Time at Suffield, pp. 1234–42

Security. Document in Personnel Jacket of R76998, LAC Cockroft, Stanley Philips, National Archives, 00–42687, R100, Microfilm Ref. WSB 804–8, p. 923

Security of Military Information Following Discharge, pp. 1004f.

Suffield Gas Veterans Group, World War II, Anonymized, December 1942, p. 694

Suffield Gas Veterans Group, World War II, p. 735, p. 746

Suffield Gas Veterans Group, World War II, Anonymized, no date, p. 750

Suffield Gas Veterans Group, World War II, RCAF, unanimous, 1941–43, p. 698

Suffield Report on Expt No. 36, Notes for CEO, 1942

Suffield Report No. 81, 'The Effect of the Lesions Produced by Mustard Spray on the Performance of Troops Engaged in a Field Exercise', 17 August 1943

The National Archive (TNA), London

AIR2/5117; AIR20/8731; AIR20/10719; AIR23/8593; AVIA22/1218; CAB4/24; CAB131/28; CAB164/789; CAB537/2711; CAB537/5346; DEFE2/1251; DEFE10/283; DEFE10/382; DEFE13/287; DEFE13/705; DEFE13/846; DEFE13/1055; DEFE55/166; DEFE68/202; FD1/279; FD1/280; FD9/592; FD9/855; FD9/3940; FD11/25; FD23/381; FD23/383; FD23/1431; FO1031/105; FO1031/239; PREM3/65; PREM3/89; PRO30/69/1273; T164/71/28; T164/72/10; WO32/19633; WO32/20162; WO32/20163; WO32/20403; WO32/20606; WO32/20843; WO32/21200; WO32/21372; WO106/4594A; WO142/241; WO142/264; WO162/507; WO188/373; WO188/429; WO188/624; WO188/666; WO188/719; WO188/785; WO188/802; WO188/2201; WO188/2307; WO188/2309; WO188/2443; WO189/122; WO189/167; WO189/357; WO189/377; WO189/1078; WO189/1079; WO189/1105; WO189/1400; WO189/1403; WO189/3238; WO189/3242; WO189/3269; WO189/3276; WO189/3293; WO189/3295; WO189/3297; WO189/3330; WO189/3364; WO189/4426; WO193/723; WO195/2778; WO195/9103; WO195/9678; WO195/10813; WO195/12139; WO195/12220; WO195/12304; WO195/14405; WO195/14846; WO195/14995; WO195/15026; WO195/15070; WO195/15381; WO195/15638; WO195/15751; WO195/16131; WO195/16134; WO195/16136; WO195/16161; WO195/16213; WO195/16214; WO195/16227; WO195/16273; WO195/16371; WO195/16427; WO195/16428; WO195/16429; WO195/16462; WO195/16529; WO195/16691; WO195/16804; WO195/16840; WO286/11; WO286/78

University of Kent (UoK), Porton Archive

A100, Porton Down Veterans, Maddison Case & Compensation
A104, Porton Down Veterans (Material of Individual Veterans)
A105, onwards, Maddison Case
A200, Great Britain Pre-Cold War
A300, United States Pre-Cold War
A400, Canada Pre-Cold War
A500, Other Countries Pre-Cold War
A501, Nazi Germany Pre-Cold War
A550, Australia Pre-Cold War
A570, Japan Pre-Cold War
B100, Tripartite Conference General 1947–70
B200, Great Britain, Cold War, Experimentation, Porton Down
B251, Great Britain, Cold War, Porton Down
B300, USA, Cold War, Experimentation
B400, Canada, Cold War, Experimentation
B500, Other Countries, Cold War, Experimentation
C100, Warsaw Pact Countries

C200, Arms Control
C300, Terrorism and Biochemical Warfare
D100, Medical Ethics & Informed Consent
  Maddison Inquest (MI) Material
MI, Transcript, Day 1 (5 May 2004)–Day 64 (15 November 2004)
MI, Exhibit, Folder 1A–Folder 2I
Folder 1A, Witness Statements
Folder 2A, Coroner's File re Maddison, 16 May 1953 and MoS, Report of a Court
  of Inquiry into Death of Maddison, May 1953
Folder 2A/I, Exhibits
Folder 2B, Exhibits
Folder 2C, Exhibits
Folder 2D, Exhibits (Two different versions of Folder 2D have been used through-
  out. Unless stated otherwise, 'Folder 2D' refers to 'Version 1'.)
Folder 2E, Exhibits
Folder 2F, Exhibits
Folder 2G, Exhibits
Folder 2H, Exhibits
Folder 2I, Exhibits
Hot Docs Alan Folder
Report by Professor Alexander R.W. Forrest
Report by Dr Alexander T. Proudfoot
Report by Dr Ulf I.D. Schmidt
Taped interview with Lord Butler of Brockwell, 15 February 2008
Taped interview with Alan Care, 3 May 2005
Taped interview with Kenneth Earl, 17 June 2005
Taped interview with Dr David Langley, 8 January 2008
Taped presentation by Dr David Langley, 5 November 2008
Taped interview with Dr Robert Maynard, 2 October 2009
  Nuremberg Doctors' Trial (NDT) Documents
frame 2/2410; frame 2/2690; frames 2/10920ff.; frame 3/1089; frames 3/1094–7;
  frame 3/1836; frame 3/2088; frames 3/2110–30; frames 3/2460–1; frames 3/2914f.;
  frame 3/2991; frame 3/3114; frame 4/2058; frame 4/2060

University of Liverpool (UoL), Special Collection and Archives

D106/2/13, Correspondence of Professor Wilson, whilst at University College
  Hospital Medical School, London, with the MoS (Porton Experimental Station)
  regarding his PF-3 research (1946–51)
D106/2/29, Distaval Clinical Trials (correspondence, completed questionnaires, and
  summaries), and correspondence regarding LSD and Ritalin (1958–62)
D106/2/29/7, four journal articles on the nature and control of clinical trials, spe-
  cifically those involving Thalidomide, and 'A Proposal for the Improvement of
  Clinical Trial Procedure' (1959–62)

D106/4/1/2, Poisoning by Drugs, Local Anaesthetics, Antagonists of ACh, Diuretics, Histamine and Anti Histamines, Action of Drugs on CNS [Central Nervous System], and Therapy of Allergic Disease, 1950–1956 and n.d. (1950–56)

D106/4/1/5, Cardiovascular System, Action of Drugs on CVS, Drugs Acting on the Heart, Respiratory Failure, Pharmacology of Respiratory System, Applied Pharmacology, 1960–71 and n.d. (1960–71)

University of Sussex (Science Policy Research Unit)

A, CBW Technology and Applicable Science (A1, Toxic Agents; A2, Infective Agents; A3, Applicable Technique; A4, Emergent CBW Technology; A5 CBW Equipment)

B, Military Aspects of CBW (B1, General; B2, Historical; B3, Utility of CW Weapons; B4, CBW Intelligence; B5, Consequences of CBW; B6 CBW Threat Reduction)

C, Countries and Alliances (C1, Overview; C2, Intergovernmental Organizations; C3, Countries)

D, Conflicts (D1, Pre World War I; D2, World War I; D3, Inter World War Period; D4, Inter World War Period; D5, 1945–60; D6, Since 1960; D7, Since 1989)

E, CBW Arms Control and Disarmament (E1, Existing Anti-CBW Regime; E2, Future Anti-CBW Regime)

F, Special Topics (F1, New History; F2, Psychological, Societal and Cultural Factors in CBW; F3, Human Exposures to CBW Agents; F9, The Chemical Industry)

G, Related Topics (GA, Scientific Topics; GB, Military Topics; GC, Country Topics; GD, Conflict Topics; GE, Arms Control Topics; GF, Special Topics; GH, Documentary Sources; GI, Author Files)

H, Documentary Sources (H6.4, Morton Papers)

I, Author Files

Wellcome Trust Library (WL), Archives and Manuscripts

GC/42/11/1, Memorandum on Gas Poisoning in Warfare with Notes on its Pathology and Treatment, 1 April 1918

M:QV662 1916G78m, Memorandum on Gas Poisoning in Warfare with Notes on its Pathology and Treatment, 20 July 1916

PP/CLE/A.9, Jodrell Chair

PP/CLE/A.11, Lovatt Evans papers

QV662 1941 G78e, Enemy Gas Attacks: Notes Prepared for the Minister of Health and the Secretary of State for Scotland on the Diagnosis and Treatment of Casualties, c. 1941

RAMC/739/6, Diary: At Bailleul with No. 8 Casualty Clearing Station, 17 June 1916

SA/SRL/M.1/2/1, CDRD, Reports 1939–50

SA/SRL/M.1/2/2, CDRD, Reports and Papers, ca 1940s

SA/SRL/M.1/4, Box 31, G.R. Cameron, F. Burgess, V.S. Trenwith, 'The Possibility of Toxic Effects from BAL in Conditions of Impaired Renal or Hepatic Function', Porton Report No. 2673, 10 March 1945

SA/SRL/M.1/4, Box 31, Lt Col H. Cullumbine, RAMC, 'The Burning Power of White Phosphorus', Addendum I to Porton Report No. 2604, 1 October 1944

World Medical Association (WMA), Archive
Tenth Meeting on International Medical Law, Working Group of IRCC, ICMMP, WMA, WHO, Monaco, 11–12 May 1964
Eighteenth World Medical Assembly, Helsinki, Finland, 13–20 June 1964, Programme
Biographies and Photos of Programme Participants, WMA 1963 Meeting
Department of National Health and Welfare, Ottawa, Canada, National Health Grants, 1948–1961 (January 1962)
First Decade Report of the WMA, 1947–1957, unpublished manuscript, c. 1957
Minutes of Ninth Annual Meeting, 16 April 1956
Minutes of Fifty-first Council Session, Helsinki, Finland, 13–14 June 1964
Minutes, Medical Ethics Committee, Forty-ninth Council Session, 21 October 1963
Pol[icies], Declaration of Helsinki, Adopted Versions, 1953 onwards
Report of the International Liaison and Medical Ethics Committees. Regulations in Time of Armed Conflict, 24 May 1957
Report of the International Liaison Committee, Symposium on International Humanitarian Law in the World Today, 28 January 1964
Summary of Activities of the WMA, Inc., 1958–71

SECONDARY MATERIAL

Academy of Medical Sciences to the Chief Scientific Adviser, Ministry of Defence, 'Report on the Zinc Cadmium Sulphide Dispersion Trials Undertaken in the United Kingdom between 1953 and 1964' (no place, 1999); <http://www.acmedsci.ac.uk/viewFile/publicationDownloads/ZincCadm.pdf>.
Ackerman, S., D. Rushe, and J. Borger, 'Senate Report on CIA Torture Claims Spy Agency Lied about "Ineffective" Program', *The Guardian*, 9 December 2014.
Adams, M.B., 'Last Judgement: The Visionary Biology of J.B.S. Haldane', *Journal of the History of Biology*, 33 (2000), pp. 457–91.
Adrian, E.D., W. Feldberg, and B.A. Kilby, 'Inhibiting Action of Fluorophosphonates on Cholinesterase', *Nature* (1946), p. 625 (Letters to Editor).
Adrian, E.D., W. Feldberg, and B.A. Kilby, 'The Cholinesterase Inhibiting Action of Fluorophosphonates', *British Journal of Pharmacology*, 2 (1947), pp. 56–8.
Aldridge, W.N., and D.R. Davies, 'Determination of Cholinesterase Activity in Human Blood', *BMJ* (1952), pp. 945–7.
Allender, S. et al., 'Symptoms, Ill-Health and Quality of Life in a Support Group of Porton Veterans', *Occupational Medicine*, 56 (2006), 5, pp. 329–37.
American Academy of Arts and Sciences, 'Ethical Aspects of Experimentation with Human Subjects', *Dædalus* (1969), 2, pp. 219–597.

Angier, C., *The Double Bond. Primo Levi. A Biography* (London, Penguin Books, 2003).

Annas, G.J., and M.A. Grodin, eds., *The Nazi Doctors and the Nuremberg Code. Human Rights in Human Experimentation* (New York, Oxford, Oxford University Press, 1992).

Arnold, L., *Britain, Australia and the Bomb: The Nuclear Tests and Their Aftermath*, second edn (Basingstoke, Palgrave Macmillan, 2006).

Arnott, S., T.W.B. Kibble, and T. Shallice, 'Maurice Hugh Frederick Wilkins', *Biographical Memoirs of Fellows of the Royal Society*, 52 (2006), pp. 455–78.

Arvidson, M.D., 'A Mustard Agent—The Air Raid on Bari', *Army Chemical Review* (1994), pp. 36–40.

Ashplant, T.G., G. Dawson, and M. Roper, *Commemorating War: The Politics of Memory* (New Brunswick, NJ, Transaction, 2004).

Avery, D., *The Science of War: Canadian Scientists and Allied Military Technology during the Second World War* (Toronto, University of Toronto Press, 1998).

Avery, D., 'The Canadian Biological Weapons Program and the Tripartite Alliance', in *Deadly Cultures: Biological Weapons since 1945*, edited by M. Wheelis, R. Lajos, and M. Dando (Cambridge, MA, London, Harvard University Press, 2006), pp. 84–107.

Avery, D., *Pathogens for War: Biological Weapons, Canadian Life Scientists, and North American Biodefence* (Toronto, University of Toronto Press, 2013).

Balfour, S., *Deadly Embrace: Morocco and the Road to the Spanish Civil War* (Oxford, Oxford University Press, 2002).

Ballantyne, B., and Beswick, F.W., 'On the Possible Relationship between Diarrhoea and o-Chlorobenzylidene Malononitrile (CS)', *Medicine, Science and the Law*, 1 (1972), 2, pp. 121–8.

Balmer, B., *Britain and Biological Warfare. Expert Advice and Scientific Policy, 1930–65* (Basingstoke, Palgrave Macmillan, 2001).

Balmer, B., 'Killing "Without the Distressing Preliminaries": Scientists' Defence of the British Biological Warfare Programme', *Minerva*, 40 (2002), 1, pp. 57–75.

Balmer, B., 'How does an Accident Become an Experiment? Secret Science and the Exposure of the Public to Biological Warfare Agents', *Science as Culture*, 13 (2004), 2, pp. 197–228.

Balmer, B., 'A Secret Formula, A Rogue Patent and Public Knowledge about Nerve Gas: Secrecy as a Spatial-Epistemic Tool', *Social Studies of Science*, 35 (2006a), 5, pp. 691–722.

Balmer, B., 'The UK Biological Weapons Program', in *Deadly Cultures: Biological Weapons since 1945*, edited by M. Wheelis, R. Lajos, and M. Dando (Cambridge, MA, London, Harvard University Press, 2006b), pp. 47–84.

Balmer, B., *Secrecy and Science: A Historical Sociology of Biological and Chemical Warfare* (Farnham, Ashgate, 2012).

Barneby, W., *The Plague Makers: The Secret World of Biological Warfare* (New York, Continuum, 2000).

Barnes, J.M., 'Toxic Hazards of Certain Pesticides to Man', *Bulletin of the World Health Organization* (1953), 8, pp. 419–90.

Barnes, J.M., and D.R. Davies, 'Blood Cholinesterase Levels in Workers Exposed to Organo-Phosphorus Insecticides', *BMJ* (1951), pp. 816–19.

Barnett, A., 'Millions Were in Germ War Tests: Much of Britain was Exposed to Bacteria Sprayed in Secret Trials', *The Observer*, 21 April 2002.

Barnett, A., 'Final Agony of RAF Volunteer Killed by Sarin—in Britain', *The Observer*, 28 September 2003.

Barnett, A., 'Revealed: The Gas Chamber Horror of North Korea's Gulag', *The Observer*, 1 February 2004.

Barrett, H.M., 'Research in Canada for National Defence', *The Engineering Journal*, 31 (1948), pp. 271–4.

Beauchamp, T.L., and J.F. Childress, *Principles of Biomedical Ethics* (New York, Oxford, Oxford University Press, 1979).

Beaumont, P., and I. Sample, 'Damascus Rocket Attack Video is Strongest Evidence Yet of Chemical Weapons Use', *The Guardian*, 22 August 2013.

Beecher, H.K., 'The Powerful Placebo', *JAMA*, 159 (1955), 17, pp. 1602–6.

Beecher, H.K., 'Experimentation in Man', *JAMA*, 169 (1959), pp. 461–78.

Beecher, H.K., 'Human Experimentation—A World Problem from the Standpoint of a Medical Investigator', *World Medical Journal*, 8 (1960), pp. 79–80.

Beecher, H.K., 'Ethics in Clinical Research', *New England Journal of Medicine*, 274 (1966a), pp. 1354–60.

Beecher, H.K., 'One Mystery Solved', *Science*, 151 (1966b), pp. 840–1.

Beecher, H.K., 'Human Studies', *Science*, 164 (1969), pp. 1256–8.

Beecher, H.K., *Research and the Individual: Human Studies* (Boston, MA, 1970).

Benison, S., *Tom Rivers: Reflections on a Life in Medicine and Science. An Oral History Memoir by Saul Benison* (Cambridge, MA, MIT Press, 1967).

Benjamin, W., 'Die Waffen von Morgen: Schlachten mit Chlorazetophenol, Diphenylaminchlorasin und Dichloräthylsulfid', in *Gesammelte Schriften*, edited by T. Rexroth, 7 vols. (Frankfurt am Main, Suhrkamp, 1972–1989), vol. 4, part 1, pp. 473–6.

Benjamin, W., *Selected Writings*, edited by M. Bullock, M.W. Jennings, and H. Eiland, translated by Rodney Livingstone et al., 4 vols. (Cambridge, MA, Belknap Press of Harvard University Press, 1996–2003).

Bergen, L. van, 'The Value of War for Medicine: Questions and Considerations Concerning and Often Endorsed Proposition', *Medicine, Conflict and Survival*, 23 (2007), 3, pp. 189–97.

Bergen, L. van, 'Medicine and War: The Value of Historical Knowledge', *Medicine, Conflict and Survival*, 24 (2008), 3, pp. 155–8.

Berger, S., and B. Niven, eds. *Writing the History of Memory* (London, Bloomsbury, 2014).

Bernard-Donals, M., 'Ethos, Witness, and Holocaust "Testimony": The Rhetoric of Fragments', *JAC*, 20 (2000), 3, pp. 565–82.

Bessel, R., 'Violence and Victimhood: Looking Back at the World Wars in Europe', in *Experience and Memory: The Second World War in Europe*, edited by J. Echternkamp and S. Martens (New York, Oxford, Berghahn, 2010), pp. 229–44.

Bevington, J.C., and B.G. Gowenlock, 'Sir Harry Work Melville, K.C.B., 27 April 1908–14 June 2000', *Biographical Memoirs of Fellows of the Royal Society*, 48 (2002), pp. 289–308.

Black, D., and J. Gray, 'Sir Harold Percival Himsworth, K.C.B., 19 May 1905–1 November 1993', *Biographical Memoirs of Fellows of the Royal Society*, 41 (1995), pp. 200–18.

Boggan, S., 'Will the Men who Fooled us into Testing Nerve Gas ever be Brought to Justice?', *Evening Standard*, 9 July 2003, p. 17.

Böhme, G., 'Rationalizing Unethical Medical Research: Taking Seriously the Case of Viktor von Weizsäcker', in: *Dark Medicine. Rationalising Unethical Medical Research*, edited by W.R. LaFleur, G. Böhme, and S. Shimazono (Bloomington, IN, Indiana University Press, 2007), pp. 15–29.

Bolton, J.P.G., and C.R.M. Foster, 'Battlefield Use of Depleted Uranium and the Health of Veterans', *Journal of the RAMC*, 148 (2002), pp. 221–30.

Bolton, J.P.G., P.H. Gilbert, and C. Tamayo, 'Heat Illness on Operation Telic in Summer 2003: The Experience of Heat Illness Treatment Unit in Northern Kuwait', *Journal of the RAMC*, 152 (2006), pp. 148–55.

Bolton, T., 'Films, Ethics and Politics at Porton Down, 1939 to 1968: A Study of Films from the Chemical Defence Experimental Establishment, Porton Down, in Relation to Medical Research Ethics in World War Two and Cold War Contexts' (University of Kent, unpublished MA thesis, 2004).

Bolton, T., '"Never Volunteer for Anything": The Concept of the "Volunteer" in Human Experimentation during the Cold War', *University of Sussex Journal of Contemporary History*, 9 (2005), pp. 1–14.

Bolton, T., 'Consent and the Construction of the Volunteer: Institutional Settings of Experimental Research on Human Beings in Britain during the Cold War' (University of Kent, unpublished PhD thesis, 2008).

Bolton, T., 'Putting Consent in Context: Military Research Subjects in Chemical Warfare Tests at Porton Down, UK', *Journal of Policy History*, 23 (2011), 1, pp. 53–73.

Botzler, R., and S.J. Armstrong, *Environmental Ethics: Divergence and Convergence* (Boston, MA, McGraw Hill, 1998).

Bowcott, O., 'New Inquest on Nerve Gas Death', *The Guardian*, 19 November 2002.

Brauch, H.G., and R.-D. Müller, eds, *Chemische Kriegsführung—Chemische Abrüstung: Dokumente und Kommentare* (Berlin, Berlin-Verlag Spitz, 1985).

Breitman, R., *Official Secrets. What the Nazis Planned. What the British and Americans Knew* (London, New York, Allen Lane, The Penguin Press, 1999).

Brophy, L.P., and G.J.B. Fisher, *The Chemical Warfare Service: Organizing for War* (Washington, DC: Department of the Army, 1959).

Brophy, L.P., W.D. Miles, and R.C. Cochrane, *The Chemical Warfare Service: From Laboratory to Field* (Washington, DC, Department of the Army, 1959).

Broszat, M., 'A Plea for the Historicization of National Socialism', in *Reworking the Past. Hitler, the Holocaust, and the Historians' Debate*, edited by P. Baldwin (Boston, MA, Beacon Press, 1990), pp. 77–87.

Broszat, M., and S. Friedländer, 'A Controversy about Historicization of National Socialism', in *Reworking the Past. Hitler, the Holocaust, and the Historians' Debate*, edited by P. Baldwin (Boston, MA, Beacon Press, 1990), pp. 102–34.

Brown, F.J., *Chemical Warfare. A Study in Restraints* (Princeton, NJ, Princeton University Press, 1968).

Brown, K., *Fighting Fit: Health, Medicine and War in the Twentieth Century* (Gloucestershire, The History Press, 2008).

Bryden, J., *Deadly Allies: Canada's Secret War, 1937–1947* (Toronto, McClelland & Stewart, 1989).

Bud, R., and P. Gummett, *Cold War, Hot Science: Applied Research in Britain's Defence Laboratories, 1945–1990* (Amsterdam, Harwood Academic Publishers & Science Museum, 1999).

Buffetaut, Y., *Ypres April 22nd 1915. The First Gas Attack*, translated by C. Cook (Louviers, Ysec Editions, 2008).

Butler Review, Lord Butler of Brockwell et al., Review of Intelligence on Weapons of Mass Destruction. Report of a Committee of Privy Counsellors (London, HMSO, 2004).

Callaway, S., D.R. Davies, and J.P. Rutland, 'Blood Cholinesterase Levels and Range of Personal Variation in a Healthy Adult Population', *BMJ* (1951), pp. 812–16.

Cameron, G.R., 'Pulmonary Oedema', *BMJ* (1948), pp. 965–72.

Campbell, P.N., and L.A. Stocken, 'Robert Henry Stewart Thompson, C.B.E., 2 February 1912–16 January 1998', *Biographical Memoirs of Fellows of the Royal Society*, 44 (1998), pp. 419–31.

Care, A., 'Poisoned by their Own People', *The Independent*, 3 October 2000.

Care, A., 'Porton Down Death—New Evidence—Did a V Nerve Agent Kill Ronald Maddison?' (press release, 7 November 2002a).

Care, A., 'The Porton Down Human Guinea Pigs—Gassed Without Consent', *APIL Newsletter*, 12 (2002b), 2, pp. 15–17.

Care, A., 'After the Inquest—Porton Revisited', *APIL PI Focus*, 15 (2005), 1, pp. 11–14.

Care, A., 'The Porton Down Settlement and the Legacy of Ronald Maddison: Cold War Human Experiments, 1940–1980', *APIL PI Focus*, 18 (2008), 3, pp. 22–5.

Care, A., 'The MI6/SIS (Secret Intelligence Services)/MoD LSD 1950s Experiments. Government Disclosure. A Retrospective' (unpublished article).

Carpenter, L.M. et al., 'Cancer Morbidity in British Military Veterans included in Chemical Warfare Agent Experiments at Porton Down: Cohort Study', *BMJ*, 338 (2009), 1–8 (b655).

Carrell, S., 'Porton Down Scientists Face Prosecution', *The Independent on Sunday*, 18 July 2001.

Carrell, S., 'High Court to Rule on Secret Nerve Gas Tests', *The Independent on Sunday*, 17 November 2002.

Carrick, D., 'The Future of Ethics Education in the Military: A Comparative Analysis', in *Ethics Education in the Military*, edited by P. Robinson, N. de Lee, and D. Carrick (Farnham, Ashgate, 2008), pp. 187–98.

Carrick, D., J. Connelly, and P. Robinson, eds., *Ethics Education for Irregular Warfare* (Farnham, Ashgate, 2009).

Carrington, A., G.J. Hills, and K.R. Webb, 'Neil Kensington Adam. 1891–1973', *Biographical Memoirs of Fellows of the Royal Society*, 20 (1974), pp. 1–26.

Carter, G.B., 'A Tale of Porton Down', *Focus*, April 1991a, pp. 10–11.

Carter, G.B., 'The Chemical and Biological Defence Establishment, Porton Down 1916–1991', *RUSI Journal*, 136 (1991b), 3, pp. 66–74.

Carter, G.B., 'The Microbiological Research Establishment and its Precursors at Porton Down: 1940–1979', *The ASA Newsletter*, 11 December 1991c, pp. 1 and 8–10.

Carter, G.B., 'The Microbiological Research Department and Establishment: 1946–1979', *The ASA Newsletter*, 1992, pp. 8–10.

Carter, G.B., 'The Old Portonians', *The Royal Engineers Journal*, 109 (1995), 2, pp. 162–7.

Carter, G.B, *Chemical and Biological Defence at Porton Down, 1916–2000* (London, HMSO, 2000).

Carter, G.B., 'Porton Down: From CDE to CBDE to DERA to DSTL', *The ASA Newsletter*, 22 February 2008, pp. 3–4.

Carter, G.B., and B. Balmer, 'Chemical and Biological Warfare and Defence, 1945–90', in *Cold War, Hot Science: Applied Research in Britain's Defence Laboratories, 1945–1990*, edited by R. Bud and P. Gummett (Amsterdam, Harwood Academic Publishers & Science Museum, 1999), pp. 295–337.

Carter, G.B., and G.S. Pearson, 'North Atlantic Chemical and Biological Research Collaboration: 1916–1995', *The Journal of Strategic Studies*, 19 (1996a), 1, pp. 74–103.

Carter, G.B., and G.S. Pearson, 'Past British Chemical Warfare Capabilities', *RUSI Journal*, 141 (1996b), pp. 59–68.

Carter, G.B., and G.S. Pearson, 'British Biological Warfare and Biological Defence, 1925–45', in *Biological and Toxin Weapons: Research, Development and Use from the Middle Ages to 1945*, edited by E. Geissler and J.E. van Courtland Moon (Oxford, Oxford University Press, 1999), pp. 168–89.

Caruth, C., *Unclaimed Experience: Trauma, Narrative, and History* (Baltimore, MD, London, The Johns Hopkins University Press, 1996).

Chang, H., and C. Jackson, eds., *An Element of Controversy: The Life of Chlorine in Science, Medicine, Technology and War* (London, BSHS Monographs, 2007).

Charcot, J.-M., *Clinical Lecture on Disease of the Nervous System* (London, New Sydenham Society, 1889).

Charles, D., *Between Genius and Genocide: The Tragedy of Fritz Haber, Father of Chemical Warfare* (London, Jonathan Cape, 2005).

Chemical Corps Association, *The Chemical Warfare Service in World War II. A Report of Accomplishments* (New York, Reinhold Publishing Corporation, 1948).

Chibnall, A.C., 'Kenneth Bailey. 1909–1963', *Biographical Memoirs of Fellows of the Royal Society*, 10 (1964), pp. 1–13.

Chick, H., M. Hume, and M. Macfarlane, *War on Disease: A History of the Lister Institute* (London, Deutsch, 1971).

Chielens, P., 'The List of Names and the Second Battle of Ypres', public lecture, University of Kent, 5 November 2014.

Chisholm, B., 'Biological Warfare: Demand for Answers', *Bulletin of the Atomic Scientists*, 15 (May 1959), 5, pp. 209–11.

Chivers, C.J., 'More Than 600 Reported Chemical Exposure in Iraq, Pentagon Acknowledges', *The New York Times*, 6 November 2014.

Chomsky, N., *Making the Future: Occupations, Interventions, Empire and Resistance* (London, Hamish Hamilton, 2012).

Chulov, M., M. Mahmoud, and I. Sample, 'Hundreds Killed in Apparent Gas Attack by Syrian Regime', *The Guardian*, 22 August 2013.

Churchill, W.S., *The World Crisis, 1915* (London, Thornton Butterworth Ltd., 1923).

Clark, R., *J.B.S.: The Life and Work of J.B.S. Haldane* (Oxford, Oxford University Press, 1984).

Cochrane, R.C., Medical Research in Chemical Warfare, vol. 30: History of Research and Development of the Chemical Warfare Service in World War II (Edgewood Arsenal, MD, unpublished manuscript, 1947).

Cole, L.A., *Clouds of Secrecy: The Army's Germ Warfare Tests over Populated Areas* (Totowa, NJ, Rowman & Littlefield, 1988).

Coleman, K., *A History of Chemical Warfare* (Basingstoke, Palgrave Macmillan, 2005).

Connelly, M., and S. Goebel, *Ypres* (Oxford: Oxford University Press, 2016, forthcoming).

Cookson, J., and J. Nottingham, *A Survey of Chemical and Biological Warfare* (London, Sydney, Sheed & War, 1969).

Corrigan, G., *Mud, Blood and Poppycock* (London, Cassell, 2003).

Corson, B.B., and R.W. Stoughton, 'Reactions of Alpha, Beta-Unsaturated Dinitriles', *Journal of the American Chemical Society*, 50 (1928), 10, pp. 2825–37.

Cotter, H., 'When the Artists Voted for the Politics of Order', *The New York Times*, 11 October 2010, pp. C1 and C7.

Court, M., 'Testing Times for New Drugs', *The Times*, 11 March 2003.

Cowell, F., X. Goh, J. Cambrook, and D. Bulley, 'Chlorine as the First Major Chemical Weapon', in *An Element of Controversy: The Life of Chlorine in Science, Medicine, Technology and War*, edited by H. Chang and C. Jackson (London, BSHS Monographs, 2007), pp. 220–54.

Craughwell, T.J. *The War Scientists: The Brains behind Military Technologies of Destruction and Defence* (2010).

Crewdson, G., *Twilight* (New York, Abrams, 2002).

Crockett, D., *German Post-Expressionism: The Art of the Great Disorder, 1918–1924* (University Park, PA, Pennsylvania State University Press, 1999).

Cullumbine, H., 'Chemical Warfare Experiments Using Human Subjects', *BMJ* (1946), pp. 576–8.

Cullumbine, H., and G.E.P. Box, 'Treatment of Lewisite Shock with Sodium Salt Solutions', *BMJ*, 1 (1946), 4450, pp. 607–8.

Curry, P., *Ecological Ethics: An Introduction* (Cambridge, Polity Press, 2006).

Dale, H.H., 'Edward Mellanby. 1884–1955', *Biographical Memoirs of Fellows of the Royal Society*, 1 (1955), pp. 192–222.

Davies, D.R., and J.D. Nicholls, 'A Field Test for the Assay of Human Whole-Blood Cholinesterase', *BMJ* (1955), pp. 1373–5.

Davison, J., 'Porton Down "Knew Tests Could be Fatal', *The Independent*, 29 October 1999.

De Bruxelles, S., 'Porton Down Faces Poison Inquest at Last', *The Times*, 6 May 2004.

De Burgh Daly, I., and R.A. Gregory, 'Charles Arthur Lovatt Evans, 1884–1968', *Biographical Memoirs of Fellows of the Royal Society*, 16 (1970), pp. 233–52.

DeFur, P.L., 'The Precautionary Principle: Application to Policies Regarding Endocrine-Disrupting Chemicals', in *Protecting Public Health and the Environment: Implementing the Precautionary Principle*, edited by C. Raffensperger and J.A. Tickner (Washington, DC, Island Press, 1999), pp. 337–48.

Dendooven, D., 'Overview: 22 April 1915—Eyewitness Accounts of the First Gas Attack', unpublished paper given at the conference *1915. Innocence Slaughtered?*, Ypres, 17–19 November 2005.

DERA, *BW and BW Defence Field Trials Conducted by the UK: 1940–1979* (HMG, 1999).

DERA, *Zinc Cadmium Sulphide (Fluorescent Particles) Field Trials Conducted by the UK: 1953–1964* (HMG, 2000).

Dörner, K., and A. Ebbinghaus, eds., *The Nuremberg Medical Trial 1946/47. Transcripts, Material of the Prosecution and Defense, Related Documents* (Munich, New York, K.G. Saur Verlag, 1999), Microfiche Edition.

Douglas, C.G., 'John Scott Haldane, 1860–1936', *Obituary Notices of Fellows of the Royal Society*, 2 (1936), 5, pp. 115–39.

Dubinin, M.M., 'Potentialities of Chemical Warfare', *Bulletin of the Atomic Scientists*, 16 (June 1960), 6, pp. 250–1.

Dudley, H., 'Tests on Volunteers at Porton Down', *BMJ*, 309 (1994), p. 1443.

Ebbinghaus, A., 'Der Prozeß gegen Tesch & Stabenow: Von der Schädlingsbekämpfung zum Holocaust', *1999. Zeitschrift für Sozialgeschichte des 20. und 21. Jahrhunderts*, 13 (1998), 2, pp. 16–71.

Ebbinghaus, A., 'Chemische Kampfstoffe in der deustchen Rüstungs- und Kriegswirtschaft', in *Krieg und Wirtschaft: Studien zur deutschen Wirtschaftsgeschichte 1939–1945*, edited by D. Eichholtz (Berlin, Metropol, 1999), pp. 171–94.

Ebbinghaus, A., and K.-H. Roth, 'Vernichtungsforschung: Der Nobelpreisträger Richard Kuhn, die Kaiser Wilhelm-Gesellschaft und die Entwicklung von

Nervenkampfstoffen während des "Dritten Reichs"', *1999. Zeitschrift für Sozialgeschichte des 20. und 21. Jahrhunderts*, 17 (2002), 1, pp. 15–50.

Echternkamp, J., and S. Martens, eds., *Experience and Memory. The Second World War in Europe* (New York, Oxford, Berghahn, 2010).

Eckart, W. U., ed., *Man, Medicine, and the State: The Human Body as an Object of Government Sponsored Medical Research in the 20th Century* (Stuttgart, Franz Steiner Verlag, 2006).

Ede, A., 'Waiting to Exhale: Chaos, Toxicity and the Origins of the U.S. Chemical Warfare Service', *Journal of Law, Medicine & Ethics*, 39 (2011), 1, pp. 28–33.

Edelson, P.J., 'Henry K. Beecher and Maurice Pappworth: Honor in the Development of the Ethics of Human Experimentation', in *Twentieth Century Ethics of Human Subject Research: Historical Perspectives on Values, Practices and Regulations*, edited by V. Roelcke and G. Maio (Stuttgart, Franz Steiner Verlag 2004), pp. 219–33.

Edgerton, D., Review of "Gassed. British Chemical Warfare Experiments on Humans at Porton Down", by Rob Evans. *The English Historical Review*, 117 (2002), 472, p. 763.

Edgerton, D., *Warfare State. Britain, 1920–1970* (Cambridge, Cambridge University Press, 2006).

Edgerton, D., *Britain's War Machine. Weapons, Resources and Experts in the Second World War* (London, Allen Lane, 2011).

Edwards, R., 'Your Country Needs You. Were 30,000 Soldiers Duped into Testing Deadly Chemical Weapons', *New Scientist*, 11 November 2000a.

Edwards, R., 'Servicemen Reveal Horror of Government's Gas Chambers', *Sunday Herald*, 12 November 2000b.

Eisner, M.A., *From Warfare State to Welfare State: World War I, Compensatory State-Building, and the Limits of the Modern Order* (University Park, PA, Pennsylvania State University Press, 2000).

Elkeles, B., *Der moralische Diskurs über das medizinische Menschenexperiment im 19. Jahrhundert* (Stuttgart, Jena, New York, Fischer, 1996).

Elliot, P.J. et al., 'The Risk to the United Kingdom Population of Zinc Cadmium Sulfide Dispersion by the Ministry of Defence during the "Cold War"', *Occupational and Environmental Medicine*, 59 (2002), 13–17.

Emsley, J., *Molecules of Murder. Criminal Molecules and Classic Cases* (Cambridge, Royal Society of Medicine, 2008).

Evans, M., 'MoD Hid Warning on Deadly Sarin Tests', *The Times*, 24 August 2004a.

Evans, M., 'Nerve Gas Death of Porton Down Guinea Pig was Unlawful Killing', *The Times*, 16 November 2004b.

Evans, M., 'Porton Down Nerve Gas Trials "Breached" Standards of Ethics', *The Times*, 15 July 2006.

Evans, R., *Gassed. British Chemical Warfare Experiments on Humans at Porton Down* (London, House of Stratus, 2000a).

Evans, R., 'The Guinea Pigs', *The Guardian*, 8 November 2000b.

Evans, R., 'Drugged and Duped', *The Guardian*, 14 March 2002.

Evans, R., 'No Charges over Porton Down "Guinea Pigs"', *The Guardian*, 8 July 2003.

Evans, R., 'MI6 Ordered LSD Tests on Servicemen. Volunteers Fed Hallucinogen in Mind Control Experiments', *The Guardian*, 22 January 2005.

Evans, R., 'MI6 Pays Out over Secret LSD Mind Control Tests', *The Guardian*, 24 February 2006a.

Evans, R., '£100,000 Payout by MoD for 1953 Nerve Gas Experiment', *The Guardian*, 26 May 2006b.

Evans, R., 'Porton Down Chemical Weapons Tests Unethical, Says Report', *The Guardian*, 15 July 2006c.

Evans, R., 'Military Scientists Tested Mustard Gas on Indians', *The Guardian*, 1 September 2007.

Evans, R., and S. Laville, 'Porton Down Unlawfully Killed Airman in Sarin Tests', *The Guardian*, 16 November 2004.

Evers, K., 'Risking Gas Warfare: Imperceptible Death and the Future of War in Weimar Culture and Literature', *The Germanic Review: Literature, Culture, Theory*, 89 (2014), 3, pp. 269–84.

Feldberg, W., 'John Henry Gaddum. 1900–1965', *Biographical Memoirs of Fellows of the Royal Society*, 13 (1967), pp. 57–77.

Felton, M., *The Devil's Doctors. Japanese Human Experiments on Allied Prisoners of War* (Barnsley, Pen & Sword Military, 2012).

Field, R., *Health Care Regulation in America: Complexity, Confrontation and Compromise* (New York, Oxford University Press, 2007).

Findings from a CDC Report on the 1946–1948 U.S. Public Health Service Sexually Transmitted Disease (STD) Inoculation Study, Based on Review of Archived Papers of John Cutler, MD, at the University of Pittsburgh (Washington, DC, U.S. Dept. of Health and Human Services, 2010).

Fletcher, J.C., 'Location of the Office for Protection from Research Risks within the National Institutes of Health: Problems of Status and Independent Authority', in: *NBAC, Ethical and Policy Issues in Research Involving Human Participants*, vol. 2: *Commissioned Papers and Staff Analysis* (Bethesda, MD, 2002), pp. B-1–B-21.

Floyd, R., *Security and the Environment. Securitisation Theory and US Environmental Security Policy* (Cambridge, Cambridge University Press, 2010).

Fluss, S., 'How the Declaration of Helsinki Developed', *Good Clinical Practice Journal*, 6 (1999), pp. 18–22.

Foulkes, C.H., '*Gas!' The Story of the Special Brigade* (Edinburgh, W. Blackwood & Sons, 1934).

Fox, J., 'Lions on the Loose and Sharks in the Channel: Rumour in Britain and Europe during the Second World War', War, Media and Society Lecture, University of Kent, 11 December 2013.

Freeman, K., 'The Unfought Chemical War', *Bulletin of the Atomic Scientists*, 47 (1991), 10, pp. 30–9.

French, R.D., *Antivivisection and Medical Science in Victorian Society* (Princeton, NJ, Princeton University Press, 1975).

Freund, P.A., 'Introduction to the Issue "Ethical Aspects of Experimentation with Human Subjects', *Dædalus*, 98 (1969), 2, pp. viii–xiv.

Frewer, A., 'Human Rights from the Nuremberg Doctors Trial to the Geneva Declaration. Persons and Institutions in Medical Ethics and History', *Medical Health Care Philosophy* (2010), 13, pp. 259–68.

Frewer, A., *Medizin und Moral in Weimarer Republik und Nationalsozialismus. Die Zeitschrift 'Ethik' unter Emil Abderhalden* (Frankfurt am Main, New York, Campus Verlag, 2000).

Frewer A., and M. Rothhaar, 'Medicine, Human Rights and Ethics: Paths to Universal Rights', *Medical Health Care Philosophy* (2010), 13, pp. 247–9.

Frewer, A., and U. Schmidt, eds, *Standards der Forschung. Historische Entwicklung und ethische Grundlagen klinischer Studien* (Frankfurt am Main, Peter Lang, 2007).

Frewer, A., and U. Schmidt, eds, *Forschung als Herausforderungen für Ethik und Menschenrechte. 50 Jahre Deklaration von Helsinki, 1964–2014* (Cologne, Deutscher Ärzteverlag, 2014).

Frewer, A., and C. Wiesemann, eds, *Medizinverbrechen vor Gericht. Das Urteil im Nürnberger Ärzteprozeß gegen Karl Brandt und andere sowie aus dem Prozeß gegen Generalfeldmarschall Erhard Milch* (Erlangen, Jena, Palm & Enke, 1999).

Friedländer, S., 'Some Reflections on the Historicization of National Socialism', in *Reworking the Past: Hitler, the Holocaust, and the Historians' Debate*, edited by P. Baldwin (Boston, MA, Beacon Press, 1990), pp. 88–101.

Friedländer, S., *Nazism and the 'Final Solution'. Probing the Limits of Representation* (Cambridge, MA, Harvard University Press, 1992).

Friedländer, S., *Memory, History and the Extermination of the Jews of Europe* (Bloomington, IN, Indiana University Press, 1993).

Friedländer, S., *Nazi Germany and the Jews*, vol. 1: *The Years of Persecution, 1933–1939* (London, Weidenfeld & Nicolson, 1997).

Friedländer, S., *The Years of Extermination. Nazi Germany and the Jews. 1939–1945* (London, Weidenfeld & Nicolson, 2007).

Friedrich, J., *Der Brand. Deutschland im Bombenkrieg 1940–1945* (Munich, Propyläen, 2002).

Fröhlich, E., ed., *Die Tagebücher von Joseph Goebbels*, part 2: *Diktate 1941–1945*, vols 1–15 (Munich, K.G. Saur Verlag, 1993–1996).

Fuchs, A., *After the Dresden Bombing. Pathways of Memory, 1945 to the Present* (Basingstoke, Palgrave Macmillan, 2012).

Furmanski, M,, and M. Wheelis, 'Allegations of Biological Weapons Use', in *Deadly Cultures: Biological Weapons since 1945*, edited by M. Wheelis, R. Lajos, and M. Dando (Cambridge, MA, London, Harvard University Press, 2006), pp. 252–83.

Galbraith, R., *Inside Outside. The Man They Can't Gag. A Biography of Tam Dalyell* (Edinburgh, London, Mainstream Publishing, 2000).

Garner, J.P., 'Some Recollections of Porton in World War I. Commentary', *Journal of the RAMC*, 149 (2003), 2, pp. 138–41.

Gassmann, M., 'Der Seltsame Investor', *Berliner Morgenpost*, 1 December 2013.

Gatton, A., 'The Acid Test', *The Big Issue*, 13 November 2000.

Geissler, E., *Biologische Waffen—nicht in Hitlers Arsenalen. Biologische und Toxin-Kampfmittel in Deutschland von 1915 bis 1945* (Münster, LIT Verlag, 1999).

Geissler, E., and J.E. van Courtland Moon, *Biological and Toxin Weapons: Research, Development and Use from the Middle Ages to 1945* (Oxford, Oxford University Press, 1999).

Gellermann, G.W., *Der Krieg, der nicht stattfand. Möglichkeiten, Überlegungen und Entscheidungen der deutschen Obersten Führung zur Verwendung chemischer Kampstoffe im Zweiten Weltkrieg* (Koblenz, Bernard & Graefe, 1986).

Gerlach, C., *Krieg, Ernährung, Völkermord. Forschungen zur deutschen Vernichtungspolitik im Zweiten Weltkrieg* (Hamburg, Hamburger Edition, 1998).

Gibbs, D.N., 'Secrecy and International Relations', *Journal of Peace Research*, 32 (1995), 2, pp. 213–28.

Gibson, C.S., 'Sir William Jackson Pope. 1870–1939', *Obituary Notices of Fellows of the Royal Society*, 3 (1941), 9, pp. 291–324.

Gilbert, M., *Finest Hour: Winston S. Churchill, 1939–1941* (London, Heinemann, 1983).

Gladstone, G.P., B.C.J.G. Knight, and G. Wilson, 'Paul Gordon Fildes. 1882–1971', *Biographical Memoirs of Fellows of the Royal Society*, 19 (1973), pp. 317–47.

Goliszek, A., *In the Name of Science. A History of Secret Programs, Medical Research, and Human Experimentation* (New York, St Martins Press, 2003).

Goodman, J., A. McElligott, and L. Marks, eds., *Useful Bodies: Humans in the Service of Medical Science in the Twentieth Century* (Baltimore, MD, London, The Johns Hopkins University Press, 2003).

Goodman, M., *Suffer and Survive: Gas Attacks, Miners' Canaries, Spacesuits and the Bends—The Extreme Life of J.S. Haldane* (London, Pocket Books, 2008).

Goodwin, B., *Keen as Mustard. Britain's Horrific Chemical Warfare Experiments in Australia* (St Lucia, University of Queensland Press, 1998).

Goodyear, M.D.E., L.A. Eckenwiler, and C. Ells, 'Thinking about the Declaration of Helsinki', *BMJ*, 337 (2008), 7678, pp. 1067–8.

Goslett, M., and J. Rentoul, 'Foul Play vs Suicide. Ten Years on, the Row Still Rages over the Death of Dr David Kelly', *The Independent on Sunday*, 14 July 2013, pp. 16–17.

Graves, C., *Mr. Punch's History of the Great War* (London, Cassell, 1919).

Gray, J., 'Making the Future by Noam Chomsky—Review. In Demonizing America, Chomsky Has Fallen into the Same Trap as the Neocons', *The Guardian*, 8 February 2012.

Grayzel, S.R., *At Home and under Fire. Air Raids and Culture in Britain from the Great War to the Blitz* (Cambridge, Cambridge University Press, 2012).

Green, F.H.K., 'The Structure and Functions of the Medical Research Council', *BMJ* (1948), pp. 462–6.

Gregory, A., *The Silence of Memory. Armistice Day 1919–1946* (Oxford, Providence, RI, Berg, 1994).

Grodin, M.A., 'Historical Origins of the Nuremberg Code', in *The Nazi Doctors and the Nuremberg Code. Human Rights in Human Experimentation*, edited by

G.J. Annas and M.A. Grodin (New York, Oxford, Oxford University Press, 1992), pp. 121–44.

Groehler, O., *Der lautlose Tod. Einsatz und Entwicklung deutscher Giftgase von 1914 bis 1945* (Reinbek, Rowohlt, 1989).

Gross, M.L., *Bioethics and Armed Conflict: Moral Dilemmas of Medicine and War* (Cambridge, MA, London, The MIT Press, 2006).

Gross, M.L. 'Teaching Military Medical Ethics: Another Look at Dual Loyalty and Triage', *Cambridge Quarterly of Healthcare Ethics*, 19 (2010), pp. 1–7.

Gross, M.L., 'Military Medical Ethics. A Review of the Literature and a Call to Arms', *Cambridge Quarterly of Healthcare Ethics*, 22 (2013), pp. 92–109.

Gross, M.L., and D. Carrick, eds, *Military Medical Ethics for the 21st Century* (Farnham, Ashgate, 2013).

Guillemin, J., *Biological Weapons: From the Invention of State-Sponsored Programs to Contemporary Bioterrorism* (New York, Columbia University Press, 2005).

Gutmann, A., 'Introduction', *Michael Ignatieff. Human Rights as Politics and Idolatry*, edited by A. Gutmann (Princeton, NJ, Woodstock, Oxon, Princeton University Press, 2001), pp. vii–xxviii.

Gutmann, A., ed., *Michael Ignatieff. Human Rights as Politics and Idolatry* (Princeton, NJ, Woodstock, Oxon, Princeton University Press, 2001).

Guttentag, O.E., 'Human Experimentation', *Science*, 145 (1964), 3634, pp. 768.

Haber, F., *Fünf Vorträge aus den Jahren 1920—1923. Über die Darstellung des Ammoniaks aus Stickstoff und Wasserstoff; Die Chemie im Krieg; Das Zeitalter der Chemie; Neue Arbeitsweisen; Zur Geschichte des Gaskrieges* (Berlin, Verlag von Julius Springer, 1924).

Haber, L.F., *The Poisonous Cloud: Chemical Warfare in the First World War* (Oxford, New York; Oxford University Press, 1986).

Haldane, J.B.S., *Callinicus: A Defence of Chemical Warfare* (London, Kegan Paul, 1925).

Haldane, J.B.S., *Possible Worlds and Other Essays* (London, Chatto & Windus, 1927).

Haldane, J.B.S., 'Future Methods of War', *The Times*, 14 October 1937, p. 9.

Haldane, J.B.S., *Heredity and Politics* (London, George Allen & Unwin, 1938).

Haldane, J.B.S., *Science in Peace and War* (London, Lawrence & Wishart, 1940).

Hammond, P.M., and G.B. Carter, *From Biological Warfare to Healthcare* (Basingstoke, Palgrave Macmillan, 2002).

Handschuh, D., 'Secret Project Results in Life of Pain', *Kelowna Daily Courier* (2004).

Hare, D., 'We Can Be Grateful There is One British Citizen Who is Not at the Mercy of the Market', *The Guardian*, 2 June 2012.

Harris, R., and J. Paxman, *A Higher Form of Killing. The Secret History of Chemical and Biological Warfare* (first edn, London, Chatto & Windus, 1982; second edn, London, Arrow Books, 2002).

Harrison, M., *The Medical War. British Military Medicine in the First World War* (Oxford, Oxford University Press, 2010).

Hayward, J., *The Bodies on the Beach. Sealion, Shingle Street and the Burning Sea Myth of 1940* (Dereham, Norfolk, CD41 Publishing, 2001).

Hazelgrove, J., 'The Old Faith and the New Science: The Nuremberg Code and Human Experimentation Ethics in Britain, 1946–73', *Social History of Medicine*, 15 (2002), pp. 109–35.

Hedgecoe A., '"A Form of Practical Machinery": The Origin of Research Ethics Committees in the UK, 1967–1972', *Medical History*, 53 (2009), 3, pp. 331–50.

Hedges, S., 'New Blow to "Guinea Pig" Ken's Fight for Justice', *Kent Messenger*, 1 August 2003, p. 35.

Hennessy, P., *The Secret State. Whitehall and the Cold War* (London, Penguin, 2003).

Hersh, S.M., *Chemical and Biological Warfare: The Hidden Arsenal* (London, Panther, 1970).

Historical Survey of the Porton Down Volunteer Programme (London, MoD, unpublished manuscript, 2006).

Hobbs, A., C. Jefferson, N. Coppeard, and C. Pitt, 'Ethics, Public Relations, and the Origins of the Geneva Protocol', in *An Element of Controversy: The Life of Chlorine in Science, Medicine, Technology and War*, edited by H. Chang and C. Jackson (London, BSHS Monographs, 2007), pp. 255–95.

Hodgkin, A., 'Edgar Douglas Adrian, Baron Adrian of Cambridge. 30 November 1889–4 August 1977', *Biographical Memoirs of Fellows of the Royal Society*, 25 (1979), pp. 1–73.

Hornblum, A.M., *Acres of Skin. Human Experimentation at Holmesburg Prison* (New York, London, Routledge, 1998).

Houghton, T., 'Chemical Offensive: British Chemical Warfare Research, 1914–1945', unpublished M.Sc. dissertation (Imperial College London, 2004).

Human, S., and S. Fluss, 'The World Medical Association's Declaration of Helsinki: Historical and Contemporary Perspectives'. Unpublished manuscript, 2001.

Huxley, A., 'Richard Hume Adrian, D.L. 2nd Baron Adrian of Cambridge. 16 October 1927–4 April 1995', *Biographical Memoirs of Fellows of the Royal Society*, 43 (1997), pp. 15–30.

Huyssen, A., *Twilight Memories. Marking Time in a Culture of Amnesia* (London, Routledge, 1995).

Ignatieff, M., 'Human Rights as Politics', in *Human Rights as Politics and Idolatry*, edited by A. Gutmann (Princeton, NJ, Princeton University Press, 2001), pp. 3–52.

IMT (International Military Tribunal), *Trial of the Major War Criminals* (New York, AMS Press, 1971).

Independent Review of the Possible Health Hazards of the Large-Scale Release of Bacteria during the Dorset Defence Trials, *House of Commons Library*, 9 February 1999.

Institution of Royal Engineers, *The Royal Engineers Corps History*, vols. 1–9 (CD-ROM, Institution of Royal Engineers, Chatham, *c.* 2005).

Irvine, R., 'Lloyd Arthur Stocken (1912–2008)', *The Biochemical Society* (2009), pp. 63–4.

Jacobs, M., *Zij, die vielen als helden . . . Inventaris van de oorlogsgedenktekens van de twee wereldoorlogen in West-Vlaanderen*, vol. 2 (Bruges, Provincie West-Vlaanderen, 1996).

Jastone, L.O., *Federal Protection for Human Research Subjects: An Analysis of the Common Rule and its Interactions with FDA Regulations and the HIPAA Privacy Rule* (New York, Novinka Books, 2006).

Jenkins, D., 'Airman's Family Wins Fight for Justice', *The Northern Echo*, 16 November 2004.

Johnson, M.K., 'Profiles in Toxicology. W. Norman Aldridge', *Toxicological Sciences*, 59 (2001), pp. 3–4.

Jonas, H., 'Philosophical Reflections on Experimenting with Human Subjects', *Dædalus*, 98 (1969), 2, pp. 219–47.

Jones, E., B. Everitt, S. Ironside, I. Palmer, and S. Wessely, 'Psychological Effects of Chemical Weapons: A Follow-up Study of First World War Veterans', *Psychological Medicine*, 38 (2008), pp. 1419–26.

Jones, G.R.N., and M.S. Israel, 'Mechanism of Toxicity of Injected CS Gas', *Nature*, 228 (1970), pp. 1315–17.

Jones, G.R.N., 'CS in the Balance', *New Scientist and Science Journal*, 50 (1971), 756, pp. 690–2.

Jones, J.J., *Bad Blood, The Tuskegee Syphilis Experiments* (London, Collier Macmillan Publishers, 1981).

Judt, T., *Reappraisals. Reflections on the Forgotten Twentieth Century* (London, Vintage Books, 2009).

Katz J., 'The Consent Principle of the Nuremberg Code: Its Significance Then and Now', in *The Nazi Doctors and the Nuremberg Code. Human Rights in Human Experimentation*, edited by G.J. Annas and M.A. Grodin (New York, Oxford, Oxford University Press, 1992), pp. 227–39.

Katz, J., 'The Nuremberg Code and the Nuremberg Trial. A Reappraisal', *JAMA*, 276 (1996), 20, pp. 1662–6.

Katz, J., 'Human Sacrifice and Human Experimentation: Reflections at Nuremberg', *Yale Journal of International Law*, 22 (1997), pp. 401–18.

Kehrl, H., *Krisenmanager im Dritten Reich. 6 Jahre Frieden—6 Jahre Krieg. Erinnerungen* (Düsseldorf, Droste, 1973).

Kennedy, I., 'An Ethical Assessment', in Historical Survey 2006, pp. 403–34.

Kent, L.H., and W.T.J. Morgan, 'David Willis Wilson Henderson. 1903–1968', *Biographical Memoirs of Fellows of the Royal Society*, 16 (1970), pp. 331–41.

Kershaw, I., *Hitler. 1889–1936: Hubris* (London, Allen Lane, 1998).

Kershaw, I., *Hitler. 1936–45: Nemesis* (London, Allen Lane, 2000).

Kidd, A., 'Limits of the Right of a Person to Consent to Experimentation on Himself', *Science*, 11 (1953), pp. 211–12.

King, N., 'Porton Down', *The Times*, 27 March 2006, p. 22.

Kirby, M.W., *Operational Research in War and Peace: The British Experience from the 1930s to 1970* (London, Imperial College Press, 2003).

Kirby, R., 'Paradise Lost: The Psycho Agents', *The CBW Conventions Bulletin* (2006), No. 71, pp. 1–5.

Kirby, R., *Selling Chemical Warfare: CWS Posters 1918–1945* (Wentzville, MO, Eximdyne, 2007).

Kirkbride, C.G. Transcript of an Interview Conducted by James J. Bohning in Washington, DC, 15 July 1993.

Klee, E., *Auschwitz. Die NS-Medizin und ihre Opfer* (Frankfurt am Main, S. Fischer Verlag, 1997).

Klever, B.E., and D. Birdsell, *The Chemical Warfare Service: Chemicals in Combat* (Washington DC, Department of the Army, 1966).

Koch, E.R., 'Folterexperten—Die geheimen Methoden der CIA'. Documentary Film. German Television SWR, released on 9 July 2007.

Kopke, C., and G. Schultz, 'Die Menschenversuche mit dem Kampfstoff Lost im KZ Sachsenhausen (1939) und die Debatte über die Rolle des Wehrmachtstoxikologen Wolfgang Wirth', in *Medizin im Zweiten Weltkrieg. Militärmedizinische Praxis und medizinische Wissenschaft im 'Totalen Krieg'*, edited by W.U. Eckart and A. Neumann (Paderborn, Munich, Vienna, Zurich, Schöningh, 2006), pp. 113–29.

Ladell, W.S.S., 'Treatment of Anticholinesterase Poisoning', *BMJ* (1958), pp. 141–2.

LaFleur, W.R., 'Refusing Utopia's Bait: Research, Rationalizations, and Hans Jonas', in *Dark Medicine. Rationalizing Unethical Medical Research*, edited by W.R. LaFleur, G. Böhme, and S. Shimazono (Bloomington, IN, Indiana University Press, 2007), pp. 233–45.

LaFleur, W.R., G. Böhme, and S. Shimazono, eds., *Dark Medicine. Rationalizing Unethical Medical Research* (Bloomington, IN, Indiana University Press, 2007).

Langer, E., 'Human Experimentation: Cancer Studies at Sloan-Kettering Stirr Public Debate on Medical Ethics', *Science*, 143 (1964), 3606, pp. 551–3.

Latour, B., and S. Woolgar, *Laboratory Life: The Construction of Scientific Facts* (Princeton, NJ, Princeton University Press, 1986).

Laville, S., 'The Dying Moments of Military Guinea Pigs', *The Guardian*, 6 May 2004a.

Laville, S., 'I'd Follow Ronnie Anywhere. I Adored Him', *The Guardian*, 16 November 2004b, p. 6.

Lawrence, C., 'Incommunicable Knowledge: Science, Technology and the Clinical Art in Britain, 1850–1914', *Journal of Contemporary History*, 20 (1985), pp. 503–20.

Lederer, S., *Subjected to Science. Human Experimentation before the Second World War* (Baltimore, MD, London, The Johns Hopkins University Press, 1995).

Lederer, S., 'Research without Borders: The Origins of the Declaration of Helsinki', in *Twentieth Century Ethics of Human Subject Research—Historical Perspectives on Values, Practices, and Regulations*, edited by V. Roelcke and G. Maio (Stuttgart, Franz Steiner Verlag, 2004), pp. 199–217.

Lederer, S., 'Research without Borders: The Origins of the Declaration of Helsinki', in *History and Theory of Human Experimentation. The Declaration of Helsinki and Modern Medical Ethics*, edited by U. Schmidt and A. Frewer (Stuttgart, Franz Steiner Verlag, 2007), pp. 145–64.

Lederer, S., 'Going for the Burn: Medical Preparedness in Early Cold War America', *Journal of Law, Medicine & Ethics*, 39 (2011), 1, pp. 48–53.

Lee, H.A., R. Gabriel, A.J. Bale, and D. Welch, 'Clinical Finding in 111 Ex-Porton Down Volunteers', *Journal of the RAMC*, 150 (2004), pp. 14–19.

Leighton, P.A., *The Stanford Fluorescent-Particle Tracer Technique: An Operational Manual.* U.S. Chemical Corps Research and Development Program. Contract DA-18-064-CML-2564 (Department of Chemistry, Stanford University, Palo Alto, CA, 1955).

Lerner, P., *Hysterical Men. War, Psychiatry, and the Politics of Trauma in Germany, 1890–1930* (Ithaca, NY, London, Cornell University Press, 2003).

Levi, P., *The Drowned and the Saved* (London, Abacus, 1989).

Levi, P., *If this is a Man* and *The Truce* (London, Abacus, 2001a).

Levi, P., *The Periodic Table* (London, Penguin, 2001b).

Levidow, L., 'Nuclear Accidents by Design', *Science as Culture*, 9 (1990), 1, pp. 99–109.

Lindee, S., 'Experimental Wounds: Science and Violence in Mid-Century America', *Journal of Law, Medicine & Ethics*, 39 (2011), 1, pp. 8–20.

Lloyd, N., *Loos 1915* (Stroud, Gloucestershire, Tempus, 2006).

Lovell, R., *Churchill's Doctor. A Biography of Lord Moran* (New York, Royal Society of Medicine, 1992).

Lucas, B.G.B., and S. Miles, 'Anticholinesterases and Muscle Relaxants', *BMJ* (1955), pp. 579–80.

Lucas, M., 'Greeting from Doom Town', *Los Angeles Times*, 19 April 1998.

Lutwick, L.I., and S.M. Lutwick, eds, *Beyond Anthrax. The Weaponization of Infectious Diseases* (New York, Springer, 2009).

MacDonald, L., *1915. The Death of Innocence* (London, Headline, 1993).

Mackay, N., 'Revealed: How Naval Intelligence Tested Lethal "Plague Bombs" off Scotland', *Sunday Herald*, 9 March 2003.

MacLean, A., 'The Ethics of Research on Humans in the United Kingdom 1939–1989', in Historical Survey 2006, pp. 351–402.

Maio, G., 'Medical Ethics and Human Experimentation in France after 1945', in *Twentieth Century Ethics of Human Subject Research: Historical Perspectives on Values, Practices and Regulations*, edited by V. Roelcke and G. Maio (Stuttgart, 2004), pp. 235–52.

Marrs, T.C., R.L. Maynard, and F.R. Sidell, *Chemical Warfare Agents. Toxicology and Treatment* (New York, John Wiley & Sons, 1996).

Mason, J.K., and G.T. Laurie, *Law and Medical Ethics* (Oxford, Oxford University Press, 2010).

Masterson, K., *The Malaria Project. The U.S. Government's Secret Mission to Find a Miracle Cure* (New York, New American Library, 2014).

McCamley, N.J., *The Secret History of Chemical Warfare* (Barnsley, Pen & Sword Military 2006).

McCoy, A.W., 'Science in Dachau's Shadow: Hebb, Beecher, and the Development of CIA Psychological Torture and Modern Medical Ethics', *Journal of the History of the Behavioral Sciences*, 43 (2007), 4, pp. 401–17.

McGehee Harvey, A., *Science at the Bedside: Clinical Research in American Medicine, 1905–1945* (Baltimore, MD, The Johns Hopkins University Press, 1981).

McKusick, Victor A., 'A. McGehee Harvey, 30 July 1911–8 May 1998', *Proceedings of the American Philosophical Society*, 144 (2000), 1, pp. 85–94.

McManus, J., et al., 'Informed Consent and Ethical Issues in Military Medical Research', *Journal of Academic Emergency Medicine*, 12 (2005), p. 1121.

Medical Ethics Committee, Draft Code of Ethics on Human Experimentation, *BMJ* (1962), 2, p. 1119.

Micale, M.S., and P. Lerner, P., eds., *Traumatic Pasts: History, Psychiatry and Trauma in the Modern Age, 1870–1930* (Cambridge, Cambridge University Press, 2001).

Michalski, S., *Neue Sachlichkeit. Malerei, Graphik und Photographie in Deutschland 1919–1933* (Cologne, Benedikt Taschen Verlag, 2003).

Milmo, C., 'Inquest Opens into 1953 Porton Down Death', *The Independent*, 6 May 2004a.

Milmo, C., 'Porton Down Volunteer "Unlawfully Killed"', *The Independent*, 16 November 2004b.

Ministry of Home Security, *The Detection and Identification of War Gases* (London, HMSO, 1943).

Ministry of Supply (MoS), 'Chief Characteristics of Nerve Gas', *BMJ* (1952a), pp. 334–5.

Ministry of Supply (MoS), 'Chief Characteristics of Nerve Gas', *The Lancet* (1952b), pp. 286–7.

Mitscherlich, A., and F. Mielke, eds., *Medizin ohne Menschlichkeit* (Frankfurt am Main, Fischer-Bücherei, 1962).

Moreno, J.D., ' "The Only Feasible Means": The Pentagon's Ambivalent Relationship with the Nuremberg Code', *Hastings Center Report*, 26 (1996), pp. 11–19.

Moreno, J.D., 'Reassessing the Influence of the Nuremberg Code on American Medical Ethics', *Journal of Contemporary Health Law and Policy*, 13 (1997), pp. 347–60.

Moreno, J.D., *Undue Risk. Secret State Experiments on Humans* (New York, W.H. Freeman, 1999).

Moreno, J.D., *Mind Wars. Brain Research and National Defence* (New York, Washington, DC, Dana Press, 2006).

Moreno, J.D., 'Helsinki into the Future. An Epilogue', in *History and Theory of Human Experimentation. The Declaration of Helsinki and Modern Medical Ethics*, edited by U. Schmidt and A. Frewer (Stuttgart, Franz Steiner Verlag, 2007), pp. 327–9.

Moreno, J.D., *The Body Politic: The Battle over Science in America* (New York, Bellevue Literary Press, 2011).

Moreno, J.D., 'Brains. The Appliance of Neuroscience', *Jane's Intelligence Review* (2013), pp. 24–8.

Morris, L., 'The Sheffield Peace Congress and Anti-Apartheid', in *Picasso. Peace and Freedom*, edited by L. Morris and C. Grunenberg (London, Tate Publishing, 2010), pp. 60–7.

Morris, L., and C. Grunenberg, 'What Picasso Stood For', in *Picasso. Peace and Freedom*, edited by L. Morris and C. Grunenberg (London, Tate Publishing, 2010), pp. 10–17.

Müller, R.-D., 'Die deutschen Gaskriegsvorbereitungen 1919–1945', *Militärgeschichtliche Mitteilungen*, 28 (1980), pp. 25–54.

Müller, R.-D., 'Albert Speer und die Rüstungspolitik im totalen Krieg', in *Das Deutsche Reich und der Zweite Weltkrieg*, vol. 5: *Organisation und Mobilisierung des deutschen Machtbereichs,* part 2: *Kriegsverwaltung, Wirtschaft und personelle Ressourcen, 1942–1944/45*, edited by B.R. Kroener, R.-D, Müller and H. Umbreit (Stuttgart, Deutsche Verlags-Anstalt, 1999), pp. 275–776.

Napier, G., *Follow the Sapper* (Institution of Royal Engineers, Chatham, 2005).

National Research Council, *Toxicological Assessment of the Army's Zinc Cadmium Sulfide Dispersion Tests* (National Academy Press, Washington DC, 1997).

Nie, J.-B., N. Guo, M. Selden, and A. Kleinman, *Japan's Wartime Medical Atrocities: Comparative Inquiries in Science, History, and Ethics* (London, New York, Routledge, 2010).

North, R., 'Mustard Gas Victim to Sue', *Yorkshire on Sunday*, 4 December 1994.

Oakley, C.L., 'Gordon Roy Cameron. 1899–1966', *Biographical Memoirs of Fellows of the Royal Society*, 14 (1968), pp. 68–116.

Office of Civilian Defense, Medical Division, *First Aid in the Prevention and Treatment of Chemical Casualties* (Washington, DC, 1941).

Oliver, M., 'Porton Down Veteran Wins Case in Strasbourg', *The Guardian*, 19 October 2005.

Ombudsman for NDCF, Final Report: Complaints Concerning Chemical Agent Testing during World War II, February 2004; <http://www.ombudsman.forces.gc.ca/assets/OMBUDSMAN_Internet/docs/en/cat-eac.pdf>.

'On Biological and Chemical Warfare', *Bulletin of the Atomic Scientists*, 15 (Oct 1959), 8, pp. 337–9.

Ord, M.G., Stocken, L.A., 'A Contribution to Chemical Defence in World War II, 1939–45', *Trends in Biochemical Sciences*, 25 (2000), pp. 253–6.

Ord, M.G., and Stocken, L.A., 'The Oxford Biochemistry Department in Wartime, 1939–45', *Notes and Records of the Royal Society*, 59 (2005), pp. 137–43.

Overy, R., *The Dictators. Hitler's Germany and Stalin's Russia* (London, Allen Lane, 2004).

Page, W.F., 'Long-Term Health Effects of Exposure to Sarin and other Anticholinesterase Chemical Warfare Agents', *Military Medicine*, 168 (2003), 3, pp. 239–45.

Page, W.F., et al., *Advisory Panel for the Study of Long-Term Health Effects of Participation in Project SHAD (Shipboard Hazard and Defence)* (Washington, DC, The National Academies Press, 2007).

Palmer, C., *Education or Catastrophe? Environmental Values and Environmental Education* (Oxford, The Farmington Institute for Christian Studies, 1997).

Palmer, C., *Environmental Ethics and Process Thinking* (Oxford, Oxford University Press, 1998).

Parker, J., *The Killing Factory: The Top Secret World of Germ and Chemical Warfare* (London, Smith Gryphon, 1996).

Pattle, R.E., and H. Cullumbine, 'Toxicity of Some Atmospheric Pollutants', *BMJ* (1956), pp. 913–16, and pp. 931–2.

Pearse, D., 'Elderly Used in Germ Test Claim', *The Universe*, 26 November 2000.

Pechura, C.M., and D.P. Rall, eds., *Veterans at Risk* (Washington, DC, National Academy Press, 1993).

Pemberton, J., 'Medical Experiments Carried out in Sheffield on Conscientious Objectors to Military Service during the 1939–45 War', *International Journal of Epidemiology*, 35 (2006), pp. 556–8.

Perley, S., et al., 'The Nuremberg Code: An International Overview', in *The Nazi Doctors and the Nuremberg Code. Human Rights in Human Experimentation*, edited by G.J. Annas and M.A. Grodin (New York, Oxford, Oxford University Press, 1992), pp. 149–73.

Perry Robinson, J.P., 'The Impact of Pugwash on the Debates over Chemical and Biological Weapons', in *Scientific Cooperation, State Conflict: The Role of Scientists in Mitigating International Discord*, edited by A.L.C. de Cerreño and Alexander Keynan (New York, The New York Academy of Science, 1998), pp. 224–52.

Peters, R.A., 'The Faith of a Master in Biochemistry', *Biochemical Journal*, 71 (1959), pp. 1–9.

Physicians for Human Rights, 'Doing Harm: Health Professionals' Central Role in the CIA Torture Program. Medical and Psychological Analysis of the 2014 U.S. Senate Select Committee on Intelligence Report's Executive Summary', December 2014.

Picardie, J., 'The Toxic Avenger', *The Independent*, 1 October 1995.

Plunkett, G., *Chemical Warfare in Australia. Australia's Involvement in Chemical Warfare 1914–1945* (Loftus, N.S.W., Australian Military History Publications, 2007).

Poems of the Great War, 1914–1918 (London, Penguin Books, 1998).

Pook, S., 'Sister Told for First Time How Sarin Killed Airman', *Daily Telegraph*, 6 May 2004a.

Pook, S., 'Porton Down Unlawful Killing Verdict Opens Gates to Claims', *Daily Telegraph*, 16 November 2004b.

Popper, K., *The Open Society and its Enemies* (London, New York, Routledge, 1994).

Porter, R., *The Greatest Benefit to Mankind. A Medical History of Humanity from Antiquity to the Present* (London, Harper Collins, 1997).

Presidential Commission for the Study of Bioethical Issues, Report 'Ethically Impossible: STD Research in Guatemala from 1946 to 1948' (Washington, DC, 2011); <http://bioethics.gov/sites/default/files/Ethically-Impossible_PCSBI.pdf>.

Presler, G., *Glanz und Elend der 20er Jahre. Die Malerei der Neuen Sachlichkeit* (Cologne, DuMont, 1992).

Proctor, R.N., *Racial Hygiene. Medicine under the Nazis* (Cambridge, MA, Harvard University Press, 1988).

Proctor, R.N., 'Nazi Doctors, Racial Medicine, and Human Experimentation', in *The Nazi Doctors and the Nuremberg Code. Human Rights in Human Experimentation*, edited by G.J. Annas and M.A. Grodin (New York, Oxford, Oxford University Press, 1992), pp. 17–31.

Pugliese, D., 'Vets Sign on to Sue over Secret Wartime Tests', *The Ottawa Citizen* (2003), p. A5.

Pulvertaft, R.J.V., 'The Individual and the Group in Modern Medicine', *The Lancet* (1952), pp. 839–42.

Quirke, V., *Collaboration in the Pharmaceutical Industry: Changing Relationships in Britain and France, 1935–1965* (London, New York, Routledge, 2007).

Rabinowitch, E., 'Pugwash—History and Outlook', *The Bulletin of the Atomic Scientists*, 13 (September 1957), 7, pp. 243–8.

Rappert, B., *Controlling the Weapons of War: Politics, Persuasion and the Prohibition of Inhumanity* (London, Routledge, 2006).

Rappert, B., *Biotechnology, Security and the Search for the Limits: An Inquiry into Research and Methods* (Basingstoke, Palgrave Macmillan, 2007).

Rappert, B., *Experimental Secrets: International Security, Codes, and the Future of Research* (Lanham, MD, University Press of America, 2009).

Rappert, B., *How to Look Good in War* (London, Pluto Press, 2012).

Rayment, S., 'Porton Nerve Gas Scientists Escape Criminal Charges', *Sunday Telegraph*, 8 June 2003.

Reagan, L.J., 'Representations and Reproductive Hazards of Agent Orange', *Journal of Law, Medicine & Ethics*, 39 (2011), 1, pp. 54–61.

Rees, A., and C. Dixon, 'Patients Died in Germ War Tests', *Daily Express*, 20 November 2000.

Reverby, S.M., ' "Normal Exposure" and Inoculation Syphilis: A PHS "Tuskegee" Doctor in Guatemala, 1946–1948', *The Journal of Policy History* (2011), 23, 1, pp. 6–28.

Reynolds, L.A., and E.M. Tansey, eds., 'Clinical Research in Britain, 1950–1980', *Wellcome Witnesses to Twentieth Century Medicine*, 7 (London, The Wellcome Trust Centre for the History of Medicine at UCL, 2000).

Reynolds, L.A., and E.M. Tansey, eds., 'Medical Ethics Education in Britain, 1963–93', *Wellcome Witnesses to Twentieth Century Medicine*, 31 (London, The Wellcome Trust Centre for the History of Medicine at UCL, 2007).

Reynolds, L.A., and E.M. Tansey, eds., 'Clinical Pharmacology in the UK, c. 1950–2000: Influences and Institutions', *Wellcome Witnesses to Twentieth Century Medicine* (London, The Wellcome Trust Centre for the History of Medicine at UCL, 2008).

Rhodes, P., 'And Not a Mere Anatomy', *BMJ*, 300 (1990), p. 1348.

Richter, D., *Chemical Soldiers: British Gas Warfare in World War I* (London, Leo Cooper, 1994).

Richter, E.D., P. Barach, T. Berman, G. Ben-David, and Z. Weinberger, 'Extending the Boundaries of the Declaration of Helsinki: A Case Study of an Unethical Experiment in a Non-Medical Setting', *Journal of Medical Ethics*, 27 (2001), 2, pp. 126–9.

Roberts, J.M., *Europe 1880–1945* (Harlow, Pearson Education, 2001).

Robins, J., 'Exposed', *The Lawyer*, 17 January 2005.

Robins, J., 'Long Road to Justice', *Institute of Legal Executives (ILEx) Journal, 17* (2008), pp. 28–9.

Roelcke, V., and G. Maio, eds., *Twentieth Century Ethics of Human Subject Research— Historical Perspectives on Values, Practices, and Regulations* (Stuttgart, Franz Steiner Verlag, 2004).

Rosenberg, J., and N. Britten, 'After 50 Years, Family Wins Inquest into Nerve Gas Case', *The Telegraph*, 19 November 2002.

Rothman, D.J., *Strangers at the Bedside. A History of how Law and Bioethics Transformed Medical Decision Making* (New York, Basic Books, 1991).

Roughton, F.J.W., 'Joseph Barcroft, 1872–1947', *Obituary Notices of Fellows of the Royal Society*, 6 (1949) 18, pp. 315–45.

Rupke, N.A., ed., *Vivisection in Historical Perspective* (London, New York, Croom Helm, 1987).

Saunders, B.C., 'Physiological Action of Di*iso*propyl Phosphorofluoridate', in *Phosphoric Esters and Related Compounds*. Report of a Symposium held at the Chemical Society Anniversary Meeting, Cambridge, 9–12 April 1957, organized by G.W. Kenner and D.M. Brown (London, The Chemical Society, 1957), pp. 165–70.

Sass, H.-M., 'Reichsrundschreiben 1931: Pre-Nuremberg German Regulations Concerning New Therapy and Human Experimentation', *The Journal of Medicine and Philosophy*, 8 (1983), pp. 99–111.

Schmaltz, F., *Kampfstoff-Forschung im Nationalsozialismus. Zur Kooperation von Kaiser-Wilhelm-Instituten, Militär und Industrie* (Göttingen, Wallstein, 2005).

Schmaltz, F., 'Neurosciences and Research on Chemical Weapons of Mass Destruction in Nazi Germany', *Journal of the History of Neurosciences*, 15 (2006a), pp. 186–209.

Schmaltz, F., 'Otto Bickenbach's Human Experiments with Chemical Warfare Agents and the Concentration Camp Natzweiler', in *Man, Medicine and the State: the Human Body as an Object of Government-Sponsored Medical Research*, edited by W.U. Eckart (Stuttgart, Franz Steiner Verlag, 2006b), pp. 139–56.

Schmaltz, F., 'Pharmakologische Nevengasforschung an der Militärärztlichen Akademie und an den Universitäten Marburg, Danzig und Leipzig im Zweiten Weltkrieg', in *Medizin im Zweiten Weltkrieg. Militärmedizinische Praxis und medizinische Wissenschaft im 'Totalen Krieg'*, edited by W.U. Eckart and A. Neumann (Paderborn, Munich, Vienna, Zurich, Schöningh, 2006c), pp. 171–94.

Schmidt, U., 'Der Ärzteprozeß als moralische Instanz? Der Nürnberger Kodex und das Problem "zeitloser Medizinethik"', in *Medizingeschichte und Medizinethik 1900–1950*, edited by A. Frewer and J. Neumann (Frankfurt am Main, New York, Campus Verlag, 2001), pp. 334–73.

Schmidt, U., *Medical Films, Ethics and Euthanasia in Nazi Germany* (Husum, Matthiesen, 2002).

Schmidt, U., *Justice at Nuremberg. Leo Alexander and the Nazi Doctors' Trial* (Basingstoke, Palgrave Macmillan, 2004).

Schmidt, U., 'Cold War at Porton Down: Informed Consent in Britain's Biological and Chemical Warfare Experiments', *Cambridge Quarterly for Healthcare Ethics*, 15 (2006), 4, pp. 366–80.

Schmidt, U., *Karl Brandt. The Nazi Doctor. Medicine and Power in the Third Reich* (London, Continuum, 2007a).

Schmidt, U., 'Medical Ethics and Human Experimentation at Porton Down: Informed Consent in Britain's Biological and Chemical Warfare Experiments', in *History and Theory of Human Experimentation. The Declaration of Helsinki and Modern Medical Ethics*, edited by U. Schmidt and A. Frewer (Stuttgart, Steiner, 2007b), pp. 283–313.

Schmidt, U., 'The Nuremberg Doctors' Trial and the Nuremberg Code', in *History and Theory of Human Experimentation. The Declaration of Helsinki and Modern Medical Ethics*, edited by U. Schmidt and A. Frewer (Stuttgart, Franz Steiner Verlag, 2007c), pp. 71–116.

Schmidt, U., *Hitlers Arzt Karl Brandt. Medizin und Macht im Dritten Reich* (Berlin, Aufbau Verlag, 2009a).

Schmidt, U., 'Medical Ethics and Nazism', in *The Cambridge World History of Medical Ethics*, edited by L.B. McCullough and R. Baker (Cambridge, New York, Cambridge University Press, 2009b), pp. 595–608.

Schmidt, U., 'Justifying Chemical Warfare. The Origins and Ethics of Britain's Chemical Warfare Programme, 1915–1939', in *Justifying War: Propaganda, Politics and the Modern Age*, edited by D. Welch and J. Fox (Basingstoke, Palgrave, 2012a), pp. 129–58.

Schmidt, U., 'Reflections on the Origins of the Declaration of Helsinki', in *Jahrbuch Medizinethik*, edited by H.J. Ehni and U. Wiesing (Cologne, Deutscher Ärzteverlag, 2012b), pp. 1–17.

Schmidt, U., 'Accidents and Experiments: Nazi Chemical Warfare Research and Medical Ethics during the Second World War', edited by D.G. Carrick and M. Gross, *Military Medical Ethics* (Farnham, Ashgate, 2013), pp. 225–44.

Schmidt, U., 'Karl Brandt, médecin de Hitler', in *Une médecine de mort. Du code de Nuremberg à l'éthique médicale contemporaine*, edited by L. Haddad and J.-M. Dreyfus (Paris, Éditions Vendémiaire, 2014), pp. 55–68.

Schmidt, U., and A. Frewer, eds., *History and Theory of Human Experimentation. The Declaration of Helsinki and Modern Medical Ethics* (Stuttgart, Franz Steiner Verlag, 2007).

Schmidt, U., and A. Frewer, 'Geschichte und Ethik der Humanforschung. 50 Jahre Deklaration von Helsinki. Zur Einführung', in *Forschung als Herausforderungen für Ethik und Menschenrechte. 50 Jahre Deklaration von Helsinki, 1964–2014*, edited by A. Frewer and U. Schmidt (Cologne, Deutscher Ärzteverlag, 2014a), pp. 9–13.

Schmidt, U., and A. Frewer, 'The Declaration of Helsinki as a Landmark for Research Ethics—Protecting Human Participants in Modern Medicine', in *The World Medical Association Declaration of Helsinki, 1964–2014. 50 Years of Evolution of Medical Research Ethics*, edited by U. Wiesing, R.W. Parsa-Parsi, and O. Kloiber (Cologne, Deutscher Ärzteverlag, 2014b), pp. 56–7.

Scholem, G., ed., *The Correspondence of Walter Benjamin and Gershom Scholem. 1932–1940* (Cambridge, MA, Harvard University Press, 1992).

Schwarz, M., 'Ypern und das Grauen des Ersten Weltkrieges', *Die Welt*, 1 July 2008.

Senate Select Committee on Intelligence, Committee Study of the Central Intelligence Agency's Detention and Interrogation Program, 9 December 2014.

Sharp, D., 'Ethics at Porton Down', *The Lancet*, 368 (2006), pp. 631–2.

Shephard, B., *A War of Nerves. Soldiers and Psychiatrists, 1914–1994* (London, Jonathan Cape, 2000).

Shevell, M., 'Neurology's Witness to History (part 2): Leo Alexander's Contribution to the Nuremberg Code', *Neurology*, 50 (1998), pp. 274–8.

Shimkin, M.B., 'The Problem of Experimentation on Human Beings, The Research Worker's Point of View', *Science* (1953), pp. 205–7.

Shuster, E., 'Fifty Years Later: The Significance of the Nuremberg Code', *The New England Journal of Medicine*, 337 (1997), pp. 1436–40.

Shuster, E., 'The Nuremberg Code: Hippocratic Ethics and Human Rights', *The Lancet*, 51 (1998), pp. 974–77.

Sigmund, E., *Rage against the Dying. Campaign against Chemical and Biological Warfare* (London, Pluto Press, 1980).

Silver, K.E., *Chaos & Classicism. Art in France, Italy, and Germany, 1918–1936* (New York, Guggenheim Museum Publications, 2010).

Simmons, I.G., *An Environmental History of Great Britain. From 10,000 Years Ago to the Present* (Edingburgh, Edingburgh University Press, 2001).

Sims, N.R.A., *The Diplomacy of Biological Disarmament: Vicissitudes of a Treaty in Force, 1975–1985* (Basingstoke, Macmillan in association with the London School of Economics and Political Science, 1986).

Sims, N.R.A., 'Commonwealth Reservations to the 1925 Geneva Protocol, 1930–92', *Round Table*, 324 (October 1992), pp. 477–99.

Sims, N.R.A., *The Evolution of Biological Disarmament* (Oxford, New York, Oxford University Press, 2001).

Sims, N.R.A., *The Future of Biological Disarmament: Strengthening the Treaty Ban on Weapons* (Abingdon, New York, Routledge, 2009).

Sinclair, D., 'The Clinical Features of Mustard-Gas Poisoning in Man', *BMJ*, 2 (1948), 4570, pp. 290–4.

Sinclair, D., 'Treatment of Skin Lesions Caused by Mustard Gas', *BMJ*, 1 (1949), 4602, pp. 476–8.

Sinclair, D., *Not a Proper Doctor* (London, Memoir Club, 1989).

Sisson, H.A., *On Guard against Gas* (London, Hutchinson & Co, 1938).

Smith, S.L., 'Mustard Gas and American Race-Based Human Experimentation in World War II', *Journal of Law, Medicine & Ethics*, 36 (2008), 3, pp. 517–21.

Smith, S.L., 'Toxic Legacy: Mustard Gas in the Sea around US', *Journal of Law, Medicine & Ethics*, 39 (2011), 1, pp. 34–40.

Smith, S.L., and S. Mawdsley, 'Alberta Advantage: A Canadian Proving Ground for American Medical Research on Mustard Gas and Polio in the 1940s and 1950s', in *Locating Health: Historical and Anthropological Investigations of Health and Place,* edited by E. Dyck and C. Fletcher (London, Pickering & Chatto, 2011), pp. 89–106.

Spector-Bagdady, K., and P.A. Lombardo, '"Something of an Adventure": Postwar NIH Research Ethos and the Guatemala STD Experiments', *Journal of Law, Medicine & Ethics*, 41 (2013), 3, pp. 697–710.

Spence, S., 'Listening to the Silence', *BMJ*, 309 (1994), p. 1024.

Spiers, E.M., *Chemical Warfare* (Basingstoke, Macmillan, 1986).

Spiers, E.M., *A History of Chemical and Biological Weapons* (London, Reaktion Books, 2010).

Sprenger, I., *Groß-Rosen. Ein Kozentrationslager in Schlesien* (Cologne, Böhlau, 1996).

Stallabrass, J., 'The Iron Cage of Boredom' [Andreas Gursky at the Tate Gallery, Liverpool], *Art Monthly*, 189 (1995), pp. 16–20.

Starling, E., *A Century of Physiology* (London, University of London Press, 1927).

Starr, P., *The Social Transformation of American Medicine. The Rise of a Sovereign Profession and the Making of a Vast Industry* (New York, Basic Book, 1982).

Stockholm International Peace Research Institute (SIPRI), *The Problem of Chemical and Biological Warfare*, vols. 1–6 (Stockholm, New York, Almqvist & Wiksell Humanities Press, 1971–1975).

Stolzenberg, D., *Fritz Haber—Chemist, Nobel Laureate, German, Jew* (Philadelphia, PA, Chemical Heritage Press, 2004).

Stone, D., *Holocaust, Fascism and Memory. Essays in the History of Ideas* (Basingstoke, Palgrave Macmillan, 2013).

Sturdy, S., 'A Co-ordinated Whole: The Life and Work of J.S. Haldane' (University of Edinburgh, unpublished PhD thesis, 1987).

Sturdy, S., 'The Meanings of "Life": Biology and Biography in the Work of J.S. Haldane (1860–1936)', *Transactions of the Royal Historical Society*, 21 (2011), pp. 171–91.

Sturdy, S., 'War as Experiment: Physiological Innovation and Administration in Britain, 1914–1918: The Case of Chemical Warfare', in *War, Medicine and Modernity*, edited by R. Cooter, M. Harrison, and S. Sturdy (Stroud: Sutton, 1998), pp. 65–84.

Suskind, R., 'Faith, Certainty and the Presidency of George W. Bush', *New York Times Magazine*, 17 October 2004.

Sutton, L.E., 'Samuel Sugden. 1892–1950', *Biographical Memoirs of Fellows of the Royal Society*, 20 (1951), pp. 492–503.

Syal, R., 'Porton Down Used Soldiers for Sarin Gas Tests in 1983', *The Sunday Telegraph*, 13 October 2002.

Syal, R., and S. Bisset, 'Ex-Ministers Face Police Inquiry on Porton Down Tests', *The Sunday Telegraph*, 29 October 2000.

Szöllösi-Janze, M., *Fritz Haber, 1868–1934: Eine Biographie* (Munich, C.H. Beck, 1998).

Tansey, E.M., D.A. Christie, and L.A. Reynolds, eds., 'Making the Human Body Transparent: The Impact of NMR and MRI. Research in General Practice. Drugs in Psychiatric Practice. The MRC Common Cold Unit', *Wellcome Witnesses to*

Twentieth Century Medicine, 2. (London, The Wellcome Trust Centre for the History of Medicine at UCL, 1998).

Terraine, J., *White Heat. The New Warfare 1914–18* (London, Leo Cooper, 1992).

'The Edgewood Arsenal', Special Edition of *Chemical Warfare*, 1 (March 1919), p. 5.

Thompson, R.H.S., and A.G. Ogston, 'Rudolph Albert Peters. 13 April 1889–29 January 1982', *Biographical Memoirs of Fellows of the Royal Society*, 29 (1983), pp. 495–523.

Thomson, I., 'Talked into Life. How "If this is a Man" Came to Be', *Times Literary Supplement*, 5700 (2012), pp. 13–15.

Thomson, L.A., *Half a Century of Medical Research*, 2 vols. (London, HMSO, 1973, 1975).

Thorpe, J.F., 'Herbert Brereton Baker, 1862–1935', *Obituary Notices of Fellows of the Royal Society*, 1 (1936) 4, pp. 523–6.

Thurlow, R., *The Secret State. British Internal Security in the Twentieth Century* (Oxford, Oxford University Press, 1994).

Travis, A., 'Nobel-winning British Scientist Accused of Spying by MI5, Papers Reveal', *The Guardian*, 26 August 2010.

Tröhler, U., and S. Reiter-Theil, eds., *Ethics Codes in Medicine* (Farnham, Ashgate, 1998).

Trotter, G., 'Balancing Pluralism and the Common Good: A Look at Open-Air Experiments with Biowarfare Agents', *Accountability in Research*, 10 (2003), 2, pp. 109–21.

Tucker, J.B., ed., *The Chemical Weapons Convention: Implementation, Challenges and Solutions* (Washington, DC, Monterey Institute of International Studies, 2001).

Tucker, J.B., *War of Nerves. Chemical Warfare from World War I to Al-Qaeda* (New York, Pantheon Books, 2006).

Tuorinski, S.D., *Medical Aspects of Chemical Warfare* (Washington, DC, Government Printing Office, 2008).

Tyrrell, D., and M. Fielder, *Cold Wars. The Fight against the Common Cold* (Oxford, Oxford University Press, 2002).

United States Advisory Committee on Human Radiation Experiments, *Final Report of the Advisory Committee on Human Radiation Experiments* (New York, NY, Oxford University Press, 1995).

Valier, H., and C. Timmermann, 'Clinical Trials and the Reorganisation of Medical Research in Post-War II Britain', *Medical History*, 52 (2008), 4, pp. 493–510.

Van Bergen, L., 'Monkey-Man, Man-Monkey: Neutrality and the Discussions about the "Inhumanity" of Poison Gas in the Netherlands and International Committee of the Red Cross', *First World War Studies*, 3 (2012), pp. 1–23.

Van Courtland Moon, J.E., 'The US Biological Weapons Program', in *Deadly Cultures: Biological Weapons since 1945*, edited by M. Wheelis, R. Lajos, and M. Dando (Cambridge, MA, London, Harvard University Press, 2006), pp. 9–46.

Vanderbilt, T., *Survival City: Adventures among the Ruins of Atomic America* (New York, Princeton Architectural Press, 2002).

Vasagar, J., 'Trust Sells Skin to Porton Down. NHS Patients Not Told of Chemical Weapons Tests', *The Guardian*, 10 February 2001.

Venables, K.M., et al., 'Mortality in British Military Participants in Human Experimental Research into Chemical Warfare Agents at Porton Down: Cohort Study', *BMJ*, 338 (2009), pp. 1–10 (b613).

Vilensky, J.A., *Dew of Death. The Story of Lewisite, America's World War I Weapon of Mass Destruction* (Bloomington, IN, Indiana University Press, 2005).

Vivian, D.T.R., 'British Scientists and Soldiers in the First World War (with Special Reference to Ballistics and Chemical Warfare)' (Imperial College London, unpublished PhD thesis, 2009).

Wachtel, C., *Chemical Warfare* (Brooklyn, New York, Chemical Publishing Company, 1941).

Wahl, M., and U. Schmidt, 'Ärzte hinter dem Eisernen Vorhang: Medizinethische Diskurse und die Deklaration von Helsinki in der ehemaligen Deutschen Demokratischen Republik, 1961–1989', in *Forschung als Herausforderungen für Ethik und Menschenrechte. 50 Jahre Deklaration von Helsinki, 1964–2014*, edited by A. Frewer and U. Schmidt (Cologne, Deutscher Ärzteverlag, 2014), pp. 71–86.

Walker, J.[oe], *Environmental Ethics* (London, Hodder & Stoughton, 2000).

Walker, J.[ohn], *Britain and Disarmament: The UK and Nuclear, Biological and Chemical Weapons Arms Control and Programmes, 1956–1975* (Farnham, Ashgate, 2012).

'War on Chemical and Biological Warfare', *Nature*, 218 (1968), pp. 905–6.

Weatherall, M.W., *Gentlemen, Scientists, and Doctors: Medicine in Cambridge 1800–1940* (Woodbridge, Boydell Press, 2000).

Weindling, P., 'Ethical Lessons from Porton Down', *The Guardian*, 18 July 2006.

Weiss, S.F., *The Nazi Symbiosis. Human Genetics and Politics in the Third Reich* (Chicago, London, The University of Chicago Press, 2010).

Welch, D., and J. Fox, eds., *Justifying War: Propaganda, Politics and the Modern Age* (Basingstoke, Palgrave, 2012).

Wells, T.C.E., et al., 'Ecological Studies on the Porton Ranges: Relationships between Vegetation, Soils and Land-Use History', *Journal of Ecology*, 64 (1976), 2, pp. 589–626.

Welsh, C.J.D., 'Op-Ed, Outlaw Nonconsensual Human Experiments Now', *Bulletin of the Atomic Scientists*, Web Edition, 16 June 2009.

Welsome, E., *The Plutonium Files: America's Secret Medical Experiments during the Cold War* (New York, Dial Press, 1999).

Wheelis, M., R. Lajos, and M. Dando, eds., *Deadly Cultures. Biological Weapons since 1945* (Cambridge, MA, London, Harvard University Press, 2006).

WHO Group of Consultants, *Health Aspects of Chemical and Biological Weapons* (Geneva, World Health Organization, 1970).

WHO Guidance, Public Health Response to Biological and Chemical Weapons (Geneva, World Health Organization, 2004).

Wightwick, A., 'Nerve-Gas "Volunteers" Seeking Justice', *The Western Mail*, 13 November 2000.

Wilkie, T., and D. Penman, 'They Shoot Pigs, Don't They', *The Independent*, 26 January 1995.

Williams, P., and D. Wallace, *Unit 731: Japan's Secret Biological Warfare in World War II* (New York, Free Press, 1989).

Williams, R.T., *The Biochemical Reactions of Chemical Warfare Agents. A Symposium Held at the London School of Hygiene and Tropical Medicine on 13 December 1947* (Cambridge, Cambridge University Press, 1948).

Willis, E.A., 'Seascape with Monkeys and Guinea-Pigs: Britain's Biological Weapons Research Programme, 1948–54', *Medicine, Conflict and Survival*, 19 (2003), 4, pp. 285–302.

Winter, J., *Sites of Memory, Sites of Mourning. The Great War in European Cultural History* (Cambridge, Cambridge University Press, 1995).

Winter, J., 'The Generation of Memory: Reflections on the "Memory Boom" in Contemporary Historical Studies', *Bulletin of the German Historical Institute Washington, D.C.*, 27 (2000), pp. 69–92.

Withnall, A., 'Nobel Peace Prize for Syria Chemical Weapons Watchdog', *The Independent*, 11 October 2013.

Witte, P., et al. eds., *Der Dienstkalender Heinrich Himmlers 1941/42* (Hamburg, Christians, 1999).

Wittmann, E., 'From the Front Line to Casualty Clearing Station: The Treatment and Management of Gas Casualties on the Western Front, 1914–1918' (University of London, unpublished BSc dissertation, 2005).

Woelk, W., 'Der Pharmakologe und Toxikologe Wolfgang Wirth (1898–1996) und die Giftgasforschung im Nationalsozialismus', in *Nach der Diktatur. Die medizinische Akademie Düsseldorf nach 1945*, edited by W. Woelk et al. (Essen, Klartext, 2003), pp. 269–87.

Woolf, M., 'Live Pigs Blown Up in Porton Down Tests', *The Independent*, 22 January 1995.

Woolf, M., 'Live Pigs Blasted in Terror Attack Experiments', *The Sunday Times*, 24 January 2010.

Wright, P., and P. Greengrass, *Spycatcher* (Victoria, Australia, William Heinemann, 1987).

Ziemann, B., *Contested Commemorations. Republican War Veterans and Weimar Political Culture* (Cambridge, Cambridge University Press, 2013).

Zuckerman, S., *Scientists and War. The Impact of Science on Military and Civil Affairs* (London, Hamish Hamilton, 1966).

Zuckerman, S., *Monkeys, Men and Missiles. An Autobiography, 1948–1988* (London, Collins, 1988).

Zweig, S., *Auf Reisen* (Frankfurt am Main, Fischer, 2004).

Index

Bold type indicates the more substantive entries. Institutions are listed under their respective nations. For specific biological, chemical and nerve agents, see 'warfare agents'; for specific hospitals, see 'hospitals'; for specific medical conditions, drugs, and treatments, see 'medical'; for specific protest groups, see 'public protest'; for specific scientific disciplines, see 'scientific'. Umlauts are ignored in alphabetization; 'ß' is sorted as 'ss'.